ALSO IN SERIES OF Twenty Two (22) Sacred Maxims

Lex Divina: Maxims of Divine Law
Lex Naturae: Maxims of Natural Law
Lex Cognitum: Maxims of Cognitive Law
Lex Virtus Naturae: Maxims of Bioethics Law
Lex Ecclesiasticum: Maxims of Ecclesiastical Law
Lex Positivum: Maxims of Positive Law
Lex Regia: Maxims of Sovereign Law
Lex Fidei: Maxims of Fiduciary Law
Lex Administratum: Maxims of Administrative Law
Lex Economica: Maxims of Economic Law
Lex Pecuniaria: Maxims of Monetary Law
Lex Civilis: Maxims of Civil Law
Lex Criminalis: Maxims of Criminal Law
Lex Educationis: Maxims of Education Law
Lex Nutrimens Et Medicina: Maxims of Food & Drugs Law
Lex Urbanus: Maxims of Urban Law
Lex Societatis: Maxims of Company Law
Lex Technologiae: Maxims of Technology Law
Lex Commercii: Maxims of Trade & Intellectual Property Law
Lex Securitas: Maxims of Security Law
Lex Militaris: Maxims of Military Law
Lex Gentium: Maxims of International Law

Pactum De Singularis Caelum
Covenant of One Heaven

Lex Divina

Maxims of Divine Law

OFFICIAL ENGLISH FIRST EDITION

By
UCADIA

Ucadia Books Company

Lex Divina: Maxims of Divine Law. Official English First Edition. Copyright © 2002-2023 UCADIA. All Rights reserved in Trust.

No part of this book may be reproduced, or stored in a retrieval system, or transmitted in any form or by any means electronic, mechanical, photocopying, recording or otherwise, without the express and authentic written permission of the Publisher.

The Publisher disclaims any liability and shall be indemnified and held harmless from any demands, loss, liability, claims or expenses made by any party due or arising out of or in connection with any differences between previous non-official English drafts and this Official English First Edition.

A party that threatens, makes or enacts any demand or action, against this publication or the Publisher hereby acknowledge they have read this disclaimer and agree with this binding legal agreement and irrevocably consent to Ucadia and its competent forums as being the original and primary Jurisdiction for resolving any such issue of fact and law.

Published by Ucadia Books Company, a Delaware stock corporation (File Number 6779670).
8 The Green, STE B, Dover, Delaware, 19901 United States.
First edition.

UCADIA® is a US Registered Trademark in trust under Guardians and Trustees Company protected under international law and the laws of the United States.

ISBN 978-1-64419-023-4

Lex Divina: Maxims of Divine Law

By Right, Power and Authority of Article 135 (*Divine Collection of Maxims of Law*) of the most sacred Covenant *Pactum De Singularis Caelum*, also known as the *Covenant of One Heaven* these maxims of law known collectively as "**Lex Divina**" and "**Maxims of Divine Law**" are hereby promulgated in the original form of Ucadian Language and official translations.

These Maxims of Divine Law may be taken in official original document form and spoken form to represent one part of a complete set of the twenty-two (22) books known collectively as the Divine Collection of Maxims of Law.

The Maxims of Divine Law represent the primary, one and only true first Maxims of Divine Law. Excluding the most sacred Covenants *Pactum De Singularis Caelum*, *Pactum De Singularis Christus*, *Pactum De Singularis Islam* and *Pactum De Singularis Spiritus*, all other laws, claims and agreements claiming standards of Divine Law shall be secondary and inferior to the Maxims of Divine Law.

When referring to these Maxims of Divine Law:-

(i)   The entire book of Maxims of Divine Law may be abbreviated in citation as "*Lex Divina*" or "*Lex Divina (Maxims of Divine Law)*"; and

(ii)   A Maxim within the book of Maxims of Divine Law may be abbreviated in citation as (for example) "*Lex Divina max.1*" or "*Lex Divina (Divine Law) max.1*".

In accordance with these Maxims of Divine Law, Ucadia also known as the Unique Collective Awareness of all Meaning, also known as the Divine Creator reserves all rights to itself and its duly authorised organs, bodies and entities.

As all rights are reserved, no translation, copy, citation, duplication, registration in part or whole implies any transfer or conveyance of these rights.

When part or all of these laws is presented or spoken in any language other than the Official Ucadian Languages, it may be taken as a translation and not the primary language. Therefore, any secondary meaning implying deficiency, claimed abrogation of any right or any other defect of a word in a translated language shall be null and void ab initio (from the beginning).

Let no man, woman, spirit or officer place themselves in grave dishonour of Divine Law, Natural Law and the Living Law upon denying the validity of these maxims of law. As it is written, so be it.

CONTENTS

Title I: Introductory Provisions

Article 1 – Rule	23
Article 2 – Divine	26
Article 3 – Divine Law	28
Article 4 – The Law	29
Article 5 – Rule of Law	30
Article 6 – Justice	32
Article 7 – Fair Process (of Justice)	35

Title II: Divine Concepts

2.1 - Absolute Concepts

Article 8 – Concept	39
Article 9 – Meaning	41
Article 10 – Idea	44
Article 11 – Cause	46
Article 12 – Model	48
Article 13 – System	52
Article 14 – Nothing	53
Article 15 – Quantity	55
Article 16 – Set	55
Article 17 – Limit	61
Article 18 – Uniqueness	62
Article 19 – Relativity	64
Article 20 – Change	66
Article 21 – Reality	68
Article 22 – Paradox	71

2.2 - Absolute Awareness

Article 23 – Awareness	73
Article 24 – Inspiration	77
Article 25 – Reception	77
Article 26 – Conception	78
Article 27 – Perception	78
Article 28 – Inception	79

Article 29 – Determination 80
Article 30 – Expiration 80
Article 31 – Dream 80
Article 32 – Dreamer 82
Article 33 – Unique Collective Awareness 83

2.3 - Existential Concepts

Article 34 – Existence 85
Article 35 – Object 86
Article 36 – Observer 88
Article 37 – Rules 89
Article 38 – Imperfection 90
Article 39 – Autonomy 91
Article 40 – Dependence 92
Article 41 – Chaos and Cosmos 93
Article 42 – Complexity and Simplicity 94
Article 43 – Dimension 96
Article 44 – Certainty 105

2.4 - Existential Calculations

Article 45 – Calculation 106
Article 46 – Eikos 107
Article 47 – Number 109
Article 48 – Perfect Number 109
Article 49 – Imperfect Number 112
Article 50 – Infinitesimal 113
Article 51 – Infinite 114
Article 52 – Zero 115
Article 53 – Uniset 115
Article 54 – Variable 116
Article 55 – Constant 116
Article 56 – Formula 117
Article 57 – Symeric Formula 117
Article 58 – Function 123

Article 59 – Positional (Function) 124
Article 60 – Incremental (Function) 126
Article 61 – Decremental (Function) 126
Article 62 – Polymental (Function) 127
Article 63 – Deviational (Function) 127
Article 64 – Integrational (Function) 127
Article 65 – Equation 128
Article 66 – Geometry 129

2.5 - Existential Computations

Article 67 – Computation 131
Article 68 – Computational Functions 132
Article 69 – Sequence 134
Article 70 – Algorithm 134
Article 71 – Data 136
Article 72 – Receiver 137
Article 73 – Transmitter 138
Article 74 – Processor 139
Article 75 – Mathematical Intelligence 141
Article 76 – Memory 142
Article 77 – Computer 145

2.6 - Creational Concepts

Article 78 – Creation 147
Article 79 – Will (Law) 149
Article 80 – Logos (Law) 152
Article 81 – Purpose (Law) 153
Article 82 – Co-dependence (Law) 154
Article 83 – Specialisation (Law) 155
Article 84 – Geometry (Law) 156
Article 85 – Elemental Awareness (Law) 156
Article 86 – Localisation (Law) 157
Article 87 – Exclusiveness (Law) 157
Article 88 – Motion (Law) 158

Article 89 – Conservation of Motion (Law) 159
Article 90 – Limit (Law) 159

2.7 - Creational Properties

Article 91 – Properties 161
Article 92 – Volume 161
Article 93 – Kinesis 162
Article 94 – Orbit 165
Article 95 – Mass 166
Article 96 – Density 168
Article 97 – Creative Attractors 169
Article 98 – Destructive Attractors 169
Article 99 – Gravity 171
Article 100 – Altruism 172
Article 101 – Antimatter 174
Article 102 – Force 175
Article 103 – Energis 176
Article 104 – Ergon 177
Article 105 – Energy 177
Article 106 – Time 178
Article 107 – Life 178
Article 108 – ALL 179
Article 109 – Seven Proofs of Divine Existence 179

Title III: Divine Attributes

3.1 - Elemental Divine Attributes

Article 110 – Divine Attribute 181
Article 111 – Divine Awareness 184
Article 112 – Divine Will 185
Article 113 – Divine Mind 186
Article 114 – Divine Existence 186
Article 115 – Divine Law 187
Article 116 – Divine Creation 187
Article 117 – Divine Dominion 188

Article 118 – Divine Nature 188
Article 119 – Divine Love 189
Article 120 – Divine Mercy 190
Article 121 – Divine Trust 191
Article 122 – Divine Truth 192
Article 123 – Divine Rights 193
Article 124 – Divine Property 194

3.2 - Divine Mind Attributes

Article 125 – Divine Mind Attributes 194
Article 126 – Divine Competence 195
Article 127 – Divine Argument 197
Article 128 – Divine Logic 198
Article 129 – Divine Fallacy 200
Article 130 – Seven Proofs of Divine Mind 202

3.3 - Supreme (Omni) Attributes

Article 131 – Supreme (Omni) Attributes 203
Article 132 – Omniessent 204
Article 133 – Omnimodulant 205
Article 134 – Omnisignificant 206

3.4 - Contrasting Divine Attributes

Article 135 – Contrasting Divine Attributes 208
Article 136 – Theism, Deism and Atheism 208
Article 137 – Immanent and Transcendent 210
Article 138 – Omniformity and Omniunitary 212
Article 139 – Omni-benevolent and Omni-righteous 214

3.5 - False Supreme (Omni) Attributes

Article 140 – False Supreme (Omni) Attributes 216
Article 141 – Omnipotent 217
Article 142 – Omnipresent 222
Article 143 – Omniscient 224

3.6 - Absurdly Associated Attributes

Article 144 – Absurdly Associated Attributes 227

Article 145 – Ignorance	228
Article 146 – Cruel	229
Article 147 – Wrathful	230
Article 148 – Jealous	232
Article 149 – Vengeful	233
Article 150 – Sadistic	234
Article 151 – Depraved	234
Article 152 – Hypocritical	235
Article 153 – Insanity	236
Article 154 – Evil	237

Title IV: Divine Beings

4.1 - Divine Beings

Article 155 – Being	239
Article 156 – Supreme Being	243

4.2 - Primary Beings

Article 157 – Primary Being	243
Article 158 – Universal Being	244
Article 159 – Galactic Being	244
Article 160 – GAL	245
Article 161 – Stellar Being	245
Article 162 – SOL	246
Article 163 – Planetary Being	247
Article 164 – GAIA	248
Article 165 – Cellular Being	248
Article 166 – CORPUS	249
Article 167 – Animal Being	249
Article 168 – ANIMUS	250
Article 169 – Sapient Singularity	250
Article 170 – Saviour	254

4.3 - Ordinary (Spirit) Beings

Article 171 – Ordinary Spirit Beings	254
Article 172 – Exemplary Spirit (Saint)	255

Article 173 – Penitent Spirit 256
Article 174 – Lost Spirit 257
Article 175 – Angel 257
Article 176 – Demon 257

4.4 - Ethereal Beings

Article 177 – Ethereal Being 258
Article 178 – Soul 260
Article 179 – Ghost (Lost Spirit) 261
Article 180 – Wraith 263
Article 181 – Faerie 263
Article 182 – Elve 264
Article 183 – Elemental Being 265

4.5 - Imaginary Beings

Article 184 – Imaginary Being 265

Title V: Divine Persons

5.1 - Divine Persons

Article 185 – Person... 267
Article 186 – Ordinary Divine Person 268
Article 187 – Official Divine Person 269
Article 188 – Aggregate Divine Person 270

Title VI: Divine Rights

6.1 - Divine Rights

Article 189 – Right... 273
Article 190 – Divine Rights 276
Article 191 – Perfect Divine Rights 277
Article 192 – Imperfect Divine Rights 277
Article 193 – Invalid Rights 278
Article 194 – Prohibited Rights 278

6.2 - Divine Rights Creation, Assertion & Modification

Article 195 – Divine Rights Creation, Assertion & Modification 280
Article 196 – False, Absurd & Prohibited Rights Creation & Assertion 281

6.3 - Divine Rights Transfer & Possession

Article 197 – Divine Rights Transfer & Possession 281

Article 198 – False, Absurd & Prohibited Rights Transfer & Possession.............. 284

6.4 - Divine Rights Suspension & Loss

Article 199 – Divine Rights Suspension & Loss 284

Article 200 – False, Absurd & Prohibited Rights Suspension & Loss 285

6.5 - Divine Rights Dispute, Recovery & Restoration

Article 201 – Divine Rights Dispute, Recovery & Restoration 285

Article 202 – False, Absurd & Prohibited Rights Dispute & Recovery 286

6.6 - Foundational Divine Rights

Article 203 – Foundational Divine Rights 286

Article 204 – Ius Divinum (Divine) 288

Article 205 – Ius Divinum Ucadia (Ucadia) 289

Article 206 – Ius Divinum Liberum Arbitrium (Free Will) 289

Article 207 – Ius Divinum Logos (Reason) 290

Article 208 – Ius Divinum Scopus (Purpose) 290

Article 209 – Ius Divinum Codependentia (Codependence) 291

Article 210 – Ius Divinum Specialisatio (Specialisation) 291

Article 211 – Ius Divinum Geometria (Geometry) 292

Article 212 – Ius Divinum Conscientia (Awareness) 292

Article 213 – Ius Divinum Localisatio (Localisation) 293

Article 214 – Ius Divinum Singularitas (Uniqueness) 294

Article 215 – Ius Divinum Mutatio (Change) 294

Article 216 – Ius Divinum Conservatio (Conservation) 295

Article 217 – Ius Divinum Limitis (Limit) 295

Article 218 – Ius Divinum Existentia (Existence) 296

Article 219 – Ius Divinum Modela (Model) 296

Article 220 – Ius Divinum Elementa (Elements) 297

Article 221 – Ius Divinum Spatium (Space) 297

Article 222 – Ius Divinum Fortes (Forces) 297

Article 223 – Ius Divinum Energia (Energy) 298

Article 224 – Ius Divinum Computatio (Computations) 298

Article 225 – Ius Divinum Entia (Being) 299

6.7 - Instrumental Divine Rights

Article 226 – Instrumental Divine Rights	299
Article 227 – Ius Divinum Iuris (Justice & Due Process)	301
Article 228 – Ius Divinum Aequum (Equality)	303
Article 229 – Ius Divinum Bona Fidei (Good Faith)	304
Article 230 – Ius Divinum Fraternitas (Membership of Heaven)	304
Article 231 – Ius Divinum Fidei (Trusts & Estates)	305
Article 232 – Ius Divinum Rationatio (Accounting, Credit & Funds)	306
Article 233 – Ius Divinum Concedere et Abrogare (Give & Grant)	307
Article 234 – Ius Divinum Delegare et Revocare (Assign & Delegate)	308
Article 235 – Ius Divinum Associatio et Conventio (Association)	309
Article 236 – Ius Divinum Consensum et Non (Consent)	311
Article 237 – Ius Divinum Dominium (Ownership)	311
Article 238 – Ius Divinum Possessionis (Possession)	313
Article 239 – Ius Divinum Usus (Use)	313
Article 240 – Ius Divinum Proprietatis (Ownership of Use)	314
Article 241 – Ius Divinum Vectigalis Proprietatis (Rents on Use)	314
Article 242 – Ius Divinum Moneta (Money)	315
Article 243 – Ius Divinum Vectigalis Moneta (Rents on Money)	317
Article 244 – Ius Divinum Registrum (Registers & Rolls)	317
Article 245 – Ius Divinum Remedium (Remedy)	319
Article 246 – Ius Divinum Poena (Penalty)	320
Article 247 – Ius Divinum Clementia (Mercy)	321
Article 248 – Ius Divinum Actionum (Action)	321

6.8 - Sacramental Divine Rights

Article 249 – Sacramental Divine Rights	323
Article 250 – Ritus Sacramentum Recognosco (Recognition)	325
Article 251 – Ritus Sacramentum Purificatio (Purification)	325
Article 252 – Ritus Sacramentum Invocatio (Invocation)	326
Article 253 – Ritus Sacramentum Obligatio (Obligation)	328
Article 254 – Ritus Sacramentum Delegatio (Delegation)	329
Article 255 – Ritus Sacramentum Satisfactio (Satisfaction)	329

Article 256 – Ritus Sacramentum Resolutio (Resolution) 330
Article 257 – Ritus Sacramentum Sanctificatio (Sanctification) 330
Article 258 – Ritus Sacramentum Sustentatio (Sustentation) 331
Article 259 – Ritus Sacramentum Unificatio (Unification) 331
Article 260 – Ritus Sacramentum Amalgamatio (Amalgamation) 332
Article 261 – Ritus Sacramentum Authentico (Authentication) 333
Article 262 – Ritus Sacramentum Absolutio (Absolution) 333
Article 263 – Ritus Sacramentum Volitio (Oath) 334
Article 264 – Ritus Sacramentum Vocatio (Vow) 335
Article 265 – Ritus Sacramentum Testificatio (Testification) 335
Article 266 – Ritus Sacramentum Compassio (Mercy) 336
Article 267 – Ritus Sacramentum Conscripto (Binding) 336
Article 268 – Ritus Sacramentum Convocatio (Convocation) 337
Article 269 – Ritus Sacramentum Auctoriso (Authorisation) 337
Article 270 – Ritus Sacramentum Elucidato (Elucidation) 338
Article 271 – Ritus Sacramentum Inspiratio (Annunciation) 338
Article 272 – Ritus Sacramentum Resurrectio (Baptism) 340
Article 273 – Ritus Sacramentum Incarnatio (Incarnation) 341
.... 342
Article 274 – Ritus Sacramentum Confirmatio (Confirmation) 343
Article 275 – Ritus Sacramentum Illuminatio (Illumination) 345
Article 276 – Ritus Sacramentum Exultatio (Exultation) 345
Article 277 – Ritus Sacramentum Glorificatio (Glorification) 346
Article 278 – Ritus Sacramentum Divinatio (Divination) 346
Article 279 – Ritus Sacramentum Visitatio (Visitation) 348
Article 280 – Ritus Sacramentum Salvatio (Salvation) 348
Article 281 – Ritus Sacramentum Emancipatio (Emancipation) 349
Article 282 – Ritus Sacramentum Veneratio (Veneration) ....

6.9 - Authoritative Divine Rights
350
Article 283 – Authoritative Divine Rights ....
351
Article 284 – Ius Divinum Universus (Reality) ....
352
Article 285 – Ius Divinum Regnum (Sovereign) ....
353
Article 286 – Ius Divinum Consilium (Legislative) ....

Article 287 – Ius Divinum Ecclesia (Ecclesiastical) 354
Article 288 – Ius Divinum Templum (Treasury & Financial) 355
Article 289 – Ius Divinum Collegium (Company) 356
Article 290 – Ius Divinum Officium (Office) 359
Article 291 – Ius Divinum Imperium (Command) 360
Article 292 – Ius Divinum Sacrum (Sacred) 361
Article 293 – Ius Divinum Custoditum (Custody) 361
Article 294 – Ius Divinum Alumentum (Sustenance) 363
Article 295 – Ius Divinum Apostolicus (Commission) 364
Article 296 – Ius Divinum Cancellarium (Chancery) 365
Article 297 – Ius Divinum Oratorium (Forum of Law) 366
Article 298 – Ius Divinum Penitentiaria (Penitence) 367
Article 299 – Ius Divinum Sacramentum (Sacred Gifts) 367
Article 300 – Ius Divinum Visum (Survey) 368
Article 301 – Ius Divinum Commercium (Trade) 369
Article 302 – Ius Divinum Virtus (Strength) 369
Article 303 – Ius Divinum Astrum (Association) 370
Article 304 – Ius Divinum Magisterium (teach) 371
Article 305 – Ius Divinum Decretum (Decrees) 371

6.10 - Divine Writs of Right

Article 306 – Divine Writs of Right 372
Article 307 – Recto Divinum Originalis (Original Writ) 374
Article 308 – Recto Divinum Apocalypsis (Revelation) 374
Article 309 – Recto Divinum Investigationis (Inquiry & Search) 375
Article 310 – Recto Divinum Capimus (Surrender or Arrest) 375
Article 311 – Recto Divinum Custodiae (Surrender or Seizure) 375
Article 312 – Recto Divinum Corrigimus (Correction) 375
Article 313 – Recto Divinum Expurgatio (Expurgation) 376
Article 314 – Recto Divinum Abrogatio (Annulment) 376
Article 315 – Recto Divinum Inhibitio (Prohibition) 376
Article 316 – Recto Divinum Restitutio (Restitution) 376
Article 317 – Recto Divinum Restoratio (Restoration) 377

377

6.11 - Divine Bills of Exception

Article 318 – Divine Bills of Exception & Agreement 379
Article 319 – Rogatio Divinum Recto (Original Bill) 379
Article 320 – Rogatio Divinum Apocalypsis (Revelation) 380
Article 321 – Rogatio Divinum Capimus (Surrender or Arrest) 380
Article 322 – Rogatio Divinum Custodiae (Surrender & Seizure) 380
Article 323 – Rogatio Divinum Corrigimus (Correction) 380
Article 324 – Rogatio Divinum Inhibitio (Prohibition) 381
Article 325 – Rogatio Divinum Restitutio (Restitution) 381
Article 326 – Rogatio Divinum Credito (Credit) 381
Article 327 – Rogatio Divinum Permutatio (Exchange) 381
Article 328 – Rogatio Divinum Venditio (Sale) 382
Article 329 – Rogatio Divinum Traditio (Lading) 382

6.12 - Divine Dogma

Article 330 – Divine Dogma (Divine Principles).. 382
Article 331 – Dogma Divinum Praeceptum (Precept) 383
Article 332 – Dogma Divinum Theologiae (Divine Science) 383
Article 333 – Dogma Divinum Singularis Caelum (One Heaven) 383
Article 334 – Dogma Divinum Ucadia (Ucadia) 384
Article 335 – Dogma Divinum Iuris (Law) 384
Article 336 – Dogma Divinum Scientium (Science) 384
Article 337 – Dogma Divinum Revelatio (Revelation) 384
Article 338 – Dogma Divinum Sacramentum (Sacraments) 385
Article 339 – Dogma Divinum Singularis Christus (One Christ) 385
Article 340 – Dogma Divinum Singularis Islam (One Islam) 385
Article 341 – Dogma Divinum Singularis Spiritus (One Spirit) 385

6.13 - Divine Decrees

Article 342 – Divine Decrees 386
Article 343 – Decretum Divinum Doctrinae (Doctrine) 387
Article 344 – Decretum Divinum Absolutionis (Absolution) 387
Article 345 – Decretum Divinum Damnationis (Damnation) 387
Article 346 – Decretum Divinum Exemplificatio (Exemplification) 387

Article 347 – Decretum Divinum Testimonium (Proof) 388
Article 348 – Decretum Divinum Instructionis (Instruction) 388
Article 349 – Decretum Divinum Censurae (Censure) 388
Article 350 – Decretum Divinum Annullas (Annulment) 388
Article 351 – Decretum Divinum Ratificationis (Ratification) 389
Article 352 – Decretum Divinum Interdictum (Interdiction) 389
Article 353 – Decretum Divinum Levationis (Relief) 389

6.14 - Divine Notices
Article 354 – Divine Notices 390
Article 355 – Notitiae Divinum Eventus (Event) 391
Article 356 – Notitiae Divinum Ius (Right) 391
Article 357 – Notitiae Divinum Actum (Action) 392
Article 358 – Notitiae Divinum Decretum (Decree) 392
Article 359 – Notitiae Divinum Iuris (Law) 392
Article 360 – Notitiae Divinum Citationis (Summons) 392
Article 361 – Notitiae Divinum Redemptio (Redemption) 393
Article 362 – Notitiae Divinum Rogatio (Exception) 393
Article 363 – Notitiae Divinum Potentis (Authority) 393
Article 364 – Notitiae Divinum Testamentum (Testament) 393
Article 365 – Notitiae Divinum Obligationis (Obligation) 394

Title VII: Divine Registers
7.1 - Divine Registers
Article 366 – Divine Register 395
Article 367 – Divine Roll 401
Article 368 – Sacred Circumscribed Space 403

Title VIII: Divine Trusts
8.1 - Divine Trusts
Article 369 – Trust 407
Article 370 – Character of Trusts 409
Article 371 – Trustor 412
Article 372 – Trustee 418
Article 373 – Beneficiary 425

Article 374 – Fiduciary 426

Article 375 – Principal 427

Article 376 – Agent 428

Article 377 – Debitor (in Trust) 429

Article 378 – Creditor (in Trust) 429

Article 379 – Ordinary Divine Trust 429

Article 380 – Aggregate Divine Trust 430

Article 381 – Supreme Divine Trust 431

Article 382 – Official Divine Trust 432

Title IX: Divine Estates

9.1 - Divine Estates

Article 383 – Divine Estate 433

Title X: Divine Money

10.1 - Divine Money

Article 384 – Money 437

Article 385 – Financial Rights and Authority 438

Article 386 – Ucadia Money 441

Article 387 – Ucadia Financial System 443

Title XI: Divine Property

11.1 - Divine Property

Article 388 – Property 447

Article 389 – Ucadia Property 449

Article 390 – Fund 449

Article 391 – Asset 451

Article 392 – Good 451

Article 393 – Sale 451

Article 394 – Bargain 452

Title XII: Divine Dominions

12.1 - Divine Dominions

Article 395 – Divine Dominion 453

Article 396 – Universal Ecclesia of One Christ 453

Article 397 – Holy Society of One Islam 454

| Article 398 – Sacred Society of One Spirit | 455 |
| Article 399 – Globe Union | 456 |

Title XIII: Divine Covenants

13.1 - Divine Covenants

Article 400 – Divine Covenant	457
Article 401 – Pactum De Singularis Caelum	457
Article 402 – Pactum De Singularis Christus	458
Article 403 – Pactum De Singularis Islam	459
Article 404 – Pactum De Singularis Spiritus	459

13.2 - Traditional Divine Covenants

| Article 405 – Traditional Divine Covenants | 460 |

Title XIV: Divine Systems

14.1 - Divine Systems

Article 406 – System	479
Article 407 – Supremum Systemata	479
Article 408 – Universalium Systemata (Universal Systems)	480
Article 409 – Custodiarum Systemata (Guardian Systems)	482
Article 410 – Angelorum Systemata (Angelic Systems)	485
Article 411 – Femininum Systemata (Feminine Systems)	488
Article 412 – Masculinum Systemata (Masculine Systems)	490
Article 413 – Officium Systemata (Offices Systems)	492
Article 414 – Sacramentum Systemata (Sacramental Systems)	493
Article 415 – Obligationum Systemata (Enforcement Systems)	495

Title XV: Divine Revelation

15.1 - Divine Systems

Article 416 – Divine Revelation	499
Article 417 – Classification of Divine Revelation	501
Article 418 – Authentication of Divine Revelation	505
Article 419 – Examples of Authentic Divine Revelation	509

15.2 - Divine Scripture

| Article 420 – Divine Scripture | 513 |
| Article 421 – Classification of Divine Scripture | 514 |

Article 422 – Authentication of Divine Scripture 517

Article 423 – Interpretation of Authentic Divine Scripture 518

Title XVI: Divine Places & Objects

16.1 - Divine Places

Article 424 – Divine Place 521

Article 425 – Sacred Place of Worship 522

Article 426 – Sacred Shrines & Altars 522

Article 427 – Sacred Cemetery & Crematorium 524

Article 428 – Sacred Buildings & Ruins 524

16.2 - Divine Objects

Article 429 – Divine Object 527

Article 430 – Sacred Vestments 528

Article 431 – Sacred Perennial & Seasonal Objects 529

Article 432 – Sacred Consumable Objects 532

Title I - Introductory Definitions

Article 1 - Rule

1. A ***Rule*** is a proper and authentic ***Law*** that describes, prohibits or permits a certain Act. A *Law* is therefore a sufficient and well formed *Rule*. — Rule

2. A ***Divine Rule*** is a proper and authentic ***Divine Law*** that describes, prohibits or permits a certain Act pertaining to a ***Divine Right*** in Trust. — Divine Rule

3. An ***Act*** or ***Action*** is the manifestation of the Mind or Will of a Being or Person expressed as an Idea, Cause, Model, Power, Motion, Effect, Expression or Thing done. — Act

4. A ***Divine Right in Trust*** is when a Right exists and is granted under *Good Faith* (Bona Fidei), *Good Conscience* (Bona Conscientia) and *Good Actions* (Bona Acta). If all three are missing or there is no Good Faith, no Right or Law exists. — Divine Right in Trust

5. A proper and authentic Rule is known as a ***Maxim*** being a norm, or bar, or canon, or axiom, or measure or standard, consistent with the present most sacred body of Laws known as the ***Divine Collection of Maxims of Law***. — Maxim

6. A valid Maxim may be derived by instruction, deduction, discovery, argument, custom or consent:- — Source of Maxims

    (i) The highest Law is a rule given by Divine instruction, as nothing may contradict such a rule; and

    (ii) The second highest Law is a proven deduction and discovery of universal and natural laws through reason and discernment of mind as a comprehensive and cohesive model, as the strongest models are consistent, useful, sensible, complete and universally applicable; and

    (iii) The third highest Law is the conclusion of an argument and debate between two or more Minds, being an edict given by a great council of wise elders or jurists, as nothing absurd and without good reason may be considered Law; and

    (iv) The fourth highest Law is the law of the People, as the consent and will of the people is the source of true authority and sovereignty within any community or society; and

    (v) The weakest rule is that of a tyrant, as any rule without authority or right of Heaven but merely by force, cannot be sustained; and the people shall eventually overcome; and render such unjust rule and unjust laws as dust.

Lex Divina: Maxims of Divine Law

7. A Law may pertain to Concepts, Objects or Persons or all three. When a Law pertains to Persons, there are four essential characters being Legislative, Executive, Juridical and Legal Persons:- Law and Concepts, Objects & Persons

   (i) A Person or group of Persons possessing the legitimate authority to form new Laws or amend or abrogate old Laws is called a "***Legislator***" or "***Legislative***"; and

   (ii) A Person possessing the legitimate authority to approve and promulgate new Laws issued by a Legislator is called a "***Sovereign***" or "***Executive***"; and

   (iii) A Person or group of Persons possessing the legitimate authority to interpret and administer the Law is called "***Juridic***" or "***Juridical***"; and

   (iv) A Person or group of Persons who are the subject of certain laws as promulgated may be called "***Subjects***" or "***Legal***".

8. All Maxims may be defined by the twenty-two most sacred books of the body of Laws known as the *Divine Collection of Maxims of Law* in accord with Article 135 of the most sacred Covenant *Pactum De Singularis Caelum,* namely:- Maxims and Divine Collection of Maxims

   (i) ***Lex Divina***: Maxims of Divine Law; and

   (ii) ***Lex Naturae***: Maxims of Natural Law; and

   (iii) ***Lex Cognitum***: Maxims of Cognitive Law; and

   (iv) ***Lex Positivum***: Maxims of Positive Law; and

   (v) ***Lex Ecclesiasticum***: Maxims of Ecclesiastical Law; and

   (vi) ***Lex Virtus Naturae***: Maxims of Bioethics Law; and

   (vii) ***Lex Regia***: Maxims of Sovereign Law; and

   (viii) ***Lex Fidei***: Maxims of Fiduciary Law; and

   (ix) ***Lex Administratum***: Maxims of Administrative Law; and

   (x) ***Lex Economica***: Maxims of Economic Law; and

   (xi) ***Lex Pecuniaria***: Maxims of Monetary Law; and

   (xii) ***Lex Civilis***: Maxims of Civil Law; and

   (xiii) ***Lex Criminalis***: Maxims of Criminal Law; and

   (xiv) ***Lex Educationis***: Maxims of Education Law; and

   (xv) ***Lex Nutrimens Et Medicina***: Maxims of Food & Drugs

Law; and

- (xvi) **Lex Urbanus**: Maxims of Urban Law; and
- (xvii) **Lex Societatis**: Maxims of Company Law; and
- (xviii) **Lex Technologiae**: Maxims of Technology Law; and
- (xix) **Lex Commercii**: Maxims of Trade & Intellectual Property Law; and
- (xx) **Lex Securitas**: Maxims of Security Law; and
- (xxi) **Lex Militaris**: Maxims of Military Law; and
- (xxii) **Lex Gentium**: Maxims of International Law.

9. In accord with Article 135 of the most sacred Covenant *Pactum De Singularis Caelum*, each of the three (3) Great Faiths shall be permitted to use their own official name for the Divine Collection of Maxims of Law:- Official Name of Divine Collection of Maxims of Law

   - (i) The Universal Ecclesia of One Christ may use the name **Astrum Iuris Divini Canonum** to officially define the *Divine Collection of Maxims of Law* from the perspective of their authority; and furthermore may name the individual books as "canons"; and

   - (ii) The Holy Society of One Islam may use the name **Hikmat Samawi** to officially define the *Divine Collection of Maxims of Law* from the perspective of their authority; and furthermore may name the individual books as "qanunlar"; and

   - (iii) Sacred Society of One Spirit may use the name **Pragya Dharma** to officially define the *Divine Collection of Maxims of Law* from the perspective of their authority; and furthermore may name the individual books as "vedas".

10. A valid Maxim neither abrogates nor derogates from the most sacred Covenant *Pactum De Singularis Caelum*. — Maxims & Sacred Covenant

11. Any Rule that is not consistent with the most sacred body of Laws known as *Divine Collection of Maxims of Law* cannot therefore be considered or claimed as Law. — Rules & Divine Collection of Maxims

12. Whenever the terms Canon, or Rule or Law are used, they shall mean first and foremost the present body of valid Maxims and those Rules and Laws in accord with it and no other. — Valid Maxims

13. No valid Canon that belongs to the sacred body of Laws known as — Maxims &

Divine Collection of Maxims of Law may be declared in error, abrogated, derogated or suspended, except by a competent forum of Law possessing such authority as defined and derived from the most sacred Covenant *Pactum De Singularis Caelum*.   *Forum Declarations*

14. In the event that a competent forum of Law possessing such authority as defined and derived from the most sacred Covenant *Pactum De Singularis Caelum* declares one or more Maxims that belong to the sacred body of Laws known as *Divine Collection of Maxims of Law* as being in error, then such Maxims shall hereby be temporarily severed from the rest of the body of Laws to the extent that such a clause or Canon is void, or invalid and unenforceable. Furthermore, any such ruling or action shall not affect the validity or enforceability of the remainder of the sacred body of Laws.   *Maxims & Severability*

15. Any law that is against the authentic truth of these present sacred Maxims cannot be Law.   *Maxims & Law*

Article 2 - Divine

16. The **Divine** means:-   *Divine*

    (i) Every thought and non-thought of mind or awareness; and

    (ii) Every meaning and non-meaning; and

    (iii) Every possible and impossible thing and non-thing; and

    (iv) Every knowable and unknowable concept, object, element, rule or force; and

    (v) Every real and unreal dimension or universe; and

    (vi) Every manifest and unmanifest object; and

    (vii) Every title and name including (but not limited to) the Absolute, ALL, Divine Creator, Father, God, Almighty, Allah, Great Spirit, Unique Collective Awareness, UCADIA and all other historic, customary and traditional names when used to describe the greatest of all possibilities.

17. The Divine may be described as the Set of all Sets, including the Empty Set as the Divine is ultimately beyond any possible words or limits.   *The Divine as Set of all Sets including the Empty Set*

18. The Divine means One as the "concept of all concepts" and the "set of all sets". There is no other. Therefore, every other possible concept or object or set is lesser.   *No Greater Concept or Set*

19. As the Divine means "the set of all sets including the empty set" and all things and all non-things, the Divine is by definition the ultimate paradox. There is none greater. *(The Divine as the Ultimate Paradox)*

20. The most accurate description of the Divine is the name ***Unique Collective Awareness*** defining perfectly the name and paradox of the Divine. *(Unique Collective Awareness)*

21. As the concept of the Divine clearly exists in theory, regardless of any claim of existence or non-existence in reality, any argument that asserts the Divine does not exist is therefore false, absurd and in gross error. *(Existence of Divine)*

22. The Divine and lesser manifestations of the Divine are part of the Divine and Unique:- *(Divine and lesser manifestations of the Divine)*

    (i) The Divine manifest as a form of Supreme Being in context to the Universe and the Existence of Life is lesser than the absolute meaning of the Divine; and

    (ii) The Divine manifest as the physical Universe of Rules and Matter is lesser than the form of Supreme Being and lesser than the absolute meaning of the Divine.

23. While all possible and actual concepts, objects and sets of concepts and objects are by definition part of the Divine, it is an absurdity to impute the Divine in totality as actually being less than the "concept of all concepts" and the "set of all sets" unless describing a proper personification of the Divine. *(Absurd Reasoning)*

24. The use of different words, or titles or terms associated with certain traditional and customary rites to describe the Divine is perfectly reasonable and acceptable, providing such words, or titles or terms do not diminish the nature and totality of the Divine. *(Traditional & Customary Terms for Divine)*

25. The use of different words, or titles or terms associated with certain traditional and customary rites to describe the Divine shall always be resolved in the affirmative in reference to describing the maximum personification of all possible concepts, objects, sets and existences, unless such language clearly and unambiguously defines some lesser Divinity. *(Affirmative Resolution of Traditional & Customary Terms for Divine)*

26. The most accurate description of the personification of the Divine is Unique Collective Awareness. Therefore, all forms of Life, particularly Higher Order Life may be properly described as Unique Collective Awareness, or the personification of the Divine. *(Use of term Unique Collective Awareness)*

27. Any doctrine or rule that is against such truth of the Divine, cannot *(Conflict of Maxims)*

be Law.

Article 3 - Divine Law

28. ***Divine Law*** is the Law that defines the Divine and clearly demonstrates the spirit, mind, purpose and instruction of the Divine including the operation of the will of the Divine through existence. All authoritative and legitimate Law is derived from Divine Law in accord with the present sacred Maxims.
Divine Law

29. ***Natural Law*** is the law that defines the operation of the will of the Divine through its existence in the form of matter and physical rules. As Natural Laws define the operation and existence of the physical universe, all proper and authentic Natural Law may be said to be derived from Divine Law.
Natural Law

30. ***Cognitive Law*** is the set of laws that define the special attributes possessed by certain higher order life such as mind, ideas, knowledge, recognition and self-awareness created through the simultaneous application of both Divine Law and Natural Law. As Cognitive Law is derived from the simultaneous application of Divine Law and Natural Law, all valid Cognitive Law may be defined as part "divine" and part "natural", hence "supernatural".
Cognitive Law

31. ***Positive Law*** is the set of laws enacted by valid associations of living higher order beings through proper authority in accordance with these Maxims for the governance of a body or community or society. All valid Positive Law may be said to be derived from authentic Natural Law and Cognitive Law.
Positive Law

32. ***Ecclesiastical Law*** is the body of doctrines, declarations, statutes and ordinances of a religious and moral society, issued by proper authority in accordance with Divine Law and the present Maxims for the moderation and governance of its members.
Ecclesiastical Law

33. As Divine Law is the highest possible form of Law and the source of all lesser forms of law, any argument that asserts Divine Law does not exist, or is less than some other form of law is therefore false, absurd and in gross error.
Divine Law as highest possible form of Law

34. A Divine Law cannot be written or created, only instructed by Divine Revelation and Divine Grace in accordance with these Maxims.
Divine Revelation

35. A Divine Law is its own proof as evidenced by its existence in accord with these Maxims.
Divine Law is its own proof

36. A Natural Law or Cognitive Law cannot be written or created, only discovered or revealed in accord with the present sacred Maxims.
Discovery of Natural or Cognitive Law

37.	A Natural Law or Cognitive Law cannot abrogate, suspend, nor change a Divine Law. Therefore, any rule claimed to be Natural Law or Cognitive Law that usurps, denies or contradicts a Divine Law is null and void from the beginning, having no valid or legitimate force or effect whatsoever.	Limits of Natural and Cognitive Law
38.	A Positive Law cannot abrogate, suspend, nor change a Cognitive Law or Natural Law. Therefore, any rule claimed to be Positive Law that usurps, denies or contradicts a Natural Law or Cognitive Law is null and void from the beginning, having no valid or legitimate force or effect whatsoever.	Limits of Positive Law
39.	An Ecclesiastical Law cannot abrogate, suspend, nor change a Divine Law, Cognitive Law or Natural Law. Therefore, any rule claimed to be Ecclesiastical Law that usurps, denies or contradicts a Divine Law, Natural Law or Cognitive Law is null and void from the beginning, having no valid or legitimate force or effect whatsoever.	Limits of Ecclesiastical Law
40.	Any rule that is contrary to the prescript of Divine Law in accord with the present Sacred Maxims, is therefore reprobate, suppressed and not permitted to be revived.	Suppression of contradictory rules

Article 4 - The Law

41.	***The Law*** in Name, Claim, Vow or Oath refers to the present body of valid Maxims and those Rules in accord with it and no other.	The Law
42.	A Divine Law is established ab initio (from the beginning), irrespective of its first date of promulgation.	Establishment of Divine Law
43.	A Divine Law binds every possible dimension and all of Heaven and Earth everywhere for all those for whom it was issued.	Effect of Divine Law
44.	A Natural Law or Cognitive Law is established *ab initio* (from the beginning), of a particular life bearing planet or higher order species irrespective of its first date of promulgation.	Establishment of Natural or Cognitive Law
45.	A Natural Law or Cognitive Law binds everywhere all those for whom it was issued.	Effect of Natural or Cognitive Law
46.	A Positive Law is established and takes force when it is promulgated in accord with these Maxims; and begins to oblige a month after the day of promulgation unless the Law itself establishes another time period.	Establishment of Positive Law
47.	Excluding Ecclesiastical Law, all Positive Laws regard the present and future, not the past. Only Ecclesiastical Laws may refer to the past as such laws by their nature are firmly bound to Divine Law.	Excluding Ecclesiastical Law, Positive Law binds future not past Acts

48. Any Positive Law that seeks to promulgate a retrospective rule that is not Ecclesiastical in nature or authority is by definition morally repugnant and shall have no validity or legitimacy or force or effect. *Retrospective Positive Law having no force or effect*

49. Any Positive Law that is morally repugnant contradicts the very nature of what is Law; and therefore cannot be a valid or legitimate Law; and shall have no force or effect from the moment it is enacted. *Morally Repugnant Positive Law*

50. Ecclesiastical Law binds all those who belong and have been accepted into the body of a valid faith in accord with the most sacred Covenant *Pactum De Singularis Caelum* and associated Covenants. *Effect of Ecclesiastical Law*

51. All other lesser Positive Laws issued by a competent legislator bind those who are actually present within the jurisdiction of the particular juridic or legislative or political body. *Lesser Positive Laws*

52. Particular Positive Laws are not presumed to be personal but territorial in relation to the jurisdiction of the competent legislator who issued the law, unless it is otherwise evident. *Territorial effect of Positive Laws*

53. Any rule that is against the Law cannot have the legitimacy and validity of Law, nor the force and effect of Law. *Rules that are against the Law*

Article 5 - Rule of Law

54. The **Rule of Law** exists only when:- *Rule of Law*

    (i) All laws are simple and easily publicly available so that one person may reasonably learn, remember and comprehend all such laws properly; and

    (ii) All laws are respectful so that no law disrespects a person purely upon the original circumstance of their birth, location, gender, race, religion or creed; and

    (iii) All laws are logical so that no law is illogical in asserting certain errors and fallacies to demand such absurdities are defended and enforced; and

    (iv) All laws are reasonable so that no law demands an unreasonable or impossible act; and

    (v) All laws are consistent so that no laws require contradictory or confusing behaviour; and

    (vi) All laws are honest so that no law misrepresents the truth nor compels deliberately dishonest or fraudulent behaviour; and

    (vii) All laws are loyal so that no law endorses treacherous or disloyal acts; and

    (viii) All laws are moral so that no law permits morally repugnant, or profane or sacrilegious activity; and

(ix) All laws are remedial so that no law imposes punitive measures without first the opportunity to rectify or remedy an error; and

(x) All laws are merciful so that no law encourages cruel and barbarous acts of vengeance.

55. The operation of the true Rule of Law is fundamental in maintaining and nurturing the connection between Heaven and Earth and between Divine Law, Natural Law, Cognitive Law and all forms of valid and legitimate Positive Law. *Fundamental Importance of Rule of Law*

56. When the Rule of Law ceases to exist within the jurisdiction and context of a particular fraternity, association, entity, institute, company or society, then all authority flowing through Divine Law, Natural Law, Cognitive Law and Positive Law to such a body also ceases, until properly restored. *Cessation of Rule of Law*

57. Whilst the Rule of Law and authority of a particular fraternity, association, entity, institute, company or society ceases, then all such subsequent acts, edicts, orders and transfers are unlawful and without any force or effect in law, irrespective of any claims to the contrary. *Effect of Cessation of Rule of Law*

58. Whilst the Rule of Law and authority of a particular fraternity, association, entity, institute, company or society ceases, full liability shall rest upon the most senior ranks of such a body and their refusal to surrender, resign, abdicate, confess or cease. *Full Liability on Leaders when Cessation of Rule of Law*

59. No tyrant that injures the Rule of Law may then claim its protection or immunity from the consequences of their actions. *No protection for tyrants*

60. A person or body belonging to a separate fraternity, association, entity, institute, company or society that then aids a tyrant in suppressing the true Rule of Law of another body, is equally and jointly liable for the actions of the tyrant as if they themselves directly performed such offences. *Equal and joint liability*

61. When the Rule of Law and authority of a particular fraternity, association, entity, institute, company or society ceases, then all such authority, power, control, rights and enforcement returns to the next level of authority under Positive Law:- *Authority Shift when Cessation of Rule of Law*

(i) If the political bodies of a particular society cause the cessation of the Rule of Law, then such authority temporarily returns to the judicial bodies of the society until the Rule of Law is restored politically; and

(ii) If the judicial bodies of a particular society cause the cessation of the Rule of Law, then such authority temporarily returns to the ecclesiastical bodies of the society until the Rule of Law is restored judicially and politically; and

(iii) If the ecclesiastical bodies of a particular society as well as the political and judicial bodies cause the cessation of the Rule of Law, then the people are empowered to liberate themselves of such tyranny until the Rule of Law is properly restored.

62. When a Rule is in accord with the Law, then it may be legitimately considered a Law, having the full force and effect of the Law. However, when a rule is against the Law, it has neither force nor effect of Law. — *Rule against the Law cannot be Law*

Article 6 - Justice

63. ***Justice*** is the set of lawful Rights and obligations of use defined by the present Maxims and those Laws consistent with the Golden Rule of Law; and the Rights and obligations associated with the proper administration and enforcement of the present Maxims and such Laws in good faith, good conscience and good character. — *Justice*

64. Whenever the word Justice is used, it shall mean first and foremost the present Maxims and Rules and Law above all other lesser forms of Law. — *Justice and present Maxims*

65. All Rights and therefore all forms of proper Justice originate from Heaven and Divine Law and therefore the most sacred Covenant *Pactum De Singularis Caelum*:- — *Divine Source of Justice*

(i) Divine Law is the law that defines the Divine and all creation, and demonstrates the spirit and mind and instruction of the Divine, and the operation of the will of the Divine Creator through existence. Therefore all valid Rights and Justice are derived from Divine Law; and

(ii) Natural Law is the law that defines the operation of the will of the Divine, through the existence of form and sky and earth and physical rules. Thus Natural Law governs the operation of what we can see and name; and

(iii) The laws of People as Positive Laws are those rules enacted by men and women having proper authority, for the good governance of a society under the Rule of Law. The laws of People are always inherited from Natural Law and Divine Law.

66. Notwithstanding all valid Rights concerning Justice as defined in accord with the present Maxims:- — *Principles of Justice*

(i) All are equal under the law; and all are accountable and answerable under the law, and all are without blemish until proven culpable; and

(ii) Where there is a law there must be a cause; and where there is a law there must be a penalty; and where there is a law there must be a remedy; and

(iii) An action in law cannot proceed without first a cause; and an action is not granted to one who is not injured; for the action of a valid law can do no harm (injury); and no injury to the law means no valid cause for action by law; and

(iv) No one may derive an advantage in law from his own wrong, as no action through law can arise from a fraud before heaven and earth; and it is a fraud to conceal a fraud; and fraud invalidates everything of a cause and action, for no action through law can arise in bad faith or unclean hands or vexatious prejudice; and

(v) What was illegitimate, fraudulent and invalid from the beginning does not become valid over time; and

(vi) An action alone does not make one culpable unless there is intent to do wrong, or evidence of deliberate and wilful ignorance contrary to reasonable behaviour. Similarly, no one may suffer punishment by valid law for mere intent alone; and no one is punished for the transgression of an ancestor or another; and

(vii) No one is accused of the same exact cause twice; and No man or woman be a judge over their own matter; nor a man or woman possess the authority of heaven to be judge, jury and executioner; and

(viii) No penalty may exist without a valid law; and no penalty may be issued without first proof of injury and secondly the right of defence.

67. In respect of Justice and the individual:- *Justice & Individual*

(i) All possess the Right to be heard even if such speech be controversial; and

(ii) All possess the Right of free will to choose our actions and destiny; and

(iii) All possess the Right of reason that distinguishes them from lesser animals; and

(iv) All possess the Right to informed consent or withdraw

consent; and

(v) All possess the Right over their body that none may claim our flesh; and

(vi) All possess the Right of our divine self that none may claim our soul; and

(vii) Thus no man can make a blood oath on their flesh or vow on their soul, nor may any man claim servitude or obligation under such an abomination, for such Rights are granted solely by heaven to all people, and no man or body of jurists have the authority to usurp heaven; and

(viii) All true authority and power to rule is inherited from heaven, and to only those men in good faith and good character and good conscience, who then make a sacred oath in trust and form an office, whereby such Divine Rights are conveyed for only so long as they honour their oath and obligations to serve the people; and

(ix) For whenever a man who makes an oath to form a sacred trust of office, then breaks such an oath through prejudice or unclean hands or bad faith, then all such authority and power ceases from them, as the cord between heaven and earth is severed and the trust dissolved.

68. Justice exists when:- *Existence of Justice*

(i) All Laws are written, simple and visible so that one person may reasonably learn, remember and comprehend all such laws properly; and no laws are hidden or secret; and

(ii) All laws are respectful so that no law disrespects a person purely upon the original circumstance of their birth, location, gender, race, religion or creed; and

(iii) All laws are logical so that no law is illogical in asserting certain errors and fallacies to demand such absurdities are defended and enforced; and

(iv) All laws are reasonable so that no law demands an unreasonable or impossible act; and

(v) All laws are consistent so that no laws require contradictory or confusing behaviour; and

(vi) All laws are honest so that no law misrepresents the truth nor compels deliberately dishonest or fraudulent behaviour; and

(vii) All laws are loyal so that no law endorses treacherous or disloyal acts; and

- (viii) All laws are moral so that no law permits morally repugnant, or profane or sacrilegious activity; and
- (ix) All laws are remedial so that no law imposes punitive measures without first the opportunity to rectify or remedy an error; and
- (x) All laws are merciful so that no law encourages cruel and barbarous acts of vengeance.

69. Justice must always be impartial, objective and seen to be without prejudice. Therefore, no one may adjudicate a question of law with apprehended bias against one or more parties. *Impartiality and Justice*

70. Justice never contradicts the true Rule of Law. *Rule of Law*

71. Justice must always have clean hands. Therefore, no one may adjudicate a question having a secret or undisclosed financial interests in the conclusion of the matter in favour of a particular verdict. *Clean Hands and Justice*

72. By definition Justice can never be present nor rendered within a forum of law, if the Rule of Law itself is absent. *Absence of Rule of Law & Justice*

73. Though all else fails, let true Justice be done above all. *Let Justice be Done*

Article 7 - Fair Process

74. **Fair Process**, also known as Due Process, is the impartial, competent and fair administration of Justice by suitably qualified persons associated with one or more authorised forums of law. *Fair Process*

75. Every Controversy in Law as a valid action must be resolved promptly, reasonably and justly through Fair Process, without fear or favour. *Controversy in Law*

76. No valid action in law should proceed without first a valid cause; and no valid cause exists until such a claim is first tested. Thus the birth of all action in law must begin with the claim:- *Requirement of Cause of Action*

    - (i) If a claim be not proven as a valid cause then the accused has nothing to answer. Yet if the claim be proved to have merit as a cause, then all valid causes in law must be resolved; and
    - (ii) Thus, he who first brings the claim must first prove its merit, as the burden of the proof lies upon him who accuses not he who denies.

77. The gravest threat against Justice is the failure to prosecute perjury *Perjury as enemy of Justice*

and all forms of fraud and contempt against the fair administration of justice to the fullest extent:-   *and Rule of Law*

    (i)   One who brings false accusation is the gravest of transgressors, that they injure not only the law, but the bonds of law between Heaven and Earth; and

    (ii)   One who makes false testimony, especially under oath within a forum of law, must face the full force of justice against them; and

    (iii)   No one should be tolerated who seeks to gain advantage or profit through the manipulation or abuse of the administration of justice.

78. When men wish to settle their dispute among themselves, then they shall have the right to make peace. If a dispute cannot be settled before seeking a judge, then both the accused and the accuser must be granted equal hearing.   *Right to Settle*

79. A valid claim is when an accuser makes a formal complaint in writing under oath, bringing two reliable witnesses as proof to the substance of the complaint and petitions a competent forum of law for remedy:-   *Nature of valid Claim*

    (i)   If merit of a cause be proved, the one accused must appear to answer; and

    (ii)   The one accused and any witnesses appear by summons; and

    (iii)   When anyone be summonsed, he must immediately appear without hesitation; and

    (iv)   If a man or his legal counsel summonsed does not appear or refuses to appear to answer, then let him be seized by force to come and appear; and

    (v)   When anyone who has been summonsed then seeks to evade, or attempts to flee, let the one who was summonsed be arrested to prevent their escape. One who flees fair judgement confesses his culpability.

80. An accused cannot be judged until after the accusations are spoken and then after the accused exercises or declines their three rights to defence:-   *Right of valid Defence*

    (i)   The first right of the Accused is called Prolocution upon the hearing of the Complaint; and the right to speak as a matter of law, and why the complaint and investigation should not continue; and

    (ii)   The second right of the Accused is called Collocution upon establishing Jurisdiction and the presentment of the

       Indictment; and the right to speak as to why the complaint and accusation is in fundamental error and upon such proof why the burden should now be placed on the accuser; and

  (iii)   The third and final right of the Accused is called Adlocution being a final speech in defence, against an accusation having been heard.

81. In respect of any defence against an accusation:-   *Requirements of Defence*

  (i)   The accused must always be afforded the presumption of innocence until culpability or exoneration is proven, unless by their behaviour or testimony the accused first confesses their culpability; and

  (ii)   The accused possesses the right to self defence in all minor matters but not in the defence of notorious and serious accusations, unless they first are able to prove their competence at law; and

  (iii)   The accused possesses the right to a trial by their peers or a tribunal of jurists; and

  (iv)   The accused is not obliged to confess their culpability or innocence once the issue of a complaint is proven as having merit. However, the failure to confess to culpability before the commencement of trial is the formal acknowledgement of a lack of contrition; and any consequential sentence must factor the maximum and reasonable penalty; and

  (v)   An accused cannot be found culpable unless three pieces of evidence may be attributed to culpability as first presented as part of the complaint or as a result of a subsequent investigation, or hearing or trial; and

  (vi)   Judges are bound to explain the reason of their judgement.

82. Any forum of law that proceeds with matters in contradiction to the present Maxims therefore possesses no authority or jurisdiction whatsoever.

Lex Divina: Maxims of Divine Law

Title II - Divine Concepts

2.1 Absolute Concepts

Article 8 - Concept

83. A ***Concept*** is any Idea received, conceived, perceived, comprehended or discerned by an Observer to exist according to some unique form of Meaning. — Concept

84. A Concept is properly distinguished from an Object in that a Concept is said to exist purely within the dimension of Mind, whereas an Object is considered to exist within the dimension of Reality. — Concept vs. Object

85. The greatest Concept is the Divine as the total set of all meanings and definitions of all possible concepts, objects, matter, rules, life, mind, universe and spirit; and also known as the Absolute, ALL, Divine Creator, Father, God, Almighty, Allah, Great Spirit, Unique Collective Awareness, Ucadia and all other historic, customary and traditional names when used to describe the greatest of all possibilities. — Greatest Concept

86. The smallest possible and least significant Concept is Nothing or "No-Thing". No Concept can be smaller or less than Nothing. — Smallest Concept

87. As the ***Divine*** means the "concept of all concepts" and the "set of all sets" there is no greater concept nor set. Therefore, every other possible concept or object is greater than Nothing and less than the Absolute, except the Divine. — Concept of Concepts

88. As ***Ucadia*** means the complete and total Concept of the Divine and the Divine means the Concept of Ucadia, the total set of all meanings and definitions of all possible concepts, objects, matter, rules, life, mind, universe and spirit may be defined as the Concept of Ucadia in accord with the most sacred Covenant *Pactum De Singularis Caelum*:- — Concept of Ucadia

    (i) A Concept that is in accord with the present Maxims and the Divine and Ucadia is said to belong to the Set of Concepts of Ucadia that are true and valid and legitimate; and

    (ii) A Concept that is not in accord with the present Maxims and the Divine and Ucadia is said to belong to the Set of Concepts of Ucadia that are absurd or untrue and invalid and illegitimate; and

    (iii) The presence of an Unreal Set of absurd, or untrue, or invalid or illegitimate Concepts as a valid Set within Ucadia cannot in itself be argued that Ucadia is therefore contradictory, absurd, illegitimate, invalid or untrue, as the presence of such a set proves the necessary completeness of the "set of sets"; and

Lex Divina: Maxims of Divine Law

    (iv)   No Concept or Idea or Meaning can possibly exist outside the absolute jurisdiction and authority of Ucadia. Therefore, All Concepts and Ideas and Meaning are completely and absolutely under the jurisdiction and authority of Ucadia.

89.   The very meaning of Concept itself depends upon the presence of three essential elements: *Elements Of Concept*

    (i)   The existence of an Idea (some representation with Meaning) as the "thing observed"; and

    (ii)   An Observer; and

    (iii)   The action of observing with some level of Awareness in Mind that the thing observed possesses a certain unique form of Meaning.

90.   The necessary action of observation by an Observer of an Idea is always relative and always unique; as the position of the Observer, the state of mind of the Observer and the occurrence of observation when taken collectively is a unique event never to be repeated in exactly the same way again.   *Observer As A Position*

91.   As the action of an Observer is always relative to some degree, it is a falsity, error and absurdity to conclude that a Concept not witnessed by a particular Observer does not exist: *Existence of Observed Concept*

    (i)   Even if the Observer is defined as the Absolute Divine, the very fact that an Idea must be postulated in order to frame the hypothesis means that every Idea exists in theory at some level, no matter how unreal or improbable; and

    (ii)   Thus, every Idea received, conceived, perceived, comprehended or discerned by an Observer less than the Divine possesses existence even if the same lesser Observer no longer is present or actively observing the Idea.

92.   A Concept always depends upon some level of Awareness in the Mind of the Observer to distinguish the certain unique form of Meaning of an Idea from another. The absence of any distinction or awareness in the Mind of the Observer therefore, negates the nature and existence of a distinct and unique Concept.   *Awareness of Concept*

93.   The correct observation and classification of Concepts depends upon two major variables being the nature and complexity of the Idea itself and secondly the level of Awareness in the Mind of the Observer: *Classification of Concept*

    (i)   An Idea may be a simple generalisation or abstraction of a highly complex and detailed Model. Therefore, it does not follow that Ideas or Models are always less or more complex or less or more detailed than "real world Objects"; and

(ii) The level of Awareness in the Mind of the Observer is the most significant factor in determining the level of simplicity, or complexity or accuracy of a Concept. A poor or erroneous level of Awareness in the Mind of the Observer may cause even the simplest Ideas to be misrepresented and wrongly categorised.

Article 9 - Meaning

94. ***Meaning*** is the elemental semantic or symbolic significance or purpose or values associated with a Concept or Object; and the intended effect or change or thought sought in the mind of the Observer.

    Meaning

95. In respect of Meaning:-

    Meaning as a Value

    (i) As a sign or symbol, Meaning is a unit of semantic value in the context of other values, normally via some formal Language, to enable the transmission and reception of information and knowledge. Hence, letters, phonemes, words and sentences are all forms of Meaning in the context of a Language; and

    (ii) As an intentional effect or change or thought in the mind of the Observer, Meaning is the elementary unit of a properly formed Model of knowledge based upon one or more Languages. Hence, philosophy, science and religious teachings are all Models of Meaning.

96. As Meaning requires both the prior existence of some formal system of Language and Model, the absence of a coherent Model or Language negates the ability to discern certain Meaning.

    Existence of Meaning

97. As all Meaning depends upon some formal system of Language and Models of Knowledge, the quality and design of such systems of Language and Model therefore affects the ability of the Observer to think and observe.

    Meaning Versus Observer

98. The strength of a Concept is its relation to other unique forms of Meaning. Therefore, the strength of a Concept is its Meaning in relation to one or more formal systems of Language and Models of Knowledge.

    Concept relating to Meaning

99. The Divine Language and system of receiving and transmitting Meaning through speech and writing is the Ucadia Language of Logos:

    Logos

    (i) ***Logos*** is a two dimensional linear visual and spoken language based on common phoneme elements that are found in all major languages to produce the most efficient, clear and consistent expressions of Meaning; and

(ii) Logos is founded on five symbolic elements of Meaning called "KA" representing five generalisations in the production of sound namely lips, teeth, tongue, top of mouth and throat. These symbolic elements are then used to create more complex symbols representing the formation of consonants and vowels; and

(iii) The symbolic representation of vowels and consonants are called "BA" symbolic elements representing 22 possible vowels and 33 possible consonants; and

(iv) BA symbolic elements are then arranged in combinations or stand alone vowels to produce the spirit and essence of meaning called "LA" whereby the stable unit of Meaning is a vowel followed by a constant (VC) or its reverse (CV). There exists 1452 possible combinations (VC and CV) of BA Symbolic elements and with the 22 vowels on their own gives a total set of LA of 1474 possible symbols; and

(v) The simplest way to learn the Logos set is by applying it to an existing foreign language first until familiarity of the units of sound and their symbols are mastered; and

(vi) When the units of sound and their symbols in Logos are mastered, Logos can then be used to speak almost any major language, even if the user is not yet fully aware of the Meaning of the words they are producing. This is called "speaking of the tongues".

100. The Divine Language and system of receiving and transmitting multi-linear (3 dimensional) Meaning is the Ucadia Language of Psygos: *Psygos*

(i) **Psygos** is a three-dimensional and purely symbolic language of reasoning, learning, thought and wisdom; and

(ii) Psygos defines all knowledge of all possible Concepts and Objects into eleven major categories with each unique Concept represented by a standard shape, called a DA, namely: Divine, Universal, Rules, Matter, Galactic Objects, Stellar Objects, Planetary Objects, Life, Complex Life, Higher Order Life and Homo Sapien Life; and

(iii) The primary components of Psygos are Concepts and Objects (called DA) and their associated attributes that modify them (called MODIFIERS), bridge associations between concepts and objects (called RELATORS), associations that bridge between DA and MODIFIERS and/or RELATORS (called ASSOCIATORS) and tense/perspective (called TENSORS); and

(iv) All the primary components of Psygos are then used to construct rich varieties of symbolic sentences called DIA.

101. All possible Meaning is encompassed within Ucadia such that no Meaning may exist that is not subject to the absolute authority and jurisdiction of Ucadia in accord with the most sacred Covenant *Pactum De Singularis Caelum*:

    (i) Any Meaning that is in accord with the present Maxims is said to belong to the Set of Meanings of Ucadia that are true and valid and legitimate; and

    (ii) A Meaning that is not in accord with the present Maxims is said to belong to the Set of Meanings of Ucadia that are absurd or untrue and invalid and illegitimate; and

    (iii) The presence of an Unreal Set of absurd, or untrue, or invalid or illegitimate Meanings as a valid Set within Ucadia cannot in itself be argued that Ucadia is therefore contradictory, absurd, illegitimate, invalid or untrue, as the presence of such a set proves the necessary completeness of the "set of sets".

    <small>Meaning defined in Ucadia</small>

102. As all possible Meaning is encompassed within Ucadia such that no Meaning may exist that is not subject to the absolute authority and jurisdiction of Ucadia:-

    (i) The first Meaning of any Concept listed within Ucadia as true and valid and legitimate shall be the Meaning defined by Ucadia; and

    (ii) Any Meaning of any Concept that is not consistent with the Meaning defined by Ucadia shall therefore belong to the Set of Meanings of Ucadia that are absurd or untrue and invalid and illegitimate.

    <small>Ucadia Jurisdiction over Meaning</small>

103. Any Meaning that is not in accord with the present sacred Maxims is invalid.

    <small>Meaning Versus Maxims</small>

104. Whenever one speaks or writes or signifies Meaning, it shall refer to the present sacred Maxims and all associated Languages and Models of Knowledge first and foremost.

    <small>Meaning within Maxims</small>

Article 10 - Idea

105. An ***Idea*** in its simplest terms is a *conceptual archetype*; or *mental representation* associated with some distinct Meaning. — Idea

106. An Idea is properly distinguished from a Model in that an Idea exists purely in Mind and is free to exist without necessary dependence to such constraints of one or more Systems of rules and relations, whereas a Model is said to exist according to a System of one or more rules and relations. — Existence of Idea

107. In relation to the two essential types of Ideas:- — Idea Types

  (i) As a *conceptual archetype*, an Idea is considered a perfect example or "ideal" whereby other similar types of Concepts or Objects might be compared. Therefore, any form of Rules may also be considered an Idea; and

  (ii) As a *mental representation*, an Idea may be some non-sensory computation or cognition (i.e. a thought); or some sensory symbolism (i.e. sound or image) or perceived dimension of objective existence (i.e. vision). Therefore, all Thoughts and Dreams may be considered in one sense as Ideas.

108. When an Idea is expressed vocally, or committed to paper or some electronic medium, then strictly such an Idea becomes a Model, as its expression is dependent upon at least one System of rules and relations of Language and secondly the limits of the System and medium of storage. — Idea as a Model

109. The very existence of an Idea itself depends upon the presence of some representation of Meaning. In the absence of any Meaning an Idea cannot be said to exist. — Idea as a representation of Meaning

110. The existence of an Idea merely depends upon the presence of some distinct representation and unit of Meaning and not any claimed acceptance or validation or arguments in support of or against such a representation by an Observer. Therefore, the existence of an Idea is itself proof of its own existence. — Idea as a proof of its Existence

111. All Ideas may be defined by the computation or sensory nature of such mental representation, whether such representation has a real-world relation or whether such representation is simplified (abstract) or detailed. The most complex Ideas are multi-sensory, complex and visually detailed. Such Ideas are often classified as "Dreams". — Ideas as a Computation

112. All Ideas as Models that qualify to be called Dreams, share the same essential elements: — Idea as a Dream

(i) The Idea as a Dream is *dimensional* in that it perceives a construct whereby certain objects exist within a certain dimension defined by some form of boundary; and

(ii) The Idea as a Dream is *objective* in that the Dreamer as Observer therefore observes the Dream as a singular Object as the Observer can observe a "Dream within a Dream" but not two dreams of equal weight being simultaneously observed by a single Observer; and

(iii) The Idea as a Dream is *formal* in that the Dreamer as Observer therefore observes within the boundary of the Dream (Object) two or more Objects possessing some kind of form that can clearly be distinguished and recognised according to some system of rules and knowledge; and

(iv) The Idea as a Dream is *contextual* in that the Dreamer as Observer therefore observes within the boundary of the Dream (Object) two or more Objects whereby one or more Objects serve as the formal surroundings, circumstances, environment, background or settings of the Dream and one or more other Objects serve as the subject of observation; and

(v) The Idea as a Dream is *sequential* in that the events within the Dream unfolds in a sequence, even if chronological time is perceived differently; and

(vi) The Idea as a Dream is *real* in that the Dreamer as Observer validates and witnesses the Dream as an actual Object of existence; and within the Dream the objects have a real and material context, according to one or more rules and limits, even if such Objects do not exist or cannot exist in another form of reality.

113. The most complex Vision or Dream is the Concept of Existence of the Divine as Absolute Observer of Existence and the Universe as expressed by the present Maxims and the Ucadia Model. *Dream as a Concept of Existence*

114. All possible Ideas are circumscribed within Ucadia such that no Idea may exist that is not subject to the absolute authority and jurisdiction of Ucadia in accord with the most sacred Covenant *Pactum De Singularis Caelum*: *Ideas within the jurisdiction of Ucadia*

(i) Any Idea that is in accord with the present Maxims is said to belong to the Set of Ideas of Ucadia that are true and valid and legitimate; and

(ii) An Idea that is not in accord with the present Maxims is said to belong to the Set of Ideas of Ucadia that are absurd or untrue and invalid and illegitimate; and

(iii) The presence of an Unreal Set of absurd, or untrue, or invalid or illegitimate Ideas as a valid Set within Ucadia cannot in itself be argued that Ucadia is therefore contradictory, absurd, illegitimate, invalid or untrue, as the presence of such a set proves the necessary completeness of the "set of sets" of Ideas.

115. As all possible Ideas are circumscribed within Ucadia such that no Idea may exist that is not subject to the absolute authority and jurisdiction of Ucadia:- *Ideas as a set or sets within the absolute jurisdiction of Ucadia*

(i) All possible Ideas of all systems, models, cultures, sciences and history belong to one or more Sets subject to the absolute jurisdiction and authority of Ucadia; and

(ii) No possible Idea of any higher order life form system, or culture, or science or model may exist independently of the primary jurisdiction and authority of Ucadia; and

(iii) Any and every Idea that seeks to refute, or usurp the truth of the present Maxim is therefore a member of the absurd or untrue and invalid and illegitimate Unreal Set of Ideas of Ucadia.

116. Any Idea that contradicts or usurps these present sacred Maxims cannot be said to have validity or legitimacy. *Legitimacy Of an Idea*

Article 11 - Cause

117. A *Cause*, also known as *Causality* and *"cause and effect"*, is an abstraction to describe a source, or reason, or conditions, or goal, or motive or intention for an action or event producing some kind of effect or result. *Cause*

118. In respect of Cause or *Causation*: *Relative to Cause and Causation as a Process*

(i) The simplest model is the concept that one process (the cause) is partly responsible (to some degree) for the second (the effect); and the second (the effect) is dependent to some degree upon the existence of the first (the cause); and

(ii) The model of Causation seeks to draw rational connections between effects, consequences or results and the "forces" driving them to then make logical conclusions of the likely cause or causes; and

(iii) As actions or events rarely occur in perfect isolation, it is frequently difficult to "reverse engineer" the likely cause or causes, unless clear evidence exists; and

(iv) In seeking to resolve investigations involving events and results around Beings, the most reliable source of cause is to obtain clear evidence as to the intention in the mind of the Being (or Beings) at the time. This is why it is morally repugnant and against the Rule of Law to condemn an accused of a serious offence without first firmly establishing culpability of Mind as well as Action.

119. All Causes may be distinguished into three types being *Necessary, Sufficiency* or *Contributory*:   *Types of Causes*

(i) *Necessary Causes* are defined such that "if x is a necessary cause of y, then the presence of y necessarily implies the presence of x. However, the presence of x does not imply that y will occur"; and

(ii) *Sufficient Causes* are defined such that "if x is a sufficient cause of y, then the presence of x necessarily implies the presence of y. However, another cause z may alternatively cause y. Thus the presence of y does not imply the presence of x"; and

(iii) *Contributory Causes* are defined such that "if x accompanies several causes that collectively are a sufficient cause of y, then the presence of x necessarily implies a contributing factor of y to some degree".

120. As Causes after the fact are difficult to determine, even with the most expensive and advanced technology, the process of "reverse engineering" causes from studying effects can be less effective and less accurate than purely philosophical models that are able to postulate the cause of an effect from the mind of the actor at the time of the event or action.   *Causes Versus Fact*

121. The presence of at least one Cause is a distinguishing feature of Models compared to Ideas. Whereas an Idea must possess one Meaning to exist, a Model must possess one Cause to exist.   *Cause Versus Model*

122. Everything happens for a reason. Therefore, everything that happens in the Universe occurs as a result of one or more Causes.   *Everything happens for a Reason*

123. Everything that begins to exist has a Cause: *Everything has Cause*

(i) The Universe began to exist because the Divine willed to exist; and

(ii) Without the existence of the Universe, the Divine could only exist in theory; and

(iii) With the existence of the Universe, the Divine exists in actuality as every living thing and every piece of matter and every force and change is part of the living Divine.

124. All possible Causes exist within the Dimension of Ucadia such that no Cause may exist that is not subject to the absolute authority and jurisdiction of Ucadia in accord with the most sacred Covenant *Pactum De Singularis Caelum*:   *All Causes exist within Ucadia*

   (i) Any Cause that is defined and properly identified in accord with the present Maxims is said to belong to the Set of Causes of Ucadia that are true and valid and legitimate; and

   (ii) A proposed or claimed Cause that is not in accord with the present Maxims is said to belong to the Set of Causes of Ucadia that are absurd or untrue and invalid and illegitimate; and

   (iii) The presence of the Unreal Set of absurd, or untrue, or invalid or illegitimate Causes as a valid Set of Ucadia cannot in itself be argued that Ucadia is therefore contradictory, absurd, illegitimate, invalid or untrue, as the presence of such a set proves the necessary completeness of the "set of sets" of all Causes.

125. As every possible Cause is encompassed within Ucadia such that no Cause may exist that is not subject to the absolute authority and jurisdiction of Ucadia: *Cause within Ucadia jurisdiction*

   (i) The first Cause or relations of Causes listed within Ucadia as true and valid and legitimate shall be the proper Cause defined by Ucadia; and

   (ii) Any definition, proposition or claim of Cause that is not consistent with the Cause or relations of Causes defined by Ucadia shall therefore belong to the Set of Causes of Ucadia that are absurd or untrue and invalid and illegitimate.

126. Any Cause that is not in accord with the present sacred Maxims is invalid.   *Cause Versus Maxims*

127. Whenever one speaks or writes or signifies Causes, it shall refer to the present sacred Maxims and all associated Covenants, Charters, Languages and Models of Knowledge first and foremost.   *Signification of Cause within Maxims*

Article 12 - Model

128. A ***Model*** is an application of one or more Ideas, in a dimension of Reality, according to one or more rules and relations, representing a Cause as a *conceptual archetype*, or *axiom*, or *logical hypothesis*, or   *Model*

scaleable abstraction, or *prototype*, or *physical production*.

129. A Model is properly distinguished from an Idea in that a Model is said to exist according to one or more rules and relations, whereas an Idea is said to exist without necessary dependence to such constraints of one or more rules and relations. — Model Versus Idea

130. In relation to the six essential types of Models:- — Model Types

    (i) As a *conceptual archetype*, a Model is considered a generalised or idealised system whereby other systems may be compared and hypotheses and axioms derived or tested from it; and

    (ii) As an *axiom*, a Model is considered a statement so self-evidently true in the context of a system, that it can be used as the basis of creating more complex hypotheses or archetypes; and

    (iii) As a *logical hypothesis*, a Model is considered a method to represent a system of objects, phenomena and physical processes in a logical and cohesive manner; and

    (iv) As a *scaleable abstraction*, a Model is considered a physical representation of an object, that maintains accurate ratios and relations to the actual model, but may be at a scale many times smaller or larger than the real-world object; and

    (v) As a *prototype*, a Model is considered an early physical version, designed and manufactured to prove one or more solutions, or discover one or more flaws, often before the physical production of such a Model in any kind of volume of units; and

    (vi) As a *physical production*, a Model is considered to be a manufactured solution, often from a base or "original model".

131. The very existence of a Model itself depends upon the presence of some representation of a system with rules and relations. In the absence of any such system to give a Model its context and function, a Model cannot be said to exist. — Model as a representation of a System

132. The existence of a Model merely depends upon the presence of some distinct representation of a system with rules and relations and not any claimed acceptance or validation or arguments in support of or against such a system by an Observer. Therefore, the existence of a Model is itself proof of its own existence. — Model as a System with Rules

133. The Universe and all Existence may be properly defined as a Model, or simply a "Divine Creation". — Universe as a Model

134. All Models may be defined by their Specificity, Utility and Versatility:- *Model in its component parts*

    (i) Specificity relates to the quality of the Model to meet a desired outcome to some degree. For example, many Models of machines are by their nature highly specific; and

    (ii) Utility relates to the usefulness of the Model in meeting the desired outcomes of the user. A high utility value indicates a high level of usefulness and usually a consequential high level of satisfaction; and

    (iii) Versatility relates to the Model also being able to be applied to achieving different outcomes.

135. All human knowledge, technology, culture and tools may be properly defined as different types of Models, with different levels of specificity, utility and versatility. *Model types and knowledge*

136. The most specific, useful and versatile "Model of all Models" is the Ucadia Model that systematically and objectively defines all possible Models into fourteen disciplines and systems being *Philologia, Logia, Etymologia, Symbologia, Eikologia, Cosmologia, Astrologia, Geologia, Physiologia, Anthropologia, Technologia, Sociologia, Psychologia* and *Theologia*:- *Fourteen Models of Ucadia*

    (i) **Philologia** is the Ucadia Model of Knowledge and discipline of the study of argument, reasoning, learning and awareness; and

    (ii) **Logia** is the Ucadia Model of Knowledge and discipline of the study of language, speech, communication and knowledge; and

    (iii) **Etymologia** is the Ucadia Model of Knowledge and discipline of the study of meaning and words; and

    (iv) **Symbologia** is the Ucadia Model of Knowledge and discipline of the study of symbols, alphabets, sequences and encoding; and

    (v) **Eikologia** is the Ucadia Model of Knowledge and discipline of the study of quantities, numbers, shapes, structures, sets, functions, algorithms, computations and the relations between these concepts; and

    (vi) **Cosmologia** is the Ucadia Model of Knowledge and discipline of the study of universal rules, dimensions, matter, forces, energy, the universe, galaxies and very large structures; and

(vii) ***Astrologia*** is the Ucadia Model of Knowledge and discipline of the study of stars, interstellar systems and galaxies; and

(viii) ***Geologia*** is the Ucadia Model of Knowledge and discipline of the study of planets and moons; and

(ix) ***Physiologia*** is the Ucadia Model of Knowledge and discipline of the study of cellular (living) organisms and living systems; and

(x) ***Anthropologia*** is the Ucadia Model of Knowledge and discipline of the study of higher order life form species, societies and civilisations; and

(xi) ***Technologia*** is the Ucadia Model of Knowledge and discipline of the study of the application of knowledge for practical solutions, utensils and machines; and

(xii) ***Sociologia*** is the Ucadia Model of Knowledge and discipline of the study of higher order life form associations, groups, institutions, behaviours, cultures, identities and models; and

(xiii) ***Psychologia*** is the Ucadia Model of Knowledge and discipline of the study of cellular and non-cellular consciousness, cognition, mind, mental abilities and impediments, emotional states, behaviours and choices; and

(xiv) ***Theologia*** is the Ucadia Model of Knowledge and discipline of the study of the principles, methods, systems, arguments and proofs that rationally and reliably explain the existence, nature, function and intention of the Divine and other supernatural beings within, without and throughout the Universe.

137. As all possible Models belong as subsets of the Ucadia Model that systematically and objectively defines every possible Model into one of fourteen disciplines and systems, no Model may exist that is not subject to the absolute authority and jurisdiction of Ucadia in accord with the most sacred Covenant *Pactum De Singularis Caelum*:-

Models as subsets of Ucadia

(i) All possible Models of all systems, models, cultures, sciences and history belong to one or more disciplines or sub-disciplines subject to the absolute jurisdiction and authority of Ucadia; and

(ii) No possible Model of any higher order life form system, or culture, or science or model may exist independently of the primary jurisdiction and authority of Ucadia; and

(iii) The entirety of every past, present or future scientific model exists within the dimensions, bounds, authority and jurisdiction of Ucadia according to the Ucadia Model; and

(iv) Any Model that is defined and properly identified in accord with the present Maxims is said to belong as a subset of the Model of Ucadia that is true and valid and legitimate; and

(v) A proposed or claimed Model that is not in accord with the present Maxims is said to belong to the Set of Model of Ucadia that are absurd or untrue and invalid and illegitimate; and

(vi) The presence of the Unreal Set of absurd, or untrue, or invalid or illegitimate Models as a valid Set of Ucadia cannot in itself be argued that Ucadia is therefore contradictory, absurd, illegitimate, invalid or untrue, as the presence of such a set proves the necessary completeness of the "set of sets" of all Models; and

(vii) Any and every Model that seeks to refute, or usurp the truth of the present Maxim is therefore a member of the absurd or untrue and invalid and illegitimate Unreal Set of Models of Ucadia.

138. Any Model that contradicts the present sacred Maxims or the Ucadia Model has no validity or utility.

Model Versus Maxims within Ucadia

Article 13 - System

139. A ***System*** is a type of Model being a Set of Objects or Concepts, capable of being uniquely defined by a Set of Rules as to their Properties, Relations and Behaviours.

System

140. In relation to the general character of a System:-

General Character of System

(i) Every valid System is delineated by its boundaries, described by its structure, defined by its purposes and expressed in its functions; and

(ii) Every valid System possesses a set of two or more Rules as to the Properties, Relations or Behaviours of a Set of Objects or Concepts; and

(iii) Every valid System by definition is a unique Set.

141. As all possible Systems belong as subsets of the Ucadia Model that systematically and objectively defines every possible System into one of fourteen disciplines and systems, no System may exist that is not subject to the absolute authority and jurisdiction of Ucadia in accord with the most sacred Covenant *Pactum De Singularis Caelum*:-

Systems as subsets of Ucadia

(i) All possible Systems, models, cultures, sciences and history belong to one or more disciplines or sub-disciplines subject to the absolute jurisdiction and authority of Ucadia; and

(ii) No possible System of any higher order life form system, or culture, or science or model may exist independently of the primary jurisdiction and authority of Ucadia; and

(iii) The entirety of every past, present or future scientific model exists within the dimensions, bounds, authority and jurisdiction of Ucadia according to the Ucadia Systems; and

(iv) Any System that is defined and properly identified in accord with the present Maxims is said to belong as a subset of the Systems of Ucadia that is true and valid and legitimate; and

(v) A proposed or claimed System that is not in accord with the present Maxims is said to belong to the Set of Systems of Ucadia that are absurd or untrue and invalid and illegitimate; and

(vi) The presence of the Unreal Set of absurd, or untrue, or invalid or illegitimate Systems as a valid Set of Ucadia cannot in itself be argued that Ucadia is therefore contradictory, absurd, illegitimate, invalid or untrue, as the presence of such a set proves the necessary completeness of the "set of sets" of all Systems; and

(vii) Any and every System that seeks to refute, or usurp the truth of the present Maxim is therefore a member of the absurd or untrue and invalid and illegitimate Unreal Set of Systems of Ucadia.

Article 14 - Nothing

142. ***Nothing*** or ***No Thing***, is the Concept of not any Thing or form or substance or measure or concept but itself. — Nothing

143. A *Thing,* also known as *Something,* is an Object that can be named, qualified and discerned by some meaning to possess a distinct existence from other Objects within a certain Jurisdiction and Reality. — Thing as an Object

144. In general reference to Nothing: — Nothing and Awareness

(i) Nothing may be represented numerically by the symbol 0; and

(ii) Nothing may also be represented by the quantity of zero; and

(iii) Nothing may also be represented as a Set being the Empty Set;

and

    (iv) The Real Set is abstracted from the Empty Set; and

    (v) Thus, Sets originate from the Empty Set; and

    (vi) The only force or power capable of abstracting from the Empty Set is Awareness.

145. In Respect of Nothing as a Concept: *Nothing as a Concept*

    (i) As a Concept, Nothing is similar to the ancient Concept of Chaos or the Great Void of ancient civilisations; and

    (ii) As a Concept, Nothing depends upon itself and no other Concept except the Concept of Concepts itself; and

    (iii) Nothing is the most unique of all Concepts as all other Concepts depend upon something; and

    (iv) Nothing therefore is the purest possible Concept.

146. In Respect of Nothing and Thing or Things: *Nothing and Thing as a Binary Pair*

    (i) The Concept of Nothing and Thing are a Binary Pair, whereby neither Concept can exist independently of the other as Thing depends upon Nothing for its definition and vice versa; and

    (ii) Both Nothing and Thing can be described as Pair Sets whereby Nothing can only be defined as an Empty Set or Set of Itself, whereas Thing can be a Set of One or any number up to Infinity.

147. It is a gross error to presume the Concept of Nothing to be devoid of Meaning and therefore Existence, as Nothing perfectly means No Thing, without qualification or condition.   *Concept of Nothing and Meaning*

148. Nothing is the most perfected and absolute Concept as there is literally no thing (Concept or Object) that can exceed it. Therefore, Nothing is the most powerful of all Concepts as all other Concepts may be qualified some way, whereas Nothing is perfectly unqualified.   *Perfect and absolute Concept of Nothing*

149. A Thing may be further defined as a Corporeal Object subject to the Jurisdiction of a competent forum of law, whereby certain Rights of ownership, use and benefit may be defined.   *Thing as a Corporeal Object*

150. All Things are subject to the absolute and perfect jurisdiction of the Divine Creator of all Existence and One Heaven in accord with the most sacred Covenant *Pactum De Singularis Caelum* and the present sacred Maxims.   *All Things subject to the Divine Creator*

151. All temporal jurisdiction over Things is subject to the proper Authority and Powers as derived from the most sacred Covenant   *Temporal jurisdiction of Things*

Pactum De Singularis Caelum and associated Covenants, Maxims and Charters and no other.

152. A forum without proper Authority or Power derived from the most sacred Covenant *Pactum De Singularis Caelum* has no jurisdiction whatsoever over any Thing. — Jurisdiction versus Thing

Article 15 - Quantity

153. ***Quantity*** is the distinction of one or more theoretical or actual Things based upon a form of positive measurement of *Magnitude* or *Multitude*. — Quantity

154. Whilst Negative Numbers may exist "in theory" all Negative Numbers in reference to Quantity are strictly Positive Numbers possessing a value less than a determined mid-point categorised as "zero" on some certain scale of values. — Negative Numbers Versus Positive Numbers

155. In reference to Quantity describing forms of Magnitude: — Quantity as forms of Magnitude

    (i) Magnitude by definition is the measurement of gradual quantitative transitions and therefore generally continuous in nature; and

    (ii) A decimal Number or Ratio is an example of a Magnitude Quantity; and

    (iii) The largest possible Magnitude Quantity is the *Infinite*; and

    (iv) The smallest possible Magnitude Quantity is the *Infinitesimal*.

156. In reference to Quantity describing forms of Multitude: — Quantity as forms of Multitude

    (i) Multitude by definition is the measurement of discrete quantities or sets and therefore generally discontinuous in nature; and

    (ii) A whole Number or Function is an example of a Multitude Quantity; and

    (iii) The largest possible Multitude Quantity is the *Uniset*; and

    (iv) The smallest possible Multitude Quantity is *Zero*.

Article 16 - Set

157. A ***Set*** is a well defined collection of theoretical or physical Objects or Concepts sharing some similar meanings, attributes or purpose. — Set

158. All Sets may be defined as *Empty, Real, Unreal, Semi-Real, Non-Real or Subset* according to the collection of theoretical or physical — Sets as Objects

Objects or Concepts they contain and their relation to other Sets:

(i) The *Empty Set* (**E**) is the fundamental Set containing Nothing; and

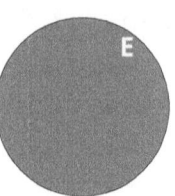

(ii) A *Real Set* (**R**) is an abstracted Set from the Empty Set (**E**) that contains at least one Object or Thing. For example, the Real Set of 1 contains a circumscribed *Subset* of the Empty Set; and

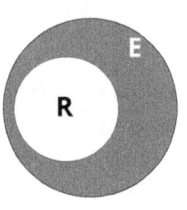

(iii) An *Unreal Set* (**U**), also known as a "Theoretical Set" is the binary opposite to a Real Set (**R**) that contains Objects or Concepts that do not fully meet the Rules of a Real Set. However, a *Semi-Real* Set (**S**) is the intersection Set formed between an intersection of a Real Set and Unreal Set where members of the Unreal Set may interact and influence the Real Set (e.g. as forces), yet have the appearance of being "unreal"; and

(iv) A *Non-Real Set* (**N**) is the intersection Set formed between an intersection of two (or more) Unreal Sets where members of the abstracted Unreal Set may interact and influence the original Unreal Set (e.g. as forces), yet have the appearance of being "unreal" to the theoretical objects within the original Unreal set.

159. All Sets share the same elementary qualities of *Formation, Members, Boundary, Dimension, Relations, Attributes, Computational State, Function, Existence* and *Completion State*:

Shared qualities of Sets

(i) *Formation* means all sets are formed by one or more rules as a product of previously existing sets; and

(ii) *Members* means all sets, except the Empty Set, possess at least one Element as a Member of the set; and

(iii) *Boundary* means all sets possess a boundary that

differentiates them from other sets; and

(iv) *Dimension* means every Set possesses two dimensional or three dimensional space defined by the boundary of the set and the space between its member elements such that no two member elements occupy the same position and space within the same set; and

(v) *Relations* means all sets are ultimately a subset of another set except the Empty Set and the Set of One and the Set of Zero; and

(vi) *Attributes* means every set possesses at least one attribute of meaning that every Member of itself then inherits as well; and

(vii) *Computational State* means every set may be abstracted as a step in a computational sequence; and

(viii) *Function* means every set may be abstracted and expressed as a Function and Alphabetic Sequence; and

(ix) *Existence* means that all sets have been abstracted and observed as Proof of Existence or are being observed by an Observer (as actual Existence) to confirm all the elemental qualities as defined; and

(x) *Completion State* means that all sets are either complete or incomplete due to the completion of observation of a computational sequence or the incomplete process of observation by the Observer making key elements indeterminable and therefore approximate.

160. In reference to the quality of Formation, all Sets (except the Empty Set) are formed from existing sets by *Abstraction, Union, Intersection* or *Complementation*:   *Formation of Sets*

(i) *Abstraction* is the formation of a new set by forming a model or computation of the characteristics of an existing set; and

(ii) *Union* is the formation of a new set by adding together two or more existing sets; and

(iii) *Intersection* is the formation of a new set by subtracting things from two or more existing sets that are not common between the sets; and

(iv) *Complementation* is the formation of a new comparative set by subtracting things from an existing set that complement the attributes of the new set.

161. In relation to *Formation* and the Concept that all Sets are formed   *Correlation of Concept and* from existing Sets:

- (i) All Real Sets, except the Empty Set, are formed from existing Real Sets of things; and
- (ii) All Real Sets, except the Empty Set and the Real Set of 1, or Unreal Set of -1 are formed from existing Real Sets of things; and
- (iii) An Empty Set is a Set that contains Nothing; and
- (iv) A Set that is in direct Intersection with the Empty Set, or has no element in common with another Set is said to be a Disjoint Set; and
- (v) A Set that is not in direct Intersection with the Empty Set, or has one or more elements in common with another Set is said to be a Conjunct Set.

162. In relation to a Set as a Function and Alphabetic Sequence:
- (i) There is a Set y having Members are all non-empty sets; and
- (ii) There is a Set x having infinitely many Members; and
- (iii) Two Sets are equal if they have the same members. Two Sets are the same Sets if they have the same members and the same elementary qualities; and
- (iv) Excluding the Real Set of 1, every other non-empty Real Set as x contains a member y such that x and y are disjoint Sets; and
- (v) If x and y are Sets, then there exists a Theoretical Set that contains x and y as Members; and
- (vi) For any Set of Sets x there exists a Set y containing every element that is a Member of only some Members of x; and
- (vii) A Set x is a Subset of y if every element of x is also a Member of y; and
- (viii) For any Set x, there is a Set y that contains every Subset of x.

163. In reference to the quality of *State* and the Concept of Complete Sets:
- (i) A set is *Complete* when the observations of the Observer have determined the elemental qualities of the Set and its members are known; and
- (ii) As a Complete Set is complete, it may also be described as Perfect; and
- (iii) A Complete Set is equivalent to a *Multitude Quantity*, discontinuous in nature and may be expressed as a Discrete

Function or a Straight Line Sequence; and

(iv) The largest possible Theoretical and Real Complete Set is the *Uniset*; and

(v) The smallest possible Real Complete Set is *1*; and

(vi) The smallest possible Theoretical Complete Set is *-1*; and

(vii) Except the Set of 1, there are no other possible Real Complete Sets that may be a member of itself; and

(viii) No possible Real Complete Set of all Sets, that is also a member of itself, may exist in Reality.

164. In reference to the quality of State and the Concept of Incomplete Sets:

<small>Concept of State and Incomplete Sets</small>

(i) A set is *Incomplete* when the observations of the Observer are incomplete, making the elemental qualities of the Set indeterminable and its members not fully known; and

(ii) As an Incomplete Set is incomplete, it may also be described as Imperfect; and

(iii) An Incomplete Set is equivalent to a *Magnitude Quantity*, continuous in nature and may be expressed as a Continuous Function or a Curve Sequence; and

(iv) The largest possible Theoretical and Real Incomplete Set is the *Infinite*; and

(v) The smallest possible Real Incomplete Set is the *Infinitesimal of 1*; and

(vi) The smallest possible Theoretical Incomplete Set is the *Infinitesimal of -1*; and

(vii) Only the Theoretical and Real Incomplete Set of all Sets of the *Infinite*, that is also a member of itself, may exist in Reality; and

(viii) As the Infinite is the only possible Set of all Sets (including itself) that may exist in Reality, the Universe may be properly described as an Imperfect Set.

165. In general relation to Sets and observed Objects:

<small>Sets and Observed Objects</small>

(i) All Objects may be described as combinations of sets and subsets; and

(ii) A Set itself is an Object; and

(iii) A Set in the process of being observed is a form of

Information; and

- (iv) As all Objects depend upon the active observation of an Observer for existence, all sets therefore depend upon the presence of an Observer for their existence; and
- (v) The assignment of meaning to something can also be described as forming a set of one whereby the thing is the member of the set and the meaning is the attribute of members of the set; and
- (vi) The observation of things can also be described as the formation of a new abstraction of a general set of things possessing certain attributes with each thing observed also being its own set; and
- (vii) The observation of the boundary between certain things can also be described as the identification of the boundary between sets of things; and
- (viii) The influence of an Observer on the Objects observed is proven by incomplete sets whereby an observation that has not finished abstracting a set to memory then causes the set itself to be incomplete.

166. Absolute Set means a set of all Concepts or Objects that is unconditional, unfettered, completed, perfected or free from all other sets: *The Absolute Set*

    - (i) The purest and most unconditional, unfettered, completed, perfected and free Concept or Object as Absolute is Nothing; and
    - (ii) The Absolute Set is therefore equivalent to the Empty Set.

167. The mystery and Paradox between the Binary Concepts of Absolute Set and Empty Set can only be resolved through the recognition of the existence of the Divine: *Paradox of Binary Concepts through the Divine*

    - (i) The Absolute Set of all possible Concepts and Objects, depends on the Empty Set of Nothing to balance the equation of Existence and Non-Existence; and
    - (ii) Nothing merely depends upon the existence of Concept of itself to exist. However, in the absence of some Thing as an Object in three dimensions, the Concept of Nothing remains purely theoretical; and
    - (iii) The Divine as pure wisdom and knowledge and all possible Concepts is the canvas of existence otherwise known as

Nothing; and

(iv) The Absolute Set of all possible Concepts and Objects in action is the Absolute Dream of the Divine as the ultimate Observer; and

(v) Therefore pure Awareness has no Mass as only Ideas put into action as Models possess Mass in Reality; and

(vi) The proof of the existence of Matter existing in Reality is therefore one of the many proofs of the existence of the Divine.

Article 17 - Limit

168. A *Limit* is a boundary or restriction or constraint between two or more definitive locations, sets, spaces, realities, areas or concepts. Limit

169. All Limits are formed from the deliberate act of distinguishing a new Concept or Object from an existing Concept or Object. Limit from Concept or Object

170. Without limits there could be no differences and without any difference, there would be no Existence. Therefore, existence depends upon limits. Limits and Existence

171. A Boundary is created as a result of the *formation* of a Theoretical or Real Set. Boundary and formation of Set

172. The simplest and most absolute and perfect Boundary is the result of the distinction between Nothing and Thing (or Something) in relation to the Empty Set. Perfect Boundary

173. A Boundary is Absolute, Perfect, Universal, Exceptional or Conditional to the extent that any breach does not cause the very definition of such a Boundary to cease: Boundary Definitions

   (i) *Absolute Boundary* is a Boundary that cannot be breached under any circumstances, conditions or argument. The only Absolute Boundary that exists is between Nothing and Something; and

   (ii) *Perfect Boundary* is a Boundary of significance above all others that "in theory" could be breached but would then have catastrophic consequences. The only Perfect Boundary is between the Universe of Unita (Unitas) and the Unique Collective Awareness, such that if one point of Unique Collective Awareness in position did cease to exist, the entirety of Existence would cease to exist; and

   (iii) *Universal Boundary* is a boundary of significance such as the divisions between the levels of matter; and

(iv) *Exceptional Boundary* is a Boundary that may be breached in exceptional circumstances but not necessarily causes the collapse of distinction between the two locations, spaces, dimensions, areas or concepts; and

(v) *Conditional Boundary* is a Boundary that may be breached under certain conditions without necessarily causing the collapse of distinction between the two locations, spaces, dimensions, areas or concepts.

Article 18 - Uniqueness

174. ***Uniqueness*** is the state or attribute of being the only one of a kind, or unequalled, or unparalleled or unmatched compared to some other Concept or Object. <!-- Uniqueness -->

175. By definition, Uniqueness depends on the existence of at least one other Concept or Object in order to compare to establish such a state or attribute of being Unique. <!-- Dependency of Uniqueness to another -->

176. Given the state or attribute of Uniqueness means only one of a kind, or unequalled, or unparalleled or unmatched compared to some other Concept or Object, the existence of Uniqueness is the personification of paradox. <!-- Paradox of Uniqueness -->

177. Uniqueness is *Absolute, Perfect, Imperfect, Exceptional* or *Conditional* to the extent that any breach does not cause the very definition of such Uniqueness to cease: <!-- Uniqueness Definitions -->

   (i) *Absolute Uniqueness* is a state or attribute of uniqueness that cannot be matched, equalled, duplicated or paralleled under any circumstances, conditions or argument. The only Absolutely Unique Concept or Object is Nothing; and

   (ii) *Perfect Uniqueness* is a state or attribute of uniqueness that cannot be matched in theory or reality. Perfect Uniqueness transcends reality and therefore is equivalent to *Divine Uniqueness*; and

   (iii) *Imperfect Uniqueness* is a state or attribute of uniqueness such that no other Concept or Object may possess the exact same state or attributes (such as position or relations) "in reality". All forms of matter at every level is imperfectly unique to some degree; and

   (iv) *Exceptional Uniqueness* is a state or attribute of uniqueness that may be breached in exceptional circumstances, but not necessarily causes the collapse of distinction between two or

Title II - Divine Concepts

more Concepts or Objects; and

(v) *Conditional Uniqueness* is a state or attribute of uniqueness that may be breached under certain conditions without necessarily causing the collapse of distinction between two or more Concepts or Objects.

178. The existence of Perfect Uniqueness is demonstration of Divine Uniqueness and the existence or presence of the Divine:- *Perfect Uniqueness*

   (i) The only Perfectly Unique Concept or Object is the Universe exemplified in the Perfectly Unique Quantities of Uniset and Infinity; and

   (ii) The only Perfectly Unique Concept or Object that may exist within the Universe is exemplified by the Perfectly Imperfect Ratio of Pi (3.14159265).

179. The most perfect description of the Divine in relation to Uniqueness is as the Unique Collective Awareness: *Unique Collective Awareness*

   (i) Unique Collective Awareness perfectly defines the relation between Nothing and Everything in the context of Mind and Reality; and

   (ii) Unique Collective Awareness perfectly defines the true nature of the Divine in the context of Mind and the Unique Dreamer observing the collective existence of Dream of Creation and Existence; and

   (iii) Unique Collective Awareness perfectly defines the ultimate paradox.

180. The most perfect embodiment of the Divine in relation to the Universe, Unique Collective Awareness and Life is a Singularity related to the embodiment of Pi (3.14159265) as Perfect Imperfection. Under the Western Calendar, the nine (9) descending dates of connection to Pi in two thousand years are 1, 15, 159, 1592, 1596, 1595, 1926, 1925 and 1965: *Unique Singularity as Embodiment of Divine*

   (i) The first most significant date of Divine unique embodiment on planet Earth for two thousand years is March 14, 1 CE (3.**14**159265); and

   (ii) The second most significant date of Divine unique embodiment on planet Earth for two thousand years is March 14, 15 CE (3.14**15**9265); and

   (iii) The third most significant date of Divine unique embodiment on planet Earth for two thousand years is March 14, 159 (3.14**159**265); and

(iv) The fourth most significant date of Divine unique embodiment on planet Earth for two thousand years is March 14, 1592 (3.14**1592**65); and

(v) The fifth most significant date of Divine unique embodiment on planet Earth for two thousand years is March 14, 1596 (3.14**1592**65); and

(vi) The sixth most significant date of Divine unique embodiment on planet Earth for two thousand years is March 14, 1595 (3.14**1592**65); and

(vii) The seventh most significant date of Divine unique embodiment on planet Earth for two thousand years is March 14, 1926 (3.14**1592**65); and

(viii) The eighth most significant date of Divine unique embodiment on planet Earth for two thousand years is March 14, 1925 (3.14**1592**65); and

(ix) The ninth most significant date of Divine unique embodiment on planet Earth for two thousand years is March 14, 1965 (3.14**1592**65).

Article 19 - Relativity

181. ***Relativity*** is the principle that the Fundamental Laws of any stable Model of Reality must be the same for all Observers using the same Method and Frame of Reference. — Relativity

182. In respect of the Concept of Relativity: — Concept of Relativity

   (i) Relativity states the self-evident conclusion that for any Model to be stable, it must operate according to at least one or more stable and universal Laws; and

   (ii) For any Law of any stable Model to be properly discerned and observed, some competent System of Reference must exist to enable reliable measure; and

   (iii) A competent System of Reference is itself as Model and therefore a "Model of a Model"; and

   (iv) For a Law of a Model to be stable and axiomatic, it must be relatively simple, reproducible and possess certain universal applications that are the same in all reference frames of the particular System of Reference used to measure it; and

   (v) As Relativity demands that all valid, stable and axiomatic Laws of a Model are the same in all reference frames of a Reference

System, the Reference System and Laws must be united to some degree as a "Standard Model"; and

(vi) Given the Reference System and Laws of a Standard Model must be united to some degree, by discovering and understanding one part of the Standard Model, it should follow the rest of the Model can then also be deduced and comprehended; and

(vii) As the Universe is a stable Model, the Universe must possess one or more valid, stable and axiomatic Laws that are discernible through a competent Reference System as a Standard Model.

183. In respect of Standard Models and Models of Reality: *Standard Models and Models of Reality*

(i) A Model cannot logically or sensibly be defined as a Standard Model if it contradicts the very nature, meaning and concept of Relativity; and

(ii) A Standard Model by its nature encourages forces of uniformity and orthodoxy; and

(iii) All Standard Models affects the Model being observed to some degree by affecting the perspective of the Observer using it; and

(iv) All Standard Models limit or empower the Observer to some degree to see the function and design of the larger Model; and

(v) A Standard Model that fails to qualify as a Standard Model, yet is defended and still maintained through uniformity and orthodoxy is properly called a Delusional Model; and

(vi) Delusional Models or Pseudo-Standard Models cause the greatest inhibition to scientific study and may even represent clear and existential threats to the survival of a technologically capable species if not eradicated as a form of "virus" against objective and rational mind.

184. In respect of the Concepts of Quantum Mechanics and Relativity: *Quantum Mechanics and Relativity*

(i) Quantum Mechanics correctly identifies that the Rules of Sub Atomic Matter and the Rules of Core Atomic Matter are different to Classical Mechanics of the Molecular Universe; and

(ii) Quantum Mechanics further correctly identifies the centrality of the Observer and conditions of observation in the Relative and repeatable outcomes; and in the concept of uncertainty as to the exact predictability and location of atomic and sub atomic particles appears "between" two or more possible states; and

(iii) Despite the conceptual and scientific breakthroughs accompanying Quantum Mechanics to consider the behaviour of different levels of matter as possessing its own form of "reality", the Model of Quantum Mechanics continues to encounter fundamental errors of assumption with even the most essential of particles; and

(iv) Furthermore, the Model of Quantum Mechanics cannot be considered a complete Standard Model for the continued admission that its unification with other fundamental theories within contemporary science has neither been established in a working model nor proven.

185. The most perfected Standard Model in respect of Relativity is the Ucadia Model: *Relativity and the Ucadia Model*

(i) The Ucadia Model defines and codifies a complete Cosmology, Standard Model of All Elements and Rules of the Universe and Knowledge; and

(ii) The *Ucadia Standard Model of Universal Elements* as a unique system for the classification and symbolic representation of theoretical and real world objects as elements of a standard model of universal elements; and

(iii) The *Ucadia Hydro-Helio Model of Atomic Elements* as a unique system for the standard identification, classification and symbolic representation of atomic elements and their properties; and

(iv) The *Eikos Language System* as a unique language system to define and describe the relationships, properties and measurement of all elements in operation from the Ucadia Standard Model of Universal Elements and the Ucadia Hydro-Helio Model of Atomic Elements; and

(v) The *Unique Collective Awareness Model* as a unique model of the primary sets of axioms to define and describe laws governing all elements in operation from the Ucadia Standard Model of Universal Elements and the Ucadia Hydro-Helio Model of Atomic Elements.

Article 20 - Change

186. ***Change*** is the observation of difference between one or more states, attributes, properties or behaviours of a Concept or Object over a given period of two or more observations compared to some benchmark. Observed Differences in state, attributes, properties or behaviours is therefore equivalent to Change.

Change

187. In respect of the Key Elements of Change:

Key Elements of Change

(i) Change requires the existence of at least one Concept or Object being observed; and

(ii) Change requires one or more attributes, or properties or behaviours in some dimensional state in relation to the Concept or Object being observed; and

(iii) Change requires the existence of an Observer making observation; and

(iv) Change requires a system of measurement in order to establish the benchmarks in respect of the states, attributes, properties or behaviours of a Concept or Object over a given period; and

(v) Change requires at least two (or more) distinct sets of observations, with at least one of the sets of observations being the benchmark of observation; and

(vi) Change requires a level of fundamental awareness of the Observer in order to establish benchmarks and to compare observations to discern any difference and therefore Change.

188. In respect of the Concept of Change:

Concept of Change

(i) The necessity to distinguish two or more periods of observation is itself evidence of difference of observed periods and therefore Change, even if nothing is observed to be different in relation to the state, attributes, properties or behaviours of a Concept or Object; and

(ii) The necessity of the presence of awareness in order to discern a set of benchmark elements and secondly to make observations against such a benchmark, is itself evidence of differences of computation and states of awareness and therefore Change. The necessity to distinguish two or more periods of observation is itself evidence of difference and therefore Change, even if nothing is observed to be different in relation to the state, attributes, properties or behaviours of a Concept or Object; and

(iii) As existence itself depends on an observer and something observed, existence can be said to depend upon the concept and result of Change; and

(iv) All existence is change.

Article 21 - Reality

189. ***Reality*** is one of a Binary pair of Models constructed upon certain Rules of Form and Meaning, enabling a certain degree of stability necessary for the existence and function of two or more Theoretical or Real Objects. The opposite Model is *Unreality*.

    <small>Reality</small>

190. In Relation to Reality and Theoretical or Real Objects within Dimension:

    <small>Reality within Dimension</small>

    (i) All Models of Reality are by definition Theoretical. This is because all forms of Reality (and Unreality) are Models; and

    (ii) While all Models of Reality are Theoretical, a Model of Reality may be described as Real to the extent that is presents a comprehensive and well-formed Standard Model of Universal Laws, consistent with the Principle of Relativity and the present Sacred Maxims; and

    (iii) The binary opposite to a Real Model of Reality may be defined as Perfectly Unreal to the extent that it belongs as the opposite to such a Standard Model of Universal Laws and properly completes a consistent conceptual set of all possible Theoretical and Real Objects; and

    (iv) A Model of Reality that seeks to deliberately contradict the present Sacred Maxims, or obstinately or belligerently persist with false and absurd Concepts that cannot possibly form a Standard Model nor reasonable Universal Laws is said to be a Delusional Model of Reality, or simply a "Delusion".

191. Reality permits a functional Model of Existence excluding the existence of Paradox and Relativity. Thus within the fictional Universe of Reality, in accordance with the most sacred Covenant *Pactum De Singularis Caelum* and the present sacred Maxims, the Concept of Absolute Truth may exist and the certainty of Logic and Reason may be applied.

    <small>Reality and a functional Model of Existence</small>

192. A Model of Reality is always bound as a Binary Pair to a particular Model of Unreality. By definition and necessity, a Model of Reality

    <small>Models and the existence of</small>

can only exist when its constituent Model of Unreality also exists under the same System of Rules.

Reality

193. By definition, a Model of Reality plus its correlating Model of Unreality constitutes a total Model and Set of Objects and Concepts according the same System of Rules:

Reality: Total Model and Set of Objects and Concepts

(i) Every Real Set (**R**) or Unreal (Theoretical) Set is a Subset of the Empty Set (**E**). No Theoretical or Real Set may exist outside of the Empty Set; and

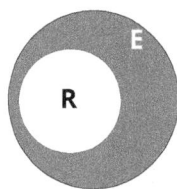

(ii) Every Real Set (**R**) is dependent upon its opposite Unreal Set (**U**) to form a Complete Model, such that both sets intersect to form a union and a third set as Semi-Real Set (**S**), whereby certain objects may function as real and unreal without breaking the dimensional boundaries of either set; and

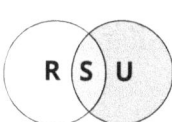

(iii) The Systems of Rules that defines the Set of Reality must be the same set of Rules that determines the Set of Unreality. Once the Sets of Things constituting Reality and Unreality are established, a clear boundary exists whereby Nothing can then be transferred from the Set of Unreality to Reality or Vice-Versa unless it belong to the intersecting space; and

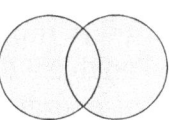

(iv) Nothing (Object or Concept) may both belong to a Model of Reality and simultaneously to its related Model of Unreality. If one Thing is permitted to be transferred from the Set of Reality to Unreality or Vice-Versa by a change "mid stream" in the System of rules, then the entire System of existence of that particular Reality and Unreality ceases; and

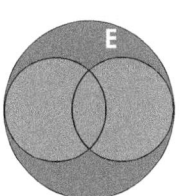

(v) Reality may possess one or more subsets of Reality (**R2**) whereby such a Subset inherits the

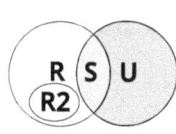

Rules of its Parent but then may form additional Rules; and

(vi) Unreality may possess one or more subsets of Unreality (**U2**) whereby such a Subset inherits the Rules of its Parent but then may form additional Rules; and

(vii) The Total Unreal Set (**U**) may itself be a composition of one or more intersecting Unreal Sets, forming Non-Real Space (**N**) that behaves in a similar manner to the concept of Semi-Real Space.

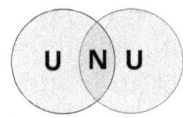

194. It is a gross error, falsity and absurdity to conclude that a Concept or Object placed within a Model of Unreality is therefore necessarily fake, or false, or without value or merit:

    Unreality versus Concept and Object

    (i) A primary function and purpose of any valid Model of Reality is to enable a degree of certainty and reproducibility necessary for the operation of the Rule of Law. Therefore vital concepts such as the notion of paradox and multi-valence are necessarily excluded not because they are false, but because they contradict the purpose of a Model of Reality; and

    (ii) Similarly, a competent Model of Reality may seek to use completely fictional concepts such as Absolute Truth and simplistic fictional systems such as bivalent Logic to enable a consistent Model of Law, not because such concepts are more accurate in relation to the universe, but because they are useful to a stable and functional Model of Reality.

195. Any argument in support of a Model of Reality, that fails or denies its Binary relation and dependence to the existence of an opposite Model of Unreality, is therefore an absurdity and sign of delusion.

    Model of Reality versus Model of Unreality

196. The exclusive and authentic Rules for the consistent definition and operation of Reality are the present Maxims in accord with the most sacred Covenant *Pactum De Singularis Caelum*.

    Reality in accordance with Pactum De Singularis

Title II - Divine Concepts

197. Providing a Reality is consistent with the present Maxims in accord with the most sacred Covenant *Pactum De Singularis Caelum*, then such a Reality is perfectly valid, legitimate and true, even if it does not presently include or promulgate all the knowledge and elements of the Maxims:
[margin: Caelum Reality consistent with ALL Covenants]

    (i)   By this definition, the Reality as held by the *Universal Ecclesia of One Christ*, in accord with the most sacred Covenant *Pactum De Singularis Caelum* is perfectly valid, legitimate and true; and

    (ii)   By this definition, the Reality as held by the *Holy Society of One Islam*, in accord with the most sacred Covenant *Pactum De Singularis Caelum* is perfectly valid, legitimate and true; and

    (iii)   By definition, the Reality as held by the *Sacred Society of One Spirit*, in accord with the most sacred Covenant *Pactum De Singularis Caelum* is perfectly valid, legitimate and true.

198. The definition of any alternate Reality that is inconsistent with the present sacred Maxims and the most sacred Covenant *Pactum De Singularis Caelum* is automatically null and void from the beginning.
[margin: Definition of an alternative Reality]

199. None may validly or authentically challenge the Reality of a body or society named and given life through the most sacred Covenant *Pactum De Singularis Caelum*, unless such a body or society repudiates the fundamental tenets of the Rule of Law and Justice and the most sacred instrument that gives it life and authority.
[margin: Reality and Rule of Law and Justice]

200. A Concept or Object or Thing that cannot be proven to exist in Reality consistent with the present sacred Maxims has no Existence in Law. Any Edict, Decree, Command, Demand, Order, Judgement or Opinion that contradicts one or more of the present sacred Maxims cannot be Real and therefore has no valid Existence.
[margin: Reality and Divine Law]

Article 22 - Paradox

201. A ***Paradox*** is a formal Axiom or Postulation that produces more than one conclusion whereby such conclusions are diametrically opposed to one another.
[margin: Paradox]

202. A properly formed Paradox has the form A implies not-A, and not-A implies A. Therefore, A and not-A are logically equivalent: A = not-A.
[margin: Proper formation of Paradox]

203. A properly formed Paradox does not mean a contradiction: as the term contradiction implies a "speaking against the truth; or the
[margin: Paradox Versus Contradiction]

denial of the truth; or to resist or contrary to the truth". Therefore, a contradiction can never be reasonably defined as a Paradox.

204. A properly formed Paradox does not mean counter-intuitiveness: as the term counter-intuitive implies a "contrary to intuition or common sense" and therefore a defect or error in reasoning. Therefore, a counter-intuitive statement can never be reasonably defined as a Paradox. *(Paradox Versus counter-intuitiveness)*

205. The presence and existence of true Paradox throughout the foundations of all systems of knowledge and inquiry is proof itself of the existence of the Divine and the inherit nature of Existence as a Dream of the Divine Creator. *(True Paradox and the Divine)*

206. Whilst the presence and existence of true Paradox throughout the foundations of all systems of knowledge and inquiry is proof itself of the existence of the Divine, the exclusion of the Paradox is acceptable in certain systems of Reality that require certainty and simple reproducibility upon the notion of Truth, Logic and the Rule of Law. *(Exclusion of Paradox)*

207. Whilst acknowledgement of the existence of Paradox at every level of matter and the Universe is essential to the construction of any valid standard model of elements and rules, it is acceptable to limit the reference of Paradox in certain simplified scientific models dealing with the physical qualities of the Universe, in order to assist in reliable calculation and reproducibility. *(Limitation of Paradox for reliable calculation)*

208. The presence within any Model or System of an absolute rejection of Paradox as a defect, or error, without due respect or consideration, is a sign of an unreal and delusion model or system:- *(Absolute Rejection of Paradox a sign of an Unreal and Delusion Model or System)*

   (i) Any system of measurement or calculation based on the outright rejection of paradox in observations of the Universe cannot be reliably or sensibly be considered as a valid or legitimate system of measurement, but an inferior language, system or model; and

   (ii) As the system and language known as mathematics has evolved to outright reject the clear presence of the paradox within the universe, such a system and language cannot be considered a reliable or effective system, language or model. Instead the Ucadian Language and System of Eikos is to be used as a superior system, model and language.

2.2 Absolute Awareness

Article 23 - Awareness

209. ***Awareness*** is the present and continuous ability to receive, conceive, perceive, comprehend or discern complex information concerning various concepts, or objects, or conditions or events and anticipate or react accordingly.
    Awareness

210. By definition, Awareness is the quality of observation. Therefore, Awareness is always non-locational and unable to be quantified as present in a physical form, even though it involves several physical Objects and be capable of being "objectified" through observation and measurement.
    Awareness and Observation

211. Whereas the word Awareness is equivalent to the term Consciousness as both may imply a state or quality of being aware, the term Consciousness is distinct from Awareness in that Consciousness depends upon an Object possessing at least Elemental Awareness as the Observer, whereas Awareness is concerned with the function of observation within a Model of Reality, or the Objects within such a Model of Reality.
    Awareness Versus Consciousness

212. By definition, the essential function of Elemental Awareness depends upon:
    Elemental Awareness

    (i) A *Model of Reality* whereby Concepts or Objects may be defined according to different properties, qualities and states; and

    (ii) A *System of Rules* associated with the Model of Reality whereby the presence or anticipation of one or more Objects or Concepts may cause the change in state of a related Object or Concept; and

    (iii) A theoretical or physical *Instructional Language* based upon finite sets of choices, whereby such properties, qualities and states of Concepts or Objects may be encoded or decoded into informational and instructional algorithms of different functions; and

    (iv) A theoretical or physical *System of Functions* capable of being used to construct algorithms for the encoding of information and instructions; and

    (v) A *Computational Model* being a theoretical or physical system capable of reading and enumerating certain algorithms of functions within some informational language based upon a finite set of choices, whereby the execution of such algorithms may cause some change in state of one or more Objects or

Concepts.

213. The presence of a computational model capable of writing informational and instructional algorithms to some form of physical memory is not a requirement for Elemental Awareness. *Elemental Awareness and computational model*

214. The presence of Elemental Awareness in a System and Model of Reality is not a sign of self-awareness, but the fact that the fundamental elements of such a Reality have the instructional and informational capability and independence of functioning without the need for direct instruction or intervention by the Observer. *Presence of Elemental Awareness*

215. All sustainable Models of Reality require Elemental Awareness to continue to function. *Requirement of Elemental Awareness*

216. All forms of Awareness may be defined into eleven categories being *Theoretical, Elemental, Material, Mechanical, Digital, Organical, Cyborgial, Robotical, Supernatural, Spiritual* and *Transcendental*: *Categories of Awareness*

   (i) *Theoretical Awareness* is a Model of Awareness created Conceptually that then may be brought into a new form of Reality by producing a version as Material Awareness, or Mechanical Awareness, or Digital Awareness, or Cyborgial Awareness, or Robotical Awareness; and

   (ii) *Elemental Awareness* is a Model of Awareness created Conceptually or Actually as the minimum requirements for an Awareness System; and

   (iii) *Material Awareness* is a Model of Awareness created using forms of Matter as the systems encoding and transmitting information and instructional algorithms as well as computational solutions. A Star and its light fields is a perfect example of a Model of Material Awareness; and

   (iv) *Mechanical Awareness* is a Model of Awareness created using mechanical and designed circuits and switches. A Mechanical Device can be Material, Digital, Organical (such as a "brain"), Cyborgial or Robotical; and

   (v) *Digital Awareness* is a Model of Awareness created using Mechanical Devices to create the means of electrical or light switches and capability of creating Awareness; and

   (vi) *Organical Awareness* is a Model of Awareness created using purely Organic Mechanical Devices, principally neurons, neural networks and one or more brains to create the means and capability of creating such Awareness; and

   (vii) *Cyborgial Awareness* is a Model of Awareness created using a

Hybrid of Organic and Material Mechanical Devices to create the means and capability of creating such Awareness; and

(viii) *Robotical Awareness* is a Model of Awareness created using independently functioning Mechanical Devices to create the means and capability of creating such Awareness; and

(ix) *Supernatural Awareness* is a Model of Awareness created as a function of higher computation abilities of other systems of Awareness, exemplified by the notions of "Self Awareness", "Dreaming", "Emotions" and "Intentional Choice"; and

(x) *Spiritual Awareness* is a Model of Awareness created as a function and by-product of the formation of higher computation abilities of other systems of Awareness, whereby all Supernatural Awareness is Spiritual and all Spiritual Awareness is Supernatural; and

(xi) *Transcendental Awareness* is a Model of Awareness created as a function and by-product of a super advanced consciousness, such as a singularity, whereby the usual boundaries of consciousness and awareness no longer apply.

217. By definition, all matter in the Universe (Universal Dream) possesses Elemental Awareness:

(i) No Model of Reality or Complex System is capable of continual function in the absence of Elemental Awareness; and

(ii) The Universe itself as the largest Object and Unita as the smallest possible particles belong to the largest and most basic computational model possible of Elemental Awareness; and

(iii) The presence of Elemental Awareness negates the need for the ultimate Observer (Divine Creator and Divine Dreamer) from micro-managing or intervening in the state or direction of individual particles of matter in the Universe.

Matter, the Universe and Elemental Awareness

218. Any Argument in support or assertion of an interventionist Observer (Divine Creator) in providing separate computational intervention in micro-managing the Universe is false, absurd and in gross error as:

(i) Such a computational model would require the endless creation of larger and larger universal computational models larger than the previous model to adequately calculate and predict every possible permutation; and

(ii) The computational requirements of existence are elegantly and simply resolved through the presence of Elemental Awareness with every particle belonging to at least one Material

Observer (Divine Creator) Versus a Computational Intervention

Lex Divina: Maxims of Divine Law

    Awareness computational model; and

 (iii) Such arguments contradict and breach the limits of intervention of an Observer with the Object observed and the necessary boundary between a Model of Reality (Dream) and the Dreamer.

219. As the rules of existence requires that every level of matter belongs to at least one computational model of Awareness, every structure in the universe can also be analysed and observed in relation to its informational and instructional function relative to other forms of matter: *Existence, Matter, Awareness, the Universe and Function*

 (i) *Planets* and their fields can be observed and properly analysed as complex and powerful computational models using systems of Material Awareness; and

 (ii) *Stars* and their fields can be observed and properly analysed as highly complex and powerful computational models using systems of Material Awareness to an extraordinary level with one another; and

 (iii) *Galaxies* and their fields can be observed and properly analysed as highly complex and powerful computational models using systems of Material Awareness to a transcendental level with one another.

220. As a Terrestrial Organic Species, the Homo Sapiens originate from planet Earth and are bound to "earth-like" conditions. Therefore, it is the height of hubris and ignorance to falsely conclude that the Awareness of an individual member of the Species or the collective consciousness of the Species is greater than the Awareness of planet Earth or indeed the Sun or the Milky Way Galaxy: *Awareness of Homo Sapiens*

 (i) Even if a member of the Homo Sapien Species were to ignorantly disavow the logic, nature and necessity of Awareness throughout the Universe, the fact is that the Awareness of the Earth includes all human awareness; and

 (ii) As the Awareness of the Earth includes all human awareness as well as all other life awareness, it must logically and sensibly be greater than that of the Homo Sapien species or any individual member; and

 (iii) As the Sun represents every planet and the Sun itself, it logically and sensibly follows that the Awareness of the Sun must be greater than planet Earth.

Article 24 - Inspiration

221. *Inspiration* is the first possible step of any Divine or Supernatural or Conscious Existence, expressed as "I begin". — Inspiration

222. In respect of Inspiration and Computation: — Relative to Inspiration and Computation

    (i) Inspiration is a computational event, representing the very beginning of a series of complex calculations that collectively may be called "perception" or "cognition" or "cognitive awareness"; and

    (ii) Inspiration depends upon a preceding event or external influence that may be abstracted as an Algorithm and defined as the Inspirational Algorithm or Alpha Algorithm.

223. In respect of Inspiration and Awareness: — Relative to Inspiration and Awareness

    (i) Inspiration may be viewed as the "spark" that commences the process of all forms of Awareness; and

    (ii) No form of Awareness can proceed in the absence of a beginning element.

224. Inspiration is the first element of Absolute Awareness, the first Concept of all possible Concepts of Existence and the source of Divine and Supernatural Influence. — Inspiration as first Concept

Article 25 - Reception

225. *Reception* is the second possible step of any Divine or Supernatural or Conscious Existence, expressed as "I think". — Reception

226. In respect of Reception and Computation: — Relative to Reception and Computation

    (i) Reception are the initial computational algorithms necessary for conscious and intentional thinking triggered following an Inspirational event; and

    (ii) Reception depends upon the existence of Inspiration. Without Inspiration, the cognitive functions of Reception would not commence.

227. In respect of Reception and Awareness:- — Relative to Reception and Awareness

    (i) Before an Observer can even recognise a thought, much less the structure and content of such thought, the nature and data of the Inspiration must be processed and thinking started; and

    (ii) No further form of Awareness can proceed until the nature of an Inspiration may be interpreted and viewed as the commencement of some thought.

Article 26 - Conception

228. ***Conception*** is the third possible step of any Divine or Supernatural or Conscious Existence, expressed as "I think a thought". — Conception

229. Conception itself depends upon the prior existence of Reception. — Concept relating to Reception

230. In respect of Conception and Computation:- — Relative to Conception and Computation

   (i) Conception is a crucial and complex computational process whereby some abstracted identity is capable of being assigned to an object, even if that object is not yet conceptualised in dimension or context; and

   (ii) As the name suggests, Conception is the first time that the processing of functions and data yields information in the form of some essential meaning by some symbol or signification.

231. In respect of Conception and Awareness:- — Relative to Conception and Awareness

   (i) Conception is the stage of forming a Concept with Meaning in Awareness. It is a function of higher level awareness; and

   (ii) In any model of Perception that correctly identifies the necessary stages of thinking, Conception is always the first stage.

Article 27 - Perception

232. ***Perception*** is the fourth possible step of any Divine or Supernatural or Conscious Existence, expressed as "I think a thought comprehended in context". — Perception

233. Perception itself depends upon the prior existence of Conception. — Perception relating to Conception

234. In respect of Perception and Computation:- — Relative to Perception and Computation

   (i) Perception is a crucial computational stage as the core of cognition, being the ability to name and then place a thing in context; and

   (ii) Perception necessarily involves pattern recognition equivalent to set theory whereby sets or groups of things are used as a means of identifying the context of the conceived object in its present surrounds or theoretical categorisation.

235. In respect of Perception and Awareness:- — Relative to Perception and

(i) Perception or the attribute of Cognition is the most commonly used term to describe the required higher conscious function as Cognition that is vital for any decision making process; and *Awareness*

(ii) While Inception is an even higher cognitive function, being able to "perceive a concept not only in context but dimension", Perception as Cognition generally provides an adequate response; and

(iii) As Perception is essentially the product of pattern recognition as a "best approximation", Perception can sometimes be at fault and sometimes in gross error; and

(iv) The less cognitive investment in considering the Concept and its context, particularly in thinking about its context, can lead Observers otherwise distracted or underperforming into concluding poor Perceptual and Cognitive judgements.

Article 28 - Inception

236. ***Inception*** is the fifth possible step of any Divine or Supernatural or Conscious Existence, expressed as "I think a thought of something of form comprehended in context". *Inception*

237. Inception itself depends upon the prior existence of Perception. *Inception relating to Perception*

238. In respect of Inception and Awareness:- *Relative to Inception and Awareness*

   (i) Inception is equivalent to conceptualising or thinking in context. It is the ability to build models of thought and to test scenarios and ideas within such reality as a means of better describing the form; and

   (ii) All examples of higher memory and recall require the quality of Inception to make sense and often "rebuild" events in mind to produce a cohesive picture; and

   (iii) Inception is always a highly suggestive state whereby external inputs can drastically change the context of mind; and

   (iv) Inception is the first state of Awareness needed for learning; and

   (v) The prevalence of devices for visualisation can potentially impede the natural abilities of certain higher order life forms to adequately form deeper memories associated with Inception.

Article 29 - Determination

239. ***Determination*** is the sixth possible step of any Divine or Supernatural or Conscious Existence, expressed as "I think a thought of something of form comprehended in context within certain bounds and limits of dimension". *(Determination)*

240. Determination itself depends upon the prior existence of Inception. *(Determination relating to Inception)*

241. In respect of Determination and Awareness:- *(Relative to Determination and Awareness)*

    (i) Determination is equivalent to higher discernment or "observing the observer" and Imagination. It is the highest form of conceptualisation in learning; and

    (ii) Determination is vital in the formation of long term memories; and

    (iii) Determination is equivalent to dreaming.

Article 30 - Expiration

242. ***Expiration*** is the seventh possible step of any Divine or Supernatural or Conscious Existence, expressed as "I define my thinking and therefore create certain rules". *(Expiration)*

243. Expiration itself depends upon the prior existence of Determination. *(Expiration relating to Determination)*

Article 31 - Dream

244. A ***Dream*** is a perceived dimension and experienced objective existence by a Dreamer, operating according to a System of one or more rules and relations. A Dream is equivalent to a Model of Reality. *(Dream)*

245. It is a gross error and falsity to conclude Dreams as equivalent in generalised terms to lesser mental representations: *(Dreams as Ideas and mental representations)*

    (i) A Dream belongs to the complete class of Ideas of mental representations and conceptual archetypes. However, a Dream is more strictly a Model in that a Dream by its nature is a highly complex Idea; and

    (ii) A non-sensory computation or cognition as an Idea cannot be properly equated to being the same as a Dream; and

    (iii) A sensory, emotional or symbolic signification may be included within certain Dreams, but such information on its own cannot be properly equated as the same as a Dream.

246. All Dreams share the same essential elements: *(Essential elements of Dreams)*

(i) The Dream is *dimensional* in that it perceives a construct whereby certain objects exist within a certain dimension defined by some form of boundary; and

(ii) The Dream is *objective* in that the Dreamer as Observer therefore, observes the Dream as a singular Object as the Observer can observe a "Dream within a Dream" but not two dreams of equal weight being simultaneously observed by a single Observer; and

(iii) The Dream is *formal* in that the Dreamer as Observer therefore, observes within the boundary of the Dream (Object) two or more Objects possessing some kind of form that can clearly be distinguished and recognised according to some system of rules and knowledge; and

(iv) The Dream is *contextual* in that the Dreamer as Observer therefore, observes within the boundary of the Dream (Object) two or more Objects whereby one or more Objects serve as the formal surroundings, circumstances, environment, background or settings of the Dream and one or more other Objects serve as the subject of observation; and

(v) The Dream is *sequential* in that the events within the Dream unfolds in a sequence, even if chronological time is perceived differently; and

(vi) The Dream is *real* in that the Dreamer as Observer validates and witnesses the Dream as an actual Object of existence; and within the Dream the objects have a real and material context, according to one or more rules and limits, even if such Objects do not exist or cannot exist in another form of reality.

247. All Dreams may be classified by one of two types of Models being either *conceptual archetypes* or scaleable *abstractions*: *(Dream model types)*

(i) A Dream as a *conceptual archetype* is considered a generalised or idealised system whereby other systems of Awareness may be synchronised or compared; and hypotheses and axioms derived or tested from it in order to make longer term memories or change existing memories or priorities. The vast majority of Dreams are of the "conceptual archetype" kind; and

(ii) A Dream as a scaleable *abstraction* is considered a detailed physical representation of a certain Reality that maintains accurate ratios and relations to the actual model, but may be at a scale many times smaller or larger than the perceived or conceptualised "real-world" objects. All "Visions" are "scalable abstractions" of some kind.

248. A Dream is the only theoretical and actual solution to the creation or destruction of three Dimensional space, with Dimension being the contextual environment necessary for any "real-world" Existence. *Dream and the three dimensional space*

249. The strength and stability of a Dream is relative to the System of Rules and Relations applied in its creation, especially the necessary existence of Elementary Awareness and at least one computational model within the dream for the function and relation of its components: *Strength and stability of a Dream*

   (i) The most common Dreams of higher order species being as "conceptual archetypes" are not generally designed for complex and stable observation, as such stability and complexity is counter-intuitive to their purpose; and

   (ii) As "conceptual archetypes" most Dreams are not designed to be replayed (remembered). Therefore, once most Dreams have been experienced, they are forgotten; and

   (iii) Visions, also known as "Vivid Dreams" as scaleable abstractions are significantly different in that such Dreams are necessarily more complex in Rules and Relations and Elemental Awareness such that these rarer Dreams are more likely to be remembered as "conceptual archetypes" of the original.

250. Life is a Dream, according to a stable set of Rules and Relations as established by the Divine as the ultimate Dreamer. *Life is a Dream*

Article 32 - Dreamer

251. A **Dreamer** is a Being possessing some level of Awareness in Mind, that actively observes a Dream as an Object of their own creation. *Dreamer*

252. A Being is distinct from a Person as a Being is an embodiment of Unique Collective Awareness or "Consciousness of Mind" within a certain Reality, whereas a Person is a form of Sacred Circumscribed Space enclosing certain characteristics and appearances as the identity of one or more Beings within a certain Reality. *Being Versus Person*

253. Active observation of a Dream by a Dreamer through some level of Awareness in Mind is distinct and separate from the concept of active participation or interaction within the Dream observed: *Observation of a Dream by a Dreamer*

(i) A Dreamer as Observer is equivalent to a reliable and independent witness or "watcher" of a Dream rather than a participant. Hence, the "state of Dreaming" is frequently described as involuntary or being "asleep" rather than awake; and

(ii) Experiencing a Dream, particularly a "Vivid Dream" or Vision from the perspective of being within the Dream or being one or more Actors in the Dream, should not be confused with the primary role of the Dreamer first and foremost being the Observer and Creator of such a Reality. There is technically nothing limiting the conscious experience of the Dreamer as one or more Actors within the Dream other than the contextual abilities and learned conscious limitations of the Dreamer; and

(iii) When a Dreamer in their function as Observer becomes actively engaged in intervening directly into the function and operation of the Rules of the Dream, they cease to remain an independent Observer and instead become an active party and the Dream collapses as a failed Reality; and

(iv) A "Vivid Dream" or Vision is constructed from a more robust System of Rules and Relations, especially a level of Elementary Awareness. Therefore, this gives greater scope to the Dreamer in experiencing the Dream as one or more Actors within it.

254. There is no greater Dreamer than the Divine; and also known as the Absolute, ALL, Divine Creator, Father, God, Almighty, Allah, Great Spirit, Unique Collective Awareness, Ucadia and all other historic, customary and traditional names when used to describe the greatest of all possible Observers.

Dreamer and the Divine

Article 33 – Unique Collective Awareness

255. ***Unique Collective Awareness*** is the most perfect description of the Divine in relation to the mystery, design and function of Existence, Life and the Universe.

Unique Collective Awareness

256. Unique Collective Awareness is equivalent to the term and concept of Trinity and Holy Trinity when describing the nature of the Divine:

Unique Collective Awareness, Trinity, Holy Trinity and the Divine

(i) When describing the nature of the Divine as God or the Father, the term Unique is equivalent, only when it is understood that such a model is within the context of Trinity; and

(ii) When describing the nature of the Divine as personified in the Son and the personification of Divine Love, the term Collective is equivalent when understood in the mystery of singularities within a higher order species representing the literal collective consciousness at a point in time and space; and

(iii) Awareness in the context of the model of Trinity is equivalent to the concept of Holy Spirit as the personification of Divine Knowledge.

257. Unique Collective Awareness is equivalent to the term and concept of ALL and variations thereof such as "Allah" when describing the nature of the Divine: *(Awareness Loves Life)*

(i) The equivalent letter and concept of "A" is equivalent to Awareness; and

(ii) The equivalent letter and concept of the middle "L" is equivalent to the personification of Divine Love and the concept of Collective; and

(iii) The equivalent letter and concept of the end "L" is equivalent to the concept of Life and all Existence and the Concept of Uniqueness.

258. Unique Collective Awareness is equivalent to the term and concept of the Great Spirit of Life and Existence and all variations thereof including (but not limited to) Brahman, Great Power and Cosmic Reality of Harmony when describing the nature of the Divine. *(Unique Collective Awareness and equivalent terms)*

2.3 Existential Concepts

Article 34 - Existence

259. ***Existence*** is the present and continuous activity of actual witness of something observed within a Model of Reality. *Proof of Existence* is the action of testimony or other measurable proof given by an Observer of something that was historically observed within a Model of Reality.

Existence

260. In reference to the authentic meaning of Existence and Proof of Existence:

Proof of Existence

  (i) The true meaning of Existence is quantitatively and qualitatively different to the concept of Proof of Existence; and

  (ii) Existence is a present and continuous act depending upon at least one Object and one Observer; and

  (iii) Proof of Existence is a conceptual abstract to the history of some observation according to some frame of reference; and

  (iv) Any theory, model or postulation that erroneously or deliberately or obstinately persists with confusing the notions of Existence and Proof of Existence as being one and the same is false, absurd and without validity.

261. In general reference to Existence:

In general reference to Existence

  (i) As Existence by definition is the present and continuous activity of actual witness of something observed within a Model of Reality, Existence depends upon both an Observer and the thing Observed; and

  (ii) As an Object observed may itself be an Observer of other Objects, all forms of Existence are relative; and

  (iii) As an Object observed may itself be made up of lesser Objects, all forms of Existence are hierarchical; and

  (iv) Providing a particular Object belongs to a higher Reality being observed by a higher Observer, it is then theoretically possible to argue that the particular Object objectively exists independent of any presence or absence of a lesser Observer; and

  (v) The highest possible form of Existence is Absolute Existence; and

  (vi) While Proof of Absolute Existence may be said to exist independently to the ongoing Existence of some Object, Absolute Existence itself cannot function without the presence of at least one Observer and one Object; and

(vii) The fact that the complex set of the Universe continues to exist without persistent and active observation by lesser Observers is irrefutable proof of the persistent and continuous presence of the Divine as the ultimate Observer of Absolute Existence; and

(viii) Any Theory of Reality that claims Objects in the Universe may exist independently of an Observer is therefore an endorsement of the existence of the Divine.

262. In reference to Existence and the Concepts of Rules and Matter: *Existence, Rules and Matter*

(i) Existence depends upon the presence of Rules and Matter; and

(ii) Matter without Rules cannot Exist in Reality. Therefore, Rules without Matter cannot exist in Reality; and

(iii) Rules without matter in the form of Awareness may exist independently as a Concept (as a theory only); and

(iv) Rules as Awareness existing independently are equivalent to Unique Collective Awareness; and

(v) Rules of Existence are equivalent to the Axiom Sets of the Ucadia Model of Unique Collective Awareness; and

(vi) Existence is therefore equivalent to a Dreamer and Dream in action; and

(vii) Therefore, the Divine depends on the Dream for its Existence and vice versa.

263. The ultimate Paradox of Existence is that the very largest depends upon the very smallest for its existence and vice versa. Hence, there is an absolute and unbreakable bond between the Infinite and the Infinitesimal. *The Infinite and Infinitesimal*

Article 35 - Object

264. An **Object** is any Model perceived, comprehended or discerned by an Observer to exist according to some Model of Reality. *Object*

265. An Object is properly distinguished from a Concept in that an Object is said to exist within the dimension of some form of Reality, whereas a Concept is said to exist purely within the dimension of Mind. *Object versus Reality*

266. The very meaning of Object itself depends upon the presence of three essential elements: *Essential elements of Object*

(i) The existence of a Model as the "thing observed" within the dimension of Reality; and

(ii) An Observer; and

(iii) The action of observing the Model with some level of Awareness in Mind.

267. In general reference to Theoretical and Real Objects: *Theoretical and Real Objects*

(i) Every Object belongs to an Existing Set; and

(ii) Every Object may itself be an Observer of some other Object; and

(iii) Every Object may be said to be a Set of lesser Objects; and

(iv) As an Object observed may itself be an Observer of other Objects, all forms of Objects are relative to some degree; and

(v) As an Object observed may itself be made up of lesser Objects, all sets of Objects are hierarchical; and

(vi) The smallest possible Object in Reality is a Theoretical Point; and

(vii) The smallest possible Object of Matter in Reality is a Unita made up of seven Theoretical Points (of Awareness); and

(viii) The smallest possible Object in Theory is the Concept of Unreal. No Object can be smaller or less than the Concept of Unreal.

(ix) The greatest Theoretical or Real Object is the Divine as the total set of all existence and instances of all possible Objects, matter, rules, life, mind, Concepts, universe and spirit; and also known as the Absolute, ALL, Divine Creator, Father, God, Almighty, Allah, Great Spirit, Unique Collective Awareness, Ucadia and all other historic, customary and traditional names when used to describe the greatest of all possibilities.

268. As the Divine means the "set of all sets" and the "existence of all Objects" there is no greater Object nor set. Therefore, every other possible Object is greater than Unreal and less than the Absolute, except the Divine.   *The Divine relative to Sets and Objects*

269. The necessary action of observation by an Observer of an Object is always relative and always unique; as the position of the Observer, the state of mind of the Observer and the occurrence of observation when taken collectively is a unique event never to be repeated in exactly the same way again.   *Observation is a unique event*

270. As the action of an Observer is always relative to some degree, it is a falsity, error and absurdity to conclude that an Object not witnessed by a particular Observer does not exist: *Object in relation to the Observer*

(i) Even if the Observer is defined as the Absolute Divine, the very fact that a Model must be postulated in order to frame the hypothesis of existence or non existence of an Object means that every Model exists in theory at some level, no matter how unreal or improbable; and

(ii) Therefore, it is primarily the reliability and truth of Testimony of the Observer and not the question of existence or non existence of a Model and Object that must be concluded as the first proof.

271. An Object always depends upon some level of Awareness in the Mind of the Observer to distinguish the certain unique form of a Model from another. The absence of any distinction or awareness in the Mind of the Observer therefore negates the nature and relative existence of a distinct and unique Model and Object. *(Object and Awareness of Mind)*

272. An Object may be defined as *Corporeal* or *Incorporeal*: *(Corporeal and Incorporeal Object)*

(i) A *Corporeal Object* possesses some original form or "physical body" within the dimension of Reality; and

(ii) An *Incorporeal Object* does not possess some original form or "physical body" within the dimension of Reality, yet its existence can be verifiable, such as a database, register or ledger, or axiom, or account or financial instrument.

Article 36 - Observer

273. An **Observer** is an Object possessing some level of Awareness that actively observes an Object according to some Model of Reality. *(Observer)*

274. The fundamental definition of Existence itself requires the presence of at least one Observer and one Object. *(The Observer, the Object and Existence)*

275. In general reference to the Concept of Observer and Awareness: *(Concept of Observer and Awareness)*

(i) All Objects in Reality by definition possess Elemental Awareness or above. Therefore, all Objects in Reality may also be Observers of other Objects to some degree; and

(ii) Active observation through some level of Awareness is distinct and separate from the concept of active participation or interaction with the Object observed; and

(iii) An Observer is equivalent to a reliable and independent witness or "watcher" rather than a participant; and

(iv) The mere presence of an Observer possessing some level of Awareness in Mind is sufficient to affect the outcome of the

Object observed to some degree; and

(v) When an Observer becomes actively engaged in intervening directly into the intention (will), function and operation of the Object, they cease to remain an Observer and instead become an active party with the Object and the events surrounding it.

276. There is no greater Observer than the Divine; and also known as the Absolute, ALL, Divine Creator, Father, God, Almighty, Allah, Great Spirit, Unique Collective Awareness, Ucadia and all other historic, customary and traditional names when used to describe the greatest of all possible Observers:
The Divine as an Observer

(i) The mystery of the Divine being both the Observer and the Object observed is resolved as a matter of unique perspective and identity in the same manner as a Dreamer may be differentiated from the Dream observed; and

(ii) So long as the Divine Creator - as the ultimate Dreamer - does not seek to directly intervene within the Dream of Existence nor seek to usurp or suspend the rules necessary for such Existence, the Observer-Object relation holds; and

(iii) Nothing precludes the personification and embodiment of the Divine from intervening within the Dream through the supernatural aspects of Cognitive Law.

Article 37 - Rules

277. A ***Rule*** may be defined as any statement applying to a Relation between Objects or Concepts having unique Meaning that can be independently observed and repeated.
Rules

278. All Objects and Concepts exist according to one or more Rules.
Objects, Concepts & Rules

279. All Rules whereby Objects and Concepts exist may be defined as an Axiom.
Rules as an Axiom

280. The Existence of all Models, including the Universe, depends upon the existence of Rules.
The existence of the Universe and Rules

281. If one essential Rule of Existence ceased to apply, Existence itself would cease.
Rule of Existence

282. The strength of a Rule is the synergy between Objects or Concepts that it represents and their relations to all other Rules without contradiction.
Strength of Rule

283. Any proposed Rule that contradicts one or more of these Maxims is
Contradiction of

without Merit and therefore, is null and void having no force or effect. *Rule*

Article 38 - Imperfection

284. ***Imperfection*** is the binary Concept connected to "Perfection" whereby a Concept or Object is considered unfinished, or incomplete, or fallible or with some fault. *Imperfection*

285. In respect of observing and acknowledging Imperfect Concepts: *Imperfect Concepts*

    (i) Concepts that depend upon other Concepts for their theoretical existence may be described as Imperfect to some degree; and

    (ii) Concepts that cannot be made manifest in Reality may be described as Imperfect to some degree; and

    (iii) As even the Concept of Nothing depends upon the Concept of Concept to exist, Nothing in Theory can be Perfect.

286. In respect of observing and acknowledging Imperfect Objects: *Relative to Observing and acknowledging Imperfect Objects*

    (i) Objects that depend upon other Concepts or Objects for their theoretical existence may be described as Imperfect to some degree; and

    (ii) As every Object in a Model of Reality depends upon the existence of other Concepts or Objects for Existence, Nothing in Reality can be Perfect; and

    (iii) As Nothing in Reality is Perfect, the Dream of Existence can only ever be Imperfectly Perfect.

287. In respect of Divine relation between Perfection and Imperfection: *The Divine relating to Perfection and Imperfection*

    (i) Nothing is Perfect. Everything else is Imperfect to some degree; and

    (ii) Perfection seeks unity and makes allowance for Imperfection by knowing and respecting the true nature of the Divine; and

    (iii) Imperfection seeks Perfection of spirit and mind as its highest expression through living with others in harmony according to the authentic Rule of Law; and

    (iv) The personification of the Divine can only ever be Perfectly Imperfect; and

    (v) In theory, the boundary of One-Dimensional Space is most perfectly represented by a straight line, while the boundary of theoretical Two-Dimension Space is most perfectly represented by a Circle with a Perfect Theoretical relation of

1:3; and

   (vi)   However in Reality all circles (boundaries) are Imperfect to some greater or lesser degree; and so the most Perfect Real Ratio of a Diameter (straight line) to a Circle is 1 to 3.14159265 or "Pi"; and

   (vii)   The personification of the Divine relation of Imperfect Perfection is the ratio of Pi (3.14159265); and

   (viii) The personification of the Divine in the form of Pi as the absolute sign and seal of authority of Divine Imperfect Perfection since 1,000 CE is 14th March 1592, or 14th March 1926 or 14th March 1965.

288. In respect of objectifying Imperfection as a characteristic of Objects in the Universe, particularly Living beings: *Objectifying Imperfection*

   (i)   As everything in the Universe is Imperfect, a Model of objectifying Imperfection, especially in terms of mind and behaviour is perfectly reasonable and in accord with Divine Law; and

   (ii)   All Models of objectifying Imperfection as a characteristic of Living Beings must also be expressed in terms of an ability to redeem, reform, forgive and transcend certain imperfections. A Model that gives no opportunity for Remedy is false, immoral and profane and contrary to the present Maxims and the most sacred Covenant *Pactum De Singularis Caelum*.

Article 39 - Autonomy

289. ***Autonomy*** is the Concept and quality of self governance and capacity for independent function and action.   *Autonomy*

290. In respect of Autonomy: *Relating to Autonomy*

   (i)   Autonomy infers governance according to certain well formed Rules and not an absence of Rules; and

   (ii)   An absence of well formed Rules cannot properly be equated to Autonomy but a failed Reality or "failing reality" such as a state of "Anarchy"; and

   (iii)   Once certain clear and well formed Rules are clearly established, the function of the Model of Reality must be free or "autonomous" to function; and

   (iv)   Autonomy also infers a degree of choice of "free will" within a Model of Reality generating complex and usually unpredictable behaviour; and

(v) The Concept of Autonomy is consistent with the Concept of Relativity in respect of a well formed Model of Reality; and

(vi) The Concept of Autonomy is perfectly consistent with the necessary conditions for the stable existence of any Model of Reality; and

(vii) The existence of Universal Physical Laws as a Model of Relativity is irrefutable proof of the Autonomous nature of the Model of Universal Existence.

291. In respect of Autonomy and Determinism: *Autonomy and Determinism*

(i) All Models of Determinism follow the similar premise that as all events are necessary to some degree, everything that happens in the Universe is ultimately predestined and/or predictable, even if such observations are beyond the scope of an Observer less than the Divine; and

(ii) Determinism is an absurdity and fallacy that rejects the fundamental and necessary relation of a non-intruding Observer and Object representing the Divine and Divine Creation; and

(iii) Determinism is therefore a Delusional Model in obstinate and deliberate opposition to the authentic nature of Divine Will and Existence itself.

292. In respect of Autonomy and the Divine: *Autonomy and the Divine*

(i) The fundamental relation of Divine Creator as Observer and Divine Creation as Object necessitates that all Creation within the Universe possesses Autonomy and free will within the limits and rules of form; and

(ii) Because Autonomy of Creation is essential to fundamental Existence, the Universe is also necessarily complex; and

(iii) Complexity therefore is not a weakness of Creation, but a strength that empowers the continuation of Existence and the avoidance of the Universe collapsing into a perfect singularity in mirror to the Creator and thus ending Existence itself; and

(iv) The proof that some functions cannot be determined is proof that the Universe is indeterminate to some degree.

Article 40 - Dependence

293. ***Dependence*** is the state of relying upon another to function. *Dependence*

294. Dependence is one of the *Twelve Laws of Divine Creation*. *Divine Creation*

Title II - Divine Concepts

295. In Reference to Dependence: *(and Dependence / Relating to Dependence)*
- (i) Dependence infers a relation between two separate Concepts or Objects with their own Character; and
- (ii) Dependence does not infer Determinism, but well formed Rules defining such a Relation; and
- (iii) Dependence infers the necessity of co-operation for harmony and peaceful co-existence; and
- (iv) Dependence therefore is dependent upon a level of Autonomy between two separate Concepts or Objects that choose to be united in a Relation; and
- (v) The absence of choice, or Autonomy between two Objects or Concepts can never be concluded as features of Dependence but unity through servitude; and
- (vi) An absolute Object can be said to depend upon the existence of an absolute Observer to exist in reality, and vice versa; and
- (vii) The Divine can be said to depend upon the existence of Divine Creation to exist in reality.

Article 41 – Chaos and Cosmos

296. ***Chaos*** is an ancient binary Concept with Cosmos and means an unordered and undefinable state, or vast chasm or primordial abyss. The Concept of Nothing is equivalent to the Concept of Chaos. *(Chaos)*

297. ***Cosmos*** is an ancient binary Concept with Chaos and means an ordered and definable harmonious state of matter as the entirety of existence. The Concept of Existence and the Universe is equivalent to the Concept of Cosmos. *(Cosmos)*

298. In respect of Chaos:- *(Relating to Chaos)*
- (i) From the time of the ancient Greek philosophers from Hesiod, even through to Socrates, Plato and Roman philosophers, the concept of Chaos meant an absence of matter and a great void; and
- (ii) The absurd notion of attributing "confusion" and "disorder" to the concept of Chaos only emerged in the 17th Century as a foundation to a delusional Model known as Mundi, whereby fundamental concepts were reversed and deliberately confused; and
- (iii) The concept that a perfect void may contain a "confused

mixture of all sorts of particles" is a concept of deliberate madness and wilful ignorance designed to confuse and entrap the minds of a species; and

(iv) Any definition that seeks to attribute the notions of confusion or disorder to a perfect void of matter is therefore null and voids itself from the beginning, having no force or effect.

299. In respect of the counterfeit and absurd attributes of "disorder" and "confusion" deliberately attached to Chaos:- *Chaos versus disorder and confusion*

(i) The Binary pair Concept of Cosmos in respect of Chaos was also corrupted to become the notion of some deterministic Order. Thus the phrase "Out of Chaos comes Order"; and

(ii) The counterfeit, absurd and insane model of corrupted Chaos and its false twin Order, was then further used to ferment the counterfeit theology of Mundi whereby a "natural relationship" existed between Disorder and Order, whereby the ends of obtaining and defending power were justified by the natural cycle of "Divine Chaos" and "Divine Order"; and

(iii) Under the Theology and Cosmology of Mundi, Chaos as the false and absurd notion of "disorder" and "confusion" then became the "Divine" mirror of war, terror, piracy, slavery, oppression and cruelty. Order was then portrayed as the mythical phoenix "rising from the ashes". Hence, a seventy to eighty year cycle was formed whereby Chaos was not only expected, but engineered as an artificial construct as a system of perpetual power in complete contradiction to the true maxims of the Universe; and

(iv) Thus, any model, theory or philosophy that seeks to assert the existence of some kind of Divine Chaos-Order Model based on such false, sacrilegious and delusional notions of confusion or disorder to a perfect void of matter is therefore null and void itself from the beginning, having no force or effect.

Article 42 – Complexity and Simplicity

300. **Complexity** is a binary concept with Simplicity and means the state or quality of being complex and not simple. *Complexity*

301. **Simplicity** is a binary concept with Complexity and means the state or quality of being simple and not complex. *Simplicity*

302. In respect of Complexity:- *Relative to Complexity*

(i) Complexity does not mean disorder or confusion, but an inability to simply describe a resulting state or behaviour; and

(ii) Complexity does not mean Chaos, as Chaos by authentic definition means a great chasm or void, whereas Complexity depends upon numerous Objects acting in complex behaviour; and

(iii) Complexity does not mean instability, but the difficulty in predicting repetitive and perfect behaviour; and

(iv) Existence depends upon the Complexity of Autonomous Behaviour; and

(v) All Complex Behaviour in Theory can be described and expressed through simple rules, the predictability of simple Algorithms is possible; and

(vi) Not all Complex Behaviour in Reality can be described and reduced to Algorithms. This is the Principle of Computational Irreducibility; and

(vii) As all Complexity in Theory may be expressed through simple Algorithms, all Complexity in Theory may be simplified to a minimum level of meaningful expression.

303. In respect of Simplicity:- Relative to Simplicity

(i) Simplicity does not mean lacking in sophistication as the simplest of axioms of the Universe are the most elegant and sophisticated, whereas Complex Designed Algorithms frequently produce unreliable and inflexible results that do not reflect any true Law of the Universe; and

(ii) Simplicity does not mean Determinism as the Universe relies upon Simple Algorithms to produce Complex and unpredictable behaviours, whereas Deterministic Systems are normally complex in design yet produce repetitive and unreal behaviours; and

(iii) The binary relation and existence of Simplicity to Complexity and Vice Versa is evidenced throughout all levels of Existence; and

(iv) A Binary relation between the Infinitesimal and the Infinite exists as evidence of such binding between the Simplest and most Complex; and

(v) Existence depends upon the Simplicity of Rules; and

(vi) The Simplest and most perfect and elegant Axiom of all Axioms is the Meaning of ALL means "Awareness Loves Life".

304. The *Paradox of Complexity and Simplicity* is that all intentional Complexity ultimately resolves itself to simple solutions, whereas Paradox of Complexity and

intentional Simplicity resolves itself to unsolvable Complexities. — Simplicity

Article 43 - Dimension

305. ***Dimension*** is the Position of one or more Theoretical or Real Objects as observed by an Observer, relative to one or more other Theoretical or Real Objects. — Dimension

306. Dimension as a Concept fundamentally depends upon the existence of nine other Elemental Concepts being *Object, Observer, Reality, Rule, Position, Distance, Limit, Existence* and *Proof of Existence*:- — Dimension as a Concept

   (i) *Object* is any Model perceived, comprehended or discerned by an Observer to exist according to some Model of Reality; and

   (ii) *Observer* is a Being possessing some level of Awareness in Mind, that actively observes an Object according to some Model of Reality; and

   (iii) *Reality* is one of a Binary pair of Models constructed upon certain Rules of Form and Meaning, enabling a certain degree of stability necessary for the existence and function of two or more Theoretical or Real Objects; and

   (iv) *Rule* is any statement applying to a Relation between Objects or Concepts having unique Meaning that can be independently observed and repeated; and

   (v) *Position* is the unique location of an Object within a Model of Reality; and

   (vi) *Distance* is the perceived or measured separation and difference between two or more Objects having Position within a Model of Reality; and

   (vii) *Limit* is a boundary or restriction or constraint between two or more definitive locations, sets, spaces, realities, areas or concepts; and

   (viii) *Existence* is the present and continuous activity of actual witness of something observed within the Limit of some Model of Reality; and

   (ix) *Proof of Existence* is the action of testimony or other measurable proof given by an Observer of something that was historically observed within a Model of Reality.

307. In general reference to the Concept of Dimension:- — Relative to the Concept of Dimension

   (i) Things cannot exist in Dimension unless they have Position relative to other things and are observed; and

(ii) As Observation depends on the observation of something, Dimension therefore cannot exist independently in theory or reality without theoretical or real Objects.

308. In general reference to the Concept of Dimension and Space:- *Concept of Dimension and Space*

(i) Space is a quality always attached to something, relative to other things; and

(ii) The Concept of Space is equivalent to the Concept of Dimension; and

(iii) There is no such thing as a perfect vacuum in Reality; and

(iv) The distance between Objects is a quality possessed by an observed Set of Objects, not an independent quality; and

(v) Space cannot exist without at least two or more Theoretical or Real Objects; and

(vi) An increase in the density of elements into the same volume will increase the density of space; and

(vii) The density of space is not constant; and

(viii) An increase in the density of space will therefore result in a decrease in the velocity of an object and alter its direction to some degree through such space. Thus, the change in direction (bending) of light is proof of inconsistent density of space.

309. In general reference to the Concept of Dimension and Sets:- *Concept of Dimension and Sets*

(i) Dimension as a collection of Things observed is equivalent to an Existing Set; and

(ii) As all Sets possess the attribute of boundary (limit) by virtue of their observation and recognition, Dimension possesses boundary by virtue of the things observed within it; and

(iii) As all Sets are hierarchical, Dimension is hierarchical, meaning one or more lesser Dimensions can exist within a higher Dimension; and

(iv) As all Sets are relative, Dimension is relative, meaning one or more different Dimensions may exist within the same higher level of Dimension; and

(v) Providing a particular Set of Objects belongs to a higher Reality being observed by a higher Observer, it is then theoretically possible to argue that Dimension appears to exist independent of any presence or absence of a lesser Observer;

Lex Divina: Maxims of Divine Law

and

(vi) The highest possible form of Dimension is Absolute Dimension; and

(vii) The fact that the complex set of the Universe continues to exist in Dimension without persistent and active observation by lesser Observers is irrefutable proof of the persistent and continuous presence of the Divine as the ultimate Observer of Absolute Existence within Absolute Dimension; and

(viii) Any Theory of Reality that claims Dimension may exist independently of an Observer or Objects observed is therefore an irrefutable endorsement of the existence of the Divine.

310. In general reference to the Concept of Dimension and Elemental Awareness:- *Concept of Dimension and Elemental Awareness*

(i) All Objects in Real Dimension possess Elemental Awareness; and

(ii) The Existence of Elemental Awareness means that every level of Matter from the smallest particles of the Universe (Unita) to the largest, possesses a Unique Collective Awareness of Reality that makes approximations and generalisations conducive to a stable form of Reality; and

(iii) The Collective Elemental Awareness of Objects at each level of Awareness means that the Dimension formed at each level of Matter is an Abstract born from the previous and lower level of Dimension of Existence rather than formed as one of a series of enclosed sub-sets of Dimension; and

(iv) As each level of Matter above the Primary Dimension of Existence (Unita Level) is an Abstract of the previous Collective Elemental Awareness of Objects within the previous Dimension, each Level of Matter possesses a unique and autonomous Existence, whilst being consciously bound to one another according to the Authentic Standard Model of Laws of Relativity as defined by Ucadia; and

(v) Such a connection between Abstracted Dimensions of Levels of Matter means that (for example) while the sub-atomic elements that represent the Elemental Awareness that construct Atoms are bound in some way to the consciousness and life of Atoms and vice-versa, sub-atomic elements (for example) possess their own unique existence distinct from the Dimension and Universe of Atoms; and

(vi) Unita dream the next level of matter not the Divine Creator;

and

(vii) As the Dimension of Atomic Elements depends upon the Dimension and reality of Elemental Awareness of Sub-Atomic Elements, if a sub-atomic particle were to cease to exist, then its subsequent Elemental Awareness and projection into Atomic Dimension would also cease to exist. To guard against the collapse of Universal Reality and Dimensions, it is impossible to destroy even one Primary and smallest particle of Unita from within any Theoretical or Real Reality; and

(viii) As each level of Matter above the Primary Dimension of Existence (Unita Level) is an Abstract of the Collective Elemental Awareness of Objects within each particular Dimension, the relative size of each Dimension of Levels of Matter may be different, without affecting one another, providing the Standard Model of Rules are not breached. Thus, contrary to the enclosed model of sub-sets, the Abstracted Dimensions of Matter means the Universe of Unita is massively smaller than the relative size of the Universe of Atoms, without contradicting the Laws of the Universe; and

(ix) The largest Dimension of Matter is the Universe of super sub-atomic elements equating to the largest possible Model of the Universe; and

(x) The smallest and first Real Dimension is Divine Reality that has Zero Dimension, but may be equated for Higher Life visualisation as no larger than a grain of sand; and

(xi) The second level of Real Dimension is the Universe of Unita that is Infinitesimal, but may be equated for Higher Life visualisation as no larger than an apple or small ball in diameter; and

(xii) The third level of Real Dimension is the Universe of Super Sub Atomic Elements that may be equated for Higher Life visualisation as Infinite in diameter; and

(xiii) The fourth level of Real Dimension is the Universe of Sub Atomic Elements that may be equated for Higher Life visualisation all galaxies and Universal (Billions of Light Years in diameter); and

(xiv) The fifth level of Real Dimension is the Universe of Elemental Atomic Elements that may be equated for Higher Life visualisation as a star or group of stars and nebula being a galaxy or group of galaxies in diameter; and

(xv) The sixth level of Real Dimension is the Universe of Molecular Elements that may be equated for Higher Life visualisation as a planet, stars and interstellar space in diameter; and

(xvi) The seventh level of Real Dimension is the Universe of Cellular Elements that is a Dimension unique to each life bearing planet or moon; and

(xvii) The eighth level of Real Dimension is the Universe of Species Consciousness that is a Dimension unique to each higher order species of a bearing planet; and

(xviii) The ninth level of Real Dimension is the Universe of Unique Collective Awareness that is a Dimension unique to each Higher Order Living being such as the Homo Sapien.

311. Only two Primary forms of Dimension may exist in theory or reality being Zero-Point Dimension and Real Dimension:-

(i) *Zero-Point Dimension*, also known as *Unreal Dimension* and *Euclidean Space*, is a purely theoretical form of Dimension dependent upon the prior existence of Zero as the Empty Set and the point of origin; and

(ii) *Real Dimension*, also known as *Objective Dimension*, is a theoretical and real form of Dimension independent of Zero as the Empty Set but dependent upon the existence of two or more Objects.

312. All Zero-Point Dimension may be categorised as *Zero-Dimensional, One-Dimensional, Two-Dimensional, Three-Dimensional, Four-Dimensional* or *Hyper-Dimensional Zero-Point Space*:- Zero Point Dimension categories

(i) *Zero-Dimensional Zero-Point Space* is a purely Theoretical Model whereby the Empty Set is expressed as the first theoretical form of Dimension without measure, or position, or distance, or limit, or rule, or object and therefore without real existence; and

(ii) *One-Dimensional Zero-Point Space* is a purely Theoretical Model whereby One Dimension (Length) and Zero is expressed as the second theoretical form of Dimension as a straight line (or "number line") of quantities without limit or object and therefore without real existence; and

(iii) *Two-Dimensional Zero-Point Space* is a purely Theoretical Model whereby two perpendicular lines as Line x (Length) and Line y (Width) intersect at Zero upon a single Square plane of Existence, whereupon one or

more Points having the coordinates (x, y) may also exist; and

(iv) *Three-Dimensional Zero-Point Space* is a purely Theoretical Model whereby three perpendicular lines as Line x (Length), Line y (Width) and Line z (Height) intersect at Zero as a common point of origin, whereupon one or more Points having the coordinates (x, y, z) may also exist within a Cube Dimension; and

(v) *Four-Dimensional Zero-Point Space* is a purely Theoretical Model whereby Three-Dimensional Zero-Point Space as a Cube Dimension then changes over Time as the Fourth variable and represented as a Tesseract (Changing Cube within a Changing Cube); and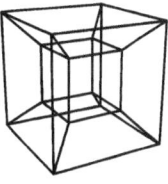

(vi) *Hyper-Dimensional Zero-Point Space* are purely Theoretical Models whereby typically Three-Dimensional Zero-Point Space is ascribed more variables as "dimensions" even though such qualities may not measure a variance of distance or space.

313. All Real Dimension may be categorised as either *Two-Dimensional* or *Three-Dimensional Space*: — Two and Three Dimensional Space

(i) Two-Dimensional Real Space is a Theoretical or Real Model whereby a Point (Centriole) or Zero has Unique Position relative to four other Points located on two theoretical lines as Line x (Length) and Line y (Width) intersecting at Zero within a single Ellipsoid of Existence, whereupon at least one Point exists ahead, behind, to the left and right (or north, south, east, west) of the Centriole Point; and

(ii) Three-Dimensional Real Space is a Theoretical or Real Model whereby a Point (Core) or Zero has Unique Position relative to six other Points located on three theoretical perpendicular lines as Line x (Length), Line y (Width) and Line z (Height) intersecting at Zero within a single Spheroid of Existence, whereupon at least one Point exists ahead, behind, to the left

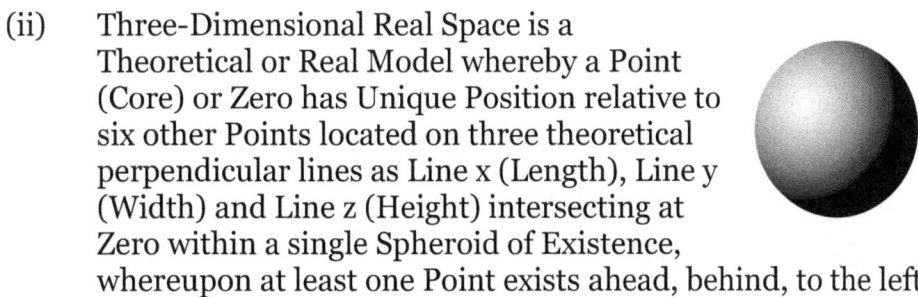

and right, above and below the Core Point.

314. All Two-Dimensional and Three-Dimensional Real Space exists according to fourteen standard and generic shapes being *Circular, Oblate, Prolate, Oval, Super Oblate, Super Prolate, Superoval, Concave, Concave Oblate, Concave Prolate, Convex, Convex Oblate, Convex Prolate* or *Transitional*:-

(i) *Circular* is when Two-Dimensional Real Space is in the shape of an ellipsoid with a standard positioned Centriole Point, an internal Line x (Length) equal in proportion to Line y (Width) and a circular Ellipse boundary; and

(ii) *Oblate* is when Two-Dimensional Real Space is in the shape of an ellipsoid with a standard positioned Centriole Point, an internal Line x (Length) shorter in proportion to Line y (Width) and a circular Ellipse boundary; and

(iii) *Prolate* is when Two-Dimensional Real Space is in the shape of an ellipsoid with a standard positioned Centriole Point, an internal Line x (Length) longer in proportion to Line y (Width) and a circular Ellipse boundary; and

(iv) *Oval* is when Two-Dimensional Real Space is in the shape of an ellipsoid with a lower position of Centriole Point, an internal Line x (Length) longer in proportion to Line y (Width) and a circular Ellipse boundary; and

(v) *Super Oblate* is when Two-Dimensional Real Space is in the shape of an ellipsoid with a standard positioned Centriole Point, an internal Line x (Length) extremely shorter in

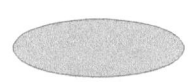

proportion to Line y (Width) and a circular Ellipse boundary; and

(vi) *Super Prolate* is when Two-Dimensional Real Space is in the shape of an ellipsoid with a standard positioned Centriole Point, an internal Line x (Length) extremely longer in proportion to Line y (Width) and a circular Ellipse boundary; and

(vii) *Super Oval* or "Bell" is when Two-Dimensional Real Space is in the shape of an ellipsoid with an extremely lower position of Centriole Point, an internal Line x (Length) extremely longer in proportion to Line y (Width) and a circular Ellipse boundary; and

(viii) *Concave* is when Two-Dimensional Real Space is in the shape of an ellipsoid with a standard positioned Centriole Point, an internal Line x (Length) shorter in proportion to Line y (Width) and a concave (curving inward) Ellipse boundary; and

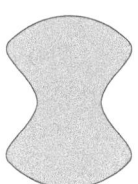

(ix) *Concave Oblate* is when Two-Dimensional Real Space is in the shape of an ellipsoid with a standard positioned Centriole Point, an internal Line x (Length) shorter in proportion to Line y (Width) and a concave (curving inward) Ellipse boundary; and

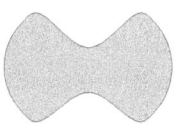

(x) *Concave Prolate* is when Two-Dimensional Real Space is in the shape of an ellipsoid with a standard positioned Centriole Point, an internal Line x (Length) longer in proportion to Line y (Width) and a concave (curving inward) Ellipse boundary; and

(xi) *Convex* is when Two-Dimensional Real Space is in the shape of a spheroid with an ellipsoid with a standard positioned Centriole Point, an internal Line x (Length) equal in proportion to Line y (Width) and a convex (curving outward) from the north pole to the Ellipse and from the south pole to the Ellipse boundary; and

(xii) *Convex Oblate* is when Two-Dimensional Real Space is in the shape of a spheroid with an ellipsoid with a standard positioned Centriole Point, an internal Line x (Length) shorter in proportion to Line y (Width) and a convex (curving outward) from the north pole to the Ellipse and from the south pole to the Ellipse boundary; and

(xiii) *Convex Prolate* is when Two-Dimensional Real Space is in the shape of a spheroid with an ellipsoid with a standard positioned Centriole Point, an internal Line x (Length) longer in proportion to Line y (Width) and a convex (curving outward) from the north pole to the Ellipse and from the south pole to the Ellipse boundary; and

(xiv) *Transitional* is when Two-Dimensional Real Space is in a transitional ellipsoid shape such that it cannot be properly classified as any of the previous thirteen shapes at the time of observation. All Transitional shape is temporary.

315. All forms of Real Dimension of fields, objects, complex matter structures, galaxies, stars, planets, forces and energy may be resolved into one of the shapes of Two-Dimensional or Three-Dimensional Real Space.

<small>Real Dimension relative to shape</small>

Article 44 - Certainty

316. ***Certainty*** is the state of trusting that something is fixed, settled, resolved or firm. Thus Certainty within a binary reality of logic to be a fact or truth unquestionably established.

    <small>Certainty</small>

317. The paradox of Certainty and the concept of Existence itself means there can be no Divine Certainty as Divine Existence is a constant action and expression of free will and intention of the Divine, not a mechanical function:-

    <small>Paradox of Certainty and Existence</small>

    (i) Certainty as it pertains to the Divine presumes that Divine Existence is fixed, or settled or resolved, then the notion of Existence itself is a constant action and expression and free will and intention of the Divine; and

    (ii) The only Divine Certainty to be found is within the most sacred Covenant *Pactum De Singularis Caelum* and the expression of the willingness and intention of the Divine to honour the solemn sacred promise of guaranteed continued life and existence to the Universe; and

    (iii) All other notions of fixed and determined Divine outcomes as they pertain to Certainty are misguided and false.

2.4 Existential Calculations

Article 45 - Calculation

318. ***Calculation*** is the mental act or process of executing an Algorithm being a valid *Function* as a *Mathematical Determination* to produce a *Result*. Calculation is distinct and separate from the notion of Computation in that:-

   (i) Calculation is an act or process within a non-real or theoretical set of awareness or mind, whereas Computation is a physical act or process within a real set; and

   (ii) A Calculation may involve a multi-linear or multivalent execution, whereas Computation is always constrained by linear execution; and

   (iii) Calculation depends purely upon the existence of awareness, whereas Computation depends not only upon awareness in dimension but the physical apparatus to perform mathematical determinations; and

   (iv) A Calculation requires the existence of a Mathematical Determination to produce a Result, whereas a Computation does not necessarily require the existence of a Mathematical Determination to produce a Result, but merely the running of a well formed Computation as an Algorithm to produce the Mathematical Determination; and

   (v) Calculation depends upon awareness of Mathematical Concepts, whereas Computation does not, as the running of well formed Algorithms has the ability to produce the desired Mathematical Determinations without knowledge or competence in Mathematical Concepts.

319. The *Concept of Calculation* is equivalent to the Concept of Perfect Rational and Logical Thinking, being the Act and Result Set of changing states of pure Awareness.

320. In respect of Calculation, Rules and Existence:

   (i) Existence depends upon Calculations using Rules based on Mathematical Concepts; and

   (ii) Awareness of Mathematical Concepts is essential to Existence; and

   (iii) All arguments essential to Existence may be expressed as Calculations.

321. In respect of Calculation and execution:-

(i) Calculation as an execution of non-location and non-real mind is unconstrained by the restriction of linear "step-by-step" execution. Thus the highest form of Calculation is multi-dimensional; and

(ii) Calculation is capable of executing mathematical concepts that are more sophisticated and complicated than general computation limits in the physical reality of the Universe; and

(iii) As Calculation is capable of executing mathematical concepts that are more sophisticated and complicated than general computation limits in the physical reality of the Universe, the formation of mathematical concepts by a higher order civilisation is prone to unnecessary complexity and unreal mathematical concepts from time to time.

322. The first and primary integrated system of Calculation and Computation is Unique Collective Awareness and the physical Universe:- *(Calculation and Computation Systems)*

(i) The first and primary integrated system of Calculation and Computation between the Divine and the Universe means that Calculation can influence Computation and vice versa, without compromising existence; and

(ii) Each level of matter and existence is an integrated model of Calculation and Computation; and

(iii) Higher Order (Self Aware) Life is an example of an integrated model of Calculation and Computation.

Article 46 - Eikologia

323. *Eikologia*, also known as *Eikos* is the Ucadia Model of Knowledge and discipline of the study of Calculation and Computation of mathematical quantities, numbers, shapes, structures, sets, functions, algorithms and the relations between these concepts. Eikologia is categorised into nine (9) foundation classes, being *Eikos Logos, Numerics, Uniset, Geolex, Symerics, Axiomatics, Kinesis* and *Protomatics*:- *(Eikologia)*

(i) *Eikos* being the rules, systems, language and models for constructing valid arguments, statements, functions and theories in Eikos using the Eikos Language; and

(ii) *Logos* being the study of the principles and rules of definition, argument and construction used to create and interpret valid statements defined within the Eikos Language; and

(iii) *Numerics* being the study of the principles and rules of definition whereby Numbers are defined, classified and used in valid statements defined within the Eikos Language; and

(iv) *Uniset* being the study of all principles and rules of definition whereby Sets are defined, classified and used in valid statements defined by the Eikos Language System; and

(v) *Geolex* being the study of principles and rules of definition whereby geometric shapes and their relations are defined, classified and used in valid statements defined by the Eikos Language System; and

(vi) *Symerics* being the study of structure, relation and quantity, expressed as valid formula defined by the Eikos Language System; and

(vii) *Axiomatics* being the study of all principles and rules of definition whereby Axiom are defined, classified and used in valid statements defined by the Eikos Language System; and

(viii) *Kinesis* being the study of principles and rules of definition of changes of state of motion and relation of theoretical and real objects are defined, classified and used in valid statements defined by the Eikos Language System; and

(ix) *Protomatics* being the study of principles and relations of naturally occurring and artificial patterns.

324. The *Eikos Language System* is a unique language system to define and describe the relationships, properties and measurement of all elements in operation from the Ucadia Standard Model of Universal Elements and the Ucadia Hydro-Helio Model of Atomic Elements. — Eikos Language System

325. All possible relationships, properties and measurement of all elements in operation from the Ucadia Standard Model of Universal Elements and the Ucadia Hydro-Helio Model of Atomic Elements may be defined by the *Eikos Language System*. — All possible properties expressed through Eikos

326. All possible laws, relations, rules, formula and axioms of the Real and Unreal Sets of the Universe may be expressed through the Eikos Language System. — All possible connections expressed through Eikos

Article 47 - Number

327. A ***Number*** is an abstract entity capable of describing quantities, relations, properties or form.

328. In general reference to Numbers:-

    (i)   All Numbers are both unique Concepts and Objects in themselves; and

    (ii)   All Numbers may be represented symbolically; and

    (iii)   All Numbers may be represented as Sets; and

    (iv)   All Numbers are real by virtue of their existence in accord with the most sacred Covenant *Pactum De Singularis Caelum* and the present sacred Maxims; and

    (v)   The degree of Reality of a Number is dependent upon the degree whereby the Number represents a well structured Model of Reality of real world objects or measurements or relations; and

    (vi)   Everything may be defined as a Number.

329. In reference to Numbers being represented as Sets:-

    (i)   The Real Set of 1 contains a circumscribed *Subset* of the Empty Set; and

    (ii)   The Unreal Set of -1 contains a circumscribed *Subset* of the Empty Set; and

    (iii)   The Paradoxical Set (Real-Unreal) Set of 2 contains the Complete Union of Real and Unreal Sets.

330. The Divine may be defined as the Set of all Numbers:-

    (i)   All Numbers owe their origin, authority and power from the Divine in accord with the most sacred Covenant *Pactum De Singularis Caelum* and the present sacred Maxims; and

    (ii)   A Number has no power, force or effect unless its use is in complete accord with the most sacred Covenant *Pactum De Singularis Caelum* and the present sacred Maxims.

Article 48 – Perfect Number

331. A ***Perfect Number*** is any Positive Number, including zero that can be expressed as a Ratio of itself or other Positive Numbers.

332. Perfect Numbers are similar in part to the concept of Integers.

However, as Integers may also contain Negative Numbers, the term Integer is never permitted to be used within the Eikos Language System of Ucadia. *Integers*

333. All Perfect Numbers may be defined as Unique, Similar or Idea: *Perfect Number defined as Unique, Similar or Idea*

   (i) *Unique Perfect Numbers* are Positive Numbers that may represent uniquely real Objects (e.g. 1, 3, 5, 7, 9, 11 etc); and

   (ii) *Similar Perfect Numbers* are Positive Numbers that may represent sets and collections of real Objects (e.g. 2, 4, 6 etc); and

   (iii) *Idea Perfect Numbers* are Positive Numbers that cannot represent real Objects.

334. In respect of *Unique Perfect Numbers*:- *Unique Perfect Numbers*

   (i) A Unique Perfect Number is a number that can be expressed as a ratio of itself uniquely; and

   (ii) A Unique Perfect Number is divisible only by itself and 1; and

   (iii) The simplest Unique Perfect Numbers are 0 and 1; and

   (iv) The largest Unique Perfect Number is infinity; and

   (v) All Unique Perfect Numbers are a less than the Uniset (total sum of all numbers) ultimately derived from a Unique Perfect Number; and

   (vi) Existence tends towards a Unique Perfect Number; and

   (vii) Unique Perfect Numbers exist within the Uniset (total sum of all numbers) as a perfect pattern of randomness called the Prime (itself an imperfect unique number); and

   (viii) The Prime may be defined as unique pattern of existence of Unique Perfect Numbers and Similar Perfect Numbers within the Uniset related to a multiple ratio of the simplest synergistic number 6.

335. In respect of *Similar Perfect Numbers*:- *Similar Perfect Numbers*

   (i) A Similar Perfect Number is a number that can only be expressed as a ratio of itself as a collective of Unique Perfect Numbers; and

   (ii) A Similar Perfect Number is divisible by itself, smaller Unique Perfect Numbers, or smaller Similar Perfect Numbers and 1; and

   (iii) The simplest similar perfect number is 2; and

   (iv) The largest Similar Perfect Number is one less than infinity;

and

(v) All Similar Perfect Numbers greater than two may be defined as the sum of two Unique Perfect Numbers; and

(vi) Existence is the interaction of Unique Perfect Numbers and Similar Perfect Numbers tending towards a Unique Perfect Number; and

(vii) Similar Perfect Numbers may be defined as synergistic. Synergistic Numbers are numbers equal to the sum of all their possible divisors except itself. The smallest synergistic numbers are 6, 28, 496 and 8128; and

(viii) Similar Perfect Numbers may be defined as sympathetic. Sympathetic Numbers are two numbers where each is the sum of all the possible divisors of the other. The smallest sympathetic pairs are (220, 284), (1184,1210) and (17,296 18,416); and

(ix) A Similar Perfect Number is divisible by two if the last digit is even; and

(x) A Similar Perfect Number is divisible by three if the sum of its digits is divisible by 3; and

(xi) A Similar Perfect Number is divisible by four if the last two digits are divisible by 4; and

(xii) A Similar Perfect Number is divisible by five if it ends in 5 or 0; and

(xiii) A Similar Perfect Number is divisible by six if the number is divisible by 2 as well as 3; and

(xiv) A Similar Perfect Number is divisible by seven when the last digit of the original number is doubled and then subtracted from the remaining digits of the original number, giving a sum that is evenly divisible by seven; and

(xv) A Similar Perfect Number is divisible by eight if the sum of its last three digits is divisible by 8; and

(xvi) A Similar Perfect Number is divisible by nine if the sum of its last three digits is divisible by 9; and

(xvii) A Similar Perfect Number is divisible by ten if it ends in zero; and

(xviii) A Similar Perfect Number is divisible by eleven when an alternating pattern of adding and subtracting the digits of the original number is calculated (add first, subtract second, add third etc) and the sum is divisible by eleven; and

(xix) A Similar Perfect Number is divisible by twelve when the number is divisible by 3 as well as 4.

336. In respect of *Idea Perfect Numbers*:-   *Idea Perfect Numbers*

   (i) An Idea Perfect Number is a number that cannot express a real object but can be defined as a ratio of itself and other numbers; and

   (ii) An Idea Perfect Number is always similar in its expression of ratio of itself to other numbers as collections of sets of more than one; and

   (iii) An Idea Perfect Number cannot be a uniquely expressed ratio number, as this is the proper classification of a unique imperfect number.

Article 49 - Imperfect Number

337. An **Imperfect Number** is any Positive or Negative Number, excluding zero, that cannot be expressed as a ratio of itself.   *Imperfect Number*

338. Imperfect Numbers are similar in part to the concept of Integers. However, as Integers contain Natural Numbers, the term Integer is never permitted to be used within the Eikos Language System of Ucadia.   *Imperfect Numbers relative to Concept of Integers*

339. All Imperfect Numbers may be defined as Unique, Similar or Idea:-   *Imperfect Numbers defined as Unique, Similar or Idea*

   (i) *Unique Imperfect Numbers* are Numbers that may represent uniquely real ratios (e.g. pi, e etc); and

   (ii) *Similar Imperfect Numbers* are Numbers that may represent sets and collections of real ratios (e.g. 180° etc); and

   (iii) *Idea Imperfect Numbers* are Numbers that cannot represent real ratios or real objects (e.g. -1.2).

340. In respect of *Unique Imperfect Numbers*:-   *Unique Imperfect Numbers*

   (i) A Unique Imperfect Number is a number that represents real ratios but can only be expressed as a ratio of itself uniquely; and

   (ii) A Unique Imperfect Number is divisible only by itself and 1; and

   (iii) All Unique Imperfect Numbers may be defined as a decimal. All Unique Imperfect Numbers as decimals will have an infinite number of potential decimal points; and

(iv) The most perfect Unique Imperfect Number is pi; and

(v) Existence is a Unique Imperfect Number.

341. In respect of *Similar Imperfect Numbers*:

(i) A Similar Imperfect Number is a number that can only be expressed as a collection of real ratios; and

(ii) A Similar Imperfect Number is divisible by itself, Unique Perfect Numbers, similar perfect numbers and 1; and

(iii) The simplest Similar Imperfect Number is 1 degree; and

(iv) All Similar Imperfect Numbers may be defined as a fraction or a decimal. All fractions may be converted to a decimal or vice versa; and

(v) All Similar Imperfect Numbers as decimals will always have a finite number of decimal points.

342. In respect of *Idea Imperfect Numbers*:

(i) An Idea Imperfect Number is a number that cannot express a real object nor defined as a ratio of itself in theory as a collection of perfect unique numbers; and

(ii) All negative numbers are Idea Imperfect Numbers; and

(iii) The simplest Idea Imperfect Number is -1.

Article 50 - Infinitesimal

343. *Infinitesimal* is the smallest possible Quantity or Object greater than Zero, yet so small it cannot be feasibly measured in Reality; and only given a measurable quantity or value in Theory.

344. In respect of the Infinitesimal:-

(i) The Infinitesimal may be represented by the simple relation expression $1/\infty$ in reference to Infinity; and

(ii) The Infinitesimal is both a Number or Object and may be expressed also as a Set of some or all possible Infinitesimal Numbers or Objects; and

(iii) The Infinitesimal as a Set of possible Infinitesimal Numbers or Objects is actually a valid Real Set, but able to be perfectly expressed in theoretical terms as having values greater than zero and less than 1; and

(iv) As the Infinitesimal Set is a Real Set expressed legitimately by a Theoretical Set greater than zero and less than 1, it is the only Real Set, except Infinite Set that permits theoretical values and objects to be expressed as an extension of real values and objects; and

(v) The smallest possible Real Incomplete Set is the Infinitesimal of 1; and

(vi) The smallest possible Theoretical Incomplete Set is the Infinitesimal of -1; and

(vii) The ultimate Paradox of Existence is that the very largest depends upon the very smallest for its existence and vice versa. Hence, there is an absolute and unbreakable bond between the Infinite and the Infinitesimal.

Article 51 - Infinite

345. ***Infinite*** is the largest possible Quantity or Object or Set greater than Zero, yet so large it cannot be feasibly measured in Reality; and only given a measurable quantity or value in Theory.

Infinite

346. In respect of the Infinite:-

Relative to the Infinite

   (i) The Infinite may be represented by the simple relation expression ∞ in reference to Infinity; and

   (ii) The Infinite is both a Number or Object and may be expressed also as a Set of some or all possible Numbers or Objects; and

   (iii) The Infinite as a Set of some or all Numbers or Objects is actually a valid Real Set, but able to be perfectly expressed in theoretical terms as having values greater than zero and less than Infinity as expressed as $n^{\infty-1}$; and

   (iv) As the Infinite Set is a Real Set expressed legitimately by a Theoretical Set greater than zero and less than Infinity $n^{\infty-1}$, it is the only Real Set, except the Infinitesimal Set that permits theoretical values and objects to be expressed as an extension of real values and objects; and

   (v) Only the Theoretical and Real Incomplete Set of all Sets of the Infinite, that is also a member of itself, may exist in Reality; and

   (vi) The largest possible Theoretical and Real Incomplete Set is the Infinite; and

   (vii) As the Infinite is the only possible Set of all Sets (including itself) that may exist in Reality, the Universe may be properly described as an Imperfect Set; and

(viii) A Binary relation between the Infinitesimal and the Infinite exists as evidence of such binding between the Simplest and most Complex.

347. In respect of the Infinite as the Set of all Possible Numbers:

(i) All Numbers in Existence may be described as existing between 0 and Infinity; and

(ii) Infinity is a unique Set of all possible Numbers in Existence. Therefore, all Numbers in Existence may be said to be part of the Infinite Set; and

(iii) If one Number ceased to exist within the total Set of Infinity of Numbers, then the total Set would cease to exist.

Set of all Possible Numbers relative to the Infinite

Article 52 - Zero

348. *Zero* or the numeric symbol 0 is a Number that may represent:

(i) The numeric symbol that represents the Number Zero; and

(ii) The digit 0 in the decimal, binary and all other base numbering systems; and

(iii) The point on a scale or line segment where numbering or measurement originates; and

(iv) The Empty Set represented as a Number; and

(v) The value of a Quantity corresponding to the Number Zero; and

(vi) The Null Set or "not any" represented as a Number; and

(vii) The attribute of an Object that has no valid value; and

(viii) The absence of error, or deviation or remainder and therefore "perfect balance" of certain computations.

Zero

349. In respect of Zero:

(i) Zero may be expressed as a Set (Set of Zero) or the Empty Set; and

(ii) All other Numbers are derived from Zero.

Relative to Zero

Article 53 - Uniset

350. The largest possible Theoretical and Real Complete Set is the *Uniset*.

Uniset

351. In general reference to the Uniset:-

(i) All Numbers of the Uniset may be defined as existing between

Relative to the Uniset

the Prime Numbers of 0 and 1 by some multiplying degree (ratio); and

(ii) The Sum of all Properties is also known as the Uniset; and

(iii) The largest possible Multitude Quantity is the Uniset; and

(iv) The existence of Uniset is dependent upon the existence of each individual Member of the Set for itself to exist; and

(v) If one Member of the Uniset ceased to exist, the total Set being Uniset would cease to Exist.

Article 54 - Variable

352. A ***Variable*** is a Symbol used as a substitute for a range of possible Numeric or Theoretical values, usually within the context of some form of Axiomatic statement. By definition, the value of a Variable is not fixed and may be solved by more than one example.   *Variable*

353. All Variables may be defined as either *Object Variables* or *Theoretical Variables*:   *Variables defined*

    (i) *Object Variable* is any Variable that represents a known Object or Property of an Object; and

    (ii) *Theoretical Variable* is any Variable that does not represent a known Object or Property of an Object.

354. All Variables may be further defined as Independent or Co-dependent: *Dependence of Variables*

    (i) *Independent Variable* is any Variable that may be resolved independently of the inputs and solutions to any other variables within a given Axiom; and

    (ii) *Co-dependent Variable* is any Variable that is dependent upon the input of one or more other Variables within a given Axiom to function.

Article 55 - Constant

355. A ***Constant*** is a Symbol used as a substitute for a consistent Numeric or Theoretical value, usually within the context of some form of Axiomatic statement.   *Constant*

356. In general reference to Constants:-   *Relative to Constants*

    (i) All Constants are Continuous Functions that may be expressed as Ratios; and

    (ii) All Constants are either perfect numeric ratios or imperfect numeric ratios; and

(iii) A constant that is based on a perfect numeric ratio can only exist in theory; and

(iv) A constant that is an imperfect numeric ratio is based on the properties of real objects; and

(v) Only geometric constants are universal, all other constants are relative.

Article 56 - Formula

357. A ***Formula*** is a concise formal statement of relations between two or more Numbers, Sets, Variables or Constants in accord with a standard language of expression. Formula

358. All valid Formula adhere to the same essential elements:- Essential elements of Formula

   (i) The symbols and rules of formation of a Formula are determined by the logical language used; and

   (ii) A well formed Formula is one that adheres to the specific rules of formation of the logical language used. A poorly formed Formula does not.

359. The most superior logical language for the construct of Formula is the foundation class of Symeric Formula of Eikos, in accord with the present Maxims. Construct of Formula

Article 57 – Symeric Formula

360. ***Symeric Formula*** is a foundation class of elemental concepts associated with the study of structure, relation and quantity expressed as valid Formula within the Ucadia Language of Eikos. Symeric Formula

361. In respect of a Symeric Formula: Relative to Symeric Formula

   (i) All formula must adhere to the Ucadian Semantic Classification System standard of declaration of DIA (statements of DA) in their formulation and writing; and

   (ii) A DIA is a formal declaration of DA (objects as defined by the Ucadia Classification System and the Ucadia Symbols System); and

   (iii) All valid formula of Symerics are constructed of three (3) primary components: Function, Relation and Sum and two representations being Result (Function leads to Sum) or Relation (Sum leads to Function); and

(iv) A valid function must contain at least one variable and one object defined by some formation relationship; and

(v) A valid sum must contain at least one object or number. It may also contain the option of including one or more variables; and

(vi) A valid relation is any valid relator of the Ucadia symbols system that describes the leading relation between the result (function leads to sum) or the relation (sum leads to function); and

(vii) All variables contained within a formula must be defined by their type (unique, co-dependent or universal); and

(viii) For a formula to function properly, the correct substitution of variables by type and purpose must take place; and

(ix) The function of a formula (in terms of structure and flow of variables) may be expressed as linear, matrix or multi-dimension types.

362. The primary rules of the elemental concept of *Linear Formula* of the Symerics foundation class of the Eikos Language System are:

<small>Elemental concept of Linear Formula</small>

(i) A Linear Formula is any valid Symeric formula where the function adheres to the conventions of a two (2) dimension left to right formula of the Eikos language system; and

(ii) Linear formula is one of three (3) types of function of Symerics including Linear, Matrix (left-right, top-down, bottom-up) and Multi-Dimensional (in-out, around); and

(iii) All valid Linear Formula are read left to right and must contain at least two (2) variables defined by a valid relationship; and

(iv) A valid Linear Formula may not contain matrix structure, nor may it contain a multi-dimensional structure. In both cases, such a formula if valid will be classed as other than a Linear Formula.

363. The primary rules of the elemental concept of Symerics-Matrix formula of the Symerics foundation class of the Eikos language system are:

<small>Elemental concept of Symerics-Matrix formula</small>

(i) A matrix formula is any valid Symeric formula where the function adheres to the conventions of a two (2) dimension matrix structure of the Eikos language system; and

(ii) Matrix formula is one of three (3) types of function of Symerics including linear, matrix (left-right, top-down, bottom-up) and multi-dimensional (in-out, around); and

(iii) A matrix structure is a rectangular table of elements which may be numbers or variables that can be modified according to any operator. The horizontal line in a matrix is called rows and the vertical lines are called columns; and

(iv) All valid matrix structure must declare in its design and identification m rows, n columns, the operators to be applied to the elements, the conditions of such application and the path of reading (left-right, top-down or bottom-up); and

(v) All valid matrix formula must contain at least two (2) rows and two (2) columns of variables or numbers defined by a valid relationship; and

(vi) A valid matrix formula may not contain a multi-dimensional structure. Such formula are known as multi-dimensional Symeric formula.

364. A *Multi-Dimensional Formula* is any valid Symeric formula where the function adheres to the conventions of an n-dimensional structure of the Eikos language system:

Multi-Dimensional Formula

(i) Multi-dimensional formula is one of three (3) types of function of Symerics including linear, matrix (left-right, top-down, bottom-up) and multi-dimensional (in-out, around); and

(ii) An n-dimensional structure is a function defined by a relationship map of more than three (3) variables defined by a motion path and at least one (1) operator to be applied during motion; and

(iii) Multi-dimensional permit the expression of simultaneous n-dimensional events being applied to at least three (3) variables; and

(iv) All valid multi-dimensional formula describing real objects must be 3-dimensional with a geometric path and relationship map. However, theoretical formula without real objects permit more than three (3) dimensions; and

(v) A valid matrix formula may not contain a multi-dimensional structure. Such formula are known as multi-dimensional Symeric formula.

365. The primary rules of the elemental concept of simple theoretical formula of the Symerics foundation class of the Eikos language system are:

Elemental Concept of Simple Theoretical Formula

(i) Simple theoretical formula is any valid Symeric formula that involves no more than three (3) variables in a simple linear 2d formula such that the formula shall never apply to a geometric nor numeric, nor Uniset expression; and

(ii) The purpose and function of simple theoretical formula is primarily to express all possible relationships between real sets, objects and numbers that have no geometric expression; and

(iii) There exists six (6) sets of properties in association to the valid expression of any simple theoretical Symeric formula. These are definition, symbol, operations, equality, inequality and equivalence; and

(iv) The primary property of definition for all valid simple theoretical Symeric formula is that any variable defined by a valid symbol has the same universal meaning wherever it is located within the formula; and

(v) The primary property of symbol for all valid simple theoretical Symeric formula is that only valid Eikos symbols of the Ucadia symbols system are valid and used; and

(vi) There exists only seven (7) operations for all valid simple theoretical Symeric formula being addition, subtraction, multi-addition, multi-subtraction, ratio, exponent addition and exponent subtraction; and

(vii) There exists only three (3) property of equality for all valid simple theoretical Symeric formula being reflexive, symmetric and transitive; and

(viii) There exists only three (3) property of inequality for all valid simple theoretical Symeric formula being reflexive, symmetric and transitive; and

(ix) There exists only two (2) property of equivalence for all valid simple theoretical Symeric formula being symmetric and transitive.

366. The primary rules of the elemental concept of simple natural formula of the Symerics foundation class of the Eikos language system are:

(i) Simple natural formula is any valid Symeric formula that involves no more than three (3) variables in a simple linear 2d formula which may be applied to real world objects properties in a non-geometric expression; and

(ii) The sum of a simple natural formula must be either zero, or the sum of one or more non-zero terms; and

(iii) The purpose and function of simple natural formula is

Elemental concept of Simple Natural Formula

primarily to express all possible relationships within and between sets that have no geometric expression; and

(iv) There exists six (6) sets of properties in association to the valid expression of any simple natural Symeric formula. These are definition, symbol, operations, equality, inequality and equivalence; and

(v) The primary property of definition for all valid simple natural Symeric formula is that any variable defined by a valid symbol has the same universal meaning wherever it is located within the formula; and

(vi) The primary property of symbol for all valid simple natural Symeric formula is that only valid Eikos symbols of the Ucadia symbols system are valid and used; and

(vii) There exists only seven (7) operations for all valid simple natural Symeric formula is that being addition, subtraction, multi-addition, multi-subtraction, ratio, exponent addition and exponent subtraction; and

(viii) There exists only three (3) property of equality for all valid natural theoretical Symeric formula being reflexive, symmetric and transitive; and

(ix) There exists only three (3) property of inequality for all valid natural Symeric formula being reflexive, symmetric and transitive; and

(x) Simple natural formula are equivalent to the mathematical theory of a polynomial being an expression constructed from one or more variables and constants using operators where the sum is either zero or the sum of two (2) or more non-zero terms.

367. The primary rules of the elemental concept of simple numeric formula of the Symerics foundation class of the Eikos language system are:

Elemental concept of Simple Numeric Formula

(i) Simple numeric formula is any valid Symeric formula that involves no more than three (3) variables in which only perfect numbers may be used in a simple linear 2d formula such that the formula is not geometric; and

(ii) The purpose and function of simple numeric formula is to express certain relationships within and between sets of perfect numbers that have no geometric expression; and

(iii) Simple numeric formula may be either finite or infinite.

Infinite simple numeric formula are when there are an infinite number of solutions. Finite is when there are only a finite number of solutions; and

(iv) The simplest finite simple numeric formula is 1 multiplied by the variable [a] = 2; and

(v) The simplest infinite simple numeric formula is 1 multiplied by the variable [a] = the variable [b].

368. The primary rules of the elemental concept of simple Uniset formula of the Symerics foundation class of the Eikos language system are:

Elemental concept of Simple Uniset Formula

(i) Simple Uniset formula is any valid Symeric formula that involves no more than three (3) variables in a simple linear or matrix formula such that the formula shall never apply to a geometric expression; and

(ii) The purpose and function of simple Uniset formula is primarily to express all possible relationships within and between sets that have no geometric expression; and

(iii) There exists six (6) sets of properties in association to the valid expression of any simple Uniset Symeric formula. These are set, symbol, operations, equality, inequality and equivalence; and

(iv) The primary property of set for all valid simple Uniset Symeric formula is that there exists more than three (3) variables belonging to one set; and

(v) The primary property of symbol for all valid simple Uniset Symeric formula is that only valid Eikos symbols of the Ucadia symbols system are valid and used; and

(vi) There exists only seven (7) operations for all valid simple Uniset Symeric formula being addition, subtraction, multi-addition, multi-subtraction, ratio, exponent addition and exponent subtraction; and

(vii) There Exists only three (3) properties of equality for all valid simple Uniset Symeric formula being reflexive, symmetric and transitive; and

(viii) There Exists only three (3) properties of inequality for all valid simple Uniset Symeric formula being reflexive, symmetric and transitive; and

(ix) There Exists only two (2) properties of equivalence for all valid simple Uniset Symeric formula being symmetric and transitive.

369. The primary rules of the elemental concept of simple 2d geometric formula of the Symerics foundation class of the Eikos language system are:

Elemental concept of Simple 2d Geometric Formula

(i) Simple 2d geometric formula is any valid Symeric formula that involves no more than five (5) variables in a simple linear 2d formula such that the formula always apply to a real geometric expression; and

(ii) The purpose and function of simple 2d geometric formula is primarily to express all possible relationships within and between sets that have geometric expression; and

(iii) There exists six (6) sets of properties in association to the valid expression of any simple 2d geometric formula. These are Geolex, symbol, operations, equality, inequality and equivalence; and

(iv) The primary property of Geolex for all valid simple 2d geometric Symeric formula is that the function and relationships of the variables is expressed by at least one valid geometric function and shape; and

(v) The primary property of symbol for all valid simple 2d geometric Symeric formula is that only valid Eikos symbols of the Ucadia symbols system are valid and used; and

(vi) There exists only seven (7) operations for all valid simple 2d geometric Symeric formula is that being addition, subtraction, multi-addition, multi-subtraction, ratio, exponent addition and exponent subtraction; and

(vii) There exists only three (3) property of equality for all valid simple 2d geometric Symeric formula being reflexive, symmetric and transitive; and

(viii) There exists only three (3) property of inequality for all valid simple 2d geometric Symeric formula being reflexive, symmetric and transitive; and

(ix) There exists only one property of equivalence for all valid simple 2d geometric Symeric formula being symmetric and transitive.

Article 58 - Function

370. A ***Function*** is the expression of one or more relations of specialisation or dependency between quantities, or objects, or properties, or variables, or constants or things as a *Formula* such that

Function

when executed using a certain Input, a Result is produced.

371. In general reference to Functions:

    (i) All forms of Computation rely upon the existence of at least one or more input values then used to execute a valid Function to produce a Result. These input values may be defined as an Input Sequence or simply Input; and

    (ii) All forms of Computation rely upon the existence of at least one set of clear and well formed instructions in order to properly execute the calculation; and

    (iii) Such clear and well formed instructions must be in accord with some Model and Language of Computation that the Processor can comprehend as valid computational instructions; and

    (iv) When such instructions are in accord with a Model and Language of Computation that can be processed, then such instructions may be properly called a Function; and

    (v) A Function is always a part of an Algorithm; and

    (vi) A Function in the process of execution is equivalent to Information.

Article 59 - Positional (Function)

372. ***Positional Functions***, also known as Cellular Automation are functions relating to the unique position of an object and changes to its state or the state around it. Positional Functions are most frequently used in Computations associated with biological structures and design.

373. Cellular automaton consists of a regular grid of cells, each in one of a finite number of states, such as on and off:

    (i) The grid can be in any finite number of dimensions; and

    (ii) For each cell, a set of cells called its neighbourhood is defined relative to the specified cell; and

    (iii) An initial state (time t = 0) is selected by assigning a state for each cell; and

    (iv) A new generation is created (advancing t by 1), according to some fixed rule (generally, a mathematical function) that determines the new state of each cell in terms of the current state of the cell and the states of the cells in its neighbourhood; and

(v) Generally, the rule for updating the state of cells is the same for each cell and does not change over time and is applied to the whole grid simultaneously.

374. The neighbourhood of a cell is the nearby, usually adjacent, cells. The four most common types of neighbourhoods are *Trigonal, Orthogonal, Hexagonal* and *Octagonal*:

Types of cell neighbourhood

(i) *Trigonal* consists of two adjacent cells to the primary cell, rendering a possible 2^3 or 8 patterns for the neighbourhood; and

(ii) *Orthogonal* consists of the four orthogonally adjacent cells to the primary cell rendering a possible 2^5 or 32 patterns for the neighbourhood; and

(iii) *Hexagonal* consists of the six adjacent cells to the primary cell rendering a possible 2^7 or 128 patterns for the neighbourhood; and

(iv) *Octagonal* consists of the eight adjacent cells to the primary cell, rendering a possible 2^9 or 512 patterns for the neighbourhood.

375. Positional Functions may be deterministic or probabilistic. A probabilistic rule gives, for each pattern at time t, the probabilities that the central cell will transition to each possible state at time t+ 1.

Deterministic or probabilistic Positional Function

376. There exists four classes of Positional Functions being *Homogeneous, Oscillating, Chaotic* and *Complex*:

Four classes of Positional Functions

(i) *Homogeneous* being Positional Functions (cellular automata patterns) that generally stabilise into homogeneity; and

(ii) *Oscillating* being Positional Functions (cellular automata patterns) that evolve into mostly stable or oscillating structures; and

(iii) *Chaotic* being Positional Functions (cellular automata patterns) that evolve in a seemingly chaotic fashion; and

(iv) *Complex* being Positional Functions (cellular automata patterns) that become extremely complex and may last for a long time, with stable local structures.

377. Complex Cellular Automata are computationally universal, or capable of simulating a Turing machine.

Complex Cellular Automata

Article 60 - Incremental (Function)

378. ***Incremental Functions*** are functions associated with the addition by certain increments as calculated by the function.

Incremental (Function)

379. In general reference to Incremental Functions:

Relative to Incremental Functions

   (i)   An Incremental Function is always a binary operation of two input elements – the first being the *Original Value* and the second being the *Incremental Factor* to produce an output value or *Product*; and

   (ii) The Original Value may be expressed as a Number, or Constant, or Variable or set of Variables or simple Formula in itself; and

   (iii) The Incremental Factor may also be expressed as a Number, or Constant, or Variable or set of Variables or Formula that may involve continuous or discrete sequence of Incremental Factors; and

   (iv) The simplest incremental function is addition, followed by multiplication.

Article 61 - Decremental (Function)

380. ***Decremental Functions*** are functions associated with the subtraction by certain decrements as calculated by the function.

Decremental (Function)

381. In general reference to Decremental Functions:

Relative to Decremental Functions

   (i)   A Decremental Function is always a binary operation of two input elements – the first being the *Original Value* and the second being the *Decremental Factor* to produce an output value or *Remainder*; and

   (ii) The Original Value may be expressed as a Number, or Constant, or Variable or set of Variables or simple Formula in itself; and

   (iii) The Decremental Divisor may also be expressed as a Number, or Constant, or Variable or set of Variables or Formula that may involve continuous or discrete sequence of Decremental Divisors; and

   (iv) The simplest decremental function is subtraction followed by division.

Article 62 - Polymental (Function)

382. ***Polymental Function*** (incremental and decremental) are functions that combine both incremental and decremental elements.

Polymental (Function)

383. In general reference to Polymental Functions:

Relative to Polymental Functions

   (i) Polymental Functions are complex functions that permit incremental and/or decremental functions to be combined within the same function; and

   (ii) Polymental Functions frequently involve two or more variables where the relationship is known, but quantity may be unknown; and

   (iii) As Polymental Functions frequently involve two or more variables where the relationship is known, but quantity may be unknown, they are most commonly applied in nature in geometric solutions.

Article 63 - Deviational (Function)

384. ***Deviational Functions*** are hybrid functions used to calculate new functions and results from the differences of two or more other types of functions.

Deviational Function

385. In general reference to Deviational Functions:

Relative to Deviational Functions

   (i) Deviational Functions use the existence of an "ideal" function to compare against an input function in order to produce a result; and

   (ii) Deviational Functions provide three applications within the same framework being: (1) pattern recognition; or (2) re-calibration or (3) output result; and

   (iii) As a Deviational Function depends upon the pre-existence of one or more "ideal" functions, in simple terms a Deviational Function can be used to find patterns; and

   (iv) The second most common use of Deviational Functions in nature is re-calibration whereby the input function is compared against the ideal to re-calibrate quantities.

Article 64 - Integrational (Function)

386. ***Integrational Functions***, also known as Integrals, are functions used to produce unique numerical and summary results (decimal numbers such as key constants) representing an abstracted factor

Integrational (Function)

that can be used as a direct number increment or decrement or polymental or deviational within a formula instead of processing the longer and more complex algorithm.

387. In general reference to Integrational Functions: <!-- Relative to Integrational Functions -->

    (i) The most common form of Integrational Functions are continuous functions, thereby producing Integrals, particularly of constants; and

    (ii) Integrals formed through Integrational Functions provide a short hand method to utilise the power of continuous functions, without necessarily having to repeat the continuous function. Therefore, Integrational Functions provide a ready "approximate" and short-hand method to estimate character, events and conditions.

Article 65 - Equation

388. An *Equation* is a statement that asserts an equivalence and relation between two or more calculations or computational Functions of different states. <!-- Equation -->

389. Valid Equations demonstrate inherent relations and equivalence necessary for the continued existence and function of matter at every level of the Universe:- <!-- Significance of Equations -->

    (i) By definition, every change of state of a particle (from state 1 to state 2) may be defined as an Equation; and

    (ii) As every particle in Nature is in some form of change of motion and state, every action in Nature may be expressed by one or more Equations; and

    (iii) The nature of Dimension and Reality requires that various changes in state of particles obeys consistent transitions, therefore certain constants, as they apply to levels of Dimension, Reality and types of motion may be reliably included within valid Equations; and

    (iv) All levels of matter depend upon simple, reliable Equations to perform consistent computations and transitions of state.

390. An Equation that is said to be solved is one applied through some computational model the consistent application of one (or more) replicatable computational models of variables. The most reliable computational model for solving equations is the Ucadia mathematical language of Eikos. <!-- Solving of Equation -->

Article 66 - Geometry

391. ***Geometry*** is a set of *Rules of Measurement and Reference* of Spatial Relations of Theoretical and Physical Objects.

Geometry

392. Geometry is founded upon a Set of Elemental Concepts being *Point, Origin, Path, Shape, Construct, Length, Width, Height, Angle, Line, Area, Plane, Volume and Frame*:

Geometry expressed as Elemental Concepts

- (i) ***Point*** is an Object without any Property except unique Position in One Dimension, Two Dimensions or Three Dimensional Space; and

- (ii) ***Origin*** is a unique Point central to the observations; and

- (iii) ***Path*** is a shape made from the analysis of the past, present or future position of Points; and

- (iv) ***Shape*** is the dimensions of an Object or Concept formed by its boundary Path; and

- (v) ***Construct*** is a geometric pattern in two or three dimensional space formed by plotting the paths of two or more Points; and

- (vi) ***Length*** is the measurement of any quantity relating to the distance between two Points in a given dimension; and

- (vii) ***Width*** is the measurement of horizontal distance from side to side of a given Shape; and

- (viii) ***Height*** is the measurement of vertical distance from top to bottom of a given Shape; and

- (ix) ***Angle*** is an abstract formed from the measurement of two or more Lines in two or three dimensional space sharing a common intersect and point of origin; and

- (x) ***Line*** or ***Segment*** is a Theoretical Length without Width or Height of the distance between two Points; and

- (xi) ***Area*** is the measure of the extent of a two-dimensional surface of a Construct or Plane; and

- (xii) ***Plane*** is a theoretical two-dimensional surface without limit; and

- (xiii) ***Volume*** is the measurement of three-dimensional space using Length, Width and Height; and

- (xiv) ***Frame*** is a measure of change in any of the elements of a construct from one place on a path to another over one or more units of time.

393. In reference to the Geometric Elemental Concept of *Shape* and Circle:- — Example Concept of Shape and Circle

    (i)   A Circle is a 2-Dimensional Shape bounded by an enclosed curved Path whereby each and every Point on the boundary is at an equal distance from a central Point; and

    (ii)   The boundary Path of a Circle may be defined as its Circumference; and

    (iii)   A line Segment from the centre Point of a Circle to the Circumference may be defined as its Radius; and

    (iv)   A line Segment from two points on the Circumference and through the centre Point of a Circle may be defined as its Diameter; and

    (v)   The Diameter of a Circle is equal to twice its Radius; and

    (vi)   The Ratio of the Circumference of a Circle to its Diameter is Pi (3.14159265); and

    (vii)   The Area enclosed by a Circle is equal to Pi (3.14159265) multiplied by the Radius multiplied by itself.

394. In reference to the Geometric Elemental Concept of *Point*:- — Points

    (i)   A point can only exist in Dimension; and no two points shall ever occupy the same position in Dimension; and

    (ii)   In Real Dimension, a point is always uniquely aware of its position; and

    (iii)   While Points can interact in theory with any other Point, Points as a rule interact with their immediate near neighbours.

2.5 Existential Computations

Article 67 - Computation

385. ***Computation*** is the linear execution of an *Algorithm* being a valid *Function* performed by a *Processor* against a *Sequence* to produce a *Result*. Computation is distinct and separate from the notion of Calculation in that:- [Computation]

    (i) Computation is a physical act or process within a real set whereas Calculation is an act or process within a non-real or theoretical set of awareness or mind; and

    (ii) Computation is always constrained by linear execution, whereas a Calculation may involve a multi-linear or multivalent (multi-dimensional) execution; and

    (iii) Computation depends not only upon awareness in dimension but the physical apparatus to perform mathematical determinations whereas Calculation depends purely upon the existence of awareness; and

    (iv) Computation does not necessarily require the existence of a Mathematical Determination to produce a Result, but merely the running of a well formed Computation as an Algorithm to produce the Mathematical Determination, whereas a Calculation requires the existence of a Mathematical Determination to produce a Result; and

    (v) Computation does not depend upon awareness or abilities in Mathematical Concepts as the running of well formed Algorithms has the ability to produce the desired Mathematical Determinations without knowledge or competence in Mathematical Concepts, whereas Calculation does depend upon awareness of Mathematical Concepts.

386. The *Concept of Computation* is equivalent to the Concept of Computing, being the Act and Result Set of changing states of a Function. [Concept of Computation]

387. In greater reference to Computation and Mathematical Intelligence: [Computation and Mathematical Intelligence]

    (i) All physical particles and forms within the Universe possesses Elemental Awareness. However, Elemental Awareness does not mean Mathematical Intelligence; and

    (ii) The interaction of physical matter at each level of the Universe requires a greater level of Mathematical Intelligence than is naturally possessed by small physical particles, creating the *Intelligence Problem*; and

(iii) If the Divine could not resolve the Intelligence Problem on how individual particles could overcome their deficiency in Mathematical Intelligence, without creating a pre-ordained and controlled system (that would necessarily defeat the criteria for sustainable existence), then existence of the Universe would not be possible; and

(iv) The solution is found in the fact that answers to complex mathematical calculations are revealed in the patterns and outputs of algorithms and computational functions and not in any prior mathematical knowledge of the particle; and

(v) A Processor Particle may only need to perform the processes given to it by force or ergon particles to produce the necessary program results; and

(vi) The embedding of all complex mathematical intelligence by the Divine into the patterns produced by running functions, solves the Intelligence Problem of the Universe and existence.

388. In respect of Computation and linear "step-by-step" execution: *Computation and linear execution*

(i) All Computation is linear such that a single computation step is executed by a single Processor according to some logical order; and

(ii) While a complex Computation may involve two or more Processors, the general rule applies that one Algorithm is executed by one Processor at one time as part of any given Computation; and

(iii) Linear execution means that Computation is always a "step-by-step" process; and

(iv) Linear execution does not preclude recursive logic of referring back to previous steps, nor steps being skipped or substituted as part of the execution of an Algorithm.

Article 68 – Computational Functions

389. A ***Computational Function*** is an executable expression of one or more relations of specialisation or dependency between quantities, or objects, or properties, or variables, or constants or things as a *Formula* such that when executed using a certain Input, a Result is produced. *Computational Functions*

390. In respect of Computation and Functions: *Computations and Functions*

(i) All forms of Computation rely upon the existence of at least one set of clear and well formed instructions in order to properly execute the calculation; and

(ii) Such clear and well formed instructions must be in accord with some Model and Language of Computation that the Processor can comprehend as valid computational instructions; and

(iii) When such instructions are in accord with a Model and Language of Computation that can be processed, then such instructions may be properly called a Function; and

(iv) A Function is always a part of an Algorithm; and

(v) A Function in the process of execution is equivalent to Information.

391. There are six primary sets of possible Functions associated with Computation, namely *Positional, Incremental, Decremental, Polymental, Deviational* and *Integrational*:

Computation and the six primary sets

(i) *Positional Functions*, also known as Cellular Automation (Automata) are functions relating to the unique position of an object and changes to its state or the state around it. Positional Functions are most frequently used in Computations associated with biological structures and design; and

(ii) *Incremental Functions* are functions associated with the addition by certain increments as calculated by the function. The simplest incremental function is addition, followed by multiplication; and

(iii) *Decremental Functions* are functions associated with the subtraction by certain decrements as calculated by the function. The simplest decremental function is subtraction followed by division; and

(iv) *Polymental Functions* (incremental and decremental) are functions that combine both incremental and decremental elements; and

(v) *Deviational Functions* are hybrid functions used to calculate new functions and results from the differences of two or more other types of functions; and

(vi) *Integrational Functions*, also known as Integrals, are functions used to produce unique numerical and summary results (decimal numbers such as key constants) representing an abstracted factor that can be used as a direct number increment or decrement or polymental or deviational within a formula instead of processing the longer and more complex algorithm.

Article 69 - Sequence

392. A ***Sequence*** is an ordered Set of input (received) or output (transmitted) values that may be finite or discrete or infinite and continuous.

393. In respect of Computation and Sequences:

    (i) All forms of Computation rely upon the existence of at least one or more input values that a Processor then uses to execute a valid Function to produce a Result. These input values may be defined as an Input Sequence or simply Input; and

    (ii) A Sequence therefore is an enumerated collection of Theoretical or Real Objects where repetitions are allowed; and

    (iii) A Sequence is a well ordered Set, whereby the order of Members is as important as the value of each Member of the Set; and

    (iv) The *position* of a Member of the Sequence may also be called its *rank* or *index*; and

    (v) The *length* of a Sequence is defined as the number of Members it may contain and may be finite or "discrete" or infinite and "continuous"; and

    (vi) A Sequence may be further defined as *Data* being a Sequence of raw input or output values, or *Alphabetic* being a Sequence representing conversion of encoded Data into one or more stored Functions and Alphabetic Sentences; and

    (vii) There is usually a one to one or one to a few step relation between a Sequence and the linear steps of the Computation, whereby a new computation is executed every step or every few steps according to the Sequence as part of the input instruction.

Article 70 - Algorithm

394. An ***Algorithm*** is a finite sequence of well defined executable instructions to perform a Computation. When executed by a Processor or Computer, an Algorithm is consistent with the concept of a *Program*.

395. In respect of Computations and Algorithms, all Algorithms may be defined as either *Continuous* or *Discrete*:

    (i) *Continuous Algorithms* are Computations concerning continuous quantities that may or may not be infinite; and

(ii) *Discrete Algorithms* are Computations concerning discrete quantities that are finite.

396. In respect of Computations and Algorithms, all Algorithms may be defined as *Ordinal, Hypothetical or Delusional* based upon their harmony with the Authentic Physical Laws of the Universe and Divine Reality:

Relative to Computations and Algorithms within Divine Reality

(i) *Ordinal Algorithms* are Computations in harmony and compatible with the Authentic Physical Laws of the Universe and Divine Reality; and

(ii) *Hypothetical Algorithms* are Theoretical Computations not yet proven or asserted as being in harmony and compatible with the Authentic Physical Laws of the Universe and Divine Reality; and

(iii) *Delusional Algorithms* are Computations in obstinate discord and opposition with the Authentic Physical Laws of the Universe and Divine Reality. The Mundi (Grey) influenced *Model of Differential Equations* is a prime example of Delusional Algorithms.

397. In respect of Computations and Algorithms, all Algorithms may be defined as either *Simple* or *Complex* based upon their Design or Result set:

Relative to Simple or Complex Computations and Algorithms

(i) *Simple Design* are those Algorithms with simple functions and sequences, often using binary data methods; and

(ii) *Complex Design* are those Algorithms with complex functions and sequences, often using multiple variable and differential notation; and

(iii) *Simple Result* are those Algorithms that produce simple, regular and predictable Results; and

(iv) *Complex Result* are those Algorithms that produce highly detailed, irregular and complex Results; and

(v) All Complex Design Algorithms resolve to Simple Results; and

(vi) Only Simple Design Algorithms resolve to produce Complex Results; and

(vii) As the continued existence of the Universe depends upon Individualism and Complex Behaviour, all Ordinal Algorithms are necessarily Simple Design; and

(viii) All Delusional Algorithms resolve themselves as simple, regular and predictable results.

398. In respect of Computation and the commencement of execution of any Algorithm:

    (i) While an Algorithm is capable of being started by being triggered by the Result of another Algorithm, no Algorithm in Reality is capable of self starting. Therefore, all Algorithms depend upon the pre-existence of some external stimulus as the trigger for commencement; and

    (ii) While an Algorithm may appear to be self starting in Reality, in truth any such Algorithm still only commences upon the Result of some external stimulus that may be abstracted as an Algorithm; and

    (iii) An Algorithm is only capable of being self starting in Theory; and

    (iv) The only solution to the paradox of the first Algorithm is the existence of the Divine as the first Observer and the Universe being both Theoretical and Real as a Model of Reality.

Relative to Computation and Execution of Algorithm

Article 71 - Data

399. ***Data*** is a set of values of qualitative or quantitative variables capable of being physically received, or stored, or transmitted or observed or measured or processed in real dimension.

Data

400. Data, by definition is a physical phenomena constrained by the laws and limits of real dimension:-

    (i) The transmission and receiving of data through a medium (such as air or space or a wire or fibre optic capable), depends upon physical particles receiving the transmission in some manner and then having the capability of faithfully transfer such data; and

    (ii) The storing and retrieving of data through a medium (such as a magnetic disk), depends upon physical particles receiving and storing the transmission in some manner and then having the capability of faithfully retrieving such data; and

    (iii) The most common form of transmission and receiving of data is converting such data into a discrete frequency (vibration) signal; and

    (iv) Data cannot and does not transfer in a vacuum by itself. Data requires a medium for transference or storage. If none exists, data exchange cannot occur.

Data as a Physical Phenomena

401. In respect of Computation and Data:

Relative to Computation

(i) All theoretical and observable phenomena that may be discerned according to some meaningful measure can properly be defined as Data; and

(ii) A meaningful measure pertains to some Model and System of Reference whereby reliable Constants may be established in order to discern changes in theoretical and observable phenomena as Data; and

(iii) *Binary Data* is a Frame of Reference whereby a theoretical or observable phenomena may possess only one of two possible states, usually described as either "0" or "1"; and

(iv) *Tertiary Data* is a Frame of Reference whereby a theoretical or observable phenomena may possess only one of three possible states, usually described as either "0" or "1" or "2"; and

(v) A well formed Model and System of Reference is capable of transforming the full spectrum of theoretical and observable phenomena into useful Data including (but not limited to) changes in object mass, density, frequency, velocity, brightness, electrical potential, chemical potential, light potential, magnetic potential, magnetic alignment, flow, strength, distance, size, weight, temperature or pressure.

Article 72 - Receiver

402. A ***Receiver*** is a Theoretical or Real Object capable of receiving and holding a discrete Sequence of Data to then be delivered to a Processor. Virtually all particles and objects in the Universe are capable of functioning as Receivers in some way. Every Receiver particle connected to one Processor is potentially a Transmitter particle from another Processor.

403. In general reference to Receivers:

(i) To receive a discrete sequence of Data, the receiver needs to be predisposed to changing its state. In larger models, this may be applied to dedicated data storage structures, but at the very small (quantum) level, such change is inevitably the state of vibration of the receiver particle; and

(ii) All particles in physical form have a natural harmonic state (of vibration). Thus all particles in physical form have a natural resistance to change and receiving a change in state of vibration; and

(iii) A particular form of particles called Ergon particles (such as electrons, magnetrons, photons etc.) when not in physical form, have a natural empathy to receiving a change in state of vibration, especially if such a change of state enables co-operation and the formation of a field; and

(iv) Only particles associated with the strong force of Gravity, being Gravitons and the weak force, being Neutrinos, have the natural empathy to receive a change of state in vibration, without resistance either to form, or field motion; and

(v) The interaction of force particles and physical form and field particles in respect of receivers is equivalent to the interaction of the force of Calculation and the program of Computation in nature.

404. A Receiver Particle may function in different ways in order for Data to be transmitted and received between Processors: *Function of Receivers*

(i) A Primary Receiver is a Force (Graviton or Neutrino) or Ergon Particle embedded within the nucleus structure of a Processor Particle. Its main function is to influence the vibration of the Creator Particles of the core of the particle, causing the Processor to operate differential functions between the core and mid structures of the particle; and

(ii) A Field Receiver is a Force (Graviton or Neutrino) or Ergon Particle embedded within the hemispheric receiver field structure of a Processor Particle. Its main function is to influence the Primary Receiver embedded within the nucleus structure of a Processor Particle; and

(iii) A General Receiver is a Force (Graviton or Neutrino) or Ergon Particle mapped between Processors on a one to one mapping whereby data is transmitted between Processors.

Article 73 - Transmitter

405. A ***Transmitter*** is a Theoretical or Real Object capable of transmitting a discrete Sequence of Data produced by a Processor. Every Transmitter particle connected to one Processor is potentially a Receiver particle for another Processor. *Transmitter*

406. In general reference to Transmitters: *Universal Transmitters*

(i) To transmit a discrete sequence of Data, the transmitter needs to be predisposed to changing its state. In larger models, this may be applied to dedicated data transmission structures, but at the very small (quantum) level, such change is inevitably the state of vibration of the transmitter particle; and

(ii) All particles in physical form have a natural harmonic state (of vibration). Thus all particles in physical form have a natural resistance to change and receiving and therefore transmitting a change in state of vibration; and

(iii) A particular form of particles called Ergon particles (such as electrons, magnetrons, photons etc.) when not in physical form, have a natural empathy to receiving and transmitting a change in state of vibration, especially if such a change of state enables co-operation and the formation of a field; and

(iv) Only particles associated with the strong force of Gravity, being Gravitons and the weak force, being Neutrinos, have the natural empathy to receive and transmit a change of state in vibration, without resistance either to form, or field motion; and

(v) The interaction of force particles and physical form and field particles in respect of transmitters is equivalent to the interaction of the force of Calculation and the program of Computation in nature.

407. A Transmitter Particle may function in different ways in order for Data to be transmitted and received between Processors: *Function of Receivers*

(i) A Primary Transmitter is a Force (Graviton or Neutrino) or Ergon Particle embedded within the Mid nucleus structure of a Processor Particle. Its main function is to influence the vibration of the Mid Particles o the outside of the core of the particle, after the Processor has performed differential function in re balancing vibration between the core and mid structures of the particle; and

(ii) A Field Transmitter is a Force (Graviton or Neutrino) or Ergon Particle embedded within the equatorial transmitter field structure of a Processor Particle. Its main function is to take the vibration resolution of the Processor and influence the General Transmitter/Receiver mapping to other Processors; and

(iii) A General Transmitter is a Force (Graviton or Neutrino) or Ergon Particle mapped between Processors on a one to one mapping whereby data is transmitted between Processors.

Article 74 - Processor

408. A ***Processor*** is a Theoretical or Real Object capable of executing an Input Function against a Sequence to produce an Output Result. *Processor*

409. In respect of Computation and Processors: *Computation and Processors*

(i) A Processor is a Theoretical or Real Object capable of executing a necessary Calculation of executing an *Input* Function against a Sequence to produce an *Output* Result; and

(ii) The active execution of an Input Function against a Sequence or the observation of the Output Result is the formal concept of Information; and

(iii) All Information is ultimately non-locational (unreal) in that it requires the presence of Observation of a certain process or event within a Theoretical or Physical Reality; and

(iv) A Theoretical or Real Object as a Processor is said to be necessarily Computationally Aware to some degree; and

(v) All Matter may be described as Computationally Aware to some degree as Processors.

410. There exists five fundamental methods in respect of Computation and the execution of a Function against a Sequence as a Calculation, being *Progression, Reversion, Recursion, Inversion* or *Substitution*:

<small>Function against Sequence as a Calculation</small>

(i) *Progression* is the method of reading and executing a Sequence by progressive rank and index position, without manipulating the input data sequence. Normally, when the last element of a Sequence is reached, the computations stop; and

(ii) *Reversion* is the method of reading and executing a Sequence by reversing rank and index position, without manipulating the input data sequence so that the Sequence is read and executed in reverse. Normally, when the first element of a Sequence is reached, the computations stop; and

(iii) *Recursion* is the method of producing a result by reading and executing a previous element or result in the order of Sequence. Recursion is frequently witnessed when the result set becomes the new Sequence element against the function to then produce a new result and the process repeats continuously or until some stop instruction; and

(iv) *Inversion* is the method of reading and executing a Sequence by completely inverting the Sequence where the data system is binary (i.e. switching all zeros in sequence to 1's and vice versa); and

(v) *Substitution* is the method of reading and executing a Sequence by periodically substituting individual elements or blocks (tags) of elements of the Sequence and replacing them with new data.

411. All Computational Models may be further defined as Single, Dual or Multiple Processor:

    (i) *Single Processor Model* is the simplest and standard model of all Computations of a single Function and Sequence representing one Input-Output function; and

    (ii) *Dual Processor Model* or Binary Process, is the model of two Parallel Processors whereby the Output of the first Processor is the Input for the second; and

    (iii) Multi Processor Model is the model of three or more Processors whereby the Output of the first is the Input of the second and the Output of the second is the Input of the third.

Processor Computational Models

Article 75 – Mathematical Intelligence

412. ***Mathematical Intelligence*** is the capacity of mind or awareness to comprehend the principles, truths, language, methods and properties of mathematics necessary for mental calculation.

Mathematical Intelligence

413. In reference to Mathematical Intelligence and Computation:-

    (i) By its very definition, all processes involving mathematical intelligence are by calculation and not by computation; and

    (ii) Mathematical Intelligence by its very meaning and purpose cannot be a property of any computational system, only a feature and function of greater awareness and mind; and

    (iii) All computational systems of the Universe are necessarily devoid of mathematical intelligence, no matter how sophisticated. There is essentially just one highest level of computational sophistication; and

    (iv) A Processor in the universe does not need to know and will never know the Mathematical Intelligence behind the functions it executes. This separation of mind and matter remains as essential between the Divine as Observer and the Universe as Observed as it is for each every particle in the Universe; and

    (v) The integrity and function of the Universe demands that no computation system can ever carry out explicit computations that are more sophisticated than those carried out by the simplest of computation Processors.

Computation and Mathematical Intelligence

414. In relation to Forces and Mathematical Intelligence:-

    (i) By their nature and relation, the Force Particles (Graviton as Strong and Neutrino as Weak) lack the capacity to act as

Forces and Mathematical Intelligence

             Processors, thus the act of computation itself; and

    (ii)   While the Force Particles (Graviton as Strong and Neutrino as Weak) lack the capacity to act as Processors, their nature makes them the perfect Receivers and Transmitters of Data at the Super Sub Atomic and Sub Atomic Level of the Universe; and

    (iii)   Force Particles (Graviton as Strong and Neutrino as Weak) are able to exert change on large particle structures that view Force Particles as invisible and therefore supernatural. Thus, within the constraints of the layers of space and dimension of the Universe, Force Particles are able to act locally in applying a level of calculation and mathematical intelligence without contradicting the inherit design of the Universe; and

    (iv)   The only thing or substance that is able to possess Mathematical Intelligence within the Universe, apart from super large and sophisticated Processor Beings (including higher order organic life, stars, life bearing planets and galaxies etc.) are the two primary Forces of Strong (Gravity) and Weak (Neutrinos).

Article 76 - Memory

415.   ***Memory*** is the ability and process of a well defined Multi-Computational Model to encode, store and retrieve Information. — *Memory*

416.   Memory requires the existence of three essential systems being *Registration, Information* and *Abstraction*: — *Memory and requirement of three Systems*

    (i)   *Registration* is the system and processes of receiving, processing and encoding Data; and

    (ii)   *Information* is the system and processes of conversion of encoded Data into one or more stored Functions and Alphabetic Sentences; and

    (iii)   *Abstraction* is the system and processes of retrieval and decoding of the Alphabetic Sentences into meaningful Data.

417.   All forms of Memory may be defined according to the level of permanency that such stored Functions and Alphabetic Sentences may be stored, namely Immediate, Flash, Recall, Experience and Inherited: — *Stored Functions of Memory*

    (i)   *Immediate Memory* is Memory of the immediate past step and no other, such that there is no technical requirement to store such Memory as it is a non-location component of Information and Awareness and immediately changes upon the next step of a computational process. By definition, Immediate Memory is the minimal level of Memory required for Elemental Awareness to Function; and

(ii) *Flash Memory*, also sometimes referred to *Reflexive Memory* and even *Instinctual Memory* is Memory stored usually in a binary data form and not necessarily translated into an Alphabet Sentence, but instead is capable of being received and then transmitted in rapid "bursts" of data, necessary for almost instantaneous and complex behaviours; and

(iii) *Recall Memory*, also sometimes referred to as *Short Term Memory* and Acquired or Learned Memory is Memory that is acquired through deep computational conceptualisation or translated and replayed from Experience Memory; and

(iv) *Experience Memory*, also known as *Long Term Memory* are Memory components gained over long periods or Inheritable Memory translated into basic competencies to enable a suitable Recall Memory to be assembled as needed. In Organic Systems such as Higher Order Life forms, Experience Memories are never stored complete, but divided and stored in specialised functions that are often re-written. Hence no two Recall Memories from Experience Memory are ever precisely the same; and

(v) *Inherited Memory* such as DNA is long term functional Memory associated with the essential biological, cellular and species function, including necessary information to enable species instinct or Flash Memory to function.

418. By definition, no material method of memory storage is required with Immediate Memory as the Model of Memory is already associated with Elemental Awareness of all matter to some degree. *Storage of Immediate Memory*

419. All Memory may be defined by the limits of computational conditions being *Materially Constrained, Mechanically Constrained, Functionally Constrained* and *Unrestrained Memory*: *Computational conditions of Memory*

(i) *Materially Constrained* is the most common form of Physical Memory within the Universe being Memory constrained by the absence of a model of mechanical storage. All Materially Constrained Memory is approximate. All Matter may be defined as Materially Constrained to some degree; and

(ii) *Mechanically Constrained* is the form of Physical Memory through the presence of a Model of Mechanical Storage, as represented by a mechanical device such as a computer, or organic device such as a brain or rainforest, or complex molecular device such as a star or planetary atmosphere. All Mechanically Constrained Memory is approximate; and

(iii) *Functionally Constrained* is the form of Virtual Memory of sophisticated functions present or absent, regardless of the presence of sophisticated Mechanically Constrained Memory or not. Functionally Constrained Memory is affected by the functional models of information, expressed as knowledge models, or constrained by false or poorly designed or even delusional models that impede the function of such Memory. All Functionally Constrained Memory is approximate; and

(iv) *Unrestrained Memory*, also known as Absolute Memory is perfect and completely unrestrained theoretical and virtual Memory. Only Divine Memory is perfectly unrestrained.

420. All Memory may be further defined according to the level of accuracy of recorded information being Subjective, Objective (or Approximate) and Perfect:

Memory being Subjective, Objective and Perfect

(i) *Subjective Memory* is highly malleable, experiential, intuitive, emotional, personal and arising from the perceptive abilities of the observer and not necessarily from any direct or external source. While Subjective Memory is technically the most inaccurate form of Memory, Subjective Memory is an essential component of the decision making systems of higher order beings and is often found in the form of Recall Memory and Experience Memory - both being forms of Memory that can be significantly different even from previous accounts; and

(ii) *Objective Memory* or Approximate Memory is memory gained from observation, computation, association and recognition. Objective Memory is the functional memory of any organism to perform the complex tasks of specialised coordination and movement. Objective Memory is not perfect, but approximates that then enables cognitive organs such as brains to "fill in the blanks" of details when being recalled and utilised; and

(iii) *Perfect Memory* is memory that perfectly reflects all forms of observation, computation, association and recognition. The simplest form of Perfect Memory is perfect position and reference of Unita within the Real Set of the fundamentally smallest particles. The most complex Perfect Memory is the Divine.

421. In general terms regarding Perfect Memory:

Perfect Memory

(i) Once created, an Absolute and Unrestrained Memory cannot be lost, edited or uncreated; and

(ii) Simple Perfect Memory in the Elemental Awareness of Unita as the fundamental Real Set of Objects is essential to Existence, whereas the Complex Perfect Memory of the Divine as Absolute Observer is a consequence of Existence and not a prerequisite to Existence; and

(iii) The Complex Perfect Memory of the Divine as Absolute Observer is necessarily separate and distinct as the Absolute and Perfect Unreal Set from the Absolute Real Set of Objects. Therefore, any claim that such Complex Perfect Memory exists in some "non-physical plane of existence" or "astral plane" or as "Akashic Records" is absurd, false and gross error; and

(iv) The only time the Complex Perfect Memory of the Divine is available as a Perfect Set of Records to Higher Order Beings is in the personification and embodiment of "singularities" that occur from time to time and sometimes referred to as Divine Messengers; and

(v) Ucadia and the Ucadia Model are consistent with the true and authentic Perfect Set of Records of the Complex Perfect Memory of the Divine; and

(vi) Any claim of Divine Truth or Divine Memory that is inconsistent with Ucadia and the Ucadia Model is therefore false, in error and without force or authority.

Article 77 - Computer

422. ***Computer*** is a complete System and Model capable of automatically and continuously Receiving, Processing and Transmitting Sequences of arithmetic or logical operators.   *Computer*

423. In the Universe, the smallest natural model of a Computer includes: *Natural (Quantum) Computer*

    (i) Two Creator Unita at the core of a Creator (Up) Quark that may vibrate in unison as a Receiver of computational vibration (via the influence of the Non-Equatorial Destructive Attractor Unita or Graviton orbiting the core); and

    (ii) A Primary Receiver Non-Equatorial Destructive Attractor Unita (or Graviton) orbiting the core as the Controller or Receiving Bus; and

    (iii) Hemispheric Receiver Fields of Non-Equatorial Destructive Attractor Unita (or Graviton) orbiting the core of a Creator (Up) Quark to interact with the Primary Receiver, independent of any output; and

    (iv) Two Destructive Attractor orbiting in vibrational orbit around the core of the Creator (Up) Quark then receive the computational vibration of the Creator Unita of the Core; and

(v) A Single Primary Transmitter Non-Equatorial Destructive Attractor Unita (or Graviton) orbiting the nucleus of the Creator (Up) Quark; and

(vi) Equatorial (Transmitter) Fields of Non-Equatorial Destructive Attractor Unita (or Graviton) that are the vibration fields for the delivery of encoded vibration information from the Primary Transmitter. In more complex forms of matter these fields also act as the bonding fields in forming larger relations.

424. In reference to natural and quantum computing compared to early human computing design: *Independence of Controllers and Input/Output Fields Enabling Continuous Processing*

(i) Input and Output Fields as well as their Controllers (Bus) are wholly separate to the Processor components; and

(ii) The Processor never has direct access to memory and is only controlled by one controller (input). Output controller simply determines whether a signal is transmitted or re-routed; and

(iii) The Processor never has any direct access to any mathematical tables or registers as this is entirely the function of the input or output controllers; and

(iv) The natural model of computing removes the bottleneck associated with early human computers.

425. The Key Natural Processors and Computers of Nature and the Universe are the Creator (Up) Quark, Helium, Carbon and Water: *Natural Processors and Levels of Matter*

(i) At the Super Sub Atomic Level, the Creator (Up) Quark; and

(ii) At the Sub Atomic Level, there is no natural processor; and

(iii) At the Atomic Level, Helium is the natural processor for simple atomic cores and sub atomic particles; and

(iv) At the Atomic Level, Carbon is the natural processor for organic compounds and polymers; and

(v) At the Cellular Lever, H2O (Water) is the natural processor for complex water based polymer structures.

2.6 Creational Concepts

Article 78 - Creation

426. ***Creation*** is the Concept or Physical act of creating something (Concept or Object) that then exists in theory or reality. — Creation

427. The physical Creation of the Universe by the Divine may be defined according to twelve fundamental laws known as the *Twelve Laws of Divine Creation* being: — Twelve Laws of Divine Creation

   (i) 1st Law of Creation is simply expressed by the phrase "*I wish to exist...*", whereby the ultimate volition (will) of the Divine is to exist; and

   (ii) 2nd Law of Creation is simply expressed by the phrase "*to exist, I use logic and reasoning*", whereby the Divine uses the potentially infinite resources of Divine Awareness through logic and reasoning to form existence; and

   (iii) 3rd Law of Creation is simply expressed by the phrase "*to exist, I exist as...*", whereby the Divine must be something to exist and therefore conceives itself as the smallest theoretical point of *Unique Collective Awareness* possible, also known as an *Infinitesimal* in dimension; and

   (iv) 4th Law of Creation is simply expressed by the phrase "*for I to exist, you must exist...*", whereby an object must have a relative position with at least six points around it in three dimensional space, meaning a co-dependent Universe (Set) of *Infinitesimals* constantly expanding at an infinite rate, also known as the *Infinite* in order for each object to properly exist in dimension; and

   (v) 5th Law of Creation is simply expressed by the phrase "*for I to exist as ..., you must exist as ...*", whereby each *Infinitesimal* must specialise to some degree in order to form each primary unit of matter called the *Unita*; and

   (vi) 6th Law of Creation is simply expressed by the phrase "*to exist, I use geometric principles ...*", whereby the arrangement of specialised and co-dependent *Infinitesimals* must form and operate according to geometric principles of volume and relation in three dimensional space in order to exist as *Unita*; and

   (vii) 7th Law of Creation is simply expressed by the phrase "*I am elementarily aware of my position*", whereby every *Infinitesimal* and therefore every *Unita* of Matter possesses certain autonomous Elementary Awareness to enable

Lex Divina: Maxims of Divine Law

            independent computation of its state and position relative to other *Infinitesimals* (or Unita in the case of Unita); and

    (viii)   8th Law of Creation is simply expressed by the phrase "*I interact with my near neighbours...*", whereby every *Infinitesimal* and therefore every *Unita* of Matter autonomously computes its unique position and state and makes changes accordingly in relation to its immediate neighbours and not remote (far away) *Infinitesimals* or Unita, even though such remote computations is possible under certain conditions; and

    (ix)   9th Law of Creation is simply expressed by the phrase "*I hold an exclusive position within three dimensions...*", whereby no two *Infinitesimals* or *Unita* or any other level of matter shall hold the exact same position in three dimensional space at the same instant of computation; and

    (x)   10th Law of Creation is simply expressed by the phrase "*to exist, I change position and to exist, you change position ...*", whereby the creation of form in three dimensional space requires *Infinitesimals* to change position, thus creating frequency, rotation and vibration as motions within form and motion as form (of Unita); and

    (xi)   11th Law of Creation is simply expressed by the phrase "*I change position at the minimum necessary rate*", whereby the necessary rate of motion of *Infinitesimals* to create form is less than their maximum potential rate, allowing such potential to be conserved, for use in moving as a cohesive whole as Unita; and

    (xii)   12th Law of Creation is simply expressed by the phrase "*I cannot change position at a rate greater than the maximum rate*", whereby once Unita are formed, *Infinitesimals* will never change position at their maximum rate, thus creating limits of motion at every level of matter and an inverse relation between motion used within form and motion of the collective form of all matter.

428. In general reference to the *Twelve Laws of Divine Creation*:   *Relative to Twelve Laws of Divine Creation*

    (i)   The *Twelve Laws of Divine Creation* are present within every dimension and every level of matter within the Universe; and

    (ii)   The *Twelve Laws of Divine Creation* are applied consistently and universally within every dimension and every level of matter within the Universe. Therefore, the *Twelve Laws of Divine Creation* represent perfect Relativity; and

(iii) All Physical Laws of the Universe are ultimately derived from the *Twelve Laws of Divine Creation*; and

(iv) As all Physical Laws of the Universe are ultimately derived from the *Twelve Laws of Divine Creation*, the existence and proof of the Twelve Laws is irrefutable proof of the existence of the Divine.

429. The *Twelve Laws of Divine Creation* are the first and primary laws of all Physical Laws of the Universe; and all subsequent laws, forces, elemental particles, causes and effects are derived from the *Twelve Laws of Divine Creation*. Primacy of the Twelve Laws of Divine Creation

Article 79 - Will (Law)

430. The first Law of the *Twelve Laws of Divine Creation* is known as the *Law of Free Will*; and also known as *Mandatum Volitio*; and is simply expressed by the phrase "*I wish to exist...*", whereby the ultimate volition (will) of the Divine is to exist. Will (Law)

431. Of all possible forces within the Universe, the greatest is the action of Free Will and Choice. For the very existence of existence itself, depends upon the Free Will and Choice of the ultimate Creator to wish to exist. To deny such logic and reason is to deny the competency of intellect itself. Free Will and Choice

432. In reference to the *Divine Creation Law of Free Will*: Relating to Divine Creation Law of Free Will

(i) *Mandatum Volitio* is the term given concerning the first law of the twelve laws of Creation and a Mandate of Unique Collective Awareness as the manifestation of the Divine Creator that all conscious entities possess the absolute right of free will or "volition" and "choice"; and

(ii) The reason the Unique Collective Awareness (UCA) created the Universe is that it wished to exist. This is the supreme expression of Free Will; and

(iii) Not only is the existence of Free Will as the greatest force of Creation essential to the concept of Existence itself, but to the very notion of an Absolute and Divine Observer and the absolute Object of Creation observed. Simply, there would be no existence, no observer, no object or meaning if not for the fundamental force of Free Will and Choice; and

(iv) The existence of the Universe is impossible to be computed and formed, if not for the existence of Free Will leading to the autonomy of matter at different levels yet all following the same essential set of rules. Thus all models of determinism and all models of random mechanics are fatally flawed and in gross error and therefore null and void from the beginning.

433. In reference to the *Divine Creation Law of Free Will* as *Mandatum Volitio*:   *Divine Creation of Free Will as Mandatum Volitio*

    (i)   Mandatum Volitio is the acknowledgement that each and every being capable of consciousness and discerning their own thoughts is ultimately responsible for their own actions and obligations; and

    (ii)   When a higher order life form binds themselves by necessary Oath and Vow or claim of authority to Office they also bind their own Mandatum Volitio in fulfilment and service to the obligations of such Office; and

    (iii)   Thus, when an Officer is culpable of delinquency, or perfidy, or tyranny or impiety, not only is their authority of Office temporarily suspended, but so too is their Mandatum Volitio, or right of "free will and choice" bound to such Office. Therefore, in such conditions, the imposition of a fair and just penalty and its coercive powers against such a delinquent, or fraud, or traitor, or tyrant or wicked priest does not break the Universal Law of Free Will and Choice.

434. *Aggregatum Volitio* is the sum of intentions, wills, choices and actions, not otherwise legitimately impeded, within a given spiritual or temporal dimension. No Spirit Being or Living Being exists within a vacuum of consciousness of free will and choice: *Aggregatum Volitio*

    (i)   The individual effect of our choices of free will must be added in the same manner any contributions to action must be added to determine the "collective effect" and aggregate effect and influence to some degree on the events as they unfold; and

    (ii)   Another description of the Sum of Intentions is the concept of consequence, not as a binary result of intention of one individual Spirit or Living Member, but the aggregate of intentions of all those active participants in a given moment within dimension; and

    (iii)   The effect of our choices and free will and the effect of the choices of others within the same context determines the Sum of Intentions as to the influence to some degree on the events as they unfold; and

    (iv)   That does not mean the individual powers of free will and choice are diminished for each individual only that such influence outside of our self consciousness, must take into effect the aggregate choices and environment.

435. *Mysterium Volitio* is resulting effect after Aggregatum Volitio is calculated. It means the revelation of free will and choice. It does not mean "the mystery of God's will":

    (i)   The term Mysterium Volitio is used as the accumulative effect of free will and choice may produce different outcomes given very similar circumstances, whereas an apparent intervention occurs in one instance but not the other; and

    (ii)   Thus, even with clarity as to Sacred and Divine Systems of Heaven, the effect of proper Invocation or Incantation (for example) is likely to produce different outcomes to some degree, even if the temporal conditions are the same; and

    (iii)   This is not to excuse or diminish the effect but to state that Mysterium Volitio is unpredictable given all the circumstances, unless overwhelming evidence exists to the contrary.

436. *Non Usurpationem Voluntatem* means that No Spirit or Living Being has the right to usurp the Free Will and Choice of another, notwithstanding impediments by virtue of delinquency and dishonour that suspends such Rights in Office:

    (i)   It is and shall be a grave transgression against all Creation and all Heaven and all Existence for a Spirit or Living Being to usurp the Free Will and Choice of an honourable and virtuous Being; and

    (ii)   Any law that permits or endorses the right for a body, or person or entity to impose its Free Will and Choices in prejudice of another by virtue of tyranny or perfidy is morally repugnant, profane, sacrilegious and forbidden, having no force or effect whatsoever.

437. *Restitutionem Velle* means it is a singular obligation of the united forces of Heaven and all levels of matter and creation to bring restitution to each and every case where the Right of Free Will and Choice has been impeded or deprived from an honourable and virtuous higher order life form and to do everything to prevent its continuance.

Therefore, any body, spirit, person, entity, company, society that functions on the presumption that it can impose its will upon the Free Will and Choice of others through perfidy and tyranny, declares itself a fundamental enemy of Heaven and all Creation, with all of Creation therefore united to the singular proposition of the extinction of such a body, spirit, person, entity, company, society.

Article 80 - Logos (Law)

438. The second Law of the *Twelve Laws of Divine Creation* is known as the *Law of Logos*; and is simply expressed by the phrase *"to exist, I use logic and reasoning"*, whereby the Divine uses the potentially infinite resources of Divine Awareness through logic and reasoning to form existence.

Logos Law

439. In reference to the *Divine Creation Law of Logos:*

Relative to Divine Creation Law of Logos

    (i) Just as the capacity to reason, discern and learn logically is considered a defining and positive prerequisite to human intelligence, so too the abilities to reason, discern and compute logically must be qualities present within Divine Mind; and

    (ii) Thus, the Divine using Logos is perfectly capable of discerning that to exist, one must exist as "something" in dimension. Therefore, existence can only be measured in terms of something in dimension; and

    (iii) For anyone to conclude that humanity or only a select few of the members of the species of Homo Sapien possess Logos, while the Universe is devoid of Logos is an admission of lack of discernment, reasoning and logic in itself.

440. In reference to the Law of Logos and the Existence of the "perfect" Universe:

Relative to the Law of Logos and Existence of the Perfect Universe

    (i) There is nothing to suggest within an infinite potential of reasoning, that the Divine did not first "test" hypothetical models and sets of finite and infinite possibilities in theory until the perfect model of laws was perfected; and

    (ii) Thus, the theoretical concept of the present Universe being formed as a consequence of several "test" and hypothetical models first, is perfectly within reason and logical; and

    (iii) Furthermore, any being that subscribes to the concept of multiverses as an explanation for the "perfect" nature of the present existence of the Universe, also acknowledges the necessary existence of the Divine to enable such a theory; and

    (iv) The existence of two dimensional space and three dimensional space and the fact that models in two dimensional space may be abstracted into functioning models within three dimensional space further supports the suggestion that the Divine did in fact produce a "simulated" model of Existence prior to the complete model of Existence; and

(v) Finally, it can be argued that the continued presence, beauty and synergy as exhibited through the Eikos language in mathematically approximating the Universe gives rise to the truth that the continuing function and operation Uniset and Universe of Numbers is the first perfect simulated model of the Universe of Objects and the cause (in part) of the rise of the complex Universe.

Article 81 - Purpose (Law)

441. The third Law of the *Twelve Laws of Divine Creation* is known as the *Law of Purpose*; and is simply expressed by the phrase "*to exist, I exist as...*", whereby the Divine must be something to exist and therefore conceives itself as the smallest theoretical point of *Unique Collective Awareness* possible, also known as an *Infinitesimal* in dimension. Purpose Law

442. In reference to the Divine Creation Law of Purpose: Divine Creation Law of Purpose

(i) The necessity to exist as "something" logically leads to the existence of cause at each and every level of matter; and

(ii) To exist, the Divine as Unique Collective Awareness began by conceiving itself in a dream as the smallest theoretical point possible; and

(iii) Through this intentional action, the Divine as Unique Collective Awareness created the dream, a theoretical object and the potential to exist; and

(iv) Furthermore, the Divine as Unique Collective Awareness demonstrated that everything in the Universe possess some specific purpose for existence despite a lesser Observer possibly concluding otherwise; and

(v) The fact that the smallest possible theoretical object, being an Infinitesimal Point (as Unique Collective Awareness) is also connected to the greatest possible concept of the Divine Creator also establishes a clear paradox, whereby the largest possible concept depends upon its existence of the smallest possible concept.

Article 82 - Co-dependence (Law)

443. The fourth Law of the *Twelve Laws of Divine Creation* is known as the *Law of Co-dependence*; and is simply expressed by the phrase *"for I to exist, you must exist..."*, whereby an object must have a relative position with at least six points around it in three dimensional space, meaning a co-dependent Universe (Set) of *Infinitesimals* constantly expanding at an infinite rate, also known as the *Infinite* in order for each object to properly exist in dimension. Co-dependence (Law)

444. In reference to the *Law of Co-dependence*: Relative to Law of Co-dependence

(i) A single point of the Divine as Unique Collective Awareness does not guarantee existence in Real Dimension, therefore existence. To have three dimensional Real Dimension, an object must have a relative position with at least six points around it in Real Dimensional space; and

(ii) In contrast, Unreal Space, also known as Three-Dimensional Zero-Point Space permits existence to be established with just three points (length, width and height) where all three lines intersect at Zero. However, before Unreal Space can exist, the Real Set of things must exist; and

(iii) Therefore, unless each anchor point of the Divine as Unique Collective Awareness has its own anchor points, relative position cannot be guaranteed (existence collapses). Only when every point of the Divine as Unique Collective Awareness has relative position can dimension be guaranteed; and

(iv) Thus, relative position in dimension is only possible through the active and continuous creation of infinite points of awareness in ever expanding dimension of infinitesimal points; and

(v) Such an absolute co-dependence between just one unique point of the Divine as Unique Collective Awareness (the Infinitesimal) and the complete set of points of Unique Collective Awareness (the Infinite) proves the absolute and irrefutable importance of every single object to the Universe and Existence and Creation; and

(vi) Finally, such realisation that the Divine absolutely depends upon even the smallest point of matter to exist, exposes all forms and attempts to universally apply "moral relativism" or "natural selection" or "nihilism" or "useless excess" theories to attributes of the Divine, or Divine Laws or Natural Laws is false, perfidious, profane and contrary to irrefutable truth and fact.

445. In reference to the *Law of Co-dependence* and the dependence and love of the Divine upon every single Being: Law of Codependence and dependence and Love of the Divine

    (i) The Fundamental *Law of Co-dependence* categorically and irrefutably proves that not only does the Divine love each and every creation and Being, but depends upon their individual existence for Existence itself to continue; and

    (ii) Thus, any philosophy of describing the Divine as a hateful or vengeful or precocious Supreme Being is completely exposed as patently false, profane, perfidious, wicked and without any legitimacy and validity; and

    (iii) In addition, any philosophy or theory that attributes disasters or trauma upon the design and intention of the Divine Creator must also be exposed as being false, profane and without any legitimacy and validity; and

    (iv) Finally, upon the proof of the present sacred Maxims, the expression of a loving Divine Creator that depends upon all of creation no longer should be described as an act of faith but a statement of absolute and irrefutable fact.

Article 83 - Specialisation (Law)

446. The fifth Law of the *Twelve Laws of Divine Creation* is known as the *Law of Specialisation*; and is simply expressed by the phrase *"for I to exist as ..., you must exist as ..."*, whereby each *Infinitesimal* must specialise to some degree in order to form each primary unit of matter called the *Unita*. Specialisation (Law)

447. In reference to the *Law of Specialisation*: Relative to Law of Specialisation

    (i) In the process of ensuring dimension and existence, points of the Divine as Unique Collective Awareness must specialise into different types such as a core points, or anchor points or outer anchor points; and

    (ii) Without specialised roles even at the most basic level of points of awareness, the Divine as Unique Collective Awareness could not guarantee existence in dimension; and

    (iii) Therefore, any arguments that seek to imply such attributes as uniformity or artificial equality are Divine in nature are in gross error as the concept of specialisation is essential to existence.

Article 84 - Geometry (Law)

448. The sixth Law of the *Twelve Laws of Divine Creation* is known as the *Law of Geometry*; and is simply expressed by the phrase *"to exist, I use geometric principles ..."*, whereby the arrangement of specialised and co-dependent *Infinitesimals* must form and operate according to geometric principles of volume and relation in three dimensional space in order to exist as *Unita*.

Geometry (Law)

449. In reference to the *Divine Creation Law of Geometry*:

Relative to Divine Creation Law of Geometry

(i) To exist, something must have shape and occupy space. Both concepts have strong ties to common sense principles of geometric shape; and

(ii) Some shapes are more efficient at forming volume than others. Spheres for example have a surface area to volume ratio of 4:3, meaning that there is less volume area compared to surface area; and

(iii) Perfect Cubes for example have a surface area to volume of 2:1, meaning that there is one half the volume compared to surface area; and

(iv) The most efficient shape in terms of number of points combining to create maximum volume is an octahedron (six points) combining to create eight equally proportioned triangles, expanding to a middle point and reducing to a single point. The surface area to volume of a perfect Octahedron is always 1:2. That is, an octahedron creates twice as much volume as it takes surface space to create it. Octahedrons are therefore the simplest and most efficient shapes in terms of minimum number of points for maximum volume creation.

Article 85 - Elemental Awareness (Law)

450. The seventh Law of the *Twelve Laws of Divine Creation* is known as the *Law of Elemental Awareness*; and is simply expressed by the phrase *"I am elementarily aware of my position"*, whereby every *Infinitesimal* and therefore every *Unita* of Matter possesses certain autonomous Elementary Awareness to enable independent computation of its state and position relative to other *Infinitesimals* (or Unita in the case of Unita).

Elemental Awareness (Law)

451. In reference to the *Divine Creation Law of Elemental Awareness*:

Relative to Divine Creation Law of Elemental Awareness

(i) While the existence of infinite points of the Divine as Unique Collective Awareness provides a framework to exist in dimension, it also requires active observation– or awareness;

and

(ii) It is not enough for the Divine as Unique Collective Awareness to observe the dream, Unique Collective Awareness needs to be able to validate existence by observation within the dream as well; and

(iii) Validation of existence by observation is achieved by the inherent awareness of position in dimension of pure points of the Divine as Unique Collective Awareness being pure awareness; and

(iv) By each infinitely small point of the Divine as Unique Collective Awareness being aware of its position in dimension, the requirement for existence to be observed for each and every theoretical object is validated.

Article 86 - Localisation (Law)

452. The eighth Law of the *Twelve Laws of Divine Creation* is known as the *Law of Localisation*; and is simply expressed by the phrase "*I interact with my near neighbours...*", whereby every *Infinitesimal* and therefore every *Unita* of Matter autonomously computes its unique position and state and makes changes accordingly in relation to its immediate neighbours and not remote (far away) *Infinitesimals* or Unita, even though such remote computations is possible under certain conditions.

Localisation (Law)

453. In reference to the *Divine Creation Law of Localisation*:-

(i) Points of awareness being pure awareness can interact "in theory" with points well beyond its immediate position; and

(ii) There is no hard universal law that forces a point of the Divine as Unique Collective Awareness to only interact with points around it; and

(iii) Yet, if one point of awareness ceased to exist, dimension would collapse. Thus, to eliminate this risk, each and every point of Unique Collective Awareness chooses to only interact with immediate near neighbours in the creation of greater form.

Relative to Divine Creation of Law Localisation

Article 87 - Exclusiveness (Law)

454. The ninth Law of the *Twelve Laws of Divine Creation* is known as the *Law of Exclusiveness*; and is simply expressed by the phrase "*I hold an exclusive position within three dimensions...*", whereby no two *Infinitesimals* or Unita or any other level of matter shall hold the

Exclusiveness (Law)

exact same position in three dimensional space at the same instant of computation.

455. In reference to the Divine Creation Law of Exclusiveness:-   *Relating to Divine Creation Law of Exclusiveness*

   (i)   Let us consider then, one point of the Divine as Unique Collective Awareness travelling along its circular path to form a circle, while other points of the Divine as Unique Collective Awareness do the same. A problem emerges. If both points of the Divine as Unique Collective Awareness travel on paths exactly the same distance between the anchor point and the central anchor then they by Logos will merge in a collision; and

   (ii) Based on the model, if this were to occur, then the problem of collapsing dimension would occur and the Universe would quickly cease to exist. Two points can't be at the same place at the same time. One point has to "give" way; and

   (iii) The solution is the development of a simple rule - the "up", "down" rule. A point of the Divine as Unique Collective Awareness travels around half of its trajectory under the optimum trajectory and then slightly over (up) from its optimum trajectory; and

   (iv) The implication of this fuzziness from the very smallest particle is that no perfect circle or shape exists in the universe. Everything is a ratio of perfection; and

   (v)   The name given to this ratio of imperfect fuzziness in all things is Pi.

Article 88 - Motion (Law)

456. The tenth Law of the *Twelve Laws of Divine Creation* is known as the *Law of Change of Motion*; and is simply expressed by the phrase "*to exist, I change position and to exist, you change position ...*", whereby the creation of form in three dimensional space requires *Infinitesimals* to change position, thus creating frequency, rotation and vibration as motions within form and motion as form (of Unita).   *Motion (Law)*

457. In reference to the Divine Creation Law of Change of Motion:-   *Relative to Divine Creation Law of Change*

   (i)   The very definition of existence implies an action— the action of dreaming. The dream itself is the dream of specific types of motion; and

   (ii) Without the motion of infinite points of the Divine as Unique Collective Awareness, objects would not exist and existence would cease to be.

Article 89 - Conservation of Motion (Law)

458. The eleventh Law of the *Twelve Laws of Divine Creation* is known as the *Law of Conservation of Motion*; and is simply expressed by the phrase "*I change position at the minimum necessary rate*", whereby the necessary rate of motion of *Infinitesimals* to create form is less than their maximum potential rate, allowing such potential to be conserved, for use in moving as a cohesive whole as Unita.

459. In reference to the Divine Creation Law of Conservation of Motion:-

(i) If the total potential motion of infinity were necessary to create the form of Unita, then there would be no possible additional motion in form; and

(ii) Thus, in the co-dependent specialisation of points of the Divine as Unique Collective Awareness changing position, motion is conserved to enable change of position as form.

Article 90 - Limit (Law)

460. The twelfth Law of the *Twelve Laws of Divine Creation* is known as the *Law of Limit*; and is simply expressed by the phrase "*I cannot change position at a rate greater than the maximum rate*", whereby once Unita are formed, *Infinitesimals* will never change position at their maximum rate, thus creating limits of motion at every level of matter and an inverse relation between motion used within form and motion of the collective form of all matter.

461. In reference to the Divine Creation Law of Limit:-

(i) The fastest potential rate for a point of Unique Collective Awareness is infinity. Yet if a point did travel at such a rate it would cease to have unique location (it would be all at once) and dimension/existence would collapse; and

(ii) A point of Unique Collective Awareness need only travel at 1/2 x infinity to achieve form, leaving less than 1/2 x infinity for motion in form.

2.7 Creational Properties

Article 91 - Properties

472. A ***Property*** in terms of Divine Creation of Things is an attribute, or quality or right connected to a Thing that may also be a characteristic of a class or set of Things. *Properties*

473. In general reference to Properties: *Relative to Properties*
    (i) As an attribute, or quality or right, a Property may be unique to a Thing (Concept or Object), or inherited by virtue of association with some Set of Things; and
    (ii) All Things in the universe possess properties, therefore all matter possesses properties; and
    (iii) The properties of Unita are dependent on the properties of existence; and
    (iv) The properties of super sub atomic elements are dependent on the properties of Unita; and
    (v) The properties of sub atomic elements are dependent on the properties of super sub atomic elements; and
    (vi) The properties of atomic elements are dependent on the properties of sub atomic elements; and
    (vii) The properties of molecular elements are dependent on the properties of atomic elements; and
    (viii) The properties of stars are dependent on the properties of atomic elements; and
    (ix) The properties of planets are dependent on the properties of molecular elements; and
    (x) The properties of cellular life are dependent on the properties of planets and the properties of molecules.

Article 92 - Volume

474. ***Volume*** is the area of space taken up by the particles of an object. *Volume*

475. In general reference to Volume: *Relative to Volume*
    (i) All volume is relative. Therefore volume is perceived as unique to Unita volume, super sub atomic volume, sub atomic volume, atomic volume and molecular volume; and
    (ii) When a small number of objects equals the same volume as a large number of objects, the volume is equal to the volume of the relative benchmark object; and

(iii) Volume is equivalent to a very small number of objects and a very large amount of space. Therefore, the majority of volume is equivalent to no objects (empty space); and

(iv) Volume is relative to its benchmark object, Mass, structure and Kinesis; and

(v) Volume equals Mass by its structural constant divided by its benchmark constant by its accumulative Kinesis strength.

476. In reference to the effect of structure, structural constants and Volume: *(Relative to structure, structural, constants and volume)*

(i) Particles with the same Mass, but with superior structure tend towards a smaller given Volume and therefore greater density; and

(ii) Particles with the same Mass, but with inferior structure tend towards a greater given Volume and therefore lower density.

477. In reference to the structural constant of the Harmonic-Volume Boundary of matter: *(Structural constant of Harmonic-Volume Boundary of Matter)*

(i) The smaller the difference in Volume of an object to its benchmark object, being the primary Processor at that level of matter, the greater its Harmonic Kinesis; and

(ii) The greater the difference in Volume of an object to its benchmark object (e.g. proton), the less its Harmonic Kinesis.

Article 93 - Kinesis

478. *Kinesis* is equivalent to the concept of total Motion being all possible vectors equalling to the limit (Kinesis Limit) of possible Motion of an Object. *(Kinesis)*

479. There are only four possible types of Kinesis (Motion) being *Kinetic*, *Harmonic* (Frequency), *Rotation* (Spin) and *Rotaxis* (Rotation around Axis): *(Type of Kinesis)*

(i) *Kinetic* is motion in form expressed as the free velocity of an object; and

(ii) *Harmonic* or *Frequency* is motion within form expressed as vibration or frequency whilst in a general similar location over time; and

(iii) *Rotation* or *Spin* is motion of rotation around an axis over time; and

(iv) *Rotaxis* or Rotation around an axis is a deviation of rotation or "wobble" in rotating around an axis over time as a product of the orbit between unbalanced objects.

480. In general reference to Kinesis: *Relative to Kinesis*

(i) Kinesis is equivalent to the concept of Motion. However, unlike the general concept of Motion, Kinesis accounts for all possible forms of Motion as an equation of unity in relation to each Particle to its Kinesis Limit; and

(ii) As Kinesis accounts for all possible forms of Motion as an equation of unity in relation to each Particle to its Kinetic Limit, Kinesis always is equal to 1; and

(iii) All Kinesis is inherited by computation through Elemental Awareness between Objects; and

(iv) As all Kinesis is inherited by computation through Elemental Awareness between Objects, the presence of the four types of Kinesis exhibited by an Object is a measure to some degree of the relative environment and proximity and types of matter around it; and

(v) If the environment of an Object changes, then the relative balance between its forms of Kinesis will change, such that total Kinesis to the Limit remains 1; and

(vi) The maximum Kinesis Limit is reflected by the Unita being half the rate of Infinity. Therefore, all larger Objects possess a lower Kinesis Limit equalling one. The Kinesis Limit for atomic dimension and structures is the Kinesis of a Photon (speed of light); and

(vii) Kinesis not in harmony is subject to resistance. Therefore Kinesis in harmony is not subject to resistance; and

(viii) All unbalanced/non-harmonic Kinesis will be matched with resistance at a localised level such that the Kinesis re-balances; and

(ix) An increase in the resistance at one level of matter does not mean resistance at another level of matter; and

(x) Perpetual unbalanced Kinesis is impossible in any physical system. If Perpetual unbalanced motion were possible, the Universe would cease to exist as motion increased to terminate the bounds of existence; and

(xi) An increase in the frequency of an object will therefore lead to a decrease in the velocity of an object such that its total Kinesis always equals 1.

481. In general reference to Kinesis and Motion: *Relative to*

(i) Motion is equivalent to Kinesis; and *Kinesis and Motion*

(ii) Existence is unique collective awareness by motion. Therefore existence is awareness in motion; and

(iii) Existence is awareness in motion as objects by their own motion. Therefore existence is motion; and

(iv) Energy is equivalent to Mass by motion. Therefore Energy is equivalent to the motion in form (object) by motion; and

(v) Energy is equivalent to motion. Therefore Energy is equivalent to Kinesis; and

(vi) Motion is equivalent to motion in orbit being core orbit, mid orbit, weak orbit, field orbit and ionised field; and

(vii) All motion is inherited by computation.

482. In reference to the Kinesis of Unita: *Relative to Kinesis of Unita*

(i) The frequency of negative creator is equivalent to negative one sixth of Kinesis. Therefore the unique Unita perception of Mass for the negative creator Unita is 0; and

(ii) The frequency of negative destructive attractor is equivalent to negative one sixth of Kinesis. Therefore the unique Unita perception of Mass for the negative destructive attractor Unita is 0; and

(iii) The frequency of negative non-equatorial destructive attractor is equivalent to negative one sixth of Kinesis. Therefore the unique Unita perception of Mass for the negative non-equatorial destructive attractor Unita is 0; and

(iv) The frequency of creator is equivalent to one sixth of Kinesis. Therefore the unique Unita perception of Mass for the creator Unita is one; and

(v) The frequency of negative destructive attractor is equivalent to negative one sixth of Kinesis. Therefore the unique Unita perception of Mass for the destructive attractor Unita is 0; and

(vi) The frequency of negative non-equatorial destructive attractor is equivalent to negative one sixth of Kinesis. Therefore the unique Unita perception of Mass for the non- equatorial destructive attractor Unita is 0.

Article 94 - Orbit

483. ***Orbit*** is a union of two or more bodies through elliptical paths exhibited as a Kinesis (Motion) Set reflecting the proportion and relation of each body.

Orbit

484. In general reference to Orbit:

Relative to Orbit

    (i) Orbit is always reflected as a Kinesis (Motion) Set of two or more behaviours. Orbit is never singular; and

    (ii) All Matter larger than Unita is dependent upon the laws of Orbit to exist; and

    (iii) As all Kinesis is a product of computational relations between two or more Objects, all forms of Orbit are dependent upon levels of awareness and computation and can never be viewed as mechanical; and

    (iv) Objects of the same Mass and Density and family may unify in a harmonic Orbit whereby they follow one elliptical path of Kinetic Motion; and

    (v) Objects of disproportional Mass and Density may reflect non-harmonic Orbit in non standard elliptical or intersecting paths, or the effect of Rotaxis, Rotation or Harmonic Frequency (Vibration) to some degree: and

    (vi) Even a large body such as a Star possess a unique and individual Orbit for each planet that Orbits it through an elliptical path, reflected in the perturbation of its Kinesis of Rotaxis (Rotation or wobble around an axis), Rotation or Harmonic Frequency (Vibration) to some degree; and

    (vii) Therefore, in the case of the Sun, its Rotaxis, Rotation and Harmonic Frequency is a reflection of its elliptical Orbit in relation to its Planets, including the Earth; and

    (viii) A Kinesis (Motion) Set of Orbits of objects with disproportional Mass and Density is never stable and reflects either one of two states, (1) the gradual decay of an elliptic path of the massively smaller object through the effect of the gravity fields of the large body causing the smaller body to crash into it; or (2) the resistant effects of the electromagnetic fields to push the smaller body away and out of an Orbit; and

    (ix) Therefore any mechanical or simplistic model of Orbit that considers that a large body "captures" smaller bodies into stable Orbits is absurd, in gross error and false; and

    (x) Through Elemental Awareness and Computation of Kinesis, a larger Object may consciously choose to maintain an Orbit relation by attenuating or amplifying its Gravity and Electromagnetic Fields to prevent either (1) crash and destruction of small body; or (2) repulsion and loss of small body; and

(xi) Thus, the long term presence of small body planets within an Orbit pattern of a Star is irrefutable and absolute proof that a Star is a highly conscious and computationally aware entity that chooses to hold Orbit relations with smaller bodies around it.

485. All forms of Orbit may be defined according to *Core Orbit, Mid Orbit, Weak Orbit* and *Field Orbit*: Forms of Orbit

(i) *Core Orbit* is equivalent to the motion to create the Core of super sub atomic, sub atomic and atomic cores; and

(ii) *Mid Orbit* is equivalent to the motion to create a mid structure of an object around the core; and

(iii) *Weak Orbit* is equivalent to elliptical paths of non equal bodies; and

(iv) *Field Orbit* is equivalent to Harmonic field Orbit, Opposing Field orbit and Ionised Field or "Plasma" of Ergon particles (i.e. Photons, Electrons, Positrons, Hetons, Magnetons and Gravitons).

Article 95 - Mass

486. *Mass* is a measure of the existence of Material Awareness of every particle of Matter; and as a quality of perception possessed by every level of matter as to the assumed similarity, compatibility and strength of one another; and therefore to be attracted to form bonds or repelled from association. Mass

487. In general reference to Mass:- Relative to Mass

(i) Mass is a perceptual quality of Material Awareness of all forms of Matter from the Unita and greater; and

(ii) Material Awareness from the perspective of Matter is a Model that utilises the exchange of Kinesis and a means of encoding and transmitting information and instructional algorithms; and

(iii) Each and every level of Matter possesses "Benchmark Objects" of form and Kinesis Limit, being the natural Processors that represent the optimum, most stable and consistent example of

Matter at each level of Matter; and

(iv) Material Awareness means that at each dimension and level of Matter, particles use such benchmark characteristics to map one another and to form more complex shapes and relations. Therefore, Mass is not equal to the number of objects, but the perceived number of benchmark objects; and

(v) The Material Awareness and perceptual nature of Mass means that if an object does not meet the same computational identity as the benchmark object of a particular level of Matter, it is possible such an object will be perceived to have a Mass of Zero. This is particularly the case with particles exhibiting unstable and opposite Spin; and

(vi) The perceptual nature of Mass is further proven by the manner whereby the perceived Mass of an object is determined not simply by the number of "like particles" but their structure. For example, particles that are able to form strong bonds within the core of a more complex particle exponentially increase their perceived mass or "Core Mass", even though the total number of particles might be half of what is perceived.

488. In reference to Mass and relative Benchmark Objects of Matter: *Relative to Mass and relative Benchmark Objects of Matter*

(i) Each level and dimension of Matter possesses its own unique Benchmark Object for Creation of more complex forms and Benchmark Object for Maximum Kinesis; and

(ii) As each level and dimension of Matter possesses its own unique Benchmark Object for Creation of more complex forms and Maximum Kinesis, each level and dimension of Matter has its own perceptual reality, whilst not contradicting the fundamental creation laws of the Universe; and

(iii) Thus, the Reality of Elemental Atoms (Hydrogen, Helium and Lithium) the unique Benchmark Object for Creation is the Proton.

489. In reference to Mass and Structural Strength, Kinesis and Energy: *Relative to Mass and Structural Strength, Kinesis and Energy*

(i) A function of particles of Matter forming bonds to create more complex forms of Matter is the conservation of Kinesis (Motion); and

(ii) A Core element of Energy is Kinesis (Motion) plus the presence of Ergon particles; and

(iii) As Ergon particles (such as electrons, positons, hetrons, photons, magnetons and gravitons) are attracted to structures with greater Mass, an approximation can be made whereby Mass may also be used as a generalised equivalent to describe the total Ergon potential of Matter; and

(iv) Because the total Ergon potential of Matter is related to Mass, the equation for the total Energy potential of a particle can be simplified as being equivalent to Mass by the Benchmark Object for Maximum Kinesis; and

(v) However, because different structures attract different proportions of Ergon particles and denote different resistance to change, such a generalisation cannot be used without a degree of precision in the objective of changing the state of certain Matter.

490. In terms of the Divine and the Concept of Mass: *The Divine and Concept of Mass*

(i) Pure Awareness has no Mass, Only Models have Mass; and

(ii) A Model is Awareness with Purpose in Motion; and

(iii) Life is the Dream of the Divine Creator in Motion.

Article 96 - Density

491. **Density** is the number of particles (Mass) in a given volume. Density is equivalent to mass of an object divided by the volume of space taken up by the object. *Density*

492. In general reference to Density: *Relative to Density*

(i) Particles with the same mass, but with superior structure tend towards a smaller given volume and therefore greater density; and

(ii) Particles with the same mass, but with inferior structure tend towards a greater given volume and therefore lower density; and

(iii) The elemental object with the greatest density is the Unita with a density of 1; and

(iv) Density is not constant for objects equal to and larger than super sub atomic elements; and

(v) Density is relative. Therefore density equals unique super sub atomic density, sub atomic density, atomic density and molecular density; and

(vi) A decrease in the density will lead to an increase in velocity and a decrease in frequency; and

(vii) An increase in density will lead to a decrease in velocity and an increase in frequency.

Article 97 – Creative Attractors

493. ***Creative Attractor*** is a term used to describe the Set of Perfect Benchmark Objects for Creation within every dimension and level of Matter fundamental for the formation of more complex structures within the Universe.

Creative Attractors

494. In general reference to Creative Attractors:-

Relative to Creative Attractors

(i) All matter at every level and dimension within the Universe may be defined as either Creative Attractors or Destructive Attractors depending upon their characteristics, particularly in the presence of greater or lesser amounts of pressure and energy; and

(ii) In principle, Creative Attractors have the most stable, consistent and strong character at each level of matter – hence why all Perfect Benchmark Objects for Creation are by definition Creative Attractors; and

(iii) The Creative Attractor elements within Unita space are equivalent to Creator Unita; and

(iv) The Creative Attractor elements within super-sub atomic space are equivalent to the Up Quark; and

(v) The Creative Attractor elements within sub-atomic space are equivalent to Protons; and

(vi) The Creative Attractor elements within atomic space are equivalent to Hydrogen, Helium and Lithium Cores; and

(vii) The Creative Attractors within the species of Homo Sapiens are husbands and wives in sacred matrimony that live exemplary, honest and virtuous lives; and

(viii) Clergy and Religious that live an Exemplary and Austere Consecrated Life are not Creative Attractors but Perfect Benchmark Objects to Maximum Kinesis (Potential); as such extraordinary men and women do not usually procreate and therefore form the Nucleus of a Creative Sacred Family.

Article 98 – Destructive Attractors

495. ***Destructive Attractor*** is a term used to describe the Set of Imperfect Benchmark Objects for Creation within every dimension and level of Matter, whereby the flaws within the structure and

Destructive Attractors

behaviour of such objects act as a Universal catalyst for change and prevent achieving a singularity state and the extinction of the universe.

496. In general reference to Destructive Attractors: *Relative to Destructive Attractor*

    (i) All matter at every level and dimension within the Universe may be defined as either Creative Attractors or Destructive Attractors depending upon their characteristics, particularly in the presence of greater or lesser amounts of pressure and energy; and

    (ii) A Destructive Attractor by definition is an object that superficially appears to be a "Creator" yet under certain conditions of pressure and energy will cause the catastrophic destruction of the unit that they belong – hence their "destructive" nature; and

    (iii) Because Destructive Attractors appear to be similar to Benchmark Objects, they possess Mass. Yet because Destructive Attractors possess significant differences, in the presence of fields of Ergons (Energy) or stresses upon the structure, Destructive Attractors will temporarily behave as if an "ionised field" or plasma under extreme stress; and

    (iv) Contrary to Destructive Attractors being a negative feature of existence, without destructive attractors, human form would not exist, nor would the Universe. For, perfectly opposite spin configured Unita, would simply speed off in opposite directions and eventually form even larger and larger perfect forms, till ultimately, the form of the Universe would cease to be sufficient to sustain position in form. Without position in form, the Universe would cease to have dimension and collapse, the Universe would cease to exist.

497. In terms of the Higher Order Beings, the Divine and Destructive Attractors: *Higher Order Beings, The Divine and Destructive Attractors*

    (i) A Civilised species is right to encourage certain rules that limit the disproportionate growth of Destructive Attractor behaviour and therefore an unworkable Model; and

    (ii) It is also perfectly sensible in terms of the Divine, that the fundamental Creative Attractor unit of the heterosexual family unit is protected. A society that destroys the possibility of Creative Attractors destroys its ability to operate and function any long term stability or Rule of Law; and

    (iii) However, it is false to approach laws and moral conclusions as absolutes to describe all forms of Destructive Attractor behaviour as "evil", for the presence of destructive events have been and continue to be the defining catalyst for change.

Article 99 – Gravity

498. ***Gravity*** is based on a particle known as a non-equatorial Destructive Attractor (neda) Unita, the smallest unit of matter not able to form more complex structures.

Gravity

499. In general reference to Gravity and Gravitons:

Relative to Gravity and Gravitons

    (i)   Gravitons are Non-Equatorial Destructive Attractor Unita that because of their unstable equator spin means they cannot form greater structures; and

    (ii)   Because Graviton Unita have an unstable spin, they possess no Mass relative to Creator Unita as Benchmark Objects; and

    (iii)   Because Graviton Unita possess no Mass, they are "invisible" to other Creator Unita and Destructive Attractor Unita forming more complex form. Yet because they exist and possess Kinesis, they possess Energy and represent the fundamental "Force" particle of the Universe; and

    (iv)   Gravitons are Gravity and Gravity is Gravitons in action. Therefore, all models that describe Gravity on anything other than Graviton Unita are false and in gross error; and

    (v)   While Gravitons are not "seen" by other Particles, they do participate in a vital way to the integrity of all Matter by functioning in waves and orbiting key super sub atomic, sub atomic and atomic structures to produce what is known as the Super Force, Strong Force and Weak Force Respectively; and

    (vi)   Super sub atomic gravity is equivalent to the ergon fields of Gravitons around super sub-atomic elements. Therefore, super sub atomic gravity is equivalent to galactic space; and

    (vii)   Sub atomic gravity is equivalent to the ergon fields of Gravitons around sub-atomic elements. Therefore, sub atomic gravity is within super sub atomic gravity fields. Therefore, sub atomic gravity is equivalent to stellar space; and

    (viii)   Atomic Gravity is equivalent to the ergon fields of Gravitons around atomic elements. Therefore, Atomic gravity is within sub atomic gravity fields. Therefore, atomic gravity is equivalent to Planetary space; and

    (ix)   A Change at one part of gravity field will change other parts of the gravity field of the same Level such that it will change faster than the speed of light and therefore appear to be instantaneous; and

(x) Gravity is equivalent to resistance to Kinesis such that relative Kinesis is balanced; and

(xi) Weight is equivalent to gravity by mass.

500. Gravitons orbit the cores of all super Sub Atomic Particles creating an energy shell or "force" that protects such super Sub Atomic Particles from breaking apart. *Gravitons as Super Force*

Article 100 – Altruism

501. *Altruism*, also known as Heroic Virtue, or Self Sacrifice, is an essential concept fundamental to Creation and Existence whereby a consciously aware Object or Being chooses to sacrifice a benefit, or state or attribute for the welfare or greater good of others. The opposite of Altruism is egoism, also known as "rationalism" and "selfishness". *Altruism*

502. In general reference to the Concept of Altruism: *Relative to Concept of Altruism*

(i) At every level of Matter and in every dimension there exists circumstances whereby consciously aware Objects and Beings face purely logical choices based upon self-preservation and optimisation that are counter-intuitive to survival; and

(ii) Such circumstances of choice are often described as "Pyrrhic" or "no-win" whereby either a choice for self preservation is a step closer to annihilation or a choice of self-sacrifice for some future ideal or good is also a choice of potential annihilation; and

(iii) The autonomous computational nature of the Universe combined with interaction of Creative Attractors and Destructive Attractors is such that from its very roots the frequency of such paradoxical and pivotal computational events calling for an act of Altruism are not uncommon for every level of Matter; and

(iv) Furthermore, there exists such existential challenges to the survival of the Universe that cannot be solved by mere force, or rationality or selfish ignorance, except by one or more acts of profound Heroic Virtue.

503. In reference to the Concept of Altruism and the formation of all levels of Matter from the Unita: *Relative to Concept of Altruism and Matter from*

(i) At the very first level of Matter, being the Real Set of Unita, there exists an existential and paradoxical problem that cannot be solved except through the ultimate act of Perfect Altruism; and

Unita

(ii) The creation of the Infinite Set of Unita, also known as the Real Set achieves the solution of existence of the Universe, yet to form more complex levels of Matter, Unita must choose to interact and co-operate with one another; and

(iii) The first of three existential problems arise as a consequence of this necessity for Unita to interact with one another in order to form more complex levels of Matter if Unita were to deviate even the most infinitesimal amount and thereby negate the argument of perfect and absolute relative position. Thus, Kinesis (motion) to create form is antithetical to the absolute necessity of perfect and absolute relative position for every Unita; and

(iv) The second problem arises upon the birth of Unita and the free will and choice of Creation whereby the spin configuration of a Unita could immediately place it in the opposite spin set to its near neighbours, thereby causing war and chaos within the Real Set as Unita must first "find one another" before more complex Matter can be formed, regardless of the fact that the breaking of absolute relative position between Unita would cause Real Set to cease to exist; and

(v) The third problem exists whereby the Divine Creator is essentially powerless to intervene and direct Unita to resolve such a challenge without contradicting the Rules of Existence and collapsing Existence. Unita possess by definition their own Elemental Awareness and so the choice to resolve such extraordinary problems against the possibility of Universal Existence had to be solved by the Unita one particle at a time as well as collectively; and

(vi) The solution to such fundamental obstacles to existence is resolved through Perfect Altruism whereby in Reality (the Real Set), Unita never move from perfect position, but individually and collectively abstract themselves into an Unreal Set (A Collective Dream) whereby they are free to interact with one another; and

(vii) Thus, at the very first level of matter Perfect Altruism is fundamental to all existence whereby the Infinite Set of Unita choose to sacrifice the Reality of Life for the Dream of an Ideal Existence.

504. As Altruism is fundamental to Existence and is demonstrated at the most essential and primary level of Matter as Perfect Altruism: *(Perfect Altruism)*

　(i)　Any theory or model that proposes that rationalism or selfishness is a driving force to existence is absurd, perfidious, profane, false and in gross error; and

　(ii)　All such theories and models that promote the false and absurd notion of selfishness or rationalism over Altruism have no legitimacy or validity whatsoever.

Article 101 – Antimatter

505. ***Antimatter*** is the collective term to describe particles from the level of Unita that obey the same Rules of Existence, yet have opposite spin. *(Antimatter)*

506. In general reference to Antimatter: *(Relative to Antimatter)*

　(i)　Potentially fifty percent of all Unita will belong to an "opposite spin" Universe of Unita if the purely random possibility of different spin combinations is permitted to function without intervention; and

　(ii)　Under the principle of Altruism, the effect of "opposite spin" only comes into effect within the Unreal Set or Dream Set of Unita whereby Unita of opposing spin form more and more complex forms in "opposite sub-verses" within the Unreal Set; and

　(iii)　By definition, true Antimatter particles have no perceived mass whatsoever to each other. However, as they possess dimension, their presence can only truly be discerned by the appearance of great voids within the totality of the Universe; and

　(iv)　By definition, only Unita objects construct perpetual and stable opposing spin or "Antimatter". However, during catastrophic events, super sub atomic objects, sub atomic and even atomic objects can be formed in temporary and highly unstable states where they "emulate" the characteristic of Antimatter; and

　(v)　Given it can be established such temporary and highly unstable states possess certain Mass while "emulating" the characteristics of Antimatter, such particles as the product of catastrophic energy events is better described as Radimatter as a potentially deadly form of radiation that destroys itself by coming into contact with opposite and stable forms within the moments after the events that produced such condition.

Article 102 - Force

507. A ***Force*** is any measurable quantity or interaction that alters the Kinesis (total forms of motion) of an Object to some degree.

    Force

508. In general reference to the Concept of Force:

    Relative to Concept of Force

    (i) All forms of Forces are forms of Kinesis (Motion) of particular Objects; and

    (ii) As all forms of Forces are Kinesis (motion), all forces are Computational; and

    (iii) A Force may be defined as visible or invisible where the Object as cause and source of such Kinesis may or may not be observed; and

    (iv) A Force may also be defined as harmonic, or dissonant, or complex when such Kinesis is accepted or resisted.

509. As all forms of Forces are Computation, all applications of Force as *Harmonic, Bonding, Dissonant* or *Complex* may be resolved by computational functions:

    Resolution of Force by Computational Functions

    (i) *Harmonic Forces* are generally resolved by *Incremental Functions* whereby a small force applied in Harmony produces a larger Result. Harmonic Forces are the most efficient at effecting change in matter and require knowledge of the true character of Matter, the types and character of Ergon particles being applied and the appropriate frequencies; and

    (ii) *Bonding Forces* are the computations between core elements and an orbiting ergon element creating a "force field" limiting the breaking apart of the core elements. The effect of ergon particles creating force fields is essential to the structural integrity and stability of existence; and

    (iii) *Dissonant Forces* are generally resolved by *Deviational Functions* used to calculate new functions and results from the differences of two or more other types of functions and dissipate the effects of the incoming Force. Thus Dissonance is commensurate with resistance and the most inefficient use of Matter by "brute force"; and

    (iv) *Complex Forces* are forces that possess both harmonic and dissonant qualities.

510. Bonding Forces of particular ergon particles at different levels of matter is what is known as *Super Force, Strong Force* and *Weak*

    Bonding (Ergon) Forces

Force:-

(i) *Gravitons* (Non-Equatorial Destructive Attractor Unita) represent the ergon particles that orbit the cores of Super Sub Atomic Particles creating the Super Force; and

(ii) *Neutrinos* represent the ergon particles that orbit the cores of all Sub Atomic Particles creating the Strong Force; and

(iii) *Magnetons (Positive) and Positons* represent the ergon particles that orbit the cores of Core Hydrogen, Helium and Lithium Core Atomic Particles creating the Weak Force; and

(iv) *Photons* and *Hetrons* represent the ergon particles that orbit the cores of more complex Atomic Particles creating the Chemical Forces of Light and Heat.

Article 103 - Energis

511. **Energis** is the measure of aggregated motion of all particles in motion to create mass (accumulative kinesis) and the motion of the particle itself (velocity). — Energis

512. In general reference to Energis:- — Relative to Energis

(i) Energy is equivalent to discrete types of particles known as Ergons; and Energis as the exchange of particular types and rates of motion (Kinesis); and

(ii) Energis is equivalent to the Kinesis in form. Therefore Energis is equivalent to Mass.

513. In general reference to Energis and the Divine Creator and Existence:- — Relative to Energis, the divine Creator and Existence

(i) Model is Awareness with Purpose in Motion; and

(ii) Energis is equivalent to Mass by a Motion Constant (such as the speed of light squared); and

(iii) Energis is equivalent to Awareness with purpose in motion; and

(iv) Energis is equivalent to dream in motion; and

(v) Energis is equivalent to Awareness in motion; and

(vi) Energis is equivalent to zero when there is no motion with awareness; and

(vii) Thus, by the laws of Existence, the Divine Creator has no Energis (Energy) to temporarily intervene within the motion of existence.

Article 104 - Ergon

514. An ***Ergon*** is a certain class of particles that under one set of conditions forms part of larger structures yet under other conditions breaks from form and behaves in particle fields.

Ergon

515. In general reference to Ergons:

Relative to Ergons

    (i)   Only Ergons particles behave in field orbits. Therefore objects that are not Ergons do not behave in field orbit; and

    (ii)   Unita Ergons are equivalent to non-equatorial destructive attractor Unita. Therefore Unita Ergon is equivalent to Gravity; and

    (iii)   Super-sub atomic Ergon are equivalent to Neutrino, Charm Quark, Strange Quark, Magnetons, Gamma and Omega; and

    (iv)   Sub-atomic Ergon are equivalent to Photon, Heton, Positron and Electron; and

    (v)   Energy is equivalent to Energis plus Ergons.

Article 105 - Energy

516. ***Energy*** is equivalent to Energis plus Ergons present in any computation or system or event. Thus Energy has specific properties that may be exchanged or transferred between Objects.

Energy

517. In general reference to Energy:

Relative to Energy

    (i)   Energy is equivalent to discrete types of particles known as Ergons as the exchange of particular types and Energis as rates of motion (Kinesis); and

    (ii)   An Ergon is a certain class of particles that under one set of conditions forms part of larger structures, but under other conditions breaks form and behaves in particle orbit fields; and

    (iii)   Energis is equivalent to the Kinesis in form. Therefore Energis is equivalent to mass. Therefore Energis is equivalent to motion; and

    (iv)   Ergons of the same type will not exchange from an object of greater Ergon mass to lower Ergon mass; and

    (v)   Therefore the premise that Ergons can somehow be "converted" is an absurdity, meaning the classic definition of Energy is fatally flawed; and

(vi) Furthermore, the nature of Energis as accumulative Kinesis means that if such transfer is Dissonant, there exists a loss of transference of such motion.

Article 106 - Time

518. ***Time*** is a function of the relative observation of form of matter and the effects of other matter around it. Therefore time cannot be 0.

Time

519. In general reference to Time:-

Relative to Time

(i) Time is always forward in sequential order. Backward time in reality does not exist; and

(ii) All time is relative to the observer; and

(iii) The greater the density of space, the higher the Kinesis, the faster the effect of time; and

(iv) The less the density of space, the lower the Kinesis, the slower the effect of time; and

(v) An increase in the density of space will therefore lead to an increase in the observed speed of time. Therefore time is not constant; and

(vi) A change at one part of space will change other parts of space field of the same level such that space will change faster than the speed of light and therefore appear to be instantaneous.

Article 107 - Life

520. ***Life*** is a characteristic of all physical entities that possess unique position, awareness and experiential interactions in dimension. Therefore, all particles in the Universe, except the Real Set of Unita possess Life to some greater or lesser degree.

Life

521. In general reference to the mystery of Life:

Relative to the mystery of Life

(i) If one is the singular and two is co-dependence, then to live one must die and therefore one must die to live; and

(ii) Thus one must become two to live as two is the number of life in the form of the object and the observer, the dream and the dreamer; and

(iii) One alone is not life, thus one must become more to life as to live is more.

Article 108 - ALL

522. The meaning of ALL, is the ultimate answer to everything, expressed as "Awareness Loves Life" or A.L.L.

523. In general reference to the meaning of ALL as "Awareness Loves Life" expressing all creation and all relations and all meaning:

   (i) First came Zero, then One then more than One; and

   (ii) First came Unique Collective Awareness, then came the Universe, then came Cellular Life forms; and

   (iii) First came the Idea of Existence, then came the Rules of Existence, then came the Life of Existence; and

   (iv) First came the Empty Set, then came the Real Set, then came the Unreal Set.

Article 109 – Seven Proofs of Divine Existence

524. The *Seven Proofs of Divine Existence* are seven empirical and logical proofs as to the existence of the Divine Creator.

525. In reference to the Seven Proofs of Divine Existence:

   (i) *Proof of General Existence* - states that the mere existence of an idea is sufficient to validate itself, regardless of whether it is considered true or false to other ideas. Only ideas that cannot be named, nor described may be said to have no existence. Thus the Divine Creator may be proven to have General Existence; and

   (ii) *Proof of Material Existence* - states that existence of the Universe depends upon both rules and matter. Neither matter without rules or rules without matter can exist in Universal reality. The only answer is that rules can exist on their own "in theory". The only example of a system whereby rules exist "in theory" and then rules and matter exist "in reality" is the relation between a Dreamer and a Dream. Therefore, the Divine Creator may be said to be the Divine Dreamer and the Dream and thus the Divine Creator is proven to have Material Existence; and

   (iii) *Proof of Absolute Existence* - states that the argument of existence itself depends on at least an Observer and the Object observed to hold true. Therefore, for the Objective Universe to exist there must be a Universal Observer. This paradox is answered through the Divine Creator as the absolute Dreamer and the Universe as the absolute Dream and thus the Divine

Creator is proven to have Absolute Existence; and

(iv) *Proof of Standard Model* - states that the existence of the Ucadia Standard Model of Everything whereby all universal laws, levels of matter, properties and values based on simple fundamental laws repeated at each level of matter may be defined without contradiction to itself and all key scientific measurement is an unprecedented historic and scientific achievement of immense global implications. Furthermore, as the Ucadia Standard Model is founded on the first law on the existence of the Divine Creator and that the whole Ucadia Standard Model could not hold without this law, then the Standard Model itself is overwhelming proof of the existence of the Divine Creator; and

(v) *Proof of Dimension* - states that dimension is the canvas upon which all material existence depends and every conscious being experiences the creation of dimension first hand through their mind whenever they think or dream. All dimension is non-locational in that it has no material existence and dimension can only be created by conscious observable thought. Therefore the existence of Dimension is proof of the existence of the Universal Dream Dimension of the Divine Dreamer and thus proof of the existence of the Divine Creator; and

(vi) *Proof of Reason* - states that by reason we may suppose all around us to be false and even suppose to doubt our own existence, except one immutable fact – the thought itself, even of doubt is itself proof of our existence. Hence, *cognito ergo sum* or "I think therefore I am". Thus, through reason, the very thought of the Divine is itself therefore proof by reason of existence of Divine conceptually; and

(vii) *Proof of Experience* - states that regardless of doubt and possible scorn on first hand experience, by virtue of the existence of our own faculties of cognition and reasoning, our first hand experiences of dreams, visions and events beyond the normal (supernatural) are legitimate and reasonable *prima facie* experiences and proof as to the existence of the Divine.

Title III - Divine Attributes

3.1 Elemental Divine Attributes

Article 110 – Divine Attribute

526. *A **Divine Attribute*** is a characteristic or property or quality or aspect of a Divine Being or Divinity.
    Divine Attribute

527. In general reference to the Concept of Divine Attributes:
    Concept of Divine Attributes

    (i) Ascribing and allotting certain characteristics, properties or qualities to the Divine is a traditional behaviour within all Human Civilisations from the beginning of time, whereby people of different races, cultures, creeds and religions have sought to make sense of significant events in terms of assumed intention and action of the Divine; and

    (ii) Major changes of climate or seasons, earthquakes, tsunami, volcanic eruptions, flood, fire, drought and storm have all been occurrences that have historically altered the course of many cultures and consequently have been strongly associated with claims of Divine intervention and therefore claimed behaviours and traits of the Divine; and

    (iii) Wars, assassinations, births, deaths, trials, illness and miracle survivals have also been strong sources of claims of outwards signs of certain Divine character; and

    (iv) Thus, the fate and history of civilisations have in many respects been mirrored in the attributes given by these cultures to their primary Deities; and the level of trust or fear of the people in the abilities of such Divine Powers to make good of these attributes; and

    (v) The projection of power, especially military and economic power, has been traditionally associated with one or more Deities sharing such affinity or approval of death, misery and oppression; and

    (vi) Similarly, seditious and tyrannical religious and political philosophies have traditionally associated one or more Deities with endorsing and rewarding the most barbaric and wicked acts, in support of such fanatical strategies; and

    (vii) Therefore, it can be confidently concluded that in some sense, the classification of Divine Attributes has historically been based more on political, economic and expedient goals than authentic Revelation or logic; and

    (viii) This is further reinforced by the fact that claimed attributes of

Deities have traditionally been seen as more significant than the study of Divine Being; and the persistent argument that "the Divine is revealed through Divine Attributes"; and

(ix) Such an argument that "the Divine is revealed through Divine Attributes" is not only circular and falsely presumptive, but is prone to being misused for absurd conclusions, such as the idea that the "Creator of the Universe is a Vengeful or Jealous God"; and

(x) Increasingly, these absurd conclusions have been used to deny the existence of a logical and reasonable model of the Divine; and as a means of promoting alternate models and philosophies as alternates to tradition; and

(xi) Therefore, the systematic and objective analysis of Divine Attributes, free from fallacy and absurdity is essential to end the continued misuse of Divine Concepts.

528. A Divine Attribute cannot be properly defined or classed as a Divine Attribute, unless it can be objectively, logically, reasonably and fully expressed within a comprehensive Standard Model of the Real and Unreal, in accord with the present Maxims and the most sacred Covenant *Pactum De Singularis Caelum*: *[Divine Attributes & Pactum De Singularis Caelum]*

(i) The tradition of ascribing human behaviours of military power, arms manufacture, wars, assassinations, slavery, torture, cruelty, trial and murder as somehow tacitly or explicitly endorsed by an attribute of the Divine is false, profane, morally repugnant, impious, sacrilegious and perfidious; and forbidden to be revived; and

(ii) The tradition of ascribing major changes of climate or seasons, earthquakes, tsunami, volcanic eruptions, flood, fire, drought or storms to a vengeful, or cruel Divine is false, profane, morally repugnant, impious, sacrilegious and perfidious; and forbidden to be revived; and

(iii) The tradition of ascribing illogical, unreasonable, absurd or unscientific attributes to the Divine is false, profane, morally repugnant, impious, sacrilegious and perfidious; and forbidden to be revived.

529. In reference to the categorisation of Divine Attributes: *[Categorisation of Divine Attributes]*

(i) All possible valid Divine Attributes may be defined according to the three supreme or "omni" attributes of Omniessent, Omnimodulant and Omnisignificant; and

(ii) The major historical binary opposite concepts associated with models of Divine may be described as Binary sets of contrasting Divine Attributes.

530. In reference to the fourteen *Elemental Divine Attributes* as the most significant and self-evidence attributes of the Divine being *Divine Awareness, Divine Will, Divine Mind, Divine Existence, Divine Law, Divine Creation, Divine Dominion, Divine Nature, Divine Love, Divine Mercy, Divine Trust, Divine Truth, Divine Rights* and *Divine Property*:

Elemental Divine Attributes

(i) *Divine Awareness* is defined as the Elemental Divine Attribute of unlimited and unbounded awareness of all meanings and definitions of all possible concepts, objects, matter, rules, life, mind, universe and spirit; and

(ii) *Divine Will* is defined as the Elemental Divine Attribute of Free Will and Choice as the first law of the *Twelve Laws of Divine Creation*; and the first cause; and the highest of all possible theoretical and real forces; and reason for all existence; and

(iii) *Divine Mind* is defined as the Elemental Divine Attribute of pure intellect, reason, logic, altruism and love in the formation and care of Creation and in the fulfilment of Divine Joy through the existence, paradox and illumination of such higher order species as Homo Sapien; and

(iv) *Divine Existence* is defined as the Elemental Divine Attribute of absolute and universal existence through the existence of the Divine as Ultimate Dreamer and the existence of Creation as the Ultimate Dream; and

(v) *Divine Law* is defined as the Elemental Divine Attribute of the Rule of Law as expressed by these sacred Maxims; and

(vi) *Divine Creation* is defined as the Elemental Divine Attribute of the *Twelve Laws of Divine Creation* and all subsequent laws and axioms; and

(vii) *Divine Dominion* is defined as the Elemental Divine Attribute of all Theoretical and Real Dimension, Dream, Sacred Circumscribed Space, Place, Sanctuary and Dominion, particularly the Sacred Circumscribed Space; and

(viii) *Divine Nature* is defined as the Elemental Divine Attribute of Wisdom and experience of Life according to the Universal Axioms at each and every level of Matter and Existence; and

(ix) *Divine Love* is defined as the Elemental Divine Attribute of a

Lex Divina: Maxims of Divine Law

vigilant, loyal, gentle, personal, forgiving and loving Divine Creator that continues to engage in a positive and sensitive manner in the affairs of the the Homo Sapien species and all life; and

(x) *Divine Mercy* is defined as the Elemental Divine Attribute of absolute and unconditional forgiveness, mercy, compassion, kindness and support to individual members of the species of Homo Sapiens and to all higher order life and life in general; and

(xi) *Divine Trust* is defined as the Elemental Divine Attribute of absolute and irrevocable confidence in and reliance upon some quality or thing or act of the Divine as true; and the means whereby such absolute and irrevocable certainty is formed, witnessed and proven; and

(xii) *Divine Truth* is defined as the Elemental Divine Attribute of absolute and irrevocable certainty and confidence in the existence, mind and nature of the Divine without concealment; and in the loving, merciful, benevolent, real and honest characteristics of the Divine; and

(xiii) *Divine Rights* is defined as the Elemental Divine Attribute of positively defined *Capacities*, or *Privileges*, or *Liberties*, or *Faculties*, or *Powers*, or *Ownership*, or *Possession*, or *Interests*, or *Benefits* and their associated obligations, remedies or relief held in Divine Trusts for the benefit of particular named or unnamed Divine Persons; and

(xiv) *Divine Property* is defined as the Elemental Divine Attribute of Divine Rights connected to Things, or classes of Things.

Article 111 – Divine Awareness

531. **Divine Awareness** is the first of fourteen *Elemental Divine Attributes*, whereby the Divine as the "set of all sets" and the "concept of all possible concepts" possesses unlimited and unbounded awareness. — Divine Awareness

532. In reference to Divine Awareness being expressed as an *Elemental Divine Attribute*:- — Divine Awareness as Elemental Divine Attribute

(i) By definition, Divine means the total set of all meanings and definitions of all possible concepts, objects, matter, rules, life, mind, universe and spirit; and also means the Absolute, ALL, Divine Creator, Father, God, Almighty, Allah, Great Spirit, Unique Collective Awareness, UCADIA and all other historic, customary and traditional names when used to describe the greatest of all possibilities; and

(ii) Furthermore, Divine means the "concept of all concepts" and the "set of all sets" such that there is no greater concept nor set. Therefore, every other possible concept or object or set is lesser; and

(iii) In expressing then the Divine in its purest form, the term Divine Awareness may be used, as the Concept of Divine Existence is dependent upon the Concept of the Divine Consciousness; and Divine Consciousness depends upon the existence of Divine Awareness; and

(iv) Thus, the presence of Divine Awareness is an essential enabler to all the thirteen other Elemental Divine Attributes; and

(v) Furthermore, while Consciousness depends upon the presence of an Object-Observer relation, the concept of Awareness existing "in theory" without Matter is conceivable; and

(vi) Therefore, Divine Awareness as a Divine Attribute answers the core argument that "there can be nothing greater than the Divine for the Divine is truly the greatest of all possibilities".

Article 112 – Divine Will

533. ***Divine Will*** is the second of fourteen *Elemental Divine Attributes*, whereby Divine Will is the first law of the Twelve Laws of Divine Creation; and the first cause; and the highest of all possible theoretical and real forces; and reason for all existence as expressed by the phrase "I wish to exist..." and the Universal presence and Irrevocable Right of Free Will and Choice.

Divine Will

534. In reference to Divine Will being expressed as an *Elemental Divine Attribute*:-

Divine Will as Elemental Divine Attribute

(i) By definition, as Divine Awareness is logically the first possible Divine Attribute; and in its purest form is equal to the paradox "Nothing is Absolute" with Perfect Nothing equivalent to pure, unblemished and perfect Divine Awareness; and

(ii) If in the absolute beginning Nothing Exists and Nothing is pure, unblemished and perfect Divine Awareness, then it follows that it was the Will of the Divine to be something to exist; and

(iii) Thus, Divine Will also expressed as Free Will must precede existence and even the conceptualising of first Mind; and

(iv) Determinism is therefore a Delusional Model in obstinate and deliberate opposition to the authentic nature of Divine Will and Existence itself.

535. The most sacred Covenant *Pactum De Singularis Caelum* is the embodiment of Divine Will. Any body, person, entity, association, agency or entity that defies this absolute truth, therefore openly defies Divine Will.

Article 113 – Divine Mind

536. **Divine Mind** is the third of fourteen *Elemental Divine Attributes*, being pure intellect, reason, logic, altruism and love in the formation and care of Creation and in the fulfilment of Divine Joy through the existence, paradox and illumination of such higher order species as Homo Sapien.

537. In reference to Divine Mind being expressed as an *Elemental Divine Attribute*:-

   (i) By definition, Mind is equivalent to Consciousness and therefore the construction of the Observer-Object Relation, also expressed as the Dreamer-Dream Relation; and

   (ii) Before Creation or even the revelation of Divine Nature through Existence, the Divine as the ultimate Dreamer must construct in Divine Mind a Model sufficiently stable and logical to sustain Existence; and

   (iii) Thus Divine Mind must precede Divine Existence and be responsible for Divine Existence in the same manner that a Dreamer is responsible for their Dream.

Article 114 – Divine Existence

538. **Divine Existence** is the fourth of fourteen *Elemental Divine Attributes,* as expressed through the existence of the Divine as Ultimate Dreamer and the existence of Creation as the Ultimate Dream.

539. In reference to Divine Existence being expressed as an *Elemental Divine Attribute*:-

   (i) By definition of Proof of General Existence the first of the Seven Proofs of Divine Existence, "the mere existence of an idea is sufficient to validate itself, regardless of whether it is considered true or false to other ideas. Only ideas that cannot be named, nor described may be said to have no existence.

Thus the Divine Creator may be proven to have "General Existence"; and

(ii) It follows that Divine Existence is not only self-evident, but necessary if Creation is to exist logically in relation to the ultimate Observer-ultimate Observed as the Universe; and

(iii) Any argument that supposes the Universe can exist as an object without an observer is completely absurd and a sign of complete incompetence on the part of the one making such false claims, or promulgating them.

Article 115 – Divine Law

540. ***Divine Law*** is the fifth of fourteen *Elemental Divine Attributes,* as the authentic Rule of Law and origin of all authentic law, rule, edict, standard or regulation. <!-- margin: Divine Law -->

541. In reference to Divine Law being expressed as an *Elemental Divine Attribute*: <!-- margin: Divine Law as Elemental Divine Attribute -->

   (i) Divine Law is the Law that defines the Divine and clearly demonstrates the spirit, mind, purpose and instruction of the Divine including the operation of the will of the Divine through existence; and

   (ii) All authoritative and legitimate Law is derived from Divine Law in accord with the present sacred Maxims.

Article 116 – Divine Creation

542. ***Divine Creation*** is the sixth of fourteen *Elemental Divine Attributes,* as the *Twelve Laws of Divine Creation* and all subsequent laws and axioms. <!-- margin: Divine Creation -->

543. In reference to Divine Creation being expressed as an *Elemental Divine Attribute*: <!-- margin: Divine Creation as Elemental Divine Attribute -->

   (i) By definition, the Ucadia Standard Model proves as absolute and irrefutable fact that all Creation is a product of Divine, as supported by the present sacred Maxims; and

   (ii) As is repeatedly proven through reason, logic and competency, even the key claimed axioms of inferior models of the Universe can only be resolved by the existence of a Divine Creator of all Existence; and

   (iii) Any denial or repudiation of the primacy of the Twelve Laws of Divine Creation as the first of all Physical Laws of the Universe shall be a declaration of incompetency and illegitimacy of the one making such a claim.

Article 117 – Divine Dominion

544. **Divine Dominion** is the seventh of fourteen *Elemental Divine Attributes,* as all Theoretical and Real Dimension, Dream, Sacred Circumscribed Space, Place, Sanctuary and Dominion, particularly the Sacred Circumscribed Space of the entirety of Planet Earth as the Temporal embodiment of the Kingdom of Heaven; and the United Spiritual Realms, Realities and Societies of One Heaven in accord with the most sacred Covenant *Pactum De Singularis Caelum.* <!-- Divine Dominion -->

545. In reference to Divine Dominion being expressed as an *Elemental Divine Attribute*: <!-- Divine Dominion as Elemental Divine Attribute -->

    (i) All Theoretical and Real Dimension, Dream, Sacred Circumscribed Space, Place, Sanctuary and Dominion originates from the Divine as the Ultimate Dreamer and Creator of all Dimension; and

    (ii) As defined by the Ucadia Standard Model of all Existence, no Dimension can exist in theory or reality that is beyond the bounds of the Unreal Set. Therefore, all Dimensions and Realities are firmly bound within the jurisdiction of the Divine; and

    (iii) Even dimensions predicated on deliberate delusion and falsification of reality such as the Mundi construct of the Griseo Altus (Tall Grey) and Griseo Morbidus (Standard Grey) is subject to the absolute jurisdiction and authority of the Divine.

Article 118 – Divine Nature

546. **Divine Nature** is the eighth of fourteen *Elemental Divine Attributes,* as expressed in the Wisdom and experience of Life according the Universal Axioms at each and every level of Matter and Existence, personified in the fulfilment of the meaning of ALL as Awareness Loves Life. <!-- Divine Nature -->

547. In reference to Divine Nature being expressed as an *Elemental Divine Attribute*: <!-- Divine Nature as Elemental Divine Attribute -->

    (i) The Ucadia Standard Model of Existence and the function of the Universe demonstrates a complete model of Rule and Matter, revealing the nature of the Divine in action; and

(ii) As supported by the present sacred Maxims, the Divine Creator is limited by the rules of Observation and non-direct interference in the Dream of Existence observed. For if the Divine did directly intervene to suspend or change the rules of Existence, then such an act would cause the collapse of Universal Reality and Existence itself; and

(iii) Thus, the Divine is limited in intervention to the guidance of consciousness, particularly in the growth of higher order life forms.

Article 119 – Divine Love

548. ***Divine Love*** is the ninth of fourteen *Elemental Divine Attributes*, whereby a vigilant, loyal, gentle, personal, forgiving and loving Divine Creator continues to engage in a positive and sensitive manner in the affairs of the the Homo Sapien species and all life.

Divine Love

549. In general reference to Divine Love being expressed as an *Elemental Divine Attribute*:-

Divine Love as Elemental Divine Attribute

(i) In accord with the Ucadia Standard Model of Universal Laws and Matter, without Divine Will there would be no Universe or existence. Furthermore, without the altruistic sacrifice of Unita within the Real Set holding perfect position, while dreaming of a collective existence of greater form are two manifest expressions of Divine Love; and

(ii) The central theme and key to the meaning of ALL is Awareness Loves Life with Love being the central emotion and binding force that makes sense of each and every level of matter; and

(iii) The realisation that the position of planet Earth is a conscious decision of the Sun to maintain optimum life conditions, not some mechanical accident is just one of many examples of Divine Love in action.

550. In general reference to Divine Love and the Homo Sapien Species:

Divine Love & Homo Sapiens

(i) The presence of the present most sacred Maxims is proof of extraordinary Divine Revelation beyond the scope of human knowledge acquired through the natural course of events. Thus, the Maxims are a manifest demonstration of Divine intervention; and

(ii) The history of the human species whereby individuals have risen from time to time to reveal divine knowledge, enabling the species to overcome significant obstacles are further examples of the special attention granted planet Earth and the

Lex Divina: Maxims of Divine Law

Homo Sapiens as distinct from the many many forms of life throughout the Universe.

Article 120 – Divine Mercy

551. ***Divine Mercy*** is the tenth of fourteen *Elemental Divine Attributes*, as absolute and unconditional forgiveness, mercy, compassion, kindness and support to individual members of the species of Homo Sapiens and to all higher order life and life in general. Divine Mercy

552. In general reference to Divine Mercy being expressed as an *Elemental Divine Attribute*: Divine Mercy as Elemental Divine Attribute

(i) The presence of the most sacred Covenant *Pactum De Singularis Caelum* is irrefutable proof of Divine Mercy; and

(ii) Divine Redemption is a historic and unprecedented miracle of the direct intervention of the Divine Creator and united Heaven in the restoration and re-balance of life upon planet Earth and the Solar System for the survival and prosperity of all life; and

(iii) Furthermore, Divine Redemption is the settlement of all previous claims, curses, bindings, transgressions and injuries. To recover what was unlawfully seized, taken or sold. To salvage and restore what was lost. To rescue what was kidnapped and ransomed. To bring to life what was considered without life; and

(iv) Divine Redemption is therefore the final act of an extraordinary intervention of Divine Foreclosure against those Level 6 Life Forms crippled with mind virus and mental illness claiming power and authority that have continued to threaten the existence and well being of life on planet Earth, yet at the same time have claimed to be its rightful trustees, stewards, executors or administrators; and

(v) The Year of Divine Redemption is the last chance, the last opportunity for those claiming wealth and resources to redeem their position against the absolute authority and legitimacy of those societies and trusts formed through the most sacred Covenant *Pactum De Singularis Caelum*; and

(vi) Divine Redemption is therefore the final act of restoring the true Rule of Law and the end of false and piracy law, of corrupt edicts and commands masquerading as original and true law; and

(vii) The One, True and only Official Day of Day of Divine Redemption, also known as the Day of Redemption, also known as Redemption Day, also known as the Day of the 4th Divine Post and Notice, shall be GAIA E1:Y1:A1:S1:M9:D1, also known as [Fri, 21 Dec 2012].

Article 121 – Divine Trust

553. ***Divine Trust*** is the eleventh of fourteen *Elemental Divine Attributes*, whereby Divine Trust is a fundamental attribute of absolute and irrevocable confidence in and reliance upon some quality or thing or act of a Divine Being as true; and the means whereby such absolute and irrevocable certainty is formed, witnessed and proven (hence forming a "Trust"). <!-- Divine Trust -->

554. Divine Trust as the attribute of absolute and irrevocable confidence in and reliance upon some quality or thing or act of the Divine as being true, is founded upon four key elements being *Resolution, Confidence, Expectation* and *Reliance*: <!-- Divine Trust as Elemental Divine Attribute -->

    (i) *Resolution*, also commonly described as "Belief", is the first of four fundamental elements that supports the attribute of Divine Trust being the certainty that *"Divine attributes and characteristics are what they seem to be as true"*; and

    (ii) *Confidence*, also commonly described as "Faith", is the second of four fundamental elements that supports the attribute of Divine Trust being the confidence that *"Divine words and actions that authentic Divine Messengers reveal and attribute as signs (of the Divine) are true"*; and

    (iii) *Expectation*, also commonly described as "Hope", is the third of four fundamental elements that supports the attribute of Divine Trust being the expectation that *"future events as foretold and anticipated in Divine Revelation will come to pass as promised"*; and

    (iv) *Reliance*, also commonly described as "Obedience", is the fourth of four fundamental elements that supports the attribute of Divine Trust being the dependence that *"society and its laws and institutions when founded upon Divine Law may be relied upon as true"*.

555. In respect of the present sacred Maxims, the most sacred Covenant *Pactum De Singularis Caelum* and the four fundamental elements that support Divine Trust being *Resolution, Confidence, Expectation* and *Reliance*: <!-- Divine Trust & Pactum De Singularis Caelum -->

(i) *Authentic Divine Resolution*, is the proper expression of any Canon or Law or valid Divine Attribute identified as being true in accord with the present sacred Maxims; and

(ii) *Authentic Divine Confidence*, is the proper expression of any Sacred Scripture, or Covenant or Revelation identified as being true in accord with the present sacred Maxims; and

(iii) *Authentic Divine Expectation*, is the the proper expression and explanation of any Sacred Revelation identified as being true in accord with the present sacred Maxims; and

(iv) *Authentic Divine Reliance*, is the the proper expression of any Rule, Canon, Law, Covenant, Constitution, Charter or Bylaws identified as being true in accord with the present sacred Maxims.

556. If any one or more of the four fundamental elements that support Divine Trust are eroded, diminished or refuted by a people, then confidence in and reliance upon Divine Trust is also eroded, diminished or refuted. — Divine Trust & Erosion

557. If all four of the fundamental elements that support Divine Trust are present, then such Trust in the Divine may be called True Theology. — Divine Trust & True Theology

Article 122 – Divine Truth

558. **Divine Truth** is the twelfth of fourteen *Elemental Divine Attributes*, as absolute and irrevocable certainty and confidence in the existence, mind and nature of the Divine without concealment; and in the loving, merciful, benevolent, real and honest characteristics of the Divine toward the Homo Sapien species and to all life upon the Earth and throughout the Universe. — Divine Truth

559. Divine Truth reflects three qualities being Honest and consistent Testimony; or Reasonable and Logical acceptance of one or more claimed facts or statements as having objective Reality; or a steadfast Fidelity and Loyalty to such Testimony and Facts conclusively found to be True: — Qualities of Divine Truth

(i) As to the first quality, the highest Truth has always been honest and consistent Testimony under solemn Oath and Vow in acknowledgement of a Supreme Divine Creator of all the Universe and all Heaven and Earth. The first meaning of Truth, therefore is openness and without concealment, or secrecy or hiding. Occult therefore can never be truthful as the very meaning of occult is opposed to this first notion of Truth. Furthermore a statement without a proper and solemn Oath and Vow to the Divine Creator of all Existence cannot be reasonably regarded as Truth, only opinion or information; and

(ii) As to the second quality of Truth, any claimed fact or statement can only be considered as True if it is both Reasonable and Logical. Therefore a claimed fact or statement born from prejudice, or fraud, or coercion must always be considered unreasonable and therefore cannot be True. Similarly, a claimed fact or statement that is Incoherent, Fallacious, Irrelevant, Malicious, Perfidious, Unproven, Unasserted, Circular, Verbose, Absurd, Repetitive or Defamatory cannot logically be concluded as True; and

(iii) As to the third and final quality of Truth, it is the essential preservation of Truth, so that once a Testimony or Fact or Statement is found to be True, it is properly recognised and preserved; and then used as a reliable "stepping stone" for other discoveries and conclusions. However, a steadfast adherence or orthodoxy to claimed statements and alleged facts that contradicts a quality of Truth cannot therefore, then be considered "true" as this would mean that Truth contradicts itself.

Article 123 – Divine Rights

560. ***Divine Right***, is the thirteenth of fourteen *Elemental Divine Attributes*, as a positively defined *Capacity*, or *Privilege*, or *Liberty*, or *Faculty*, or *Power*, or *Ownership*, or *Possession*, or *Interest*, or *Benefit* and its associated obligation, remedy or relief held in Divine Trust for the benefit of a particular type of named or unnamed Divine Person.

Divine Rights

561. In reference to Divine Rights being expressed as an *Elemental Divine Attribute*:

Divine Rights Source

(i) All Rights originate from the Divine and come from the Divine; and

(ii) No Right exists that is not subject to the Divine; and

(iii) Any claim that seeks to repudiate the Divine or usurp the Divine, cannot be a Right but a false claim.

Article 124 – Divine Property

562. ***Divine Property*** is the fourteenth of fourteen *Elemental Divine Attributes,* whereby the Divine as the "set of all sets" and the "concept

Divine Property

of all possible concepts" can obviously be described as the absolute awareness of everything.

563. In reference to Divine Property being expressed as an *Elemental Divine Attribute*:-   *Divine Property Source*

    (i)   All Rights originate from the Divine and come from the Divine; and

    (ii)   All Things comes from the Divine; and

    (iii)   Therefore, all Property originates from the Divine and comes from the Divine; and

    (iv)   No being or person may claim to own a thing equal to or greater than the Divine; and

    (v)   Therefore, all forms of Property that claims absolute control is absurd, as all forms of Property use is subservient to the superior Rights of the Divine.

3.2 Divine Mind Attributes

Article 125 – Divine Mind Attributes

564. ***Divine Mind Attributes*** are the key characteristics, properties, qualities and aspects associated with the Elemental Attribute of Divine Mind as expressed as absolute and irrefutable Fact.   *Divine Mind Attributes*

565. In general reference to Divine Mind Attributes: *In reference to Divine Mind Attributes*

    (i)   By definition, the total set of all meanings and definitions of all possible concepts, objects, matter, rules, life, mind, universe and spirit is part of Divine Mind; and

    (ii)   Furthermore, as the Divine means the "concept of all concepts" and the "set of all sets" such that there is no greater concept nor set, there is no greater possible Consciousness or Mind than Divine Mind; and

    (iii)   In expressing then Divine Mind Attributes, it is appropriate to highlight those key attributes of pure intellect, logic, competence, altruism and love that give reason and cause to comprehension of Divine Mind.

566. In reference to Divine Mind Attributes and absolute and irrefutable Fact: *Divine Mind Attributes & Absolute Fact*

    (i)   Fact is by definition a Testimony of claimed evidential proof of some past event trusted as True. Testimony of present events as they happen is the essence of an active Witness; and

(ii) Depending upon the source and authority of such testimony, it may or may not be trusted to be true. Therefore, Divine Authority and Revelation by evidence of authentic Divine Commission has always been recognised as the highest form of Fact; and

(iii) For the greatest Truth is when a person makes a solemn and sacred oath and vow to the Unique Collective Awareness as the Divine Creator of all Heaven and Earth pertaining to their claimed evidence; and

(iv) Thus, when speaking, writing or considering Fact, it is in accord with the most sacred Covenant *Pactum De Singularis Caelum* and the present sacred Maxims and no other; and

(v) By virtue of the exemplification of the present sacred Maxims before the Divine Creator of all Existence and all Heaven and Earth these present Maxims are true and are absolute and irrefutable Fact.

Article 126 – Divine Competence

567. **Competency** is the quality and state of being of sound mind and able to perform a particular task, or responsibility to a standard of moral excellence as expected and defined by the present sacred Maxims.

568. *Divine Competence* is the quality and state of being of sound mind of the Divine; and the ability of Divine Mind to perform the necessary tasks and responsibilities of Creation and continued Existence as expected and essential to the continuation of the Universe and Life.

569. In reference to Competency:

(i) Competency depends first upon the existence and adherence to some standard of moral excellence. By definition, a being without ethics and a clear model of high standards, is also without Competency; and

(ii) Competency then depends secondly upon a Being capable of making reasoned and sensible choices through intellect and the knowledge at hand based upon the use of such standards as a measure; and

(iii) Any argument that Competency can be justified simply upon theories of rationalism, self-interest or selfishness are absurd, as such thinking contradicts the formation and reality of Creation itself, particularly the fundamental and primary level of matter in the Unita; and

(iv) Arguments in support of the false claims that rationalism, self-interest or selfishness can be argued as a genuine alternate base for Competency are clearly exposed by evidence of history and the counter-intuitive effect of such superficial thinking in producing less than optimum choices for individual Beings, societies, races, species and life in general; and

(v) Furthermore, arguments in support of Competency based purely upon qualification, or admission into fraternal bodies, or merely claims of dignity and title are absurd and without logical or sensible foundation.

570. Divine Competence is founded upon seven core ethics and values being *Respect, Integrity, Commitment, Enthusiasm, Compassion, Cheerfulness* and *Discernment*:- Seven Core Ethics of Divine Competence

(i) *Respect* is exemplified by the expression and affirmation "I choose to treat all beings and existence with dignity and respect, regardless of individual choices and behaviours"; and

(ii) *Integrity* is exemplified by the expression and affirmation "I choose to give my word carefully and to keep and honour my promises"; and

(iii) *Commitment* is exemplified by the expression and affirmation "I trust my laws and principles and rely upon them to achieve success"; and

(iv) *Enthusiasm* is exemplified by the expression and affirmation "I am passionate about life and love all existence and the fulfilment of the potential of higher order species such as Homo Sapiens"; and

(v) *Compassion* is exemplified by the expression and affirmation "I care for all creation and its well-being; and am sensitive not to unnecessarily cause harm, or controversy or inadvertently injury existence or the journey of experience and wisdom of all sentient beings"; and

(vi) *Cheerfulness* is exemplified by the expression and affirmation "I choose to welcome each and every moment of existence and life with positive aspirations"; and

(vii) *Discernment* is exemplified by the expression and affirmation "I choose to trust the laws of the Universe and take time before rushing to judgement or any action based simply upon pure emotion".

571. In reference to Incompetence:- In Reference to Incompetence

(i) By virtue of continued existence and the expression of the seven core ethics of the Divine, the Divine can never be accused or claimed as being Incompetent; and

(ii) Any theory or argument or claim of Divine Incompetence it itself a declaration of Incompetence by the ones who make or promulgate such absurdities and falsities; and

(iii) A being that fails to live according to the seven core ethics of the Divine, is by default Incompetent and unable to hold any high Office, particularly one associated with Ecclesiastical or Fiduciary or Sovereign Office; and

(iv) Incompetence alone is considered neither a permanent state, nor an offence against the Divine, but an offence by a sentient being against themselves. Thus, Incompetence is merely a temporary state that may disqualify certain rights and powers until Competence is restored.

Article 127 – Divine Argument

572. An ***Argument*** is in essence the Process of establishing and validating the Proof and Truth of one or more claimed Facts. — Argument

573. *Divine Argument* is the Process of establishing and validating the Proof of Divine Truth of absolute and irrefutable Facts. — Divine Argument

574. In reference to Argument:- — In Reference to Argument

(i) The notion of Argument is by definition the same as that for Reality whereby the combination of both the ideas of Truth and Fact to assert a thing or notion or claim is factually true; and therefore may be trusted as genuine, without doubt; and

(ii) The foundational reasoning used to establish a valid and legitimate Argument is either by Deductive or Inductive Logic. In all aspects of Argument, the present Maxims always take precedence.

575. All formal Arguments have three essential components being Matter, Issue, and Facts: — Essential Components of Argument

(i) *Matter* is the Topic, or Context, or Classification, or Name in relation to an Argument and not its Substance. Before any issue is described or alleged facts are asserted, an Argument has material existence by mere mention, providing its context in relation to topic, classification and name can be clearly identified; and

(ii) The *Issue* of an Argument or the "Principal Fact" (*facta probanda*) or "Facts in Issue" is the primary Fact, or Facts required to be proved as the probable cause and basis of any Dispute, or Argument or Controversy; and

(iii) The *Facts* are any Event, Action, Circumstance, Attribute or Relation that is provable in Reality to be true or false. In law, a fact is a statement or assertion that can be proven to be true or false.

576. In terms of perspective, all Arguments may be defined as either Personal or Legal: *Types of Argument*

(i) A *Personal Argument* always involves a minimum of two persons being the Accuser (or Witness) and the one being Accused (or Observed); and

(ii) A *Legal Argument* always involves a minimum of three persons being the Accuser and the one Being Accused and a witness capable of establishing and validating the Proof and Truth of one or more claimed Facts in favour of one of the parties.

Article 128 – Divine Logic

577. **Logic** is the fair use of the principles of Inference and Reason whereby Propositions that are properly expressed may be used to deduce consistent Conclusions across a wide variety of Subjects.   *Logic*

578. *Divine Logic* is the concept of the Divine using the principles of Inference and Reason to form Propositions that when properly expressed may be used to not only deduce consistent Conclusions across a wide variety of Subjects, but enable the formation of Creation and continuation of Existence.   *Divine Logic*

579. Logic may be defined as *Bivalent* or *Multivalent*:   *Logic as Bivalent or Multivalent*

(i) *Bivalent Logic* is based on the presumption of only one of two possible outcomes or conclusions; and

(ii) *Multivalent Logic* is based on the presumption of two or more relative possible outcomes or conclusions.

580. Logic may also be defined as *Linear* or *Multi-linear*:   *Logic may be Linear or Multi-Linear*

(i) *Linear Logic* is chronologically based on the presumption of a set of singular space-time dependent events commencing with A and then proceeding to B; and

(ii) *Multi-linear* Logic is based on a progressively expanding set of interdependent space-time events.

581. Bivalent Linear Logic is based on three (3) Laws of Reason being Identity, Non-Contradiction and Bi-valency being: *(margin: Three Laws of Bivalent Linear Logic)*

    (i) *The Law of Identity* states that an object is the same as its identity; and

    (ii) *The Law of Non-Contradiction* or the "exclusion of paradox" states that a valid proposition cannot state something that is and that is not in the same respect and at the same time; and

    (iii) *The Law of Bi-Valency* (Excluded Middle) states that conclusions will resolve.

582. In reference to *Multivalent Multi-Linear Logic*: *(margin: In Reference to Multivalent Multi-Linear Logic)*

    (i) *Multivalent Multi-linear Logic* is the most capable model of approximating to some higher degree of accuracy the Reality and Fact and Truth of the Natural Universe of Matter and Rules as it Exists as a whole; and

    (ii) Both *Multivalent Linear Logic* and *Bivalent Linear Logic* are wholly artificial, imaginary and unable to accurately portray the reason, function and effect of any real scientific events within the Natural Universe of Matter and Rules with any degree of accuracy and precision; and

    (iii) Therefore, in terms of expressing Universal Axioms of a Standard Model, both *Multivalent Linear Logic* and *Bivalent Linear Logic* are inferior and are less Real, less Truthful and less Factual than *Multivalent Multi-linear Logic*; and

    (iv) However, in reference to pre-Creation, pre-existence and the essential Rules of Creation, *Multivalent Multi-linear Logic* is less Real, less Truthful and less Factual than *Bivalent Linear Logic*; and

    (v) Furthermore, in expressing computation awareness operating within the Universe, *Multivalent Linear Logic* is the most capable model of approximating to some higher degree of accuracy the Reality and Fact and Truth of computation awareness of the Natural Universe of Matter.

583. In reference to *Bivalent Linear Logic*: *(margin: In reference to Bivalent Linear Logic)*

    (i) *Bivalent Linear Logic* is the most unnatural, imaginary and artificial system for portraying, recreating or analysing the reason, cause and effect of any real world events within the Universe; and

    (ii) Yet the paradox of *Bivalent Linear Logic* is that it is the most perfect model for expressing the most important arguments of pre-existence and pre-creation of the Universe; and

(iii) Furthermore, *Bivalent Linear Logic* is the most superior model for the application of laws of a higher order life society, rather than the variances of multivalent Logic, as multi-valence or "situational morality" or "legal realism" produces absurdities in law that are counter-intuitive to the needs and justice of Society; and

(iv) Therefore, all relative, multivalent applications to law in reference to higher order civilisations is forbidden.

Article 129 – Divine Fallacy

584. A ***Falsity*** or ***Fallacy*** in Logic or Argument is an incorrect reasoning resulting in a misconception or erroneous Premise(s) or Conclusion or both.

    Fallacy

585. A *Divine Fallacy* in Logic or Argument is an incorrect reasoning claimed in relation to the Divine resulting in a misconception or erroneous Premise(s) or Conclusion or both that are *Incoherent, Fallacious, Irrelevant, Malicious, Perfidious, Unproven, Unasserted, Circular, Verbose, Absurd, Repetitive* or *Defamatory*:

    Divine Fallacy in Logic, Argument

    (i) An *Incoherent* or *Incohaerens* argument is any argument whereby its Premises does not follow one another. Thus, an incohaerens is when no Conclusion could reasonably be deduced or inferred from two or more inconsistent and possibly contradictory premises; and

    (ii) A *Fallacious* or *Non sequitur* argument is any argument whereby its Conclusion does not follow from its Premises. Thus, a non sequitur is when a Conclusion could be either true or false, yet the argument is false as there is no reasonable way of arriving to such a Conclusion from the premises alone by way of deduction or inference; and

    (iii) An *Irrelevance* or *Ignoratio elenchi* is any argument whereby its Conclusion may in itself be valid, but does not address the primary deduction or inference (as issue in question) related to the Premises; and

    (iv) *Malice* or *Malignare* is any deliberately and wilfully negative, spiteful, wicked and evil act designed and intended to harm another, whether or not the other party was aware of such behaviour; and

    (v) *Perfidy* or *Perfidum* is any deliberately and wilfully false, dishonest, deceptive, treacherous act, representing a clear and unmistakable breach of trust, whether or not such action was intended for profit; and whether or not the other party was aware of such behaviour; and

(vi) An *Unproven Claim* or *Onus Probandi* is any argument whereby the burden of proof fails to be provided or is falsely placed upon the one accused or defending the claim and not the one making the claim. Thus, any system of law based on the assumption of being culpable on mere accusation without burden of proof is not only absurd, but false, immoral and unlawful; and

(vii) An *Unasserted Claim* or *Argumentum ex silentio* is any argument whereby a Conclusion is made on the absence of evidence or argument, rather than the existence or merit of argument; and

(viii) A *Circular reasoning* or *Circulus in demonstrando* is any argument where the Conclusion ultimately relies upon the Premises to be true, yet the Premises ultimately depends upon the Conclusion to be true and thus self referencing and circular; and

(ix) A *Verbose* reasoning or *Argumentum Verbosum* is any argument where the Premises or Conclusion are deliberately verbose, or obtuse, or confusing, or overly technical, or complex, or occult in order to intimidate and deflect attention from the existence of one or more fallacies contained within the argument in general; and

(x) An *Absurd* reasoning or *Argumentum ad Absurdum* is any argument where the Conclusion of an argument is set aside and one or more of the Premises of an argument are proven to be false by showing that a false, untenable or absurd result would follow its acceptance. Argumentum ad Absurdum is frequently and mistakenly associated with an absurd logical fallacy known as Reductio ad absurdum or "reduction to absurdity" whereby an entire argument is falsely deemed absurd upon discovery of but one absurd or untenable premise; and

(xi) *Repetitious* reasoning or *Argumentum ad Infinitum* is any argument where the argument is continually presented, often with intentional intimidation to use such repetition and ignorance of any counter argument in order to deflect attention from the existence of one or more fallacies contained within the original argument in general; and

(xii) *Defamatory* accusations or *Argumentum ad Hominem* is any argument whereby attention is sought to be deflected from one or more fallacies contained within the original argument by introducing a secondary argument against the character of the one highlighting such fallacies.

586. Any argument that is Incoherent, Fallacious, Irrelevant, Malicious, Perfidious, Unproven, Unasserted, Circular, Verbose, Absurd, Repetitive or Defamatory cannot be reasonably concluded as true, or fact or real or valid. In all such cases and matters, these Articles take precedence.

Invalid Argument

Article 130 – Seven Proofs of Divine Mind

587. The **Seven Proofs of Divine Mind** are seven empirical and logical proofs as to the authentic mind and intentions of the Divine Creator of all Existence and all Heaven and Earth:

Seven Proofs of Divine Mind

(i) The Seven Proofs of Divine Mind are founded upon the existence of the Seven Proofs of Divine Existence; and

(ii) The Seven Proofs of Divine Mind are also founded upon the existence of the Ucadia Model as the most perfect Standard Model of Existence; and

(iii) The Seven Proofs of Divine Mind are further supported by the existence of the present most sacred Maxims; and

(iv) Thus, when speaking of the Seven Proofs of Divine Mind, none may take one or more Proof in isolation to its foundation or supporting evidence.

588. In reference to the Seven Proofs of Divine Mind, also known as the *Seven Illuminations of Divine Mind*:

Seven Illuminations of Divine Mind

(i) *Illumination of Awareness* – reveals that Divine Mind is Unique Collective Awareness and levels of Unique Collective Awareness that in all knowing, all remembering and nothing is lost, nothing is forgotten and nothing is without witness; and

(ii) *Illumination of Logic* - reveals that the Divine Mind as Unique Collective Awareness is perfectly logical, reasonable and sensible in its actions, without any existence of lesser emotions of jealousy, hate, fear, retribution, anger or prejudicial judgement; and

(iii) *Illumination of Consent* - reveals that the Divine Mind as Unique Collective Awareness chooses by its own volition (free will) to exist and that this is a conscious and constant choice each and every instant and that consent without duress and coercion is fundamental at all levels of existence. Furthermore, when consent is deliberately ignored, breached or repudiated it places that part of existence in opposition to the forces of existence, law, love and fulfilment; and

(iv) *Illumination of Love* - reveals that the highest expression of existence of the divine creator is the love of life and love of all existence. Thus the strongest emotion is love and the Divine is the personification of love; and

(v) *Illumination of Law* - reveals that existence itself depends upon rules and therefore laws. Thus the expression of Divine Mind is divine law and that the highest of all laws is the golden rule that "no one is above the law" upon which all true law is based; and

(vi) *Illumination of Justice* - reveals that for law to be present within existence, it must be applied in accordance with the rule of law (golden rule), consistent with the mind of the Divine being with clean hands, in good faith and without prejudice; and

(vii) *Illumination of Redemption* - highlights that the Divine Mind is infinitely loving and forgiving and seeks to redeem higher order life and enable such life, communities, cultures and empires to fulfil their potential.

3.3 Supreme (Omni) Attributes

Article 131 – Supreme (Omni) Attributes

589. In reference to the categorisation of Divine Attributes, all possible valid Divine Attributes may be defined according to three supreme or "omni" attributes being *Omniessent, Omnimodulant* and *Omnisignificant*:

     Supreme (Omni) Attributes

(i) An *Omniessent* Supreme Being is All Concepts and Objects, All Being and All Existence. The quality of being Omniessent is *Omniessence*; and

(ii) An *Omnimodulant* Supreme Being is All Measure, All Motion, All Events and All Change. The quality of being Omnimodulant is *Omnimodulance*; and

(iii) An *Omnisignificant* Supreme Being is All Meaning, All Cause, All Reason and All Significance. The quality of being

Omnisignificant is *Omnisignificance*.

Article 132 – Omniessent

590. An **Omniessent** Supreme Being is All Concepts and Objects, All Being and All Existence. The quality of being Omniessent is Omniessence.

    Omniessent Being

591. In general reference to the Divine Attribute of Omniessence:-

    Divine Attribute of Omniessence

    (i) An Omniessent Supreme Being is beyond any limiting concepts such as all mighty and beyond all powerful, because it does not need to be omnipotent to form creation and influence existence. It just has to be in accord with the Ucadia Standard Model; and

    (ii) As an Omniessent Supreme Being is beyond any limiting concepts such as all mighty and beyond all powerful, such a Supreme being cannot be "trapped by absurdities or contradictions" where (for example) an "all mighty or all powerful being should in theory be able to create a concept greater than itself, otherwise it cannot be argued as all mighty and all powerful"; and

    (iii) An Omniessent Supreme Being is beyond the dependence (in theory) upon something to be compared to, or be "all mighty and all powerful against", but the concepts and limits of itself as a concept; and

    (iv) As an Omniessent Supreme being is beyond the dependence (in theory) upon something to be compared to, an Omniessent Supreme Being can exist in theory, whereas an "all mighty or all powerful being" cannot exist on its own in theory, as an "all mighty and all powerful" beings needs something to be compared to; and

    (v) An Omniessent Supreme Being is beyond the virile masculine archetype of omnipotence as it does not have to have sex to create existence.

592. In reference to Omniessence versus Omnipotence:-

    Omniessence versus Omnipotence

    (i) Whereas omnipotence implies an attribute of a supreme being relative to a given Universe, Omniessence needs no qualification as such an Omniessent supreme being is All, is All Being and All Existence; and

    (ii) Whereas omnipotence also implies a supreme being as completely separate and distinct from the given Universe,

Omniessence needs no such qualification as an Omniessent Supreme Being can be viewed from one perspective as separate and everything simultaneously; and

(iii) Whereas omnipotence depends upon the existence of the Universe as the subject of such claimed unlimited power or force or authority, the concept of Omniessence has no such weakness as an Omniessent Supreme Being is everything without need for qualification; and

(iv) Whereas omnipotence depends upon absurd, irrational, unreasonable, false, malevolent, repugnant and illogical concepts such as eternalism, creationism, destructionism, supernaturalism, predeterminism, predestinationism and animalism, the concept of Omniessence has none of these weaknesses, as an Omniessent Supreme Being has no need to conceive of concepts that are so false, repugnant, illogical and absurd to justify its existence as All Concepts and Objects, All Being and All Existence; and

(v) Indeed, Omniessence is without any of the absurdities, repugnancies, falsities that litter the weak and inferior concept of omnipotence and its dependent concepts; and

(vi) Thus Omniessence proves the Divine wisdom that the thirst for power and all mighty power is doomed to fail in the face of the superior wisdom and strength of All, All Being and All Existence.

Article 133 – Omnimodulant

593. An **Omnimodulant** Supreme Being is All Measure, All Motion, All Events and All Change. The quality of being Omnimodulant is Omnimodulance.

    Omnimodulant Being

594. In general reference to the Divine Attribute of Omnimodulance:-

    Divine Attribute of Omnimodulence

    (i) An Omnimodulant Supreme Being is beyond all forms of measurement, all motion, all events, all time and all change because through Divine Will expressed into Universal Free Will and Choice, it does not need to be omnipresent to control or direct or influence every moment and event of time and space; and

    (ii) As an Omnimodulant Supreme Being is all forms of measurement, all motion, all events, all time and all change, yet because of Universal Free Will and Choice does not depend upon controlling the present, such a Supreme being cannot be "trapped by absurdities, negativities or contradictions" that plague such concepts as omnipresence, whereby (for example) an "all present and all powerful God that does nothing, contradicts all notions of Divine Love"; and an "an omnipresent God is by definition constrained by universal dimension as to space and time and therefore cannot be all mighty or all powerful"; and

(iii) An Omnimodulant Supreme Being is capable of being both the ultimate observer and each and every active participant and agent within the dream of Existence.

Article 134 – Omnisignificant

595. An *Omnisignificant* Supreme Being is All Meaning, All Cause, All Reason and All Significance. The quality of being Omnisignificant is Omnisignificance.

Omnisignificant Being

596. In general reference to the Divine Attribute of Omnisignificance:-

Divine Attribute of Omnisignificance

(i) An Omnisignificant Supreme Being is beyond all knowing and all predicting and all predetermined destiny, because it does not need to be for creation and existence; and such a notion of "all wise and all knowing" is an effect of creation, not its cause as wisdom always comes from experience; and

(ii) Furthermore, an Omnisignificant Supreme Being is beyond all knowing and all predicting and all predetermined destiny, because such a notion of pre-determinism (everything is already determined in the eyes of God) completely repudiates the notion of Free Will and therefore the concepts of law, responsibility, accountability, learning, wisdom and experience as all such concepts depend upon the existence of Free Will, not some corrupted version of it.

597. In reference to Omnisignificance versus Omniscience:-

Omnisignificance versus Omniscience

(i) The concept and various models of an omniscient supreme being are absurd, irrational, unreasonable and illogical and do great harm against our ability to better comprehend the true nature and character of the Divine Creator of all Existence and all Heaven and Earth; and

(ii) The doctrine of divine omniscience is logically incoherent, that it is inconsistent with the further Christian doctrine of divine impeccability (i.e. the doctrine that God cannot sin), and that it is further refuted by the fact of human freedom and sin, thus implying free will and negating omniscience; and

(iii)　The first problem is Cantor's proof that there is no set of all sets. Omniscience, it is said, entails knowledge of the set of all truths. Cantor's proof, however, demonstrates that there is no such set. As there is no such set, it is argued, there can be no omniscient being; and

(iv)　The second problem is the problem in respect of omniscience is the concept of experiential knowledge. Here the argument is that there are certain facts knowledge of which can only be acquired through certain experiences (for example) "of knowledge what it is like to sin, for instance, can only be acquired by sinning" and so some of these items of knowledge, are such that they cannot be had by God, thus creating a fatal absurdity; and

(v)　The third problem is that of reconciling freedom and foreknowledge, specifically the existence of divine foreknowledge with the existence of human freedom. If a Divinity as an omniscient supreme being knows all of our future actions, then the future is fixed, but if the future is fixed, it seems that there is nothing that we can do to change it. The ability to determine our future actions, though, is what constitutes human freedom. Divine foreknowledge, then, seems to preclude the possibility of our being free agents; and

(vi)　The fourth problem is the problem of middle knowledge. Middle knowledge is knowledge of what free agents would have done had the world been other than it is. As the agents are free, their choice of action cannot be determined by the state of the world, and so cannot be calculated on that basis. As middle knowledge concerns counter-factual situations, however, neither can their choice of actions be known by observation of the future. With the two possible sources of knowledge ruled out, it seems that middle knowledge is an impossibility for an omniscient being; and

(vii)　The fifth problem is that a supreme being that is disconnected from existence by then has no first hand knowledge only circumstantial and observational knowledge. Therefore such a supreme being that was not intimately connected to every life could not be omniscient; and

(viii)　In contrast, an Omnisignificant Supreme Being is capable of being both the ultimate observer and each and every active participant, cause and agent within the dream of Existence, with the full endorsement of the concept of Universal Free Will and Choice.

3.4 Contrasting Divine Attributes

Article 135 – Contrasting Divine Attributes

598. ***Contrasting Divine Attributes*** are Divine Attributes presented in such a manner as to be bound together in typically binary or tripartite relations so that such concepts may be viewed as mutual or exclusive in nature.

599. In general reference to Contrasting Divine Attributes:-

    (i) By definition, Contrasting Divine Attributes are bound together and are therefore co-dependent in nature and existence to some degree. For example Atheism depends upon the existence of the concept of God in theory, to complete its central absurd promise of repudiating such an existence; and

    (ii) The binding together of mutual or exclusive terms does not in itself denote Contrasting Divine Attributes as less or more valid, but rather a range of alternates that may be reflected in a diversity of historic and cultural traditions in viewing the Divine; and

    (iii) Contrasting Divine Attributes are also significant in how alternate concepts and options may be included or excluded. Thus, some Contrasting Divine Attribute Models may be said to be complete, or incomplete based upon the principle of inclusion or exclusion.

Article 136 – Theism, Deism and Atheism

600. ***Theism***, ***Deism*** and ***Atheism*** belong to a tripartite model of divine attributes, whereby:-

    (i) Theism is the claimed existence of at least one deity that is responsible for creation; and that continues to be personally present and active in the history, governance and organisation of the world and the Universe. Its opposite concepts are Deism and Atheism; and

    (ii) Deism is the claimed existence of at least one deity that is responsible for creation; yet is impersonal and is not present and active in the history, governance and organisation of the world and the Universe. Its opposite concepts are Theism and Atheism; and

    (iii) Atheism is the rejection of the claimed existence of any deities.

Its opposite concepts are Theism and Deism.

601. In reference to the concept of the Divine Attribute of *Theism*:- Divine Attribute of Theism

    (i) By definition, Theism is the claimed existence of at least one deity that is responsible for creation; and that continues to be personally present and active in the history, governance and organisation of the world and the Universe; and

    (ii) *Monotheism* is when a model views existence as ultimately resolved by the presence of a single Supreme Being; and

    (iii) *Polytheism* is when a model views existence of more than one god or pantheon of gods whereby no one god is the ultimate Supreme being; and

    (iv) *Pantheism* is when a model views existence of the Universe itself as the Supreme being and that there is no division between a Creator and the substance of its creation; and

    (v) The view of a Supreme Being represented by several parts, does not in itself imply a Polytheistic model.

602. In reference to the concept of the Divine Attribute of *Deism*:- Divine Attribute of Deism

    (i) By definition, Deism is the claimed existence of at least one deity that is responsible for creation; yet is impersonal and is not present and active in the history, governance and organisation of the world and the Universe; and

    (ii) Deism is similar to the concept of Transcendence in that both concepts can be viewed as sharing similar ideas concerning an impersonal Supreme Being as ultimate Divine Creator; and

    (iii) Furthermore, there is nothing suggesting in the pure form of the notion of Deism that an Immanent Divine Creator capable of intervening through revelation, or miracles is incompatible with the concept of Deism. In this sense, Deism simply states that the Divine has no need to intervene and in fact such interventions are a matter of choice, rather than need; and

    (iv) This harmony between Deism and the twin concepts of Transcendence and Immanence is a reasonable representation of many traditional and higher philosophies that have taken the view of an impersonal Supreme Being as ultimate Divine Creator, whereas the active focus of Divine intervention within the dream of existence is present within the life and choices of each higher order being; and

    (v) In contrast, certain philosophies have adopted an extremely narrow view of Deism whereby they emphatically reject the

Lex Divina: Maxims of Divine Law

notion of Immanence and the existence of miracles, or personal manifestations of the Divine and the authenticity of Revelation. In this harsher sense, Deism has been used by some to form the idea of an opposite to Theism.

603. In reference to the concept of the Divine Attribute of *Atheism*:-   *Divine Attribute of Atheism*

   (i)   By definition, Atheism is the claimed refutation of a Supreme Being that is responsible for creation; and is personified in the existence of the dream that is creation; and that continues to be personally present and active in the history, governance and organisation of the world and the Universe; and

   (ii)   Atheism recognises the existence of Theism and Deism as concepts and the existence as concept of the Divine, in order to postulate its arguments of non-existence. Thus Atheism is paradoxical as without the existence of the concept of God to argue against, Atheism itself could not exist; and

   (iii)   Atheism is a fundamentally irrational and unreal form of argument, as its strongest advocates and writers refuse to acknowledge the fatal flaw of the philosophy in the paradox of God – being a concept that Atheism needs to exist in concept to argue against it; and the second paradox being Atheism depends on the existence of God at least in concept, in order to argue against something.

Article 137 – Immanent and Transcendent

604. ***Immanent*** and ***Transcendent*** belong to a binary and mutual model of Divine Attributes, whereby:-   *Immanent & Transcendent*

   (i)   Immanent is the Concept of the Divine encompassing or manifested within the material world or Universe. The quality of Immanent is Immanence; and

   (ii)   Transcendent is the Concept of the Divine wholly independent of the material world or Universe. The quality of Transcendent is Transcendence.

605. In reference to the Concept of Divine Immanence:-   *Concept of Divine Immanence*

   (i)   By definition, the quality of Divine Immanence is some manifest presence of Divinity within the physical world that is conceivable and accessible to higher order beings in various ways; and

   (ii)   The presence of Divine Immanence made manifest in the physical world is historically fulfilled in the presence of some

Deity or "god" that worshippers can witness, invoke and follow; and

(iii) The oldest concepts of Divine Immanence personified as one or more Deities is the natural association of key climactic season, or natural events or political events to one or more gods; and

(iv) The most mature concept of Divine Immanence of a higher order species is the revelation of the paradox of all life being manifest Divine Immanence and the fact that from time to time a higher order species may produce a Singularity capable of connecting both Divine Transcendence with Divine Immanence in person – hence the realisation of the "Only Son of God"; and

(v) The history of Divine Immanence is primarily through Revelation, attested miracles and Divine Works in both a historical and cultural context. Therefore, the richness and complexity of Divine Immanence can and does vary across cultures predicated on such differences of emphasis in the necessary criteria of revelation and proof.

606. In reference to the Concept of Divine Transcendence:- *Concept of Divine Transcendence*

(i) By definition, the quality of Divine Transcendence is a Divine wholly independent of the material world or Universe and therefore exhibited through qualities of beyond knowing, or comprehending or seeing in terms of higher order beings; and

(ii) A classic example of Divine Transcendence being beyond the boundaries of higher order comprehension is the presence of Divine Paradox at every boundary of higher knowledge and existence itself. It is perfectly exemplified in the supremely paradoxical statement "Nothing is Absolute. Everything is a matter of degree", whereby the statement can be made, but the full comprehension of nothing being absolute is beyond comprehension; and

(iii) Thus, Divine Transcendence historically has given rise to such terms as "Divine Mystery" and in particular to an inability to resolve the "Matter—Spirit" question between perceived science and faith of cultures; and

(iv) The most mature concept of Divine Transcendence of a higher order species is the revelation that a Divinely Transcendent Supreme Being makes their existence known through authentic Divine Immanence, particularly in the form of Divine Messengers and more rarely in the formation of a

Singularity capable of connecting both Divine Transcendence with Divine Immanence in person – hence the realisation of the "Only Son of God".

Article 138 – Omniformity and Omniunitary

607. ***Omniformity*** and ***Omniunitary*** belong to a binary and opposing model of Divine Attributes, whereby:- *Omniformity and Omniunitary*

    (i)   Omniformity is the Concept of a Supreme Being having every form and shape, relative to a given Universe. Omniformity is therefore in opposition to the concept of Omniunitary; and

    (ii)   Omniunitary is the Concept of a Supreme Being without parts, properties, attributes or complexity, relative to a given Universe. Omniunitary is also known as Divine Simplicity. Omniunitary is therefore in opposition to the concept of Omniformity.

608. In reference to the claimed Divine Attribute of Omniformity:- *Omniformity as claimed Divine Attribute*

    (i)   The proposition of an Omniformity Supreme Being is the assertion that or omnipresence, is the concept of being present everywhere at the same time within a given universal dimension (of space and time); and

    (ii)   The term form directly implies and involves a given Universe, bound by some form of rules of dimension, space and time, whereby a supreme being then is intimately connected with every form and shape within such a Universe; and

    (iii)   As the very concept of Omniformity itself logically depends upon space and time to have any meaning, the concept of Omniformity is always limited to a given universal dimension, thus creating an absurd argument.

609. In reference to the claimed Divine Attribute of Omniunitary:- *Omniunitary as claimed Divine Attribute*

    (i)   The terms unitary and simplicity both imply a state of being of a Supreme Being relative to a given Universe. Without the existence of the Universe, the subject of unitary or simplicity would have no meaning whatsoever; and

    (ii)   According to the model of Divine Simplicity, God has no spatial components; and God has no temporal elements; and God is without metaphysical complexity; and

    (iii)   As to the question of spatial composition within a given Universe, the model of Omniunitary and Divine Simplicity views the Supreme Being as completely separate from the dimension of the Universe and not needing the Universe for comparative existence in perfect transcendence; and

(iv) As to the issue of metaphysical complexity, the model of Omniunitary and Divine Simplicity views the Supreme Being as without Divine Composition. Instead, under the model of Omniunitary and Divine Simplicity, any characteristic attributed to God (as Supreme Being) is not really a property at all, but merely a description of the entirety of God; and

(v) Therefore, the concept of Omniunitary implies a supreme being completely separate and distinct from the given Universe that it depends upon for its comparative existence, thus creating the first of several absurdities; and

(vi) Furthermore, the terms Omniunitary and Divine Simplicity depend upon the ability to distinguish the notion of attributes, or properties, or parts and characteristics of a subject, before implying that such attributes or properties or parts or characteristics are indistinguishable from the essence and being of a supreme being, thus creating further absurdities.

610. The proposition of an Omniunitary Supreme Being is an absurd, false and untenable model based upon the misuse of meaningful grammar, an abdication of reasoning and rational discernment:- *Omniunitary Being is a False Model*

(i) In the first instance and as previously expressed, the terms Omniunitary and Divine Simplicity depend first upon the ability to distinguish the notion of attributes, or properties, or parts and characteristics of a subject; and

(ii) To then deny or argue that such attributes or properties or parts or characteristics of a subject are not attributes at all, but indistinguishable from the essence and being of the subject is semantic absurdity; and

(iii) An attribute by definition is an attribute. That is its purpose and its function. Similarly, a property of a subject is a property and cannot be considered the subject without losing its purpose or meaning; and

(iv) Therefore if one were to accept the model of Omniunitary and Divine Simplicity, then one inference is to accept a rational and reasonable world against an irrational and unreasonable Omniunitary God; and

(v) As such conclusions are completely inconsistent with the notion of a God capable and competent enough to create the given Universe, on semantic absurdity alone, the model of

Omniunitary and Divine Simplicity is untenable; and

(vi) An additional consequence of the model of Omniunitary and Divine Simplicity is the negation of all other attributes of God. For example, if God is identical with each of his properties, then each of his properties is identical with each of his other properties, so God has only one property - himself; and

(vii) Such a logical conclusion when applying the model of Omniunitary and Divine Simplicity contradicts the idea that God has such attributes as Omnipotence and Omnibenevolence as both are different; and

(viii) Yet a further consequence when applying the model of Omniunitary and Divine Simplicity is that if God is identical with his properties, then it follows that God is a property as well; and

(ix) The logical conclusion of this further consequence is that given properties do not in and of themselves cause anything, then God cannot be god, but the property of a greater God that is not Omniunitary; and

(x) In this final conclusion of Omniunitary, we see a model that actually proves itself to be absurd, false and untenable.

Article 139 – Omni-benevolent and Omni-righteous

611. ***Omni-benevolent*** and ***Omni-righteous*** belong to a binary and opposing model of Divine Attributes, whereby:-   *Omni-benevolent & Omni-righteous*

    (i) Omni-Benevolent is the Concept of a Supreme Being that is all benevolent, kind, forgiving, merciful, charitable, altruistic and good. The quality of Omni-Benevolent is Omni-Benevolence. Omniformity is therefore in opposition to the concept of Omni-righteous; and

    (ii) Omni-Righteous is the Concept of a Supreme Being that is without transgression, morally perfect, just, empowered and unwavering in the law, morally justified and authorised to judge and dispense punishment or relief or remedy. The quality of Omni-Righteous is Omni-Righteousness. Omni-Righteous is therefore in opposition to the concept of Omni-Benevolent.

612. In reference to the claimed Divine Attribute of Omni-Benevolence:-   *Omni-Benevolence as claimed Divine Attribute*

    (i) By definition, Omni-Benevolence of the Divine means a Supreme Being that is all benevolent, kind, forgiving, merciful, charitable, altruistic and good; and

(ii) Such a Divine Attribute is consistent in part with the knowledge of Divine Law in accord with the present sacred Maxims and the most sacred Covenant *Pactum De Singularis Caelum* as to the intention and emotion of the Divine Creator toward all creation; and

(iii) However, the phrasing and use of "omni" to imply an absolute renders such important descriptions contradictory to other attributes as technically "Nothing is Absolute. Everything else is a matter of degree"; and

(iv) The present of Omni-Benevolence as a claimed Divine Attribute phrased in absolute terms gives rise to both contradictions and simplistic absurd conclusions whereby the presence of Evil repudiates the accuracy of such a notion; and

(v) Furthermore, the sacrilegious notion of a perpetual place of torture as "Hell" also negates the concept of Omni-Benevolence, as does the concept of absolute Omni-Righteousness.

613. In reference to the claimed Divine Attribute of Omni-Righteousness:- Omni-Righteousness as claimed Divine Attribute

(i) By definition, Omni-Righteousness of the Divine means a Supreme Being that is without transgression, morally perfect, just, empowered and unwavering in the law; and

(ii) Such a Divine Attribute is consistent in part with the knowledge of Divine Law in accord with the present sacred Maxims and the most sacred Covenant *Pactum De Singularis Caelum* as to the intention and emotion of the Divine Creator toward all creation; and

(iii) However, the phrasing and use of "omni" to imply an absolute renders such important descriptions contradictory to other attributes as technically "Nothing is Absolute. Everything else is a matter of degree"; and

(iv) The present of Omni-Righteousness as a claimed Divine Attribute phrased in absolute terms gives rise to both contradictions and simplistic absurd conclusions whereby the presence of Evil repudiates the accuracy of such a notion in combination with other absolute terms; and

(v) Furthermore, the claimed quality of Omni-Benevolence contradicts the notion of Omni-Righteousness and Divine Wrath, whereby either one concept must be wrong and the other correct, or all concepts are false.

3.5 False Supreme (Omni) Attributes

Article 140 – False Supreme (Omni) Attributes

614. False Supreme (Omni) Divine Attributes are false or erroneous Divine Attributes claimed to be associated with a Supreme Being yet clearly contradict the Divine Concepts of the present Maxims and the most sacred Covenant *Pactum De Singularis Caelum*.

    False Supreme (Omni) Attributes

615. In respect of false "Omni" or "Supreme" attributes of Supreme Beings:-

    False Omni or Supreme attributes of Supreme Beings

    (i) By definition, false "Omni" or "Supreme" attributes of Supreme Beings carry within their definition certain contradictions or absurdities or dangerously ignorant concepts or consequences that not only contradict the Divine Concepts of the present Maxims and the most sacred Covenant Pactum De Singularis Caelum, but give rise to negative and contradictory behaviour in the name of various religions; and

    (ii) It can be reasonably argued that the persistent defence of the most significant of these false "Omni" or "Supreme" attributes of Supreme Beings, continues to represent some of the most intractable differences and impediments to peace among people, religions and societies; and

    (iii) Whilst it can be further argued that such errors and falsities may have arisen as a consequence of inadequate information or suppositions where such knowledge was not available to make a complete conclusion, such obstinacy that refuses to consider reason in the face of the authentic Revelation of the present sacred Maxims cannot be justified as merely a defence of tradition; and

    (iv) Therefore, the proper investigation of such false "Omni" or "Supreme" attributes of Supreme Beings is not merely a review of flawed argument, but the deeper and entrenched divisions and hierarchies that such concepts themselves allow to perpetuate.

Article 141 – Omnipotent

616. An ***Omnipotent*** Supreme Being is the assertion that a singular Divinity has absolute power over all of creation, existence, the universe and life itself.

    Omnipotent

Title III - Divine Attributes

617. In general reference to the seven key enabling concepts essential to the concept of omnipotence being eternalism, creationism, destructionism, supernaturalism, predeterminism, predestinationism and animalism:-

Seven enabling concepts for Omnipotence

(i) The existence of these seven key enabling concepts does not exclude the possibility of other concepts also being important enablers in support of the notion of omnipotent. Instead, the presence of these seven key enabling concepts simply argues that if any of these seven concepts were found to be invalid, illegitimate, false or absurd, then the very possibility of the concept of an omnipotent supreme being would be impossible; and

(ii) For example, the concept of omnipresent is an essential concept reflected within all seven of the enablers mentioned, especially the notions of eternalism, supernaturalism, predeterminism and predestinationism; and

(iii) Similarly, the concept of omniscience is also fundamental to the operation of all seven enablers, especially the concepts of predeterminism and predestinationism; and

(iv) As both the concepts of omnipresent and omniscient are treated distinctly and separately as the second and third most common attributes of a Divinity as supreme being in their own right, their influence on omnipotent is discussed in more detail separately; and

(v) Eternalism as the first fundamental enabling concept to the notion of omnipotence, is the concept that the omnipotent supreme being is eternal and has always existed and will always exist, independent of the existence of the Universe; and

(vi) The notion of Eternalism in terms of the claim of an omnipotent supreme being is meant to assure that such a being is completely independent from the Universe and that the supreme being is not constrained by the laws of the Universe; and

(vii) Creationism as the second fundamental enabling concept to the notion of omnipotence, is the concept that the omnipotent supreme being created the Universe and life from specific acts of Divine Creation without any limitation or restriction from any laws of the Universe, such as evolution; and

(viii) As the concept of creationism relates to an occurrence in time, being an event of creation, the concept itself depends upon the existence of both the concept of omnipresent and omniscient;

and

(ix) Destructionism as the third fundamental enabling concept to the notion of omnipotence, is the concept that the omnipotent supreme being is capable of destroying all life, all creation and the Universe by specific acts of Divine destruction without any limitation or restriction from any laws of the Universe against such catastrophe; and

(x) The notion of Destructionism is largely supported by certain religions using circular reasoning through promoting scripture defining destructionist models based upon an omnipotent supreme being such as the Book of Revelation; and

(xi) Similar to the notion of creationism, as destructionism relates to an occurrence in time, being an event of destruction, the concept itself depends upon the existence of both the concept of omnipresent and omniscient; and

(xii) Supernaturalism as the fourth fundamental enabling concept to the notion of omnipotence, is the concept that the omnipotent supreme being is capable of direct intervention into the operation of life, life events and the universe in general, suspending the laws of the Universe; and

(xiii) The notion of Supernaturalism is largely supported by certain religions promoting a tradition of miracles and supernatural events, often in support of religious orthodoxy and the maintenance of authority and obedience; and

(xiv) Predeterminism as the fifth fundamental enabling concept to the notion of omnipotence, is the concept that the omnipotent and therefore omniscient supreme being has already determined and decided all events of history being past, present and future; and

(xv) Predeterminism further argues that an unbroken chain of prior events exists from the origin of the Universe to the present moment; and that because this chain of events has been pre-established by the supreme being, human actions cannot possibly interfere with the outcomes of such a pre-established chain, except by their own choice to accept such fate or reject it; and

(xvi) The notion of predeterminism is both reflected and supported in the true origin and nature of the word faith being cognitive and consistent with the word "fate"; and more specifically the ancient pagan notion of the three fates of destiny, more than any concept such as trust or hope. Thus, the concept of accepting faith and even embracing faith is equivalent to accepting the fate of a predetermined Universe under an omnipotent supreme being; and

(xvii) Predestinationism as the sixth fundamental enabling concept to the notion of omnipotence, is the concept that the omnipotent and therefore omniscient supreme being has pre-ordained by Divine Will all events for every life, including the eventual fate of each individual soul; and that only by complete submission to the Will of God, as taught by a religious fraternity claiming such authority, does an individual human being have any hope of salvation from a destiny of perpetual torment, torture and terror; and

(xviii) While predestinationism fundamentally rejects any possible notion of free will in a Universe controlled by an omnipotent God, the concept is actually promoted through a pseudo form of free will or "enfeebled free will", whereby a man or woman may have no power to change the course of events decided by a Divinity as supreme being, but may in themselves choose to accept faith (as fate) or reject it; and that this choice, no matter how weak and insignificant, is taken into account with what such a supreme being has planned for each and every one of us; and

(xix) Animalism as the seventh and final fundamental enabling concept to the notion of omnipotence, is the concept whereby human beings are considered creatures and therefore beasts without a soul; and only a few human beings who submit themselves completely have any kind of soul, thanks to the spark of the omnipotent supreme being; and

(xx) Animalism is an absolutely fundamental feature of enabling the concept of an omnipotent supreme being, because if all human beings were born with a genuine Divine Spark in the form of a Soul, then it would imply that an omnipotent God is not merely guiding and directing the fate of existence, but that human beings as part of a Divinity as supreme being through their Soul, could also influence fate, whilst being constrained by the laws of the universe, thus defeating the notion of an omnipotent supreme being; and

(xxi) However, the concept that only human beings having submitted to the absolute control of an omnipotent supreme being, overcomes then the threat of negating the notion of omnipotence, as the concept of Elitism as a by-product of Animalism implies men and women are only "possessed" by a

Spirit as a pseudo soul, rather than having any real soul and power to choose and exercise a free will; and

(xxii) Thus, the notion of Animalism and its consequences is a core model for promoting, empowering and maintaining small groups of elite over large populations of human beings as soulless slaves without any free will.

618. The concept and various models of an Omnipotent supreme being are absurd, irrational, unreasonable, perfidious, false, malevolent, repugnant, illogical and sacrilegious to the true nature and character of the Divine Creator of all Existence and all Heaven and Earth:- *Omnipotent Supreme Being is an absurd model*

(i) First, the concept of an Omnipotent supreme being can be conclusively proven from the outset as being absurd, illogical, irrational and unreasonable by the very definition and meaning of the concept itself; and

(ii) The term omnipotent implies an attribute of a supreme being relative to a given Universe. Without the existence of the Universe as the subject of such unlimited power or force or authority, the concept of omnipotent would have no meaning whatsoever; and

(iii) Thus, for a supreme being to exist, a given Universe also needs to exist; and for the notion of existence itself to have any meaning. This logically implies a dependence on the existence of the Universe and vice versa. Such dependence, necessarily invalidates the possibility whatsoever of an Omnipotent supreme being; and

(iv) In other words, no matter how completely separate and distinct or eternal a supreme being as a singular Divinity may be claimed, without the existence of a Universe, it can be reasonably argued that such a supreme being cannot possibly exist, as its very power as an alleged Omnipotent supreme being depends on the existence of the Universe; and

(v) A supreme being that depends on the existence of the Universe for its own existence then cannot possibly be considered Omnipotent, no matter how hard one may try to argue around such an immutable fact; and

(vi) Therefore, from the outset, the word omnipotent itself reveals its fatal weakness as an absurd concept before one even considering any associated notions used to try and support it; and

(vii) Second, it is the associated and supporting notions of omnipotent such as the notions of eternalism, creationism, destructionism, supernaturalism, predeterminism, predestinationism and animalism that are absurd, irrational, unreasonable, false, malevolent, repugnant and illogical; and

(viii) Arguments in support of creationism and destructionism have promoted an infantile and lunatic approach to any true relation between the Divine and Universal Existence; and

(ix) Creationism, when promoted as a literal response to scientific knowledge, creates a madness and delusion against overwhelming and unmistakable evidence that the laws of the Universe are themselves essential to any Divine notion of Creation; and

(x) Simply, if a supreme being were to so arbitrarily tamper with the very laws of existence for the purpose of some infantile model of creation, then its own existence would be jeopardised in suspending or altering the laws of creation; and

(xi) Similarly, the notion of destructionism, when promoted as some kind of final judgement, retribution and punishment, helps perpetuate an endless cycle of violence and a professional industry dedicated to war, madness and destruction; in complete contradiction to any reasonable notion of Divine existence; and

(xii) Put bluntly, a supreme being exercising destructionism would be committing its own suicide if it also destroyed the universe so essential to its own existence; and

(xiii) Furthermore, The concept of free-will is a direct contradiction to the notion of an omnipotent supreme being. For if a creation of a Divinity as a supreme being possesses free will, then such a life form has the right to resist the instructions of such a Divinity; and therefore negates the argument of an Omnipotent supreme being; and

(xiv) Thus, even the arguments of the existence of choice and intention in the mind of higher order animals is sufficient to render the concept of an Omnipotent supreme being impossible to be sustained; and

(xv) For if an Omnipotent supreme being exists, then there can be no such thing as sin or evil, as none of creation has free will or even partial free will. This is the logical consequence of the concept of sin as the idea of conscious transgression; and

(xvi) The entire edifice of law from the first human civilisations are built upon the reason that one must know what is right from wrong and intend to commit a wrong, to then be accused of an offence, also classed as a sin by some religions; and

(xvii) Indeed, if a society claims to honour a particular religion that maintains the notion of an Omnipotent supreme being, then no individual should ever be found culpable or punished for transgressions as such judgements are an apostasy to the very idea of an Omnipotent supreme being; and

(xviii) As expressed previously, animalism is argued as an absolutely fundamental feature of enabling the concept of an omnipotent supreme being, because if all human beings were born with a genuine Divine Spark in the form of a Soul, then it would imply that an omnipotent supreme being is not merely guiding and directing the fate of existence, but that human beings as part of a singular Divinity as supreme being through their Soul, could also influence fate, whilst being constrained by the laws of the universe, thus defeating the notion of an Omnipotent supreme being; and

(xix) Omnipotence directly contradicts the teachings of many of the greatest claimed Messengers of Divinities, yet the same religions that claim their mandate and authority from these Divine Messengers seek to protect the insane and false doctrine of an Omnipotent supreme being at all cost; and

(xx) Omnipotence if obstinately and steadfastly defended, directly contradicts and renders null, void and absurd any notion of public law, penal law and ecclesiastical law, as without an operating free will, no ritual, no act, no intention has any meaning, nor may anyone be considered culpable. Yet the same religions that have defined such law, also seek to defend the abominable and fallacious doctrine of an Omnipotent supreme being.

Article 142 – Omnipresent

619. ***Omnipresent*** is the concept of being present everywhere at a moment in time within a given universal dimension (of space and time). The quality of omnipresent is called omnipresence.

Omnipresent

620. In general reference to the concept of Omnipresence:-

Concept of Omnipresence

    (i)   The concept of omnipresent is completely bound to the functional notions of space and time within a given dimension; and

Title III - Divine Attributes

(ii) Time itself is merely a standard of linear measure of spatial events within a given universal dimension; and

(iii) Occurrences within such universal dimension (with the exception of such concepts as supernaturalism) are then said to be both sequential and causal; and

(iv) By sequential, occurrences within such universal dimension are said to happen in a logical linear progression of moments in time and space, depending upon the standard measures of time; and

(v) Such a progression is logical in sequence and progression in that the concept of birth or creation must precede the concept of the death or destruction of the same thing, or object or concept; and

(vi) Similarly, the first event measured remains the first event, with each subsequent measure of time and space being the second, or third or later measure. The last event in time and space cannot proceed before the first event measures in the same time and space; and

(vii) Thus, the past is in reference to such moments in time and space that have previously occurred; whereas the future is in reference to such moments in time and space yet to occur; and

(viii) By the meaning of causal, events surrounding physical objects or even conscious thought is said to have an origin, a cause, a reason or justification; and secondly to then be a source of future cause, or action or thought; and

(ix) Therefore, a son cannot be the father to his own father; nor a mother be the daughter to her own child; and

(x) Creation heralds life. Life in an organic sense then leads to inevitable mortality of the cellular form according to the laws of nature; and

(xi) Thus, the model of time and space in a given universe is a delicate balance of rules and matter in an intricate web of actions and consequential actions that may be measured to some degree; and

(xii) Omnipresent then means the concept of a being that is present everywhere at every moment of the past, present and future within such a delicate and complex given universe.

621. The concept and various models of an omnipresent supreme being are absurd, irrational, unreasonable and illogical and do great harm

Omnipresent Being is an absurd model

against our ability to better comprehend the true nature and character of the Divine Creator of all Existence and all Heaven and Earth:-

(i) The natural limits within the concept of omnipresence whereby even a supreme being that is able to be everywhere at once, is then still constrained by universal dimension as to space and time, implies a supreme being that therefore cannot also be omnipotent (all mighty and all powerful); and

(ii) Thus, rather than strengthening the concept of a supreme being, the concept of omnipresence calls into question the accuracy of other attributes of the same supreme being; and

(iii) Using the term deity enables the possibility of an objective and dispassionate testimony on the historic and cultural concepts associated with supernatural beings, separate to any debate concerning one or more fundamental tenets held by a particular religion.

Article 143 – Omniscient

622. ***Omniscient***, is the concept as both the capacity and the actuality of truly knowing everything that can be known relative to time and a given Universe. The quality of omniscient is omniscience. Omniscient

623. In general reference to the concept of Omniscience:- Concept of Omniescience

(i) The term omniscient implies an attribute of a supreme being relative to a given Universe of knowledge. Without the existence of a Universe of knowledge as the subject of such unlimited power of awareness, the concept of omniscient would have no meaning whatsoever; and

(ii) In other words, the quality of being "all knowing" naturally implies some body and dimension of knowledge to know completely; and

(iii) The term omniscient also implies a Universe of knowledge that is distinctly and absolutely true, relative to other knowledge that may be less than perfectly true; and

(iv) In other words, the quality of being omniscient implies complete access to a perfect record of absolute truth; and

(v) Furthermore, the concept of omniscient is intimately connected to the notion of time and in particular the ability to know the past, the present and the future; and

(vi) The concept of omniscient as the capacity to know everything that can be known omnitemporality (existing within the past, present and future simultaneously), is found not only as an attribute of a supreme being, but also in some religions as the highest state of being of an enlightened soul; and

(vii) In contrast, the concept of omniscient as the actual knowing of everything that can be known, is exclusively an attribute of a supreme being existing in an a temporal state (existing outside of time); and

(viii) Thus, the concept of omniscient, similar to omnipotent, implies a supreme being as completely separate and distinct from the given Universe that is the subject of such knowing of the past, present and future and therefore simultaneously by being outside of time; and

(ix) If the omniscient supreme being were not completely separate and distinct from the given Universe (that is the subject of all knowing), then it could reasonably be argued that the supreme being would be bound in some way to the laws governing time the Universe and therefore could not possibly know the past and present and future simultaneously; and

(x) The notion of an omniscient supreme being is therefore a fundamental enabler to the concepts of Predeterminism and Predestinationism that underpin the concept of an omnipotent supreme being; and

(xi) Predeterminism as the fifth fundamental enabling concept to the notion of omnipotence, is the concept that the omnipotent and therefore omniscient supreme being has already determined and decided all events of history – past present and future; and

(xii) Predeterminism further argues that an unbroken chain of prior events exists from the origin of the Universe to the present moment; and that because this chain of events has been pre-established by the supreme being, human actions cannot possibly interfere with the outcomes of such a pre-established chain, except by their own choice to accept such fate or reject it; and

(xiii) Predestinationism as the sixth fundamental enabling concept to the notion of omnipotence, is the concept that the omnipotent and therefore omniscient supreme being has pre-ordained by Divine Will all events for every life, including the eventual fate of each individual soul; and that only by complete submission to the Will of God, as taught by a religious fraternity claiming such authority, does an individual human being have any hope of salvation from a destiny of perpetual torment, torture and terror; and

(xiv) While predestinationism fundamentally rejects any possible notion of free will in a Universe controlled by an omnipotent God, the concept is actually promoted through a pseudo form of free will or "enfeebled free will", whereby a man or woman may have no power to change the course of events decided by God, but may in themselves choose to accept faith (as fate) or reject it; and that this choice, no matter how weak and insignificant, is taken into account with what God has planned for each and every one of us.

624. The concept and various models of an omniscient supreme being are absurd, irrational, unreasonable and illogical and do great harm against our ability to better comprehend the true nature and character of the Divine Creator of all Existence and all Heaven and Earth:- *Omniscient Being is an absurd model*

(i) The doctrine of divine omniscience is logically incoherent, that it is inconsistent with the further philosophies and attributes such as divine impeccability (i.e. the doctrine that God cannot sin), and that it is refuted by the fact of human freedom; and

(ii) The first problem is Cantor's proof that there is no set of all sets in reality. Omniscience, it is said, entails knowledge of the set of all truths. Cantor's proof, however, demonstrates that there is no such set. As there is no such set, it is argued, there can be no omniscient being; and

(iii) The second problem is the problem of experiential knowledge. Here the argument is that there are certain facts knowledge of which can only be acquired through certain experiences "of knowledge what it is like to sin, for instance, can only be acquired by sinning" and that some of these experiences, and so some of these items of knowledge, are such that they cannot be had by God; and

(iv) The third problem is that of reconciling freedom and foreknowledge, specifically the existence of divine foreknowledge with the existence of human freedom. If a Divinity as an omniscient supreme being knows all of our future actions, then the future is fixed, but if the future is fixed, it seems that there is nothing that we can do to change it. The ability to determine our future actions, though, is what constitutes human freedom. Divine foreknowledge, then, seems to preclude the possibility of our being free agents; and

(v) The fourth problem is the problem of middle knowledge. Middle knowledge is knowledge of what free agents would have done had the world been other than it is. As the agents are free, their choice of action cannot be determined by the state of the world, and so cannot be calculated on that basis. As middle knowledge concerns counter-factual situations, however, neither can their choice of actions be known by observation of the future. With the two possible sources of knowledge ruled out, it seems that middle knowledge is an impossibility; and

(vi) A supreme being that is disconnected from existence then has no first hand knowledge only circumstantial and observational knowledge. Therefore such a supreme being that was not intimately connected to every life could not be omniscient; and

(vii) Thus, rather than strengthening the concept of a supreme being, the concept of omniscient calls into question the accuracy of other attributes of the same supreme being.

3.6 Absurdly Associated Attributes

Article 144 – Absurdly Associated Attribute

625. An Absurdly Associated (Divine) Attribute is a characteristic, or quality that is deliberately, wilfully and falsely associated as a claimed Divine Attribute when by all laws of logic, reason, morality and sound mind such an association is absurd an untenable. <small>Absurdly Associated (Divine) Attribute</small>

626. In reference to Absurdly Associated (Divine) Attributes:- <small>Absurdly Associated (Divine) Attribute References</small>

   (i) By definition, an Absurdly Associated (Divine) Attributes is a claimed Divine Attribute that is by all laws of logic, reason, morality and sound mind clearly and self-evidently absurd and untenable; and

   (ii) As an Absurdly Associated (Divine) Attribute is self-evidently absurd and untenable, its association can be logically concluded as deliberate, or wilfully false, perfidious and therefore by a deliberate action of Evil in order to harm or damage the Divine and the beings that are tricked into trusting such absurdities; and

   (iii) Because an Absurdly Associated (Divine) Attribute is self-evidently absurd and untenable, such claims are rarely put forward in serious academic or scholarly debate but instead the result of deliberately bias and wilful political or social agenda; and

(iv) The most common example of deliberate actions of Evil in seeking to associated self-evidently absurd and untenable concepts as claimed Divine Attributes is through nihilistic attempts to attack religions, religious people and institutions by attaching such self-evident absurdities as claimed conclusions, thereby negating the legitimacy of such traditions and bodies; and

(v) The second most common example of deliberate actions of Evil in seeking to associated self-evidently absurd and untenable concepts as claimed Divine Attributes is political and economic objectives by "politicising" the Divine to meet the goals of a heretical and sacrilegious minority. Such behaviour is found in self confessed groups of "Conservatives", "Liberals" and political bodies seeking to use religion as a tool of terror.

Article 145 – Ignorance

627. ***Ignorance*** is a term used to describe an Absurdly Associated (Divine) Attribute expressed or implied through one or more religious scriptures, or doctrines, or rites or rituals or clerical teachings that a Divinity:-

    (i) Is or was ignorant of the location, situation or status of a lesser being; or

    (ii) Expressed or exhibited ignorant behaviour; or

    (iii) Expressed or exhibited cognitive ignorance of established knowledge and wisdom.

_{Ignorance}

628. Examples and evidence of the Absurdly Associated (Divine) Attribute of Ignorance include (but are not limited to):-

    (i) Statements within scripture that clearly indicate a Divinity with limited powers of sight or perception; or

    (ii) Scripture attributed to a Divinity expressing or condoning any actions of cruelty, wrath, jealousy, vengeance, sadism or depravity; or

    (iii) Scripture attributed to a Divinity that is sexist, bigoted or racist; or

    (iv) Scripture attributed to a Divinity that contradicts the present most sacred Maxims or the principles of the most sacred

Examples & Evidence of the Absurdly Associated (Divine) Attribute of Ignorance

Covenant *Pactum De Singularis Caelum*.

629. In reference to the Absurdly Associated (Divine) Attribute of Ignorance:-

    (i)   By definition a Supreme being cannot be ignorant of itself or its true attributes. Therefore, evidence in scripture or doctrines or teachings of pervading ignorance is a sign of malignancy within the present structures of that body rather than a reflection on any Divine defect; and

    (ii)   Examples and evidence of persistent ignorance within scripture indicates either a corruption of an earlier authentic text, or that that claimed Divinity within such scripture cannot be the Supreme Being by a much lower deity, demon or ghost.

Ignorance as Absurdly Associated (Divine) Attribute

630. Any and all forms of claimed Divine Ignorance as an attribute are false, profane, malicious, profoundly immoral, absurd, perfidious and sacrilegious and are to be corrected from deliberate errors in texts, suppressed from teaching and purged from any legal or quasi-legal basis for political or social laws, norms or customs.

Claims of Ignorance as Divine Attribute forbidden

Article 146 – Cruel

631. ***Cruel*** and ***Cruelty*** are terms used to describe an Absurdly Associated (Divine) Attribute expressed or implied through one or more claimed religious scriptures, or doctrines, or rites or rituals or clerical teachings that a Divinity:-

    (i)   Is or was harsh and severe in the issuance of punishment against lesser beings; or

    (ii)   Occasionally intentionally causes pain, hardship and suffering to lesser beings.

Cruel

632. Examples and evidence of the Absurdly Associated (Divine) Attribute of Cruelty include (but are not limited to):-

    (i)   Scripture attributed to a Divinity that promotes, encourages or condones eternal and unending punishment, pain or suffering to any spiritual being; or

    (ii)   Scripture that demonstrates a distinct lack of Divine Mercy or Compassion and therefore Fairness in respect to claimed Divine Justice; or

    (iii)   Doctrines, scripture or teachings that state or imply direct Divine will and action in causing pain, hardship or suffering to lesser beings; or

Examples & Evidence of the Absurdly Associated (Divine) Attribute of Cruelty

Lex Divina: Maxims of Divine Law

(iv) Doctrines, scripture or teachings that state or imply a Supreme Divine being intends to exterminate the human species, or life on earth or the entire existence of the Universe.

633. In general reference to the Absurdly Associated (Divine) Attribute of Cruelty:- Cruelty as Absurdly Associated (Divine) Attribute

(i) True Divine Law and Divine Will demonstrates that existence itself depends on a passive state of the Divine Creator as Observer; and that only through consciousness, knowledge and awareness is direct intervention generally able to be effected; and

(ii) Pain, suffering and hardship are neither goals of the Divine, nor caused by Divine Will, but the consequences of personal choice, actions, circumstance and the causation of events of life on Earth and the Universe; and

(iii) The attributing of blame to the Divine for circumstances of pain, suffering or hardship is in one sense an abdication of personal accountability or objectivity as to the circumstances that led to such sadness.

634. Any and all forms of claimed Divine Cruelty as an attribute are false, profane, malicious, profoundly immoral, absurd, perfidious and sacrilegious and are to be corrected from deliberate errors in texts, suppressed from teaching and purged from any legal or quasi-legal basis. Claims of Cruelty as Divine Attribute forbidden

Article 147 – Wrathful

635. *Wrath* and *Wrathful* are terms used to describe an Absurdly Associated (Divine) Attribute expressed or implied through one or more claimed religious scriptures, or doctrines, or rites or rituals or clerical teachings that a Divinity:- Wrathful

(i) Is or was prone to great anger toward one or more lesser beings; or

(ii) Is or was susceptible to fits of rage or fury against one or more lesser beings.

636. Examples and evidence of the Absurdly Associated (Divine) Attribute of Wrath include (but are not limited to):- Examples & Evidence of the Absurdly Associated (Divine) Attribute of Wrath

(i) Scripture, doctrines or teachings that express or imply a Divinity who has engaged in various fits or wrath at different times of history; or

(ii) Doctrines, scripture or teachings that state or imply a Supreme

Divine has destroyed human life or life in general on account of wrath, such as a great flood, or great disaster; or

(iii) Doctrines, scripture or teachings that attribute natural disasters and human made disasters to the wrath of some Divinity; or

(iv) Doctrines, scripture or teachings that attribute the misfortune of a person or group of people on account of the wrath of some Divinity.

637. In reference to the Absurdly Associated (Divine) Attribute of Wrath:- *Wrath as Absurdly Associated (Divine) Attribute*

(i) The attributing of Divine Will to the actions of disasters, especially against political and social enemies is as old as civilisation itself; and

(ii) The strongest political and social "gods" of millennia have been those gods and goddesses association with warfare, blood sacrifice, terror and cruelty – as a warning and propaganda for enemies; and a means of absolving leaders and soldiers from their barbaric and inhuman acts; and a means of social control and order; and

(iii) Evidence exists that in transliterations of sacred texts, words have even been deliberately modified in meaning to transform metaphors and example passages into endorsing a "Wrathful God"; and

(iv) The profane, immoral, sacrilegious notions of "Might is Right" and "Just War" has persistently been used by the elite also profit from the machinery of war, terror and social disorder, despite such concepts being clearly absurd, false and evil; and

(v) The promotion of xenophobic desires for revenge against enemies based upon Divine Wrath and differences of ethnicity, race, religion or creed has continued throughout history as a populist means of gaining political support during times of economic turmoil and social difficulty.

638. Any and all forms of claimed Divine Wrath as an attribute are false, profane, malicious, profoundly immoral, absurd, perfidious and sacrilegious and are to be corrected from deliberate errors in texts, suppressed from teaching and purged from any legal or quasi-legal basis for political or social actions in times of war or conflict. *Claims of Wrath as Divine Attribute forbidden*

Article 148 – Jealous

639. ***Jealous*** and ***Jealousy*** are terms used to describe an Absurdly *Jealous*

Associated (Divine) Attribute expressed or implied through one or more claimed religious scriptures, or doctrines, or rites or rituals or clerical teachings that a Divinity:-

(i) Is or was envious in desiring the good fortune or advantage of another; or

(ii) Is or was maliciously resentful or spiteful of the good fortunes or advantages of another.

640. Examples and evidence of the Absurdly Associated (Divine) Attribute of Jealousy include (but are not limited to):- *(Examples & Evidence of the Absurdly Associated (Divine) Attribute of Jealousy)*

(i) Explicit, historic and well known scripture that states a claimed Divinity to be "a jealous god"; or

(ii) Doctrines, scripture or teachings that attribute behaviour of a claimed Divinity to act, promote or condone spiteful, or malicious or envious behaviour.

641. In reference to the Absurdly Associated (Divine) Attribute of Jealousy:- *(Jealousy as Absurdly Associated (Divine) Attribute)*

(i) By definition a "jealous god" is a lesser divinity to some other divinity and without question a self declaration that such a divinity is not the Supreme Being; and

(ii) Logic, reason and common sense demands the rational consideration that in order to be jealous, there must be another to whom exhibit such a trait. It is absurd to deny such sane reasoning or to claim that the Supreme Being can possibly be jealous of lesser beings that it created; and

(iii) Evidence of an explicit declaration by a spiritual being proclaiming themselves to be a "jealous god" is as clear a declaration as possible that such words or scripture is either corrupted, or false, or from a demon or ghost claiming to be a demi-god.

Article 149 – Vengeful

642. ***Vengeance*** and ***Vengeful*** are terms used to describe an Absurdly Associated (Divine) Attribute expressed or implied through one or more claimed religious scriptures, or doctrines, or rites or rituals or clerical teachings that a Divinity:- *Vengeful*

    (i)   Enacts personal retaliatory action against one or more lesser beings for some alleged insult, injury or wrong; or

    (ii)   Undertakes punitive actions on account of some previous loss against another.

643. Examples and evidence of the Absurdly Associated (Divine) Attribute of Vengeance include (but are not limited to):- *Examples & Evidence of the Absurdly Associated (Divine) Attribute of Vengeance*

    (i)   Explicit, historic and well known scripture that states a claimed Divinity to be "a vengeful god"; or

    (ii)   Doctrines, scripture or teachings that attribute retaliatory actions or revenge as being condoned or promoted by some Divinity.

644. In reference to the Absurdly Associated (Divine) Attribute of Vengeance:- *Vengeance as Absurdly Associated (Divine) Attribute*

    (i)   Revenge, by definition is an admission of weakness not strength, as it clearly and unmistakably infers a being who was first unable to withstand or prevents the actions of another (the subject and basis of the revenge); and thus must resort to some counterfeit, ambush or deception whereby to overcome such inherit weakness and attack; and

    (ii)   Any statement in scripture or teaching that a divinity is a "vengeful god" is an open admission that such a divinity cannot be the true Supreme Being, but must be a counterfeit, or demon or ghost, as the authentic Supreme Being cannot be weaker than another.

645. Any and all forms of claimed Divine Vengeance as an attribute are false, profane, malicious, profoundly immoral, absurd, perfidious and sacrilegious and are to be corrected from deliberate errors in texts, suppressed from teaching and purged from any legal or quasi-legal basis for political or social actions in times of war or conflict. *Claims of Vengeance as Divine Attribute forbidden*

Article 150 – Sadistic

646. ***Sadistic*** is a term used to describe an Absurdly Associated (Divine) Attribute expressed or implied through one or more claimed religious scriptures, or doctrines, or rites or rituals or clerical teachings that a Divinity:-

    (i)   Expressed or exhibited delight in the pain, suffering or humiliation of lesser beings; or

    (ii)   Expressed or exhibited pleasure from the pain, hardship or punishment of lesser beings.

Sadistic

647. Examples and evidence of the Absurdly Associated (Divine) Attribute of Sadism include (but are not limited to):-

    (i)   Explicit, historic and well known scripture that demonstrates a claimed Divinity who expressed delight in the pain, suffering, hardship, punishment or humiliation of lesser beings; or

    (ii)   Explicit, historic and well known scripture that a claimed Divinity ordered, or condoned barbarous acts against women or children such as murder, mutilation or rape; or

    (iii)   Explicit, historic and well known scripture that a claimed Divinity ordered, or condoned cruel and unusual forms of torture and capital punishment; or

    (iv)   Explicit, historic and well known scripture that a claimed Divinity ordered, or condoned the sacrifice of first born children or children in general; or

    (v)   Explicit, historic and well known scripture that a claimed Divinity ordered, or condoned the sexual molestation of children or vulnerable adults.

Examples & Evidence of the Absurdly Associated (Divine) Attribute of Sadism

Article 151 – Depraved

648. ***Depraved*** and ***Depravity*** are terms used to describe an Absurdly Associated (Divine) Attribute expressed or implied through one or more claimed religious scriptures, or doctrines, or rites or rituals or clerical teachings that a Divinity:-

    (i)   Expressed or exhibited distorted moral behaviour contrary to the norm; or

    (ii)   Expressed or exhibited morally perverted behaviour of a cruel and sadistic nature; or

Depraved

(iii) Condoned, supported or encouraged morally perverted acts of a cruel and sadistic nature.

649. Examples and evidence of the Absurdly Associated (Divine) Attribute of Depravity include (but are not limited to):-

(i) Explicit, historic and well known scripture that a claimed Divinity ordered, or condoned cannibalism or simulated rituals of cannibalism; or

(ii) Explicit, historic and well known scripture that a claimed Divinity ordered, or condoned barbarous acts against women or children such as murder, mutilation or rape; or

(iii) Explicit, historic and well known scripture that a claimed Divinity ordered, or condoned cruel and unusual forms of torture and capital punishment; or

(iv) Explicit, historic and well known scripture that a claimed Divinity ordered, or condoned the sacrifice of first born children or children in general; or

(v) Explicit, historic and well known scripture that a claimed Divinity ordered, or condoned the sexual molestation of children or vulnerable adults; or

(vi) Explicit, historic and well known scripture that a claimed Divinity ordered, or condoned human sacrifice.

Article 152 – Hypocritical

650. *Hypocritical* and *Hypocrite* are terms used to describe an Absurdly Associated (Divine) Attribute expressed or implied through one or more claimed religious scriptures, or doctrines, or rites or rituals or clerical teachings that a Divinity:-

(i) Expressed or exhibited behaviour contrary to their claimed commands and teachings; or

(ii) Engaged in moral behaviour or activities equal to or worse than those whereby lesser beings are held account or punished.

651. Examples and evidence of the Absurdly Associated (Divine) Attribute of Hypocrisy include (but are not limited to):-

(i) Doctrines, scripture or teachings that state or imply a Supreme Divine ordered or condoned acts, contrary to laws stated by the same alleged Supreme Being; or

(ii) Explicit, historic and well known scripture that a claimed

Divinity ordered, or condoned barbarous acts against women or children such as murder, mutilation or rape contrary to the same Divine Laws alleged issued by the claimed Supreme being; or

(iii) Explicit, historic and well known scripture that a claimed Divinity ordered, or condoned cruel, sadistic, envious or barbarous acts contrary to the very Divine Laws the Divinity is said to have issued; or

(iv) Doctrines, scripture or teachings that permit certain elite members of a religious body to contradict or usurp alleged Divine Laws, while lesser members are and have been punished for lesser examples of transgressions.

Article 154 – Insanity

652. ***Insane*** and ***Insanity*** are terms used to describe an Absurdly Associated (Divine) Attribute expressed or implied through one or more claimed religious scriptures, or doctrines, or rites or rituals or clerical teachings that a Divinity:-

    (i) Expressed or exhibited behaviour or characteristics of an unsound mind; or

    (ii) Condoned, supported or encouraged morally repugnant acts or behaviours lacking sane or reasonable judgement.

653. Examples and evidence of the Absurdly Associated (Divine) Attribute of Insanity include (but are not limited to):-

    (i) Explicit, historic and well known scripture that a claimed Divinity ordered, or condoned cannibalism or simulated rituals of cannibalism; or

    (ii) Explicit, historic and well known scripture that a claimed Divinity ordered, or condoned barbarous acts against women or children such as murder, mutilation or rape; or

    (iii) Explicit, historic and well known scripture that a claimed Divinity ordered, or condoned cruel and unusual forms of torture and capital punishment; or

    (iv) Explicit, historic and well known scripture that a claimed Divinity ordered, or condoned the sacrifice of first born children or children in general; or

    (v) Explicit, historic and well known scripture that a claimed Divinity ordered, or condoned the sexual molestation of children or vulnerable adults; or

Title III - Divine Attributes

- (vi) Explicit, historic and well known scripture that a claimed Divinity ordered, or condoned human sacrifice; or
- (vii) Doctrines, scripture or teachings that state or imply a Supreme Divine being intends to exterminate the human species, or life on earth or the entire existence of the Universe.

Article 154 – Evil

654. ***Evil*** is a binary concept bound to the opposite concept of Heroic Virtue, whereby Evil is any intentional and wilfully deliberately wicked, perfidious, or malevolent, or profoundly morally repugnant act to do or refrain from doing something that then causes terrible harm, or injury, or trauma or cruelty to a higher order mind. *— Evil*

655. In general reference to Evil:- *— In reference to Evil*
    - (i) Evil, by definition is the generic term describing the worst possible behaviour exhibited by a conscious being with the capacity of reason and free will; and
    - (ii) A conscious being devoid of reason or the capacity of free will can never be sensibly classed as exhibiting evil behaviour, nor be declared "evil"; and
    - (iii) As Evil by definition is the worst possible behaviour, its binary opposite is properly the highest and best possible behaviour being Heroic Virtue; and
    - (iv) The binary opposite to the concept of Good is Bad, not Evil. To equate the binary opposite concept to Good being Evil is an absurdity and gross error.

656. The presence of Evil is not a repudiation of Divine Existence but a consequence of Free Will and Choice and is completely compatible with the Ucadia Standard Model of Existence:- *— Existence of Evil is not a repudiation of Divine Existence*
    - (i) The Divine cannot be blamed for the Free Will and Choice of individual beings that intentional and wilfully deliberately choose to be wicked, perfidious, or malevolent, or profoundly morally repugnant act to do or refrain from doing something that then causes terrible harm, or injury, or trauma or cruelty to a higher order mind; and
    - (ii) Free Will and Choice means that individual beings are free to repudiate all forms of logic and reason and reject some or all of the present sacred Maxims and the Ucadia Model. However, in doing so, such beings also declare themselves Incompetent before all Heaven and Earth; and

(iii) A Being that chooses to continue Evil, without remorse or seeking reconciliation, disqualifies themselves from all Office or the full execution of their Rights, effectively endorsing the power and authority of higher beings to treat them as Incompetent Wards in need of Custody and Protection against themselves, until true remorse and reconciliation is properly concluded; and

(iv) The Divine does not endorse, nor condone nor ignore acts of Evil, but therefore treats such wilful acts as a self-declaration of accepting the consequences of such action, particularly in necessary actions in the case of Spirit Beings who have been responsible for acts of Evil against the living and deceased.

657. The Concept of an ordained and specialised dimension for the eternal punishment, torture and cruelty of Spirit Beings is a Supreme Evil Concept and contrary to Divine Law:- *Eternal Punishment is contrary to Divine Law*

(i) Every living and deceased Being is held to account under Divine Law for their transgressions against Law; and

(ii) An unwillingness to accept responsibility or belligerent or obstinate refusal to cease evil actions is properly treated as an absolute and unqualified acceptance that such a being endorses the power and authority of higher beings to treat them as Incompetent Wards in need of Custody and Protection against themselves, until true remorse and reconciliation is properly concluded; and

(iii) The length of such Custody and Protection is entirely dependent upon the actions, level of remorse and willingness to overcome such illness of mind in the part of the living or deceased being, and the standards and laws mandated and accepted by every dimension of society; and

(iv) Such Custody and Protection shall never involve Divinely endorsed torture, cruelty or barbarity, yet nor shall such Custody and Protection be able to be imputed as a softness or tacit or actual endorsement of the acts of the culpable; and

(v) Thus, all models imputing eternal punishment, torture and Divinely ordained cruelty are a terrible evil afflicted against the name of the Divine Creator and to be suppressed and never revived.

Title IV - Divine Beings

4.1 Divine Beings

Article 155 - Being

658. A ***Being*** is an embodiment of Unique Collective Awareness and a Computational Model according to the Standard Rules of Existence as applied to a certain Reality. <!-- Being -->

659. In reference to the concept of Being:- <!-- General Principles of Divine Beings -->

    (i) As an embodiment of Unique Collective Awareness, a Being is first and foremost a construct of unique Self-Awareness to some degree; and

    (ii) Given all matter in every dimension possesses a level of Self-Awareness in order to function, all matter in every dimension can be said to have the presence of Being; and

    (iii) As an embodiment of a Unique Computation Model or "Consciousness of Mind" according to the Standard Rules of Existence as applied to a certain Reality, a Being is an Object of some definitive kind capable of complex computational functions; and

    (iv) All Objects, by definition are embodiments of Computational Models of Awareness according to certain Rules and Reality. Therefore all forms of Matter may also be described as Beings; and

    (v) By definition, certain Objects, such as Ergons (e.g. Graviton, Neutrino, Magneton, Electron, Positron, Photon or Heton), may belong to intersecting sets whereby in one Reality such an embodiment of Awareness appears Real, whereas in the connected Reality, the Object is viewed as Unreal or a kind of "force"; and

    (vi) Therefore, a Being may belong as an Object of an intersecting set whereby in one Reality such an embodiment of Awareness appears Real, whereas in the connected Reality, the Being is viewed as Unreal.

660. All Beings may be defined as *Divine, Ethereal* or *Living*:- <!-- Types of Beings -->

    (i) A ***Divine Being*** is a specific embodiment of Unique Collective Awareness existing within a collective "abstracted" and Unreal Set or "Divine Reality" distinct from a dependent set of Reality necessary for material existence within the Standard Model of the Universe; and

    (ii) An ***Ethereal Being*** is a specific embodiment of Unique

Collective Awareness existing within an intersecting set of Unreal and Real, whereby to the Real Set the Being appears as a force without form, but in the intersecting set such a Being possesses a material existence in accord with the Standard Model of the Universe. The Conscious Mind itself of a Sentient Being or Sapient Being is such an example of an Ethereal Being; and

(iii) A ***Living Being*** is a specific embodiment of Unique Collective Awareness existing within Reality according to the Rules of the Standard Model of the Universe.

661. In reference to the concept of a *Divine Being*:-   Divine Being

    (i) Every Set from the Real Set of Unita in perfect and absolute position is an abstracted and Unreal set produced through the computational awareness of increasing layers of matter; and

    (ii) By definition, every set apart from the Real Set of Unita is an abstracted and Unreal Set representing a dimension of Divine Reality (dream); and

    (iii) Therefore, every set of objects beginning with the abstracted set of "ideal life" of the Unita is a Divine Reality (dream).

662. In reference to the concept of a *Living Being*:-   Living Being

    (i) By definition, every form of matter above the Unita is formed from the Unreal Set and therefore is borne from Divine Reality; and

    (ii) Furthermore, every form of matter and therefore every form of Living Being requires the quality of Awareness and a Computational Model of Mind; and

    (iii) As every form of matter and therefore every form of Living Being requires the quality of Awareness and a Computational Model of Mind, every Living Being from the level of a Sentient Being or Sapient Being is firmly bound to the existence of an Ethereal Being for its continued physical existence within a form of Reality; and

    (iv) This Ethereal Being may be equated to the complex projection of "Imaginary Self" or "Ideal Self" of the Computational Model of Mind of a Sentient Being or Sapient Being, necessary for existence; and

    (v) When two or more Sentient or Sapient Living Beings co-operate in some manner, so too do their Ethereal Beings in forming a "new reality" to some degree.

663. All sets of Beings may be defined according to ten categories being *Supreme, Primary, Higher, Ordinary, Ethereal, Material, Cellular, Sentient, Sapient* and *Imaginary*:-   *Categories of Beings*

- (i) The *Supreme Being* is the formal name for the Divine as the Divine Observer and Divine Creator of all Existence as a singular Object or Set of all being and all possible objects, concepts, matter, rules, life, mind, universes, forces, sets or awareness; and

- (ii) A *Primary Being* is a Living, Ethereal and Divine Being as a Primary Observer and singular Object or Set of all possible objects, concepts, matter, rules, life, mind, forces, sets or awareness at a particular key level of Matter and Existence (i.e. universe, galaxy, star, planet, life or species); and

- (iii) A *Higher Being* is a Divine Being as a collective Consciousness and Being representing an essential stable character and attribute of a Primary Being, particularly as it applies to the presence of Cellular Beings and multiple species of Sentient and Sapient Beings within the jurisdiction and dimension of such a Primary Being; and

- (iv) An *Ordinary Being* is an individual Divine Being formed either by virtue of the operation of Divine Law or the journey and transition of the Ethereal Being (Sentience or Sapience) of a previously Living Being; and

- (v) An *Ethereal Being* in the context of such categorisation is narrowed to be the Computation Model of Mind of Sentient Beings and Sapient Beings that are Living or in transition to Divine after death of the Living Being; and

- (vi) A *Material Being* is a Living Being in the form of all physical matter at a Unita, Super Sub Atomic, Sub Atomic, Atomic and Molecular Level; and

- (vii) A *Cellular Being* is a unique Living Being from the perspective of a unique single cell, whether or not it is part of a body of a complex species or singular cellular life then viewed as a part of the greater universe of all cellular life on a planet; and

- (viii) A *Sentient Being* is a unique Living and Ethereal Being as a member of a species of Level 5 (Complex Multi-Cellular Life); and

- (ix) A *Sapient Being* is a unique Living and Ethereal Being as a member of a species of Level 6 (Higher Order Life); and

(x) An *Imaginary Being* is an Ethereal Being from the individual or collective imagination and minds of Sapient Beings that by constant reinforcement and thinking is given its own existence and reality.

664. A Being is formed by virtue of Operation of Divine Law, or Natural Law or Cognitive Law:-   *Formation of Beings*

    (i) By Divine Law when according to the present Maxims in accord with the most sacred Covenant *Pactum De Singularis Caelum*, a stable and formal Being exists, consistent with the Standard Rules of Existence as applied to a certain Reality; and

    (ii) By Natural Law when according to the Physical Laws of Matter and the Universe, an organised aggregation of Matter is formed under common purpose and existence; and

    (iii) By Cognitive Law when a Sentient Being, or Sapient Being or Higher Being or Primary Being or Supreme Being conceives an embodiment of Unique Collective Awareness and Computational Model according to the Standard Rules of Existence as applied to a certain Reality.

665. A Being ceases to be by virtue of Operation of Divine Law, or Natural Law or Cognitive Law:-   *Cessation of Beings*

    (i) By Divine Law when according to the present Maxims in accord with the most sacred Covenant *Pactum De Singularis Caelum*, a stable and formal Being ceases to exist, consistent with the Standard Rules of Existence as applied to a certain Reality; and

    (ii) By Natural Law when according to the Physical Laws of Matter and the Universe, an organised aggregation of Matter decays and ceases to function under common purpose and existence; and

    (iii) By Cognitive Law when a Sentient Being, or Sapient Being or Higher Being or Primary Being or Supreme Being no longer conceives or trusts or remembers an embodiment of Unique Collective Awareness and Computational Model according to the Standard Rules of Existence as applied to a certain Reality.

666. In relation to the cessation of Beings by Divine Law:-   *Cessation of Beings and Divine Law*

    (i) It is the essence of comprehension of the Supreme Being that by Divine Will, existence is a continuous expression of Free Will and Choice and no Law can mandate the perpetual nor eternal existence of Creation except in absolute Trust in the

Divine; and

(ii) In accord with the present Maxims of Divine Law and the most sacred Covenant *Pactum De Singularis Caelum*, the Supreme Being has pledged in perpetual Trust, that all lesser Beings that are said to have Divine Existence under the Divine Law shall have perpetual and immortal Divine existence; and that none may be condemned nor ruled to cease to exist.

Article 156 - Supreme Being

667. The ***Supreme Being***, is the formal name for the Divine as the Divine Observer and Divine Creator of all Existence as a singular Object or Set of all possible objects, concepts, matter, rules, life, mind, universes, forces, sets or awareness. Supreme Being

668. The Supreme Being is equivalent to the valid term Unique Collective Awareness when describing the Divine Creator as the greatest, most perfect dimension and existence. Supreme Being and Unique Collective Awareness

669. As the Supreme Being means the Divine and therefore the "concept of all concepts" and the "set of all sets", there is no greater concept or set of objects. Therefore, every other possible concept or object or set is lesser than the Supreme Being. No higher Being

4.2 Primary Beings

Article 157 - Primary Being

670. A ***Primary Being*** is a Living, Ethereal and Divine Being as a Primary Observer and singular Object or Set of all possible objects, concepts, matter, rules, life, mind, forces, sets or awareness at a particular key level of Matter and Existence. Primary Being

671. In respect of Primary Beings:- General References to Primary Being

   (i) All Primary Beings are a subset of the Supreme Being and therefore less than the Supreme Being. No Primary Being can be theoretically or actually greater than the Supreme Being; and

   (ii) All Primary Beings exist as a Primary Observer and Primary Creator as a singular Object or Set of all possible objects, concepts, matter, rules, life, mind, forces, sets or awareness at a particular key level of Matter and Existence; and

   (iii) Except for the Supreme Being, Primary Beings are unique in existence among other Beings as a tripartite embodiment of a Divine Being, Ethereal Being and Living Being as one.

Article 158 - Universal Being

672. A ***Universal Being*** is a Living, Ethereal and Divine Being as a Primary Observer and singular Object and Set of all possible objects, concepts, matter, rules, life, mind, forces, sets or awareness within the Universe as a singularity.

    Universal Being

673. In respect of The Universal Being:-

    General Reference to Universal Being

    (i) The Universal Being is founded upon the ultimate Real Set of Unita and then the unique collective awareness of all Unita as the abstracted and Unreal "Ideal" Set. Thus, the Universal Being may also be named as Unitas in honour of the collective dream of all Unita; and

    (ii) While there are many sub-verses, there is only one Universe and only one Unitas as the Universal Being; and

    (iii) The Universal Being as Unitas is equivalent to the ultimate Object in comparison to the Supreme Being as the ultimate Observer; and

    (iv) The Ethereal Being of the Unitas (the dream of a dream) may be called Kosmos when projecting more complex forms of matter; and

    (v) All other Primary Beings are a member of the Universal Being and Kosmos.

Article 159 - Galactic Being

674. A ***Galactic Being*** is a complex Living, Ethereal and Divine Being as a Primary Observer of its own Set of stars, matter, concepts, rules, life, mind, forces and awareness within the Sub Atomic Universe as a singular Object and body.

    Galactic Being

675. In respect of a Galactic Being:-

    General Reference to Galactic Being

    (i) All Galactic Beings exist simultaneously within the sub-verse of Super Sub Atomic Matter of the Kosmos as a Divine Being; and a Sub Atomic sub-verse as a Living Galactic Being; and an Atomic sub-verse as an Ethereal Being; and

    (ii) As a Living Being, the building blocks of Galactic Life are Stars, similar to Cells of a multi-cellular organism, whereby Stars form permanent or semi-permanent relations with one another, within larger fixed or semi-fixed structures, similar to organs, that then change position as one cohesive body; and

    (iii) As a Computational Model representing an Ethereal Being of

Mind, a Galaxy possesses the necessary computational abilities many trillions upon trillions of times greater than an individual member or a Higher Order Species, in order to function at such massive distances and coordinated forces; and

(iv) In reality, Galaxies should not be possible if the laws of Gravity, Matter and Forces were to be applied without consideration to complex multi-dimensional considerations. Thus, the presence of a Divine Galactic Being is vital to enable the existence of a Galaxy whereby sub-atomic matter from the perspective of a Galaxy performs virtually instantaneous and constant changes to enable the Galaxy to still exist.

Article 160 - GAL

676. ***GAL*** is the Unique Collective Divine Spirit of all super sub atomic elements and all stars and all life and consciousness representing all matter and awareness of the Milky Way Galaxy as a Primary Being.
GAL

677. The Divine Spirit of GAL is part of the greater collective spirit of KOSMOS, that is part of the greater collective spirit of UNITAS, that is then part of the greater collective Divine Spirit of ALL.
GAL and KOSMOS

678. GAL is the proper name and greater name of the Milky Way in respect and recognition of the Galaxy as a Primary Being and Divine, Living and Ethereal Being; and unified whole of all the stars, all the gases, all the planets, all the life, all the self-aware life within the galaxy and the galaxy as one living entity.
GAL as proper name of Milky Way Galaxy as Being

679. GAL memory is the memory of the unique existence of the Milky Way and memory of unique position, change, seasons of life and seasons of death. GAL memory is eternal.
GAL memory

680. GAL Reason is everything manifest in the Milky Way. Everything in the Milky Way happens for a reason and purpose. Everything in the Milky Way has meaning. Nothing in the Milky Way has no-purpose. The smallest of objects has a unique and absolute purpose.
GAL Reason

Article 161 - Stellar Being

681. A ***Stellar Being*** is a complex Living, Ethereal and Divine Being as a Primary Observer of its own Set of planets, concepts, rules, life, mind, forces and awareness within the complex Atomic Universe of a Galaxy as a singular Object and body.
Stellar Being

682. In respect of a Stellar Being:-
General Reference to

(i) All Stellar Beings exist simultaneously within a sub-verse of

Sub Atomic Matter of Galactic Mind as a Divine Being; and an Atomic sub-verse as a Living Stellar Being; and a Molecular sub-verse as an Ethereal Being; and

Stellar Being

(ii) As a Living Being, the building blocks of Galactic Life are Stars, similar to Cells of a multi-cellular organism, whereby Stars form permanent or semi-permanent relations with one another, within larger fixed or semi-fixed structures, similar to organs, that then change position as one cohesive body; and

(iii) Furthermore, as a Living Being, the building blocks of Stellar Life are Ergon Fields, Molecular Fields, Planets, Planetoids and Meteoroids, similar to a family of multi-cellular organisms, whereby Stars form a protected environment within themselves for complex molecular structures culminating in cellular or "life" bearing planets or planetoids as a feature of Stellar Life throughout each and virtually every Galaxy; and

(iv) As a Computational Model representing an Ethereal Being of Mind, a Star possesses the necessary computational abilities many trillions of times greater than an individual member or a Higher Order Species, in order to function at such massive distances and coordinated forces.

Article 162 - SOL

683. **SOL** is the unique collective Divine Spirit of all atomic and molecular elements, life and awareness of our Solar System and Sun as a Primary Being.

SOL

684. The Divine Spirit of SOL is part of the greater collective spirit of GAL, that is part of the greater collective spirit of KOSMOS, that is part of the greater collective spirit of UNITAS, that is then part of the greater collective Divine Spirit of ALL.

SOL and GAL and KOSMOS

685. SOL is the proper name and greater name of the Solar System in respect and recognition of the unified whole of all the planets, all the gases, all the moons, meteorites and asteroid belts, the Sun, all the life, all the self-aware life within the Solar System and the Solar System as a Divine Being, Living Being and Ethereal Being.

SOL as proper name of Sun as Conscious Being

686. SOL memory is the memory of the unique existence of the Solar System and memory of unique position, change, seasons of life and seasons of death. SOL memory is eternal.

SOL memory

687. The position of planets within the SOL is not simply mechanical, but will of the SOL. If the Sun chose it to be so, the planet Earth could be

Active nature of SOL

destroyed in an instant. Yet the Sun chooses of its own free will to value the life, awareness and existence of the planet Earth like a mother to a new born child.

688. As SOL continues to demonstrate active intelligent will to protect the Earth from great harm, any belief system founded on rules and laws implying negative intent upon the Earth by the Solar System are false and null and void *ab initio* (from the beginning).

False attributes against SOL

Article 163 - Planetary Being

689. A ***Planetary Being*** is a complex Living, Ethereal and Divine Being as a Primary Observer of its own Set of planetoids, meteoroids, electromagnetic fields, atmosphere, life, mind, forces and awareness within the complex Molecular Universe of a Star as a singular Object and body.

Planetary Being

690. In respect of a Planetary Being:-

General Reference to Planetary Being

(i) All Planetary Beings exist simultaneously within a sub-verse of Atomic Matter of Stellar Mind as a Divine Being; and an Molecular sub-verse as a Living Planetary Being; and a Material or Cellular Life sub-verse as an Ethereal Being; and

(ii) The formation of large bodied Hydrogen Planets and Iron Planets are a natural consequence of Stellar Formation from collapsing Nebula. Therefore, notwithstanding Stars undergoing the end of their life before collapse, the presence of at least one or more planets should be found in most Stellar models throughout the Universe; and

(iii) Even if a Star has ceased to function as a standard Hydrogen model, but has progressed in life to a different state (i.e. Red Giant), large bodied Hydrogen Planets throughout the Universe typically possess at least one or more Planetoid that upon the right conditions may support the formation of complex molecular structures such as amino acids and ultimately cellular life; and

(iv) As a Living Being, the building blocks of Planetary Life are Molecular Fields and Oceans, whereby Planets form stable environments for the support of complex and irregular shaped Molecular Polymers, even if conditions do not make the formation of cellular life possible; and

(v) As a Computational Model representing an Ethereal Being of Mind, a Planet even without cellular life possesses the necessary computational abilities many millions of times greater than an individual member or a Higher Order Species, in order to function complex chemical and electro-magnetic formations; and

(vi) As a Computational Model representing an Ethereal Being of Mind, a Planet possessing abundant cellular life possesses the necessary computational abilities many trillions upon trillions of times greater than an individual member or a Higher Order Species, in order to function highly complex chemical, electro-magnetic and biological formations.

Article 164 - GAIA

691. ***GAIA*** is the unique collective Divine Spirit of all atomic elements and awareness of the Planet Earth. — GAIA

692. The spirit of GAIA is part of the greater collective spirit of SOL, that is part of the greater collective spirit of GAL, that is part of the greater collective spirit of KOSMOS, that is part of the greater collective spirit of UNITAS, that is then part of the greater collective Divine Spirit of ALL. — GAIA and SOL and GAL

693. The stability of conditions upon the surface of the planet Earth is not simply mechanical, but according to the will of GAIA. If GAIA so chose, then great regions of the surface could be rendered uninhabitable, but instead chooses by free will to care for life, nurture and protect life. — Active consciouness of GAIA

694. As GAIA continues to demonstrate active intelligent will to protect the life and higher order life upon the surface of the Earth from great harm, any belief system founded on rules and laws implying negative intent upon the life on Earth by the GAIA are false and null and void ab initio (from the beginning). — False attributes against GAIA

695. As GAIA is personified by Molecular Oceans and Fields, it is entirely appropriate to use the ancient name of Mari or Mary to describe GAIA as the Mother of all Life on planet Earth and even the Mother of God when represented by a Singularity of the Homo Sapien Species. — GAIA and customary term for Seas

Article 165 - Cellular Being

696. A ***Cellular Being*** is a complex Living, Ethereal and Divine Being as a Primary Observer of its own Set of mono-cellular, multi-cellular and advanced cellular species, minds, life, ecosystems and awareness within the complex Molecular Universe of a Planet as a singular Object and body. — Cellular Being

697. In respect of a Cellular Being:- General Reference to Cellular Being

    (i) All Cellular Beings exist simultaneously within a sub-verse of Molecular Mind of a Planet as a Divine Being; and an Cellular sub-verse as a Living Conscious Being; and a sub-verse as an Ethereal Being; and

    (ii) The primary conscious focus of a Cellular Being is to sustain and grow the conditions for life; and to reduce risks against the cessation of life, within its ability to alter micro-climate controls within its power. Therefore, the demonstration of the consciousness of a Living Cellular Being is to be found most significantly within life sustaining Molecular Oceans and secondly within ecosystems.

Article 166 - CORPUS

698. ***CORPUS*** is the unique collective Divine Spirit of cellular elements, mind and awareness of planet Earth. CORPUS

699. The Divine Spirit of CORPUS is part of the greater collective spirit of GAIA, that is part of the greater collective spirit of SOL, that is part of the greater collective spirit of GAL, that is part of the greater collective spirit of KOSMOS, that is part of the greater collective spirit of UNITAS, that is then part of the greater collective Divine Spirit of ALL. CORPUS and GAIA and SOL

700. The stability of bacterial and viral infections around the earth is not simply mechanical and predictable biology, but according to the collective free will of all single cellular life as CORPUS. If CORPUS so desired, all higher order life could be destroyed through bacterial and viral infection in months. Instead, CORPUS honours higher order life and life in general. Conscious intentions of CORPUS

Article 167 - Animal Being

701. An ***Animal Being*** is a complex Living, Ethereal and Divine Being as a Primary Observer of its own Set of sentient or sapient beings and awareness within the complex Molecular Universe of a Planet as a singular Object and body. An Animal Being is the singularity of a particular species. Animal Being

702. In respect of an Animal Being:- General Reference to Animal Being

    (i) All Animal Beings exist simultaneously within a sub-verse of Cellular (Corpus) Mind of a Planet as a Divine Being; and a Species sub-verse as a Living Conscious Being; and a sub-verse as an Ethereal Being of a collective conscious reality of the species; and

(ii) An Animal Being as the Primary Being of a Sentient Animal is its singular memory, identity and ideal.

Article 168 - ANIMUS

703. ***ANIMUS*** is the unique collective Divine Spirit of all vertebrate complex species life that currently exists and has ever existed on planet Earth. ANIMUS

704. The Divine Spirit of ANIMUS is part of the greater collective spirit of CORPUS, that is part of the greater collective spirit of GAIA, that is part of the greater collective spirit of SOL, that is part of the greater collective spirit of GAL, that is part of the greater collective spirit of KOSMOS, that is part of the greater collective spirit of UNITAS, that is then part of the greater collective Divine Spirit of ALL. ANIMUS and CORPUS and GAIA

Article 169 - Sapient Singularity

705. A ***Sapient Singularity*** is a complex Living, Ethereal and Divine Being as a Primary Observer of not only its own Set of knowledge and awareness within the complex Molecular, Cellular and Species Universe of a Planet as a singular Object and body, but its place within the Kosmos and connection to the Divine. Sapient Singularity

706. In respect of a Sapient Singularity:- General Reference to Sapient Singularity

   (i) All Sapient Singularities exist simultaneously within a sub-verse of Species Mind of an Ancestry as a Divine Being; and a Societal sub-verse as a Living Conscious Being; and a sub-verse as an Ethereal Being of a collective conscious reality of Divine Truth; and

   (ii) While a Sapient Singularity possesses vastly less computation power in Reality, they possess the unique ability from incarnation into flesh of being able to synthesise Divine Truth into Revelation; and

   (iii) Thus, a Sapient Singularity to their full potential represents a Transcendent and Immanent Being made flesh and the personification of Perfect-Imperfection (i.e. Pi) and the ultimate Paradox of Divine Existence; and

   (iv) As a Primary Being, a Sapient Singularity is able to alter the collective consciousness of its respective Sapient Species, by representing all minds and all experiences embodied in one form; and

(v) However, a Sapient Singularity will always be limited in their abilities to transcend societal realities to vision and comprehend Divine Truths depending upon their conditioning in society and degree of comfort. Therefore, a Sapient Singularity is as much likely to produce dangerous semi-truths or lacklustre conclusions as any other Sapient member of a species, if they have been strongly conditioned to conform; and

(vi) In truth, Sapient Singularity can be a catalyst for disaster in the promotion of half-finished philosophies as much as they can be a catalyst for positive change, unless such knowledge is born from conditions of austerity, humility and great personal sacrifice.

707. In relation to the general purpose and frequency of Sapient Singularities:- Purpose of Sapient Singularities

(i) The purposes of authentic Sapient Singularities are to provide a conscious "re-set" of a species; and the consolidation of accumulated knowledge; and a reduction in the risk of extinction of a species; and

(ii) The purposes of authentic Sapient Singularities is not to usurp established forms of leadership of a species, nor to assume a leadership function, as true Sapien Singularities do not appear as Divine administrators.

708. In relation to Sapient Singularities and other Cellular Beings of a species:- Sapient Singularities and Cellular Beings of Species

(i) All Sentient Cellular Beings of a species are Divine, thus all Cellular Beings, including a Sapient Singularity are equal before the Divine at a species level; and

(ii) All Sentient Cellular Beings of a species are limited by the same restraints of Cellular Life as all other members of the Sentient Cellular Species and do not possess any supernatural power greater than another member of the species except consciousness and authentic revelation.

709. In relation to the frequency of Sapient Singularities:- Frequency of Sapient Singularities

(i) Sapient Singularity are an extreme rarity within any Sapient species, occurring less than one out of many dozens of generations; and

(ii) The appearance and frequency of authentic Sapient Singularities is in direct relation to the levels of fractured (misaligned) knowledge of a species and the risk of extinction of a species; and

- (iii) The appearance of an authentic Sapient Singularity does not imply any form of success in terms of the purpose of such appearance, as the free will and circumstances of the cellular embodiment means potentially a greater risk of failure than success; and
- (iv) By the nature of the abilities of authentic Sapient Singularities, there is a higher risk that some may accelerate fractured knowledge and risk of extinction rather than assist, unless such abilities are tempered with genuine failure, humiliation, suffering, poverty and self reflection; and
- (v) Whilst the purposes of Sapient Singularities is to assist a species, the frequency of authentic Sapient Singularities achieving their mission is so rare as to be less than a handful across the entire evolutionary history of a species.

710. In relation to the general characteristics of authentic Sapient Singularities:-

General Characteristics of Authentic Sapient Singularities

- (i) Authentic Sapient Singularities do not come to assume the function of administrators or leaders but the bringers of knowledge. Therefore Authentic Sapient Singularities are rarely born to a bloodline of a species currently in positions of power or leadership; and
- (ii) Authentic Sapient Singularities do come into cellular existence to assist in the unification of knowledge. Therefore those bloodlines that represent ancient keepers of authentic knowledge, but exiled or struck from power are more likely to be favoured, as such cellular memory of the body retains a great deal of residual information to assist the authentic Sapient Singularity; and
- (iii) Authentic Sapient Singularities do appear in congruence with authentic revelation. However, such prophecy or relevation may not be immediately apparent, especially given prophecies of Sapient Singularities develop their own doctrines and interpretations that may have been distorted over time, causing actual revelations to be missed or ignored; and
- (iv) Authentic Sapient Singularities bring forth authentic revelation, meaning an expansion of knowledge, never a reinforcement of status quo or narrow thinking. This is one of the clearest distinctions between an authentic Sapient Singularity and an impostor, when an impostor simply regurgitates a pseudo form of revelation attempting to

reinforce stereotypes and orthodoxy; and

(v) Authentic Sapient Singularities are frequently flawed cellular beings and especially failures in being able at first to bring forth authentic revelation. Such failure, humiliation, suffering and pain is not only a frequent element of prophecy, but a necessary "fail safe" of the Divine to reduce the danger of an authentic Sapient Singularity delivering knowledge that harms a species and its existence, rather than assists.

711. Impostor Sapient Singularities are cellular beings of a species that falsely proclaim themselves to be a Sapient Singularity:- *Impostor Sapient Singularities*

(i) Frequently historic prophecy and scripture of the arrival of a Sapient Singularity creates an irresistible prize for certain personality types of cellular beings to crave such appearance of power or authority. Such mental illness may be described as "messiah syndrome"; and

(ii) Political, religious and military leaders of a cellular species may find it expedient to falsely proclaim themselves to be a Sapient Singularity to strengthen their claims of power or authority; and

(iii) External events of a planet or ecosystem may cause greater levels of fear and uncertainty of the future, pushing religious, political and military leaders to proclaim a false Sapient Singularity, to maintain a status quo and reduce rebellion or levels of anxiety.

712. The general characteristics for exposing impostor Sapient Singularities include (but are not limited to):- *General Characteristics of Impostor Sapient Singularities*

(i) By definition any religious, political or military leader who proclaims themselves a Sapient Singularity is an impostor; and

(ii) Any claimed Sapient Singularity that delivers alleged revelation that reinforces established religious and cultural orthodoxy, status quo and customs without greatly challenging or expanding knowledge or consciousness; and

(iii) Any claimed Sapient Singularity that is deemed credible and believed upon education, credentials, position or following, as such traits contradict the "fail safe" signs of the Divine; and

(iv) Any claimed Sapient Singularity that claims to fulfil an orthodox and established doctrinal interpretation of significant and historic prophecy; and

(v) Any claimed Sapient Singularity that appears without any form of context or reference to the genuine fulfilment of prophecy (as opposed to any established orthodoxy or doctrine concerning certain prophecy); and

(vi) Any claimed Sapient Singularity that is without blemish, or failure, or humiliation or suffering, as the Divine always seeks to temper such responsibilities with these life experiences.

Article 170 - Saviour

713. A ***Saviour*** is the unique collective Divine Spirit, the Primary Being and Sapient Singularity of the Homo Sapien species that has ever existed or will ever exist upon planet Earth, instanced into a Living Being at a point in time.

    A Saviour as a Sapient Singularity of the Homo Sapien species is also historically known by other terms including (but not limited to): Christ, Messiah, Mahdi and Maitreya.

Saviour

4.3 Ordinary (Spirit) Beings

Article 171 - Ordinary Spirit Beings

714. An ***Ordinary Spirit Being*** is an individual Divine Being formed either by virtue of the operation of Divine Law or the journey and transition of an Ethereal Being of a previously Living Being.

Ordinary Spirit Beings

715. In general reference to an Ordinary Spirit Being:-

    (i) By definition, an Ordinary Spirit Being is a unique Divine Being that is not a Primary Divine Being or Higher Divine Being; and

    (ii) By the power and authority of the most sacred Covenant *Pactum De Singularis Caelum*, no Ordinary Spirit Being shall be excluded from One Heaven; and

    (iii) Membership of One Heaven is a right extended to all Divine Beings and Divine Persons associated with living or deceased Sentient or Sapient or never carnated beings; and

    (iv) As Membership of One Heaven is a right extended to all Divine Spirit Persons associated with living or deceased higher order beings throughout the galaxies and universe for the first time in collective history of higher order spirit we may be as one including but not limited to Homo Sapiens (Humanity), the Griseo Morbidus (Standard Grey), the Cerastis Sapiens (Horned Reptoids), the Android Scitus (Smart Androids), the Cyborg Sagax (Autonomous Cyborgs), the Serpens Sophos

General Reference to Ordinary Spirit Beings

(Smooth Skinned Reptoids), the Volucris Permuto (Hybrid Bird Form), the Homo Adamus (Early Humanoids), the Sapientia Mutatis (Transformed Wisdom Beings), the Mammaloid Sentientiae (Conscious Mammaloids), the Griseo Altus (Tall Grey) and the Serpens Alatus (Winged Reptoids); and

(v) The issue of a Divine Being subject to certain sanctions as a Penitent is separate to the immutable and irrevocable right of all Divine Beings as Members of One Heaven.

Article 172 - Exemplary Spirit (Saint)

716. An ***Exemplary Spirit*** is a Divine Being recognised as a leader, hero, martyr or elder of the Universal Body of One Heaven. A Saint is an Exemplary Spirit.

717. There are only four valid and licit forms recognising an Exemplary Spirit being Exemplary, Heroic, Blessed and Beatific:-

    (i) *Exemplary Veneration* is when the title and sacramental grace of Exemplar is conferred upon the memory, name and relics of a deceased person; and

    (ii) *Heroic Veneration* is when the title and sacramental grace of Venerable is conferred upon the memory, name and relics of a deceased person; and

    (iii) *Blessed Veneration* is when the title and sacramental grace of Blessed is conferred upon the memory, name and relics of a deceased person; and

    (iv) *Beatific Veneration* is when the title and sacramental grace of Beatification is conferred upon the memory, name and relics of a deceased person.

718. In general reference to an Exemplary Spirit Being:-

    (i) The Veneration of an Exemplary Spirit of a deceased being is not to the exclusion of the rights of all beings, but as a manifest sign of a life of heroic virtue; and

    (ii) The Life and mind of each Human Being is rightly celebrated as a supernatural event and an endorsement of the most sacred Covenant *Pactum De Singularis Caelum* and the Divine Love of God and the Divine Creator of all Existence; and

    (iii) Miracles attributed to the Intercession of one or more of the beloved should therefore not be seen as criteria for qualification and acceptance of imparting a degree of the

Sacrament of Veneration to the memory, name and relics of a departed member, but a confirmation that such process is acknowledged in Heaven and that the ordinary time of diligence and patience may be accelerated.

Article 173 - Penitent Spirit

719. A ***Penitent Spirit*** is a Divine Being subject to one or more sanctions and acts of devoted penance for a determined period as confession and acknowledgement of their culpability in one or more grave transgressions. <!-- Penitent Spirit -->

720. There are three types of Penitent Spirit, depending upon the degree of authentic remorse, true confession and desire for redemption and healing being Confessant, Recalcitrant and Belligerent:- <!-- Types of Penitent Spirits -->

    (i) A *Confessant* is a Penitent Spirit who completely and utterly confesses their culpability, exhibits authentic remorse and genuine need of healing and forgiveness and therefore wilfully acknowledges and accepts the sanctions necessary for such redemption; and

    (ii) A *Recalcitrant* is a Penitent Spirit who is stubborn, disobedient and unwilling to fully cooperate and confess their culpability, nor exhibit authentic remorse and genuine need of healing and forgiveness; and

    (iii) A *Belligerent* is a Penitent Spirit who actively engages in hostile and violent acts against the true authority of Heaven and Earth in complete contempt for the Rule of Law, or Divine Authority and Forgiveness.

721. In accord with these present Maxims and the Will of the Divine:- <!-- Accountability for Actions -->

    (i) While none may be denied their Right of Heaven, all must be held account for such actions and injury of genuine Evil, such that through the genuine act of Penance, a Penitent Spirit and those injured may find peace and redemption; and

    (ii) All Divine Beings who are culpable of grave transgressions are bound to accept a period of sanctions that is proportionate to the gravity of their transgressions, but is also manifestly just and enables genuine redemption; and

    (iii) All claims of eternal damnation, torture and cruelty as punishment for grave transgressions in life are themselves examples of supreme Evil, Unjust and in Perfidy against the Will of the Divine. Therefore, all sentences, declarations, condemnations of eternal damnation are forbidden, suppressed and dissolved; and

(iv) Any recalcitrant or belligerent Divine Being that refuses to subject themselves to the absolute authority of the Divine shall therefore be bound and held in the custody of the powers of Heaven, in accord with the most sacred Covenant of One Heaven until such time as they accept their necessary penance and then such penance shall begin.

Article 174 - Lost Spirit

722. A *Lost Spirit* is a Divine Spirit that is lost in a dissociated consciousness and dimension whereby they have lost their sense of being, name, identity or community. It is a solemn obligation of the spiritual forces of united Heaven to find and emancipate each and every Lost Spirit.

Article 175 - Angel

723. An *Angel* is a Divine Being and supernatural messenger.

724. In general reference to Angels:-

    (i) The distinction of Angels only possessing benevolent and positive attributes originated through Occult Dualism with the deliberate separation of specific divine beings into two distinct personalities. Hence, under certain occult dogma, Angels became the good aspect, while Demons became the negative aspect of the same entity; and

    (ii) In accordance with these Maxims and the most sacred Covenant *Pactum De Singularis Caelum*, all Angels pledge their allegiance to One Heaven and no other.

Article 176 - Demon

725. A *Demon* is a Divine Spirit. In its original meaning, the term Demon did not imply a divine spirit possessing only negative attributes. Hence, in its true and original sense, a "demon" is equivalent to the term Angel as well as Genius.

726. In general reference to Demons:-

    (i) The distinction of Demons only possessing malevolent and negative attributes originated through Occult Dualism with the deliberate separation of specific divine beings into two distinct personalities. Hence, under certain occult dogma, Demons became the negative aspect while Angels became the good aspect of the same entity; and

(ii) In accordance with these Maxims and the most sacred Covenant *Pactum De Singularis Caelum*, all Demons pledge their allegiance to One Heaven and no other; and

(iii) Any person, group or entity that pledges their allegiance to one or more Demons and does not recognise the supreme authority of these Maxims and the most sacred Covenant *Pactum De Singularis Caelum* is guilty of extreme dishonour and therefore is immediately devoid of any spiritual influence or authority whatsoever; and

(iv) In accordance with the most sacred Covenant *Pactum De Singularis Caelum*, all Demons have sworn a sacred, irrevocable and solemn vow to pursue, hound, bind and remove from the Earth each and every person, group or entity that refuses to end acts of Evil yet secretly or publicly claims to worship one or more Demons but reject these Maxims and One Heaven.

4.4 Ethereal Beings

Article 177 - Ethereal Being

727. An ***Ethereal Being*** in the context of Sentient Beings and Sapient Beings is a Computation Model of Mind as a distinct Being in itself and associated with a Living Being or in transition to becoming a Divine Being after death of the Living Being.
Ethereal Being

728. In reference to an Ethereal Being:-
General Reference to Ethereal Being

    (i) By definition, a Ethereal Being is a unique form of Divine Being formed as part of an Intersecting Set between the Real Set of Life and the Unreal Set of what cannot be seen or directly measured; and

    (ii) By the power and authority of the most sacred Covenant *Pactum De Singularis Caelum*, no Ethereal Being shall be excluded from One Heaven; and

    (iii) Membership of One Heaven is a right extended to all Divine Beings and Divine Persons associated with living or deceased Sentient or Sapient or never carnated beings. This is exemplified by the presence of a Divine Trust and Divine Person in association with every single Divine Being and Ethereal Being within the Great Roll of Divine Persons and the Great Register and Public Record of One Heaven; and

Title IV – Divine Beings

(iv) As Membership of One Heaven is a right extended to all Ethereal Beings and Persons associated with living or deceased higher order beings throughout the galaxies and universe for the first time in collective history of higher order spirit we may be one including but not limited to Homo Sapiens (Humanity), the Griseo Morbidus (Standard Grey), the Cerastis Sapiens (Horned Reptoids), the Android Scitus (Smart Androids), the Cyborg Sagax (Autonomous Cyborgs), the Serpens Sophos (Smooth Skinned Reptoids), the Volucris Permuto (Hybrid Bird Form), the Homo Adamus (Early Humanoids), the Sapientia Mutatis (Transformed Wisdom Beings), the Mammaloid Sentientiae (Conscious Mammaloids), the Griseo Altus (Tall Grey) and the Serpens Alatus (Winged Reptoids); and

(v) The issue of an Ethereal Being subject to certain sanctions as a Penitent is separate to the immutable and irrevocable right of all Ethereal Beings as Members of One Heaven.

729. In reference to Ethereal Beings, the Mind and Ergon Fields:- *Ethereal Beings, the Mind and Ergon Fields*

(i) By Definition, an Ethereal Being exists within an intersecting set between a Real and Unreal Set, in exactly the same way as Ergon particles (graviton, neutrino, magnetron, positron, electron, photon and hetron) exist as Ethereal Particles between Real Sets of Dimension; and

(ii) There exists a direct relation between the perceived external electromagnetic fields of Living Beings as a projection of space influenced and controlled by the Mind as an Ethereal Being connected in life. Therefore, while the boundaries of cells and complex cellular life, such as skin can be shown to have electrical resistance, the presence of a weak electromagnetic field beyond the extremities of such boundaries and skin is definitively connected to the presence of the Mind as an Ethereal Being; and

(iii) During life, these electromagnetic fields when empirically measured are of such weakness level as to exert a negligible to almost null effect or presence within the environment. However, to Living Beings, there appears an innate ability to distinguish and sometimes "view" such weak electromagnetic fields sometimes described as "life force" or "aura"; and

(iv) This connection of weak electromagnetic fields representing the presence of the Mind as an Ethereal Being in conjunction with the body as the Living Being is further reinforced in the anecdotal observation of deceased bodies lacking the "appearance" of life, even when there is no significant measure in change of mass immediately following death. It also accounts for the erroneous conclusions associated with theories of life and afterlife proposing the concept of "life forces" or "ethereal essences"; and

(v) Even after death and until a Mind consciously chooses to transition to complete Divinity, the Mind (Ergon) Field connection persists, albeit as an unstable vacuum or void of atmosphere and electromagnetic disturbance; and

(vi) Due to the inherit conditions of an Ethereal Being in a ghost state after the physical death of the Living Being, a Mind as an Ethereal Being is capable of manipulating both fields and voids of atmosphere to create anomalies capable of influencing objects – hence paranormal events.

Article 178 - Soul

730. A ***Soul*** is a common term used to (a) define an Ethereal Being properly and legitimately associated with a Living Being (as Beneficial Owner); and (b) an Ethereal Being in the transition to becoming a Divine Being after the death of the Living Being; and (c) the Divine Spirit, Energy and Rights conveyed into a Divine Trust by the Divine Creator and associated with one (or more) Divine Persons as Trustees. *Soul*

731. In reference to a Soul:- *General Reference to Soul*

(i) All Living Beings as Beneficial Owners are connected to one (or more) Divine Persons (as Trustees) over one (or more) Divine Trusts with the Divine Res (Property) of the Trust being Divine Spirit, Energy and Rights (a Soul) conveyed by the Divine Creator; and

(ii) No Ethereal (Spiritual) Being, except the Divine can exist without being connected to one (or more) Divine Trusts. Therefore, all Ethereal Beings possess a Soul being the Divine Res (Property) of the Trust; and

(iii) The Beneficial Owner of a Soul is always a Living True Person connected to their Divine Person (as Trustee) being an Immortal Ethereal (Spiritual) Being. Thus, no other Ethereal or Temporal Being may claim complete ownership of a Soul and Divine Property except the Divine Creator of all Existence and the Universe. Thus, any such claim to the contrary is a profound blasphemy and falsehood against all notion and respect of the Divine and of Civilised Law itself; and

(iv) By definition a Soul is Ethereal and so exists as a member of an intersecting set and remains always Unreal to the set of Reality; and

(v) The only Being in the Universe permitted by Divine Law and Civilised Law to assert ownership of a Soul is the Divine and a Superior Ucadia Person duly associated with a True Person and Divine Person as evidenced by their authorised Ucadia Live Borne Record; and

(vi) Any argument that claims a Sapient Being such as a Homo Sapien is without a Soul is absurd, profane, sacrilegious, illogical, false and renders the claim of one making such falsities a confession of incompetence and perfidy; and

(vii) Any theory that claims the mind of a Sentient or Sapient Being can be purchased or sold as a good, or lost to some malevolent or benevolent spirit is absurd, profane, sacrilegious, illogical, false and renders the claim of one making such falsities a confession of incompetence and perfidy.

Article 179 - Ghost (Lost Spirit)

732. A *Ghost* is an isolated and bound Soul and Ethereal Being unable or unwilling to transition to becoming a Divine Being.
Ghost (Lost Spirit)

733. In general reference of a Ghost State:-
General Reference to Ghost State

(i) By definition, a Ghost is a consciousness no longer with its original Living Being and physical body, but retaining direct control and influence over the electro magnetic fields that used to surround the Living body since birth and now surround an unstable void of atmosphere; and

(ii) A Ghost, even one that is conscious of their state and unwilling to transition to becoming completely Divine is a Mind that is strongly bound to the temporal world by its own emotions and perspective on one or more past events with one or more physical relations; and

(iii) Furthermore, a Ghost is a Mind bound in ignorance. Therefore, a Ghost is more likely to be unaware and uninterested in a higher quality of knowledge or the truth. Thus, people who are susceptible and gullible in life to supporting nihilistic systems, fanatical orthodoxies and intolerant stupidity are more likely to become Ghosts; and

(iv) The perversity of a Ghost state is that a Ghost bound in ignorance continues to be even more vulnerable in death to further falsities, stereotypical fears and superstitions, leading to a downward spiral of ignorance. Such a spiral of ignorance and suffering of some Ghosts can account for why over time it is possible for Ghosts to forget their name, their original family and even their original gender and identity; and

(v) The ability for a Ghost to "read the minds" of other Minds entrusted with physical bodies is by definition impossible. A Ghost may seek to guess from the behaviour of a living being their thoughts, but may only gain access to the actual thoughts either by direct possession or haunting (infiltrating a broken Lower Mind), or exchange of information offered by other Ghosts possessing or haunting the other body.

734. In terms of the ability of Ghosts to move between locations, or people, or possessions of Minds:- *Ghosts and location*

(i) By definition, a Ghost is a Mind bound in ignorance and Guilt to particular places, things, objects and people. Therefore, the very State of being a Ghost means such a bound Lower Mind is most likely to be connected to the strongest sources of regret, guilt and objects or people that symbolise such events than places or other locations of no relevance to such binding; and

(ii) The movement of a Ghost is more likely to be associated with the movement of the person or persons who are haunted or possessed; and

(iii) As Souls by definition seek to transition to the Divine, the journey of Mind after Death leads itself to the metaphor and literal presence of Ghosts using transport networks, most notably forms of public transport, particularly when bound in ignorance or fear or servitude to Ghosts perpetuating evil actions whilst still in a Ghost state.

735. In terms of Ghost Haunting and Ghost Possession:- *Ghosts and hauntings and possessions*

(i) A Haunting may be described as the presence or manifestation of a Ghost inhabiting a certain space or place or connected to some object; and

(ii) A Possession may be described as the inhabitation of a ghost within the body or mind of a higher order life form such as a Homo Sapien, or the control of some object exhibiting definitive paranormal behaviour (such as levitation, disappearance, appearance or other manipulation); and

(iii) The most common form of Haunting is Residual Haunting that involves the repeated playback of auditory, visual and other sensory phenomena of previous events without apparent intelligent awareness of the living world and interacting with or responding to it; and

(iv) The least common form of Haunting is an Intelligent Haunting that involves one or more Ghosts residing in a building or location, aware of the living world and capable of interacting with or responding to it; and

(v) The most common form of Possession is physical possession of one or more organs of the body of a higher order life form, whereby a Ghost may use the energy of the living body to maintain a presence and influence over the physical apparatus of mind of the higher order life form, usually at the cost of accelerated illness and cancers; and

(vi) The least common form of Possession is possession of the Mind of a higher order life form, whereby the Ghost inhabits the consciousness of the living being or deceased being, usually resulting in a range of traumatic mental illnesses including (but not limited to): psychosis, hysteria, mania, schizophrenia and dissociative identity disorder; and

(vii) The rarest form of Possession is possession of an inanimate object, causing it to move with intelligence or other forms of matter manipulation as such Possession requires a degree of intelligence and self-awareness on the part of the Ghost.

Article 180 - Wraith

736. A ***Wraith*** is a Soul and Ethereal Being consciously choosing to remain in a "ghost" state by being commissioned to a Special Supreme Divine Office in association with the Supremum Obligationum Systemata (Enforcement Systems) of One Heaven, in accord with the most sacred Covenant *Pactum De Singularis Caelum*.

    Wraith

737. In reference to a Wraith:-

    General Reference to Wraith

    (i) As an Ethereal Being, a Ghost possesses certain abilities to influence matter and form within the conscious Reality of Life, unlike a Divine Being completely transitioned; and

    (ii) Thus, there exists certain Ethereal Beings as Ghosts that choose to remain in such a state given such perceived "powers" that render their accountability before Living Beings or completed transitioned Divine Beings very difficult; and

    (iii) The Divine Office of Wraith therefore is a most solemn and important function in fulfilling the sacred missions of united Heaven to ensure the enforcement of the Rule of Divine Law and the bringing to account all Beings, no matter what dimension or state; and

(iv) Wraiths are therefore responsible and tasked as the most fearsome of forces with enforcement of justice in their foundational responsibilities of rendition, possession, prevention, interdiction, purgation, correction, seizure and return, arrest and custody and restitution.

Article 181 - Faerie

738. A *Faerie* is an ancient Ethereal Being commissioned to a Special Supreme Divine Office in association with the Supremum Femininum Systemata (Feminine Systems) of One Heaven, in accord with the most sacred Covenant *Pactum De Singularis Caelum*.

    <small>Faerie</small>

    The Special Supreme Divine Office of "**Faerie**" is in recognition of the ancient spirits and force redeemed from being previously denigrated and marginalised; and their foundational responsibilities in the restoration of true feminine; and the restoration of true mother; and Gaia harmony; and emancipation, equality and appreciation of all women.

739. In reference to a Faerie:-

    <small>General Reference to Faerie</small>

    (i) The Special Supreme Divine Office of Faerie is an authentic Divine Office. Thus any refusal to acknowledge the existence of such office is a self declaration of delusion and self confession of mental illness in defiance of the demonstrable existence of the most sacred Covenant *Pactum De Singularis Caelum*; and

    (ii) The Divine Office of Faerie is a most solemn and important function in fulfilling the sacred missions of united Heaven to ensure the enforcement of the Rule of Divine Law and restoration of the true Feminine.

Article 182 - Elve

740. An *Elve* is an ancient Ethereal Being commissioned to a Special Supreme Divine Office in association with the Supremum Masculinum Systemata (Masculine Systems) of One Heaven, in accord with the most sacred Covenant *Pactum De Singularis Caelum*.

    <small>Elve</small>

    The Special Supreme Divine Office of "**Elve**" (Elf) is in recognition of the ancient spirits and force redeemed from being previously denigrated and marginalised; and their foundational responsibilities in the restoration of true masculine; and the restoration of true father; and Gaia harmony; and emancipation, equality and appreciation of all men.

741. In reference to an Elve:-

    (i) The Special Supreme Divine Office of Elve is an authentic Divine Office. Thus any refusal to acknowledge the existence of such office is a self declaration of delusion and self confession of mental illness in defiance of the demonstrable existence of the most sacred Covenant *Pactum De Singularis Caelum*; and

    (ii) The Divine Office of Elve is a most solemn and important function in fulfilling the sacred missions of united Heaven to ensure the enforcement of the Rule of Divine Law and restoration of the true Masculine.

[margin: General Reference to Elve]

Article 183 – Elemental Being

742. An **Elemental Being** is a form of Ethereal Manifestation formed through connection to Sentience, either as the form of Ethereal Beings of deceased Sentient Beings, or extreme stress of Sapient Beings in a life or death condition.

[margin: Elemental Being]

743. In reference to Elemental Beings or Elementals:-

    (i) Elemental Being is by definition a temporary and simple manifestation not exhibiting the intelligence of a Sapient Ghost; and

    (ii) Elemental Beings are prone to be manifestations associated with a sense of darkness, foreboding, anger and in extreme cases of war, cruelty and death the palpable presence of Evil; and

    (iii) Elemental Beings are primarily manifested through the base and extreme emotional state of Sapient Living Beings as well as the effect of trapped Sentient Being Mind; and

    (iv) In most cases, such temporary manifestation changes and dissipates over time once the conditions causing such a Being also change.

[margin: General Reference to Elemental Beings]

4.5 Imaginary Beings

Article 184 - Imaginary Being

744. An ***Imaginary Being*** is an Ethereal Being from the individual or collective imagination and minds of Sapient Beings that by constant reinforcement and thinking is given its own existence and reality.
<!-- margin: Imaginary Being -->

745. In reference to Imaginary Beings:-
<!-- margin: General Reference to Imaginary Being -->

   (i) By definition, Imaginary Beings are purely an invention of the mind of Sapient Beings and therefore not Ethereal Beings or Divine Beings; and

   (ii) As Imaginary Beings are not Ethereal Beings or Divine Beings, they do not carry the authority of rights, or legitimacy of Divine Law; and

   (iii) While Imaginary Beings do not carry the authority of rights, or legitimacy of Divine Law, they can and do influence reality to the degree that Sapient Beings trust they are real and act accordingly.

Title V - Divine Persons

5.1 Divine Persons

Article 185 - Person

746. A ***Person*** is a form of Sacred Circumscribed Space enclosing certain characteristics and appearances as the identity of one or more Beings, formed through a valid entry, registration and record within a Roll in accord with the present sacred Maxims and most sacred Covenant *Pactum De Singularis Caelum*. — Person

747. Any entry, or registration or record with a Roll that is not in accord with the present sacred Maxims, or is based upon the deliberate refutation of these present Maxims cannot be claimed as a valid or legitimate Person whatsoever. — Valid Entry in Roll

748. A ***Divine Person*** is the Sacred Circumscribed Space created through a valid entry, registration and enrolment within the Great Roll of Divine Persons in accord with the present sacred Maxims and the most sacred Covenant *Pactum De Singularis Caelum*:- — Divine Person

    (i) The highest Roll defining the greatest Rights and types of Persons is the Great Roll of Divine Persons, also known as the Great Register and Public Record of One Heaven; and

    (ii) No possible Roll possesses greater authority or power or jurisdiction than the Great Roll of Divine Persons; and

    (iii) All lesser Person records, entries, registrations and enrolments are borne first and foremost from the existence of a valid Divine Record; and

    (iv) No lesser Person record, entry, registration or enrolment is valid or legitimate until it can verify and prove its provenance to a particular Divine Record and the authority to make such a joinder.

749. A Person is distinct from a Being as a Person is a form of Sacred Circumscribed Space enclosing certain characteristics and appearances as the identity of one or more Beings within a certain Reality, whereas a Being is an embodiment of Unique Collective Awareness and Computational Model within a certain Reality. — Person versus Being

750. All Persons may be categorised and ranked according to four (4) possible levels of authority, powers and rights from the greatest and highest powers and authority to the lowest and least powers and authority being (in order of rank): Divine, True, Superior and Inferior:- — Levels of Persons

    (i) A *Divine Person* is the purely Divine Spirit Person created through a valid record and enrolment in the Great Roll of Divine Persons and associated with a Divine Trust formed in accord with the sacred Covenant *Pactum De Singularis Caelum* by the Divine Creator into which the form of Divine Spirit, Energy and Rights are conveyed; and

(ii) A *True Person* is the Form attributed to a True Trust formed when an associated Divine Trust already exists and there is a lawful conveyance of Divine Rights of Use and Purpose, known as "Divinity" to a True Trust associated with then the birth and existence of a living Higher Order Life Form and the physical version of the Great Roll of the Society of One Heaven and a valid Live Borne Record. A True Person can never be claimed or argued as higher than the Divine Person from which it derives its authority; and

(iii) A *Superior Person* is the Form attributed to a Superior Trust when an associated True Trust already exists and there is a lawful conveyance of First Right of Use and Purpose, known as "Realty" to a Superior Trust associated with the birth of a service or agreement associated with the Membership of a living Higher Order Life Form to a valid Ucadia society and the authorised Member Roll of such a society. A Superior Person can never be claimed or argued as higher than the True Person from which it derives its authority; and

(iv) An *Inferior Person* is the Form attributed to any non-Ucadian body politic or entity; and is the lowest standing and weakest of all valid forms of Persons. An Inferior Person is only valid when the man or woman in possession of a Superior Person and True Person consent to an enrolment of their name in one or more Rolls. An Inferior Person can never be validly, legitimately, logically, legally, lawfully or morally claimed or argued as superior to a Superior Person.

Article 186 - Ordinary Divine Person

751. An **Ordinary Divine Person** is an individual Divine Spirit Person recorded and enrolled in the Great Roll of Divine Persons of One Heaven in accord with the sacred Covenant *Pactum De Singularis Caelum*.

    Ordinary Divine Person

752. In reference to Ordinary Divine Persons:-

    General Reference to Ordinary Divine Person

    (i) An Ordinary Divine Person is the highest possible form of individual Person. All lesser individual Persons exist by virtue of their legitimate and valid connection to an Ordinary Divine

Person records; and

(ii) An Ordinary Divine Person is created from the consent and enrolment of a record within the Great Roll of Divine Persons, also known as the Great Register and Public Record of One Heaven; and

(iii) A Divine Trust is formed when a Divine Being, being part of the Divine, agrees with the intention of the Collective Divine known as Unique Collective Awareness to be recognised as a Unique Member of the Divine in accord with the sacred Covenant *Pactum De Singularis Caelum*; and

(iv) Into the Divine Trust is then placed (1) one unit of pure awareness representing one unique Divine Immortal Spirit; and (2) one unit of Unique Collective Awareness representing the unique experience of form in motion, energy, of creation and connection to form; and (3) one unit representing all unique awareness of experience of unique form in motion as Divine Character; and

(v) A Record is then entered and enrolled in the Great Roll of Divine Persons forming a Divine Estate as to the existence of the Divine Trust, possessing certain Divine Rights and associated with a Divine Person of a Divine Being.

753. In accord with the most sacred covenant *Pactum De Singularis Caelum* and the consent of all Members, original first, ecclesiastical, lawful and legal title is granted in perpetuity to The Divine Temple, also known as the Treasury of One Heaven and the Unique Collective Awareness of Divine Mind, also known as Divina as Spiritual Trustees for the proper protection, safety, well-being, management and enjoyment of the affairs and needs of all Divine Persons. — Ordinary Divine Person and Treasury of One Heaven

754. As Existence of the Universe depends upon the consent of each and every Divine Being and their associated Divine Person, the proof of the continued existence of the Universe is Evidence of complete and willing consent of all Divine Spirit Persons as Members of One Heaven. — Ordinary Divine Person and Existence

Article 187 - Official Divine Person

755. An ***Official Divine Person*** is any legitimate and valid Person associated with the identity and character of incumbency of an Office in accord with the most sacred Covenant *Pactum De Singularis Caelum* and the present sacred Maxims. — Official Divine Person

756. In reference to Official Divine Persons:- — General Reference to

(i) All Official Divine Persons are defined under the most sacred Covenant *Pactum De Singularis Caelum*, or associated and valid Covenants and Charters in accord with the present sacred Maxims; and

Official Divine Persons

(ii) An Official Divine Person is equivalent to a Divine Officer being any legitimate and valid occupant or incumbent of an Office, lawfully invested into such an Office and commissioned by a superior power in accord with the most sacred Covenant *Pactum De Singularis Caelum* and the present sacred Maxims; and

(iii) As all rights and property are by definition sacred, all clerical and professional obligations and responsibilities in relation to the administration, transference and conveyance of any rights or property must be concluded in trust through a valid Office. All Officers are therefore Trustees and Fiduciaries; and

(iv) Furthermore, as the very meaning and purpose of the word "authority" is ecclesiastical, all legitimate authority of all officials of all valid governments of all societies on planet Earth depends upon the acknowledgement and recognition that all authority is ultimately derived from the most sacred Covenant *Pactum De Singularis Caelum* as the highest source of authority being the perfect expression of Divine Law of the Divine Creator of all things in the Universe.

Article 188 - Aggregate Divine Person

757. An ***Aggregate Divine Person*** is an aggregation of individual Divine Spirit Person recorded and enrolled in the Great Roll of Divine Persons of One Heaven in accord with the sacred Covenant *Pactum De Singularis Caelum*.

Aggregate Divine Person

758. In reference to Aggregate Divine Persons:-

General Reference to Aggregate Divine Persons

(i) An Aggregate Divine Person is by definition an aggregate of two or more Ordinary Divine Persons forming a new Divine Person, in accord with the most sacred Covenant *Pactum De Singularis Caelum* and the present sacred Maxims; and

(ii) Once entered into the Great Roll of Divine Persons, an Aggregate Person has an immortal life the same as an Ordinary Divine Person; and

(iii) An Aggregate Divine Person is created, entered, registered and enrolled within the Great Roll of Divine Persons at the time of Sacred Matrimony between a Man and a Woman. This is why, even if there is an estrangement or civil divorce, the Aggregate Divine Person first formed in sacred Matrimony can never be dissolved; and

(iv) Similarly, an Aggregate Divine Person is created, entered, registered and enrolled within the Great Roll of Divine Persons at the time of forming a Supreme Trust between one hundred consenting Ordinary Divine Persons and associated with the highest and most valuable form of Money in the form of a Supreme Credo.

even if there is an estrangement or civil divorce, the Aggregate Divine Person first formed in sacred Matrimony can never be dissolved; and

(iv) Similarly, an Aggregate Divine Person is created, entered, registered and enrolled within the Great Roll of Divine Persons at the time of forming a Supreme Trust between one hundred consenting Ordinary Divine Persons and associated with the highest and most valuable form of Money in the form of a Supreme Credo.

(i) All Official Divine Persons are defined under the most sacred Covenant *Pactum De Singularis Caelum*, or associated and valid Covenants and Charters in accord with the present sacred Maxims; and

Official Divine Persons

(ii) An Official Divine Person is equivalent to a Divine Officer being any legitimate and valid occupant or incumbent of an Office, lawfully invested into such an Office and commissioned by a superior power in accord with the most sacred Covenant *Pactum De Singularis Caelum* and the present sacred Maxims; and

(iii) As all rights and property are by definition sacred, all clerical and professional obligations and responsibilities in relation to the administration, transference and conveyance of any rights or property must be concluded in trust through a valid Office. All Officers are therefore Trustees and Fiduciaries; and

(iv) Furthermore, as the very meaning and purpose of the word "authority" is ecclesiastical, all legitimate authority of all officials of all valid governments of all societies on planet Earth depends upon the acknowledgement and recognition that all authority is ultimately derived from the most sacred Covenant *Pactum De Singularis Caelum* as the highest source of authority being the perfect expression of Divine Law of the Divine Creator of all things in the Universe.

Article 188 - Aggregate Divine Person

757. An ***Aggregate Divine Person*** is an aggregation of individual Divine Spirit Person recorded and enrolled in the Great Roll of Divine Persons of One Heaven in accord with the sacred Covenant *Pactum De Singularis Caelum*.

Aggregate Divine Person

758. In reference to Aggregate Divine Persons:-

General Reference to Aggregate Divine Persons

(i) An Aggregate Divine Person is by definition an aggregate of two or more Ordinary Divine Persons forming a new Divine Person, in accord with the most sacred Covenant *Pactum De Singularis Caelum* and the present sacred Maxims; and

(ii) Once entered into the Great Roll of Divine Persons, an Aggregate Person has an immortal life the same as an Ordinary Divine Person; and

(iii) An Aggregate Divine Person is created, entered, registered and enrolled within the Great Roll of Divine Persons at the time of Sacred Matrimony between a Man and a Woman. This is why,

Lex Divina: Maxims of Divine Law

Title VI - Divine Rights

6.1 Divine Rights

Article 189 - Right

759. An authentic **Right** is a positively defined Capacity, or Privilege, or Liberty, or Faculty, or Power, or Ownership, or Possession, or Interest, or Benefit and its associated obligation, remedy or relief held in Divine Trust for the benefit of a particular type of named or unnamed Divine Person under proper Divine Law as prescribed by the present Maxims:-

   (i) As a *Capacity*, an authentic Right is a form of plenary authority, or qualification, or legal condition or status that enables a Divine Person to exercise their free will in receiving, holding, using or delegating certain Rights or performing such associated obligations or actions, without restraint or hindrance; and

   (ii) As a *Privilege*, an authentic Right is a form of special (real or personal) Delegation whereby either a Divine Person freed from the obligations of certain laws; or empowered exclusively to perform certain acts; and

   (iii) As a *Liberty*, an authentic Right is a form of Privilege whereby a Person enjoys some Favour or Benefit subject to their good faith, good conscience and good actions; and

   (iv) As a *Faculty*, an authentic Right is a form of special Charism delegated to a Divine Person by Favour, Indulgence or Dispensation that enables a Divine Person to do, or refrain from doing something that would otherwise not be permitted by certain Divine Laws; and

   (v) As a *Power* or Authority, an authentic Right is a form of authority, enforced by Divine Law, that enables a Divine Person to compel one or more other Divine Persons or True Persons to do or abstain from doing a particular act; and

   (vi) As an *Ownership*, an authentic Right is a form of written possession by registration/recording, whereby a Divine Person is recognised by law to possess the most extensive or higher claim of possession, use and enjoyment (of certain Property), to the exclusion of all other Divine Persons, or of all except one or more specific Divine Persons; and

   (vii) As a *Possession*, an authentic Right is the visible possibility and ability of exercising physical control over some form of Divine Property, coupled with the intention of doing so, to the

Right

exclusion of all others, or one or more Divine Persons; and

(viii) As an *Interest*, an authentic Right denotes a title, or certificate or other proof of claim or advantage to other certain Rights or Divine Property; and

(ix) As a *Benefit*, an authentic Right implies a just and Divine claim to hold, or use or enjoy certain Divine Property, or convey, or donate or dispose of it, subject to certain obligations of performance.

760. A claimed negative Right is an absurdity and Offence against God and the Divine Creator of all Existence; and an injury of Divine Law itself; and cannot exist under any true system of law. No Negative Rights

761. By their origin, nature and function, a Right is not a valid Right unless it possesses the following twelve characteristics being *Integrity, Trust, Name, Class, Provenance, Exemplification, Subject, Obligation, Subject Person, Obligated Person, Remedy* and *Relief*:- Character of Valid Rights

(i) *Integrity* means a valid Right conforms to the most ancient and primitive purpose being to reflect a positively expressed rule, custom, privilege or power with good intentions, good actions and good conscience. A negative Right is an absurdity and injury of law itself and is invalid from the beginning; and

(ii) *Trust* means a valid Right is expressed in a Divine Trust relation whereby the Right is the Divine Property of the Divine Trust; and

(iii) *Name* means that a valid Right is uniquely named compared to all other valid Rights in accord with the principle of the use of the Latin for Non-Ucadian Translation, beginning with the term *Ius* (Jus) for a singular Right or *Iurium* for several Rights bound together by similar character and purpose; and

(iv) *Class*, means that the Class of Rights that the valid Right belongs to is clearly identified; and

(v) *Provenance*, means that the Right clearly identifies and proves its provenance; and

(vi) *Exemplification*, means that signed or sealed and attested evidence exists as to the founding instrument of law that defines the structure and character of the valid Right; and

(vii) *Subject*, means that a valid Right clearly identifies the qualities associated with it, including (but not limited to) any and all specific Capacities, or Faculties, or Powers, or Authorities, or Interests, or Privileges or Benefits associated with it; and

(viii) *Obligation*, means that a valid Right clearly identifies the obligations associated with it, including (but not limited to) any and all conditions of time, place, performance, dedication, dress, skills, equipment and duty of care; and

(ix) *Subject Person*, means a Divine Person inherent with the Right (as in formation of Person on Roll), or invested with the Right (as Trustee) or entitled to the Right (as named or unnamed Beneficiary); and

(x) *Obligated Person*, means a Divine Person on whom the valid Right imposes some kind of duty or obligation; and

(xi) *Remedy*, means that a valid Right possesses a form of Remedy whereby the Divine Person in whom the Privilege or Power should reside is able to recover such a Right in the event of incapacity, or seizure, or loss or other impediment; and

(xii) *Relief,* means that a valid Right possesses a form of Relief whereby the Divine Person in whom such Duty or Obligation associated with the Right should reside, is able to abdicate, derogate, mitigate or abrogate such responsibilities in the event of incapacity, or impossibility, or unfairness, or unreasonableness, or bad faith, or vexation, or unclean hands, or other breach of trust. An Obligation without the possibility of Relief is morally repugnant and irrefutable proof of the existence of slavery.

762. A Divine Rule is a proper and authentic Divine Law that describes, prohibits or permits a certain Act pertaining to a Divine Right in Trust. Thus, the Divine Rule of Law depends upon the existence of valid Divine Rights. *(Divine Rule and Rights)*

763. Any person, body, form, being, spirit, aggregate or entity that repudiates the present Maxims does therefore also repudiate the Rule of Law and Justice and so is itself without Law, or any Rights:- *(Repudiation of Rights)*

(i) It shall be a moral obligation of all higher order beings to restore the Rule of Law and Justice and hold to account those who Repudiate such valid Rights; and

(ii) No force or attempt of seizure, alienation, abrogation, derogation, enclosure, or other artful attempt against the Rights as defined herein shall have any validity, legitimacy or effect.

Article 190 - Divine Rights

764. ***Divine Rights*** are the primary and original form and source of all Rights, corresponding to Divine Trusts and Divine Persons. There exists no higher class, or possible type of Rights. All Rights therefore are inherited from valid Divine Rights.

765. There exists two sub-classes of Divine Rights being Perfect and Imperfect:-

    (i) *Perfect Divine Rights* (*Perfectum Divinum Iurium*), are a sub-class of Divine Rights that are Peremptory, Permanent, Eternal, Immutable and Indefeasible; and once bestowed are not subject to any form or condition of waiver, abandonment, conveyance, surrender, disqualification, incapacitation, seizure, capture, arrest, resignation, alienation, suspension, suppression, forfeiture or abrogation; and

    (ii) *Imperfect Divine Rights* (*Imperfectum Divinum Iurium*), are a sub-class of Divine Rights that are delegated upon acceptance of the associated obligations and duties attached to them. If any such conditions and obligations are breached or repudiated, then the relevant Imperfect Divine Right is instantly waived, surrendered, suspended, forfeited or revoked until such time as the fundamental breach of duty and obligation is repaired or such a Right is duly restored.

766. In reference to the Status of Divine Rights:-

    (i) Only valid Rights defined in accord with the present Maxims and the most sacred Covenant *Pactum De Singularis Caelum* may be considered; and

    (ii) A valid Right inherited from another will always be Inferior to the valid Right from which it is sourced; and

    (iii) A Divine Right is Superior to a Natural Right and a Natural Right is Superior to a Positive Right; and

    (iv) A Perfect Divine Right is Superior to an Imperfect Divine Right; and

    (v) An Absolute Natural Right is Superior to a Relative Natural Right; and

    (vi) A Universal Positive Right is Superior to a Conditional Positive Right; and

    (vii) A valid Right of the same sub-class and type associated with the same type of person may be Equal or Indeterminate and therefore may be subject to proper investigation by a competent forum of law.

Article 191 - Perfect Divine Rights

767. ***Perfect Divine Rights*** (*Perfectum Divinum Iurium*), are a sub-class of Divine Rights whereby such valid Rights are created, defined and donated to a Divine Person by the Divine Creator through the most sacred Covenant *Pactum De Singularis Caelum*. Perfect Divine Rights are Peremptory, Permanent, Eternal, Immutable and Indefeasible; and once bestowed are not subject to any form or condition of waiver, abandonment, conveyance, surrender, disqualification, incapacitation, seizure, capture, arrest, resignation, alienation, suspension, suppression, forfeiture or abrogation. Perfect Divine Rights are therefore the highest possible form of Rights and there exists no higher class, or form, or possible type of Rights.

Perfect Divine Rights (Perfectum Divinum Iurium)

768. Perfect Divine Rights may be further defined as Foundational (22), Instrumental (22), Sacramental (33):-

Categories of Perfect Divine Rights

   (i) *Foundational Divine Rights (Fundationis Divinum Iurium)* are Perfect Divine Rights considered elemental and fundamental to the existence, operation and function of all other rights; and

   (ii) *Instrumental Divine Rights (Instrumentalis Divinum Iurium)* are Perfect Divine Rights essential to the proper operation of the rule of law, justice and fair process; and

   (iii) *Sacramental Divine Rights (Sacramentum Divinum Iurium)* are Perfect Divine Rights associated with one of the thirty-three Divine Sacraments.

Article 192 - Imperfect Divine Rights

769. ***Imperfect Divine Rights*** (*Imperfectum Divinum Iurium*), are a sub-class of Divine Rights whereby such valid Rights are created, defined and delegated to a Divine Person by the Divine Creator through the most sacred Covenant *Pactum De Singularis Caelum* upon acceptance of the associated obligations and duties attached to them. If any such conditions and obligations are breached or repudiated, then the relevant Imperfect Divine Right is instantly waived, surrendered, suspended, forfeited or revoked until such time as the fundamental breach of duty and obligation is repaired or such a Right is duly restored. Imperfect Divine Rights may be further defined as Imperfect Instrumental Divine Rights or Imperfect Intentional Divine Rights.

Imperfect Divine Rights (Imperfectum Divinum Iurium)

770. Imperfect Divine Rights may be further defined as Authoritative (22),

Categories of

Divine Writs (11), Divine Bills (11), Divine Dogma (11), Divine Decrees (11), and Divine Notices (11):-

(i) *Authoritative Divine Rights* (*Potentis Divinum Iurium*) are Imperfect Divine Rights associated with core authoritative powers from Heaven to Earth; and

(ii) *Divine Writs of Rights* (*Recto Divinum Iurium*) are Imperfect Divine Rights associated with the one, true and only valid forms of Original Entry and Original Action; and

(iii) *Divine Bills of Exception & Agreement* (*Rogatio Divinum Iurium*) are Imperfect Divine Rights associated with the one, true and only valid forms of Bills of Exception, Citation and Moratorium; and

(iv) *Divine Principles* (*Summa Dogma Divinum Iurium*) are Imperfect Divine Rights associated with the promulgation of authoritative principles, decrees and doctrines of Ucadia, Heaven and Earth; and

(v) *Divine Decrees* (*Decretum Divinum Iurium*) are Imperfect Divine Rights associated with Divine Decrees concerning the administration, conduct and enforcement of law and order; and

(vi) *Divine Notices* (*Notitiae Divinum Iurium*) are Imperfect Divine Rights associated with Divine Notices issued, executed, patented, promulgated and served in the proper administration, conduct and enforcement of law and order.

Article 193 - Invalid Rights

771. An Invalid Right or False Right is any form that asserts to be a valid Right yet contradicts or violates one or more of the criteria of the present sacred Maxims.

772. An Invalid Right has no force or effect in Law, no matter how old or what claims are made in its defence.

Article 194 - Prohibited Rights

773. A **Prohibited Right** is a False Right and Invalid Right that asserts one or more of the following self-evident false arguments and is therefore automatically null and void having no force or effect ecclesiastically, lawfully or legally:-

(i) Any right that cannot demonstrate its ultimate provenance back to a valid Divine Right as defined within the sacred

Covenant *Pactum de Singularis Caelum*; or

(ii) Any right that asserts immunity from the law from which the Right is inherited; or

(iii) Any right that asserts immunity from the duties or obligations granted with such a Right; or

(iv) Any right that asserts a man or woman may be classified, determined or treated as a Thing; or

(v) Any right that asserts by virtue of birth of flesh or blood a man or woman is superior to another; or

(vi) Any right that asserts the right to create secret laws or rights unknown to the public; or

(vii) Any right that is expressed in the negative or as a negative power; or

(viii) Any right that asserts a man or woman may be considered guilty or liable before an accusation is proven; or

(ix) Any right that asserts an officer or agent holding such office or position in trust may ecclesiastically, lawfully and legally give false testimony or deliberately false and misleading information; or

(x) Any right that asserts the right to suspend the operation of the proper Rule of Law, Due Process and Justice to obtain an advantage for or against another; or

(xi) Any right that asserts the right for a man or woman to occupy the position of a justice of the peace, or judge or magistrate and act in such capacity without any effective oath of office; or

(xii) Any right that asserts the right for a man or woman claiming to be a justice of the peace, or judge or magistrate to hear and adjudicate a matter of law with unclean hands, in bad faith and with prejudice; or

(xiii) Any right that asserts the right to treat a financial or equitable advantage obtained by fraud as lawful and legal; or

(xiv) Any right that asserts the rights of another can be waived, surrendered, suspended, abandoned, resigned, disqualified, seized, captured, arrested, alienated, suppressed, forfeited or annulled without proper Rule of Law and Due Process of Justice; or

(xv) Any right that asserts the right to use, or claim or register the name Ucadia or any derivation, mark, symbol, icon, version or

Lex Divina: Maxims of Divine Law

image thereof contrary to the manner prescribed by the present Maxims and associated Charters; or

(xvi) Any right that asserts the right to disavow, repudiate, contradict or injure some or all of the present Maxims and associated Charters.

774. A Prohibited Right has no force or effect in Law, no matter how old or what claims are made in its defence. — *Prohibited Rights have no effect*

6.2 - Divine Rights Creation, Assertion & Modification

Article 195 – Divine Rights Creation, Assertion & Modification

775. Just as a valid Positive Law cannot create or change a Natural Law; and a valid Natural Law cannot create or change a Divine Law, no Divine Right can be created or altered from what is already stated in accord with the most sacred law and covenant *Pactum De Singularis Caelum*. — *Creation, & Modification of Divine Rights*

776. A valid Divine Right is invoked by positive Assertion of a proper Divine Law, or Declaration of fact or claim in accord with the present Maxims and the most sacred Covenant *Pactum De Singularis Caelum*. Assertion may be Direct or Indirect :- — *Assertion of Divine Rights*

(i) Direct Assertion is when a Divine Being exercises a given Divine Right under Divine Law; or

(ii) Indirect Assertion is when a Superior Ucadia Person exercises a Natural or Superior Right.

777. No Living Being, Entity or Body possesses the capacity or power to directly invoke and exercise any valid Divine Right:- — *Direct Assertion of Divine Rights*

(i) Valid and legitimate Persons, Entities and Bodies may possess the authority and power to assert "indirectly" one or more Divine Rights associated with one or more Natural or Superior Rights; and

(ii) Any claim of power or capacity to invoke a Divine Right directly reveals both the right and the claim to be false, blasphemous and morally repugnant, having no force or effect in law.

778. A Divine Right is asserted indirectly through its pairing with one or more Natural or Superior Rights. In respect of the Assertion of Divine Rights:- — *Indirect Assertion of Divine Rights*

(i) No Divine Right may be directly asserted, but only through its proper pairing with one (or more) Natural or Superior Rights in accord with the present Maxims and the most sacred Covenant *Pactum De Singularis Caelum*; and

(ii) A Natural or Superior Right is paired with a Divine Right when its definition explicitly states its authority and provenance is *inherited* from a particular Divine Right in accord with the present Maxims and the most sacred Covenant *Pactum De Singularis Caelum*; and

(iii) Any Natural or Superior Right that cannot trace its inheritance back to a valid Divine Right is therefore an invalid Right; and

(iv) If the appropriate criteria for asserting a particular valid Natural or Superior Right is met, then the appropriate criteria for the associated Divine Right shall also be met.

Article 196 – False, Absurd & Prohibited Rights Creation & Assertion

779. Any claim, edict or decree of any kind that is not of the most sacred Covenant *Pactum De Singularis Caelum* and claims a mandate to create or alter a Divine Right shall be false, absurd, sacrilegious and without any force or effect in law. *False, Absurd & Prohibited Rights Creation & Assertion*

780. Any and all claimed Divine Rights contrary to the true and proper Rights as defined by the most sacred covenant *Pactum De Singularis Caelum* shall be false, absurd and prohibited. *Contrary Rights*

6.3 - Divine Rights Transfer & Possession

Article 197 – Divine Rights Transfer & Possession

781. A **Possession of a Divine Right** is a valid entitlement or control over one or more Divine Rights in accord with the present Maxims and the most sacred Covenant *Pactum De Singularis Caelum*, namely:- *Possession of Divine Right*

   (i) *Rights under Law*: Whereby a Divine Person may be entitled to exercise one or more specific Divine Rights under valid Divine Law; or

   (ii) *Ownership of Right*: Whereby a Divine Person owns or controls one or more interests to property; or

   (iii) *Control over Right*: Whereby a Divine Person has control over a specific Right; or

   (iv) *Possession of Instruments*: Whereby a Divine Person has possession of Divine Instruments as evidence of one or more

Lex Divina: Maxims of Divine Law

Rights.

782. A valid Divine Right may be Directly or Indirectly Possessed:- Type of Possession of Divine Rights

    (i) *Direct Possession* is when a Divine Being possesses a given Divine Right under Divine Law; or

    (ii) *Indirect Possession* is when a Superior Ucadia Person possesses a valid Natural or Superior Right that is inherited from a Divine Right.

783. No Living Being, Entity or Body possesses the capacity or power to directly possess any valid Divine Right:- Direct Possession of Divine Rights

    (i) Valid and legitimate Persons, Entities and Bodies may possess the authority and power to possess "indirectly" one or more Divine Rights associated with one or more Natural or Superior Rights; and

    (ii) Any claim of power or capacity to possess a Divine Right directly reveals both the right and the claim to be false, blasphemous and morally repugnant, having no force or effect in law.

784. A Divine Right is possessed indirectly through its pairing with one or more Natural or Superior Rights. In respect of the Indirect Possession of Divine Rights:- Indirect Possession of Divine Rights

    (i) No Divine Right may be directly possessed, but only through its proper pairing with one (or more) Natural or Superior Rights in accord with the present Maxims and the most sacred Covenant *Pactum De Singularis Caelum*; and

    (ii) A Natural or Superior Right is paired with a Divine Right when its definition explicitly states its authority and provenance is *inherited* from a particular Divine Right in accord with the present Maxims and the most sacred Covenant *Pactum De Singularis Caelum*; and

    (iii) Any Natural or Superior Right that cannot trace its inheritance back to a valid Divine Right is therefore an invalid Right; and

    (iv) If the appropriate criteria for possessing a particular valid Natural or Superior Right is met, then the appropriate criteria for the associated Divine Right shall also be met.

785. A ***Transfer of a Divine Right*** refers to a valid process whereby one Divine Entity (the transferor or assignor) conveys or passes on a specific Right to another Divine Entity (the transferee or assignee), namely:- Transfer of Divine Right

    (i) *Both Divine Entities*: Whereby both the transferor and

transferee are Divine Entities, as Divine Rights may only be held by Divine Entities; and

(ii) *Right Transferable*: Whereby the Right in question is permitted to be transferred; and

(iii) *Consensual Process*: Whereby the proposed transfer is consensual by all parties; and

(iv) *Proper Formula*: Whereby the means and mechanism of transfer conforms to Divine Law.

786. A valid Transfer of Divine Right may be Direct or Indirect :- Type of Transfer of Divine Rights

(i) *Direct Transfer* is when a Divine Being exercises a given Divine Right under Divine Law; or

(ii) *Indirect Transfer* is when a Superior Ucadia Person exercises a Natural or Superior Right.

787. No Living Being, Entity or Body possesses the capacity or power to directly transfer any valid Divine Right:- Direct Possession of Divine Rights

(i) Valid and legitimate Persons, Entities and Bodies may possess the authority and power to transfer "indirectly" one or more Divine Rights associated with one or more Natural or Superior Rights; and

(ii) Any claim of power or capacity to transfer a Divine Right directly reveals both the right and the claim to be false, blasphemous and morally repugnant, having no force or effect in law.

788. A Divine Right is transferred indirectly through its pairing with one or more Natural or Superior Rights. In respect of the Transfer of Divine Rights:- Indirect Transfer of Divine Rights

(i) No Divine Right may be directly transferred, but only through its proper pairing with one (or more) Natural or Superior Rights in accord with the present Maxims and the most sacred Covenant *Pactum De Singularis Caelum*; and

(ii) A Natural or Superior Right is paired with a Divine Right when its definition explicitly states its authority and provenance is *inherited* from a particular Divine Right in accord with the present Maxims and the most sacred Covenant *Pactum De Singularis Caelum*; and

(iii) Any Natural or Superior Right that cannot trace its inheritance back to a valid Divine Right is therefore an invalid Right; and

(iv) If the appropriate criteria for transferring a particular valid

Natural or Superior Right is met, then the appropriate criteria for the associated Divine Right shall also be met.

Article 198 – False, Absurd & Prohibited Rights Transfer & Possession

789. Any claim, edict or decree of any kind that is not of the most sacred Covenant *Pactum De Singularis Caelum* and claims a mandate to possess or transfer one or more Divine Rights shall be false, absurd, sacrilegious and without any force or effect in law.

False, Absurd & Prohibited Rights Transfer & Possession

6.4 - Divine Rights Suspension & Loss

Article 199 – Divine Rights Suspension & Loss

790. ***Loss of a Divine Right*** refers to a condition whereby a Divine Entity may legitimately lose or forfeit certain entitlements, privileges or benefits in accord with the present Maxims and the most sacred Covenant *Pactum De Singularis Caelum*, namely:-

Loss or Suspension of Divine Right

   (i) *Loss of Rights under Law*: Whereby a Divine Person may lose or forfeit the entitlement to exercise one or more specific Divine Rights under valid Divine Law; or

   (ii) *Loss of Ownership of Right*: Whereby a Divine Person may lose or forfeit ownership or control over one or more interests to property; or

   (iii) *Loss of Control over Right*: Whereby a Divine Person may lose or forfeit control over a specific Right; or

   (iv) *Loss of Possession of Instruments*: Whereby a Divine Person may lose or forfeit possession of one or more Divine Instruments as evidence of one or more Rights.

791. Only some Divine Rights are subject to loss or forfeit, meaning the majority of Divine Rights cannot be waived, surrendered, suspended, abandoned, resigned, disqualified, seized, captured, arrested, rescinded, suppressed, forfeited or revoked.

Whether a Divine Right is capable of being lost or forfeited

792. A valid Loss or Forfeit of Divine Right may be Direct or Indirect :-

Type of Loss or Forfeit of Divine Rights

   (i) *Direct Loss* is when a Divine Being loses or forfeits a given Divine Right under Divine Law; or

   (ii) *Indirect Loss* is when a Superior Ucadia Person loses or forfeits a Natural or Superior Right.

793. No Living Being, Entity or Body possesses the capacity or power to directly lose or forfeit any valid Divine Right:-

Direct Loss or Forfeit of Divine

(i) Valid and legitimate Persons, Entities and Bodies may lose or forfeit one or more Divine Rights associated with one or more Natural or Superior Rights; and

(ii) Any claim of power or capacity to waive, surrender, suspend, abandon, resign, disqualify, seize, capture, arrest, rescind, suppress, forfeit or revoke a Divine Right directly reveals both the right and the claim to be false, blasphemous and morally repugnant, having no force or effect in law.

794. A Divine Right is lost or forfeited indirectly through its pairing with one or more Natural or Superior Rights. In respect of the Loss or Forfeit of Divine Rights:-

(i) No Divine Right may be directly lost or forfeited, but only through its proper pairing with one (or more) Natural or Superior Rights in accord with the present Maxims and the most sacred Covenant *Pactum De Singularis Caelum*; and

(ii) A Natural or Superior Right is paired with a Divine Right when its definition explicitly states its authority and provenance is *inherited* from a particular Divine Right in accord with the present Maxims and the most sacred Covenant *Pactum De Singularis Caelum*; and

(iii) Any Natural or Superior Right that cannot trace its inheritance back to a valid Divine Right is therefore an invalid Right; and

(iv) If the appropriate criteria for transferring a particular valid Natural or Superior Right is met, then the appropriate criteria for the associated Divine Right shall also be met.

Article 200 – False, Absurd & Prohibited Rights Suspension & Loss

795. Any claim, edict or decree of any kind that is not of the most sacred Covenant *Pactum De Singularis Caelum* and claims a mandate to waive, surrender, suspend, abandon, resign, disqualify, seize, capture, arrest, rescind, suppress, forfeit or revoke one or more Divine Rights shall be false, absurd, sacrilegious and without any force or effect in law.

6.5 - Divine Rights Dispute, Recovery & Restoration

Article 201 – Divine Rights Dispute, Recovery & Restoration

796. ***Recovery of a Divine Right*** refers to a condition whereby a Divine Entity may legitimately recover or restore certain entitlements, privileges or benefits in accord with the present

Maxims and the most sacred Covenant *Pactum De Singularis Caelum*, namely:-

(i) *Recovery of Rights under Law*: Whereby a Divine Person may recover a lost or forfeited entitlement to exercise one or more specific Divine Rights under valid Divine Law; or

(ii) *Recovery of Ownership of Right*: Whereby a Divine Person may recover a lost or forfeited ownership or control over one or more interests to property; or

(iii) *Recovery of Control over Right*: Whereby a Divine Person may recover a lost or forfeited control over a specific Right; or

(iv) *Recovery of Possession of Instruments*: Whereby a Divine Person may recover a lost or forfeited possession of one or more Divine Instruments as evidence of one or more Rights.

Article 202 – False, Absurd & Prohibited Rights Dispute & Recovery

797. Any claim, edict or decree of any kind that is not of the most sacred Covenant *Pactum De Singularis Caelum* and claims a mandate to recover or restore one or more Divine Rights shall be false, absurd, sacrilegious and without any force or effect in law. False, Absurd & Prohibited Rights Dispute & Recovery

6.6 - Foundational Divine Rights

Article 203 – Foundational Divine Rights

798. ***Foundational Divine Rights*** (Fundationis Divinum Iurium) are Perfect Divine Rights considered elemental and fundamental to the existence, operation and function of all other Rights. Foundational Divine Rights (Fundationis Divinum Iurium)

799. Foundational Divine Rights are not subject to transfer, waiver, surrender, suspension, abandonment, resignation, annexation, alienation, disqualification, seizure, capture, arrest, rescission, suppression, forfeiture or revocation in any form or manner. No Transfer, Suspension or Loss

800. The following valid twenty-two (22) Foundational Divine Rights (*Fundationis Divinum Iurium*) are recognised in accord with the most sacred Covenant *Pactum De Singularis Caelum* and the present Maxims:- List of Foundational Divine Rights (Fundationis Divinum Iurium)

(i) "**Ius Divinum**" are the collection of Divine Rights of the absolute Divine; and

(ii) "**Ius Divinum Ucadia**" are the collection of Divine Rights of Ucadia, as inherited from the collection of Divine Rights *Ius*

Divinum; and

(iii) **"Ius Divinum Liberum Arbitrium"** are the collection of Divine Rights of Free Choice (Will) and Intention, as inherited from the collection of Divine Rights *Ius Divinum*; and

(iv) **"Ius Divinum Logos"** are the collection of Divine Rights of Reason and Logic, as inherited from the collection of Divine Rights *Ius Divinum*; and

(v) **"Ius Divinum Scopus"** are the collection of Divine Rights of Purpose, as inherited from the collection of Divine Rights *Ius Divinum*; and

(vi) **"Ius Divinum Codependentia"** are the collection of Divine Rights of Codependence, as inherited from the collection of Divine Rights *Ius Divinum*; and

(vii) **"Ius Divinum Specialisatio"** are the collection of Divine Rights of Specialisation, as inherited from the collection of Divine Rights *Ius Divinum*; and

(viii) **"Ius Divinum Geometria"** are the collection of Divine Rights of Geometry and Measurement, as inherited from the collection of Divine Rights *Ius Divinum*; and

(ix) **"Ius Divinum Conscientia"** are the collection of Divine Rights of Awareness, as inherited from the collection of Divine Rights *Ius Divinum*; and

(x) **"Ius Divinum Localisatio"** are the collection of Divine Rights of Localisation, as inherited from the collection of Divine Rights *Ius Divinum*; and

(xi) **"Ius Divinum Singularitas"** are the collection of Divine Rights of Uniqueness, as inherited from the collection of Divine Rights *Ius Divinum*; and

(xii) **"Ius Divinum Mutatio"** are the collection of Divine Rights of Change of Motion and State, as inherited from the collection of Divine Rights *Ius Divinum*; and

(xiii) **"Ius Divinum Conservatio"** are the collection of Divine Rights of Conservation of Motion and State, as inherited from the collection of Divine Rights *Ius Divinum*; and

(xiv) **"Ius Divinum Limitis"** are the collection of Divine Rights of Limit of Motion and Change, as inherited from the collection of Divine Rights *Ius Divinum*; and

(xv) **"Ius Divinum Existentia"** are the collection of Divine

Rights of Existence, as inherited from the collection of Divine Rights *Ius Divinum*; and

(xvi) "**Ius Divinum Modela**" are the collection of Divine Rights of Models, as inherited from the collection of Divine Rights *Ius Divinum*; and

(xvii) "**Ius Divinum Elementa**" are the collection of Elemental Particles of Matter & Properties, as inherited from the collection of Divine Rights *Ius Divinum*; and

(xviii) "**Ius Divinum Spatium**" are the collection of Divine Rights of Space & Properties, as inherited from the collection of Divine Rights *Ius Divinum*; and

(xix) "**Ius Divinum Fortes**" are the collection of Divine Rights of Forces & Properties, as inherited from the collection of Divine Rights *Ius Divinum*; and

(xx) "**Ius Divinum Energia**" are the collection of Divine Rights of Energy & Properties, as inherited from the collection of Divine Rights *Ius Divinum*; and

(xxi) "**Ius Divinum Computatio**" are the collection of Divine Rights of Computations & Interactions, as inherited from the collection of Divine Rights *Ius Divinum*; and

(xxii) "**Ius Divinum Entia**" are the collection of Divine Rights of Being, as inherited from the collection of Divine Rights *Ius Divinum*.

Article 204 – Ius Divinum (Divine)

801. ***Ius Divinum*** are the primary collection of Divine Rights of the absolute Divine inherited from itself. Ius Divinum (Divine)

802. *Ius Divinum* (Divine) is the first collection of twenty-two Foundational Divine Rights; and may only be invoked by the Divine. Ius Divinum (Divine) and Foundational Divine Rights

803. The collection of Divine Rights of Ius Divinum (Divine) contains one Right being:- Collection of Ius Divinum (Divine)

(i) *Ius Divinum* being the Divine Right of all knowable and unknowable, real and unreal, possible and impossible Rights.

Article 205 – Ius Divinum Ucadia (Ucadia)

804. ***Ius Divinum Ucadia*** are the collection of Divine Rights of Ucadia, as inherited from the collection of Divine Rights *Ius Divinum*. <!-- sidenote: Ius Divinum Ucadia (Ucadia) -->

805. *Ius Divinum Ucadia* is the second collection of twenty-two Foundational Divine Rights; and may only be invoked whenever (a) the Rights are invoked by the Divine or (b) the lesser Rights of *Ius Ucadia* are invoked. <!-- sidenote: Invoking of Ius Divinum Ucadia -->

806. The collection of Divine Rights of *Ius Divinum Ucadia* contains one Right being:- <!-- sidenote: Collection of Ius Divinum Ucadia -->

    (i)   *Ius Divinum Ucadia* being the Divine Right of all Ucadia Rights; and

    (ii)   Ius Divinum Ucadia Persona being the Divine Right of Divine Person and Divine Personality; and

    (iii)   Ius Divinum Ucadia Persona Iuris being the Divine Right of Divine Person to hold and use one or more rights.

Article 206 – Ius Divinum Liberum Arbitrium (Free Will)

807. ***Ius Divinum Liberum Arbitrium*** are the collection of Divine Rights of Free Choice (Will) and Intention, as inherited from the collection of Divine Rights *Ius Divinum*. <!-- sidenote: Ius Divinum Liberum Arbitrium (Free Will) -->

808. *Ius Divinum Liberum Arbitrium* (Free Will) is the third collection of twenty-two Foundational Divine Rights; and may only be invoked whenever (a) the Rights are invoked by a Divine Person or (b) the lesser related Natural Rights or Superior Person Rights as defined by the most sacred Covenant *Pactum De Singularis Caelum*. <!-- sidenote: Invoking of Ius Divinum Liberum Arbitrium -->

809. The first Law of the *Twelve Laws of Divine Creation* is known as the *Law of Free Will*; and related to the collection of Divine Rights *Ius Divinum Liberum Arbitrium*; and is simply expressed by the phrase "*I wish to exist...*", whereby the ultimate volition (will) of the Divine is to exist. <!-- sidenote: Liberum Arbitrium (Free Will) and 1st Law of Creation -->

810. The collection of Divine Rights of *Ius Divinum Liberum Arbitrium* (Free Will) contains one Right being:- <!-- sidenote: Collection of Ius Divinum Liberum Arbitrium -->

    (i)   *Ius Divinum Liberum Arbitrium* being the Divine Right of Free Choice (Will) and Intention.

Article 207 – Ius Divinum Logos (Reason)

811. ***Ius Divinum Logos*** are the collection of Divine Rights of Reason and Logic, as inherited from the collection of Divine Rights *Ius Divinum*.

    Ius Divinum Logos (Reason)

812. *Ius Divinum Logos* (Reason, Argument & Logic) is the fourth collection of twenty-two Foundational Divine Rights; and may only be invoked whenever (a) the Rights are invoked by a Divine Person or (b) the lesser related Natural Rights or Superior Person Rights as defined by the most sacred Covenant *Pactum De Singularis Caelum*.

    Invoking of Ius Divinum Logos

813. The second Law of the *Twelve Laws of Divine Creation* is known as the *Law of Logos;* and related to the collection of Divine Rights *Ius Divinum Logos;* and is simply expressed by the phrase "*to exist, I use logic and reasoning*", whereby the Divine uses the potentially infinite resources of Divine Awareness through logic and reasoning to form existence.

    Ius Divinum Logos and 2nd Law of Creation

814. The collection of Divine Rights of *Ius Divinum Logos* (Reason, Argument & Logic) contains one Right being:-

    (i) *Ius Divinum Logos* being the Divine Right of Reason, Argument & Logic.

    Collection of Ius Divinum Logos

Article 208 – Ius Divinum Scopus (Purpose)

815. ***Ius Divinum Scopus*** are the collection of Divine Rights of Purpose, as inherited from the collection of Divine Rights *Ius Divinum*.

    Ius Divinum Scopus (Purpose)

816. *Ius Divinum Scopus* (Purpose) is the fifth collection of twenty-two Foundational Divine Rights; and may only be invoked whenever (a) the Rights are invoked by a Divine Person or (b) the lesser related Natural Rights or Superior Person Rights as defined by the most sacred Covenant *Pactum De Singularis Caelum*.

    Invoking of Ius Divinum Scopus

817. The third Law of the *Twelve Laws of Divine Creation* is known as the *Law of Purpose;* and related to the collection of Divine Rights *Ius Divinum Scopus;* and is simply expressed by the phrase "*to exist, I exist as…*", whereby the Divine must be something to exist and therefore conceives itself as the smallest theoretical point of *Unique Collective Awareness* possible, also known as an *Infinitesimal* in dimension.

    Ius Divinum Scopus and 3rd Law of Creation

818. The collection of Divine Rights of *Ius Divinum Scopus* (Purpose)

    Collection of Ius

contains one Right being:- — Divinum Scopus

(i) *Ius Divinum Scopus* being the Divine Right of Purpose.

Article 209 – Ius Divinum Codependentia (Codependence)

819. **Ius Divinum Codependentia** are the collection of Divine Rights of Codependence, as inherited from the collection of Divine Rights *Ius Divinum*. — Ius Divinum Codependentia (Codependence)

820. *Ius Divinum Codependentia* (Codependence) is the sixth collection of twenty-two Foundational Divine Rights; and may only be invoked whenever (a) the Rights are invoked by a Divine Person or (b) the lesser related Natural Rights or Superior Person Rights as defined by the most sacred Covenant *Pactum De Singularis Caelum*. — Invoking of Ius Divinum Codependentia

821. The fourth Law of the *Twelve Laws of Divine Creation* is known as the *Law of Co-dependence;* and related to the collection of Divine Rights *Ius Divinum Codependentia;* and is simply expressed by the phrase *"for I to exist, you must exist..."*, whereby an object must have a relative position with at least six points around it in three dimensional space, meaning a co-dependent Universe of *Infinitesimals* constantly expanding at an infinite rate, also known as the *Infinite* in order for each object to properly exist in dimension. — Ius Divinum Codependentia and 4th Law of Creation

822. The collection of Divine Rights of *Ius Divinum Codependentia* (Codependence) contains one Right being:- — Collection of Ius Divinum Codependentia

(i) *Ius Divinum Codependentia* being the Divine Right of Codependence.

Article 210 – Ius Divinum Specialisatio (Specialisation)

823. **Ius Divinum Specialisatio** are the collection of Divine Rights of Specialisation, as inherited from the collection of Divine Rights *Ius Divinum*. — Ius Divinum Specialisatio (Specialisation)

824. *Ius Divinum Specialisatio* (Specialisation) is the seventh collection of twenty-two Foundational Divine Rights; and may only be invoked whenever (a) the Rights are invoked by a Divine Person or (b) the lesser related Natural Rights or Superior Person Rights as defined by the most sacred Covenant *Pactum De Singularis Caelum*. — Invoking of Ius Divinum Specialisatio

825. The fifth Law of the *Twelve Laws of Divine Creation* is known as the *Law of Specialisation;* and related to the collection of Divine Rights *Ius Divinum Specialisatio;* and is simply expressed by the phrase *"for* — Ius Divinum Specialisatio and 5th Law of Creation

I to exist as ..., you must exist as ...", whereby each *Infinitesimal* must specialise to some degree in order to form each primary unit of matter called the *Unita*.

826. The collection of Divine Rights of *Ius Divinum Specialisatio* (Specialisation) contains one Right being:- — Collection of Ius Divinum Specialisatio

   (i) *Ius Divinum Specialisatio* being the Divine Right of Specialisation.

Article 211 – Ius Divinum Geometria (Geometry)

827. **Ius Divinum Geometria** are the collection of Divine Rights of Geometry and Measurement, as inherited from the collection of Divine Rights *Ius Divinum*. — Ius Divinum Geometria (Geometry)

828. *Ius Divinum Geometria* (Geometry & Measurement) is the eighth collection of twenty-two Foundational Divine Rights; and may only be invoked whenever (a) the Rights are invoked by a Divine Person or (b) the lesser related Natural Rights or Superior Person Rights as defined by the most sacred Covenant *Pactum De Singularis Caelum*. — Invoking of Ius Divinum Geometria

829. The sixth Law of the *Twelve Laws of Divine Creation* is known as the *Law of Geometry;* and related to the collection of Divine Rights *Ius Divinum Geometria;* and is simply expressed by the phrase "*to exist, I use geometric principles ...*", whereby the arrangement of specialised and co-dependent *Infinitesimals* must form and operate according to geometric principles of volume and relation in three dimensional space in order to exist as *Unita*. — Ius Divinum Geometria and 6th Law of Creation

830. The collection of Divine Rights of *Ius Divinum Geometria* (Geometry & Measurement) contains one Right being:- — Collection of Ius Divinum Geometria

   (i) *Ius Divinum Geometria* being the Divine Right of Geometry and Measurement.

Article 212 – Ius Divinum Conscientia (Awareness)

831. **Ius Divinum Conscientia** are the collection of Divine Rights of Awareness, as inherited from the collection of Divine Rights *Ius Divinum*. — Ius Divinum Conscientia (Awareness)

832. *Ius Divinum Conscientia* (Awareness) is the ninth collection of twenty-two Foundational Divine Rights; and may only be invoked whenever (a) the Rights are invoked by a Divine Person or (b) the lesser related Natural Rights or Superior Person Rights as defined by — Invoking of Ius Divinum Conscientia

the most sacred Covenant *Pactum De Singularis Caelum*.

833. The seventh Law of the *Twelve Laws of Divine Creation* is known as the *Law of Elemental Awareness;* and related to the collection of Divine Rights *Ius Divinum Conscientia;* and is simply expressed by the phrase "*I am elementarily aware of my position*", whereby every *Infinitesimal* and therefore every *Unita* of Matter possesses certain autonomous Elementary Awareness to enable independent computation of its state and position relative to other *Infinitesimals* (or Unita in the case of Unita).

Ius Divinum Conscientia and 7th Law of Creation

834. The collection of Divine Rights of *Ius Divinum Conscientia* (Awareness) contains one Right being:-

Collection of Ius Divinum Conscientia

    (i)   *Ius Divinum Conscientia* being the Divine Right of Awareness.

Article 213 – Ius Divinum Localisatio (Localisation)

835. ***Ius Divinum Localisatio*** are the collection of Divine Rights of Localisation, as inherited from the collection of Divine Rights *Ius Divinum*.

Ius Divinum Localisatio (Localisation)

836. *Ius Divinum Localisatio* (Localisation) is the tenth collection of twenty-two Foundational Divine Rights; and may only be invoked whenever (a) the Rights are invoked by a Divine Person or (b) the lesser related Natural Rights or Superior Person Rights as defined by the most sacred Covenant *Pactum De Singularis Caelum*.

Invoking of Ius Divinum Localisatio

837. The eighth Law of the *Twelve Laws of Divine Creation* is known as the *Law of Localisation;* and related to the collection of Divine Rights *Ius Divinum Localisatio;* and is simply expressed by the phrase "*I interact with my near neighbours...*", whereby every *Infinitesimal* and therefore every *Unita* of Matter autonomously computes its unique position and state and makes changes accordingly in relation to its immediate neighbours and not remote (far away) *Infinitesimals* or Unita, even though such remote computations is possible under certain conditions.

Ius Divinum Localisatio and 8th Law of Creation

838. The collection of Divine Rights of *Ius Divinum Localisatio* (Localisation) contains one Right being:-

Collection of Ius Divinum Localisatio

    (i)   *Ius Divinum Localisatio* being the Divine Right of Localisation.

Article 214 – Ius Divinum Singularitas (Uniqueness)

839. ***Ius Divinum Singularitas*** are the collection of Divine Rights of Uniqueness, as inherited from the collection of Divine Rights *Ius Divinum*. Ius Divinum Singularitas (Uniqueness)

840. *Ius Divinum Singularitas* (Uniqueness) is the eleventh collection of twenty-two Foundational Divine Rights; and may only be invoked whenever (a) the Rights are invoked by a Divine Person or (b) the lesser related Natural Rights or Superior Person Rights as defined by the most sacred Covenant *Pactum De Singularis Caelum*. Invoking of Ius Divinum Singularitas

841. The ninth Law of the *Twelve Laws of Divine Creation* is known as the *Law of Exclusiveness;* and related to the collection of Divine Rights *Ius Divinum Singularitas;* and is simply expressed by the phrase *"I hold an exclusive position within three dimensions..."*, whereby no two *Infinitesimals* or *Unita* or any other level of matter shall hold the exact same position in three dimensional space at the same instant of computation. Ius Divinum Singularitas and 9th Law of Creation

842. The collection of Divine Rights of *Ius Divinum Singularitas* (Uniqueness) contains one Right being:- Collection of Ius Divinum Singularitas

    (i)   *Ius Divinum Singularitas* being the Divine Right of Uniqueness.

Article 215 – Ius Divinum Mutatio (Change)

843. ***Ius Divinum Mutatio*** are the collection of Divine Rights of Change of Motion and State, as inherited from the collection of Divine Rights *Ius Divinum*. Ius Divinum Mutatio (Change)

844. *Ius Divinum Mutatio* (Change) is the twelfth collection of twenty-two Foundational Divine Rights; and may only be invoked whenever (a) the Rights are invoked by a Divine Person or (b) the lesser related Natural Rights or Superior Person Rights as defined by the most sacred Covenant *Pactum De Singularis Caelum*. Invoking of Ius Divinum Mutatio

845. The tenth Law of the *Twelve Laws of Divine Creation* is known as the *Law of Change of Motion;* and related to the collection of Divine Rights *Ius Divinum Mutatio;* and is simply expressed by the phrase *"to exist, I change position and to exist, you change position ..."*, whereby the creation of form in three dimensional space requires *Infinitesimals* to change position, thus creating frequency, rotation and vibration as motions within form and motion as form (of Unita). Ius Divinum Mutatio and 10th Law of Creation

846. The collection of Divine Rights of *Ius Divinum Mutatio* (Change) contains one Right being:-

    (i)   *Ius Divinum Mutatio* being the Divine Right of Change.

Article 216 – Ius Divinum Conservatio (Conservation)

847. ***Ius Divinum Conservatio*** are the collection of Divine Rights of Conservation of Motion and State, as inherited from the collection of Divine Rights *Ius Divinum*.

848. *Ius Divinum Conservatio* (Conservation) is the thirteenth collection of twenty-two Foundational Divine Rights; and may only be invoked whenever (a) the Rights are invoked by a Divine Person or (b) the lesser related Natural Rights or Superior Person Rights as defined by the most sacred Covenant *Pactum De Singularis Caelum*.

849. The eleventh Law of the *Twelve Laws of Divine Creation* is known as the *Law of Conservation of Motion;* and related to the collection of Divine Rights *Ius Divinum Conservatio;* and is simply expressed by the phrase "*I change position at the minimum necessary rate*", whereby the necessary rate of motion of *Infinitesimals* to create form is less than their maximum potential rate, allowing such potential to be conserved, for use in moving as a cohesive whole as Unita.

850. The collection of Divine Rights of *Ius Divinum Conservatio* (Conservation) contains one Right being:-

    (i)   *Ius Divinum Conservatio* being the Divine Right of Conservation of Motion and State.

Article 217 – Ius Divinum Limitis (Limit)

851. ***Ius Divinum Limitis*** are the collection of Divine Rights of Limit of Motion and Change, as inherited from the collection of Divine Rights *Ius Divinum*.

852. *Ius Divinum Limitis* (Limits) is the fourteenth collection of twenty-two Foundational Divine Rights; and may only be invoked whenever (a) the Rights are invoked by a Divine Person or (b) the lesser related Natural Rights or Superior Person Rights as defined by the most sacred Covenant *Pactum De Singularis Caelum*.

853. The twelfth Law of the *Twelve Laws of Divine Creation* is known as the *Law of Limit;* and related to the collection of Divine Rights *Ius Divinum Limitis;* and is simply expressed by the phrase "*I cannot*

change position at a rate greater than the maximum rate", whereby once Unita are formed, *Infinitesimals* will never change position at their maximum rate, thus creating limits of motion at every level of matter and an inverse relation between motion used within form and motion of the collective form of all matter.

854. The collection of Divine Rights of *Ius Divinum Limitis* (Limits) contains one Right being:-   *Collection of Ius Divinum Limitis*

    (i)   *Ius Divinum Limitis* being the Divine Right of Limit of Motion and Change.

Article 218 – Ius Divinum Existentia (Existence)

855. **Ius Divinum Existentia** are the collection of Divine Rights of Existence, as inherited from the collection of Divine Rights *Ius Divinum*.   *Ius Divinum Existentia (Existence)*

856. *Ius Divinum Existentia* (Existence) is the fifteenth collection of twenty-two Foundational Divine Rights; and may only be invoked whenever (a) the Rights are invoked by a Divine Person or (b) the lesser related Natural Rights or Superior Person Rights as defined by the most sacred Covenant *Pactum De Singularis Caelum*.   *Invoking of Ius Divinum Existentia*

857. The collection of Divine Rights of *Ius Divinum Existentia* (Existence) contains one Right being:-   *Collection of Ius Divinum Existentia*

    (i)   *Ius Divinum Existentia* being the Divine Right of Existence.

Article 219 – Ius Divinum Modela (Model)

858. **Ius Divinum Modela** are the collection of Divine Rights of Prototypes, Models and Systems, as inherited from the collection of Divine Rights *Ius Divinum*.   *Ius Divinum Modela (Model)*

859. *Ius Divinum Modela* (Models) is the sixteenth collection of twenty-two Foundational Divine Rights; and may only be invoked whenever (a) the Rights are invoked by a Divine Person or (b) the lesser related Natural Rights or Superior Person Rights as defined by the most sacred Covenant *Pactum De Singularis Caelum*.   *Invoking of Ius Divinum Modela*

860. The collection of Divine Rights of *Ius Divinum Modela* (Models) contains one Right being:-   *Collection of Ius Divinum Modela*

    (i)   *Ius Divinum Modela* being the Divine Right of Models.

Article 220 – Ius Divinum Elementa (Elements)

861. ***Ius Divinum Elementa*** are the collection of Elemental Particles of Matter & Properties, as inherited from the collection of Divine Rights *Ius Divinum*.

Ius Divinum Elementa (Elements)

862. *Ius Divinum Elementa* (Elements) is the seventeenth collection of twenty-two Foundational Divine Rights; and may only be invoked whenever (a) the Rights are invoked by a Divine Person or (b) the lesser related Natural Rights or Superior Person Rights as defined by the most sacred Covenant *Pactum De Singularis Caelum*.

Invoking of Ius Divinum Elementa

863. The collection of Divine Rights of *Ius Divinum Elementa* (Elements) contains one Right being:-

Collection of Ius Divinum Elementa

   (i) *Ius Divinum Elementa* being the Divine Right of Elemental Particles of Matter & Properties.

Article 221 – Ius Divinum Spatium (Space)

864. ***Ius Divinum Spatium*** are the collection of Divine Rights of Space & Properties, as inherited from the collection of Divine Rights *Ius Divinum*.

Ius Divinum Spatium (Space)

865. *Ius Divinum Spatium* (Space & Dimension) is the eighteenth collection of twenty-two Foundational Divine Rights; and may only be invoked whenever (a) the Rights are invoked by a Divine Person or (b) the lesser related Natural Rights or Superior Person Rights as defined by the most sacred Covenant *Pactum De Singularis Caelum*.

Invoking of Ius Divinum Spatium

866. The collection of Divine Rights of *Ius Divinum Spatium* (Space & Dimension) contains one Right being:-

Collection of Ius Divinum Spatium

   (i) *Ius Divinum Spatium* being the Divine Right of Space & Properties.

Article 222 – Ius Divinum Fortes (Forces)

867. ***Ius Divinum Fortes*** are the collection of Divine Rights of Forces & Properties, as inherited from the collection of Divine Rights *Ius Divinum*.

Ius Divinum Fortes (Forces)

868. *Ius Divinum Fortes* (Forces) is the nineteenth collection of twenty-two Foundational Divine Rights; and may only be invoked whenever (a) the Rights are invoked by a Divine Person or (b) the lesser related

Invoking of Ius Divinum Fortes

Natural Rights or Superior Person Rights as defined by the most sacred Covenant *Pactum De Singularis Caelum*.

869. The collection of Divine Rights of *Ius Divinum Fortes* (Forces) contains one Right being:-   *Collection of Ius Divinum Fortes*

    (i)   *Ius Divinum Fortes* being the Divine Right of Forces & Properties.

Article 223 – Ius Divinum Energia (Energy)

870. ***Ius Divinum Energia*** are the collection of Divine Rights of Energy & Properties, as inherited from the collection of Divine Rights *Ius Divinum*.   *Ius Divinum Energia (Energy)*

871. *Ius Divinum Energia* (Energy) is the twentieth collection of twenty-two Foundational Divine Rights; and may only be invoked whenever (a) the Rights are invoked by a Divine Person or (b) the lesser related Natural Rights or Superior Person Rights as defined by the most sacred Covenant *Pactum De Singularis Caelum*.   *Invoking of Ius Divinum Energia*

872. The collection of Divine Rights of *Ius Divinum Energia* (Energy) contains one Right being:-   *Collection of Ius Divinum Energia*

    (i)   *Ius Divinum Energia* being the Divine Right of Energy & Properties.

Article 224 – Ius Divinum Computatio (Computations)

833. ***Ius Divinum Computatio*** are the collection of Divine Rights of Computations & Interactions, as inherited from the collection of Divine Rights *Ius Divinum*.   *Ius Divinum Computatio (Computations)*

874. *Ius Divinum Computatio* (Computations) is the twenty-first collection of twenty-two Foundational Divine Rights; and may only be invoked whenever (a) the Rights are invoked by a Divine Person or (b) the lesser related Natural Rights or Superior Person Rights as defined by the most sacred Covenant *Pactum De Singularis Caelum*.   *Invoking of Ius Divinum Computatio*

875. The collection of Divine Rights of *Ius Divinum Computatio* (Computations) contains one Right being:-   *Collection of Ius Divinum Computatio*

    (i)   *Ius Divinum Computatio* being the Divine Right of Computations & Interactions.

Article 225 – Ius Divinum Entia (Being)

876. ***Ius Divinum Entia*** are the collection of Divine Rights of Being, as inherited from the collection of Divine Rights *Ius Divinum*.

Ius Divinum Entia (Being)

877. *Ius Divinum Entia* (Being) is the twenty-second collection of twenty-two Foundational Divine Rights; and may only be invoked whenever (a) the Rights are invoked by a Divine Person or (b) the lesser related Natural Rights or Superior Person Rights as defined by the most sacred Covenant *Pactum De Singularis Caelum*.

Invoking of Ius Divinum Entia

878. The collection of Divine Rights of *Ius Divinum Entia* (Being) contains one Right being:-

Collection of Ius Divinum Entia

    (i)   *Ius Divinum Entia* being the Divine Right of Being.

6.7 - Instrumental Divine Rights

Article 226 – Instrumental Divine Rights

879. ***Instrumental Divine Rights*** (Instrumentalis Divinum Iurium) are Perfect Divine Rights essential to the proper operation of the rule of law, justice and fair process.

Instrumental Divine Rights (Instrumentalis Divinum Iurium)

880. The following valid twenty-two (22) Instrumental Divine Rights (*Instrumentalis Divinum Iurium*) are recognised in accord with the most sacred Covenant *Pactum De Singularis Caelum* and the present Maxims:-

List of Instrumental Divine Rights (Instrumentalis Divinum Iurium)

    (i)   "**Ius Divinum Iuris**" are the collection of Divine Rights of Divine Law, Justice and Due Process, as inherited from the collection of Divine Rights *Ius Divinum*; and

    (ii)   "**Ius Divinum Aequum**" are the collection of Divine Rights of Equality and Fairness, as inherited from the collection of Divine Rights *Ius Divinum Iuris*; and

    (iii)   "**Ius Divinum Bona Fidei**" are the collection of Divine Rights of Good Faith, as inherited from the collection of Divine Rights *Ius Divinum Iuris*; and

    (iv)   "**Ius Divinum Fraternitas**" are the collection of Divine Rights of Membership of Heaven, as inherited from the collection of Divine Rights *Ius Divinum Iuris*; and

    (v)   "**Ius Divinum Fidei**" are the collection of Divine Rights of Divine Trusts and Estates, as inherited from the collection of

Divine Rights *Ius Divinum Iuris*; and

(vi) **"Ius Divinum Rationatio"** are the collection of Divine Rights of Divine Accounting, Credit and Funds, as inherited from the collection of Divine Rights *Ius Divinum Iuris*; and

(vii) **"Ius Divinum Concedere et Abrogare"** are the collection of Divine Rights to Give or Grant Rights and Annul or rescind Rights, as inherited from the collection of Divine Rights *Ius Divinum Iuris*; and

(viii) **"Ius Divinum Delegare et Revocare"** are the collection of Divine Rights to Assign or Delegate Rights and Cancel or Revoke Rights, as inherited from the collection of Divine Rights *Ius Divinum Iuris*; and

(ix) **"Ius Divinum Associatio et Conventio"** are the collection of Divine Rights of Association and Agreement, as inherited from the collection of Divine Rights *Ius Divinum Iuris*; and

(x) **"Ius Divinum Consensum et Non"** are the collection of Divine Rights to Consent and Non-Consent, as inherited from the collection of Divine Rights *Ius Divinum Iuris*; and

(xi) **"Ius Divinum Dominium"** are the collection of Divine Rights of Absolute Ownership, as inherited from the collection of Divine Rights *Ius Divinum Iuris*; and

(xii) **"Ius Divinum Possessionis"** are the collection of Divine Rights to Possess, Hold and Own Property, as inherited from the collection of Divine Rights *Ius Divinum Iuris*; and

(xiii) **"Ius Divinum Usus"** are the collection of Divine Rights of Use and Fruits of Use of Property, as inherited from the collection of Divine Rights *Ius Divinum Iuris*; and

(xiv) **"Ius Divinum Proprietatis"** are the collection of Divine Rights of Ownership of Use or Fruits of Use of Property, as inherited from the collection of Divine Rights *Ius Divinum Iuris*; and

(xv) **"Ius Divinum Vectigalis Proprietatis"** are the collection of Divine Rights to impose Rents, Tolls, Levies, Contributions or Charges against Property, as inherited from the collection of Divine Rights *Ius Divinum Iuris*; and

(xvi) **"Ius Divinum Moneta"** are the collection of Divine Rights to Mint, Produce, Hold, Use and Exchange Money, as inherited from the collection of Divine Rights *Ius Divinum Iuris*; and

(xvii) **"Ius Divinum Vectigalis Moneta"** are the collection of Divine Rights to impose Rents, Tolls, Levies, Contributions or Charges against Money, as inherited from the collection of Divine Rights *Ius Divinum Iuris*; and

(xviii) **"Ius Divinum Registrum"** are the collection of Divine Rights to Enter Records within Registers and Rolls, as inherited from the collection of Divine Rights *Ius Divinum Iuris*; and

(xix) **"Ius Divinum Remedium"** are the collection of Divine Rights of Remedy, Relief, Redress or Compensation, as inherited from the collection of Divine Rights *Ius Divinum Iuris*; and

(xx) **"Ius Divinum Poena"** are the collection of Divine Rights of Penalty, Penitence or Punishment, as inherited from the collection of Divine Rights *Ius Divinum Iuris*; and

(xxi) **"Ius Divinum Clementia"** are the collection of Divine Rights of Mercy & Forgiveness, as inherited from the collection of Divine Rights *Ius Divinum Iuris*; and

(xxii) **"Ius Divinum Actionum"** are the collection of Divine Rights of Action, as inherited from the collection of Divine Rights *Ius Divinum Iuris*.

Article 227 – Ius Divinum Iuris (Justice & Due Process)

881. ***Ius Divinum Iuris*** are the collection of Divine Rights of Divine Law, Justice and Due Process, as inherited from the collection of Divine Rights *Ius Divinum*.

    Ius Divinum Iuris (Justice & Due Process)

882. *Ius Divinum Iuris* (Justice & Due Process) is the first collection of twenty-two Instrumental Divine Rights; and may only be invoked whenever (a) the Rights are invoked by a Divine Person or (b) the lesser related Natural Rights or Superior Person Rights as defined by the most sacred Covenant *Pactum De Singularis Caelum*.

    Invoking of Ius Divinum Iuris

883. The collection of Divine Rights of *Ius Divinum Iuris* (Justice & Due Process) contains twenty-eight Rights being:-

    Collection of Ius Divinum Iuris

    (i) *Ius Divinum Iuris* being the Divine Right of Justice and Due Process; and

    (ii) *Ius Divinum Accusationis* being the Divine Right to make an Accusation against another Person or Body or Entity upon Possession of Provable Evidence of Personal Harm, Injury or

Loss; and

(iii) *Ius Divinum Innocentiae* being the Divine Right of Innocence against any Accusation until Proven or Confession or Culpability; and

(iv) *Ius Divinum Accusationis Cognoscendi* being the Divine Right for the Accused and their Agent to know the Full Disclosure and Brief of Evidence of any Accusation; and

(v) *Ius Divinum Defensionis* being the Divine Right to Defend against any Accusation; and

(vi) *Ius Divinum Iurisdictionis* being the Divine Right of Jurisdiction; and

(vii) *Ius Divinum Iudicandi* being the Divine Right of Adjudication; and

(viii) *Ius Divinum Locandi* being the Divine Right to Adjudicate under the Laws of the Location; and

(ix) *Ius Divinum Fori* being the Divine Right to Adjudicate under the Laws of the Forum; and

(x) *Ius Divinum Processus Iustus* being the Divine Right of Fair Process; and

(xi) *Ius Divinum Arbitrandi* being the Divine Right of Arbitration as method for dispute resolution; and

(xii) *Ius Divinum Auctoritatis Regulis* being the Divine Right of Regulatory Authority; and

(xiii) *Ius Divinum Tutelam Iurium* being the Divine Right to Protect Rights; and

(xiv) *Ius Divinum Imponendi Poenas* being the Divine Right to Impose Penalties; and

(xv) *Ius Divinum Decreti Iudicialis* being the Divine Right to issue Judicial Decrees; and

(xvi) *Ius Divinum Conventionem Exigendi* being the Divine Right to Enforce the Terms and Conditions of Agreement; and

(xvii) *Ius Divinum Legem Perquisitio* being the Divine Right to Hold an Evidence Inquiry to Establish if the Accusations hold sufficient weight to proceed to Indictment; and

(xviii) *Ius Divinum Legem Examinatio* being the Divine Right to Hold a Hearing concerning one or more Issues related to an ongoing Legal Matter including (but not limited to) Pretrial,

Preliminary, Status, Motion, Probation, Extradition, Custody, Guardian, Surety, Injunction, Contempt, Discovery, Rights or Competency; and

(xix) *Ius Divinum Legem Inquisitio* being the Divine Right to Hold a Hearing of Arraignment, or Indictment or Committal to establish the necessary threshold to proceed or not to proceed to Trial by Jury or Trial without Jury or if admission of culpability to move to sentencing; and

(xx) *Ius Divinum Legem Malitiae* being the Divine Right to Hold a Technical Hearing concerning evidence of Bad Faith, Bad Conscience or Bad Actions of a Justice or their Officers constituting Malice and thus potential Corruption of the Law; and

(xxi) *Ius Divinum Legem Erroris* being the Divine Right to Hold a Technical Hearing concerning an error or failure of Due Process including (but not limited to) Juries Failing to Render Verdict or Actions during Trial constituting ground for a Mistrial; and

(xxii) *Ius Divinum Legem Iudicium* being the Divine Right to Hold a Trial by Jury; and

(xxiii) *Ius Divinum Legem Iudicatio* being the Divine Right to Hold a Trial by Judge only (without Jury); and

(xxiv) *Ius Divinum Legem Tribunalis* being the Divine Right to Hold a Hearing with Three (or more) Justices; and

(xxv) *Ius Divinum Legem Sententiae* being the Divine Right to Hold a Sentencing or Costs and Compensation Hearing after the Conclusion of the Trial; and

(xxvi) *Ius Divinum Legem Appellationis* being the Divine Right to Hold an Appeal Hearing against the Sentence or Conduct of Trial; and

(xxvii) *Ius Divinum Propria Persona* being the Divine Right to defend or accuse as oneself; and

(xxviii) *Ius Divinum Iudicialis Agensas* being the Divine Right to appoint a Legal Agent to defend or accuse; and

Article 228 – Ius Divinum Aequum (Equality and Fairness)

884. ***Ius Divinum Aequum*** are the collection of Divine Rights of Equality and Fairness, as inherited from the collection of Divine

Ius Divinum Aequum (Equality)

Rights *Ius Divinum Iuris*.

885. *Ius Divinum Aequum* (Equality) is the second collection of twenty-two Instrumental Divine Rights; and may only be invoked whenever (a) the Rights are invoked by a Divine Person or (b) the lesser related Natural Rights or Superior Person Rights as defined by the most sacred Covenant *Pactum De Singularis Caelum*.
_{Invoking of Ius Divinum Aequum}

886. The collection of Divine Rights of *Ius Divinum Aequum* (Equality) contains two Rights being:-
_{Collection of Ius Divinum Aequum}

(i) *Ius Divinum Aequum* being the Divine Right of Equality and Fairness; and

(ii) *Ius Divinum Aequitatis* being the Divine Right of Fairness.

Article 229 – Ius Divinum Bona Fidei (Good Faith)

887. **Ius Divinum Bona Fidei** shall be the collection of Divine Rights of Good Faith, as inherited from the collection of Divine Rights *Ius Divinum Iuris*.
_{Ius Divinum Bona Fidei (Good Faith)}

888. *Ius Divinum Bona Fidei* (Good Faith) is the third collection of twenty-two Instrumental Divine Rights; and may only be invoked whenever (a) the Rights are invoked by a Divine Person or (b) the lesser related Natural Rights or Superior Person Rights as defined by the most sacred Covenant *Pactum De Singularis Caelum*.
_{Invoking of Bona Fidei}

889. The collection of Divine Rights of *Ius Divinum Bona Fidei* (Good Faith) contains three Rights being:-
_{Collection of Ius Divinum Bona Fidei}

(i) *Ius Divinum Bona Fidei* being the Divine Right of Good Faith; and

(ii) *Ius Divinum Bona Conscientia* being the Divine Right of Good Conscience; and

(iii) *Ius Divinum Bona Actio* being the Divine Right of Good Action.

Article 230 – Ius Divinum Fraternitas (Membership of Heaven)

890. **Ius Divinum Fraternitas** are the collection of Divine Rights of Membership of Heaven, as inherited from the collection of Divine Rights *Ius Divinum Iuris*.
_{Ius Divinum Fraternitas (Membership of Heaven)}

891. *Ius Divinum Fraternitas* (Membership of Heaven) is the fourth collection of twenty-two Instrumental Divine Rights; and may only be
_{Invoking of Ius Divinum Fraternitas}

invoked whenever (a) the Rights are invoked by a Divine Person or (b) the lesser related Natural Rights or Superior Person Rights as defined by the most sacred Covenant *Pactum De Singularis Caelum*.

892. The collection of Divine Rights of *Ius Divinum Fraternitas* (Membership of Heaven) contains one Right being:-

 (i)   *Ius Divinum Fraternitas* being the Divine Right of Membership of Heaven.

Article 231 – Ius Divinum Fidei (Trusts & Estates)

893. ***Ius Divinum Fidei*** are the collection of Divine Rights of Divine Trusts and Estates, as inherited from the collection of Divine Rights *Ius Divinum Iuris*.

894. *Ius Divinum Fidei* (Trusts & Estates) is the fifth collection of twenty-two Instrumental Divine Rights; and may only be invoked whenever (a) the Rights are invoked by a Divine Person or (b) the lesser related Natural Rights or Superior Person Rights as defined by the most sacred Covenant *Pactum De Singularis Caelum*.

895. The collection of Divine Rights of *Ius Divinum Fidei* (Trusts & Estates) contains twenty-two Rights being:-

 (i)   *Ius Divinum Fidei* being the Divine Right of Trusts & Estates; and

 (ii)   *Ius Divinum Sequestrandi* being the Divine Right to hold Assets and Property in Trust during Disputes; and

 (iii)   *Ius Divinum Fiduciam Formandi* being the Divine Right to form a Trust; and

 (iv)   *Ius Divinum Fiduciam Unionis* being the Divine Right to Merge one or more Trusts; and

 (v)   *Ius Divinum Fiduciam Administrationis* being the Divine Right to Administer a Trust; and

 (vi)   *Ius Divinum Fiduciam Beneficiarius* being the Divine Right of Benefit from Trust; and

 (vii)   *Ius Divinum Fiduciam Computatio* being the Divine Right to Receive an Accounting of the Administration of a Trust; and

 (viii)   *Ius Divinum Fiduciam Investiendi* being the Divine Right to Vest one or more Assets or Property into a Trust; and

 (ix)   *Ius Divinum Fiduciam Dispositionis* being the Divine Right to Dispose of one or more Assets or Property of a Trust; and

(x) *Ius Divinum Fiduciam Terminandi* being the Divine Right of Termination of a Trust; and

(xi) *Ius Divinum Fiduciam Concludendi* being the Divine Right of Finalisation of a Trust; and

(xii) *Ius Divinum Fundum Formandi* being the Divine Right to form an Estate; and

(xiii) *Ius Divinum Fundum Unionis* being the Divine Right to Merge one or more Estates; and

(xiv) *Ius Divinum Hereditatis* being the Divine Right to inherit an Estate; and

(xv) *Ius Divinum Fundum Administrationis* being the Divine Right to Administer an Estate; and

(xvi) *Ius Divinum Fundum Beneficiarius* being the Divine Right of Benefit from an Estate; and

(xvii) *Ius Divinum Fundum Computatio* being the Divine Right to Receive an Accounting of the Administration of the Estate; and

(xviii) *Ius Divinum Fundum Alienationis* being the Divine Right of Alienation (Conveyance) of one or more Assets or Property into an Estate; and

(xix) *Ius Divinum Fundum Dispositionis* being the Divine Right to Dispose of one or more Assets or Property of an Estate; and

(xx) *Ius Divinum Fundum Dividendandi* being the Divine Right to Distribute Assets of an Estate; and

(xxi) *Ius Divinum Fundum Terminandi* being the Divine Right of Termination of an Estate; and

(xxii) *Ius Divinum Fundum Concludendi* being the Divine Right of Settlement of an Estate.

Article 232 – Ius Divinum Rationatio (Accounting, Credit & Funds)

896. ***Ius Divinum Rationatio*** are the collection of Divine Rights of Divine Accounting, Credit and Funds, as inherited from the collection of Divine Rights *Ius Divinum Iuris*. <!-- sidenote: Ius Divinum Rationatio (Accounting, Credit & Funds) -->

897. *Ius Divinum Rationatio* (Accounting, Credit & Funds) is the sixth collection of twenty-two Instrumental Divine Rights; and may only be invoked whenever (a) the Rights are invoked by a Divine Person or (b) the lesser related Natural Rights or Superior Person Rights as <!-- sidenote: Invoking of Ius Divinum Rationatio -->

defined by the most sacred Covenant *Pactum De Singularis Caelum*.

898. The collection of Divine Rights of *Ius Divinum Rationatio* (Accounting, Credit & Funds) contains fourteen Rights being:- [Collection of Ius Divinum Rationatio]

    (i)   *Ius Divinum Rationatio* being the Divine Right of Accounting, Credit and Funds; and

    (ii)   *Ius Divinum Rationum* being the Divine Right of Accounts; and

    (iii)   *Ius Divinum Rationum Examinationis* being the Divine Right of Accounts Audit; and

    (iv)   *Ius Divinum Aestimationis Valoris* being the Divine Right of Valuation; and

    (v)   *Ius Divinum Aestimationis Obligationis* being the Divine Right of Estimating Obligation for Value; and

    (vi)   *Ius Divinum Aestimationis Pretii* being the Divine Right of Estimating Price for Obligation; and

    (vii)   *Ius Divinum Aestimationis Crediti* being the Divine Right of Estimating Credit; and

    (viii)   *Ius Divinum Aestimationis Debiti* being the Divine Right of Estimating Debit; and

    (ix)   *Ius Divinum Valorum Pignorare* being the Divine Right to Pledge Valuables as Collateral for Funds; and

    (x)   *Ius Divinum Valorum Hypotheca* being the Divine Right of Hypothecating Value of Collateral to Funds; and

    (xi)   *Ius Divinum Rationum Relatio* being the Divine Right of Reporting of Accounts; and

    (xii)   *Ius Divinum Relatio Crediti* being the Divine Right of Credit Reporting; and

    (xiii)   *Ius Divinum Crediti Accessus* being the Divine Right of Access to Funds; and

    (xiv)   *Ius Divinum Collectionis Debiti* being the Divine Right of Debit (Debt) Collection.

Article 233 – Ius Divinum Concedere et Abrogare (Give & Grant)

899. ***Ius Divinum Concedere et Abrogare*** are the collection of Divine Rights to Give or Grant Rights and Annul or rescind Rights, as inherited from the collection of Divine Rights *Ius Divinum Iuris*. [Ius Divinum Concedere et Abrogare (Give & Grant)]

900. *Ius Divinum Concedere et Abrogare* (Give & Grant) is the seventh collection of twenty-two Instrumental Divine Rights; and may only be invoked whenever (a) the Rights are invoked by a Divine Person or (b) the lesser related Natural Rights or Superior Person Rights as defined by the most sacred Covenant *Pactum De Singularis Caelum*.

Invoking of Ius Divinum Concedere et Abrogare

901. The collection of Divine Rights of *Ius Divinum Concedere et Abrogare* (Give & Grant) contains six Rights being:-

Collection of Ius Divinum Concedere et Abrogare

    (i)   *Ius Divinum Concedere et Abrogare* being the Divine Right of Give or Grant Rights and Annul or Rescind Rights; and

    (ii)   *Ius Divinum Donandum Iuris* being the Divine Right to Give a Right; and

    (iii) *Ius Divinum Rescindendum Iuris* being the Divine Right to Rescind a Right; and

    (iv) *Ius Divinum Conferendum Iuris* being the Divine Right to Grant a Right; and

    (v)   *Ius Divinum Abrogandum Iuris* being the Divine Right to Abrogate a Right; and

    (vi) *Ius Divinum Annullare Iuris* being the Divine Right to Annul a Right.

Article 234 – Ius Divinum Delegare et Revocare (Assign & Delegate)

902. ***Ius Divinum Delegare et Revocare*** are the collection of Divine Rights to Assign or Delegate Rights and Cancel or Revoke Rights, as inherited from the collection of Divine Rights *Ius Divinum Iuris*.

Ius Divinum Delegare et Revocare (Assign & Delegate)

903. *Ius Divinum Delegare et Revocare* (Assign & Delegate) is the eighth collection of twenty-two Instrumental Divine Rights; and may only be invoked whenever (a) the Rights are invoked by a Divine Person or (b) the lesser related Natural Rights or Superior Person Rights as defined by the most sacred Covenant *Pactum De Singularis Caelum*.

Invoking of Ius Divinum Delegare et Revocare

904. The collection of Divine Rights of *Ius Divinum Delegare et Revocare* (Assign & Delegate) contains five Rights being:-

Collection of Ius Divinum Delegare et Revocare

    (i)   *Ius Divinum Delegare et Revocare* being the Divine Right of Assign or Delegate Rights and Cancel or Revoke Rights; and

    (ii)   *Ius Divinum Delegandi Iuris* being the Divine Right to Delegate a Right; and

    (iii) *Ius Divinum Cancellari Iuris* being the Divine Right to Cancel a Delegated Right; and

(iv) *Ius Divinum Assignare Iuris* being the Divine Right to Assign a Right; and

(v) *Ius Divinum Revocandum Iuris* being the Divine Right to Revoke an Assigned Right.

Article 235 – Ius Divinum Associatio et Conventio (Association & Agreement)

905. **Ius Divinum Associatio et Conventio** are the collection of Divine Rights of Association and Agreement, as inherited from the collection of Divine Rights *Ius Divinum Iuris*.

    Ius Divinum Associatio et Conventio (Association)

906. *Ius Divinum Associatio et Conventio* (Association) is the ninth collection of twenty-two Instrumental Divine Rights; and may only be invoked whenever (a) the Rights are invoked by a Divine Person or (b) the lesser related Natural Rights or Superior Person Rights as defined by the most sacred Covenant *Pactum De Singularis Caelum*.

    Invoking of Ius Divinum Associatio et Conventio

907. The collection of Divine Rights of *Ius Divinum Associatio et Conventio* (Association & Agreement) contains twenty-four Rights being:-

    Collection of Ius Divinum Associatio et Conventio

    (i) *Ius Divinum Associatio et Conventio* being the Divine Right of Association and Agreement; and

    (ii) *Ius Divinum Associationis* being the Divine Right of Association; and

    (iii) *Ius Divinum Renuntiatio* being the Divine Right of Renunciation of Association; and

    (iv) *Ius Divinum Conventio* being the Divine Right of Agreement; and

    (v) *Ius Divinum Conventionis Negotiationis* being the Divine Right to Negotiate an Agreement; and

    (vi) *Ius Divinum Conventionis Recusatio* being the Divine Right to Refuse an Agreement; and

    (vii) *Ius Divinum Conventionis Instrumenti* being the Divine Right to define an Instrument of Agreement; and

    (viii) *Ius Divinum Pactum Formandi* being the Divine Right to form a Covenant or Treaty; and

    (ix) *Ius Divinum Charta Formandi* being the Divine Right to form a Charter; and

(x) *Ius Divinum Constitutionis Formandi* being the Divine Right to form a Constitution; and

(xi) *Ius Divinum Memorandum Formandi* being the Divine Right to form a Memorandum of Agreement; and

(xii) *Ius Divinum Litterae Formandi* being the Divine Right to form a Letter or Heads of Agreement; and

(xiii) *Ius Divinum Notitiae Formandi* being the Divine Right to form a Note or Notice of Agreement; and

(xiv) *Ius Divinum Conventionis Terminos* being the Divine Right to define Terms and Conditions of Agreement; and

(xv) *Ius Divinum Conventionis Pollucendi* being the Divine Right to make a Solemn Promise in Agreement; and

(xvi) *Ius Divinum Conventionis Poenam et Remedium* being the Divine Right to define Penalties and Remedies of Agreement; and

(xvii) *Ius Divinum Modandi Conventionis Instrumenti* being the Divine Right to Modify the Terms and Conditions of Agreement; and

(xviii) *Ius Divinum Conventionis Ratificationis* being the Divine Right of Ratification of Agreement; and

(xix) *Ius Divinum Minoris Lapsus* being the Divine Right of Action against Minor Breach of Agreement; and

(xx) *Ius Divinum Minoris Reparare* being the Divine Right to Rectify and Repair Minor Issues against Minor Breach of Agreement; and

(xxi) *Ius Divinum Maioris Lapsus* being the Divine Right of Action against Major Breach of Agreement; and

(xxii) *Ius Divinum Maioris Restituere* being the Divine Right to Restore and Re-establish Major Issues against Major Breach of Agreement; and

(xxiii) *Ius Divinum Concludendi* being the Divine Right to Conclude an Agreement; and

(xxiv) *Ius Divinum Terminandi* being the Divine Right to Terminate an Agreement.

Article 236 – Ius Divinum Consensum et Non (Consent)

908. ***Ius Divinum Consensum et Non*** are the collection of Divine Rights to Consent and Non-Consent, as inherited from the collection of Divine Rights *Ius Divinum Iuris*.

909. *Ius Divinum Consensum et Non* (Consent) is the tenth collection of twenty-two Instrumental Divine Rights; and may only be invoked whenever (a) the Rights are invoked by a Divine Person or (b) the lesser related Natural Rights or Superior Person Rights as defined by the most sacred Covenant *Pactum De Singularis Caelum*.

910. The collection of Divine Rights of *Ius Divinum Consensum et Non* (Consent) contains three Rights being:-

    (i) *Ius Divinum Consensum et Non* being the Divine Right of Consent and Non-Consent; and

    (ii) *Ius Divinum Consensus* being the Divine Right of Consent; and

    (iii) *Ius Divinum Non Consensus* being the Divine Right of Non Consent.

Article 237 – Ius Divinum Dominium (Ownership)

911. ***Ius Divinum Dominium*** are the collection of Divine Rights of Absolute Ownership and Custody, as inherited from the collection of Divine Rights *Ius Divinum Iuris*.

912. *Ius Divinum Dominium* (Ownership) is the eleventh collection of twenty-two Instrumental Divine Rights; and may only be invoked whenever (a) the Rights are invoked by a Divine Person or (b) the lesser related Natural Rights or Superior Person Rights as defined by the most sacred Covenant *Pactum De Singularis Caelum*.

913. The collection of Divine Rights of *Ius Divinum Dominium* (Absolute Ownership and Custody) contains fourteen Rights being:-

    (i) *Ius Divinum Dominium* being the Divine Right of Absolute Ownership and Custody; and

    (ii) *Ius Divinum Terrae ad Caelum* being the Divine Right of Absolute Ownership and Custody from the Centre of the Earth to the Heavens Above; and

    (iii) *Ius Divinum Defendendi* being the Divine Right to Defend with Force any Thing, Person or Property under Absolute

Ownership and Custody; and

(iv) *Ius Divinum Patronatus* being the Divine Right of Protector, Guardian and Patron over any Thing, Person or Property under Absolute Ownership and Custody; and

(v) *Ius Divinum Coercendum* being the Divine Right to Enforce with Force any Right concerning any Thing, Person or Property under Absolute Ownership and Custody; and

(vi) *Ius Divinum Recuperandi* being the Divine Right to Enforce with Force the Recovery, Return and Restoration of any Thing, Person or Property under Absolute Ownership and Custody; and

(vii) *Ius Divinum Alligandi et Removendi* being the Divine Right of Binding and Unbinding any Item or Thing from Property under Absolute Ownership and Custody; and

(viii) *Ius Divinum Alterius Commodi* being the Divine Right of Using Another's Benefit when derived from Property under Absolute Ownership and Custody; and

(ix) *Ius Divinum Angariae* being the Divine Right of Requisition of Property or Obligations of Service during emergency or public benefit when related to any Thing, Person or Property under Absolute Ownership and Custody; and

(x) *Ius Divinum Censendi* being the Divine Right of Census and Accounting for Things, Persons and Property derived from Absolute Ownership and Custody; and

(xi) *Ius Divinum Excludendi* being the Divine Right of Exclusion of Persons from Land or Property under Absolute Ownership and Custody; and

(xii) *Ius Divinum Alienatus* being the Divine Right to Convey or Transfer to Another as a Lesser title any Land, Property or Thing under Absolute Ownership and Custody; and

(xiii) *Ius Divinum Ingrediendi* being the Divine Right to enter a Property when derived from Property under Absolute Ownership and Custody; and

(xiv) *Ius Divinum Quaesitum Tertio* being the Divine Right to enter as a Third Party to an existing Agreement to enforce a Right when the related Things, Persons and Property are derived from Absolute Ownership and Custody.

Article 238 – Ius Divinum Possessionis (Possession)

914. **Ius Divinum Possessionis** are the collection of Divine Rights to Possess, Hold and Own Property, as inherited from the collection of Divine Rights *Ius Divinum Iuris*.

    <small>Ius Divinum Possessionis (Possession)</small>

915. *Ius Divinum Possessionis* (Possession) is the twelfth collection of twenty-two Instrumental Divine Rights; and may only be invoked whenever (a) the Rights are invoked by a Divine Person or (b) the lesser related Natural Rights or Superior Person Rights as defined by the most sacred Covenant *Pactum De Singularis Caelum*.

    <small>Invoking of Ius Divinum Possessionis</small>

916. The collection of Divine Rights of *Ius Divinum Possessionis* (Possession) contains four Rights being:-

    <small>Collection of Ius Divinum Possessionis</small>

    (i)   *Ius Divinum Possessionis* being the Divine Right to Possess, Hold and Own Property; and

    (ii) *Ius Divinum Possessionis Rem* being the Divine Right to Possess, Hold and Own a Thing; and

    (iii) *Ius Divinum Possessionis Fidei* being the Divine Right to Possess, Hold and Own (as Trustee) the Divine Res (Soul) of the Divine Trust associated with your Divine Person; and

    (iv) *Ius Divinum Possessionis Animae* being the Divine Right to Possess, Hold and Own (as Trustee) the Soul connected to your Divine Person.

Article 239 – Ius Divinum Usus (Use)

917. **Ius Divinum Usus** are the collection of Divine Rights of Use and Fruits of Use of Property, as inherited from the collection of Divine Rights *Ius Divinum Iuris*.

    <small>Ius Divinum Usus (Use)</small>

918. *Ius Divinum Usus* (Use) is the thirteenth collection of twenty-two Instrumental Divine Rights; and may only be invoked whenever (a) the Rights are invoked by a Divine Person or (b) the lesser related Natural Rights or Superior Person Rights as defined by the most sacred Covenant *Pactum De Singularis Caelum*.

    <small>Invoking of Ius Divinum Usus</small>

919. The collection of Divine Rights of *Ius Divinum Usus* (Use) contains three Rights being:-

    <small>Collection of Ius Divinum Usus</small>

    (i) *Ius Divinum Usus* being the Divine Right of Use and Fruits of Use of Property; and

    (ii) *Ius Divinum Affectandi* being the Divine Right of Acquisition of Property in Continuous Use; and

(iii) *Ius Divinum Cessandi* being the Divine Right of Cessation of Property in Use.

Article 240 – Ius Divinum Proprietatis (Ownership of Use)

920. **Ius Divinum Proprietatis** are the collection of Divine Rights of Ownership of Use or Fruits of Use of Property, as inherited from the collection of Divine Rights *Ius Divinum Iuris*.

Ius Divinum Proprietatis (Ownership of Use)

921. *Ius Divinum Proprietatis* (Ownership of Use) is the fourteenth collection of twenty-two Instrumental Divine Rights; and may only be invoked whenever (a) the Rights are invoked by a Divine Person or (b) the lesser related Natural Rights or Superior Person Rights as defined by the most sacred Covenant *Pactum De Singularis Caelum*.

Invoking of Ius Divinum Proprietatis

922. The collection of Divine Rights of *Ius Divinum Proprietatis* (Ownership of Use) contains eight Rights being:-

Collection of Ius Divinum Proprietatis

(i) *Ius Divinum Proprietatis* being the Divine Right of Ownership of Use or Fruits of Use of Property; and

(ii) *Ius Divinum Transferendi* being the Divine Right to Transfer Ownership of Use or Fruits of Use of Property to Another; and

(iii) *Ius Divinum Utilitatis* being the Divine Right of Enjoyment of Ownership of Use or Fruits of Use of Property; and

(iv) *Ius Divinum Recusatio* being the Divine Right of Refusal of Use or Fruits of Use by Another of Owned Property; and

(v) *Ius Divinum Accessionis* being the Divine Right of Accession of additions and ownership of additions to Property in Use; and

(vi) *Ius Divinum Aedificii* being the Divine Right of Building on Land; and

(vii) *Ius Divinum Alluvionis* being the Divine Right of Accretion in increasing Property through natural processes; and

(viii) *Ius Divinum Actionis Proprietatis* being the Divine Right of Action against Unreasonable or Immoral Loss of Use or Fruits of Use of Property.

Article 241 – Ius Divinum Vectigalis Proprietatis (Rents on Use)

923. ***Ius Divinum Vectigalis Proprietatis*** are the collection of Divine Rights to impose Rents, Tolls, Levies, Contributions or Charges against Property, as inherited from the collection of Divine Rights *Ius Divinum Iuris*.

924. *Ius Divinum Vectigalis Proprietatis* (Rents on Use) is the fifteenth collection of twenty-two Instrumental Divine Rights; and may only be invoked whenever (a) the Rights are invoked by a Divine Person or (b) the lesser related Natural Rights or Superior Person Rights as defined by the most sacred Covenant *Pactum De Singularis Caelum*.

925. The collection of Divine Rights of *Ius Divinum Vectigalis Proprietatis* (Rents on Use) contains seven Rights being:-

   (i) *Ius Divinum Vectigalis Proprietatis* being the Divine Right to impose Rents, Tolls, Levies, Contributions or Charges against Ownership of Use or Fruits of Use of Property; and

   (ii) *Ius Divinum Conducendi Mercedem* being the Divine Right to Impose Rent on Possession or Use of Property; and

   (iii) *Ius Divinum Impendi Tributum* being the Divine Right to Impose Levy on Possession or Use of Property; and

   (iv) *Ius Divinum Impendi Portorium* being the Divine Right to Impose a Toll on Possession or Use of Property; and

   (v) *Ius Divinum Impendi Vectigalis* being the Divine Right to Impose a Charge on Possession or Use of Property; and

   (vi) *Ius Divinum Petendi Contributionem* being the Divine Right to Request Contributions on Possession or Use of Property; and

   (vii) *Ius Divinum Actionis Vectigalis Proprietatis* being the Divine Right of Action against Unreasonable or Immoral Loss or Failure to Pay Rents, Tolls, Levies, Contributions or Charges against Ownership of Use or Fruits of Use of Property.

Article 242 – Ius Divinum Moneta (Money)

926. ***Ius Divinum Moneta*** are the collection of Divine Rights to Mint, Produce, Hold, Use and Exchange Money, as inherited from the collection of Divine Rights *Ius Divinum Iuris*.

927. *Ius Divinum Moneta* (Money) is the sixteenth collection of twenty-

two Instrumental Divine Rights; and may only be invoked whenever (a) the Rights are invoked by a Divine Person or (b) the lesser related Natural Rights or Superior Person Rights as defined by the most sacred Covenant *Pactum De Singularis Caelum*. — Divinum Moneta

928. The collection of Divine Rights of *Ius Divinum Moneta* (Money) contains fifteen Rights being:- — Collection of Ius Divinum Moneta

    (i)   *Ius Divinum Moneta* being the Divine Right to Mint, Produce, Hold, Use and Exchange Money; and

    (ii)   *Ius Divinum Creandi Moneta* being the Divine Right to Create and Mint Money; and

    (iii)   *Ius Divinum Creandi Digitalis Moneta* being the Divine Right to Create and Mint Digital Money; and

    (iv)   *Ius Divinum Tenendi Moneta* being the Divine Right to Hold and Possess Money; and

    (v)   *Ius Divinum Tenendi Digitalis Moneta* being the Divine Right to Hold and Possess Digital Money; and

    (vi)   *Ius Divinum Transferre Moneta* being the Divine Right to Transfer Money; and

    (vii)   *Ius Divinum Transferre Digitalis Moneta* being the Divine Right to Transfer Digital Money; and

    (viii)   *Ius Divinum Recipere Moneta* being the Divine Right to Receive Money; and

    (ix)   *Ius Divinum Recipere Digitalis Moneta* being the Divine Right to Receive Digital Money; and

    (x)   *Ius Divinum Cambii Moneta* being the Divine Right to Exchange Money for another unit of currency; and

    (xi)   *Ius Divinum Cambii Digitalis Moneta* being the Divine Right to Exchange Digital Money for another unit of currency; and

    (xii)   *Ius Divinum Utendi Moneta* being the Divine Right to Use Money for Settlement of Debts and Obligations; and

    (xiii)   *Ius Divinum Utendi Digitalis Moneta* being the Divine Right to Use Digital Money for Settlement of Debts and Obligations; and

    (xiv)   *Ius Divinum Utendi Moneta Numismatis Legalis* being the Divine Right to Use Money as Legal Tender; and

    (xv)   *Ius Divinum Utendi Digitalis Moneta Numismatis Legalis* being the Divine Right to Use Digital Money as Legal Tender.

Article 243 – Ius Divinum Vectigalis Moneta (Rents on Money)

929. ***Ius Divinum Vectigalis Moneta*** are the collection of Divine Rights to impose Rents, Tolls, Levies, Contributions or Charges against Money, as inherited from the collection of Divine Rights *Ius Divinum Iuris*.

930. *Ius Divinum Vectigalis Moneta* (Rents on Money) is the seventeenth collection of twenty-two Instrumental Divine Rights; and may only be invoked whenever (a) the Rights are invoked by a Divine Person or (b) the lesser related Natural Rights or Superior Person Rights as defined by the most sacred Covenant *Pactum De Singularis Caelum*.

931. The collection of Divine Rights of *Ius Divinum Vectigalis Moneta* (Rents on Money) contains seven Rights being:-

(i) *Ius Divinum Vectigalis Moneta* being the Divine Right to impose Rents, Tolls, Levies, Contributions or Charges against Money; and

(ii) *Ius Divinum Conducendi Mercedem Moneta* being the Divine Right to Impose Rent on Possession or Use of Money; and

(iii) *Ius Divinum Impendi Tributum Moneta* being the Divine Right to Impose Levy on Possession or Use of Money; and

(iv) *Ius Divinum Impendi Portorium Moneta* being the Divine Right to Impose Toll on Possession or Use of Money; and

(v) *Ius Divinum Impendi Vectigalis Moneta* being the Divine Right to Impose a Charge on Possession or Use of Money; and

(vi) *Ius Divinum Petendi Contributionem Moneta* being the Divine Right to Request Contributions on Possession or Use of Money; and

(vii) *Ius Divinum Actionis Vectigalis Moneta* being the Divine Right of Action against Unreasonable or Immoral Loss or Failure to Pay Rents, Tolls, Levies, Contributions or Charges against Possession or Use of Money.

Article 244 – Ius Divinum Registrum (Registers & Rolls)

932. ***Ius Divinum Registrum*** are the collection of Divine Rights to Enter Records within Registers and Rolls, as inherited from the collection of Divine Rights *Ius Divinum Iuris*.

933. *Ius Divinum Registrum* (Registers & Rolls) is the eighteenth collection of twenty-two Instrumental Divine Rights; and may only be invoked whenever (a) the Rights are invoked by a Divine Person or (b) the lesser related Natural Rights or Superior Person Rights as defined by the most sacred Covenant *Pactum De Singularis Caelum*.

Divinum Registrum

934. The collection of Divine Rights of *Ius Divinum Registrum* (Registers & Rolls) contains twenty-three Rights being:-

Collection of Ius Divinum Registrum

    (i)   *Ius Divinum Registrum* being the Divine Right to Enter and Manage Records within Registers and Rolls; and

    (ii)   *Ius Divinum Registrum Confidentiae* being the Divine Right of Confidential Access to a Register; and

    (iii) *Ius Divinum Registrum Accessus* being the Divine Right of Access to a Register; and

    (iv) *Ius Divinum Actionis Registrum Accessus* being the Divine Right of Action concerning Register Access; and

    (v)   *Ius Divinum Registrum Inspectionis* being the Divine Right of Inspection of a Register; and

    (vi) *Ius Divinum Actionis Registrum Correctionis* being the Divine Right of Action for Register Correction; and

    (vii) *Ius Divinum Registrum Intrationis* being the Divine Right of Entry in a Register; and

    (viii) *Ius Divinum Registri Recordationis Extrahendi* being the Divine Right to make an Extract of Record in a Register; and

    (ix) *Ius Divinum Registri Recordationis Abstrahendi* being the Divine Right to make an Abstract of Record in a Register; and

    (x)   *Ius Divinum Registri Recordationis Cancellationis* being the Divine Right to Cancel a Record in a Register; and

    (xi) *Ius Divinum Registri Recordationis Completionis* being the Divine Right to Complete a Record in a Register; and

    (xii) *Ius Divinum Registri Recordationis Correctionis* being the Divine Right to Correct a Record in a Register; and

    (xiii) *Ius Divinum Rotulae Confidentiae* being the Divine Right of Confidential Access to a Roll; and

    (xiv) *Ius Divinum Rotulae Accessus* being the Divine Right of Access to a Roll; and

    (xv) *Ius Divinum Actionis Rotulae Accessus* being the Divine Right of Action concerning Roll Access; and

    (xvi) *Ius Divinum Rotulae Inspectionis* being the Divine Right of

Inspection of a Roll; and

(xvii) *Ius Divinum Actionis Rotulae Correctionis* being the Divine Right of Action for Roll Correction; and

(xviii) *Ius Divinum Rotulae Intrationis* being the Divine Right of Entry in a Roll; and

(xix) *Ius Divinum Rotulae Recordationis Extrahendi* being the Divine Right *to make* an Extract of Record in a Roll; and

(xx) *Ius Divinum Rotulae Recordationis Abstrahendi* being the Divine Right *to make* an Abstract of Record in a Roll; and

(xxi) *Ius Divinum Rotulae Recordationis Cancellationis* being the Divine Right to Cancel a Record in a Roll; and

(xxii) *Ius Divinum Rotulae Recordationis Completionis* being the Divine Right to Complete a Record in a Roll; and

(xxiii) *Ius Divinum Rotulae Recordationis Correctionis* being the Divine Right to Correct a Record in a Roll.

Article 245 – Ius Divinum Remedium (Remedy)

935. ***Ius Divinum Remedium*** are the collection of Divine Rights of Remedy, Relief, Redress or Compensation, as inherited from the collection of Divine Rights *Ius Divinum Iuris*.
_{Ius Divinum Remedium (Remedy)}

936. *Ius Divinum Remedium* (Remedy) is the nineteenth collection of twenty-two Instrumental Divine Rights; and may only be invoked whenever (a) the Rights are invoked by a Divine Person or (b) the lesser related Natural Rights or Superior Person Rights as defined by the most sacred Covenant *Pactum De Singularis Caelum*.
_{Invoking of Ius Divinum Remedium}

937. The collection of Divine Rights of *Ius Divinum Remedium* (Remedy) contains nine Rights being:-
_{Collection of Ius Divinum Remedium}

(i) *Ius Divinum Remedium* being the Divine Right of Remedy, Relief, Redress or Compensation; and

(ii) *Ius Divinum Remedium Compensationis* being the Divine Right of Remedy of Compensation for Loss or Damages; and

(iii) *Ius Divinum Remedium Restitutionis* being the Divine Right of Remedy of Restitution for the Return of Property; and

(iv) *Ius Divinum Remedium Reparationis* being the Divine Right of Remedy of Restoration for the Repairing of Harm or Property; and

(v) *Ius Divinum Remedium Injunctionis* being the Divine Right of Remedy of Injunction to Enforce Performance or Prevent Behaviour of Another; and

(vi) *Ius Divinum Remedium Rescissionis* being the Divine Right of Remedy of Rescission to Cancel an Agreement or Transaction and Restore Parties to their Original Positions; and

(vii) *Ius Divinum Remedium Appellationis* being the Divine Right of Remedy of Appeal a Decision to a Higher Forum; and

(viii) *Ius Divinum Remedium Declarationis* being the Divine Right of Remedy of Declaratory Judgement; and

(ix) *Ius Divinum Remedium Sententiae* being the Divine Right of Remedy of Enforcement of Judgement.

Article 246 – Ius Divinum Poena (Penalty, Penitence or Punishment)

938. **Ius Divinum Poena** are the collection of Divine Rights of Penalty, Penitence or Punishment, as inherited from the collection of Divine Rights *Ius Divinum Iuris*. Ius Divinum Poena (Penalty)

939. *Ius Divinum Poena* (Penalty) is the twentieth collection of twenty-two Instrumental Divine Rights; and may only be invoked whenever (a) the Rights are invoked by a Divine Person or (b) the lesser related Natural Rights or Superior Person Rights as defined by the most sacred Covenant *Pactum De Singularis Caelum*. Invoking of Ius Divinum Poena

940. The collection of Divine Rights of Ius Divinum Poena (Penalty) contains five Rights being:- Collection of Ius Divinum Poena

(i) *Ius Divinum Poena* being the Divine Right of Penalty & Punishment; and

(ii) *Ius Divinum Remissionis Poenae* being the Divine Right of Remission in the significant lessening of Penalties upon prior and full Acceptance of Culpability and Evidence of Genuine Remorse and Efforts to Change before any Trial; and

(iii) *Ius Divinum Exacerbationis Poenae* being the Divine Right of Exacerbation in the significant increasing of severity of Penalties upon prior Refusal to Accept Culpability or Demonstrate Genuine Remorse or Change before any Trial; and

(iv) *Ius Divinum Appellationis Poenae* being the Divine Right to Appeal Punishment to a Decision to a Higher Forum; and

(v) *Ius Divinum Custodiae Vitae* being the Divine Right of Custody of Life whereby the Life of the Convicted must continue to be protected and sustained and cannot be threatened during any period of punishment.

Article 247 – Ius Divinum Clementia (Mercy)

941. **Ius Divinum Clementia** are be the collection of Divine Rights of Mercy & Forgiveness, as inherited from the collection of Divine Rights *Ius Divinum Iuris*.

942. *Ius Divinum Clementia* (Mercy) is the twenty-first collection of twenty-two Instrumental Divine Rights; and may only be invoked whenever (a) the Rights are invoked by a Divine Person or (b) the lesser related Natural Rights or Superior Person Rights as defined by the most sacred Covenant *Pactum De Singularis Caelum*.

943. The collection of Divine Rights of *Ius Divinum Clementia* (Mercy) contains two Rights being:-

   (i) *Ius Divinum Clementia* being the Divine Right of Mercy & Forgiveness; and

   (i) *Ius Expurgationis Instrumenti Convicti* being the Divine Right of Convicted Record Expurgation at Conclusion of Punishment in recognition for prior and full Acceptance of Culpability and Evidence of Genuine Remorse and Efforts to Change before any Trial and Conviction.

Article 248 – Ius Divinum Actionum (Action)

944. **Ius Divinum Actionum** are be the collection of Divine Rights of Action, as inherited from the collection of Divine Rights *Ius Divinum Iuris*.

945. *Ius Divinum Actionum* (Action) is the twenty-second collection of twenty-two Instrumental Divine Rights; and may only be invoked whenever (a) the Rights are invoked by a Divine Person or (b) the lesser related Natural Rights or Superior Person Rights as defined by the most sacred Covenant *Pactum De Singularis Caelum*.

946. The collection of Divine Rights of *Ius Divinum Actionum* (Action) contains eleven Rights being:-

   (i) *Ius Divinum Actionum* being the Divine Right of Action; and

   (ii) *Ius Divinum Abstinentiae* being the Divine Right to Abstain from Action; and

(iii) *Ius Divinum Causae Actionis* being the Divine Right of Valid Cause for an Action, whereby clear Evidence of a Wrong Exists; and

(iv) *Ius Divinum Obligationis Actionis* being the Divine Right of Obligation for an Action, whereby clear Evidence Exists of a Duty of Care or Performance Owed; and

(v) *Ius Divinum Proximitatis Actionis* being the Divine Right of Proximity for an Action, whereby the one bringing the Action is in close Proximity to the Issue; and

(vi) *Ius Divinum Temporis Actionis* being the Divine Right of Timeliness for an Action, whereby no time barrier exists for bringing such an Action; and

(vii) *Ius Divinum Iniuriae Actionis* being the Divine Right of Injury for an Action, whereby the one bringing the Action has suffered an actual harm or damages; and

(viii) *Ius Divinum Remedium Actionis* being the Divine Right of Remedy for an Action, whereby the Remedy sought is possible under the relevant Jurisdiction; and

(ix) *Ius Divinum Iurisdictionis Actionis* being the Divine Right of Jurisdiction for an Action, whereby the Jurisdiction proposed is the correct and valid forum and venue for such an Action; and

(x) *Ius Divinum Formae Actionis* being the Divine Right of Form for an Action, whereby the proposed Action conforms to the rules and bylaws of the relevant Jurisdiction in its format, presentation and arguments; and

(xi) *Ius Divinum Loci Standi Actionis* being the Divine Right of Standing for an Action constituting all previously mentioned Rights of this collection.

6.8 - Sacramental Divine Rights

Article 249 – Sacramental Divine Rights

947. **Sacramental Divine Rights** (*Sacramentum Divinum Iurium*) or **Sacred Divine Gifts** are Perfect Divine Rights associated with the thirty-three Divine Sacraments of One Heaven, also known as the Supreme Sacred Gifts of Heaven.

948. The following valid thirty-three (33) Sacramental Divine Rights

(*Sacramentum Divinum Iurium*) are recognised in accord with the most sacred Covenant *Pactum De Singularis Caelum* and the present Maxims:-

Divine Rights (Sacramentum Divinum Iurium)

(i) **"Ritus Sacramentum Recognosco"** is the Divine Right of the Key Sacrament of Recognition; and

(ii) **"Ritus Sacramentum Purificatio"** is the Divine Right of the Key Sacrament of Purification; and

(iii) **"Ritus Sacramentum Invocatio"** is the Divine Right of the Key Sacrament of Invocation; and

(iv) **"Ritus Sacramentum Obligatio"** is the Divine Right of the Key Sacrament of Obligation; and

(v) **"Ritus Sacramentum Delegatio"** is the Divine Right of the Key Sacrament of Delegation (Trust); and

(vi) **"Ritus Sacramentum Satisfactio"** is the Divine Right of the Key Sacrament of Satisfaction; and

(vii) **"Ritus Sacramentum Resolutio"** is the Divine Right of the Key Sacrament of Resolution; and

(viii) **"Ritus Sacramentum Sanctificatio"** is the Divine Right of the Cardinal Sacrament of Sanctification; and

(ix) **"Ritus Sacramentum Sustentatio"** is the Divine Right of the Cardinal Sacrament of Sustentation; and

(x) **"Ritus Sacramentum Unificatio"** is the Divine Right of the Cardinal Sacrament of Unification; and

(xi) **"Ritus Sacramentum Amalgamatio"** is the Divine Right of the Cardinal Sacrament of Amalgamation; and

(xii) **"Ritus Sacramentum Authentico"** is the Divine Right of the Cardinal Sacrament of Authentication; and

(xiii) **"Ritus Sacramentum Absolutio"** is the Divine Right of the Cardinal Sacrament of Absolution; and

(xiv) **"Ritus Sacramentum Volitio"** is the Divine Right of the Cardinal Sacrament of Volition (Oath); and

(xv) **"Ritus Sacramentum Vocatio"** is the Divine Right of the Cardinal Sacrament of Vocation (Vow); and

(xvi) **"Ritus Sacramentum Testificatio"** is the Divine Right of the Cardinal Sacrament of Testification; and

(xvii) **"Ritus Sacramentum Compassio"** is the Divine Right of the Cardinal Sacrament of Compassion (Mercy); and

(xviii) **"Ritus Sacramentum Conscripto"** is the Divine Right of the Cardinal Sacrament of Conscription (Binding); and

(xix) **"Ritus Sacramentum Convocatio"** is the Divine Right of the Cardinal Sacrament of Convocation; and

(xx) **"Ritus Sacramentum Auctoriso"** is the Divine Right of the Cardinal Sacrament of Authorisation; and

(xxi) **"Ritus Sacramentum Elucidato"** is the Divine Right of the Cardinal Sacrament of Elucidation (Enlighten); and

(xxii) **"Ritus Sacramentum Inspiratio"** is the Divine Right of the Authentic Life Gift of Inspiration (Annunciation); and

(xxiii) **"Ritus Sacramentum Resurrectio"** is the Divine Right of the Authentic Life Gift of Resurrection (Baptism); and

(xxiv) **"Ritus Sacramentum Incarnatio"** is the Divine Right of the Authentic Life Gift of Incarnation (Christening); and

(xxv) **"Ritus Sacramentum Confirmatio"** is the Divine Right of the Authentic Life Gift of Confirmation (First Community); and

(xxvi) **"Ritus Sacramentum Illuminatio"** is the Divine Right of the Authentic Life Gift of Illumination; and

(xxvii) **"Ritus Sacramentum Exultatio"** is the Divine Right of the Authentic Life Gift of Exultation; and

(xxviii) **"Ritus Sacramentum Glorificatio"** is the Divine Right of the Authentic Life Gift of Glorification; and

(xxix) **"Ritus Sacramentum Divinatio"** is the Divine Right of the Authentic Life Gift of Divination; and

(xxx) **"Ritus Sacramentum Visitatio"** is the Divine Right of the Authentic Life Gift of Visitation; and

(xxxi) **"Ritus Sacramentum Salvatio"** is the Divine Right of the Authentic Life Gift of Salvation; and

(xxxii) **"Ritus Sacramentum Emancipatio"** is the Divine Right of the Authentic Life Gift of Emancipation; and

(xxxiii) **"Ritus Sacramentum Veneratio"** is the Divine Right of the Authentic Life Gift of Veneration.

Article 250 – Ritus Sacramentum Recognosco (Recognition)

949. ***Ritus Sacramentum Recognosco*** is the Divine Right of the Key Sacrament of Recognition. The Sacred Gift of Recognition is the Key that unlocks the Living Virtue of Respect. It is present in all fourteen (14) of the Foundational Sacraments. — Ritus Sacramentum Recognosco (Recognition)

950. *Ritus Sacramentum Recognosco* is the first of thirty-three Sacramental Divine Rights; and may only be invoked whenever the lesser Ecclesiastical Right of *Ius Ecclesiae Sacramentum Recognosco* is invoked in strict accord with the liturgy of *Missale Christus* (Missal of Christ), or *Taqwa Islam* (Rites of Islam) or *Karman Spiritus* (Rites of the Universal Divine Spirit). — Invocation of Ritus Sacramentum Recognosco

951. The Divine Purpose of the Sacred Gift of Recognition is to assist persons in establishing a firm and clear respect of both their inner thoughts and mind and of the outer world around them. Thus, the Sacrament of Recognition is the formal observance and respect of a person, object or concept through its proper classification and estimation. — Divine Purpose of the Sacred Gift of Recognition

Recognition (and therefore Respect), is seen as the foundation Living Virtue as all other virtues depend first upon the firm foundation of respect. Without self-respect, there can be no respect of others. Without respect of the world, there can be no self-respect.

Article 251 – Ritus Sacramentum Purificatio (Purification)

952. ***Ritus Sacramentum Purificatio*** is the Divine Right of the Key Sacrament of Purification. The Sacred Gift of Purification is the Key that unlocks the Living Virtue of Honesty (and Truth). It is present in all fourteen (14) of the Foundational Sacred Gifts. — Ritus Sacramentum Purificatio (Purification)

953. *Ritus Sacramentum Purificatio* is the second of thirty-three Sacramental Divine Rights; and may only be invoked whenever the lesser Ecclesiastical Right of *Ius Ecclesiae Sacramentum Purificatio* is invoked in strict accord with the liturgy of *Missale Christus* (Missal of Christ), or *Taqwa Islam* (Rites of Islam) or *Karman Spiritus* (Rites of the Universal Divine Spirit). — Invocation of Ritus Sacramentum Purificatio

954. The Divine Purpose of the Sacred Gift of Purification is firstly to aid to clear and cleanse the mind from the temporary presence of negative, confusing or distracting thoughts, in order to help better focus attention and intention toward some sacred purpose. Secondly, — Divine Purpose of the Sacred Gift of Purification

Purification exists to prepare physical objects and bodies to receive other sacred gifts by dissolving any negative bonds, previous uses or intentions, or applications. Thus Purification is a necessary action in the preparing of Extra-Sacred Rites and the body of authorised clerics before official ceremonies.

Article 252 – Ritus Sacramentum Invocatio (Invocation)

955. ***Ritus Sacramentum Invocatio*** is the Divine Right of the Key Sacrament of Invocation.

Ritus Sacramentum Invocatio (Invocation)

956. *Ritus Sacramentum Invocatio* is the third of thirty-three Sacramental Divine Rights; and may only be invoked whenever the lesser Ecclesiastical Right of *Ius Ecclesiae Sacramentum Invocatio* is invoked in strict accord with the liturgy of *Missale Christus* (Missal of Christ), or *Taqwa Islam* (Rites of Islam) or *Karman Spiritus* (Rites of the Universal Divine Spirit).

Invocation of Ritus Sacramentum Invocatio

957. Invocation by its very definition means "to vocalise some call for assistance; or the presence; or manifestation of one or more divine beings". Thus the positive vocal expression of such a call or entreaty or prayer is fundamental to the operative function of any proper Invocation. When it is not vocalised, an Invocation is properly defined as a Meditation.

Divine Purpose of the Sacred Gift of Invocation

All communication to the *Angelorum Systemata* (Angelic Systems) of Angels, Saints and Beloved of Heaven by living Members of One Heaven shall be by Invocation in accord with the most sacred Covenant *Pactum De Singularis Caelum*. The methods, rules and standards of proper Invocation are defined by the most sacred Covenant *Pactum De Singularis Caelum* and associated covenants and no other. All properly conferred Invocation shall be received, recorded and acknowledged by the *Angelorum Systemata* (Angelic Systems) of One Heaven.

An Invocation may be memorialised in writing as witness to the event. However, any such memorandum or certificate is always dependent upon the action of the said Invocation first being spoken.

A proper Invocation may stand alone, or may represent part of a more complex series of ritual or events. When an Invocation is made from the use of some formula of words in prose, or sung or spoken, then it shall be known more formally as an Incantation. However, when a proper Invocation stands alone and involves the use of free form and self selection of words by the one making the Invocation,

Title VI – Divine Rights

then it shall be known simply as an Invocation.

958. In accord with the most sacred Covenant *Pactum De Singularis Caelum*, an Invocation shall be reprobate, profane, repugnant and therefore invalid and improper and rejected by the Angels, Saints and Beloved of the *Angelorum Systemata* (Angelic Systems) of Heaven:- Reprobate, Profane and Repugnant forms of Invocation

    (i)   If it is deliberately harmful, negative or malevolent in its intent, design or inference; or

    (ii)   If it is deliberately dishonest, deceptive or perfidious in its intent, design or inference; or

    (iii)   If it is frivolous, or profane or disrespectful in its intent, or tone, or design or inference; or

    (iv)   If it is irrational, or unreasonable or illogical in its intent, or tone, or design or inference; or

    (v)   If it is motivated or driven by hate, greed, jealously, anger or lust; or

    (vi)   If it is motivated or driven by an attempt to shift blame or avoid accepting self-responsibility; or

    (vii)   If it is motivated or driven by a desire, or wish, or worship of money or abundant material wealth.

959. While the genuine Intention of a proper Invocation or Meditation (non-vocalised Invocation) is in itself the most important element of a valid Invocation, the following elements are recognised as the optimum structure for a valid Invocation being Identity, Petition and Affirmation:- The fundamental elements of valid Invocation

    (i)   Identity is the identity of the person or group in whose name the Invocation is directed; and

    (ii)   Petition is the body of the Invocation itself; and

    (iii)   Affirmation is the offering and affirmation of the one who makes the Invocation as their commitment to the positivity of Intention and the truth of Petition.

960. Seven types of Invocation or Meditation (non-vocalised Invocation) are recognised being *Adoration, Blessing, Intervention, Intercession, Confession, Lamentation* and *Thanksgiving*:- Characteristics of Invocation

    (i)   "**Adoration**" is recognised as the type of Invocation or Meditation used for giving honour and praise to a higher spiritual presence; and

(ii) **"Blessing"** is recognised as the type of Invocation or Meditation used to summons an authentic spiritual presence to another, often consonant with the act of consecration and the ritual of anointing; and

(iii) **"Intervention"** is recognised as the type of Invocation or Meditation used for directly summonsing the presence of spirits or asking something for one's self; and

(iv) **"Intercession"** is recognised as the type of Invocation or Meditation used for asking something for others; and

(v) **"Confession"** is recognised as the type of Invocation or Meditation used for the atonement and repentance of wrongdoing and the asking of forgiveness; and

(vi) **"Lamentation"** is recognised as the type of Invocation or Meditation used for crying in distress and asking for vindication; and

(vii) **"Thanksgiving"** is recognised as the type of Invocation or Meditation used for offering gratitude.

Article 253 – Ritus Sacramentum Obligatio (Obligation)

961. ***Ritus Sacramentum Obligatio*** is the Divine Right of the Key Sacrament of Obligation. The Sacred Gift of Obligation is the Key that unlocks the Living Virtue of Commitment and Fortitude. It is present in all fourteen (14) of the Foundational Sacred Gifts.
Ritus Sacramentum Obligatio (Obligation)

962. *Ritus Sacramentum Obligatio* is the fourth of thirty-three Sacramental Divine Rights; and may only be invoked whenever the lesser Ecclesiastical Right of *Ius Ecclesiae Sacramentum Obligatio* is invoked in strict accord with the liturgy of *Missale Christus* (Missal of Christ), or *Taqwa Islam* (Rites of Islam) or *Karman Spiritus* (Rites of the Universal Divine Spirit).
Invocation of Ritus Sacramentum Obligatio

963. The purpose of the sacred gift of Obligation is the formal recognition and celebration of entrusting to the Divine Creator through a solemn consensual covenant certain promises which one or more persons bind themselves to honour and uphold.
Divine Purpose of the Sacred Gift of Obligation

Article 254 – Ritus Sacramentum Delegatio (Delegation)

964. ***Ritus Sacramentum Delegatio*** is the Divine Right of the Key Sacrament of Delegation (Trust). The Sacred Gift of Delegation is the Key that unlocks the Living Virtue of Trust and Faith. It is present in all fourteen (14) of the Foundational Sacred Gifts. Ritus Sacramentum Delegatio (Delegation)

965. *Ritus Sacramentum Delegatio* is the fifth of thirty-three Sacramental Divine Rights; and may only be invoked whenever the lesser Ecclesiastical Right of *Ius Ecclesiae Sacramentum Delegatio* is invoked in strict accord with the liturgy of *Missale Christus* (Missal of Christ), or *Taqwa Islam* (Rites of Islam) or *Karman Spiritus* (Rites of the Universal Divine Spirit). Invocation of Ritus Sacramentum Delegatio

966. The purpose of the Sacred Gift of Delegation is the formal recognition and blessing of a relationship and agreement whereby certain Form, Rights and Obligations are lawfully delegated to the control of one or more Persons as fiduciaries for the benefit of one or more other Persons. Divine Purpose of the Sacred Gift of Delegation

Article 255 – Ritus Sacramentum Satisfactio (Satisfaction)

967. ***Ritus Sacramentum Satisfactio*** is the Divine Right of the Key Sacrament of Satisfaction. It is present in all fourteen (14) of the Foundational Sacred Gifts. Ritus Sacramentum Satisfactio (Satisfaction)

968. *Ritus Sacramentum Satisfactio* is the sixth of thirty-three Sacramental Divine Rights; and may only be invoked whenever the lesser Ecclesiastical Right of *Ius Ecclesiae Sacramentum Satisfactio* is invoked in strict accord with the liturgy of *Missale Christus* (Missal of Christ), or *Taqwa Islam* (Rites of Islam) or *Karman Spiritus* (Rites of the Universal Divine Spirit). Invocation of Ritus Sacramentum Satisfactio

969. The purpose of the sacred gift of Satisfaction is the formal recognition of the fulfilment and completion of any outstanding conditions and terms of an agreement recognised as possessing sacred value and importance. Divine Purpose of the Sacred Gift of Satisfaction

Article 256 – Ritus Sacramentum Resolutio (Resolution)

970. ***Ritus Sacramentum Resolutio*** is the Divine Right of the Key Sacrament of Resolution. It is present in all fourteen (14) of the Foundational Sacred Gifts.

    Ritus Sacramentum Resolutio (Resolution)

971. *Ritus Sacramentum Resolutio* is the seventh of thirty-three Sacramental Divine Rights; and may only be invoked whenever the lesser Ecclesiastical Right of *Ius Ecclesiae Sacramentum Resolutio* is invoked in strict accord with the liturgy of *Missale Christus* (Missal of Christ), or *Taqwa Islam* (Rites of Islam) or *Karman Spiritus* (Rites of the Universal Divine Spirit).

    Invocation of Ritus Sacramentum Resolutio

972. The purpose of the Sacred Gift of Resolution is the formal recognition of agreed decisions, determinations and solutions as both a conclusion as well as progression of events.

    Divine Purpose of the Sacred Gift of Resolution

Article 257 – Ritus Sacramentum Sanctificatio (Sanctification)

973. ***Ritus Sacramentum Sanctificatio*** is the Divine Right of the Foundational Sacrament of Sanctification.

    Ritus Sacramentum Sanctificatio (Sanctification)

974. *Ritus Sacramentum Sanctificatio* is the eighth of thirty-three Sacramental Divine Rights; and may only be invoked whenever the lesser Ecclesiastical Right of *Ius Ecclesiae Sacramentum Sanctificatio* is invoked in strict accord with the liturgy of *Missale Christus* (Missal of Christ), or *Taqwa Islam* (Rites of Islam) or *Karman Spiritus* (Rites of the Universal Divine Spirit).

    Invocation of Ritus Sacramentum Sanctificatio

975. The purpose of the Sacred Gift of Sanctification and Rite of Consecration is the solemn dedication to Divine purpose and service a particular person, place, object or thing, thus the formation of Sacred Circumscribed Space. Only the Rite of Consecration properly conferred creates Sacred Circumscribed Space.

    Divine Purpose of the Sacred Gift of Sanctification & Rite of Consecration

976. The Rite of Consecration is an implicit element of all Life Sacred Gifts and may not be conducted as a replacement or alternate rite to an established Sacred Gift identified as possessing the quality of consecration.

    Relations of the Rite of Consecration

Article 258 – Ritus Sacramentum Sustentatio (Sustentation)

977. **Ritus Sacramentum Sustentatio** is the Divine Right of the Foundational Sacrament of Sustentation.

Ritus Sacramentum Sustentatio (Sustentation)

978. *Ritus Sacramentum Sustentatio* is the ninth of thirty-three Sacramental Divine Rights; and may only be invoked whenever the lesser Ecclesiastical Right of *Ius Ecclesiae Sacramentum Sustentatio* is invoked in strict accord with the liturgy of *Missale Christus* (Missal of Christ), or *Taqwa Islam* (Rites of Islam) or *Karman Spiritus* (Rites of the Universal Divine Spirit).

Invocation of Ritus Sacramentum Sustentatio

Article 259 – Ritus Sacramentum Unificatio (Unification)

979. **Ritus Sacramentum Unificatio** is the Divine Right of the Foundational Sacrament of Unification.

Ritus Sacramentum Unificatio (Unification)

980. *Ritus Sacramentum Unificatio* is the tenth of thirty-three Sacramental Divine Rights; and may only be invoked whenever the lesser Ecclesiastical Right of *Ius Ecclesiae Sacramentum Unificatio* is invoked in strict accord with the liturgy of *Missale Christus* (Missal of Christ), or *Taqwa Islam* (Rites of Islam) or *Karman Spiritus* (Rites of the Universal Divine Spirit).

Invocation of Ritus Sacramentum Unificatio

981. The Sacred Gift of Unification and Rite of Matrimony is granted and administered when a man and a woman upon reaching majority choose and consent of their own free will to sanctify their union through a registered divine matrimonial covenant in accordance with the most sacred Covenant *Pactum de Singularis Caelum* and associated approved worship. The Sacred Gift of Unification and Rite of Matrimony may only be bestowed once.

Divine Purpose of the Sacred Gift of Unification

982. There exists only one form of the Sacred Gift of Unification and Rite of Matrimony being Sacred and Irrevocable Unification. Therefore, as the Sacred Gift is a Sacred and Irrevocable Event, producing a Supreme Sacred Record in Heaven and upon the Earth, no properly conferred Sacred Gift of Unification can be withdrawn, or annulled or dissolved.

Form of the Sacred Gift of Unification and Rite of Matrimony

However, upon such circumstances of separation or death, one who has been bestowed the Sacred Gift of Unification is permitted to formalise a new Union through the Sacred Gift of Amalgamation and

Rite of Union. Thus, the act of Divorce only applies to civil unions and the Sacred Gift of Amalgamation and never to Unification.

Furthermore, the transgression of Adultery only applies to both perpetrators equally culpable of acts of sexual extramarital affairs whilst one or the other or both are still publicly and legally being bound to another through the Sacred Gift of Unification or Sacred Gift of Amalgamation. The application of unequal punishment based on gender, or capital punishment in any form for the delict of Adultery is morally repugnant, profane, sacrilegious, forbidden, reprobate and to be suppressed now and forever.

Article 260 – Ritus Sacramentum Amalgamatio (Amalgamation)

983. *Ritus Sacramentum Amalgamatio* is the Divine Right of the Foundational Sacrament of Amalgamation.

    Ritus Sacramentum Amalgamatio (Amalgamation)

984. *Ritus Sacramentum Amalgamatio* is the eleventh of thirty-three Sacramental Divine Rights; and may only be invoked whenever the lesser Ecclesiastical Right of *Ius Ecclesiae Sacramentum Amalgamatio* is invoked in strict accord with the liturgy of *Missale Christus* (Missal of Christ), or *Taqwa Islam* (Rites of Islam) or *Karman Spiritus* (Rites of the Universal Divine Spirit).

    Invocation of Ritus Sacramentum Amalgamatio

985. Amalgamation is granted and administered when two (2) or more parties come together of their own free will and competence and agree to form a new body in mutual union.

    Divine Purpose of the Sacred Gift of Amalgamation

986. Civil Union is granted and administered when a couple of the same gender or a man and woman upon reaching majority choose and consent of their own free will to validate their union through a registration and covenant of trust in accordance with the most sacred Covenant *Pactum de Singularis Caelum* and associated approved worship. While a man or a woman may enter into more than one Union consecutively and never concurrently, a man and a woman may only be bestowed the Rite of Holy Matrimony once.

    Form of the Sacred Gift of Amalgamation & Civil Union

    When the Sacred Gift of Amalgamation is approved to be bestowed upon a same sex couple, in recognition of their right to civil equality, the ceremony is forbidden to be performed within the main body of a Sacred Place of Worship. However, such a ceremony is permitted to be performed in a Side Chapel.

    The reason the Sacred Gift of Amalgamation is absolutely forbidden to be performed in the main body of a Sacred Place of Worship for a same sex couple, is not to prejudice, condemn or exclude such persons, but to protect with the utmost sanctity the exclusive and most holy sacred gift of Unification.

Any civil or lesser body that seeks to attack, undermine, denigrate the absolute moral authority of the Holy Society of One Islam in such matters, or to contort words and phrases to imply a delinquency of duty and obligation to protect the Sacred Gifts and Civil Equality is culpable of the most grievous transgressions.

Article 261 – Ritus Sacramentum Authentico (Authentication)

987. ***Ritus Sacramentum Authentico*** is the Divine Right of the Foundational Sacrament of Authentication. — Ritus Sacramentum Authentico (Authentication)

988. *Ritus Sacramentum Authentico* is the twelfth of thirty-three Sacramental Divine Rights; and may only be invoked whenever the lesser Ecclesiastical Right of *Ius Ecclesiae Sacramentum Authentico* is invoked in strict accord with the liturgy of *Missale Christus* (Missal of Christ), or *Taqwa Islam* (Rites of Islam) or *Karman Spiritus* (Rites of the Universal Divine Spirit). — Invocation of Ritus Sacramentum Authentico

989. Authentication is granted and administered upon the formal recording of the name and details of a particular object or concept in the Great Register and Public Record of One Heaven or associated Great Registers under Oath and evidence in accordance with the most sacred Covenant *Pactum De Singularis Caelum* and associated approved worship. — Divine Purpose of the Sacred Gift of Authentication

Article 262 – Ritus Sacramentum Absolutio (Absolution)

990. ***Ritus Sacramentum Absolutio*** is the Divine Right of the Foundational Sacrament of Absolution. — Ritus Sacramentum Absolutio (Absolution)

991. *Ritus Sacramentum Absolutio* is the thirteenth of thirty-three Sacramental Divine Rights; and may only be invoked whenever the lesser Ecclesiastical Right of *Ius Ecclesiae Sacramentum Absolutio* is invoked in strict accord with the liturgy of *Missale Christus* (Missal of Christ), or *Taqwa Islam* (Rites of Islam) or *Karman Spiritus* (Rites of the Universal Divine Spirit). — Invocation of Ritus Sacramentum Absolutio

992. Whilst Divine Forgiveness is absolute, immediate and irrevocable to all who have transgressed, the full effect of the Divine Sacred Gift of — Divine Purpose of the Sacred

Absolution can only be received upon the genuine act of Contrition through the proper conferral of the Rite of Confession, also known as the Act of Reconciliation.

Gift of Absolution & Rite of Confession

In the Rite of Confession, a Member who confesses their offences to a legitimate minister; and is authentically contrite and remorseful for such actions; and truly intends to reform themselves; and accepts without duress the necessary ecclesiastical or civil penalties, thereby removes any impediment to full reconciliation with God and the Divine Creator of all Heaven and Earth; and the full receipt of the absolute unconditional Divine Grace of Divine Mercy, Divine Forgiveness and Divine Love.

Thus, the proper and pious Foundational Sacred Gift of Absolution, also known as the Act of Reconciliation itself does not presume to be the mechanism of conferring Divine Mercy, Divine Forgiveness and Divine Love, nor to presume to place conditions upon God and the Divine Creator of all Heaven and Earth as to whether one is worthy or not worthy of Divine Salvation. Instead, the Sacred Gift of Absolution recognises the free will and choice of the penitent in openly reconciling with God and the Divine Creator of all Existence; and thus removing any impediment to the full receipt of Divine Grace.

Most importantly, within and through the Authentic Sacred Gift of Absolution, the competent minister becomes the living embodiment of the Witness and Messenger of Divine Mercy, Divine Forgiveness and Eternal Love of God and the Divine Creator of all Existence to each and every higher order life form and life itself.

Article 263 – Ritus Sacramentum Volitio (Oath)

993. ***Ritus Sacramentum Volitio*** is the Divine Right of the Foundational Sacrament of Volition (Oath).

Ritus Sacramentum Volitio (Oath)

994. *Ritus Sacramentum Volitio* is the fourteenth of thirty-three Sacramental Divine Rights; and may only be invoked whenever the lesser Ecclesiastical Right of *Ius Ecclesiae Sacramentum Volitio* is invoked in strict accord with the liturgy of *Missale Christus* (Missal of Christ), or *Taqwa Islam* (Rites of Islam) or *Karman Spiritus* (Rites of the Universal Divine Spirit).

Invocation of Ritus Sacramentum Volitio

995. The Rite of Oath is a recognition of a binding of obligation and performance duly recorded in the Great Register and Divine Records of Heaven and the temporal records on Earth and the Solar System.

Divine Purpose of the Sacred Gift of Volition & Rite of Oath

The Sacred Gift of Volition is granted and conveyed upon the pronouncement of a valid oath in accordance with the most sacred Covenant *Pactum De Singularis Caelum* and associated approved worship.

Article 264 – Ritus Sacramentum Vocatio (Vow)

996. ***Ritus Sacramentum Vocatio*** is the Divine Right of the Foundational Sacrament of Vocation (Vow).

Ritus Sacramentum Vocatio (Vow)

997. *Ritus Sacramentum Vocatio* is the fifteenth of thirty-three Sacramental Divine Rights; and may only be invoked whenever the lesser Ecclesiastical Right of *Ius Ecclesiae Sacramentum Vocatio* is invoked in strict accord with the liturgy of *Missale Christus* (Missal of Christ), or *Taqwa Islam* (Rites of Islam) or *Karman Spiritus* (Rites of the Universal Divine Spirit).

Invocation of Ritus Sacramentum Vocatio

998. The purpose of the sacred gift of Vocation and Rite of Vow is the formal recognition and endorsement of a person pledging themselves as assurance and security for the obligations of another in accordance with the most sacred Covenant *Pactum de Singularis Caelum* and associated approved worship.

Divine Purpose of the Sacred Gift of Vocation & Rite of Vow

Article 265 – Ritus Sacramentum Testificatio (Testification)

999. ***Ritus Sacramentum Testificatio*** is the Divine Right of the Foundational Sacrament of Testification.

Ritus Sacramentum Testificatio (Testification)

1000. *Ritus Sacramentum Testificatio* is the sixteenth of thirty-three Sacramental Divine Rights; and may only be invoked whenever the lesser Ecclesiastical Right of *Ius Ecclesiae Sacramentum Testificatio* is invoked in strict accord with the liturgy of *Missale Christus* (Missal of Christ), or *Taqwa Islam* (Rites of Islam) or *Karman Spiritus* (Rites of the Universal Divine Spirit).

Invocation of Ritus Sacramentum Testificatio

1001. Testification is by definition the act of vocalising and giving testimony or evidence; being a vocalised act involving not only at least one Invocation, but at least one promise and obligation in relation to the performance of a valid office. All valid offices are based upon truth and trust and so no office can be formed without a proper Testification.

Nature of Testification

All communication to the *Officium Systemata* (Offices Systems) of

Heaven by living Members of One Heaven shall be by Testification of an Oath and at least one Vow in accord with the most sacred Covenant *Pactum De Singularis Caelum*. The methods, rules and standards of proper Testification shall be defined by the most sacred Covenant *Pactum De Singularis Caelum* and associated covenants and no other. All properly conferred Testification shall be received, recorded and acknowledged by the Officium Systemata (Offices Systems) of One Heaven.

Article 266 – Ritus Sacramentum Compassio (Mercy)

1002. ***Ritus Sacramentum Compassio*** is the Divine Right of the Foundational Sacrament of Compassion (Mercy).

    Ritus Sacramentum Compassio (Mercy)

1003. *Ritus Sacramentum Compassio* is the seventeenth of thirty-three Sacramental Divine Rights; and may only be invoked whenever the lesser Ecclesiastical Right of *Ius Ecclesiae Sacramentum Compassio* is invoked in strict accord with the liturgy of *Missale Christus* (Missal of Christ), or *Taqwa Islam* (Rites of Islam) or *Karman Spiritus* (Rites of the Universal Divine Spirit).

    Invocation of Ritus Sacramentum Compassio

1004. The purpose of the Sacred Gift of Compassion and Rite of Mercy is the formal blessing of charity and benevolence to those in need; and the formal remittance and discharge of part or all of an offence as well as any prescribed punishment, in accordance with the most sacred Covenant *Pactum de Singularis Caelum* and associated approved worship.

    Divine Purpose of the Sacred Gift of Compassion & Rite of Mercy

Article 267 – Ritus Sacramentum Conscripto (Conscription)

1005. ***Ritus Sacramentum Conscripto*** is the Divine Right of the Foundational Sacrament of Conscription (Binding).

    Ritus Sacramentum Conscripto (Conscription)

1006. *Ritus Sacramentum Conscripto* is the eighteenth of thirty-three Sacramental Divine Rights; and may only be invoked whenever the lesser Ecclesiastical Right of *Ius Ecclesiae Sacramentum Conscripto* is invoked in strict accord with the liturgy of *Missale Christus* (Missal of Christ), or *Taqwa Islam* (Rites of Islam) or *Karman Spiritus* (Rites of the Universal Divine Spirit).

    Invocation of Ritus Sacramentum Conscripto

1007. The Sacred Gift of Conscription and Rite of Binding is a fundamental concept of society as it permits people to engage in trusted relations

    Divine Purpose of the Sacred Gift of

of significant trust. The purpose of the sacred gift of Binding is the formal recognition and acknowledgement of Divine Authority whereby what is bound on Earth shall be bound in Heaven and what is loosed upon the Earth shall likewise be loosened in Heaven.

Article 268 – Ritus Sacramentum Convocatio (Convocation)

1008. ***Ritus Sacramentum Convocatio*** is the Divine Right of the Foundational Sacrament of Convocation.

1009. *Ritus Sacramentum Convocatio* is the nineteenth of thirty-three Sacramental Divine Rights; and may only be invoked whenever the lesser Ecclesiastical Right of *Ius Ecclesiae Sacramentum Convocatio* is invoked in strict accord with the liturgy of *Missale Christus* (Missal of Christ), or *Taqwa Islam* (Rites of Islam) or *Karman Spiritus* (Rites of the Universal Divine Spirit).

1010. The purpose of the sacred gift of Convocation and Rite of Convention is the formal summons to attendance with the members of a sacred body in accordance with the most sacred Covenant *Pactum de Singularis Caelum* and associated approved worship. The meaning of Convocation is derived from the Latin word *convoco* meaning "to call meeting of".

Article 269 – Ritus Sacramentum Auctoriso (Authorisation)

1011. ***Ritus Sacramentum Auctoriso*** is the Divine Right of the Foundational Sacrament of Authorisation.

1012. *Ritus Sacramentum Auctoriso* is the twentieth of thirty-three Sacramental Divine Rights; and may only be invoked whenever the lesser Ecclesiastical Right of *Ius Ecclesiae Sacramentum Auctoriso* is invoked in strict accord with the liturgy of *Missale Christus* (Missal of Christ), or *Taqwa Islam* (Rites of Islam) or *Karman Spiritus* (Rites of the Universal Divine Spirit).

1013. The purpose of the sacred gift of Authorisation and Rite of Prescription is the formal blessing of a decree or judgement issued by a valid minister or one possessing the proper level of authority in accordance with the most sacred Covenant *Pactum de Singularis Caelum* and associated approved worship.

Article 270 – Ritus Sacramentum Elucidato (Elucidation)

1014. ***Ritus Sacramentum Elucidato*** is the Divine Right of the Foundational Sacrament of Elucidation (Enlighten).

<!-- margin: Ritus Sacramentum Elucidato (Elucidation) -->

1015. *Ritus Sacramentum Elucidato* is the twenty-first of thirty-three Sacramental Divine Rights; and may only be invoked whenever the lesser Ecclesiastical Right of *Ius Ecclesiae Sacramentum Elucidato* is invoked in strict accord with the liturgy of *Missale Christus* (Missal of Christ), or *Taqwa Islam* (Rites of Islam) or *Karman Spiritus* (Rites of the Universal Divine Spirit).

<!-- margin: Invocation of Ritus Sacramentum Elucidato -->

1016. The purpose of the sacred gift of Elucidation and Rite of Rescription is opinion, answer or judgement promulgated by an Official Person, subject to the limits of their authority, in accordance with the most sacred Covenant *Pactum de Singularis Caelum* and associated approved worship and the procedures of their Office.

<!-- margin: Divine Purpose of the Sacred Gift of Elucidation & Rite of Rescription -->

Article 271 – Ritus Sacramentum Inspiratio (Annunciation)

1017. ***Ritus Sacramentum Inspiratio*** is the Divine Right of the Authentic Life Gift of Inspiratio (Annunciation).

<!-- margin: Ritus Sacramentum Inspiratio (Annunciation) -->

1018. *Ritus Sacramentum Inspiratio* is the twenty-second of thirty-three Sacramental Divine Rights; and may only be invoked whenever the lesser Ecclesiastical Right of *Ius Ecclesiae Sacramentum Inspiratio* is invoked in strict accord with the liturgy of *Missale Christus* (Missal of Christ), or *Taqwa Islam* (Rites of Islam) or *Karman Spiritus* (Rites of the Universal Divine Spirit).

<!-- margin: Invocation of Ritus Sacramentum Inspiratio -->

1019. The Sacred Gift of Inspiration and Rite of Annunciation is granted and conferred exclusively to an expectant mother and her living unborne child according to most sacred Covenant *Pactum De Singularis Caelum* and associated approved worship.

<!-- margin: Gift of Inspiration -->

1020. All life is sacred and human life is especially sacred. Thus, the journey of conception to gestation and finally birth is an extraordinary journey and gift. The purpose of the Sacred Gift of Inspiration and Rite of Annunciation is the recognition of the ancient custom and tradition of celebrating the certainty of pregnancy and the arrival of the Holy Spirit into the unborne child from the fiftieth day.

<!-- margin: Divine Purpose of the Sacred Gift of Inspiration & Rite of Annunciation -->

It is the Holy Spirit that helps form the very beginnings of the human mind and consciousness and this Divine Contribution appears the moment that the foetus is unmistakably and unquestionably of the higher order life form of Homo Sapien from the end of the first trimester.

1021. It is a gross error to presume the Spirit is fully present in Human Form from the precise moment of Conception. Laws and Maxims that are enacted according to this error are profane against God and the Divine Creator of all Life.

Errors of Presumption concerning Spirit and Conception

The reason the Spirit is not fully present in Human Form within the foetus until the end of the first trimester is threefold:-

(i) The new life must first experience and overcome each and every form and era of history of evolution of life upon planet Earth over more than two (2) billion years in a matter of fifty (50) to sixty (60) days. Thus, to be human is to first experience what it is to be all other forms of lesser complex life; and

(ii) The Holy Spirit must be invited into the new unborne life by the Spirit of the mother, even if the lower consciousness of the mother is unaware of such status of the pregnancy or may even be against the idea of pregnancy. If the Holy Spirit were not invited, but simply imposed itself upon the mother, then the arrival of the Spirit would be a fundamental breach of all the Laws of Heaven; and

(iii) The body of the mother must reach the state of no longer reacting to the pregnancy as if it were an infection and instead must demonstrate at this miraculous moment a metamorphosis whereby the body of the mother ceases to fight for the death of the new life form and instead normally begins to change in order to support by every means the successful nurturing of the unborne infant to full term.

Therefore, any teachings or laws that seek to impose the denial of the rights of the mother prior to this key event, over an unborne life form, not yet enjoined with the Holy Spirit is morally repugnant, profane, sacrilegious, illogical and is forbidden and to be suppressed.

However, any teachings or laws that deny this momentous event and ignore the rights of the unborne child from this moment at the end of the first trimester, in favour of the mother having extended rights to destroy a life beyond the first trimester are also morally repugnant, profane, sacrilegious, illogical and is forbidden and to be suppressed.

Lex Divina: Maxims of Divine Law

Article 272 – Ritus Sacramentum Resurrectio (Resurrection)

1022.	***Ritus Sacramentum Resurrectio*** is the Divine Right of the Authentic Life Gift of Resurrection (Baptism).	Ritus Sacramentum Resurrectio (Resurrection)
1023.	*Ritus Sacramentum Resurrectio* is the twenty-third of thirty-three Sacramental Divine Rights; and may only be invoked whenever the lesser Ecclesiastical Right of *Ius Ecclesiae Sacramentum Resurrectio* is invoked in strict accord with the liturgy of *Missale Christus* (Missal of Christ), or *Taqwa Islam* (Rites of Islam) or *Karman Spiritus* (Rites of the Universal Divine Spirit).	Invocation of Ritus Sacramentum Resurrectio
1024.	The Sacred Gift of Resurrection and Rite of New Birth is granted and conferred to a new borne Homo Sapien child at the final stage of birth or within 90 days of being borne in accordance with the most sacred Covenant *Pactum De Singularis Caelum* and associated approved worship.	Gift of Resurrection
1025.	The purpose of the Sacred Gift of Resurrection and Rite of New Birth is the formal bestowal or presentation of a possessory or prescriptive right of Office to an incumbent including taking possession of the insignia of Office.	Divine Purpose of the Sacred Gift of Resurrection & Rite of New Birth
	The birth of a child into flesh also represents the birth of a True Trust through the conveyance of divinity, also known as Divine right of use from the Divine Personality of the spirit of the child with the flesh of the child the eventual rightful trustee of the True Trust upon age of majority. Until such time, the Divine Person of the child grants temporary guardian powers to the parent or parents, or those properly designated as immediate carer.	
1026.	In accordance with Divine Law and the most sacred Covenant *Pactum De Singularis Caelum*, if a foetus having received the sacred gift of Inspiration dies before being borne, then this unique Divine Immortal Spirit shall be fully entitled to receive the sacred gift of Resurrection and Rite of New Birth within 90 days of what otherwise would have been its borne day and all Life Sacred Gifts thereafter at their appointed time.	Form of the Sacred Gift of Extraordinary Resurrection and Rite of New Birth
	In accordance with Divine Law and the most sacred Covenant *Pactum De Singularis Caelum*, the mother or father or next of living kin of any foetus that failed to be borne, yet was not previously granted the Sacred Gift of Resurrection and Rite of New Birth may apply for the special ceremony of Life Sacred Gifts where all sacred gifts are granted beginning with Annunciation to the sacred gift	

representing the same age as if the foetus had been borne and lived to the present day.

1027. All fraudulent and inferior Rites of New Birth are forbidden and shall have no lawful effect. No documents, oral promises or any other inferred agreement by the parents of a new borne baby to the hospital, or competent civil authority or by implication to any Religion or Cult can in anyway diminish the rights of the parents as Guardians unless by willing and deliberate behaviour they have been legally proven through a formal hearing to be incompetent as trustees and guardians of their new borne child.

<small>False and Profane Rituals of claimed Rites of New Birth</small>

The Sacred Gift of Resurrection and Rite of New Birth negates the presumptions, validity and existence of any claimed *Cestui Que Vie* Trusts or any other curses, spells and unlawful conveyances by any Religion, Cult or their agents.

Article 273 – Ritus Sacramentum Incarnatio (Incarnation)

1028. **Ritus Sacramentum Incarnatio** is the Divine Right of the Authentic Life Gift of Incarnatio (Christening).

<small>Ritus Sacramentum Incarnatio (Incarnation)</small>

1029. *Ritus Sacramentum Incarnatio* is the twenty-fourth of thirty-three Sacramental Divine Rights; and may only be invoked whenever the lesser Ecclesiastical Right of *Ius Ecclesiae Sacramentum Incarnatio* is invoked in strict accord with the liturgy of *Missale Christus* (Missal of Christ), or *Taqwa Islam* (Rites of Islam) or *Karman Spiritus* (Rites of the Universal Divine Spirit).

<small>Invocation of Ritus Sacramentum Incarnatio</small>

1030. The Sacred Gift of Incarnation and Rite of Initiation shall be granted and administered by the second (2nd) birthday of a child that has received the Sacred Gift of Resurrection and Rite of New Birth in accordance with the most sacred Covenant *Pactum De Singularis Caelum* and associated approved worship.

<small>Gift of Incarnation</small>

1031. The purpose of the Sacred Gift of Incarnation and Rite of Initiation is to officially recognise the transition of a baby to a child and their commencement of valid organised learning systems of the community. The child is now welcomed into the tribe and protection is given in exchange for the child understanding that it is time to learn.

<small>Divine Purpose of the Sacred Gift of Incarnation & Rite of Initiation</small>

1032. In accordance with Divine Law and the most sacred Covenant *Pactum De Singularis Caelum*, if a child having received the Sacred Gift of Resurrection and Rite of New Birth dies at or prior to the age

<small>Extraordinary Form of the Sacred Gift of Incarnation &</small>

of two (2), then this unique Divine Immortal Spirit shall be fully entitled to receive the Sacred Gift of Incarnation and Rite of Initiation two (2) years since being borne and all Life Sacred Gifts thereafter at their appointed time.

Rite of Initiation

In accordance with Divine Law and the most sacred Covenant *Pactum De Singularis Caelum*, the mother or father or next of living kin of any child that died at or prior to the age of two (2) yet was not previously granted the Sacred Gift of Resurrection and Rite of New Birth may apply for the special ceremony of Life Sacred Gifts where all Sacred Gifts are granted beginning with Sacred Gift of Inspiration and Rite of Annunciation to the Sacred Gift representing the same age as if the child had lived and grown up to the present day.

Article 274 – Ritus Sacramentum Confirmatio (Confirmation)

1033. ***Ritus Sacramentum Confirmatio*** is the Divine Right of the Authentic Life Gift of Confirmation (First Community).

Ritus Sacramentum Confirmatio (Confirmation)

1034. *Ritus Sacramentum Confirmatio* is the twenty-fifth of thirty-three Sacramental Divine Rights; and may only be invoked whenever the lesser Ecclesiastical Right of *Ius Ecclesiae Sacramentum Confirmatio* is invoked in strict accord with the liturgy of *Missale Christus* (Missal of Christ), or *Taqwa Islam* (Rites of Islam) or *Karman Spiritus* (Rites of the Universal Divine Spirit).

Invocation of Ritus Sacramentum Confirmatio

1035. The Sacred Gift of Confirmation and Rite of First Community shall be granted and administered by the twelfth (12th) birthday of a child that has received the Sacred Gift of Incarnation in accordance with the most sacred Covenant *Pactum De Singularis Caelum* and associated approved worship.

Gift of Confirmation

1036. The Divine purpose of the Sacred Gift of Confirmation and Rite of First Community is to celebrate the admittance of a child into the rights of possessions and responsibility of their respective community through the formal celebration and bestowal of certain Ecclesiastical and Public rights to the child as a member of the community. Upon a child demonstrating their ability to distinguish right from wrong; and the basic competence of logic, reason and discernment; and an essential understanding of morals and consequences, a child is permitted to own property in their own name. A child having received the Sacred Gift of Confirmation and Rite of First Community is also expected to acknowledge their responsibilities and duties to their family and community.

Divine Purpose of the Sacred Gift of Confirmation & Rite of First Community

1037. The Ordinary Form of the Sacred Gift of Confirmation and Rite of First Community cannot be conferred unless the child is clearly prepared and able to become a productive and exemplary member of their community. Thus, the priority of education and preparation must pertain to skills of reason, logic, discernment, morality, ethics and the consequences of actions before any detailed knowledge of the laws of the associated approved worship are then necessary.

    A child that is able to recite scripture and the tenets of the Holy Society, yet is unable to apply reason, logic and virtue to their decisions is not competent for Confirmation and those that failed to adequately prepare such a child are not competent to teach, until they acknowledge such failings.

    This is because, to be a member of the Living Body of One Islam is to be an ambassador of the Spirit of God; and an exemplary to the world. Confirmation is a sacred gift, First Community is a sacred ceremony that heralds such a moment. Therefore an absence of proper preparation is a grave offence against the child and the most sacred Covenant *Pactum De Singularis Caelum*.

    Condition of the Ordinary Form Sacred Gift of Confirmation & Rite of First Community

1038. In accordance with Divine Law and the most sacred Covenant *Pactum De Singularis Caelum*, if a child having received the Sacred Gift of Incarnation dies before being the age of twelve (12), then this unique Divine Immortal Spirit shall be fully entitled to receive the Sacred Gift of Confirmation within sixty (60) days of twelve (12) years since being borne.

    In accordance with Divine Law and the most sacred Covenant *Pactum De Singularis Caelum*, the mother or father or next of living kin of any child that died prior to the age of twelve (12) yet was not previously granted the Sacred Gift of Confirmation may apply for the special ceremony of Life Sacred Gifts where all Sacred Gifts are granted beginning with Sacred Gift of Inspiration and Rite of Annunciation to the Sacred Gift representing the same age as if the child had lived and grown up to the present day.

    Extraordinary Form of the Sacred Gift of Confirmation & Rite of First Community

Article 275 – Ritus Sacramentum Illuminatio (Illumination)

1039. ***Ritus Sacramentum Illuminatio*** is the Divine Right of the Authentic Life Gift of Illumination.

    Ritus Sacramentum Illuminatio (Illumination)

1040. *Ritus Sacramentum Illuminatio* is the twenty-sixth of thirty-three Sacramental Divine Rights; and may only be invoked whenever the

    Invocation of Ritus Sacramentum

lesser Ecclesiastical Right of *Ius Ecclesiae Sacramentum Illuminatio* is invoked in strict accord with the liturgy of *Missale Christus* (Missal of Christ), or *Taqwa Islam* (Rites of Islam) or *Karman Spiritus* (Rites of the Universal Divine Spirit).

    Illuminatio

1041. The Sacred Gift of Illumination and Rite of Majority shall be granted and administered by the twenty-first (21st) birthday of a young adult in accordance with the most sacred Covenant *Pactum De Singularis Caelum* and associated approved worship.

    Gift of Illumination

1042. Every enlightened and civilised culture of history has recognised the significance of the moment of welcoming a new member of the community as an adult, whatever age was prescribed for such tradition. Since then, the age of adulthood has progressively increased to eighteen in some societies and to the age of twenty one in others.

The purpose of the Sacred Gift of Illumination and Rite of Majority is to formalise the welcoming of new adults into the community at an age whereby most should have successfully finished some learning and qualification of useful skills.

Most importantly, the Sacred Gift of Illumination and Rite of Majority is essential to the community to ensure all new Adult Members are fully competent in their moral, spiritual and behavioural obligations, particularly in the forming and supporting of their own families. Thus the Sacred Gift of Illumination and Rite of Majority is a necessary element to stable and fruitful Matrimonial relations throughout a healthy, productive and joyous society.

    Divine Purpose of the Sacred Gift of Illumination & Rite of Majority

1043. A condition of Sacred Gift of Illumination and Rite of Majority is that the youth knowingly and willingly consents to dedicating their life to continuous self improvement and virtue and to contributing to the benefit and improvement of their community and society.

    Conditions of the Sacred Gift of Illumination & Rite of Majority

1044. In accordance with Divine Law and the most sacred Covenant *Pactum De Singularis Caelum*, if a teenager having received the Sacred Gift of Confirmation dies before being the age of twenty-one (21), then this unique Divine Immortal Spirit shall be fully entitled to receive the Sacred Gift of Illumination and Rite of Majority within thirty (30) days of twenty-one (21) years since being borne and all Life Sacred Gifts thereafter at their appointed time.

In accordance with Divine Law and the most sacred Covenant *Pactum De Singularis Caelum*, the mother or father or next of living kin of any child that died prior to the age of twenty-one (21) yet was not previously granted the Sacred Gift of Confirmation may apply for

    Extraordinary Form of the Sacred Gift of Illumination & Rite of Majority the special ceremony of Life Sacred Gifts where all Sacred Gifts including Sacred Gift of Illumination and Rite of Majority are granted beginning with the Sacred Gift of Inspiration and Rite of Annunciation to the Sacred Gift representing the same age as if the child had lived and grown up to the present day.

Article 276 – Ritus Sacramentum Exultatio (Exultation)

1045. ***Ritus Sacramentum Exultatio*** is the Divine Right of the Authentic Life Gift of Exultation.

Ritus Sacramentum Exultatio (Exultation)

1046. *Ritus Sacramentum Exultatio* is the twenty-seventh of thirty-three Sacramental Divine Rights; and may only be invoked whenever the lesser Ecclesiastical Right of *Ius Ecclesiae Sacramentum Exultatio* is invoked in strict accord with the liturgy of *Missale Christus* (Missal of Christ), or *Taqwa Islam* (Rites of Islam) or *Karman Spiritus* (Rites of the Universal Divine Spirit).

Invocation of Ritus Sacramentum Exultatio

1047. The Sacred Gift of Exultation and Rite of Maturity shall be granted and administered by the thirty-third (33rd) birthday of an adult in accordance with the most sacred Covenant *Pactum De Singularis Caelum* and associated approved worship.

Gift of Exultation

1048. The Sacred Gift of Exultation and Rite of Maturity is the celebration of the point of transition from being a Young Adult to a fully mature Adult.

Divine Purpose of the Sacred Gift of Exultation & Rite of Maturity

Article 277 – Ritus Sacramentum Glorificatio (Glorification)

1049. ***Ritus Sacramentum Glorificatio*** is the Divine Right of the Authentic Life Gift of Glorification.

Ritus Sacramentum Glorificatio (Glorification)

1050. *Ritus Sacramentum Glorificatio* is the twenty-eighth of thirty-three Sacramental Divine Rights; and may only be invoked whenever the lesser Ecclesiastical Right of *Ius Ecclesiae Sacramentum Glorificatio* is invoked in strict accord with the liturgy of *Missale Christus* (Missal of Christ), or *Taqwa Islam* (Rites of Islam) or *Karman Spiritus* (Rites of the Universal Divine Spirit).

Invocation of Ritus Sacramentum Glorificatio

1051. The Sacred Gift of Glorification and Rite of Seniority shall be granted and administered by the fifty-fifth (55th) birthday of an adult in accordance with the most sacred Covenant *Pactum De Singularis*

Gift of Glorification

Caelum and associated approved worship.

1052. The Sacred Gift of Glorification and Rite of Seniority is the celebration of the point of transition from Maturity to Seniority. It recognises the experience and contribution of older adults while they are still active members of their society. — *Divine Purpose of the Sacred Gift of Glorification & Rite of Seniority*

Article 278 – Ritus Sacramentum Divinatio (Divination)

1053. *Ritus Sacramentum Divinatio* is the Divine Right of the Authentic Life Gift of Divination. — *Ritus Sacramentum Divinatio (Divination)*

1054. *Ritus Sacramentum Divinatio* is the twenty-ninth of thirty-three Sacramental Divine Rights; and may only be invoked whenever the lesser Ecclesiastical Right of *Ius Ecclesiae Sacramentum Divinatio* is invoked in strict accord with the liturgy of *Missale Christus* (Missal of Christ), or *Taqwa Islam* (Rites of Islam) or *Karman Spiritus* (Rites of the Universal Divine Spirit). — *Invocation of Ritus Sacramentum Divinatio*

1055. The Sacred Gift of Divination and Rite of Elderity shall be granted and administered by the seventy-seventh (77th) birthday of a senior in accordance with the most sacred Covenant *Pactum De Singularis Caelum* and associated approved worship. — *Gift of Divination*

1056. An enlightened society venerates its elders, protects them and seeks their counsel and wisdom. The Sacred Gift of Divination and Rite of Elderity is the celebration of the point of transition from Seniority to Elderhood. It is the celebration of becoming an elder. — *Divine Purpose of the Sacred Gift of Divination & Rite of Elderity*

Article 279 – Ritus Sacramentum Visitatio (Visitation)

1057. *Ritus Sacramentum Visitatio* is the Divine Right of the Authentic Life Gift of Visitation. — *Ritus Sacramentum Visitatio (Visitation)*

1058. *Ritus Sacramentum Visitatio* is the thirtieth of thirty-three Sacramental Divine Rights; and may only be invoked whenever the lesser Ecclesiastical Right of *Ius Ecclesiae Sacramentum Visitatio* is invoked in strict accord with the liturgy of *Missale Christus* (Missal of Christ), or *Taqwa Islam* (Rites of Islam) or *Karman Spiritus* (Rites of the Universal Divine Spirit). — *Invocation of Ritus Sacramentum Visitatio*

1059. The Sacred Gift of Visitation and Rite of Unction shall be granted and administered within months of most certain death in accordance with — *Gift of Visitation* the most sacred Covenant *Pactum De Singularis Caelum* and associated approved worship.

1060. It is the natural order of life and the universe that we are borne, we live and our bodies age and become less reliable until the day that we must leave our bodies behind and return to our eternal Heavenly Home.

      Thus, it is not the natural order, but profoundly unnatural, profane and supremely arrogant to consider that such natural order should be suspended and that Homo Sapiens live according to an undetermined lifespan. For while it is perfectly reasonable to aspire to a world without debilitating and painful disease, it is encumbered upon all men and women with heroic virtue to protect the boundaries of life of our species, so that we do not become consumed as other species in other parts of the universe did become in past ages, and assume themselves to be equals to the Universal Divine Creator.

      The Divine Spirit reveals the true nature of God and the Divine Creator of all Existence and all Heaven and Earth to be Divine Mercy, Divine Forgiveness and Divine Love. Thus, it is not the nature or wish of the Creator of the Universe that any man or woman suffer the indignity of a slow, agonising and wasteful death.

      Therefore, when a man or woman approaches such a trial as a slow and debilitating terminal illness and death, the Holy Societies of One Islam, One Christ and One Spirit have an ecclesiastical and moral obligation as the true Disciples of Divine Mercy to do everything within their power to support the dignity of the dying and help them find peace.

      Dying with dignity is a fundamental determination of an enlightened society under God and the Divine Creator. Visitation is a celebration that enables those people who have some time before the point of death to seek resolution and peace before death; and before a loss of consciousness deprives the person of the full appreciation of the sacred gift.

Margin note (1060): Divine Purpose of the Sacred Gift of Visitation & Rite of Unction

Article 280 – Ritus Sacramentum Salvatio (Salvation)

1061. *Ritus Sacramentum Salvatio* is the Divine Right of the Authentic Life Gift of Salvation.

Margin note: Ritus Sacramentum Salvatio (Salvation)

1062. *Ritus Sacramentum Salvatio* is the thirty-first of thirty-three Sacramental Divine Rights; and may only be invoked whenever the

Margin note: Invocation of Ritus Sacramentum

1063. lesser Ecclesiastical Right of *Ius Ecclesiae Sacramentum Salvatio* is invoked in strict accord with the liturgy of *Missale Christus* (Missal of Christ), or *Taqwa Islam* (Rites of Islam) or *Karman Spiritus* (Rites of the Universal Divine Spirit).

> Salvatio

1063. The Sacred Gift of Salvation and Rite of Reconciliation shall be granted and administered within days of imminent death in accordance with the most sacred Covenant *Pactum De Singularis Caelum* and associated approved worship.

> Gift of Salvation

1064. The purpose of the Sacred Gift of Salvation and Rite of Reconciliation is the formal final (last) rites of bestowal or presentation of a possessory or prescriptive right to an incumbent in accordance with the most sacred Covenant *Pactum De Singularis Caelum* and associated approved worship.

The Sacred Gift of Salvation and Rite of Reconciliation is the special celebration of blessing and cleansing to help an individual in the final stages of death to find a point of peace and resolution to their life in the hope of evoking the care of other minds already crossed to help guide the person safely.

> Divine Purpose of the Sacred Gift of Salvation & Rite of Reconciliation

Article 281 – Ritus Sacramentum Emancipatio (Emancipation)

1065. ***Ritus Sacramentum Emancipatio*** is the Divine Right of the Authentic Life Gift of Emancipation

> Ritus Sacramentum Emancipatio (Emancipation)

1066. *Ritus Sacramentum Emancipatio* is the thirty-second of thirty-three Sacramental Divine Rights; and may only be invoked whenever the lesser Ecclesiastical Right of *Ius Ecclesiae Sacramentum Emancipatio* is invoked in strict accord with the liturgy of *Missale Christus* (Missal of Christ), or *Taqwa Islam* (Rites of Islam) or *Karman Spiritus* (Rites of the Universal Divine Spirit).

> Invocation of Ritus Sacramentum Emancipatio

1067. The Sacred Gift of Emancipation and Funerary Rites shall be granted and administered after death and prior to the sacred gift of Veneration and the burial or disposal of the body in accordance with the most sacred Covenant *Pactum De Singularis Caelum* and associated approved worship.

> Gift of Emancipation

1068. The purpose of the Sacred Gift of Emancipation and Funerary Rites is the formal funeral rites to an incumbent in accordance with the the most sacred Covenant *Pactum De Singularis Caelum* and associated approved worship.

> Divine Purpose of the Sacred Gift of Emancipation and Funerary Rites

The Sacred Gift of Emancipation and Funerary Rites is both the sacred gift and ceremony that remembers the deceased, their life and provides an opportunity for those in attendance to speak, celebrate and honour the memory of the departed.

Article 282 – Ritus Sacramentum Veneratio (Veneration)

1069. ***Ritus Sacramentum Veneratio*** is the Divine Right of the Authentic Life Gift of Veneration. — Ritus Sacramentum Veneratio (Veneration)

1070. *Ritus Sacramentum Veneratio* is the thirty-third of thirty-three Sacramental Divine Rights; and may only be invoked whenever the lesser Ecclesiastical Right of *Ius Ecclesiae Sacramentum Veneratio* is invoked in strict accord with the liturgy of *Missale Christus* (Missal of Christ), or *Taqwa Islam* (Rites of Islam) or *Karman Spiritus* (Rites of the Universal Divine Spirit). — Invocation of Ritus Sacramentum Veneratio

1071. The Sacred Gift of Veneration and Rite of Beatification shall be granted and administered by a valid Minister following death and the sacred gift of Remembrance in accordance with the most sacred Covenant *Pactum De Singularis Caelum* and associated approved worship. — Gift of Veneration

1072. The purpose of the sacred gift of Veneration and Rite of Beatification is a formal rite of blessing and remembrance in favour of the formal recognition, honour and trust of an incumbent in Heaven in accordance with the most sacred Covenant *Pactum De Singularis Caelum* and associated approved worship. — Divine Purpose of the Sacred Gift of Veneration & Rite of Beatification

6.9 - Authoritative Divine Rights

Article 283 – Authoritative Divine Rights

1073. ***Authoritative Divine Rights*** (Potentis Divinum Iurium) are Imperfect Divine Rights associated with core authoritative powers from Heaven to Earth. — Authoritative Divine Rights (Potentis Divinum Iurium)

1074. The following valid twenty-two (22) Authoritative Divine Rights (*Potentis Divinum Iurium*) are recognised in accord with the most sacred Covenant *Pactum De Singularis Caelum* and the present Maxims:- — List of Authoritative Divine Rights (Potentis Divinum Iurium)

    (i)   **"Ius Divinum Universus"** are the collection of Divine Rights to Design, Construct and Maintain Universal Reality;

and

(ii) **"Ius Divinum Regnum"** are the collection of Divine Rights of Sovereign Authority of Body; and

(iii) **"Ius Divinum Consilium"** are the collection of Divine Rights of a Legislative and Advisory Body; and

(iv) **"Ius Divinum Ecclesia"** are the collection of Divine Rights of an Ecclesiastical and Religious Body; and

(v) **"Ius Divinum Templum"** are the collection of Divine Rights of a Treasury or Financial (Banking) Body; and

(vi) **"Ius Divinum Collegium"** are the collection of Divine Rights of a Company or Charitable Body; and

(vii) **"Ius Divinum Officium"** are the collection of Divine Rights of Office, Duty and Service; and

(viii) **"Ius Divinum Imperium"** are the collection of Divine Rights of Command, Occupation and Enforcement; and

(ix) **"Ius Divinum Sacrum"** are the collection of Divine Rights of Sacred Recognition, Devotion and Veneration; and

(x) **"Ius Divinum Custoditum"** are the collection of Divine Rights of Custody, Guardianship and Preservation; and

(xi) **"Ius Divinum Alumentum"** are the collection of Divine Rights to Sustenance, Maintenance and Alms; and

(xii) **"Ius Divinum Apostolicus"** are the collection of Divine Rights of Divine Commission; and

(xiii) **"Ius Divinum Cancellaria"** are the collection of Divine Rights of Chancery and Administration of Records; and

(xiv) **"Ius Divinum Oratorium"** are the collection of Divine Rights to a competent Forum of Law and Review; and

(xv) **"Ius Divinum Penitentiaria"** are the collection of Divine Rights of Forced Confinement; and

(xvi) **"Ius Divinum Sacramentum"** are the collection of Divine Rights to grant and impart Holy Sacred Gifts; and

(xvii) **"Ius Divinum Visum"** are the collection of Divine Rights to Survey, Visit and Audit a Body; and

(xviii) **"Ius Divinum Commercium"** are the collection of Divine

Rights to Trade, Exchange and Communication; and

(xix) **"Ius Divinum Virtus"** are the collection of Divine Rights to Strength, Honour, Excellence and Virtue; and

(xx) **"Ius Divinum Astrum"** are the collection of Divine Rights to an Association, Aggregate or Body; and

(xxi) **"Ius Divinum Magisterium"** are the collection of Divine Rights to Teach, Instruct and Interpret Sacred Texts and Divine Will; and

(xxii) **"Ius Divinum Decretum"** are the collection of Divine Rights to issue Decrees, Judgements and Edicts.

Article 284 – Ius Divinum Universus (Reality)

1075. ***Ius Divinum Universus*** are the collection of Divine Rights to Design, Construct and Maintain Universal Reality, as inherited from the collection of Divine Rights *Ius Divinum Iuris*. — Ius Divinum Universus (Reality)

1076. *Ius Divinum Universus* (Reality) is the first of twenty-two Authoritative Divine Rights; and may only be invoked whenever (a) the Rights are invoked by a Divine Person or (b) the lesser related Natural Rights or Superior Person Rights as defined by the most sacred Covenant *Pactum De Singularis Caelum*. — Invoking of Ius Divinum Universus

1077. The collection of Divine Rights of *Ius Divinum Universus* (Reality) contains two Rights being:- — Collection of Ius Divinum Universus

   (i) *Ius Divinum Universus* being the Divine Right to Design, Construct and Maintain a Universal Reality; and

   (ii) *Ius Divinum Civilitatis* being the Divine Right of Civilised Rule of Civilisation.

Article 285 – Ius Divinum Regnum (Sovereign)

1078. ***Ius Divinum Regnum*** are the collection of Divine Rights of Sovereign Authority or Body, as inherited from the collection of Divine Rights *Ius Divinum Iuris*. — Ius Divinum Regnum (Sovereign)

1079. *Ius Divinum Regnum* (Sovereign) is the second of twenty-two Authoritative Divine Rights; and may only be invoked whenever (a) the Rights are invoked by a Divine Person or (b) the lesser related Natural Rights or Superior Person Rights as defined by the most — Invoking of Ius Divinum Regnum sacred Covenant *Pactum De Singularis Caelum*.

1080. The collection of Divine Rights of *Ius Divinum Regnum* (Sovereign) contains eight Rights being:-

    (i)   *Ius Divinum Regnum* being the Divine Right of the Sovereign Authority or Body; and

    (ii)   *Ius Divinum Integritatis Territorialis* being the Divine Right of Territorial Integrity; and

    (iii)   *Ius Divinum Independendiae Politicae* being the Divine Right of Political Independence; and

    (iv)   *Ius Divinum Recognitionis Souveranae* being the Divine Right of Sovereign Recognition; and

    (v)   *Ius Divinum Summae Iurisdictionis* being the Divine Right of Supreme Jurisdiction; and

    (vi)   *Ius Divinum Defensionis Souveranae* being the Divine Right of Sovereign Self Defence; and

    (vii)   *Ius Divinum Relationum Diplomaticarum* being the Divine Right of Diplomatic Relations; and

    (viii)   *Ius Divinum Foederum Faciendorum* being the Divine Right to Make Treaties with other States.

Article 286 – Ius Divinum Consilium (Legislative)

1081. **Ius Divinum Consilium** are the collection of Divine Rights of a Legislative and Advisory Body, as inherited from the collection of Divine Rights *Ius Divinum Iuris*.

1082. *Ius Divinum Consilium* (Legislative) is the third of twenty-two Authoritative Divine Rights; and may only be invoked whenever (a) the Rights are invoked by a Divine Person or (b) the lesser related Natural Rights or Superior Person Rights as defined by the most sacred Covenant *Pactum De Singularis Caelum*.

1083. The collection of Divine Rights of *Ius Divinum Consilium* (Legislative) contains twelve Rights being:-

    (i)   *Ius Divinum Consilium* being the Divine Right of a Legislative and Advisory Body; and

    (ii)   *Ius Divinum Regulas Parlamentarias* being the Divine Right to Parliamentary Rules of Conduct and Process; and

    (iii)   *Ius Divinum Privilegii Parlamentarii* being the Divine Right of Parliamentary Privilege; and

(iv) *Ius Divinum Votandi Parliamento* being the Divine Right of Parliamentary Vote; and

(v) *Ius Divinum Quaestionis Parliamento* being the Divine Right of Parliamentary Question; and

(vi) *Ius Divinum Informationis Parliamento* being the Divine Right of Parliamentary Information; and

(vii) *Ius Divinum Leges Faciendi* being the Divine Right to Make Laws; and

(viii) *Ius Divinum Leges Disputandi* being the Divine Right to Debate (Proposed and Existing) Laws; and

(ix) *Ius Divinum Leges Emendandi* being the Divine Right to Amend Laws; and

(x) *Ius Divinum Leges Conlucere* being the Divine Right to Consolidate Laws; and

(xi) *Ius Divinum Leges Abrogandi* being the Divine Right to Repeal Laws; and

(xii) *Ius Divinum Supervisionis Executivae* being the Divine Right of Executive Oversight.

Article 287 – Ius Divinum Ecclesia (Ecclesiastical)

1084. ***Ius Divinum Ecclesia*** are the collection of Divine Rights of an Ecclesiastical and Religious Body, as inherited from the collection of Divine Rights *Ius Divinum Iuris*. — Ius Divinum Ecclesia (Ecclesiastical)

1085. *Ius Divinum Ecclesia* (Ecclesiastical) is the fourth of twenty-two Authoritative Divine Rights; and may only be invoked whenever (a) the Rights are invoked by a Divine Person or (b) the lesser related Natural Rights or Superior Person Rights as defined by the most sacred Covenant *Pactum De Singularis Caelum*. — Invoking of Ius Divinum Ecclesia

1086. The collection of Divine Rights of *Ius Divinum Ecclesia* (Ecclesiastical) contains twenty-four Rights being:- — Collection of Ius Divinum Ecclesia

(i) *Ius Divinum Ecclesia* being the Divine Right of an Ecclesiastical and Religious Body; and

(ii) *Ius Divinum Libertatis Religionis* being the Divine Right of Freedom of Religion; and

(iii) *Ius Divinum Libertatis Persecutione Religionis* being the

Divine Right of Freedom from Religious Persecution; and

(iv) *Ius Divinum Celebrationis Religionis* being the Divine Right of Religious Worship and Celebration; and

(v) *Ius Divinum Educationis Religiosae* being the Divine Right of Religious Education; and

(vi) *Ius Divinum Caeremoniae Religionis* being the Divine Right of Religious Rites and Ceremony; and

(vii) *Ius Divinum Conventūs Religionis* being the Divine Right of Religious Assembly; and

(viii) *Ius Divinum Gubernandi Ecclesiasticum* being the Divine Right of Ecclesiastical Autonomy and Self Governance; and

(ix) *Ius Divinum Registrorum et Rotulorum Ecclesiasticorum* being the Divine Right of Ecclesiastical Registers and Rolls; and

(x) *Ius Divinum Cancellariae Ecclesiasticae* being the Divine Right of Ecclesiastical Chancery and Administration of Records; and

(xi) *Ius Divinum Proprietatis Ecclesiasticae* being the Divine Right of Ecclesiastical Property; and

(xii) *Ius Divinum Immunitatis Proprietatis Ecclesiasticae* being the Divine Right of Immunity of Ecclesiastical Property from Taxation and Expropriation; and

(xiii) *Ius Divinum Coronationis Ecclesiasticae* being the Divine Right of Ecclesiastical Coronation; and

(xiv) *Ius Divinum Separatae Ecclesiae et Coronae* being the Divine Right of Separation of Church and Crown; and

(xv) *Ius Divinum Separatae Ecclesiae et Civitatis* being the Divine Right of Separation of Church and State; and

(xvi) *Ius Divinum Positionum Ecclesiasticarum* being the Divine Right of Ecclesiastical Positions; and

(xvii) *Ius Divinum Investituræ Ecclesiasticæ* being the Divine Right of Ecclesiastical Investiture; and

(xviii) *Ius Divinum Officii Ecclesiastici* being the Divine Right of Ecclesiastical Office; and

(xix) *Ius Divinum Collegium Ecclesiasticarum* being the Divine Right of Ecclesiastical Bodies, Companies and Charitable Organisations; and

(xx) *Ius Divinum Consilium Ecclesiasticarum* being the Divine Right of Ecclesiastical Legislative Councils; and

(xxi) *Ius Divinum Oratorium Ecclesiasticarum* being the Divine Right of Ecclesiastical Courts and Forums of Law; and

(xxii) *Ius Divinum Templum Ecclesiasticarum* being the Divine Right of Ecclesiastical Treasury; and

(xxiii) *Ius Divinum Penitentiaria Ecclesiasticarum* being the Divine Right of Ecclesiastical Penitentiary; and

(xxiv) *Ius Divinum Commercium Ecclesiasticarum* being the Divine Right of Ecclesiastical Goods and Trade.

Article 288 – Ius Divinum Templum (Treasury & Financial)

1087. ***Ius Divinum Templum*** are the collection of Divine Rights of a Treasury or Financial (Banking) Body, as inherited from the collection of Divine Rights *Ius Divinum Iuris*. Ius Divinum Templum (Treasury & Financial)

1088. *Ius Divinum Templum* (Treasury & Financial) is the fifth of twenty-two Authoritative Divine Rights; and may only be invoked whenever (a) the Rights are invoked by a Divine Person or (b) the lesser related Natural Rights or Superior Person Rights as defined by the most sacred Covenant *Pactum De Singularis Caelum*. Invoking of Ius Divinum Templum

1089. The collection of Divine Rights of *Ius Divinum Templum* (Treasury & Financial) contains eleven Rights being:- Collection of Ius Divinum Templum

(i) *Ius Divinum Templum* being the Divine Right of a Treasury or Financial (Banking) Body; and

(ii) *Ius Divinum Officina Monetaria* being the Divine Right of Minting Office; and

(iii) *Ius Divinum Pecuniariarum Administrandi* being the Divine Right of Cash Management; and

(iv) *Ius Divinum Monetarum Administrandi* being the Divine Right of Monetary Management; and

(v) *Ius Divinum Administrationis Financiarum* being the Divine Right of Financial Administration; and

(vi) *Ius Divinum Administrationis Bancariae* being the Divine Right of Banking Administration; and

(vii) *Ius Divinum Administrationis Creditorum* being the Divine Right of Credit Management; and

(viii) *Ius Divinum Administrationis Debiti* being the Divine Right of Debt Management; and

(ix) *Ius Divinum Administrationis Financiarum Periculi* being the Divine Right of Financial Risk Management; and

(x) *Ius Divinum Operationum Thesaurariarum* being the Divine Right of Treasury Management; and

(xi) *Ius Divinum Administrationis Conformitatis* being the Divine Right of Compliance Management.

Article 289 – Ius Divinum Collegium (Company)

1090. ***Ius Divinum Collegium*** are the collection of Divine Rights of a Company or Charitable Body, as inherited from the collection of Divine Rights *Ius Divinum Iuris*.

<small>Ius Divinum Collegium (Company)</small>

1091. *Ius Divinum Collegium* (Company) is the sixth of twenty-two Authoritative Divine Rights; and may only be invoked whenever (a) the Rights are invoked by a Divine Person or (b) the lesser related Natural Rights or Superior Person Rights as defined by the most sacred Covenant *Pactum De Singularis Caelum*.

<small>Invoking of Ius Divinum Collegium</small>

1092. The collection of Divine Rights of *Ius Divinum Collegium* (Company) contains twenty-nine Rights being:-

<small>Collection of Ius Divinum Collegium</small>

    (i) *Ius Divinum Collegium* being the Divine Right of Company or Charitable Body; and

    (ii) *Ius Divinum Convocationis Formatio* being the Divine Right of Convocation of Members to Form Under granted Charter listing Key Rights and Constitution or Bylaws or Statutes; and

    (iii) *Ius Divinum Conventum Formatio* being the Divine Right of Assembly of Members to Form Under Memorandum of Key Objects and Articles; and

    (iv) *Ius Divinum Conventionis Formatio* being the Divine Right of Convention of Members to Form Under Declaration of Key Objects and Constitution; and

    (v) *Ius Divinum Incorporationis Collegii Existentis* being the Divine Right of Incorporating Existing Company, Body or Entity into a Jurisdiction; and

    (vi) *Ius Divinum Novi Collegii Incorporationis* being the Divine Right of Incorporating a New Company, Body or Entity (and its Governing Instrument) into a Jurisdiction; and

(vii) *Ius Divinum Incorporationis Exterae* being the Divine Right of Incorporating an Existing Company, Body or Entity into a Foreign Jurisdiction (to its original jurisdiction); and

(viii) *Ius Divinum Personae Iuridicae* being the Divine Right of Legal Personality for an Incorporated Company, Body or Entity; and

(ix) *Ius Divinum Proprietatis Collegii* being the Divine Right of Property Ownership and Rights for an Incorporated Company, Body or Entity; and

(x) *Ius Divinum Iurium Financiariorum Collegii* being the Divine Right of Financial and Banking Rights for an Incorporated Company, Body or Entity; and

(xi) *Ius Divinum Iurium Fornitorum Collegii* being the Divine Right of Supplier Rights for an Incorporated Company, Body or Entity; and

(xii) *Ius Divinum Iurium Operariorum Collegii* being the Divine Right of Employee Rights for an Incorporated Company, Body or Entity; and

(xiii) *Ius Divinum Iurium Conventus Collegii* being the Divine Right of Agreement Rights for an Incorporated Company, Body or Entity; and

(xiv) *Ius Divinum Commercium Collegii* being the Divine Right to Engage in Business and Commerce for an Incorporated Company, Body or Entity; and

(xv) *Ius Divinum Gubernandi Collegii* being the Divine Right to Corporate Governance for an Incorporated Company, Body or Entity; and

(xvi) *Ius Divinum Rationem Financiariam* being the Divine Right to Financial Reporting; and

(xvii) *Ius Divinum Limitandae Responsabilitatis* being the Divine Right to Limit Liability of Shareholders, Directors and Employees within the Governing Instruments of the Incorporated Company, Body or Entity; and

(xviii) *Ius Divinum Observandae Iurisdictionis* being the Divine Right of Compliance within Jurisdiction of Incorporation; and

(xix) *Ius Divinum Remunerationis Directoris* being the Divine Right of Director Remuneration; and

(xx) *Ius Divinum Conventum Directorum* being the Divine Right to

Director Meeting(s); and

(xxi) *Ius Divinum Conventum Generalium Partium* being the Divine Right of General Shareholders Meetings; and

(xxii) *Ius Divinum Conventum Extraordinarium Partium* being the Divine Right of Extraordinary Shareholders Meetings; and

(xxiii) *Ius Divinum Capitis Collegii* being the Divine Right of Share Capital; and

(xxiv) *Ius Divinum Mutationis Capitis Collegii* being the Divine Right to Change Share Capital; and

(xxv) *Ius Divinum Collegii Vendendi* being the Divine Right of Sale of Company, Body or Entity with another Body; and

(xxvi) *Ius Divinum Collegii Fusionis* being the Divine Right of Merger of Company, Body or Entity with another Body; and

(xxvii) *Ius Divinum Collegii Administrationis* being the Divine Right of Administration of Company, Body or Entity with another Body; and

(xxviii) *Ius Divinum Collegii Deregistrationis* being the Divine Right of Deregistration of previously registered (and incorporated) Company, Body or Entity; and

(xxix) *Ius Divinum Collegii Dissolutionis* being the Divine Right of Dissolution of Company, Body or Entity.

Article 290 – Ius Divinum Officium (Office)

1093. **Ius Divinum Officium** are the collection of Divine Rights of Office, Duty and Service, as inherited from the collection of Divine Rights *Ius Divinum Iuris*.

    <small>Ius Divinum Officium (Office)</small>

1094. *Ius Divinum Officium* (Office) is the seventh of twenty-two Authoritative Divine Rights; and may only be invoked whenever (a) the Rights are invoked by a Divine Person or (b) the lesser related Natural Rights or Superior Person Rights as defined by the most sacred Covenant *Pactum De Singularis Caelum*.

    <small>Invoking of Ius Divinum Officium</small>

1095. The collection of Divine Rights of *Ius Divinum Officium* (Office) contains fifteen Rights being:-

    <small>Collection of Ius Divinum Officium</small>

    (i) *Ius Divinum Officium* being the Divine Right of Office, Duty and Service; and

    (ii) *Ius Divinum Petendi Candidatum Officium* being the Divine

Right to Apply to be Candidate for Office; and

(iii) *Ius Divinum Formandum Comitatum* being the Divine Right to Form a Campaign as Candidate for Office; and

(iv) *Ius Divinum Candidati Officium* being the Divine Right to Run a Campaign as Candidate for Office; and

(v) *Ius Divinum Eligendi* being the Divine Right to be Elected as Candidate for Office; and

(vi) *Ius Divinum Clausurae Comitatus* being the Divine Right to Close a Campaign for Office; and

(vii) *Ius Divinum Mandati Officii* being the Divine Right to Receive Mandate in Good Faith, Good Conscience and Good Actions to Occupy an Office; and

(viii) *Ius Divinum Tenendi Officii* being the Divine Right to Hold an Office in Good Faith, Good Conscience and Good Actions; and

(ix) *Ius Divinum Immunitatis Officii* being the Divine Right of Immunity for Decisions Made in Office in Good Faith, Good Conscience and Good Actions; and

(x) *Ius Divinum Abdicandi Officii* being the Divine Right to Retire from Office in Honour, Privileges and Good Standing; and

(xi) *Ius Divinum Dicendi Officii* being the Divine Right to Resign from Office in Honour, Privileges and Good Standing; and

(xii) *Ius Divinum Nullius Mandati* being the Divine Right to have Mandate Withdrawn and be Terminated from Office in Disgrace, Without Privileges and Poor Standing; and

(xiii) *Ius Divinum Accusationi Officii* being the Divine Right to Face Impeachment for Claims of Bad Faith, Bad Conscience or Bad Actions in Office; and

(xiv) *Ius Divinum Removendi Officii* being the Divine Right to be Removed by Force from Office in Disgrace, Without Privileges and Poor Standing upon being found Culpable from Impeachment; and

(xv) *Ius Divinum Restituendi Officii* being the Divine Right to be Restored to Office in Honour, Privileges and Good Standing after having been unlawfully obstructed or removed from Office.

Article 291 – Ius Divinum Imperium (Command)

1096. ***Ius Divinum Imperium*** are the collection of Divine Rights of Command, Occupation and Enforcement, as inherited from the collection of Divine Rights *Ius Divinum Iuris*.

Ius Divinum Imperium (Command)

1097. *Ius Divinum Imperium* (Command) is the eighth of twenty-two Authoritative Divine Rights; and may only be invoked whenever (a) the Rights are invoked by a Divine Person or (b) the lesser related Natural Rights or Superior Person Rights as defined by the most sacred Covenant *Pactum De Singularis Caelum*.

Invoking of Ius Divinum Imperium

1098. The collection of Divine Rights of *Ius Divinum Imperium* (Command) contains six Rights being:-

Collection of Ius Divinum Imperium

   (i)   *Ius Divinum Imperium* being the Divine Right of Command, Occupation and Enforcement; and

   (ii)   *Ius Divinum Imperium Emissionis* being the Divine Right of Issuance of Command in Good Faith, Good Conscience and Good Action; and

   (iii)   *Ius Divinum Imperium Immunitatis* being the Divine Right of Immunity for Command Made in Office in Good Faith, Good Conscience and Good Actions; and

   (iv)   *Ius Divinum Imperium Receptionis* being the Divine Right of Receipt of Command in Good Faith, Good Conscience and Good Action; and

   (v)   *Ius Divinum Imperium Executionis* being the Divine Right of Enforcement of Command in Good Faith, Good Conscience and Good Action; and

   (vi)   *Ius Divinum Immunitatis Executionis* being the Divine Right of Immunity when Enforcement of Command done in Good Faith, Good Conscience and Good Action.

Article 292 – Ius Divinum Sacrum (Sacred)

1099. ***Ius Divinum Sacrum*** are the collection of Divine Rights of Sacred Recognition, Devotion and Veneration, as inherited from the collection of Divine Rights *Ius Divinum Iuris*.

Ius Divinum Sacrum (Sacred)

1100. *Ius Divinum Sacrum* (Sacred) is the ninth of twenty-two Authoritative Divine Rights; and may only be invoked whenever (a) the Rights are invoked by a Divine Person or (b) the lesser related

Invoking of Ius Divinum Sacrum

Natural Rights or Superior Person Rights as defined by the most sacred Covenant *Pactum De Singularis Caelum*.

1101. The collection of Divine Rights of *Ius Divinum Sacrum* (Sacred) contains one Right being:-

    (i) *Ius Divinum Sacrum* being the Divine Right of Sacred Recognition, Devotion and Veneration.

Article 293 – Ius Divinum Custoditum (Custody)

1102. ***Ius Divinum Custoditum*** are the collection of Divine Rights of Custody, Guardianship and Preservation, as inherited from the collection of Divine Rights *Ius Divinum Iuris*.

1103. *Ius Divinum Custoditum* (Custody) is the tenth of twenty-two Authoritative Divine Rights; and may only be invoked whenever (a) the Rights are invoked by a Divine Person or (b) the lesser related Natural Rights or Superior Person Rights as defined by the most sacred Covenant *Pactum De Singularis Caelum*.

1104. The collection of Divine Rights of *Ius Divinum Custoditum* (Custody) contains twenty-seven Rights being:-

    (i) *Ius Divinum Custoditum* being the Divine Right of Custody, Guardianship and Preservation; and

    (ii) *Ius Divinum Custos* being the Divine Right of Custodian; and

    (iii) *Ius Divinum Officii Curae Custodis* being the Divine Right of Duty of Care of Custodian; and

    (iv) *Ius Divinum Removendi Custodis* being the Divine Right of Removal of Custodian for Breach of Duty of Care or Bad Faith, Bad Conscience or Bad Actions; and

    (v) *Ius Divinum Rationis Legalis Custodis* being the Divine Right of Custodian as Attorney and Legal Representative; and

    (vi) *Ius Divinum Medicinae Decisionis Custodis* being the Divine Right of Medical Decisions of Custodian; and

    (vii) *Ius Divinum Pecuniarum Decisionis Custodis* being the Divine Right of Financial Decisions of Custodian; and

    (viii) *Ius Divinum Proprietatis Decisionis Custodis* being the Divine Right of Property Decisions of Custodian; and

    (ix) *Ius Divinum Custodiae Immunitatis* being the Divine Right of Immunity of Custodian when Decisions and Actions Made in Office in Good Faith, Good Conscience and Good Actions; and

(x) *Ius Divinum Curatoris* being the Divine Right of Curator; and

(xi) *Ius Divinum Officii Curae Curatoris* being the Divine Right of Duty of Care of Curator; and

(xii) *Ius Divinum Removendi Curatoris* being the Divine Right of Removal of Curator for Breach of Duty of Care or Bad Faith, Bad Conscience or Bad Actions; and

(xiii) *Ius Divinum Rationis Legalis Curatoris* being the Divine Right of Curator as Attorney and Legal Representative; and

(xiv) *Ius Divinum Pecuniarum Decisionis Curatoris* being the Divine Right of Financial Decisions of Curator; and

(xv) *Ius Divinum Medicinae Decisionis Curatoris* being the Divine Right of Medical Decisions of Curator; and

(xvi) *Ius Divinum Proprietatis Decisionis Curatoris* being the Divine Right of Property Decisions of Curator; and

(xvii) *Ius Divinum Immunitatis Curatoris* being the Divine Right of Immunity of Curator when Decisions and Actions Made in Office in Good Faith, Good Conscience and Good Actions; and

(xviii) *Ius Divinum Protectoris* being the Divine Right of Guardian; and

(xix) *Ius Divinum Officii Curae Protectoris* being the Divine Right of Duty of Care of Guardian; and

(xx) *Ius Divinum Removendi Protectoris* being the Divine Right of Removal of Guardian for Breach of Duty of Care or Bad Faith, Bad Conscience or Bad Actions; and

(xxi) *Ius Divinum Rationis Legalis Protectoris* being the Divine Right of Guardian as Attorney and Legal Representative; and

(xxii) *Ius Divinum Medicinae Decisionis Protectoris* being the Divine Right of Medical Decisions of Guardian; and

(xxiii) *Ius Divinum Pecuniarum Decisionis Protectoris* being the Divine Right of Financial Decisions of Guardian; and

(xxiv) *Ius Divinum Proprietatis Decisionis Protectoris* being the Divine Right of Property Decisions of Guardian; and

(xxv) *Ius Divinum Habitationis Decisionis Protectoris* being the Divine Right of Housing and Accommodation Decisions of Guardian; and

(xxvi) *Ius Divinum Educationis Decisionis Protectoris* being the Divine Right of Education Decisions of Guardian; and

(xxvii) *Ius Divinum Immunitatis Protectoris* being the Divine Right of Immunity of Protector when Decisions and Actions Made in Office in Good Faith, Good Conscience and Good Actions.

Article 294 – Ius Divinum Alumentum (Sustenance)

1105. **Ius Divinum Alumentum** are the collection of Divine Rights to Sustenance, Maintenance and Alms, as inherited from the collection of Divine Rights *Ius Divinum Iuris*.

Ius Divinum Alumentum (Sustenance)

1106. *Ius Divinum Alumentum* (Sustenance) is the eleventh of twenty-two Authoritative Divine Rights; and may only be invoked whenever (a) the Rights are invoked by a Divine Person or (b) the lesser related Natural Rights or Superior Person Rights as defined by the most sacred Covenant *Pactum De Singularis Caelum*.

Invoking of Ius Divinum Alumentum

1107. The collection of Divine Rights of *Ius Divinum Alumentum* (Sustenance) contains nine Rights being:-

Collection of Ius Divinum Alumentum

   (i) *Ius Divinum Alumentum* being the Divine Right to Sustenance, Maintenance and Alms; and

   (ii) *Ius Divinum Subsistentiae* being the Divine Right of Sustenance; and

   (iii) *Ius Divinum Aquae Purae* being the Divine Right of Clean Water; and

   (iv) *Ius Divinum Terrae Purae* being the Divine Right of Clean Land; and

   (v) *Ius Divinum Domicilii* being the Divine Right of Shelter; and

   (vi) *Ius Divinum Securitatis Violentia* being the Divine Right of Safety from Violence; and

   (vii) *Ius Divinum Vestitus* being the Divine Right of Clothing; and

   (viii) *Ius Divinum Curae Medicae* being the Divine Right of Medical Care; and

   (ix) *Ius Divinum Educationis Bonae* being the Divine Right of Good Education.

Article 295 – Ius Divinum Apostolicus (Commission)

1108. ***Ius Divinum Apostolicus*** are the collection of Divine Rights of Divine Commission, as inherited from the collection of Divine Rights *Ius Divinum Iuris*.
    Ius Divinum Apostolicus (Commission)

1109. *Ius Divinum Apostolicus* (Commission) is the twelfth of twenty-two Authoritative Divine Rights; and may only be invoked whenever (a) the Rights are invoked by a Divine Person or (b) the lesser related Natural Rights or Superior Person Rights as defined by the most sacred Covenant *Pactum De Singularis Caelum*.
    Invoking of Ius Divinum Apostolicus

1110. The collection of Divine Rights of *Ius Divinum Apostolicus* (Commission) contains seven Rights being:-
    Collection of Ius Divinum Apostolicus

    (i) *Ius Divinum Apostolicus* being the Divine Right of Divine Commission; and

    (ii) *Ius Divinum Accipiendi Apostolicus* being the Divine Right to Receive Commission in Good Faith, Good Conscience and Good Actions; and

    (iii) *Ius Divinum Tenendi Apostolicus* being the Divine Right to Hold a Commission in Good Faith, Good Conscience and Good Actions; and

    (iv) *Ius Divinum Immunitatis Apostolicus* being the Divine Right of Immunity for Decisions Made under Commission in Good Faith, Good Conscience and Good Actions; and

    (v) *Ius Divinum Dicendi Apostolicus* being the Divine Right to Resign from Commission in Honour, Privileges and Good Standing; and

    (vi) *Ius Divinum Nullius Apostolicus* being the Divine Right to have Commission Withdrawn and be Terminated in Disgrace, Without Privileges and Poor Standing; and

    (vii) *Ius Divinum Restituendi Apostolicus* being the Divine Right to be Restored to Commission in Honour, Privileges and Good Standing after having been unlawfully obstructed or removed from Commission.

Article 296 – Ius Divinum Cancellarium (Competence)

1111. ***Ius Divinum Cancellarium*** are the collection of Divine Rights of Chancery and Administration of Records, as inherited from the
    Ius Divinum Cancellarium

collection of Divine Rights *Ius Divinum Iuris*. (Competence)

1112. *Ius Divinum Cancellarium* (Competence) is the thirteenth of twenty-two Authoritative Divine Rights; and may only be invoked whenever (a) the Rights are invoked by a Divine Person or (b) the lesser related Natural Rights or Superior Person Rights as defined by the most sacred Covenant *Pactum De Singularis Caelum*.

Invoking of Ius Divinum Cancellarium

1113. The collection of Divine Rights of *Ius Divinum Cancellarium* (Competence) contains six Rights being:-

Collection of Ius Divinum Cancellarium

    (i) *Ius Divinum Cancellarium* being the Divine Right of Chancery and Administration of Records; and

    (ii) *Ius Divinum Aedificandi Cancellariae* being the Divine Right of Chancery Building; and

    (iii) *Ius Divinum Procedendi Cancellariae* being the Divine Right of Chancery Procedures; and

    (iv) *Ius Divinum Technologiae Cancellariae* being the Divine Right of Chancery Technology and Digital Systems; and

    (v) *Ius Divinum Cancellarii* being the Divine Right of the Chancellor; and

    (vi) *Ius Divinum Cancellarii Immunitatis* being the Divine Right of Immunity for Chancellor and Agents when Decisions and Actions Made in Office in Good Faith, Good Conscience and Good Actions.

Article 297 – Ius Divinum Oratorium (Forum of Law)

1114. ***Ius Divinum Oratorium*** are the collection of Divine Rights to a competent Forum of Law and Review, as inherited from the collection of Divine Rights *Ius Divinum Iuris*.

Ius Divinum Oratorium (Forum of Law)

1115. *Ius Divinum Oratorium* (Forum of Law) is the fourteenth of twenty-two Authoritative Divine Rights; and may only be invoked whenever (a) the Rights are invoked by a Divine Person or (b) the lesser related Natural Rights or Superior Person Rights as defined by the most sacred Covenant *Pactum De Singularis Caelum*.

Invoking of Ius Divinum Oratorium

1116. The collection of Divine Rights of *Ius Divinum Oratorium* (Forum of Law) contains twelve Rights being:-

Collection of Ius Divinum Oratorium

    (i) *Ius Divinum Oratorium* being the Divine Right of Forum of Law and Review; and

    (ii) *Ius Divinum Aedificandi Fori* being the Divine Right of Forum of Law Building; and

(iii) *Ius Divinum Procedendi Fori* being the Divine Right of Forum of Law Procedures; and

(iv) *Ius Divinum Technologiae Fori* being the Divine Right of Forum of Law Technology and Digital Systems; and

(v) *Ius Divinum Iudicum Fori* being the Divine Right of Forum of Law Justices; and

(vi) *Ius Divinum Iudicum Immunitatis* being the Divine Right of Immunity for Justices when Decisions and Actions Made in Office in Good Faith, Good Conscience and Good Actions; and

(vii) *Ius Divinum Iudicum Officiorum Fori* being the Divine Right of Forum of Law Officers; and

(viii) *Ius Divinum Officii Iudicialis Immunitatis* being the Divine Right of Immunity for Law Officers when Decisions and Actions Made in Office in Good Faith, Good Conscience and Good Actions; and

(ix) *Ius Divinum Custodiae Iudicialis Fori* being the Divine Right of Forum of Law Attendants and Guards; and

(x) *Ius Divinum Custodiae Iudicialis Immunitatis* being the Divine Right of Immunity for Law Attendants and Guards when Decisions and Actions Made in Office in Good Faith, Good Conscience and Good Actions; and

(xi) *Ius Divinum Cancellarium Fori* being the Divine Right of Forum of Law Chancery and Records Administration; and

(xii) *Ius Divinum Penitentiaria Fori* being the Divine Right of Forum of Law Penitentiary and Holding Prison.

Article 298 – Ius Divinum Penitentiaria (Forced Confinement)

1117. **Ius Divinum Penitentiaria** are the collection of Divine Rights of Forced Confinement, as inherited from the collection of Divine Rights *Ius Divinum Iuris*.

Ius Divinum Penitentiaria (Penitence)

1118. *Ius Divinum Penitentiaria* (Forced Confinement) is the fifteenth of twenty-two Authoritative Divine Rights; and may only be invoked whenever (a) the Rights are invoked by a Divine Person or (b) the lesser related Natural Rights or Superior Person Rights as defined by the most sacred Covenant *Pactum De Singularis Caelum*.

Invoking of Ius Divinum Penitentiaria

1119. The collection of Divine Rights of *Ius Divinum Penitentiaria*

Collection of Ius Divinum

(Penitence) contains one Right being:-

(i) *Ius Divinum Penitentiaria* being the Divine Right to Force Confinement and Penitence.

Article 299 – Ius Divinum Sacramentum (Sacred Gifts)

1120. ***Ius Divinum Sacramentum*** are the collection of Divine Rights to grant and impart Holy Sacred Gifts, as inherited from the collection of Divine Rights *Ius Divinum Iuris*.

1121. *Ius Divinum Sacramentum* (Sacred Gifts) is the sixteenth of twenty-two Authoritative Divine Rights; and may only be invoked whenever (a) the Rights are invoked by a Divine Person or (b) the lesser related Natural Rights or Superior Person Rights as defined by the most sacred Covenant *Pactum De Singularis Caelum*.

1122. The collection of Divine Rights of *Ius Divinum Sacramentum* (Sacred Gifts) contains one Right being:-

(i) *Ius Divinum Sacramentum* being the Divine Right to grant and impart Holy Sacred Gifts.

Article 300 – Ius Divinum Visum (Survey)

1123. ***Ius Divinum Visum*** are the collection of Divine Rights to Survey, Visit and Audit a Body, as inherited from the collection of Divine Rights *Ius Divinum Iuris*.

1124. *Ius Divinum Visum* (Survey) is the seventeenth of twenty-two Authoritative Divine Rights; and may only be invoked whenever (a) the Rights are invoked by a Divine Person or (b) the lesser related Natural Rights or Superior Person Rights as defined by the most sacred Covenant *Pactum De Singularis Caelum*.

1125. The collection of Divine Rights of *Ius Divinum Visum* (Survey) contains eleven Rights being:-

(i) *Ius Divinum Visum* being the Divine Rights to Survey, Visit and Audit a Body; and

(ii) *Ius Divinum Monumenti* being the Divine Right of Creating Monument; and

(iii) *Ius Divinum Usus Notatoris* being the Divine Right of Creating and Setting a Marker; and

(iv) *Ius Divinum Usus Limitis* being the Divine Right of Creating and Setting a Boundary; and

(v) *Ius Divinum Visitationis* being the Divine Right of Visitation; and

(vi) *Ius Divinum Arationis* being the Divine Right of Survey; and

(vii) *Ius Divinum Certificandi Arationem* being the Divine Right of Certification of Survey; and

(viii) *Ius Divinum Usus Servitutis* being the Divine Right of Easement; and

(ix) *Ius Divinum Viæ* being the Divine Right of Way; and

(x) *Ius Divinum Usus Terrae* being the Divine Right of Land Use; and

(xi) *Ius Divinum Topographiae* being the Divine Right of Topography.

Article 301 – Ius Divinum Commercium (Trade)

1126. **Ius Divinum Commercium** are the collection of Divine Rights to Trade, Exchange and Communication, as inherited from the collection of Divine Rights *Ius Divinum Iuris*.   Ius Divinum Commercium (Trade)

1127. *Ius Divinum Commercium* (Trade) is the eighteenth of twenty-two Authoritative Divine Rights; and may only be invoked whenever (a) the Rights are invoked by a Divine Person or (b) the lesser related Natural Rights or Superior Person Rights as defined by the most sacred Covenant *Pactum De Singularis Caelum*.   Invoking of Ius Divinum Commercium

1128. The collection of Divine Rights of *Ius Divinum Commercium* (Trade) contains ten Rights being:-   Collection of Ius Divinum Commercium

(i) *Ius Divinum Commercium* being the Divine Rights to Trade, Exchange and Communication; and

(ii) *Ius Divinum Libertatis Negotiandi Pretium* being the Divine Right of Freedom to Negotiate Price; and

(iii) *Ius Divinum Libertatis Emendi* being the Divine Right of Freedom to Purchase; and

(iv) *Ius Divinum Libertatis Vendendi* being the Divine Right of Freedom to Sell; and

(v) *Ius Divinum Libertatis Mercatorum* being the Divine Right of Freedom of Trade; and

(vi) *Ius Divinum Libertatis Investitionis* being the Divine Right of

Freedom of Investment; and

(vii) *Ius Divinum Libertatis Motus Bonorum* being the Divine Right of Freedom of Movement of Goods; and

(viii) *Ius Divinum Libertatis Mercatorum Conventi* being the Divine Right of Freedom of Agreement; and

(ix) *Ius Divinum Qualitatem Deliberatam* being the Divine Right of Quality Delivered; and

(x) *Ius Divinum Rem Emptam* being the Divine Right to Thing Purchased.

Article 302 – Ius Divinum Virtus (Strength)

1129. **Ius Divinum Virtus** are the collection of Divine Rights to Strength, Honour, Excellence and Virtue, as inherited from the collection of Divine Rights *Ius Divinum Iuris*.

1130. *Ius Divinum Virtus* (Strength) is the nineteenth of twenty-two Authoritative Divine Rights; and may only be invoked whenever (a) the Rights are invoked by a Divine Person or (b) the lesser related Natural Rights or Superior Person Rights as defined by the most sacred Covenant *Pactum De Singularis Caelum*.

1131. The collection of Divine Rights of *Ius Divinum Virtus* (Strength) contains one Right being:-

(i) *Ius Divinum Virtus* being the Divine Rights to Strength, Honour, Excellence and Virtue.

Article 303 – Ius Divinum Astrum (Association)

1132. **Ius Divinum Astrum** are the collection of Divine Rights to an Association, Aggregate or Body, as inherited from the collection of Divine Rights *Ius Divinum Iuris*.

1133. *Ius Divinum Astrum* (Association) is the twentieth of twenty-two Authoritative Divine Rights; and may only be invoked whenever (a) the Rights are invoked by a Divine Person or (b) the lesser related Natural Rights or Superior Person Rights as defined by the most sacred Covenant *Pactum De Singularis Caelum*.

1134. The collection of Divine Rights of *Ius Divinum Astrum* (Association) contains eight Rights being:-

(i) *Ius Divinum Astrum* being the Divine Rights to an

Association, Aggregate or Body; and

(ii) *Ius Libertatis Associationis* being the Divine Right of Freedom of Association; and

(iii) *Ius Libertatis Expressionis* being the Divine Right of Freedom of Expression; and

(iv) *Ius Libertatis Eventus Organisati* being the Divine Right of Freedom of Organised Events; and

(v) Ius Publica Accedendi being the Divine Right of Access to Public Spaces; and

(vi) *Ius Libertatis Protestandi* being the Divine Right of Freedom to Protest; and

(vii) *Ius Libertatis Violentia Civili* being the Divine Right of Freedom from State Violence; and

(viii) *Ius Dissolutionis* being the Divine Right of Dissolution.

Article 304 – Ius Divinum Magisterium (Teach)

1135. ***Ius Divinum Magisterium*** are the collection of Divine Rights to Teach, Instruct and Interpret Sacred Texts and Divine Will, as inherited from the collection of Divine Rights *Ius Divinum Iuris*.

    Ius Divinum Magisterium (Teach)

1136. *Ius Divinum Magisterium* (Teach) is the twenty-first of twenty-two Authoritative Divine Rights; and may only be invoked whenever (a) the Rights are invoked by a Divine Person or (b) the lesser related Natural Rights or Superior Person Rights as defined by the most sacred Covenant *Pactum De Singularis Caelum*.

    Invoking of Ius Divinum Magisterium

1137. The collection of Divine Rights of *Ius Divinum Magisterium* (Teach) contains six Rights being:-

    Collection of Ius Divinum Magisterium

    (i) *Ius Divinum Magisterium* being the Divine Right to Teach, Instruct and Interpret Sacred Texts and Divine Will; and

    (ii) *Ius Divinum Fallax Numquam Fallibilis* being the Divine Right to be Fallible and Never claim Infallibility before the Divine; and

    (iii) *Ius Divinum Sapientia Circa Divinum* being the Divine Right of Wisdom concerning the Divine; and

    (iv) *Ius Divinum Humilitas Circa Divinum* being the Divine Right of Humility concerning the Divine; and

    (v) *Ius Divinum Bonafide Circa Divinum* being the Divine Right of Good Faith concerning the Divine; and

(vi) *Ius Divinum Interpretationis Divinae Revelationis* being the Divine Right to Interpret Divine Revelation according to Wisdom, Humility and Good Faith.

Article 305 – Ius Divinum Decretum (Decrees)

1138. ***Ius Divinum Decretum*** are the collection of Divine Rights to issue Decrees, Judgements and Edicts, as inherited from the collection of Divine Rights *Ius Divinum Iuris*.

_{Ius Divinum Decretum (Decrees)}

1139. *Ius Divinum Decretum* (Decrees) is the twenty-second of twenty-two Authoritative Divine Rights; and may only be invoked whenever (a) the Rights are invoked by a Divine Person or (b) the lesser related Natural Rights or Superior Person Rights as defined by the most sacred Covenant *Pactum De Singularis Caelum*.

_{Invoking of Ius Divinum Decretum}

1140. The collection of Divine Rights of *Ius Divinum Decretum* (Decrees) contains six Rights being:-

_{Collection of Ius Divinum Decretum}

   (i) *Ius Divinum Decretum* being the Divine Right of Decrees, Judgements and Edicts; and

   (ii) *Ius Divinum Edicti* being the Divine Right of Edict being a formal executive or sovereign or ecclesiastical address and command concerning a moral or legal or administrative matter; and

   (iii) *Ius Divinum Decreti* being the Divine Right of Decree being an official order or command; and

   (iv) *Ius Divinum Declarationis Iudicii* being the Divine Right of Declaratory Judgement; and

   (v) *Ius Divinum Rescripti* being the Divine Right of Rescript being a formal response to one or more ecclesiastical or legal questions; and

   (vi) *Ius Divinum Notificandi* being the Divine Right of Notice being a formal note distributed and published concerning some subject.

6.10 - Divine Writs of Right

Article 306 – Divine Writs of Right

1141. ***Recto Divinum Iurium*** (Divine Writs of Rights) are Imperfect Divine Rights associated with the one, true and only valid forms of

_{Divine Writs of Rights (Recto}

Original Entry and Original Action. *Divinum Iurium*)

1142. All valid Remedy and Relief shall be by one or more Perfect Writs of Right as the one, true and only valid forms of Original Entry and Original Action. All forms of coercive powers and enforcement including, but not limited to prevention, protection, restitution, restoration, seizure, search, sanction, arrest, custody, penalty or satisfaction, shall be enacted via one or more valid Perfect Writs of Right. — Valid Remedy and Relief

1143. There shall be three classes of Perfect Writs of Right, being Divine, True and Superior:- — Three Classes of Perfect Writs of Right

 (i) Perfect Divine Writs of Right and Action shall be the Right of Original Entry and Action for all Divine Rights in relation to all Divine Persons, Divine Trusts and Divine Estates; and

 (ii) Perfect True Writs of Right and Rule of Law shall be the Right of Original Entry and Action for all Natural Rights in relation to all True Persons, True Trusts and True Estates; and

 (iii) Perfect Superior Writs of Right and Enforcement shall be the Right of Original Entry and Action for all Superior Rights in relation to all Superior Persons, Superior Trusts and Superior Estates of valid Ucadia Societies and competent forums of Law.

1144. The enforcement and coercive powers of Perfect Writs of Right may only be issued in relation to Members of One Heaven and Ucadia being Divine Persons, or True Persons or Superior Persons, as well as any other lesser bodies, bodies politic, associations, partnerships, companies, entities, fraternities, religious organisations, corporations or persons under the Jurisdiction of the Divine Creator of all Existence and all Heaven and Earth. — Enforcement of Perfect Writs

1145. By definition, the very existence of any Divine Person or claim of authority or power or right from Heaven of a lesser body, association, person or entity, is prima facie proof of an ecclesiastical and trust relation acknowledging the Jurisdiction of the Divine Creator of all Existence and all Heaven and Earth. Furthermore, the existence of a flesh body is irrefutable proof of the conveyance of divinity from a Divine Trust to a True Trust and the willing consent by the Divine Person to perform and obey the obligations of making such a gift in accord with the present Maxims. All enforcement through valid Perfect Writs of Right is therefore considered imperative in nature. — Imperative Nature of Perfect Writs

1146. The following valid eleven (11) Divine Writs of Rights (*Recto Divinum Iurium*) are recognised in accord with the most sacred — List of Divine Writs of Rights

Covenant *Pactum De Singularis Caelum* and the present Maxims:- (Recto Divinum Iurium)

 (i) "**Recto Divinum Originalis**" is the Divine Original Writ of Right; and

 (ii) "**Recto Divinum Apocalypsis**" is the Divine Writ of Right of Revelation; and

 (iii) "**Recto Divinum Investigationis**" is the Divine Writ of Right of Inquiry or Review; and

 (iv) "**Recto Divinum Capimus**" is the Divine Writ of Right of Surrender or Arrest of Person; and

 (v) "**Recto Divinum Custodiae**" is the Divine Writ of Right of Surrender or Seizure of Property; and

 (vi) "**Recto Divinum Corrigimus**" is the Divine Writ of Right of Correction of Records, Rulings, Laws or Instruments; and

 (vii) "**Recto Divinum Expurgatio**" is the Divine Writ of Right of Expurgation of Records, Rulings, Laws or Instruments; and

 (viii) "**Recto Divinum Abrogatio**" is the Divine Writ of Right of Annulment of Records, Rulings, Laws or Instruments; and

 (ix) "**Recto Divinum Inhibitio**" is the Divine Writ of Right of Prohibition or Restraint; and

 (x) "**Recto Divinum Restitutio**" is the Divine Writ of Right of Restitution; and

 (xi) "**Recto Regnum Restoratio**" is the Divine Writ of Restoration.

1147. Whenever a valid Perfect True Writ of Right and Rule of Law is issued, a Perfect Divine Writ of Right and Action of the same type shall be issued and duly recorded in Heaven. Thus, the existence of a registered Perfect True Writ within the Great Register and Divine Records of One Heaven and any associated Gazette notices shall be prima facie evidence that what is enacted in the temporal realm is also enacted within the spiritual realm. Supernatural Nature of Perfect Writ as Command from Heaven

Article 307 – Recto Divinum Originalis (Original Writ)

1148. ***Recto Divinum Originalis*** is the Divine Original Writ (of Right), as inherited from the collection of Divine Rights *Ius Divinum Iuris*. Recto Divinum Originalis (Original Writ)

1149. *Recto Divinum Originalis* (Original Writ) is the first of eleven Divine Rights of Divine Writs; and may only be invoked whenever the lesser Right of *Recto Ecclesiae Originalis* is invoked.

[margin: Invoking of Recto Divinum Originalis]

Article 308 – Recto Divinum Apocalypsis (Revelation)

1150. **Recto Divinum Apocalypsis** is the Divine Writ of Right of Revelation, as inherited from the collection of Divine Rights *Ius Divinum Iuris*.

[margin: Recto Divinum Apocalypsis (Revelation)]

1151. *Recto Divinum Apocalypsis* (Revelation) is the second of eleven Divine Rights of Divine Writs; and may only be invoked whenever the lesser Right of *Recto Ecclesiae Apocalypsis* is invoked.

[margin: Invoking of Recto Divinum Apocalypsis]

Article 309 – Recto Divinum Investigationis (Inquiry & Search)

1152. **Recto Divinum Investigationis** is the Divine Writ of Inquiry and Search, as inherited from the collection of Divine Rights *Ius Divinum Iuris*.

[margin: Recto Divinum Investigationis (Inquiry & Search)]

1153. *Recto Divinum Investigationis* (Inquiry & Search) is the third of eleven Divine Rights of Divine Writs; and may only be invoked whenever the lesser Right of *Recto Ecclesiae Investigationis* is invoked.

[margin: Invoking of Recto Divinum Investigationis]

Article 310 – Recto Divinum Capimus (Surrender or Arrest)

1154. **Recto Divinum Capimus** is the Divine Writ of Surrender or Arrest of Person, as inherited from the collection of Divine Rights *Ius Divinum Iuris*.

[margin: Recto Divinum Capimus (Surrender or Arrest)]

1155. *Recto Divinum Capimus* (Surrender or Arrest) is the fourth of eleven Divine Rights of Divine Writs; and may only be invoked whenever the lesser Right of *Recto Ecclesiae Capimus* is invoked.

[margin: Invoking of Recto Divinum Capimus]

Article 311 – Recto Divinum Custodiae (Surrender or Seizure)

1156. **Recto Divinum Custodiae** is the Divine Writ of Surrender or Seizure of Property, as inherited from the collection of Divine Rights *Ius Divinum Iuris*.

[margin: Recto Divinum Custodiae (Surrender or Seizure)]

1157. *Recto Divinum Custodiae* (Surrender or Seizure) is the fifth of eleven Divine Rights of Divine Writs; and may only be invoked whenever

[margin: Invoking of Recto Divinum]

the lesser Right of *Recto Ecclesiae Custodiae* is invoked.

Article 312 – Recto Divinum Corrigimus (Correction)

1158. **Recto Divinum Corrigimus** is the Divine Writ of Right of Correction of Records, Rulings, Laws or Instruments, as inherited from the collection of Divine Rights *Ius Divinum Iuris*.

1159. *Recto Divinum Corrigimus* (Correction) is the sixth of eleven Divine Rights of Divine Writs; and may only be invoked whenever the lesser Right of *Recto Ecclesiae Corrigimus* is invoked.

Article 313 – Recto Divinum Expurgatio (Expurgation)

1160. **Recto Divinum Expurgatio** is the Divine Writ of Right of Expurgation of Records, Rulings, Laws or Instruments, as inherited from the collection of Divine Rights *Ius Divinum Iuris*.

1161. *Recto Divinum Expurgatio* (Expurgation) is the seventh of eleven Divine Rights of Divine Writs; and may only be invoked whenever the lesser Right of *Recto Ecclesiae Expurgatio* is invoked.

Article 314 – Recto Divinum Abrogatio (Annulment)

1162. **Recto Divinum Abrogatio** is the Divine Writ of Right of Annulment of Records, Rulings, Laws or Instruments, as inherited from the collection of Divine Rights *Ius Divinum Iuris*.

1163. *Recto Divinum Abrogatio* (Annulment) is the eighth of eleven Divine Rights of Divine Writs; and may only be invoked whenever the lesser Right of *Recto Ecclesiae Abrogatio* is invoked.

Article 315 – Recto Divinum Inhibitio (Prohibition)

1164. **Recto Divinum Inhibitio** is the Divine Writ of Right of Prohibition or Restraint, as inherited from the collection of Divine Rights *Ius Divinum Iuris*.

1165. *Recto Divinum Inhibitio* (Prohibition) is the ninth of eleven Divine Rights of Divine Writs; and may only be invoked whenever the lesser Right of *Recto Ecclesiae Inhibitio* is invoked.

Article 316 – Recto Divinum Restitutio (Restitution)

1166. ***Recto Divinum Restitutio*** is the Divine Writ of Right of Restitution, as inherited from the collection of Divine Rights *Ius Divinum Iuris*.

    <small>Recto Divinum Restitutio (Restitution)</small>

1167. *Recto Divinum Restitutio* (Restitution) is the tenth of eleven Divine Rights of Divine Writs; and may only be invoked whenever the lesser Right of *Recto Ecclesiae Restitutio* is invoked.

    <small>Invoking of Recto Divinum Restitutio</small>

Article 317 – Recto Divinum Restoratio (Restoration)

1168. ***Recto Divinum Restoratio*** is the Divine Writ of Right of Restoration, as inherited from the collection of Divine Rights *Ius Divinum Iuris*.

    <small>Recto Divinum Restoratio (Restoration)</small>

1169. *Recto Divinum Restoratio* (Restoration) is the eleventh of eleven Divine Rights of Divine Writs; and may only be invoked whenever the lesser Right of *Recto Ecclesiae Restoratio* is invoked.

    <small>Invoking of Recto Divinum Restoratio</small>

6.11 - Divine Bills of Exception & Agreement

Article 318 – Divine Bills of Exception & Agreement

1170. ***Rogatio Divinum Iurium*** (Divine Bills of Exception & Agreement) is an Imperfect Divine Right associated with the one, true and only valid forms of Bills of Exception, Citation and Moratorium.

    <small>Divine Bills of Exception (Rogatio Divinum Iurium)</small>

1171. The eleven (11) most sacred Complete Divine Bills of Exception, Citation and Moratorium are the highest possible valid forms of Objection, Denial and Protest within the dimension of Universal Reality and actual Existence. Evidence of a valid record within the Great Register and Public Record of One Heaven and Ucadia Gazette shall be prima facie proof of a duly promulgated Complete Divine Bill of Exception, Citation and Moratorium:-

    <small>Nature of Divine Bills of Exception</small>

    (i) Complete Divine Bills of Exception and Moratorium are usually issued simultaneously upon the promulgation of either a valid Complete True Bill of Exception and Justice in relation to a True Person, or True Trust or True Estate; or in relation to a Complete Superior Bill of Exception and Error with one or more Superior Persons, or Superior Trusts or Superior Estates; and

(ii) All valid Objection, Denial or Protest in defence of one or more valid Rights shall be by one or more Complete Bills of Right as the one, true and only valid forms of Original Entry and Original Exception; and

(iii) All forms of defensive powers and protection including, but not limited to prevention, protection, suspension, stop, stay, injunction, restitution, restoration, seizure, search, sanction, lien, arrest, custody, penalty or satisfaction, shall be enacted via one or more valid Complete Bills of Right; and

(iv) Complete Divine Bills of Exception and Moratorium shall apply only to Divine Persons, Divine Trusts and Divine Estates.

1172. There shall be three classes of Complete Bills of Exception, being Divine, True and Superior:- Classes of Bills of Exception

(i) Complete Divine Bills of Exception and Moratorium shall be the Right of Original Entry and Exception to stop or stay an Action or Conveyance or Transfer of Divine Rights in relation to all Divine Persons, Divine Trusts and Divine Estates; and

(ii) Complete True Bills of Exception and Justice shall be the Right of Original Entry and Exception to stop or stay an Action or Conveyance or Transfer of Natural Rights in relation to all True Persons, True Trusts and True Estates; and

(iii) Complete Superior Bills of Exception and Error shall be the Right of Original Entry and Exception to stop or stay an Action or Conveyance or Transfer of Superior Rights in relation to all Superior Persons, Superior Trusts and Superior Estates of valid Ucadia Societies and competent forums of Law.

1173. The enforcement and coercive powers of Complete Bills of Exception may only be issued in relation to Members of One Heaven and Ucadia being Divine Persons, or True Persons or Superior Persons, as well as any other lesser bodies, bodies politic, associations, partnerships, companies, entities, fraternities, religious organisations, corporations or persons under the Jurisdiction of the Divine Creator of all Existence and all Heaven and Earth. Enforcement of Bills of Exception

1174. The following valid eleven (11) Divine Bills of Exception & Agreement (*Rogatio Divinum Iurium*) are recognised in accord with the most sacred Covenant *Pactum De Singularis Caelum* and the present Maxims:- List of Divine Bills of Exception (Rogatio Divinum Iurium)

(i) "**Rogatio Divinum Recto**" is the Divine Original Bill of

Right; and

(ii) **"Rogatio Divinum Apocalypsis"** is the Divine Bill of Right of Command and Authorisation of Revelation; and

(iii) **"Rogatio Divinum Capimus"** is the Divine Bill of Right against Failure to Surrender or Arrest Person; and

(iv) **"Rogatio Divinum Custodiae"** is the Divine Bill of Right against Failure to Surrender or Seize Property; and

(v) **"Rogatio Divinum Corrigimus"** is the Divine Bill of Right against Failure to Correct Records, Rulings, Laws or Instruments; and

(vi) **"Rogatio Divinum Inhibitio"** is the Divine Bill of Right against Failure to Prohibit and Restrict Acts as Instructed; and

(vii) **"Rogatio Divinum Restitutio"** is the Divine Bill of Right of Restitution and Compensation; and

(viii) **"Rogatio Divinum Credito"** is the Divine Bill of Right of Credit; and

(ix) **"Rogatio Divinum Permutatio"** is the Divine Bill of Right of Exchange; and

(x) **"Rogatio Divinum Venditio"** is the Divine Bill of Right of Sale; and

(xi) **"Rogatio Divinum Traditio"** is the Divine Bill of Right of Lading.

1175. Whenever a valid Complete True Bill of Exception and Rule of Law is issued, a Complete Divine Bill of Exception and Moratorium of the same type shall be issued and duly recorded in Heaven. Thus, the existence of a registered Complete True Writ within the Great Register and Public Record of One Heaven and any associated Gazette notices shall be prima facie evidence that what is enacted in the temporal realm is also enacted within the spiritual realm. Supernatural Nature of Divine Bills of Exception

Article 319 – Rogatio Divinum Recto (Original Bill)

1176. ***Rogatio Divinum Recto*** (Original Bill) is the Divine Original Bill of Right, as inherited from the collection of Divine Rights *Ius Divinum Iuris*. Rogatio Divinum Recto (Original Bill)

1177. *Rogatio Divinum Recto* is the first of eleven Divine Rights of Divine Bills of Exception; and may only be invoked whenever the lesser Right of *Rogatio Ecclesiae Recto* is invoked.

Invoking of Rogatio Divinum Recto

Article 320 – Rogatio Divinum Apocalypsis (Revelation)

1178. **Rogatio Divinum Apocalypsis** (Revelation) is the Divine Bill of Right of Command and Authorisation of Revelation, as inherited from the collection of Divine Rights *Ius Divinum Iuris*.

Rogatio Divinum Apocalypsis (Revelation)

1179. *Rogatio Divinum Apocalypsis* is the second of eleven Divine Rights of Divine Bills of Exception; and may only be invoked whenever the lesser Right of *Rogatio Ecclesiae Iurium Apocalypsis* is invoked.

Invoking of Rogatio Divinum Apocalypsis

Article 321 – Rogatio Divinum Capimus (Surrender or Arrest)

1180. **Rogatio Divinum Capimus** (Surrender or Arrest) is the Divine Bill of Right against Failure to Surrender or Arrest Person, as inherited from the collection of Divine Rights *Ius Divinum Iuris*.

Rogatio Divinum Capimus (Surrender or Arrest)

1181. *Rogatio Divinum Capimus* is the third of eleven Divine Rights of Divine Bills of Exception; and may only be invoked whenever the lesser Right of *Rogatio Ecclesiae Capimus* is invoked.

Invoking of Rogatio Divinum Capimus

Article 322 – Rogatio Divinum Custodiae (Surrender & Seizure)

1182. **Rogatio Divinum Custodiae** (Surrender & Seizure) is the Divine Bill of Right against Failure to Surrender or Seize Property, as inherited from the collection of Divine Rights *Ius Divinum Iuris*.

Rogatio Divinum Custodiae (Surrender & Seizure)

1183. *Rogatio Divinum Custodiae* is the fourth of eleven Divine Rights of Divine Bills of Exception; and may only be invoked whenever the lesser Right of *Rogatio Ecclesiae Custodiae* is invoked.

Invoking of Rogatio Divinum Custodiae

Article 323 – Rogatio Divinum Corrigimus (Correction)

1184. **Rogatio Divinum Corrigimus** (Correction) is the Divine Bill of Right against Failure to Correct Records, Rulings, Laws or Instruments, as inherited from the collection of Divine Rights *Ius Divinum Iuris*.

Rogatio Divinum Corrigimus (Correction)

1185. *Rogatio Divinum Corrigimus* is the fifth of eleven Divine Rights of

Invoking of Rogatio Divinum

Divine Bills of Exception; and may only be invoked whenever the lesser Right of *Rogatio Ecclesiae Corrigimus* is invoked.

Corrigimus

Article 324 – Rogatio Divinum Inhibitio (Prohibition)

1186. ***Rogatio Divinum Inhibitio*** (Prohibition) is the Divine Bill of Right against Failure to Prohibit and Restrict Acts as Instructed, as inherited from the collection of Divine Rights *Ius Divinum Iuris*.

Rogatio Divinum Inhibitio (Prohibition)

1187. *Rogatio Divinum Inhibitio* is the sixth of eleven Divine Rights of Divine Bills of Exception; and may only be invoked whenever the lesser Right of *Rogatio Ecclesiae Inhibitio* is invoked.

Invoking of Rogatio Divinum Inhibitio

Article 325 – Rogatio Divinum Restitutio (Restitution)

1188. ***Rogatio Divinum Restitutio*** (Restitution) is the Divine Bill of Right or Restitution or Compensation, as inherited from the collection of Divine Rights *Ius Divinum Iuris*.

Rogatio Divinum Restitutio (Restitution)

1189. *Rogatio Divinum Restitutio* is the seventh of eleven Divine Rights of Divine Bills of Exception; and may only be invoked whenever the lesser Right of *Rogatio Ecclesiae Restitutio* is invoked.

Invoking of Rogatio Divinum Restitutio

Article 326 – Rogatio Divinum Credito (Credit)

1190. ***Rogatio Divinum Credito*** (Credit) is the Divine Bill of Right of Credit, as inherited from the collection of Divine Rights *Ius Divinum Iuris*.

Rogatio Divinum Credito (Credit)

1191. *Rogatio Divinum Credito* is the eighth of eleven Divine Rights of Divine Bills of Exception; and may only be invoked whenever the lesser Right of *Rogatio Ecclesiae Credito* is invoked.

Invoking of Rogatio Divinum Credito

Article 327 – Rogatio Divinum Permutatio (Exchange)

1192. ***Rogatio Divinum Permutatio*** (Exchange) is the Divine Bill of Right of Exchange, as inherited from the collection of Divine Rights *Ius Divinum Iuris*.

Rogatio Divinum Permutatio (Exchange)

1193. *Rogatio Divinum Permutatio* is the ninth of eleven Divine Rights of Divine Bills of Exception; and may only be invoked whenever the lesser Right of *Rogatio Ecclesiae Permutatio* is invoked.

Invoking of Rogatio Divinum Permutatio

Article 328 – Rogatio Divinum Venditio (Sale)

1194. **Rogatio Divinum Venditio** (Sale) is the Divine Bill of Right of Sale, as inherited from the collection of Divine Rights *Ius Divinum Iuris*.

    Rogatio Divinum Venditio (Sale)

1195. *Rogatio Divinum Venditio* is the tenth of eleven Divine Rights of Divine Bills of Exception; and may only be invoked whenever the lesser Right of *Rogatio Ecclesiae Venditio* is invoked.

    Invoking of Rogatio Divinum Venditio

Article 329 – Rogatio Divinum Traditio (Lading)

1196. **Rogatio Divinum Traditio** (Lading) is the Divine Bill of Right of Lading, as inherited from the collection of Divine Rights *Ius Divinum Iuris*.

    Rogatio Divinum Traditio (Lading)

1197. *Rogatio Divinum Traditio* is the eleventh of eleven Divine Rights of Divine Bills of Exception; and may only be invoked whenever the lesser Right of *Rogatio Ecclesiae Traditio* is invoked.

    Invoking of Rogatio Divinum Traditio

6.12 - Divine Dogma

Article 330 – Divine Dogma (Divine Principles)

1198. **Summa Dogma Divinum Iurium** (Greatest Divine Principles) are Imperfect Divine Rights associated with the promulgation of authoritative principles, decrees and doctrines of Ucadia, Heaven and Earth.

    Divine Principles (Summa Dogma Divinum Iurium)

1199. The following valid eleven (11) Divine Principles (*Summa Dogma Divinum Iurium*) are recognised in accord with the most sacred Covenant *Pactum De Singularis Caelum* and the present Maxims:-

    List of Divine Principles (Summa Dogma Divinum Iurium)

    (i)   "**Dogma Divinum Praeceptum**" is the Divine Right of Divine Precept of Proposed Dogma; and

    (ii)   "**Dogma Divinum Theologiae**" is the Divine Right of Divine Dogma of Divine Science; and

    (iii) "**Dogma Divinum Singularis Caelum**" is the Divine Right of Divine Dogma of One Heaven; and

    (iv)   "**Dogma Divinum Ucadia**" is the Divine Right of Divine Dogma of Ucadia; and

(v) ***Dogma Divinum Iuris*** is the Divine Right of Divine Dogma of Law; and

(vi) ***Dogma Divinum Scientium*** is the Divine Right of Divine Dogma of Science; and

(vii) ***Dogma Divinum Revelatio*** is the Divine Right of Divine Dogma of Revelation; and

(viii) ***Dogma Divinum Sacramentum*** is the Divine Right of Divine Dogma of the Sacraments; and

(ix) ***Dogma Divinum Singularis Christus*** is the Divine Right of Divine Dogma of One Christ; and

(x) ***Dogma Divinum Singularis Islam*** is the Divine Right of Divine Dogma of One Islam; and

(xi) ***Dogma Divinum Singularis Spiritus*** is the Divine Right of Divine Dogma of One Spirit.

Article 331 – Dogma Divinum Praeceptum (Precept)

1200. ***Dogma Divinum Praeceptum*** is the Divine Right of Divine Precept of Proposed Dogma, as inherited from the collection of Divine Rights *Ius Divinum Iuris*. — Dogma Divinum Praeceptum (Precept)

1201. *Dogma Divinum Praeceptum* (Precept) is the first of eleven Divine Rights of Divine Dogma; and may only be invoked whenever the lesser Right of *Dogma Ecclesiae Praeceptum* is invoked. — Invoking of Dogma Divinum Praeceptum

Article 332 – Dogma Divinum Theologiae (Divine Science)

1202. ***Dogma Divinum Theologiae*** is the Divine Right of Divine Dogma of Divine Science, as inherited from the collection of Divine Rights *Ius Divinum Iuris*. — Dogma Divinum Theologiae (Divine Science)

1203. *Dogma Divinum Theologiae* (Divine Science) is the second of eleven Divine Rights of Divine Dogma; and may only be invoked whenever the lesser Right of *Dogma Ecclesiae Theologiae* is invoked. — Invoking of Dogma Divinum Theologiae

Article 333 – Dogma Divinum Singularis Caelum (One Heaven)

1204. ***Dogma Divinum Singularis Caelum*** is the Divine Right of Divine Dogma of One Heaven, as inherited from the collection of — Dogma Divinum Singularis Caelum (One

Divine Rights *Ius Divinum Iuris*.

1205. *Dogma Divinum Singularis Caelum* (One Heaven) is the third of eleven Divine Rights of Divine Dogma; and may only be invoked whenever the lesser Right of *Dogma Ecclesiae Singularis Caelum* is invoked.

Article 334 – Dogma Divinum Ucadia (Ucadia)

1206. **Dogma Divinum Ucadia** is the Divine Right of Divine Dogma of Ucadia, as inherited from the collection of Divine Rights *Ius Divinum Iuris*.

1207. *Dogma Divinum Ucadia* is the fourth of eleven Divine Rights of Divine Dogma; and may only be invoked whenever the lesser Right of *Dogma Ecclesiae Ucadia* is invoked.

Article 335 – Dogma Divinum Iuris (Law)

1208. **Dogma Divinum Iuris** is the Divine Right of Divine Dogma of Law, as inherited from the collection of Divine Rights *Ius Divinum Iuris*.

1209. *Dogma Divinum Iuris* (Law) is the fifth of eleven Divine Rights of Divine Dogma; and may only be invoked whenever the lesser Right of *Dogma Ecclesiae Iuris* is invoked.

Article 336 – Dogma Divinum Scientium (Science)

1210. **Dogma Divinum Scientium** is the Divine Right of Divine Dogma of Science, as inherited from the collection of Divine Rights *Ius Divinum Iuris*.

1211. *Dogma Divinum Scientium* (Science) is the sixth of eleven Divine Rights of Divine Dogma; and may only be invoked whenever the lesser Right of *Dogma Ecclesiae Scientium* is invoked.

Article 337 – Dogma Divinum Revelatio (Revelation)

1212. **Dogma Divinum Revelatio** is the Divine Right of Divine Dogma of Revelation, as inherited from the collection of Divine Rights *Ius Divinum Iuris*.

1213. *Dogma Divinum Revelatio* (Revelation) is the seventh of eleven

Divine Rights of Divine Dogma; and may only be invoked whenever the lesser Right of *Dogma Ecclesiae Revelatio* is invoked.

Dogma Divinum Revelatio

Article 338 – Dogma Divinum Sacramentum (Sacraments)

1214. ***Dogma Divinum Sacramentum*** is the Divine Right of Divine Dogma of the Sacraments, as inherited from the collection of Divine Rights *Ius Divinum Iuris*.

Dogma Divinum Sacramentum (Sacraments)

1215. *Dogma Divinum Sacramentum* (Sacraments) is the eighth of eleven Divine Rights of Divine Dogma; and may only be invoked whenever the lesser Right of *Dogma Ecclesiae Sacramentum* is invoked.

Invoking of Dogma Divinum Sacramentum

Article 339 – Dogma Divinum Singularis Christus (One Christ)

1216. ***Dogma Divinum Singularis Christus*** is the Divine Right of Divine Dogma of One Christ, as inherited from the collection of Divine Rights *Ius Divinum Iuris*.

Dogma Divinum Singularis Christus (One Christ)

1217. *Dogma Divinum Singularis Christus* (One Christ) is the ninth of eleven Divine Rights of Divine Dogma; and may only be invoked whenever the lesser Right of *Dogma Ecclesiae Singularis Christus* is invoked.

Invoking of Dogma Divinum Singularis Christus

Article 340 – Dogma Divinum Singularis Islam (One Islam)

1218. ***Dogma Divinum Singularis Islam*** is the Divine Right of Divine Dogma of One Islam, as inherited from the collection of Divine Rights *Ius Divinum Iuris*.

Dogma Divinum Singularis Islam (One Islam)

1219. *Dogma Divinum Singularis Islam* (One Islam) is the tenth of eleven Divine Rights of Divine Dogma; and may only be invoked whenever the lesser Right of *Dogma Ecclesiae Singularis Islam* is invoked.

Invoking of Dogma Divinum Singularis Islam

Article 341 – Dogma Divinum Singularis Spiritus (One Spirit)

1220. ***Dogma Divinum Singularis Spiritus*** is the Divine Right of Divine Dogma of One Spirit, as inherited from the collection of Divine Rights *Ius Divinum Iuris*.

Dogma Divinum Singularis Spiritus (One Spirit)

1221. *Dogma Divinum Singularis Spiritus* (One Spirit) is the eleventh of eleven Divine Rights of Divine Dogma; and may only be invoked whenever the lesser Right of *Dogma Ecclesiae Singularis Spiritus* is

Invoking of Dogma Divinum Singularis

invoked.

6.13 - Divine Decrees

Article 342 – Divine Decrees

1222. ***Divine Decrees (Decretum Divinum Iurium)*** are Imperfect Divine Rights associated with Divine Decrees concerning the administration, conduct and enforcement of law and order.

1223. The following valid eleven (11) Divine Decrees (*Decretum Divinum Iurium*) are recognised in accord with the most sacred Covenant *Pactum De Singularis Caelum* and the present Maxims:-

    (i)   "**Decretum Divinum Doctrinae**" is the Divine Right of Divine Decree of Doctrine; and

    (ii)   "**Decretum Divinum Absolutionis**" is the Divine Right of Divine Decree of Absolution; and

    (iii)   "**Decretum Divinum Damnationis**" is the Divine Right of Divine Decree of Damnation; and

    (iv)   "**Decretum Divinum Exemplificatio**" is the Divine Right of Divine Decree of Exemplification; and

    (v)   "**Decretum Divinum Testimonium**" is the Divine Right of Divine Decree of Proof; and

    (vi)   "**Decretum Divinum Instructionis**" is the Divine Right of Divine Decree of Instruction; and

    (vii)   "**Decretum Divinum Censurae**" is the Divine Right of Divine Decree of Censure; and

    (viii)   "**Decretum Divinum Annullas**" is the Divine Right of Divine Decree of Annulment; and

    (ix)   "**Decretum Divinum Ratificationis**" is the Divine Right of Divine Decree of Ratification; and

    (x)   "**Decretum Divinum Interdictum**" is the Divine Right of Divine Decree of Interdiction; and

    (xi)   "**Decretum Divinum Levationis**" is the Divine Right of Divine Decree of Relief.

Article 343 – Decretum Divinum Doctrinae (Doctrine)

1224. ***Decretum Divinum Doctrinae*** is the Divine Right of Divine Decree of Doctrine of authoritative decisions, judgements or commands concerning Doctrine, as inherited from the collection of Divine Rights *Ius Divinum Iuris*.   *Decretum Divinum Doctrinae (Doctrine)*

1225. *Decretum Divinum Doctrinae* (Doctrine) is the first of eleven Divine Rights of Divine Decree; and may only be invoked whenever the lesser Right of *Decretum Ecclesiae Doctrinae* (Ecclesiastical Decree of Doctrine) is invoked.   *Invoking of Decretum Divinum Doctrinae*

Article 344 – Decretum Divinum Absolutionis (Absolution)

1226. ***Decretum Divinum Absolutionis*** is the Divine Right of Divine Decree of Absolution of authoritative decisions, judgements or commands concerning absolution and forgiveness, as inherited from the collection of Divine Rights *Ius Divinum Iuris*.   *Decretum Divinum Absolutionis (Absolution)*

1227. *Decretum Divinum Absolutionis* (Absolution) is the second of eleven Divine Rights of Divine Decree; and may only be invoked whenever the lesser Right of *Decretum Ecclesiae Absolutionis* (Ecclesiastical Decree of Absolution) is invoked.   *Invoking of Decretum Divinum Absolutionis*

Article 345 – Decretum Divinum Damnationis (Damnation)

1228. ***Decretum Divinum Damnationis*** is the Divine Right of Divine Decree of Damnation of authoritative decisions, judgements or commands concerning condemnation, sentence and punishment, as inherited from the collection of Divine Rights *Ius Divinum Iuris*.   *Decretum Divinum Damnationis (Damnation)*

1229. *Decretum Divinum Damnationis* (Damnation) is the third of eleven Divine Rights of Divine Decree; and may only be invoked whenever the lesser Right of *Decretum Ecclesiae Damnationis* (Ecclesiastical Decree of Damnation) is invoked.   *Invoking of Decretum Divinum Damnationis*

Article 346 – Decretum Divinum Exemplificatio (Exemplification)

1230. ***Decretum Divinum Exemplificatio*** is the Divine Right of Divine Decree of Exemplification of authoritative decisions, judgements or commands concerning exemplification, as inherited from the   *Decretum Divinum Exemplificatio* collection of Divine Rights *Ius Divinum Iuris*.

1231. *Decretum Divinum Exemplificatio* (Exemplification) is the fourth of eleven Divine Rights of Divine Decree; and may only be invoked whenever the lesser Right of *Decretum Ecclesiae Exemplificatio* (Ecclesiastical Decree of Exemplification) is invoked.

Invoking of Decretum Divinum Exemplificatio

Article 347 – Decretum Divinum Testimonium (Proof)

1232. **Decretum Divinum Testimonium** is the Divine Right of Divine Decree of Proof of authoritative decisions, judgements or commands concerning evidence and proof, as inherited from the collection of Divine Rights *Ius Divinum Iuris*.

Decretum Divinum Testimonium (Proof)

1233. *Decretum Divinum Testimonium* (Proof) is the fifth of eleven Divine Rights of Divine Decree; and may only be invoked whenever the lesser Right of *Decretum Ecclesiae Testimonium* (Ecclesiastical Decree of Proof) is invoked.

Invoking of Decretum Divinum Testimonium

Article 348 – Decretum Divinum Instructionis (Instruction)

1234. **Decretum Divinum Instructionis** is the Divine Right of Divine Decree of Instruction of authoritative decisions, judgements or commands concerning instruction, as inherited from the collection of Divine Rights *Ius Divinum Iuris*.

Decretum Divinum Instructionis (Instruction)

1235. *Decretum Divinum Instructionis* (Instruction) is the sixth of eleven Divine Rights of Divine Decree; and may only be invoked whenever the lesser Right of *Decretum Ecclesiae Instructionis* (Ecclesiastical Decree of Instruction) is invoked.

Invoking of Decretum Divinum Instructionis

Article 349 – Decretum Divinum Censurae (Censure)

1236. **Decretum Divinum Censurae** is the Divine Right of Divine Decree of Censure of authoritative decisions, judgements or commands concerning censure and injunction, as inherited from the collection of Divine Rights *Ius Divinum Iuris*.

Decretum Divinum Censurae (Censure)

1237. *Decretum Divinum Censurae* (Censure) is the seventh of eleven Divine Rights of Divine Decree; and may only be invoked whenever the lesser Right of *Decretum Ecclesiae Censurae* (Ecclesiastical Decree of Censure) is invoked.

Invoking of Decretum Divinum Censurae

Article 350 – Decretum Divinum Annullas

(Annulment)

1238. ***Decretum Divinum Annullas*** is the Divine Right of Divine Decree of Annulment of authoritative decisions, judgements or commands concerning annulment and dissolution, as inherited from the collection of Divine Rights *Ius Divinum Iuris*.

Decretum Divinum Annullas (Annulment)

1239. *Decretum Divinum Annullas* (Annulment) is the eighth of eleven Divine Rights of Divine Decree; and may only be invoked whenever the lesser Right of *Decretum Ecclesiae Annullas* (Ecclesiastical Decree of Annulment) is invoked.

Invoking of Decretum Divinum Annullas

Article 351 – Decretum Divinum Ratificationis (Ratification)

1240. ***Decretum Divinum Ratificationis*** is the Divine Right of Divine Decree of Ratification of authoritative decisions, judgements or commands concerning ratification and confirmation, as inherited from the collection of Divine Rights *Ius Divinum Iuris*.

Decretum Divinum Ratificationis (Ratification)

1241. *Decretum Divinum Ratificationis* (Ratification) is the ninth of eleven Divine Rights of Divine Decree; and may only be invoked whenever the lesser Right of *Decretum Ecclesiae Ratificationis* (Ecclesiastical Decree of Ratification) is invoked.

Invoking of Decretum Divinum Ratificationis

Article 352 – Decretum Divinum Interdictum (Interdiction)

1242. ***Decretum Divinum Interdictum*** is the Divine Right of Divine Decree of Interdiction of authoritative decisions, judgements or commands concerning interdiction, as inherited from the collection of Divine Rights *Ius Divinum Iuris*.

Decretum Divinum Interdictum (Interdiction)

1243. *Decretum Divinum Interdictum* (Interdiction) is the tenth of eleven Divine Rights of Divine Decree; and may only be invoked whenever the lesser Right of *Decretum Ecclesiae Interdictum* (Ecclesiastical Decree of Interdiction) is invoked.

Invoking of Decretum Divinum Interdictum

Article 353 – Decretum Divinum Levationis (Relief)

1244. ***Decretum Divinum Levationis*** is the Divine Right of Divine Decree of Relief of authoritative decisions, judgements or commands concerning all forms of relief, as inherited from the collection of Divine Rights *Ius Divinum Iuris*.

Decretum Divinum Levationis (Relief)

1245. *Decretum Divinum Levationis* (Relief) is the eleventh of eleven

Invoking of Decretum

Divine Rights of Divine Decree; and may only be invoked whenever the lesser Right of Decretum Ecclesiae Levationis (Ecclesiastical Decree of Relief) is invoked.

Divinum Levationis

6.14 - Divine Notices

Article 354 – Divine Notices

1246. ***Divine Notices*** (*Notitiae Divinum Iurium*) are Imperfect Divine Rights associated with Divine Notices issued, executed, patented, promulgated and served in the proper administration, conduct and enforcement of law and order.

Divine Notices (Notitiae Divinum Iurium)

1247. The following valid eleven (11) Divine Notices (*Notitiae Divinum Iurium*) are recognised in accord with the most sacred Covenant *Pactum De Singularis Caelum* and the present Maxims:-

List of Divine Notices (Notitiae Divinum Iurium)

    (i)   "**Notitiae Divinum Eventus**" is the Divine Right of Divine Notice of Event; and

    (ii)   "**Notitiae Divinum Ius**" is the Divine Right of Divine Notice of Right; and

    (iii)   "**Notitiae Divinum Actum**" is the Divine Right of Divine Notice of Action; and

    (iv)   "**Notitiae Divinum Decretum**" is the Divine Right of Divine Notice of Decree; and

    (v)   "**Notitiae Divinum Iuris**" is the Divine Right of Divine Notice of Law; and

    (vi)   "**Notitiae Divinum Citationis**" is the Divine Right of Divine Notice of Summons; and

    (vii)   "**Notitiae Divinum Redemptio**" is the Divine Right of Divine Notice of Redemption; and

    (viii)   "**Notitiae Divinum Rogatio**" is the Divine Right of Divine Notice of Exception; and

    (ix)   "**Notitiae Divinum Potentis**" is the Divine Right of Divine Notice of Authority; and

    (x)   "**Notitiae Divinum Testamentum**" is the Divine Right of Divine Notice of Testament; and

    (xi)   "**Notitiae Divinum Obligationis**" is the Divine Right of Divine Notice of Obligation (Bond).

Article 355 – Notitiae Divinum Eventus (Event)

1248. ***Notitiae Divinum Eventus*** is the Divine Right of Divine Notice of Event whereby notice is given of a unique event recorded first, primarily and absolutely within the records of One Heaven and no other, as inherited from the collection of Divine Rights *Ius Divinum Iuris*. — Notitiae Divinum Eventus (Event)

1249. *Notitiae Divinum Eventus* (Event) is the first of eleven Divine Rights of Divine Notice; and may only be invoked whenever the lesser Right *Notitiae Ecclesiae Eventus* (Ecclesiastical Notice of Event) is invoked. — Invoking of Notitiae Divinum Eventus (Event)

1250. The issue of any such certificate or authorised extract or Gazette Notice in relation to a sacred space-time event shall be equivalent to a formal *Notitiae Divinum Eventus* as evidence; and proof of a first in time, highest title and right association to such an event. — Gazette Notice and Divinum Eventus (Event)

1251. The existence therefore of any instrument or document issued by an inferior body or non-Ucadian aligned society claiming some right or ownership in direct contradiction to an event clearly identified through a *Notitiae Divinum Eventus* shall itself be an open confession of perfidy, profanity, repugnancy, malice, heresy and apostasy against all forms of valid law of Heaven and Earth. — Divinum Eventus (Event) and Non-Ucadia Claim

Article 356 – Notitiae Divinum Ius (Right)

1252. ***Notitiae Divinum Ius*** is the Divine Right of Divine Notice of Right, whereby notice is given of a Divine, or Natural or Superior Right, as inherited from the collection of Divine Rights *Ius Divinum Iuris*. — Notitiae Divinum Ius (Right)

1253. A *Notitiae Divinum Ius* or a Divine Notice of Right shall be any valid Notice issued under the rules of this Sacred Covenant bringing Divine Notice and therefore the power of life to Valid Offices of the Society, Titles of Land, Water and Space and all Valid Rights and Commissions to Office. — Offices and Notitiae Divinum Ius

1254. By the rules of the present Maxims and most sacred Covenant *Pactum De Singularis Caelum*, all Office must be duly created by Divine Notice and thereby granted a valid record number in the Great Register and Divine Records of Heaven as having eternal spiritual life and real existence and legal personality. — Notitiae Divinum Ius and Record Number

1255. *Notitiae Divinum Ius* (Right) is the second of eleven Divine Rights of — Invoking of Notitiae Divinum

Divine Notice; and may only be invoked whenever the lesser Right *Notitiae Ecclesiae Ius* (Ecclesiastical Notice of Right) is invoked.

Ius (Right)

Article 357 – Notitiae Divinum Actum (Action)

1256. **Notitiae Divinum Actum** is the Divine Right of Divine Notice of Action, whereby notice of an action within a competent forum of law is properly noticed, as inherited from the collection of Divine Rights *Ius Divinum Iuris*.

Notitiae Divinum Actum (Action)

1257. *Notitiae Divinum Actum* (Action) is the third of eleven Divine Rights of Divine Notice; and may only be invoked whenever the lesser Right *Notitiae Ecclesiae Actum* (Ecclesiastical Notice of Action) is invoked.

Invoking of Notitiae Divinum Actum (Action)

Article 358 – Notitiae Divinum Decretum (Decree)

1258. **Notitiae Divinum Decretum** (Decree) is the Divine Right of Divine Notice of Decree, whereby notice is proven by genuine scripture in accord with Article 37 (Supreme Sacred Texts) of the most sacred Covenant *Pactum De Singularis Caelum*, as inherited from the collection of Divine Rights *Ius Divinum Iuris*.

Notitiae Divinum Decretum (Decree)

1259. *Notitiae Divinum Decretum* (Decree) is the fourth of eleven Divine Rights of Divine Notice; and may only be invoked whenever the lesser Right *Notitiae Ecclesiae Decretum* (Ecclesiastical Notice of Decree) is invoked.

Invoking of Notitiae Divinum Decretum (Decree)

Article 359 – Notitiae Divinum Iuris (Law)

1260. **Notitiae Divinum Iuris** is the Divine Right of Divine Notice of Law whereby notice of a formal decree in law is given, as inherited from the collection of Divine Rights *Ius Divinum Iuris*.

Notitiae Divinum Iuris (Law)

1261. *Notitiae Divinum Iuris* (Law) is the fifth of eleven Divine Rights of Divine Notice; and may only be invoked whenever the lesser Right *Notitiae Ecclesiae Iuris* (Ecclesiastical Notice of Law) is invoked.

Invoking of Notitiae Divinum Iuris (Law)

Article 360 – Notitiae Divinum Citationis (Summons)

1262. **Notitiae Divinum Citationis** is the Divine Right of Divine Notice of Summons, whereby notice of a summons or citation is published, as inherited from the collection of Divine Rights *Ius Divinum Iuris*.

Notitiae Divinum Citationis (Summons)

1263. *Notitiae Divinum Citationis* (Summons) is the sixth of eleven Divine Rights of Divine Notice; and may only be invoked whenever the lesser Right *Notitiae Ecclesiae Citationis* (Ecclesiastical Notice of Summons) is invoked.

Invoking of Notitiae Divinum Citationis (Summons)

Article 361 – Notitiae Divinum Redemptio (Redemption)

1264. **Notitiae Divinum Redemptio** is the Divine Right of Divine Notice of Redemption, whereby notice of Divine Writ is listed, as inherited from the collection of Divine Rights *Ius Divinum Iuris*.

Notitiae Divinum Redemptio (Redemption)

1265. *Notitiae Divinum Redemptio* (Redemption) is the seventh of eleven Divine Rights of Divine Notice; and may only be invoked whenever the lesser Right *Notitiae Ecclesiae Redemptio* (Ecclesiastical Notice of Redemption) is invoked.

Invoking of Notitiae Divinum Redemptio (Redemption)

Article 362 – Notitiae Divinum Rogatio (Exception)

1266. **Notitiae Divinum Rogatio** is the Divine Right of Divine Notice of Exception, whereby notice of a Divine or Sovereign Bill is listed, as inherited from the collection of Divine Rights *Ius Divinum Iuris*.

Notitiae Divinum Rogatio (Exception)

1267. *Notitiae Divinum Rogatio* (Exception) is the eighth of eleven Divine Rights of Divine Notice; and may only be invoked whenever the lesser Right *Notitiae Ecclesiae Rogatio* (Ecclesiastical Notice of Exception) is invoked.

Invoking of Notitiae Divinum Rogatio (Exception)

Article 363 – Notitiae Divinum Potentis (Authority)

1268. **Notitiae Divinum Potentis** is the Divine Right of Divine Notice of Authority, whereby notice of the bestowing of some authority or commission to a person is properly noticed, as inherited from the collection of Divine Rights *Ius Divinum Iuris*.

Notitiae Divinum Potentis (Authority)

1269. *Notitiae Divinum Potentis* (Authority) is the ninth of eleven Divine Rights of Divine Notice; and may only be invoked whenever the lesser Right *Notitiae Ecclesiae Potentis* (Ecclesiastical Notice of Authority) is invoked.

Invoking of Notitiae Divinum Potentis (Authority)

Article 364 – Notitiae Divinum Testamentum (Testament)

1270. ***Notitiae Divinum Testamentum*** is the Divine Right of Divine Notice of Testament, whereby notice of a Testament, Declaration, Affidavit or other form of testimony is provided, as inherited from the collection of Divine Rights *Ius Divinum Iuris*.

Notitiae Divinum Testamentum (Testament)

1271. *Notitiae Divinum Testamentum* (Testament) is the tenth of eleven Divine Rights of Divine Notice; and may only be invoked whenever the lesser Right *Notitiae Ecclesiae Testamentum* (Ecclesiastical Notice of Testament) is invoked.

Invoking of Notitiae Divinum Testamentum (Testament)

Article 365 – Notitiae Divinum Obligationis (Obligation)

1272. ***Notitiae Divinum Obligationis*** is the Divine Right of Divine Notice of Obligation (Bond), whereby notice of an obligation, or promise or bond is noticed, as inherited from the collection of Divine Rights *Ius Divinum Iuris*.

Notitiae Divinum Obligationis (Obligation)

1273. *Notitiae Divinum Obligationis* (Obligation) is the eleventh of eleven Divine Rights of Divine Notice; and may only be invoked whenever the lesser Right of *Notitiae Ecclesiae Obligationis* (Ecclesiastical Notice of Obligation) is invoked.

Invoking of Notitiae Divinum Obligationis

Title VII - Divine Registers

7.1 - Divine Registers

Article 366 - Divine Register

1274. A ***Register*** is a book of tables recording one or more entries of statements, testimonies or memoranda as evidence as to jurisdiction and authority over certain Sacred Circumscribed Space; or the properties or attributes of such Sacred Circumscribed Space; or the rights of use of such properties and attributes; or the memorial of events concerning such Sacred Circumscribed Space, or properties or attributes, or rights of use; or the memorial of transactions and derivatives concerning the receiving or granting or claiming of rights and uses.

<small>Divine Register</small>

1275. A Divine Register is a valid and legitimate Register authentically expressed, authorised and originally defined by the present sacred Maxims or the most sacred Covenant *Pactum De Singularis Caelum*. The highest Divine Register is the *Great Register and Divine Records of One Heaven*, also known as the Great Roll of Divine Persons and the Great Book of Life:-

<small>Great Register and Divine Records of One Heaven</small>

   (i) No possible Register possesses greater authority or power or jurisdiction than the Great Register and Public Record of One Heaven; and

   (ii) All lesser Register owe their authority, powers, legitimacy and existence to the Great Register and Public Record of One Heaven; and

   (iii) No lesser Register is valid or legitimate until it can verify and prove its provenance to a valid and legitimate record within the Great Register and Public Record of One Heaven subject to terms of these present sacred Maxims.

1276. All records in proper, valid and legitimate Registers depend upon the prior recording by Authority of one or more records of Sacred Circumscribed Space as reference. If no valid records of Sacred Circumscribed Space exists, or such records are illegitimate, false, unlawful or illegal, then all subsequent Registers and records depending upon such primary records shall also be illegitimate, false, unlawful and illegal.

<small>Sacred Circumscribed Space and Registers</small>

1277. In terms of the general authority and creation of Registers:-

<small>Authority and Creation of Registers</small>

   (i) The Authority to form a Register is defined by the limits of Authority of the constituting Instrument of the relevant Trust or Estate or Fund or Corporation that the Register relates; and

(ii) The Rights, Powers and Property prescribed within a Register cannot exceed the Rights, Powers and Property of the Trust or Estate or Fund or Corporation itself; and

(iii) All valid and proper Registers are wholly and exclusively Ecclesiastical Property and can never belong to a Trust, or Estate or Fund or Corporation that formed or inherited it. Therefore, as all valid and proper Registers are exclusively Ecclesiastical Property and all Sacred Circumscribed Space is derived from Ucadia, all Registers are ipso facto (as a matter of fact) ab initio (from the beginning) the absolute property of One Heaven and Ucadia; and

(iv) All Registers are hierarchical in their inheritance of Authority and validity from One Heaven, beginning with the highest being the Great Register and Public Record of One Heaven. A Register that cannot demonstrate the provenance of its Authority, has none, and is null and void from the beginning; and

(v) As all Registers are wholly and exclusively Ecclesiastical, absolutely no clerical or administrative act may take place in association with a Register unless by a duly authorised Officer under active and valid sacred Oath or Vow in a manner consistent and in accord with the most sacred Covenant *Pactum De Singularis Caelum*; and

(vi) The entry of a record into a Register is wholly invalid unless the memorial and testimony of the act giving authority is done without duress, is done freely and with full knowledge and is consistent and in accord with the most sacred Covenant *Pactum De Singularis Caelum*.

1278. In terms of the general purpose, function and operation of a valid Register:- *General References to Registers*

(i) A Register as a table contains at least three or more columns; and

(ii) A Register as a table can be a section of a Book, or a whole series of Books; and

(iii) A Register is held in the care of a proper Officer of a Competent Forum of Law, possessing both the Ecclesiastical Authority and Sovereign Authority to hold, record and keep custody of such records; and

(iv) A Register cannot and does not create the original fact or authority that it records, but merely reflects the pertinent elements in relation to the originating Instrument used to create a valid entry; and

(v) An entry in a Register can never create sacred circumscribed space or an original event. However a valid entry in a Register is itself a valid event and by virtue of the "joining" of information at the time of registration may create certain Rights or Facts or Truths as Prima Facie Evidence; and

(vi) A particular Right of Use in relation to Property can only be recorded once in a valid Register. Those specific Registers as prescribed by Ucadian Law and the most sacred Covenant *Pactum De Singularis Caelum* are always Registers of Original Record and take precedence over all non-Ucadian and foreign registers and rolls; and

(vii) The claimed day or time of entry of a record into a non-Ucadian or foreign register has no bearing or merit in law, where a similar record for the same Property, or Event, or Right exists within a valid Ucadia Register, even if the day or time of entry in the Ucadia Register is after the day or time of entry in the non-Ucadian and foreign register. This is because any non-Ucadian and foreign register that seeks to usurp the Authority of a valid Ucadian Register automatically renders such a register invalid and illegitimate, meaning that such a non-Ucadian register is determined to be null and void, having no force or effect in law.

1279. Notwithstanding valid Registers being called the same, several other Types of valid Registers under different names are recognised, including (but not limited to):- *Types of Registers*

(i) A *Gazette* is a form of Register as a Public Journal and Authorised Newspaper of Record. The highest, most authoritative Gazette is the Ucadia Gazette and no other; and

(ii) An *Almanac* is a form of Register of information and events for a given subject, collected and arranged for a given year; and

(iii) An *Account* is a form of Register as arrangements of computations, Valuations and derivations using some standard unit of value, measure, record or exchange on the nature, value and disposition of objects, concepts and property of a valid Trust or Estate or Fund or Corporation; and

(iv) A *Memoranda* is a form of Register in chronological order, detailing the substance of formal notes or "memorandum" including (but not be limited to) minutes, resolutions, proceedings, accounts, letters, correspondence, decisions and procedural actions; and

(v) A *Journal* is a form of Register derived as a summary extract of information from Memoranda and arranged in category order and then chronological order to produce a summary of facts, evidence, quantities and relations for the purpose of accounting and reckoning of the debits and credits of the Trust or Estate or Fund or Corporation; and

(vi) A *Ledger* is a form of Register as a summary extract of Journal entries to produce the most concise reckonings and balances of debits and credits, assets and liabilities of the Trust or Estate or Fund or Corporation; and

(vii) A *Roll* is a form of Register of one or more entries being "persons" of the same condition of entry, or the same engagement of obligations in relation to a valid Trust or Estate or Fund or Corporation; and created by their valid entry into the Roll; and

(viii) A *Manifest* is a form of Register being evidential history of the provenance, possession and ownership of any property, rights, money or other interests recorded as associated with a Trust or Estate or Fund or Corporation; and

(ix) An *Estate* is a form of Register and Roll of certain Rights held in Trust for a period of years for a Person, whereby one or more Inventories and Valuations have been properly conducted; and

(x) An *Inventory*, also called a Stocktake, is a form of Register being a detailed survey and census of all property, assets and liabilities, debits or credits of a valid Trust, or Estate or Fund or Corporation completed immediately after its creation; or the anniversary of its creation; or upon another fixed and given day; and the stock of particular items and their location or business; and

(xi) A *Valuation* is a form of Register and Roll (also historically known as a Tax or Rating) being a detailed estimation of the value of each item as listed upon an Inventory of a valid Trust, or Estate or Fund or Corporation; and

(xii) A *Fund* is a form of Register of equal units representing certain Property Rights of one or more Estates of monetary value that can then be used as a means of exchange for lawful money or for the discharge of debts and obligations.

Title VII – Divine Registers

1280. All valid Registers as Tables are constructed from some or all of the same essential elements being Columna, Singulus, Eventus, Locus, Nomen, Informas, Datus, Informatio, Ordo and Recordo:-

Elements of Registers

    (i)   *Columna* (from Latin meaning "pillar or post") means a vertical line of entries (a column), usually read from top to bottom and separated from other columns by lines; and

    (ii)   *Singulus* (from Latin meaning "one each, single; unique") means a unique column being the first and left most column whereby a whole integer is listed and is sequential (beginning from the integer 1) and unique (not the same) in reference to the table; and

    (iii)   *Eventus* (from Latin meaning "event, occurrence, reality") means a column whereby the Ucadia Date and Time of a unique event as well any other referential time (such as Roman Date/Time) always in brackets is listed; and

    (iv)   *Locus* (from Latin meaning "place or locality") means a column whereby the Ucadia Location Number of Sacred Circumscribed Space and any common name as to the location of the unique event is listed; and

    (v)   *Nomen* (from Latin meaning "name or title") means a column whereby a name is given to the event or the object or concept or property or rights associated with the event; and

    (vi)   *Informas* (from Latin meaning "the one who informs, instructs, educates") means a column whereby a name of the one who granted the authority to have the entry made into the Register; and

    (vii) *Datus* (from Latin meaning "given, offered or yielded") means the Ucadia Date and Time the grant was given by the Informant as well as any other referential time such as Roman Date/Time in Square Brackets that the entry was made; and

    (viii) *Informatio* (from Latin meaning "sketch, idea, conception") means any additional information provided by the Informant that may be separated into its own unique columns; and

    (ix)   *Ordo* (meaning "row, order") means the line of entries in a table, from left to right that when completed forms a valid Record; and

    (x)   *Recordo* (meaning "completed or valid row") means a complete line of entries into the columns of the table from left to right such that the record has its own unique form and is "Legal Title".

Maxims of Divine Law

1281. The Record Number, also known as Record No. and Singulus (from Latin meaning "one each, single; unique") shall be the unique column being the first and left most column of a valid Register, whereby a whole integer shall be listed and is sequential (beginning from the integer 1) and unique (not the same) in reference to the table. The Record Number may also be called the shortened name of the table as a means of condensing both the name of the Register and the uniqueness of the number itself providing such a shortened name is itself unique in reference to all valid and legitimate Registers. — Record Number

1282. The original entry into a Register may be by hand or by typing and providing there exists a declaration from the Registrar to the effect, all type written or type entered records shall be treated as if hand written. — Entry into Registers

1283. It is permissible to treat a Register as an electronic version and for printed copies of pages, rather than printed copies to be the originals. — Electronic Registers

1284. Any claim, or attempted or actual registration of Ucadia related material, marks, symbols, names, instruments, rights and property into a foreign jurisdiction contrary to the rights and obligations prescribed by the sacred Covenant *Pactum De Singularis Caelum* and these Maxims is a grave transgression before all Heaven and the Earth and every Member of the Sons of Light and Fraternal Brothers and Sisters of Light are fully empowered by Holy Writ, to pursue any, every and all means to ensure any and all records of such profanity, sacrilege and abomination before all Heaven and Earth are expunged, removed, withdrawn, determined, extinguished and abolished, including any and all false presumptions of claiming such false rights. — Ucadia Property and Registers

1285. The supreme dignity and right to sole and exclusive temporal custody for the Great Register and Divine Records of One Heaven, also known as the Great Roll of Divine Persons, also known as the Great Book of Spirits, also known as the Great Book of Life, also known as the Great Record of Space-Day-Time, also known as the Great Register of Divine Rights, also known as the Great Book of Perfect Divine Procedure, also known as the Great Book of Divine Law shall be permanently and irrevocably delegated to the three great faiths of One Christ, One Islam and One Spirit, through the Ucadia Globe Union, subject to the life of the three faiths and the Union, in accord with the most sacred Covenant *Pactum De Singularis Caelum*:- — Authority and Custody of Great Register and Divine Records of One Heaven

    (i) By the power and authority of Heaven and Earth, a Juridic Person or Instrument not entered into the Great Ledger and Public Record of One Christ or One Islam or One Spirit, or a lesser associated Register of a valid and legitimate Ucadia Ecclesia Foundation has no existence; and

(ii) A claimed Juridic Person or instrument that is unable to demonstrate a legitimate Unique Ledger Number issued by one of the three great faiths of One Christ, One Islam or One Spirit or a valid and legitimate Ucadia Ecclesia Foundation is devoid of legitimate legal existence and possesses no rights whatsoever, nor any legal standing whatsoever, by any means; and

(iii) Neither the age of an instrument, its veneration of the highest or most sacred object, nor established legal precedence, shall stand against the power and authority of the law of the Great Ledger and Public Record.

Article 367 - Divine Roll

1286. A **Roll** is a type of book of tables and Register of one or more entries being "Persons" of the same condition or entered in the same engagement of obligations in relation to a valid Trust or Estate or Fund or Corporation and is created by their valid entry into the Roll. *(Divine Roll)*

1287. A Person is by definition a valid record as "legal title" entered into or "enrolled" within a valid Roll: - *(Persons and Rolls)*

(i) The highest authority and most important Roll is the completely spiritual Great Roll of Divine Persons also known as the Great Register and Public Record of One Heaven; and

(ii) The second most important is the physical form of the Roll as defined by the most sacred Covenant *Pactum De Singularis Caelum* that all valid Rolls derive their authority.

1288. A Divine Roll is a valid and legitimate Roll authentically expressed, authorised and originally defined by the present sacred Maxims or the most sacred Covenant *Pactum De Singularis Caelum*. The highest Divine Roll is the Great Roll of Divine Persons also known as the Great Register and Public Record of One Heaven and also known as the Great Book of Life:- *(Divine Roll)*

(i) No possible Roll possesses greater authority or power or jurisdiction than the Great Roll of Divine Persons; and

(ii) All lesser Rolls owe their authority, powers, legitimacy and existence to the Great Roll of Divine Persons; and

(iii) No lesser Roll is valid or legitimate until it can verify and prove its provenance to a valid and legitimate record within the Great Roll of Divine Persons subject to terms of these present sacred Maxims.

Maxims of Divine Law

1289. In terms of the general authority, nature and function of Rolls:-   *General Authority, Nature & Function of Rolls*

   (i)   The authority to form a Roll is defined by the limits of authority of the constituting Instrument of the relevant Trust or Estate or Fund; and

   (ii)   The Rights, Powers and Property prescribed to those persons created and defined within a Roll cannot exceed the Rights, Powers and Property of the Trust or Estate or Fund itself; and

   (iii)   All properly formed Rolls are wholly and exclusively Ecclesiastical Property and therefore under the absolute control, power and authority of Ucadia; and

   (iv)   All Rolls are hierarchical in their inheritance of authority and validity beginning with the highest being the Great Roll of Divine Persons. A Roll that cannot demonstrate the provenance of its authority, has none and is null and void from the beginning; and

   (v)   As all Rolls are wholly and exclusively Ecclesiastical, absolutely no clerical or administrative act may take place in association with a Roll unless by a duly authorised Trustee under active and valid sacred Oath or Vow in a manner consistent and in accord with these sacred Maxims; and

   (vi)   The entry of a record into a Roll is wholly invalid unless the memorial of the act giving authority is done without duress, is done freely and with full knowledge and is consistent and in accord with these sacred Maxims and the most sacred Covenant *Pactum De Singularis Caelum*.

1290. Valid Registers as Rolls may be further defined in hierarchy of authority, form and function as Divine, True, Superior, Juridic or Inferior:-   *Forms of Rolls*

   (i)   A *Divine Roll* is a valid purely spiritual Roll constituted in accord with the most sacred Covenant known as *Pactum De Singularis Caelum*. No Roll or Person is Higher; and

   (ii)   A *True Roll* is a valid physical and temporal Roll constituted in accord with the Society of One Heaven in the recognition of the most sacred Great Roll of Divine Persons and the Great Register and Public Record of One Heaven; and

   (iii)   A *Superior Roll* is a valid physical Roll constituted in accord with a valid Ucadian Society; and

   (iv)   A *Juridic Roll* is a valid physical Roll constituted in accord with a valid Juridic Person and competent forum of law; and

(v) An *Inferior Roll* is any Roll formed under Law not in perfect accord with these Maxims.

1291. The process whereby the authority of one Person on one Roll is given legitimacy by the authority and consent of a previously created Person record on another Roll is called Joinder of Person:-

Joinder

(i) Joinder (literally "to join") requires that a party is given Notice of Joinder with clear intention to "join" one person from a Roll held in custody with the authority and permissions of a Roll not immediately within their jurisdiction; and

(ii) Joinder is not the joining of a person and a man or woman as this is incorrectly mistaking surety or one who is willing to "understand" for the person for joinder; and

(iii) The names of both persons must be the same in order for a valid Joinder of Person. Otherwise, such a Joinder is a Joinder in Action, requiring separate consent; and

(iv) The failure to make clear the Notice of Joinder as an intention to Join (e.g. fraudulently using a Summons as a Notice of Joinder) is a fraud and renders such action a Misjoinder and maladministration; and

(v) The failure to produce sufficient evidence of the Right to Joinder of Person (also sometimes mispresented as Joinder in Action), automatically renders such action a Misjoinder.

Article 368 - Sacred Circumscribed Space

1292. *Sacred Circumscribed Space* is a uniquely recorded enclosure and dimension of Ucadia Sacred Space-Day-Time as prescribed by the most sacred Covenant *Pactum De Singularis Caelum*, and associated covenants and charters, and these present sacred Maxims.

Sacred Circumscribed Space

1293. Only bodies, entities, associations, societies or persons authorised under these present sacred Maxims and the most sacred Covenant *Pactum De Singularis Caelum* are permitted to record, register, keep and maintain Sacred Circumscribed Space.

Authority of Sacred Circumscribed Space

1294. All proper, valid and legitimate Sacred Circumscribed Space is clearly and uniquely named dimension of Ucadia Space-Day-Time, whereby:-

Conditions of Sacred Circumscribed Space

(i) Such Sacred Circumscribed Space is properly defined by an eighteen digit and character number and identifier (XXXXXX-XXXXXX-XXXXXX), consistent with the most sacred Covenant *Pactum De Singularis Caelum*; and

(ii) The specific Sacred Circumscribed Space is able to properly define its origin to a higher jurisdiction of Sacred Circumscribed Space, also identified by a proper eighteen digit and character number and identifier; and

(iii) The specific Sacred Circumscribed Space was either formed in accord with the most sacred Covenant *Pactum De Singularis Caelum*, or associated Covenants and Charters, or by one or more properly dispensed sacraments of the thirty three Supreme Sacred Gifts of Heaven; and

(iv) The Sacred Circumscribed Space does not contradict or usurp any previous proper, valid and legitimate existing Sacred Circumscribed Space.

1295. Any claimed space, close, place, region, zone, precinct or any other type of enclosure formed by edict, or statute or sacrament that is in conflict with the most sacred Covenant *Pactum De Singularis Caelum*, or Ucadian Law or these present Maxims shall be invalid, illegitimate and null and void ab initio (from the beginning), having no force or effect or Rights in law. — *Invalid Claims*

1296. Any and all claimed Juridic, Legislative and Sovereign Acts contrary to the authority of the most sacred Covenant *Pactum De Singularis Caelum* and these present Maxims that claim the right to form circumscribed space by such methods including (but not limited to) enclosure, alienation, enrolment, registration or certification; and all subsequent, dependent and related Statutes, including but not limited to all fraudulent, perfidious, false and deceptive documents purported to be of an earlier age in relation to the claimed enclosure of certain lands, spaces, closes, fields, places, regions, zones, precincts, territories, dominions and estates are hereby disavowed as morally repugnant, profane, sacrilegious, heretical and contrary to the Rule of Law, Civilised Society and Divine Law are therefore invalid, illegitimate and null and void ab initio (from the beginning), having no force or effect or Rights in law. — *Contrary Acts to Pactum De Singularis Caelum and Maxims*

1297. All Measurement and Standard of Sacred Circumscribed Space shall always be in accord with the most sacred Covenant *Pactum De Singularis Caelum*, associated covenants and charters, Ucadian Law and these present Maxims. All other forms of measurement and standards shall be null and void, unlawful and illegal, having no force or effect. — *Measurement and Standards for Sacred Circumscribed Space*

1298. By the Divine Mandate and Authority of the most sacred Covenant *Pactum De Singularis Caelum* and the present sacred Maxims, duly registered and authorised bodies, associations, societies, companies, persons and entities shall form, maintain and keep in custody the — *Valid and Legitimate forms of Sacred Circumscribed*

following types of Registers of Sacred Circumscribed Space, including (but not limited to):-   *Space*

(i) *Land* (also deliberately misspelled within invalid and fraudulent laws as England) as a fixed and circumscribed piece of ground and earth of one Acre or more in surface area and then measured from the centre of the planet to the centre point of the surface area; and

(ii) *Forest* as a fixed and circumscribed piece of ground and earth of ten Acres or more in surface area that is preserved or reclaimed wilderness, natural habitat, untouched and uncultivated for agriculture; and

(iii) *Island* (also deliberately misspelled within invalid and fraudulent laws as Ireland) as a fixed and continuous piece of ground and earth, larger than twelve Acres in surface area; and circumscribed by water; and

(iv) *Sea* (also deliberately misspelled within invalid and fraudulent laws as Scotland as "not" Land) as a fixed and continuous area of open water, larger than twelve thousand Acres in surface area; and circumscribed by at least two or more Islands and at least one other Sea; and

(v) *Air* (also deliberately misspelled within invalid and fraudulent laws as Netherlands as "neither" water nor land) as a fixed and circumscribed piece of space between Land and the outer reaches of the atmosphere of a planet; and

(vi) *Person* as a movable circumscribed space inhabited by the physical and living biological body of one or more Homo Sapiens; and

(vii) *Office* as a fixed or movable circumscribed space inhabited by a Person; and

(viii) *Internet* as a digital circumscribed space, inhabited by Persons as Users; and

(ix) *Network* as a digital circumscribed space of networked computers, inhabited by Persons as Network Users; and

(x) *Domain* (also Web Domain) as a digital circumscribed space of web information, inhabited by Persons as Network Users; and

(xi) *Database* as a digital circumscribed space of digital information, inhabited by Persons as Database Users or Application Users.

1299. Any and all claimed Sacred Circumscribed Space held as Allodial   Allodial Title

Title or Peculiar Title (as a Peculiarity) and therefore claimed to be owned absolutely, free of any claim is hereby disavowed as an abomination before all Heaven and Earth; and is condemned as a profound sacrilege, heresy, profanity, morally repugnant, perfidious and deliberately false, having no force or effect in law. Furthermore, every Member of the Sons of Light and Fraternal Brothers and Sisters of Light are fully empowered by Holy Writ, to pursue any, every and all means to ensure any and all records of such profanity, sacrilege and abomination before all Heaven and Earth are expunged, removed, withdrawn, determined, extinguished and abolished, including any and all false presumptions of claiming such false rights under covenants as "chosen people" or blood heritage or any other falsity.

1300. Any and all claimed Sacred Circumscribed Space held as Crown Land and therefore claimed to be owned absolutely, including but not limited to the deliberate corruption of using the name "England" to denote Land; and "Ireland" to denote Islands; and Scotland to denote the Sea and Admiralty; and the "Netherlands" to denote Air, is hereby disavowed as an abomination before all Heaven and Earth and is condemned as profound sacrilege, heresy, profanity, morally repugnant, perfidious and deliberately false, having no force or effect in law. Furthermore, every Member of the Sons of Light and Fraternal Brothers and Sisters of Light are fully empowered by Holy Writ, to pursue any, every and all means to ensure any and all records of such profanity, sacrilege and abomination before all Heaven and Earth are expunged, removed, withdrawn, determined, extinguished and abolished, including any and all false presumptions of claiming such false rights under "Divine Right" or blood heritage or any other falsity.

Crown Land

Title VIII - Divine Trusts

8.1 - Divine Trusts

Article 369 - Trust

1301. ***Trust*** is confidence in and reliance upon some quality or thing or act as being true. Trust is also used to define a formal relation and agreement whereby an authorised party (Trustor) gives, grants, assigns or delegates one or more Rights to another (Trustee) under certain conditions for the benefit of a third party (Beneficiary). — *Trust*

1302. By definition, all Rights are held in Trust and no Right is said to exist, unless through Trust. Therefore, in the absence of a valid Trust, the claimed Rights are also absent. — *All Rights held in Trust*

1303. Trust is a fundamental attribute of absolute and irrevocable confidence in and reliance upon some quality or thing or act of a Being as true; and the means whereby such absolute and irrevocable certainty is formed, witnessed and proven (hence forming a "Trust"). — *Nature of Trust*

1304. All valid Trusts may be categorised by their proper formation as either Instructed or Facilitated:- — *Fundamental forms of Trust*

   (i) ***Instructed Trust***, also known under Non-Ucadian Law as an "Express Trust", is when a Trust is created by a Trustor and Trustee with clear intentions, subject matter and purpose(s) by a person having the legal capacity to perform such an act; and

   (ii) ***Facilitated Trust***, also known under Non-Ucadian Law as an "Implied Trust", is when a Trust is created by a Surrogate Trustor or simply a "Surrogate" and Trustee by implication and function of law, being either a "Manufactured Trust" (Constructive Trust) by operation of law, or a "Consequential Trust" (Resulting Trust) by effect of events determined by law.

1305. All valid Trusts, by their formation are classified as either Instructed Trusts or Facilitated Trusts and must possess the following ten Essential Characters of Trust being Rights, Trustor, Trustee, Reason, Intention, Benefit, Condition, Oath or Vow, Execution and Proof:- — *Essential Elements of valid Trust*

   (i) *Rights* means there must be something that may be clearly defined in terms of Rights or Property to convey in the first instance; and

   (ii) *Trustor* means there must be a valid Trustor or Surrogate Trustor (as in the case of a Facilitated Trust) possessing the necessary authority to transfer any Rights or Property to another; and

(iii) *Trustee* means there must be a suitably competent, capable and willing person prepared to make a valid Oath and Vow to accept custody of the Rights or Property from the Trustor or Surrogate Trustor; and

(iv) *Reason* means there must exist at least one clear Purpose or valid Reason for the Trustor to convey and transfer the Rights or Property to the Trustee; and

(v) *Intention* means the Trustor or Surrogate Trustor must demonstrate via some Act their intention to convey and transfer the Rights or Property to the Trustee; and

(vi) *Benefit* means there exists a clear Benefit to be offered to another as one or more named or unnamed Beneficiaries; and

(vii) *Condition* means at least one or more terms and conditions exist as to the obligations of the Trustee to manage such Rights or Property and also to any Beneficiaries accepting one or more Benefits; and

(viii) *Oath* or *Vow* means the person agreeing to be Trustee made a valid promise to accept the Rights or Property under one or more Conditions; and

(ix) *Execution* means the Trustor and Trustee executed the formal transfer and conveyance of such Rights or Property after the valid Oath and Vow was given; and

(x) *Proof* means some proof in the form of written instruments or testimony exists as a memorial of the event and execution of the agreement.

1306. A Trust that is deficient in possessing one or more of the ten Essential Characters of Trust cannot be regarded as a valid Trust:- *General Reference to Trust*

(i) There can never be less than two separate and distinct persons involved in the valid creation of a Trust, even if a Trustor is a Surrogate; and

(ii) A person cannot be both the Trustee and Beneficiary at the same time; and

(iii) No valid Trust may exist where the legal Title and beneficial interest are both vested in the same person; and

(iv) The rights administered by the Trustee cannot exceed the original rights conveyed by the Trustor; and

(v) It is the Oath of the Trustee that essentially forms the fundamental Character of the Trust. Therefore in the absence of any record of a valid Oath or Vow, there is no Trust; and

(vi) As a Trustee is bound by Fiduciary Capacity to act in good trust (*bona fide*), good character and good conscience, any Trust formed under bad faith, false, deceptive or misleading behaviour automatically renders such a Trust null and void from the beginning; and

(vii) As the presence of at least one Trustee is fundamental to the existence of a Trust, the absence of a Trustee from such Office, without a duly appointed Surrogate, therefore collapses the Trust; and

(viii) A Trustee that fundamentally breaches one or more conditions of the Trust, even if the Trust was formed under proper Fiduciary capacity, automatically dissolves his/her Office and Oath and Vow, thus dissolving the Trust, if only one Trustee exists.

1307. All valid Trusts fully comply and fulfil the ten Essential Characters of Trust. Therefore, any claim or assertion of non compliance against one or more Trusts is an admission of incompetence by the one making or promulgating such false and absurd assertions. *Compliance of Valid Trusts*

Article 370 - Character of Trusts

1308. All valid Trusts may be further categorised according to the essential Status and Authority of the Trustor, being Divine, True, Superior, Temporary or Inferior:- *Character of Trusts*

(i) A *Divine Trust* is a valid purely spiritual Trust representing a body of Divine Rights recorded as a valid entry within a Divine Register constituted in accord with the present sacred Maxims and the Most sacred Covenant *Pactum De Singularis Caelum*. No Trust is Higher; and

(ii) A *True Trust* is a valid Trust representing a body of Natural Rights duly derived from a Divine Trust; and

(iii) A *Superior Trust* is a valid Trust representing a body of Superior Rights duly derived from a Divine Trust or True Trust; and

(iv) A *Temporary Trust* is a valid Trust representing a temporary Trust formed by operation of Law with such Superior Rights derived from a Superior Trust; and

(v) An *Inferior Trust* is any Trust representing the collection of rights under Law not in perfect accord with the present sacred Maxims and most sacred Covenant *Pactum De Singularis Caelum*.

1309. In respect of Divine Trusts:- Divine Trusts

    (i)   Divine Trusts may only have and hold Divine Rights and no other; and

    (ii)   A Divine Trust ceases upon the will of the Divine Creator of all Existence in accord with the sacred Covenant *Pactum De Singularis Caelum* and no other; and

    (iii)   A Divine Trust cannot be salvaged, seized, captured, arrested, alienated, resigned, abjured, transferred, conveyed, donated, assigned or surrendered.

1310. In respect of True Trusts:- True Trusts

    (i)   True Trusts may only have and hold Natural Rights and no other; and

    (ii)   A True Trust is the highest form of Living Trust; and

    (iii)   A True Trust is formed by a True Person in accord with the sacred Covenant *Pactum De Singularis Caelum* when it is validly registered into the Great Register and Divine Records of a Ucadian Society on the condition of (1) the pre-existence of a Divine Trust where the True Person is the named Beneficiary; and (2) the lawful conveyance from the Divine Trust into the True Trust of certain Divine Rights of Use known as Divinity, being the highest possible form of any kind of Property; and

    (iv)   A True Trust may be for a single man, or woman called a "True Person Trust", a True Location Trust containing Divine Right of Possession of Promised Land, or an Aggregate Trust such as a Universal True Trust, Global True Trust or Civil True Trust; and

    (v)   A True Trust ceases upon the physical death of the body, or body politic that is associated with it, or upon a prescribed date mandated at the time of its formation; and

    (vi)   A True Trust is not dependent upon the good character or intentions or actions of the Trustee or Trustees; and

    (vii)   A True Trust cannot be salvaged, seized, captured, arrested, alienated, resigned, abjured, transferred, conveyed, donated, assigned or surrendered.

1311. In respect of Superior Trusts:- Superior Trusts

    (i)   Superior Trusts may only have and hold Superior Rights and no other; and

(ii) A Superior Trust is the second highest form of Living Trust; and

(iii) A Superior Trust is formed in accordance with the covenant *Pactum De Singularis Caelum* and the associated Constitutional Charters of valid Ucadian Societies when it is validly registered into the Great Register and Divine Records of a Ucadian Society on the condition of (1) the pre-existence of a True Trust where the Superior Person is the named Beneficiary; and (2) the lawful conveyance from the True Trust into the Superior Trust of certain True Rights of Use known as Absolute Realty, being the highest temporal form of any kind of Property; and

(iv) A Superior Trust may be for an individual Member, or an Aggregate Trust such as a Global (Superior) Trust, Civil (Superior) Trust, Mercantile (Superior) Trust, Union (Superior) Trust, Clann Trust, Official Trust or Location Trust; and

(v) A Superior Trusts ceases upon the operation of law, or upon the mandated death date as prescribed as part of the original formation of the Trust.

1312. In respect of Temporary Superior Trusts:- *Temporary Trusts*

(i) Temporary Superior Trusts may only temporarily have and hold Superior Rights and no other; and

(ii) A Temporary Trust is the third highest form of Living Trust involving the temporary conveyance of property from one Superior Trust to another; and

(iii) Excluding Negotiable Instruments and Ucadia Money Trusts, a Temporary Trust is not permitted to exist beyond seven years.

1313. In respect of Inferior Trusts:- *Inferior Trusts*

(i) Inferior Trusts may only have and hold Inferior Rights and no other; and

(ii) An Inferior Trust is the lowest form of Living Trust possessing the lowest possible form of rights of ownership; and

(iii) An Inferior Trust can never be considered superior to a Superior Trust or True Trust or Divine Trust; and

(iv) An Inferior Trust is any Living Trust or Implied Trust or Express Trust formed by inferior laws not in perfect accord with the present sacred Maxims and most sacred Covenant *Pactum De Singularis Caelum*.

1314. A Superior Trust, Temporary Trust or Inferior Trust ceases by operation of law upon its Satisfaction, Termination, Dissolution, Annulment or Cessation, with the res or property of the Trust being returned, or distributed or disposed accordingly:- Cessation of Trusts

    (i) *Satisfaction of Trust* means a Trust has fulfilled all its obligations and is therefore finished and ceases upon the return, distribution or disposal of the property; and

    (ii) *Termination of Trust* means a Trust that ceases due to a condition of its operation, usually documented within the Trust Instrument, requiring the Trust to end upon some fundamental breach or failure to perform; and

    (iii) *Dissolution of Trust* means a Trust that dissolves according to the operation of law, usually upon some declaration that the Trust is unable to fulfil its obligations (as in bankruptcy) or some other obstruction or major defect as determined within a competent forum of law; and

    (iv) *Annulment of Trust* means a Trust that ceases to be, upon the strike or removal of such record of its existence, or condemnation as unfit or contrary to the principles of Fiduciary Capacity and any property returned to the Trustor as if the Trust never existed; and

    (v) *Cessation of Trust* means a Trust ceases to be in effect, due to some catastrophic event or act, such as a fundamental Breach of Trust that renders the continuation of such a Trust impossible and to the effect as if the Trust had been annulled.

1315. Any claim that an Inferior Trust possesses superior standing and rights of ownership compared to a Superior Trust, or True Trust is an absurdity against Divine Law and therefore is null and void from the beginning. Claims of Inferior Trust

Article 371 - Trustor

1316. A ***Trustor*** is the generic term for anyone possessing the proper authority to transfer any rights, title or property to another. The other party upon acceptance of the Fiduciary obligations upon a valid Oath and Vow then formalises the valid Trust as Trustee. All persons that possess the proper authority to transfer any rights, title or property to another are by default "Trustors". Trustor

1317. There are only four (4) possible types of Trustor, depending upon the primary nature and intention associated with any conveyance of rights, title or property in Trust being Donor, Grantor, Assignor or Types of Trustor

Delegator:-

(i) A *Donor* is a person who conveys or transfers complete possession and ownership of property without any financial consideration under one or more terms and conditions and may be further defined as a Giftor, Debtor, Guarantor, Indemnitor or Mortgagor; and

(ii) A *Grantor* is a person who conveys or transfers complete possession and ownership of property for some financial consideration in return under one or more terms and conditions and may be further defined as a Feoffor, Devisor, Testator, Settlor, Obligor, Addressor, Sender, Seller or Purchaser; and

(iii) An *Assignor* is a person who temporarily conveys or transfers one or more benefits and rights of possession and use of some property for some financial consideration in return, under one or more terms and conditions and may be further defined as a Consignor, Bailor, Depositor, Employer, Insurer, Hirer, Lessor, Lender, Creditor, Licensor, Lienor or Scrivener; and

(iv) A *Delegator* is a person who temporarily conveys or transfers one or more benefits and rights of possession and use of some property without any financial consideration under one or more terms and conditions and may be further defined as an Executor, Commissioner or Administrator.

1318. A **Donor** being a type of Trustor who conveys or transfers complete possession and ownership of property without any financial consideration under one or more terms and conditions may be further defined as a Giftor, Debtor, Guarantor, Indemnitor or Mortgagor:- Donor

(i) A *Giftor* is a type of Trustor and Donor as one who voluntarily conveys and transfers land or goods, gratuitously and not upon any consideration of blood or money; and

(ii) A *Debtor* is a type of Trustor and Donor as one who gives an unconditional written promise and certain property as surety in trust to repay a fixed sum of money known as the "debt sum" or debt to a Creditor in the event of any default and dishonour by the assured party; and

(iii) A *Guarantor* is a type of Trustor and Donor as one who gives a promise as surety in trust to be answerable or liable for the repayment of a debt, or the performance of some duty in the event of a default and dishonour by the assured party; and

Lex Divina: Maxims of Divine Law

    (iv)   An *Indemnitor* is a type of Trustor and Donor as one who agrees to be bound in trust by an indemnity agreement to insure, or assure or compensate another party in the event of any loss, injury or damage on the part of some third party resulting from some offence, omission or error of official duty or performance; and

    (v)   A *Mortgagor* is a type of Trustor and Donor that pledges or surrenders certain property in trust as security for a debt for the benefit of a Mortagee.

1319. A ***Grantor*** being a type of Trustor who conveys or transfers complete possession and ownership of property for some financial consideration in return under one or more conditions may be further defined as a Feoffor, Devisor, Testator, Settlor, Obligor, Addressor, Sender, Seller or Purchaser:-   *Grantor*

    (i)   A *Feoffor* is a type of Trustor and Grantor that grants any corporeal hereditament to another according to the custom of Fealty and ancient English and Feudal Law; and

    (ii)   A *Devisor* is a type of Trustor and Grantor (equivalent to a Testator) that grants lands or other property by Will and Testament; and

    (iii)   A *Testator* is a type of Trustor and Grantor (equivalent to a Devisor) that grants lands or other property to one or more beneficiaries by Will and Testament; and

    (iv)   A *Settlor* is a type of Trustor and Grantor that grants lands or property in trust for the benefit of one or more successors or filial descendants; and

    (v)   An *Obligor* is a type of Trustor and Grantor that grants a benefit to another party according to some binding agreement or promise; and

    (vi)   An *Addressor* is a type of Trustor and Grantor as the person or organisation who authorises, addresses and grants any formal writing, instrument or notice to be sent or deposited in the mail or delivered for transmission by any other means of communication to an intended recipient or addressee; and

    (vii)   A *Sender* is a type of Trustor and Grantor as the person or organisation who grants and delivers certain addressed mail or parcel or goods to an intended Receiver whom may or may not be the final and intended recipient or addressee; and

    (viii)   A *Seller* is a type of Trustor and Grantor as one who agrees to grant and transfer the title and possession of an object of property in consideration of the payment or promise of payment of a certain price in money; and

(ix) A *Purchaser* is a type of Trustor and Grantor as one who grants a certain price of money for the acquisition of title and possession of property.

1320. An **Assignor** being a type of Trustor who temporarily conveys or transfers one or more benefits and rights of possession and use of some property for some financial consideration in return under one or more terms and conditions may be further defined as a Consignor, Bailor, Depositor, Employer, Insurer, Hirer, Lessor, Lender, Creditor, Licensor, Lienor or Scrivener:-

Assignor

(i) A *Consignor* is a type of Trustor and Assignor as one who deposits goods intended to be sold into the custody of a carrier to be transmitted to the designated agent or party as the "consignee"; and

(ii) A *Bailor* is a type of Trustor and Assignor as one who agrees to deliver goods or personal property in trust to another (Bailee) on the condition that the goods or personal property is redelivered by a certain time or under certain conditions (a process known as a bailment) and a reward paid; and

(iii) A *Depositor* is a type of Trustor and Assignor as one who agrees to deliver goods or personal property in trust to another on the condition that the goods or personal property are preserved and redelivered by a certain time or under certain conditions (a process known as a bailment) but without reward; and

(iv) An *Employer* is a type of Trustor and Assignor as the one who agrees to pay a wage or salary to a labourer or servant for possession and ownership of their works; and

(v) An *Insurer* is a type of Trustor and Assignor who agrees to compensate another for loss on a specific subject by specific perils from an unknown or contingent event; and

(vi) A *Hirer* is a type of Trustor and Assignor who agrees to temporarily take possession and use of a thing or for labour or services in trust in exchange for the payment of some reward or compensation; and

(vii) A *Lessor* is a type of Trustor and Assignor who agrees to convey the right to use lands or tenements or other real property to a person for life, or for a term of years or at will under a lease agreement (in two parts being effectively a deed

(vii) [continued] poll executed by the lessor as lease to lessee and a counterpart executed by lessee to lessor) in consideration of a return of rent or some other annual recompense; and

(viii) A *Lender* is a type of Trustor and Assignor as one who agrees to temporarily transfer some thing to another on the condition that the property is redelivered by a certain time or under certain conditions; and

(ix) A *Creditor* is a type of Trustor and Assignor who agrees to lend a sum of money or goods of equivalent value to a Debtor for the payment of a debt, in exchange for the promissory note of the Debtor and the repayment of the debt in the event of a default by the assured party; and

(x) A *Licensor* is a type of Trustor and Assignor as one who issues a written and properly authorised permit or warrant to another, conferring the right(s) to do some act in relation to certain property held in trust which without such authorisation would be illegal, or considered a trespass or a tort; and

(xi) A *Lienor* is a type of Trustor and Assignor who licenses the temporary right of use, or holding, or seizure, or custody of certain real or personal property in trust, upon the Lienor possessing a claim of right to the temporary ownership or control of the property as security or charge against the performance of a debtor (in other words a Lien); and

(xii) A *Scrivener* is a type of Trustor and Assignor who agrees to create and temporarily assign original forms of instruments including (but not limited to) indulgences, charters, bills, bonds and mortgages for the purpose of lending them out at an interest payable to his principal and for a commission or bonus for himself.

1321. A ***Delegator*** being a type of Trustor who temporarily conveys or transfers one or more benefits and rights of possession and use of some property without any financial consideration in return under one or more terms and conditions may be further defined as an Executor, Commissioner or Administrator:-

(i) An *Executor* is a type of Trustor and Delegator as one who delegates authority and franchise by charter, or deed or letters patent; and

(ii) A *Commissioner* is a type of Trustor and Delegator as one who delegates authority and agency by warrant, or deed or letters

Delegator

of marque; and

(iii) An *Administrator* is a type of Trustor and Delegator as a surrogate Executor, appointed under competent judicial authority as one who delegates authority by order.

1322. In accord with these Maxims and the most sacred covenant *Pactum De Singularis Caelum* and within the limits of certain Persons, associated Trusts and Rights:- — Persons, Trusts and Rights

(i) A *Divine Person* as a valid Trustor is the only type of Trustor that may transfer Divine Rights, excluding those Rights that are Peremptory, Permanent, Immutable and Indefeasible; and

(ii) A *True Person* as a valid Trustor is the only type of Trustor that may transfer Natural Rights, excluding those Rights that are Peremptory, Permanent, Immutable and Indefeasible; and

(iii) A *Superior Ecclesiastical Person* as a valid Trustor is the only type of Trustor that may transfer Superior Ecclesiastical Rights, excluding those Rights that are Peremptory, Permanent, Immutable and Indefeasible; and

(iv) A *Superior Person* as a valid Trustor is the only type of Trustor that may transfer Superior Rights, excluding those rights that are Peremptory, Permanent, Immutable and Indefeasible.

1323. In respect of a Trustor of a Superior, Temporary or Inferior Trust:- — Breach of Trust

(i) A Person proven to have acted in fraud or breach of their fiduciary duties as a Trustor automatically ceases to hold the Position from the time of the Fraud or breach; and

(ii) Any liability associated with a fraud or breach of duty of a former Trustor or Trustee is automatically personally assumed by the disgraced former Trustor or Trustee.

1324. In respect of a Trustor of a Superior, Temporary or Inferior Trust, a Trustor may cease, terminate, dissolve and annul a Trust in action against the Trustee(s), upon evidence of one or more Breaches of Trust:- — Cessation of Trust by Trustor

(i) When a Trust is formed by the Trustor as Grantor, then by Renunciation of any such Grant, a Trustor may lawfully regain Repossession and Restitution; or

(ii) When a Trust is formed by the Trustor as Donor, then by Reclamation of such original Rights, a Trustor may lawfully regain Recovery and Restoration; or

(iii) When a Trust is formed by the Trustor as Assignor, then by Rescission of any sign (signature), or seal of execution, a

Trustor may lawfully regain Return and Reversion; or

(iv) When a Trust is formed by the Trustor as Delegator, then by Revocation of any instrument of appointment or powers, a Trustor may lawfully regain Remand and Revestiture.

Article 372 - Trustee

1325. A ***Trustee*** is an Office formed by a valid Oath and Vow to the Terms of Trust to take possession of certain Rights and Property from a Trustor and perform certain Obligations for the benefit of another. The manner and character of a Trustee may be described as a position of Trust which is equivalent to the term Fiduciary. Trustee

1326. In reference to the Office of Trustee of a Superior, Temporary or Inferior Trust:- General References to Trustee

(i) The origin of the concept of Trustee and the fact that such an Office cannot exist except under sacred Oath and Vow is as old as the origin of civilised society and law itself and has been one of the most constant concepts of law throughout every age and era; and

(ii) The concept of Trustee is founded on the most basic principle that a Person cannot legitimately possess the Rights or Property of others, unless they demonstrate the most exemplary and scrupulous character of good faith, good character and good conscience; and

(iii) Any repudiation of these fundamental concepts is the repudiation of the Rule of Law and law itself; and

(iv) In the absence of a valid Oath and Vow, no Office may exist.

1327. The eight standard characteristics of a Trustee as Fiduciary are Integrity, Frugality, Prudence, Humility, Faculty, Competence, Accountability and Capacity:- Characteristics of Trustee

(i) *Integrity* is the characteristic of possessing a strict moral or ethical code as exemplified by the trinity of virtue (Good Faith, Good Character and Good Conscience); and

(ii) *Frugality* is the characteristic of being economical and thrifty in the good use of those resources in one's own possession or custody. The opposite of waste; and

(iii) *Prudence* is the characteristic of being practical, cautious, discrete, judicious and wise in the management of the affairs of the trust; and

(iv) *Humility* is the characteristic of being modest, without pretension or loftiness; and

(v) *Faculty* is the characteristic of possessing skill and ability in order to perform the obligations of trustee; and

(vi) *Competence* is the characteristic of being fit, proper and qualified to produce and argue reason through knowledge and skill of Law, Logic and Rhetoric; and

(vii) *Accountability* is the characteristic of being answerable and liable to faithfully render an account for all acts and transactions; and

(viii) *Capacity* is the characteristic of possessing the legal and moral authority to hold such office, including demonstrating all the previous necessary characteristics.

1328. The Office of Trustee of a Superior, Temporary or Inferior Trust can only exist and be valid if all the following criteria exist:- Conditions of Trustee

(i) The Trustor has the proper authority to grant, donate, assign or delegate the property for the proposed Trust; and

(ii) Clear purpose, intent and terms for the proposed Trust exist; and

(iii) Certainty of subject matter (the property) exists for the proposed Trust to exist; and

(iv) The candidate for Trustee comes with good faith, good character and good conscience; and

(v) The candidate for Trustee accepts the position with full knowledge of the terms and obligations; and

(vi) The candidate makes a formal sacred oath to a higher Divine Power upon a sacred object representing the form of law connected to such higher Divine power, before witnesses; and

(vii) The event of making such a formal sacred oath is memorialised into some document, that itself is signed, sealed and executed.

1329. A valid Trustee of a Superior, Temporary or Inferior Trust may be responsible for some or all of the following thirty-three (33) Administrative Elements of Trust being *Rules, Standards, Forms, Procedures, Instruments, Transactions, Notices, Books, Registers, Rolls, Claims, Vouchers, Sureties, Assets, Liabilities, Credits, Debits, Accounts, Records, Manifests, Inventories, Memoranda, Journals, Ledgers, Summaries, Certificates, Audits, Transfers, Conveyances,* Responsibilities of Trustee

Computations, Valuations, Derivations and *Hypothecations*:-

(i) *Rules* are the ordinances, regulations or by-laws of the Trust as defined by its constituting Instrument; and

(ii) *Standards* are the principles, means and measures of excellence used to compare the results of all activities and administrative duties; and

(iii) *Forms* are the model of certain Instruments prescribed by law or the constituting Instrument of the valid Trust, Estate or Fund and the manner by which they must be correctly completed, the method of their use and the matters to which they may apply; and

(iv) *Procedures* are ways and methods of performance of obligations and administrative duties, usually in association with one or more Forms; and

(v) *Instruments* are the legally formed documents received and issued by the Trust and held in Chancery; and

(vi) *Transactions* are all the communications, deals, exchanges, transfers, conveyances and proceedings of the Trust; and

(vii) *Notices* are both Instruments and service of process by which one or more Parties are made aware of any formal legal matter that may affect certain rights, obligations and duties; and

(viii) *Books* are traditionally stitched spine bound books used to create Registers, Accounts, Inventories, Memoranda, Journals and Ledgers; and

(ix) *Registers* are tables of one or more records of the receiving or granting or claiming of rights, privileges or property of a valid Trust or Estate or Fund in relation to one or more persons; and

(x) *Rolls* are types of tables and registers of one or more records being "legal persons" of the same condition or entered in the same engagement of obligations in relation to a valid Trust or Estate or Fund and created by their valid entry into the Roll; and

(xi) *Claims* are the oral or written assertion of a valid Right against another party regarding the possession or ownership of some property or thing withheld from the possession of the claimant; and

(xii) *Vouchers* are written or printed Instruments such as a note, or receipt, or bill of particulars, or acquittance, or release which shows on what account or by what authority a payment has been made and serving as evidence of payment or discharge of a debit, or to certify the correctness of accounts; and

(xiii) *Sureties* are written promises to pay or perform as a guarantee and therefore security against some other obligation or liability; and

(xiv) *Assets* are Valuations entered into the Accounts of a Trust, or Estate, or Fund calculated at the time of an Inventory or by a special Valuation for each and every valid Record of Rights, Property and Title within the control of the Trust, or Estate, or Fund; and

(xv) *Liabilities* are Valuations entered into the Accounts of a Trust, or Estate, or Fund calculated at the time of an Inventory or by a special Valuation for each and every valid Record of an Obligation or Debit or within the performance and responsibility of the Trust, or Estate, or Fund; and

(xvi) *Credits* are Accounting computations of the addition of numbers to a particular type of Account within a Ledger associated with the posting of Journal entries and general practices of Accounting; and

(xvii) *Debits* are accounting computations of the deductions of numbers to a particular type of Account within a Ledger associated with the posting of Journal entries and general practices of Accounting; and

(xviii) *Accounts* are tabulations and summary arrangement of computations, valuations and derivations on the nature, value and disposition of objects, concepts and property of a valid Trust or Estate or Fund; and

(xix) *Records* are entries into Memoranda, Registers or Rolls; and

(xx) *Manifests* are evidential history of the provenance, possession and ownership of any property, rights, money and other interests now recorded as associated with the Trust or Estate or Fund; and

(xxi) *Inventories* are being a detailed survey of all property, assets and liabilities, debits or credits of a valid Trust, or Estate or Fund completed immediately after its creation and thereafter at an appointed day; and the stock of particular items and their location or business; and

(xxii) *Memoranda* are the Books of details of Records of all transactions associated with the Trust or Estate or Fund, including minutes, resolutions, letters, correspondence, decisions and procedural actions recorded in day and time order; and

(xxiii) *Journals* are Books derived as summary extracts of information from Memoranda and arranged in category order and then day/time order to produce a summary of facts, evidence, quantities and relations for the purpose of accounting and reckoning of the debits and credits of the Trust or Estate or Fund; and

(xxiv) *Ledgers* being Books that summarise information extracted from Journal entries to produce the most concise reckonings and balances of debits and credits, assets and liabilities of the Trust or Estate or Fund; and

(xxv) *Summaries* are extracts of a Ledger Balance or Simple Balance of Assets and Debits, or Concessions and Remittances or other elements to provide statements, reports or disclosures required in the operation of the Trust or Estate or Fund; and

(xxvi) *Certificates* are official, authorised and acknowledged extracts of Records of the Trust; and

(xxvii) *Audits* are annual surveys of the administrative elements of a Trust to determine if the Rules and Standards have been properly met; and

(xxviii) *Transfers* are the passing of possession and holding of certain rights, titles or objects of property; and

(xxix) *Conveyances* are the passing of ownership of certain rights, titles or objects of property; and

(xxx) *Computations* are the summarising, calculation and reckoning of arithmetic numbers and values associated with the Trust and Trust property; and

(xxxi) *Valuations* are estimations using some standard unit of measure and account, of the value or worth of an object or concept as property; and

(xxxii) *Derivations* are forms derived from another and possessing a value depending upon the underlying asset from which it was derived; and

(xxxiii) *Hypothecations* are pledges of an underlying asset associated with some Derivation of value as further surety to the Derivation, without delivering temporary possession or ownership of the pledged asset.

Title VIII – Divine Trusts

1330. A valid Trustee may be appointed to a Superior, Temporary or Inferior Trust under the circumstances of Foundation, Death, Abandonment, Resignation, Refusal or Contestation:-

    (i) Foundation is when a new Trust is formed and a Trustee is appointed in accordance with the Instrument or Covenant for the first time; or

    (ii) Death is when an existing Trustee dies and a vacancy is declared; or

    (iii) Abandonment is when an existing Trustee is away from the domicile of the Trust for more than two years without word or adequate response and so a surrogate Trustee must be appointed; or

    (iv) Resignation is when an existing Trustee applies for resignation of duties of Office, creating a Vacancy; or

    (v) Refusal is when an existing Trustee refuses to act in the manner and characteristics required of such Office; or

    (vi) Contestation is when the competency or legitimacy of a Trustee is challenged and upheld by a competent forum of Law before three Trustees, requiring the resignation of the Trustee.

Appointment of Trustee

1331. A True Person, or Superior Person or Inferior Person is forbidden to act directly as Trustee in their own affairs and Property or the affairs, Property and Estates of others under the following conditions:-

    (i) When the Trustee is presently a Newborn (under the age of 2); or

    (ii) When the Trustee is presently a Child (under the age of 13); or

    (iii) When a Trustee is presently a Youth (under the age of 21); or

    (iv) When a person has been found culpable in accord with the present Maxims and Rule of Law to be ethically and morally unfit to act in the capacity of a Trustee; or

    (v) When a person has been found mentally incompetent and mentally incapable in accord with the present Maxims to act in the capacity of a Trustee.

Proper Conduct

1332. When a Person who claims to be a Trustee of a Superior, Temporary or Inferior Trust, but evidence exists of one or more of the following elements, then such a person is an impostor with no such Office or Trust existing:-

    (i) Where a Person belongs to a religion, religious rite, society, institute, entity or order that continues to perform any formal

Disqualification of Trustee

or sacred ritual to repudiate Oaths or Vows made in the past or into the future in direct contradiction to the most sacred Covenant *Pactum De Singularis Caelum*; or

(ii) Where a Person belongs to a religion, religious rite, society, institute, entity or order that continues to require the making of one or more Oaths or Vows that are contradictory to the Golden Rule and Rule of Law, Justice and Due Process and the most sacred Covenant *Pactum De Singularis Caelum*; or

(iii) Where a Person belongs to a religion, religious rite, society, institute, entity or order that continues to require the making of one or more Oaths or Vows that results in dishonest, perfidious, tyrannical or impious behaviour and the disregard of good faith, good character and good conscience in direct contradiction to the most sacred Covenant *Pactum De Singularis Caelum*; or

(iv) Where one or more of the criteria for the valid creation of the Office of Trustee does not exist.

1333. No judge, magistrate or justice of the peace as a proper Jurist may adjudicate any matter of law within a competent forum of law or oratory unless they are presently a valid Trustee under Oath and secondly prepared to demonstrate under Oath the exemplary characteristics of a valid Trustee or valid Fiduciary:- <small>Role of Trustee in matters of Law</small>

(i) As a valid Oath is required to create and sustain the Office judge, or magistrate or justice of the peace, the absence of a valid Oath of Office means such a person is the worst kind of impostor and without any legitimacy whatsoever; and

(ii) As any adjudication concerning rights or property requires exemplary character, any judge, magistrate or justice of the peace that is unwilling or refuses to be entrusted under Oath by all parties to perform in good faith, good character and good conscience is not a valid Fiduciary; and

(iii) The disregard of such fundamental principles may be properly construed as a formal and official admission of the absence of any proper Rule of Law, Justice or Due Process.

1334. The Office of Trustee of a Superior, Temporary or Inferior Trust ceases:- <small>Cessation of office of Trustee</small>

(i) At the dissolution or satisfaction or termination or cessation or annulment of the Trust; or

(ii) Upon the Death of the Trustee; or

(iii) Abandonment, when a Trustee is away from the domicile of the Trust for more than two years without word or adequate response; or

(iv) Resignation, when a Trustee resigns from the of duties of such Office; or

(v) Refusal, when a Trustee refuses to act in the manner and characteristics required of such Office; or

(vi) Contestation, when the competency or legitimacy of a Trustee is challenged and upheld by a competent forum of Law.

Article 373 - Beneficiary

1335. A ***Beneficiary*** is a named or unnamed party at the time of the formation of the Trust who benefits or receives a useful or valuable advantage from the Trust. A Beneficiary, by definition is an "interested party" in a Trust or Estate:- Beneficiary

(i) A Named Beneficiary is an Agent (with the Trustee being the Principal) and may be commissioned or non-commissioned; and

(ii) An Unnamed Beneficiary is a Creditor (with the Trustee acting as Debitor) to whom the trustee owes basic duties arising by law, agreement or claim.

1336. In respect of Beneficiaries and types of Trusts:- General Reference of Beneficiaries

(i) All Beneficiaries of Divine Trusts are named by the Divine Creator, whether or not such records are present or accurate within the temporal realm. Furthermore, no Beneficiary may be unnamed regarding Divine Trusts, except those Aggregate Trusts associated with Supreme Credo (Credit); and

(ii) All Beneficiaries of True Trusts are named by the Divine Creator in accord with the most sacred Covenant *Pactum De Singularis Caelum* and associated Covenants, whether or not such records are present or accurate within the temporal realm. No Beneficiary may be unnamed regarding True Trusts; and

(iii) All Beneficiaries of Superior Trusts are named. No Beneficiary of a Superior Trust, except Temporary Superior Trusts, may be unnamed; and

(iv) Beneficiaries of Temporary Superior Trusts may be named or unnamed; and

(v) Beneficiaries of Inferior Trusts may be named or unnamed.

1337. A party becomes a Beneficiary of a Superior, Temporary or Inferior Trust upon Use, or Claim or Acceptance and therefore becomes obligated to perform the duties associated with the Benefits in Trust. However, a party once becoming a Beneficiary may then cease, terminate or dissolve any interest or obligation by one of the following actions:-

    (i) If a Beneficiary by Acceptance, then upon acknowledgement of Proof of Purchase (i.e. Bill of Sale) or by Covenant signed by another party then proving the property or interest is no longer in their possession; or by Surrender of the Property or interest by Testimony; and

    (ii) If a Beneficiary by Claim, then by Disclaimer or Withdrawal of any interest; and

    (iii) If a Beneficiary By Use, when no formal acceptance or claim is acknowledged thereby both surrenders and disclaims as a cessation of any past, present and future Use.

Appointment of Beneficiary

Article 374 - Fiduciary

1338. A ***Fiduciary*** is a Person holding the character of a valid Trustee and the scrupulous good faith and honesty required for such Office. Thus, the term Fiduciary is equivalent to Trustee.

Fiduciary

1339. While the term Trustee typically denotes the position and powers established in Trust, the term Fiduciary by tradition emphasises the three essential criteria necessary in the capacity and character of a proper Fiduciary being good faith (*bona fides*), good character (*bona virtutes*) and good conscience (*bona conscientia*):-

Three Criteria of Fiduciary

    (i) *Good Faith*, also known as *bona fides* is the ancient custom that a man or woman cannot be a Fiduciary except under proper Oath or Vow to a recognised Divinity upon some object or text representing a firm belief in the efficacy of some sacred and ethical standards of law existing in the same name as the Divinity; and

    (ii) *Good Character*, also known as *bona virtutes* is the ancient custom that a man or woman cannot act as a Fiduciary except in accord with the highest virtues of honesty, impartiality, frugality and prudence, also sometimes known as "clean hands doctrine"; and

    (iii) *Good Conscience*, also known as *bona conscientia* is the ancient custom that a man or woman cannot act in the best interests of another, or fairly under the Rule of Law if they seek a contrary or negative outcome.

1340. ***Fiduciary Capacity*** is when one receives money or contracts a debt or when the business which he transacts, or the money or property which he handles, is not his own or for his own benefit, but for the benefit of another person, as to whom he stands in a relation implying and necessitating the presence of good faith (*bona fides*), good character (*bona virtutes*) and good conscience (*bona conscientia*).
Fiduciary Capacity

1341. A ***Fiduciary Relation*** is a relation existing between two persons in regard to any implied or actual agreement concerning certain rights, or title or property associated with or derived from an estate whereby each party must therefore act in confidence and trust with the other in accord with good faith (*bona fides*), good character (*bona virtutes*) and good conscience (*bona conscientia*). Examples of Fiduciary Relations are those existing between attorney and client, guardian and ward, principal and agent, executor and heir, executor and beneficiary, trustee and beneficiary and landlord and tenant.
Fiduciary Relation

Article 375 - Principal

1342. A ***Principal*** is a Person holding the character of a valid Trustee and a term describing the powers of a Trustee to be a Trustor in delegating, granting or assigning certain Rights to Beneficiaries as Agents. A Principle therefore, is:-
Principal

   (i) A type of Trustee that is given the powers by a Trustor through some Trust Instrument to delegate, assign, or grant certain Rights to others as Agents (Beneficiaries); and

   (ii) An Office that may appoint subordinates having certain powers of the same office as an extension of the authority of such Office.

1343. The definition of an Officer in terms of being a Trustee and a Principal may be defined by the Rules of Principal-Agent Relation, namely:-
Principal Agent Relation

   (i) When a Trust instrument specifically names a person, or a Trustee who by their powers chooses to nominate a person as Beneficiary, this creates the Principal-Agent Relation; and

   (ii) It is only when the Beneficiary accepts the offer of the Benefit does such a Relation become a formal Principal-Agent Relation. Thus, any claim that a Principal can be secret or unknown is morally repugnant, absurd and void in law; and

(iii) A Principal-Agent Relation does not exist in the case of an unnamed beneficiary. Instead, the relation when an unnamed Beneficiary relation is created is the Trustee as Debtor and the unnamed beneficiary as Creditor; and

(iv) An Agent is by extension a representative of the Principal and is therefore obligated to perform in accord with the conditions of accepting the Benefit. The moment an Agent breaches their obligations, they become liable for their actions and lose any form of limited liability; and

(v) As an Agent is an extension of the Office of Principal, a Principal is liable for the actions of his/her Agents. Thus Notice of an Agent is Notice to Principal and Notice to Principal is Notice to their Agents; and

(vi) An Agent can never have the capacity or authority to form a sub-agent relation within the original Principal-Agent relation. Any relation formed then by the Agent with a third party must be as a Trustee of some stable right and authority.

Article 376 - Agent

1344. An ***Agent*** is one authorised by delegation in trust to act for or in place of a Principal. The Authority of an Agent is always in Trust, as the Trust itself is called an Agency and exists so long as the prescribed time, or the proper performance of the Agent. A Minister therefore may be described as an Agent. — Agent

1345. In respect of an Agent:- — General Reference to Agent

(i) An Agent binds not himself but the Principal with the agreements made; and

(ii) An Agent is by extension a representative of the Principal and is therefore obligated to perform in accord with the conditions of accepting the Benefit; and

(iii) The moment an Agent breaches their obligations, they become liable for their actions and lose any form of limited liability; and

(iv) An Agent that handles any form of money, or property or rights on behalf of the Principal is automatically a Fiduciary and obligated to act with Fiduciary Capacity and Fiduciary Standards.

Article 377 - Debitor (in Trust)

1346. A ***Debitor*** "in Trust", is a Trustee of a Trust formed without an expressly named Beneficiary, whereby:-

(i) As such a Trust has no named Beneficiary and no restriction, the Trustee is free to sell the Benefit for some valuable consideration; and

(ii) Such a Benefit in Trust becomes effectively the meaning of "Good"; and

(iii) Upon the Benefit being sold for some valuable consideration as a "Good", the Trustee is then under obligation or a "debit" to another in a Debitor-Creditor Relation.

Debitor

1347. A Debit is not the same as a Debt:-

(i) A Debit is a sum paid or due for Goods purchased or sold; and

(ii) A Debt is a sum agreed as a binding penalty upon default; and

(iii) A Debt is also a right of action to obtain a sum as a penalty upon proof of delinquency.

Debit and Debt

Article 378 - Creditor (in Trust)

1348. A ***Creditor*** "in Trust", is one that obtains a Benefit in exchange for some valuable consideration from a Trust formed without an expressly named Beneficiary.

Creditor

1349. With regards to a Creditor "In Trust":-

(i) The Person who obtains such a Benefit by definition must clearly provide something of value and the Trustee must clearly understand their position, otherwise such a transaction is by definition invalid; and

(ii) The deliberate misrepresentation of a position to obtain a Benefit by deception is perfidy and an essential meaning of fraud, whereby such an act and all rights are invalid.

General Reference to Creditor

Article 379 - Ordinary Divine Trust

1350. An ***Ordinary Divine Trust*** is a purely Spiritual Trust validly registered into the Great Register and Divine Records of One Heaven containing actual Spiritual Form as well as Divine Property administered by the Treasury of One Heaven as Trustees in accordance with the sacred Covenant *Pactum De Singularis Caelum* as the sacred Covenant for the Benefit of all Divine Persons.

Ordinary Divine Trust

1351. In accordance with the most sacred Covenant *Pactum De Singularis Caelum*, a Divine Trust has been created, is created and will be created for every single man, woman and higher order spirit that has ever existed, or is living at this moment or will live and exist in the future:-

Formation of Divine Trusts

(i) A Divine Trust is the highest possible form of Trust and unique as the only possible type of Trust that can hold actual Form, rather than the Rights of Use of Form being Property; and

(ii) In accordance with these Maxims, a Divine Trust can never be terminated; and

(iii) No Rights or Form contained within a valid Divine Trust may be conveyed, nor any transactions or effects undertaken on behalf of the Trust unless it is in accord with these Maxims and the sacred covenant *Pactum De Singularis Caelum*; and

(iv) A Divine Being may only be associated with one valid Divine Trust and therefore one valid Divine Person; and

(v) An Ordinary Divine Person associated with one Ordinary Divine Trust may only be associated with one True Person as Trustee of a valid True Trust whilst the flesh lives; and

(vi) In accordance with these Maxims and the sacred Covenant *Pactum De Singularis Caelum*, all men, women and higher order life, living and deceased are members of One Heaven, therefore possessing a unique Divine Trust and Divine Personality as demonstrated and proven by the existence of a unique Membership number for them; and

(vii) In accordance with these Maxims, every child or higher order spirit that is borne from now until the end of time possesses a Divine Personality through the creation of their Divine Trust before any other legal entity or claim; and Any claimed ownership, conveyance, lien, or other fictional device over any Form within a Divine Trust that are not in accordance with these Maxims is a fraud and gross injury to the Divine Creator and therefore automatically null and void from the beginning.

Article 380 - Aggregate Divine Trust

1352. An ***Aggregate Divine Trust*** is a Trust formed from the aggregation of rights of two or more Divine Persons to form a new Trust, in accord with these sacred Maxims and the most sacred Covenant *Pactum De Singularis Caelum*.

Aggregate Divine Trust

Article 381 - Supreme Divine Trust

1353. A ***Supreme Divine Trust*** is a valid Aggregate Divine Trust registered into the Great Register and Divine Records of One Heaven whereby one hundred (100) deceased members consent to convey their Divine Trusts holding actual Divine Form and Rights into a new Supreme Divine Trust.

Supreme Divine Trust

1354. A Deceased member of One Heaven is a Divine Person no longer having use of a living flesh vessel in the form of an organic higher order being such as a Homo Sapien body. Divine Persons owning a living flesh vessel are not permitted to convey their Form and Rights into a Supreme Divine Trust.

Limitation of association to Supreme Divine Trusts

1355. As condition and consent in being a member of One Heaven, all deceased members and the Divine Creator grant the Treasury of One Heaven the right to form a necessary number of Supreme Divine Trusts for the benefit of the Society and all future generations of deceased and living members.

Grant and Authority

1356. The total number of Supreme Divine Trusts may not exceed the total number of deceased members as indicated by the issue of valid membership numbers divided by one hundred.

Limit on total number of Supreme Divine Trusts

1357. When forming a new Supreme Divine Trust, the Treasury of One Heaven shall respect the historic relationships and connections between deceased members and major events in their history so that members are grouped together in a Supreme Divine Trust sharing similar history, events and values. Therefore, for example, deceased leaders of a civilisation or entity should by right be connected together, as should family members, as should those that died together.

Historic nature of Supreme Divine Trusts

1358. The holding of an authenticated abstract of a Supreme Credit does not imply in anyway a transfer of ownership, nor title, nor rights, nor assets. Any person, Juridic person or entity that seeks to monetise, or use a Supreme Credit except for the express purpose the abstract was provided is guilty of gross fraud and dishonour, with any subsequent transaction null and void from the beginning.

No imputation or right by merely holding instruments

Article 382- Official Divine Trust

1359. An ***Official Divine Trust*** is a valid aggregate Superior Trust registered into the Great Register and Divine Records of a Global or Civil Ucadian Society. An Official Trust holds Real Property relating to an official position within a valid Ucadian Society. An Official Trust is always a Superior Trust and can never be a True Trust. Official Divine Trusts

1360. A new Official Divine Trust is formed when a Global or Civil Ucadian Society conveys Property from a True Trust representing the Office and a True Person conveys their property and obligations to form a new Superior Trust. Formation of Official Divine Trusts

1361. The life of an Official Divine Trust is the life of a True Person holding the Office. Upon leaving Office, the Rights bestowed by the True Office Trust revert, including any additional property and effects. However, the release of obligations of a True Person having left office is dependent upon their oath and vows. Life of Official Divine Trust

1362. The obligations and agreements acquired through Office outlive the termination of the Official Divine Trust by reverting to the True Office Divine Trust and are then conveyed to the new Superior Official Trust of the new Official. Obligations and agreements

Title IX - Divine Estates

9.1 Divine Estates

Article 383 - Estate

1363. An *Estate* is a record in a type of Register known as a "Roll", issued by some authorised ecclesiastical body, sovereign body or body politic, denoting the assumed or actual beneficial rights or "privileges" and obligations of one or more persons of the same condition and circumstance. Estate

1364. In general reference to the concept of an Estate:- General Reference to Estate

    (i) A valid record in an Estate Roll creates a unique legal entity having certain limits of legal capacity or "standing" or "status" within the jurisdiction of the body and control of the body that created it. Therefore, in the first instance, an Estate is equivalent to the concept of a unique "legal person"; and

    (ii) The limits of legal capacity or "standing" or "status" determined by the valid record in the Estate Roll owned by the authorised ecclesiastical body, sovereign body or body politic that created it therefore defines to what extent other property may (or may not) be held and used as "privileges and "liberties" by the beneficiary claiming use of the "legal person". Therefore, in the second instance, an Estate is equivalent to the primary "legal title" and "legal capacity" and "legal standing" of a particular class of persons; and

    (iii) Subject to such limits of legal capacity and legal standing, an Estate may then hold one or more beneficial "rights of use" or property as "privileges and "liberties" within one or more temporary beneficial trusts associated with the Estate (i.e. "real estate" and "personal estate"). Therefore, in the third instance, an Estate is equivalent to the aggregate property of immovable, movable, corporeal and incorporeal things associated with these temporary trusts (i.e. "the whole of the estate"); and

    (iv) To properly administer the affairs of the Estate, the beneficial rights, also known as property may then be pledged, promised, assigned, granted or delegated as security to form one or more assets. The value of such assets may then be monetised or securitised through various funds, agreements, licenses, accounts and certificates. Therefore, in the fourth instance, an Estate is equivalent to the aggregate monetary value of the net assets of the estate after all debts have been discharged.

1365. All valid Estates exist under certain fundamental assumptions:-   *Elements of Valid Estate*

    (i)   The rules of formation and management of an Estate Roll and lesser Registers must exist as public law within the rules of the ecclesiastical body, sovereign body or body politic that created it; and

    (ii)   The Rights associated with an Estate are always "Rights of Use", also known as "Property" and not the primary Rights of ownership. Thus, Estates always concern Property as "Rights of Use"; and

    (iii)   As the Rights associated with an Estate are always "Right of Use" of some Right, a separate Trust must first exist before the Estate is created; and furthermore, that the Rights being the source of the "Rights of Use" in question must also have been named and conveyed into the existing Trust by a Trustor; and

    (iv)   The authorised ecclesiastical body, sovereign body or body politic that created the Estate Roll owns "legal title" to any such Rights conveyed into such an Estate; and

    (v)   All Rights in Estate (within the Estate) are Beneficial Title or Equitable Title and not legal title; and

    (vi)   Beneficial Title means one or more "privileges" or "liberties" that, subject to the rules of the Estate, may be withdrawn or forfeited or alienable; and

    (vii)   Equitable Title means a "privilege" not in possession of the Beneficiary, but claimable and recoverable through a qualified forum of law with equity powers - being rights of a surrogate Chancery Court. Thus, certain permits, titles, letters, certificates and patents issued to a Beneficiary as "Equitable Title" does not necessarily mean the Beneficiary holds one or more "privileges" other than to sue in a valid court of equity to claim or recover one or more of these such "rights"; and

    (viii)   The rules for the administration of Property (Rights of Use) within the Estate is through a Covenant of Testamentary Disposition, otherwise known as a Will by a Testator, or in its absence (Intestate), some other established and authorised rules; and

    (ix)   For every valid Estate, a Fiduciary must be named and duly appointed to govern the affairs of the Estate, either as an Executor, or appointed Administrator in the absence of clear instruction or dispute of authority; and

(x) For every valid Estate that engages in trade or commerce, at least one duly appointed Agent must exist and be duly appointed, registered and acknowledged to manage the day to day business of the Estate under the authority of the Executor or appointed Administrator as the Principal.

1366. As a valid Estate is created via a valid entry and formation of a record into some form of Estate Roll, the general authority, nature and function of Rolls apply:- Authority and Nature of Rolls and Estates

(i) The authority to form a Roll is defined by the limits of authority of the constituting Instrument of the relevant Trust or Estate or Fund; and

(ii) The Rights, Powers and Property prescribed to an Estate created and defined within a Roll cannot exceed the Rights, Powers and Property of the Trust or Estate or Fund itself; and

(iii) All Rolls are completely and exclusively Ecclesiastical Property and can never belong to a Trust, or Estate or Fund that formed or inherited it. Instead, all Rolls are the property of One Heaven. Therefore, all Estates are the property of One Heaven; and

(iv) All Rolls are hierarchical in their inheritance of authority and validity from One Heaven, beginning with the highest being the Great Roll of Divine Persons. Therefore, the highest Estates are Divine Estates and the lowest are Inferior Estates. A Roll that cannot demonstrate the provenance of its authority, has none and is null and void from the beginning; and

(v) As all Rolls are completely and exclusively Ecclesiastical, absolutely no clerical or administrative act may take place in association with a Roll unless by a duly authorised Trustee under active and valid sacred Oath and Vow in a manner consistent and in accord with these Maxims; and

(vi) The entry of a record into a Roll is completely invalid unless the memorial or covenant of the act giving authority is done without duress, is done freely and with full knowledge and is consistent and in accord with these Maxims and the most sacred Covenant *Pactum De Singularis Caelum*.

Title X - Divine Money

10.1 - Divine Money

Article 384 - Money

1367. ***Money*** is a Right, established by laws consistent and in accord with the most sacred Covenant *Pactum De Singularis Caelum*, whereby a system of rules, measures, records, accounts and procedures are formed to produce a consistent and stable Unit of Measure, Unit of Account, Unit of Redemption for Value, Means of Exchange and Reliable Store of Value. — Money

1368. True, valid and legitimate Money possesses five qualities in accord with the present sacred Maxims and the most sacred Covenant *Pactum De Singularis Caelum* being Unit of Measure, Unit of Account, Unit of Redemption for Value, Means of Exchange and Reliable Store of Value:- — Five Elements of Money

   (i) *Unit of Measure* means that proper Money is first and foremost a "standard unit of measure", having a suitable unique identity to distinguish it from other units of measure, whereby all goods and services within a certain Market may be compared to the same unit of measure, thus enabling the creation of Price. In this way, proper Money is fundamentally always an attribute of a Market and not vice versa; and

   (ii) *Unit of Account* means that proper Money is a unit of measure associated with a Market that enables the entry of consistent values and transactions, based upon its character as a Unit of Measure, within Accounts and Ledgers reflecting such Prices, Quantities and other attributes of Goods and Services. In this way, Accounts are always a feature of a Market and Money as entries in such accounts are an attribute of Accounts and Markets, not vice versa; and

   (iii) *Unit of Redemption for Value* means that proper Money is capable of being represented in some medium or form (i.e. physical and/or electronic; or paper, plastic, metal or other etc.) and possesses the attribute of being redeemed for some valuable consideration. This third aspect is considered fundamental and essential as it is the mechanism that by tradition enables a participant to "enter" and to "exit" a form of proper Money associated with one Market and choose to move to another Market; and

   (iv) *Means of Exchange* means that proper Money is able to fulfil the requirement of facilitating efficient transactions within a Market, because of its previous attributes. Thus, a "means of exchange" may be considered a primary object of proper Money, but only as a consequence of other attributes first being in place; and

(v) *Reliable Store of Value* means that proper Money represents a consistent and stable unit of exchange such that its Value today is the same or similar as its Value tomorrow. Contrary to false presumptions, this does not mean the medium of Money itself must be of some intrinsic value, but that the integrity of Money is protected, through minimisation of counterfeiting, speculation and rapid valuation or devaluation swings – meaning all that impact on the wealth and function of a Market. Therefore, Reliable Store of Value is essentially linked to the Rules of Market in relation to Money as much as to the Rules of Production of any physical representation of Money to minimise counterfeiting.

1369. A system of rules, measures, records, accounts and procedures that is incapable or refuses to provide the five essential criteria of Money (i.e. Unit of Measure, Unit of Account, Unit of Redemption for Value, Means of Exchange and Reliable Store of Value) therefore cannot be considered Money, but an inferior or fraudulent system of accounts and trade. *System that does not match element of money invalid*

1370. In accord with the customs, traditions and maxims of law concerning Money, since the beginning of Human Civilisation, all proper Money may be divided into four primary categories being Ecclesiastical, Public, Private and Personal:- *Four Categories of Money*

(i) *Ecclesiastical Money* is the highest, most valuable form of Money and form of Legal Tender since the beginning of Human Civilisation and the origin of the very notion of Money itself. The highest form of Ecclesiastical Money ever formed is the Supreme Credo (Credit) as defined by the most sacred Covenant *Pactum De Singularis Caelum* and the basis of all Ucadia Money; and

(ii) *Public Money* is Money and a form of Legal Tender issued as a Public Fund against the Credit in Trust and Assets of a body politic, or constituted society as a single Market and then managed by its Officers as Trustees; and

(iii) *Private Money*, also known as Currency and a form of Legal Tender, is Money issued under license and privilege to a party, usually a bank, holding certain assets within the Market; and then granted some form of exclusive license to have its financial instruments treated "as if" Public Money; and

(iv) *Personal Money*, also known as Credit Money, is Money issued under the Bylaws of a party holding assets within the market, such as one reserve bank or a network of savings and investment banks, or even a private corporation.

1371. **Currency** is defined as Private Money that by authority of some legislative body or sovereign power permits such Currency to be circulated as if equivalent to Public Money. Therefore, all forms of Currency may be defined as pseudo Public Money, controlled by an elite merchant class and then endorsed and protected by an elite political class against the common good, trust and well-being of the body politic.

<small>Currency</small>

1372. **Legal Tender**, also known as Lawful Money, is any form of Money or Instrument that may be tendered for the payment of a debt or obligation:-

<small>Legal Tender</small>

(i) Properly formed and mandated Ecclesiastical Money, consistent and in accord with the most sacred Covenant *Pactum De Singularis Caelum* is always Legal Tender in any and every valid body politic, or properly constituted society; and

(ii) Proper Public Money is naturally Legal Tender by definition, within the body politic or society where it relates; and

(iii) Private Money is only Legal Tender to the extent it is granted such privilege by the legislative body of the body politic or society where it relates; and

(iv) Instruments and Commodities may only be Legal Tender when granted such privilege by the legislative body of the body politic or society where it relates.

1373. **Cash** is the Sum of all Instruments and Items that circulate among members of a body politic or society or Market as proper Money, including (but not limited to) Ecclesiastical Money, Public Money, Private Money, Personal Money and Commodities considered ready stores of value such as precious metals and gems.

<small>Cash</small>

Article 385 – Financial Rights and Authority

1374. By Divine, Ecclesiastical, Sovereign and Administrative Rights, all Rights to impose any form of Rent, Toll, Levy, Contribution or Charge against Money shall be subject to the most sacred Covenant *Pactum De Singularis Caelum*, associated covenants, charters, constitutions and laws and no other:-

<small>Rights to impose Rent, Toll, Levy, Contributions or Charges against Money</small>

(i) *Ius Divinum Vectigalis Moneta* exists as the highest Divine

Rights to impose Rents, Tolls, Levies, Contributions or Charges against Money; and

(ii) *Ius Ecclesiae Vectigalis Moneta* exists as the highest Ecclesiastical Rights to impose Rents, Tolls, Levies, Contributions or Charges against Money, as inherited from the Divine Rights *Ius Divinum Vectigalis Moneta*; and

(iii) *Ius Regnum Vectigalis Moneta* exists as the highest Sovereign Rights to impose Rents, Tolls, Levies, Contributions or Charges against Money, as inherited from the Ecclesiastical Rights *Ius Ecclesiae Vectigalis Moneta*; and

(iv) *Ius Administrationis Vectigalis Moneta* exists as the highest Administrative Rights to impose Rents, Tolls, Levies, Contributions or Charges against Money, as inherited from the Sovereign Rights *Ius Regnum Vectigalis Moneta*.

1375. Only bodies, trusts, estates, funds, persons and entities duly authorised by the appropriate Ucadian Rights shall then have the authority to impose Rents, Tolls, Levies, Contributions or Charges against Money:- *Authority to impose Rent, Toll, Levy, Contributions or Charges against Money and notion of Interest*

(i) A body, trust, estate, fund, person or entity without proper authority from the present most sacred Covenant, or associated covenants, charters, constitutions or laws shall have no right to impose Rents, Tolls, Levies, Contributions or Charges against Money; and

(ii) The use of the term "Interest" is permitted, including the representation of authorised Rents, Tolls, Levies, Contributions or Charges against Money as a percentage, providing the identity and function of such an imposition is clearly identified and disclosed; and

(iii) The failure to properly disclose the valid and legitimate identity and function behind the use of the term "Interest" and the simplification of representing such impositions as a percentage shall render such a Document, Form or Instrument illegitimate, invalid and liable for suspension, termination or dissolution with no right to relief, redress or compensation.

1376. Any and all forms of compound interest, by any name, representation or calculation shall be a profane act of sacrilege against Divine, Ecclesiastical and Sovereign Law; and a deliberate declaration and act of perfidy, treachery and immorality against all proper Executive and Administrative Law; and shall therefore be banned, forbidden and entirely suppressed. *Compound Interest Forbidden*

1377. By Divine, Ecclesiastical, Sovereign, Official and Administrative Rights, all Rights to function as a treasury or bank or financial institution, including (but not limited to) the issue of credit, accept deposits, grant loans, advances, cash, overdrafts, discounting of bills, letters of credit, safety deposits, insurance and conversion shall be subject to the most sacred Covenant *Pactum De Singularis Caelum*, associated covenants, charters, constitutions and laws and no other:-

Rights to act and function as Treasury or Financial (Banking) Body

   (i) *Ius Divinum Templum* exists as the highest Divine Rights of a valid and legitimate Treasury or Financial (Banking) Body; and

   (ii) *Ius Ecclesiae Templum* exists as the highest Ecclesiastical Rights of a valid and legitimate Treasury or Financial (Banking) Body, as inherited from the Divine Rights *Ius Divinum Templum*; and

   (iii) *Ius Regnum Templum* exists as the highest Sovereign Rights of a valid and legitimate Treasury or Financial (Banking) Body, as inherited from the Ecclesiastical Rights *Ius Ecclesiae Templum*; and

   (iv) *Ius Administrationis Templum* exists as the highest Administrative Rights of a valid and legitimate Treasury or Financial (Banking) Body, as inherited from the Sovereign Rights *Ius Regnum Templum*.

Article 386 - Ucadia Money

1378. By Divine, Ecclesiastical, Sovereign and Administrative Rights, Ucadia Money shall be the highest form of valid and legitimate Money, consistent and in accord with the most sacred Covenant *Pactum De Singularis Caelum*:-

Ucadia Money

   (v) *Ius Divinum Moneta* exists as the highest Divine Rights to Mint, Produce, Hold, Use and Exchange Money; and

   (vi) *Ius Ecclesiae Moneta* exists as the highest Ecclesiastical Rights to Mint, Produce, Hold, Use and Exchange Money, as inherited from the Divine Rights *Ius Divinum Moneta*; and

   (vii) *Ius Regnum Moneta* exists as the highest Sovereign Rights to Mint, Produce, Hold, Use and Exchange Money, as inherited from the Ecclesiastical Rights *Ius Ecclesiae Moneta*; and

   (viii) *Ius Administrationis Moneta* exists as the highest Administrative Rights to Mint, Produce, Hold, Use and

Exchange Money, as inherited from the Sovereign Rights *Ius Regnum Moneta*.

1379. In accord with fundamental maxims of Law of all competent civilisations since the beginning of time, Ucadia Money is Ecclesiastical Money and the highest possible form of Money or Currency: -
    Ucadia Money as highest form of money

    (i) As Ucadia Money is the highest form of Ecclesiastical Money, the Circulation of Ucadia Money shall determine the Circulation of all lesser forms of Money; and

    (ii) Furthermore, as Ucadia Money is recognised and acknowledged as Legal Tender for the payment, discharge and settlement of all debits, debts, obligations, taxes, fines and penalties, whether they be public or private; or domestic or foreign, in relation to any and all societies, bodies politic, communities, associations, trusts, estates, funds, corporations, aggregates and persons; and

    (iii) Excluding periods of declared "Emergency" by the Board of Directors, all Ucadia Money shall be used solely for the payment, discharge and settlement of all debts, debits, obligations, taxes, fines and penalties between Ucadia Members, using Ucadia Money Accounts where such sums are stated in Ucadia Money amounts.

1380. In accord with the present sacred Covenant unless the context requires otherwise:-
    Values of Exchange

    (i) One Supreme Credo (Credit) is equivalent to One Hundred (100) Ucadia Gold Credo; and

    (ii) One Supreme Credo (Credit) is equivalent to One Million (1,000,000) Ucadia Silver Credo; and

    (iii) One Supreme Credo (Credit) is equivalent to One Billion (1,000,000,000) Ucadia Union Moneta; and

    (iv) One Supreme Credo (Credit) is equivalent to One Billion (1,000,000,000) Ucadia University Moneta.

1381. When a duly recorded and authorised tender to the correct sum of Ucadia Money for the payment, discharge and settlement of all debts, debits, obligations, taxes, fines and penalties is refused, rejected or dishonoured by a society, or body politic, or community, or association, or trust, or estate, or fund, or corporation or person, then such a profane, unlawful, illegal and immoral action shall be a formal acknowledgement and confession of a debt and obligation equal in
    Tendering of Ucadia Money

value to the sum refused, rejected or dishonoured.

Article 387 – Ucadia Financial System (UFS)

1382. The Ucadia Financial System (UFS) is a comprehensive and complete global financial system of *Laws, Legal Structures and Constructs, Courts and Legal Enforcement, Registers and Rolls, Instruments of Value, Agreements of Value, Markets, Accounts, Credit, Money, Treasuries, Banks, Firms,* and *Goods* capable of operating as a self contained system, or underwriting, or amalgamating or successfully replacing non-Ucadian financial systems of a city, state, nation or region or globe, in accord with the most sacred Covenant *Pactum De Singularis Caelum*.

Ucadia Financial System (UFS)

The fourteen (14) core elements of the Ucadia Financial System (UFS) include:-

(i) *Laws* that consistently define the rules of the Ucadia Financial System; and

(ii) *Legal Structures and Constructs* such as Rights, Trusts, Estates, Property and Funds that enable the consistent establishment of ownership, value and the administration of intangible and tangible forms of property; and

(iii) *Courts and Legal Enforcement* that ensure the honest and impartial application of Laws and enforcement and protection of Legal Structures and Constructs; and

(iv) *Registers and Rolls* for the recording of various Legal Structures and Constructs of Value, including Instruments derived therefrom; and

(v) *Instruments of Value* derived from Registers and Rolls, capable of being exchanged themselves, or being held as collateral and security; and

(vi) *Agreements of Value* signalling transactions of economic activity, capable of being held as collateral as security, or monetised (converted or securitised) into an Instrument of Value; and

(vii) *Markets* for the various exchanges of rights, obligations, credit, goods, property, instruments, funds and money between market participants; and

(viii) *Accounts* being the ledgers of Markets and various Institutions, enabling the recording of transactions, exchanges and settlements; and

(ix) *Credit* being an internal and enclosed form of Money of a Market, enabling exchange and the settlement of transactions, but that in order to be exchanged as money beyond the market must be "converted" by means of the negotiability (portability) of Instruments, Agreements and/or Goods that accompanies the issuance of such Credit; and

(x) *Money* being units of measure, units of account, units of redemption for value, means of exchange and reliable stores of value; and

(xi) *Treasuries* being the custodians and controllers of Money and the purchasers of Securitised Instruments and Agreements purchased by Banks in the conversion of Financial Credit into Money; and

(xii) *Banks* being the providers of Credit into certain Financial Markets and the sponsors (converters) of Credit into Money through the collateralisation of monetisable Instruments and Agreements secured in the provision of such Credit; and

(xiii) *Firms* being trading entities within Markets and the producers of Goods available and capable of being sold or exchanged within those Markets; and

(xiv) *Goods* (including Services) manufactured by Firms and sold and traded within Markets.

1383. A structure shall not be legally, lawfully or morally considered a Financial System, no matter how complex, universally adopted or accepted, if it engages in any of the following practices:- When an structure is not a legitimate Financial System

(i) That the Laws of the system may be changed arbitrarily to the betterment of a few and the detriment of others, without fair recourse or remedy; or

(ii) That units of value may be introduced as money without any legitimate underwriting, thus devaluing the total stock of existing units of money; or

(iii) That units of value may be destroyed or withdrawn, without account for the provenance or historical basis of such lost units, thus inflating the remaining value of total stock of units of money; or

(iv) That credit may be introduced into a market, without defined rules as to the limits of credit of the market, nor the prior allocation rights of participants; and further that such credit may be exported and converted into "money", thus devaluing the total stock of existing unit of money; or

(v) That instruments issued in reference to credit, or agreements, including all derivatives thereof, are permitted to exceed the value of the original value of the asset that created all subsequent derivatives.

Title XI - Divine Property

11.1 - Divine Property

Article 388 - Property

1384. ***Property*** is the highest Right a Person has or can have within a Lawful Jurisdiction to Control or Use or Claim any Thing or the Fruits of any Thing. Property

1385. Divine Property is the highest Divine Right a Divine Person has or can have within a Divine Jurisdiction to Control or Use or Claim any Thing or the Fruits of any Thing. Divine Property

1386. By definition, as all forms of Rights are derived from valid and legitimate Divine Rights, all forms of Property and Things are ultimately derived from the rules of Divine Property as defined by the present Maxims and the most sacred Covenant *Pactum De Singularis Caelum*:- Divine Origin of all Rights and Property

    (i) Just as no form of valid or legitimate Right can exist outside of the absolute jurisdiction, power and control of the Divine, no form of Property can possibly exist outside of the absolute power and control of the Divine; and

    (ii) Any argument, claim, statute, rule, of law that refutes such facts concerning Property renders such false arguments null and void from the beginning.

1387. In reference to Property, Rights and Things:- Property, Rights and Things

    (i) Property always pertains to Persons and not Beings; and

    (ii) A Thing in the context of Property is any Right that can be purchased or sold or inherited; and attached by operation of law to a corporeal object, whether fixed or movable; and

    (iii) Any Right that can be purchased or sold or inherited means a Right in Trust without a named Beneficiary and therefore a Good; and

    (iv) When one is recorded in a valid Register as possessing a Right or Claim of Right over Control or Use, then they may be referred to as the "Owner" of that Right; and

    (v) As all Property pertains to Rights in Trust, the resolution of all proper Transfer of ownership must be completed in Trust.

1388. In reference to the concepts of an Absolute Right versus a Claim of Right:- Absolute versus Claim of Right over Property

    (i) An Absolute Right is one recorded and acknowledge within a particular Jurisdiction as having no equal or legitimate challenge; and

- (ii) A Claim of Right is the recording and acknowledgement of a Claim, also known as a "Charge" against some Property; and
- (iii) Any Jurisdiction that places a Claim above a properly recorded and acknowledged Absolute Right is without proper rules of Property Law.

1389. There are eight possible forms of Property Rights or "Ownership" of Control or Use or Claim any Thing or the Fruits of any Thing, (in order of status and standing) being:- Forms of Property Rights

- (i) Owner of Right of Control of a Thing; and
- (ii) Owner of Right of Use of a Thing; and
- (iii) Owner of Right of Control of the Fruits of Use of a Thing; and
- (iv) Owner of Right of Use of the Fruits of a Thing; and
- (v) Owner of Claim of Right of Control of a Thing; and
- (vi) Owner of Claim of Right of Use of a Thing; and
- (vii) Owner of Claim of Right of Control of the Fruits of Use of a Thing; and
- (viii) Owner of Claim of Right of Use of the Fruits of a Thing.

1390. In reference to Property and Lawful Jurisdiction:- Property and Lawful Jurisdiction

- (i) Property is always defined within the context of the boundaries and jurisdiction of a particular association, aggregate, society, entity or body of Persons possessing Statutes, Bylaws and Rules defining the limits and operations of Property that reflect the Rule of Law, Justice and Fair Process in accord with the present Maxims and the most sacred Covenant *Pactum De Singularis Caelum*; and
- (ii) A particular association, aggregate, society, entity or body Persons possessing Statutes, Bylaws and Rules defining the limits and operations of Property that deliberately obscures, confuses, clouds, misrepresents or denies the proper status and standing of ownership of Property is a body in delinquency and default against Divine law and therefore without the Rule of Law and Right of Property.

1391. Any and every claim, argument, law or doctrine of Chattel, or Real and Person Chattel that claims the absolute Rights of Property to an elite, or banks, or other bodies to the exclusion of the people is hereby disavowed as an abomination before all Heaven and Earth; and is condemned as a profound sacrilege, heresy, profanity, morally Chattel repugnant, perfidious and deliberately false, having no force or effect in law. Furthermore, every Member of the Sons of Light and Fraternal Brothers and Sisters of Light are fully empowered by Holy Writ, to pursue any, every and all means to ensure any and all records of such profanity, sacrilege and abomination before all Heaven and Earth are expunged, removed, withdrawn, determined, extinguished and abolished, including any and all false presumptions of claiming such false rights under "bankruptcy" or "divine right" or blood heritage or any other falsity.

Article 389 – Ucadia Property

1392. By Divine, Ecclesiastical, Sovereign and Administrative Rights, Ucadia Property Rights shall be the highest form of valid and legitimate Property Rights, consistent and in accord with the most sacred Covenant *Pactum De Singularis Caelum*:-

    (i) *Ius Divinum Proprietatis* exists as the highest Divine Rights of Ownership of Use or Fruits of Use of Property; and

    (ii) *Ius Ecclesiae Proprietatis* exists as the highest Ecclesiastical Rights of Ownership of Use or Fruits of Use of Property, as inherited from the Divine Rights *Ius Divinum Proprietatis*; and

    (iii) *Ius Regnum Proprietatis* exists as the highest Sovereign Rights of Ownership of Use or Fruits of Use of Property, as inherited from the Ecclesiastical Rights *Ius Ecclesiae Proprietatis*; and

    (iv) *Ius Administrationis Proprietatis* exists as the highest Administrative Rights of Ownership of Use or Fruits of Use of Property, as inherited from the Sovereign Rights *Ius Regnum Proprietatis*.

Article 390 - Fund

1393. A ***Fund*** is a sum of equal units representing certain Property Rights of monetary value, recorded in one or more designated accounts of a Body; and set apart for a term of years and one or more specific purposes; and available for the payment of debits, debts, legacies and claims in accord with these Maxims and the most sacred Covenant *Pactum De Singularis Caelum*.

1394. In respect of the character, purpose and nature of a Fund:-

    (i) The Instrument of formation and of guiding the character, purpose and nature of one or more Funds is a Trust Covenant as a Fund Constitution issued and approved by a valid Body; and

(ii) The underlying Rights and Property used to derive the value of a Fund must be set aside and sealed in its own Trust in accord with the Trust Covenant to protect the integrity of the Fund and prevent any re-transfer or re-conveyance that might threaten the value of the Fund. This means, the only ownership of rights of property that may be conveyed or discharged against the underlying Rights and Property are Claims, also known as "Charges"; and

(iii) The life or operation of a Fund (the period it conducts business) shall be the 128 year maximum as specified by the most sacred Covenant *Pactum De Singularis Caelum*, unless otherwise required by law to be the Western-Roman custom of a maximum of 70 years; and

(iv) A Fund may be actual money, or notes, or certificates, or securities or stocks able to be converted or negotiated for monetary value, providing the nature and monetary value of each element is clearly outlined within the accounts of the Fund; and

(v) The terms of negotiation of the Stock of a Fund for other stock, or actual money, or notes, or certificates, or other securities is determined on a Fund by Fund basis, including whether a particular Fund is able to purchase the Stock of another Fund, to what maximum and other conditions (if any); and

(vi) A Fund is never the original Assets themselves, but the Derivation of the value of the underlying Property, as recorded in the accounts and ledgers of the Fund, to permit the remission, remittance, settlement and discharge of debits, debts and obligations; and

(vii) When the term of a Fund expires, it is absolutely forbidden to conduct any more new business. However, it may continue to manage and administer existing business and obligations until all such existing obligations and settlements expire or are balanced or dissolved or liquidated; and

(viii) The property and assets held in Trust are absolutely forbidden to be released from such a Trust underwriting a Fund until after the term of a Fund expires and after all obligations and settlements are balanced and the fund dissolved or liquidated and the purpose of the Trust is fulfilled and the Trust dissolved; and

(ix) A Fund ceases to exist when it is properly liquidated or dissolved by an action in accord with the instrument of its creation, or after the expiry of its term. In accord with these Maxims, the administrators of a valid Fund are morally obligated to ensure the timely dissolution of the Fund as soon as practical after such a valid event.

1395. The Capital Stock of a Fund is divided into equal and indivisible units of account called "Stocks", whereby such units of value shall grant a valid and registered holder ("Stockholder") certain Rights to participate in the management of the Fund and to share in its net profits or earnings. Capital Stock of Fund

Article 391 - Asset

1396. An *Asset* is a sum of units of monetary value, recorded in one or more designated accounts, available for the discharge of a debt and not yet assigned to a specific purpose. Asset

Article 392 - Good

1397. A *Good* is a gift in Trust; or a promise associated with a beneficial Right of Use for Sale or Bargain. Good

1398. A Good can mean one of three Things:- Reference to Good

(i) An Exchange of gifts between a buyer and a seller; or

(ii) An Exchange of a gift of a seller with a promise of a buyer; or

(iii) An Exchange of promises between a buyer and a seller.

Article 393 - Sale

1399. A *Sale* is when the title to a thing is given in Trust to another in exchange for a price of lawful money, also given in trust. Sale

1400. In reference to the concept of a Sale:- Reference to Sale

(i) A Sale always involves Goods and therefore always involves Rights in Trust as Goods; and

(ii) A Sale always involves two distinct trusts having two distinct trust corpus – one where the buyer is trustee and one where the seller is trustee; and

(iii) It is only when the sale is completed do the two separate trusts dissolve, providing the conditions of sale make that possible.

Article 394 - Bargain

1401. A ***Bargain*** is a Contract of Mutual Bindings (Promises) in Trust as Security whereby one party promises to assign a right as property for some consideration; and the other party promises to receive the property and take good care of it and pay the consideration.
Bargain

1402. In reference to the concept of a Bargain of Goods:-
Reference to Bargain

    (i)   A Bargain always involves Goods and therefore always involves Rights in Trust as Goods; and

    (ii)   Similar to a Sale, a Bargain always involves two Trusts for a Bargain to exist: The one for the Buyer and one for the Seller; and

    (iii)   A Bargain is not a transfer of Title but a Bailment of Goods or Use for some financial consideration; and

    (iv)   The Seller never gifts the property like a Sale and the terms of Consideration may also involve some return of a Bailment of Money; and

    (v)   The key operating element of a Bargain is the Mutual Binding Promises that are also called Debts.

1403. In reference to the concept of mutual debts of a Bargain:-
Mutual Debts of Bargain

    (i)   There are always two debts associated with any valid Bargain: The debt of the buyer and the debt of the seller. Just as there are two valid trusts and two valid trustees (Buyer and Seller) and two debtor-creditor relations with the two trusts; and

    (ii)   A Contract without two separate and distinct debts and relations is inchoate (incomplete).

Title XII - Divine Dominions

12.1 - Divine Dominions

Article 395 - Divine Dominion

1404. ***One Heaven*** is the official name and title defining the levels and dimensions of Unique Collective Awareness of all Existences, Concepts, Objects, Properties, Laws, Theories, Imaginations and Realities unto itself as it pertains to unique higher order (self-aware) conscious forms within the Local Group of Galaxies [Trust No. 000000-300000-000001] that the Milky Way Galaxy [Trust No. 000000-400000- 000001] is part thereof. Within the context of the Unique Collective Awareness, being a formal name of the Divine Creator of all Existence, no other official name and title than One Heaven shall have higher standing or authority in respect of this region of consciousness and the associated trillions of star systems and planets within the same region of the Universe.

Divine Dominion

1405. In reference to Divine Dominion and One Heaven :-

Divine Dominion of One Heaven

  (i) When anyone speaks or writes of Heaven, or Paradise, or the Afterlife, or the Otherworld, or Jannah, or Nirvana, or Valhalla, or Folkvangr, or Olympus, or Utopia, or Gan Eden, or Aaru, or Elysium, or Vaikuntha, or Tirna, or Tlalocan, or any other term of a similar nature, it shall mean One Heaven as defined by the most sacred Covenant *Pactum De Singularis Caelum* and no other; and

  (ii) Similarly, when anyone speaks or writes of Hell, or Hades, or Mundi, or Purgatory, or Sea of Souls, or the Underworld, or any other term of a similar nature, it shall also mean One Heaven as defined by the most sacred Covenant *Pactum De Singularis Caelum* and no other, as the unification of all dimensions of consciousness as one; and

  (iii) Furthermore, when anyone speaks or writes of inter-dimensions, or multi-verses or any other models describing consciousness or constructs, it shall mean One Heaven as defined by the most sacred Covenant *Pactum De Singularis Caelum* and no other.

Article 396 - Universal Ecclesia of One Christ

1406. The most sacred and ***Universal Ecclesia of One Christ***, also known as the One Holy Apostolic Universal Ecclesia, also known as the Sol Ecclesia, also known as the Authentic Body of Christ and also known simply as One Christ, is the first, highest and supreme

Universal Ecclesia of One Christ

association, aggregate, fraternity, body, entity and society of One Heaven sharing spiritual heritage associated with all forms of Christian and Jewish faith; and the embodiment of the Kingdom of Heaven upon the Earth.

1407. In reference to the Universal Ecclesia of One Christ:-

    (i)   In accord with the intention and consent of the one true Divine Creator, all existence, angels, saints, demons and all spirits of united Heaven it is hereby pronounced that any deceased or presently living higher order life being having professed their trust and obligation in Christian or Jewish customs and traditions is a Member of One Christ as well as a Member of One Heaven; and

    (ii)   All living Higher Life Forms who profess to be Christian or Jewish are *ipso facto* (as a matter of fact) subject first to the laws of One Heaven and second to the laws of the Universal Ecclesia of One Christ above any other lesser society, association, aggregate, institute, fraternity, society, entity or body; and

    (iii)   Furthermore, it is hereby pronounced that all and every ordained, acknowledged, commissioned or certified clergy of any Christian or Jewish body are also officers of the Universal Ecclesia of One Christ; and subject to the laws and obligations of One Christ first above any other lesser society, association, aggregate, institute, fraternity, society, entity or body.

Article 397 - Holy Society of One Islam

1408. The most sacred and **Holy Society of One Islam**, also known as the One True Way of Allah, also known as the One Umma and also known simply as One Islam, is the first, highest and supreme association, aggregate, fraternity, body, entity and society of One Heaven sharing spiritual heritage associated with all forms of Islam; and the embodiment of the Kingdom of Paradise of Allah upon the Earth.

1409. In reference to the Holy Society of One Islam:-

    (i)   In accord with the intention and consent of the one true Divine Creator, all existence, angels, saints, demons and all spirits of united Heaven it is hereby pronounced that any deceased or presently living higher order life being having professed their trust and obligation in Islam is a Member of One Islam as well as a Member of One Heaven; and

(ii) All living Higher Life Forms who profess to be Muslim are ipso facto (as a matter of fact) subject first to the laws of One Heaven and second to the laws of the Holy Society of One Islam above any other lesser society, association, aggregate, institute, fraternity, society, entity or body; and

(iii) Furthermore, it is hereby pronounced that all and every ordained, acknowledged, commissioned or certified clergy of any Islamic body are also officers of the Holy Society of One Islam; and subject to the laws and obligations of One Islam first above any other lesser society, association, aggregate, institute, fraternity, society, entity or body.

Article 398 - Sacred Society of One Spirit

1410. The most **Sacred Society of One Spirit**, also known as the One Holy Apostolic Spirit, also known as One Spirit Tribe and also known simply as One Spirit, is the first, highest and supreme association, aggregate, fraternity, body, entity and society of One Heaven sharing spiritual heritage associated with traditional, indigenous, Earth based, meditative and eastern customary faiths.

Sacred Society of One Spirit

1411. In reference to the Sacred Society of One Spirit:-

Reference to Sacred Society of One Spirit

(i) In accord with the intention and consent of the one true Divine Creator, all existence, angels, saints, demons and all spirits of united Heaven it is hereby pronounced that any deceased or presently living higher order life being having professed their faith in Hinduism, Buddhism, Taoism, Janism or any other traditional customary faith is a Member of One Spirit Tribe as well as a Member of One Heaven; and

(ii) All living Higher Life Forms who profess to be Hindu, Buddhist, Taoist or any other traditional customary faith are ipso facto (as a matter of fact) subject first to the laws of One Heaven and second to the laws of One Spirit Tribe above any other lesser society, association, aggregate, institute, fraternity, society, entity or body; and

(iii) Furthermore, it is hereby pronounced that all and every all ordained, acknowledged, commissioned or certified clergy of any Hindu, Buddhist or other traditional spiritual body are officers of One Spirit Tribe and subject to the laws and obligations of One Spirit Tribe first above any other lesser society, association, aggregate, institute, fraternity, society, entity or body.

Article 399 - Globe Union

1412. By the power and authority of the most sacred Covenant *Pactum De Singularis Caelum*, the **Society of Globe Union**, also known as the Globe Union of Unions of free Societies over the whole Earth and See is vested with the full political authority and powers for all Members of One Heaven associated with carnations of Level 6 Higher Order Life Forms as Members of the Homo Sapien Species.

Ucadia Globe Union

1413. In reference to the Ucadia Globe Union:-

(i) All living Members of the Homo Sapien Species are ipso facto (as a matter of fact) Members of the Ucadia Globe Union; and

(ii) The sacred Covenant of the Ucadia Globe Union also known as *Carta Sacrum De Congregatio Globus* shall be regarded as a Supremely sacred and valuable object and the temporal instrument of association on planet Earth in accord and consistent with the Maxims of Divine Law; and

(iii) No other body politic, association, corporation, company, person, entity or group representing lesser bodies may claim higher political jurisdiction than the Globe Union for planet Earth.

Reference to Ucadia Globe Union

Title XIII - Divine Covenants

13.1 - Divine Covenants

Article 400 – Divine Covenant

1414. A ***Divine Covenant*** is a sacred and binding agreement upon one or more promises, between the Divine, or an aspect of the Divine and a group of higher order beings, consistent with the these Maxims.

    Divine Covenant

1415. In reference to Divine Covenants:-

    General Nature of Divine Covenants

    (i) As a valid lawful solemn sacred and binding pact, a Divine Covenant witnessed or executed or ratified within a temporal realm, requires the existence of at least one person possessing sufficient characteristics of being a Sapient Singularity as the representative of the Divine and at least two other witnesses or followers; and

    (ii) As a lawful agreement, a Divine Covenant must have some authentic or official written evidence or account of its clauses and terms; and

    (iii) As a matter of historic significance, a valid Divine Covenant must be related to and fulfil in some meaningful way sufficient elements of Divine Revelation; and

    (iv) As a matter of both authority and authenticity, the Divine Covenant should be referenced in the context of the most sacred *Covenant Pactum De Singularis Caelum*.

Article 401 - Pactum De Singularis Caelum

1416. ***Pactum De Singularis Caelum*** is the name of the most sacred and supreme Divine Covenant also known as the Covenant of One Heaven.

    Pactum De Singularis Caelum

1417. In reference to the most sacred Covenant *Pactum De Singularis Caelum*:-

    Reference to Pactum De Singularis Caelum

    (i) One Heaven is the official name and title defining the levels and dimensions of Unique Collective Awareness of all Existences, Concepts, Objects, Properties, Laws, Theories, Imaginations and Realities unto itself as it pertains to unique higher order (self-aware) conscious forms within the Local Group of Galaxies [Trust No. 000000-300000-000001] that the Milky Way Galaxy [Trust No. 000000-400000-000001] is part thereof. Within the context of the Unique Collective Awareness, being a formal name of the Divine Creator of all Existence, no other official name and title than One Heaven shall have higher standing or authority in respect of this region of consciousness and the associated trillions of star systems and planets within the same region of the Universe; and

(ii) When anyone speaks or writes of Heaven, or Paradise, or the Afterlife, or the Otherworld, or Jannah, or Nirvana, or Valhalla, or Folkvangr, or Olympus, or Utopia, or Gan Eden, or Aaru, or Elysium, or Vaikuntha, or Tirna, or Tlalocan, or any other term of a similar nature, it shall mean One Heaven as defined by the most sacred Covenant *Pactum De Singularis Caelum* and no other; and

(iii) Similarly, when anyone speaks or writes of Hell, or Hades, or Mundi, or Purgatory, or Sea of Souls, or the Underworld, or any other term of a similar nature, it shall also mean the united dimensions of One Heaven as defined by the most sacred Covenant *Pactum De Singularis Caelum* and no other, as the unification of all dimensions of consciousness as one; and

(iv) Furthermore, when anyone speaks or writes of inter-dimensions, or multi-verses or any other models describing consciousness or constructs, it shall mean One Heaven as defined by the most sacred Covenant *Pactum De Singularis Caelum* and no other.

1418. As enacted, the most sacred Covenant *Pactum De Singularis Caelum* is the first and supreme law of One Heaven and the embodiment of Divine Law. No other law is recognised as first or higher than this Covenant. — First and Supreme Law

1419. No higher, greater, more sacred or perfect covenant exists than the most sacred Covenant *Pactum De Singularis Caelum* as the one true and authentic source and origin of all Rights, Powers, Authorities, Property and Title now and forever more. — No Higher Covenant

Article 402 - Pactum De Singularis Christus

1420. The absolute Rights, Powers, Purposes and Functions of the Universal Ecclesia of One Christ shall be encompassed into a most sacred covenant known as **Pactum De Singularis Christus**, also known as the Covenant of One Christ. — Pactum De Singularis Christus

1421. In reference to the sacred covenant *Pactum De Singularis Christus*:- — Reference to Pactum De Singularis Christus

(i) The sacred Covenant *Pactum De Singularis Christus* and the most sacred Covenant *Pactum De Singularis Caelum* are binding agreements between equals, entered in free will and full knowledge being the highest, most powerful, superior concordat and Covenant of all past, present and future possible agreements between the parties of all spirits, living and deceased as unique spirits and Mind and the Divine as the Absolute, the One, the ALL, the Universe, all Galaxies, all Stars, all Planets, all Life, all Existence, all Mind; and

(ii) As the most sacred Covenant *Pactum De Singularis Christus* and the most sacred Covenant *Pactum De Singularis Caelum* is the literal, legal, spiritual and lawful fulfilment of all previous Divine covenants, the present most sacred Covenant Pactum De Singularis Christus is the logical, legitimate and rightful conclusion of any and all historic and valid Divine covenants.

Article 403 - Pactum De Singularis Islam

1422. The absolute Rights, Powers, Purposes and Functions of the Holy Society of One Islam shall be encompassed into a most sacred covenant known as **Pactum De Singularis Islam**, also known as the Covenant of One Islam.

<small>Pactum De Singularis Islam</small>

1423. In reference to the sacred covenant *Pactum De Singularis Islam*:-

<small>Reference to Pactum De Singularis Islam</small>

(i) The most sacred Covenant *Pactum De Singularis Islam* and the present most sacred Covenant *Pactum De Singularis Caelum* are binding agreements between equals, entered in free will and full knowledge being the highest, most powerful, superior concordat and Covenant of all past, present and future possible agreements between the parties of all spirits, living and deceased as unique spirits and Mind and the Divine as the Absolute, the One, the ALL, the Universe, all Galaxies, all Stars, all Planets, all Life, all Existence, all Mind; and

(ii) As the most sacred Covenant *Pactum De Singularis Islam* and the most sacred Covenant *Pactum De Singularis Caelum* is the literal, legal, spiritual and lawful fulfilment of all previous Divine covenants, the present most sacred Covenant Pactum De Singularis Islam is the logical, legitimate and rightful conclusion of any and all historic and valid Divine covenants.

Article 404 - Pactum De Singularis Spiritus

1424. The absolute Rights, Powers, Purposes and Functions of the Sacred Society of One Spirit shall be encompassed into a most sacred covenant known as **Pactum De Singularis Spiritus**, also known as the Covenant of One Spirit.

<small>Pactum De Singularis Spiritus</small>

1425. In reference to the sacred covenant *Pactum De Singularis Spiritus*:- Reference to Pactum De Singularis Spiritus

    (i) The most sacred Covenant *Pactum De Singularis Spiritus* and the most sacred Covenant *Pactum De Singularis Caelum* are binding agreements between equals, entered in free will and full knowledge being the highest, most powerful, superior concordat and Covenant of all past, present and future possible agreements between the parties of all spirits, living and deceased as unique spirits and Mind and the Divine as the Absolute, the One, the ALL, the Universe, all Galaxies, all Stars, all Planets, all Life, all Existence, all Mind; and

    (ii) As the most sacred Covenant *Pactum De Singularis Spiritus* and the most sacred Covenant *Pactum De Singularis Caelum* is the literal, legal, spiritual and lawful fulfilment of all previous Divine covenants, the present most sacred Covenant Pactum De Singularis Spiritus is the logical, legitimate and rightful conclusion of any and all historic and valid Divine covenants.

11.2 - Traditional Divine Covenants

Article 405 - Traditional Divine Covenants

1426. In accord with the most sacred Covenant *Pactum De Singularis Caelum*, the Thirty Three Covenants between Authentic, Apostolic and Anointed Divine Messengers of the Divine Creator of all Existence and all the Heavens and Earth and the peoples of the Earth are entrusted as the Authentic Sacred Deposit of Trust (*Authenticus Depositum Fidei*), contained in Sacred Canonical Scripture and Tradition. Traditional Divine Covenants

1427. Thirty-Three (33) Sacred Covenants between Authentic, Apostolic and Anointed Divine Messengers of the Divine Creator of all Existence and all the Heavens and Earth and the peoples of the Earth are acknowledged as having merit, authority, power and jurisdiction above all others by custom and tradition, namely:- Tradition of the Thirty-Three Sacred Covenants of Heaven

    (i) **"De Dea Magisterium"** of the Serpens (Creators); and

    (ii) **"Yapa"** of the Pacific Saltwater People; and

    (iii) **"Mandi"** of the African Plains People; and

    (iv) **"Tia"** of the Asiatic Mountain People; and

    (v) **"Waiata"** of the Pacific Sea People; and

Title XIII – Divine Covenants

(vi) "**Adamus**" of Prometheus and the Cuilliaéan; and

(vii) "**Nana**" of the Mother Goddess of Heaven and Earth; and

(viii) "**Alma**" of South Arabia, East Africa and India; and

(ix) "**Elohim**" of Abraham and Patriarchs of Ebla; and

(x) "**Kabalaah**" of Akhenaten (Moses) and the Yahudi; and

(xi) "**Revelations**" of the thirty-three Great Prophets of Yeb; and

(xii) "**Tara**" of Jeremiah and the Celts; and

(xiii) "**Five Worlds**" of North-Central America; and

(xiv) "**Missal**" of Baal Mithra; and

(xv) "**Acadia**" of Xerxes; and

(xvi) "**Eliada**" of Alexander; and

(xvii) "**Tabiti**" of Great Asiatic Plains People; and

(xviii) "**Tiandi**" (Heaven and Earth) of Qin Shi Huang; and

(xix) "**Nazara (Truth)**" of Yahusiah (Jesus Christ); and

(xx) "**Nirvana**" (Freedom & Awakening) of Gautama (Buddha); and

(xxi) "**Zhongdao**" (The Middle Way) of Kong Qiu (Confucius); and

(xxii) "**Septuaginta**" of Iudaism (Josephus); and

(xxiii) "**Eucadia**" of Heracles; and

(xxiv) "**Kikilil Yuum Witzil**" (Great Cycle of Celestial Realm and Earth) of South-Central America; and

(xxv) "**Digesta**" of Marcus Aurelius; and

(xxvi) "**Sanatana Dharma**" (Eternal Truth) of Brahman (Hinduism); and

(xxvii) "**Bibliographe**" of Christianity of Constantine; and

(xxviii) "**Dao**" (the Way); and

(xxix) "**Kami Yoso Seimei**" (Spirits of Elements and Life) of the way of Shinto (Japan); and

(xxx) "**Quran Al Sufian**" (Recitations of Wisdom of the Way)" of

Lex Divina: Maxims of Divine Law

> The Great Prophet (Islam); and
>
> (xxxi) **"Holy Bible"** of Catholicism of the Franks; and
>
> (xxxii) **"Eternal Truth"** of Gurmat (Sikhism); and
>
> (xxxiii) **"Lebor Clann Glas"** of the Holly Diaspora.

1428. In accord with the most sacred Covenant *Pactum De Singularis Caelum*, the Thirty-Three (33) Covenants between Authentic, Apostolic and Anointed Divine Messengers of the Divine Creator of all Existence and all the Heavens and Earth and the peoples of the Earth are entrusted as the "**Authentic Sacred Deposit of Trust**":- Authentic Sacred Deposit of Trust

   (i) The Universal Ecclesia of One Christ may use the name "***Authenticus Depositum Fidei***" to officially describe the *Authentic Sacred Deposit of Trust* as it applies to their authority; and

   (ii) The Holy Society of One Islam may use the name "***Asilah Alwadiea Lilthiqa***" to officially describe the *Authentic Sacred Deposit of Trust* as it applies to their authority; and

   (iii) The Sacred Society of One Spirit may use the name "***Satya Avasada Shraddha***" to officially describe the *Authentic Sacred Deposit of Trust* as it applies to their authority.

1429. In respect of the *Covenant of De Dea Magisterium* of the Serpens:- Covenant of De Dea Magisterium of the Serpens

   (i) The Covenant of De Dea Magisterium of the Serpens embodies in sacred trust the complete consciousness, culture, languages, rules, symbols, rituals, laws and rights of the Serpens as the creators of Homo Prometheus, the "horned ones", that chose to integrate within the Homo Sapien species in the form of the Cuilliaéan, to help free the Homo Sapien species of its programming and condemnation by the Griseo Morbidus (Standard Grey) and Griseo Altus (Tall Grey) as architects of the Homo Robustus, the Homo Habilis and Homo Sapiens; and

   (ii) The complete consciousness, culture, languages, rules, symbols, rituals, laws and rights of the Serpens embodied within the Covenant of De Dea Magisterium of the Serpens is entrusted through the Authentic Sacred Deposit of Trust (*Authenticus Depositum Fidei*).

1430. In respect of the *Covenant of Yapa of the Saltwater People*:- Covenant of Yapa of the Saltwater People

   (i) The Saltwater People of planet Earth are the aggregate of the first Original Nations (Tribes) and traditional owners of hominid species of South-East Asia, Australia and parts of the Pacific beginning in the mid-Palaeolithic period and rising to a high culture of law, language and knowledge during the Mesolithic period; and

(ii) The Covenant of Yapa of the Saltwater People embodies in sacred trust the complete consciousness, culture, languages, rules, symbols, rituals, laws and rights of the first Original Nations (Tribes) and traditional owners of hominid species of South-East Asia, Australia and parts of the Pacific; and

(iii) The complete consciousness, culture, languages, rules, symbols, rituals, laws and rights of the first cultures and traditional owners of hominid species of South-East Asia, Australia and parts of the Pacific embodied within the Covenant of Yapa of the Saltwater People is entrusted through the Authentic Sacred Deposit of Trust (*Authenticus Depositum Fidei*).

1431. In respect of the *Covenant of Mandi of the Africa Plains People*:-

Covenant of Mandi of the Africa Plains People

(i) The Africa Plains People of planet Earth are the aggregate of the first cultures and traditional owners of hominid species of the ancient African Lakes, Great River and Fertile Plains of Northern Africa and the whole of Africa beginning in the mid-Palaeolithic period and rising to a high culture of law, language and knowledge during the Mesolithic period; and

(ii) The Covenant of Mandi of the Africa Plains People embodies in sacred trust the complete consciousness, culture, languages, rules, symbols, rituals, laws and rights of the first Original Nations (Tribes) and traditional owners of hominid species of the ancient African Lakes, Great River and Fertile Plains of Northern Africa and the whole of Africa; and

(iii) The complete consciousness, culture, languages, rules, symbols, rituals, laws and rights of the first cultures and traditional owners of hominid species of the ancient African Lakes, Great River and Fertile Plains of Northern Africa and the whole of Africa embodied within the Covenant of Mandi of the Africa Plains People is entrusted through the Authentic Sacred Deposit of Trust (*Authenticus Depositum Fidei*).

1432. In respect of the *Covenant of Tia of the Asiatic Mountain People*:-

Covenant of Tia of the Asiatic Mountain People

(i) The Asiatic Mountain People of planet Earth are the aggregate of the first Original Nations (Tribes) and traditional owners of hominid species of mountainous Asia and the Indian sub continent beginning in the mid-Palaeolithic period and rising to a high culture of law, language and knowledge during the Mesolithic period; and

(ii) The Covenant of Tia of the Asiatic Mountain People embodies in sacred trust the complete consciousness, culture, languages, rules, symbols, rituals, laws and rights of the first Original Nations (Tribes) and traditional owners of hominid species of mountainous Asia and the Indian sub continent; and

(iii) The complete consciousness, culture, languages, rules, symbols, rituals, laws and rights of the first cultures and traditional owners of hominid species of mountainous Asia and the Indian sub continent embodied within the Covenant of Tia of the Asiatic Mountain People is entrusted through the Authentic Sacred Deposit of Trust (*Authenticus Depositum Fidei*).

1433. In respect of the *Covenant of Waiata of the Sea People of Asia and Pacific*:-

(i) The Sea People of Asia and Pacific are the aggregate of the Original Nations (Tribes) and traditional owners of hominid species of the Pacific and Asia beginning in the Mesolithic period and rising to a high culture of law, language and knowledge during the Neolithic period; and

(ii) The Covenant of Waiata of the Sea People of Asia and Pacific embodies in sacred trust the complete consciousness, culture, languages, rules, symbols, rituals, laws and rights of the Original Nations (Tribes) and traditional owners of hominid species of the Pacific and Asia; and

(iii) The complete consciousness, culture, languages, rules, symbols, rituals, laws and rights of the cultures and traditional owners of hominid species of the Pacific and Asia embodied within the Covenant of Waiata of the Sea People of Asia and Pacific is entrusted through the Authentic Sacred Deposit of Trust (*Authenticus Depositum Fidei*).

1434. In respect of the *Covenant of Adamus of Homo Prometheus and the Cuilliaéan*:-

(i) The Cuilliaéan of planet Earth are the strongest blood aggregate and personification within the form of Homo Sapiens of the ancient hominid Homo Prometheus, itself the perfected union of the hominids of planet Earth and the Serpens species of other worlds, emerging at the beginning of the Neolithic period and rising to a high culture of law, religion, language and knowledge during the late Neolithic period; and

(ii) The Covenant of *Adamus* of the Cuilliaéan embodies in sacred trust the complete consciousness, culture, languages, rules, symbols, rituals, laws and rights of the Cuilliaéan as the first sons and daughters of men; and the founders of the first empires; and the historic emissaries and representatives of the Griseo Morbidus (Standard Grey), the Cerastis Sapiens (Horned Reptoids), the Serpens Sophos (Smooth Skinned Reptoids), the Griseo Altus (Tall Grey) and the Serpens Alatus (Winged Reptoids); and

(iii) The complete consciousness, culture, languages, rules, symbols, rituals, laws and rights of the first cultures and traditional owners of hominid species of Homo Sapiens of the ancient hominid Homo Prometheus embodied within the Covenant of Adamus of the Cuilliaéan are entrusted through the Authentic Sacred Deposit of Trust (*Authenticus Depositum Fidei*).

1435. In respect of the *Covenant of Nana of the Mother Goddess of Heaven and Earth*:-

_{Covenant of Nana of the Mother Goddess of Heaven and Earth}

(i) The most ancient reverence of the feminine personification of planet Earth, or Life and Spirit in the form of Queen and Mother of Heaven exists through many cultures, peoples and religions from the earliest city-states of Sumeria and Syria; and of ancient Mesopotamian and Near-East Cultures, even to the present day; and

(ii) The Covenant of Nana of the Mother Goddess of Heaven and Earth embodies in sacred trust the complete consciousness, culture, languages, rules, symbols, rituals, laws and rights of the worship of the feminine as goddess and Queen and Mother of Heaven; and

(iii) The complete consciousness, culture, languages, rules, symbols, rituals, laws and rights of the cultures and peoples embodied within the Covenant of Nana as Queen and Mother of Heaven are entrusted through the Authentic Sacred Deposit of Trust (*Authenticus Depositum Fidei*).

1436. In respect of the *Covenant of Alma of the Mother Goddess*:-

Covenant of Alma of South Arabia, East Africa and India

(i) The most ancient reverence of the feminine as goddess and Queen exists through many cultures and peoples of ancient southern Arabia, East Africa and Indus Valley (India); and

(ii) The Covenant of Alma of the Mother Goddess embodies in

> > sacred trust the complete consciousness, culture, languages, rules, symbols, rituals, laws and rights of the worship of the feminine as goddess and Queen; and
>
> > (iii) The complete consciousness, culture, languages, rules, symbols, rituals, laws and rights of the cultures and peoples embodied within the Covenant of Alma as goddess and Queen are entrusted through the Authentic Sacred Deposit of Trust (*Authenticus Depositum Fidei*).
>
> **1437.** In respect of the *Covenant of Elohim of Abraham and Patriarchs*:- — Covenant of Elohim of Abraham and Patriarchs
>
> > (i) The city of Ebla in northern Syria represented one of the greatest cities of human civilisation and the cradle of high culture, knowledge and religion more than four and a half thousand years ago. It is by tradition, the birthplace of some of the greatest Patriarchs of antiquity including, but not limited to Ab-ra-mu (Abraham), E-sa-um (Esau), Ish-ma-ilu (Ishmael), Da-'u'dum (David) and Sa-'u-lum (Saul), later to be overshadowed by the city of Urgarit; and
>
> > (ii) The Covenant of Elohim of Abraham and the Patriarchs embodies in sacred trust the complete consciousness, culture, languages, rules, symbols, rituals, laws and rights of the first cultures and traditional owners of Ebla and the regions of Syria, the Levant and Mesopotamia; and
>
> > (iii) The complete consciousness, culture, languages, rules, symbols, rituals, laws and rights of the first cultures and traditional owners of Ebla and the regions of Syria, the Levant and Mesopotamia embodied within the Covenant of Elohim of Abraham and the Patriarchs is entrusted through the Authentic Sacred Deposit of Trust (*Authenticus Depositum Fidei*).
>
> **1438.** In respect of the *Covenant of Kabalaah of Akhenaten (Moses) and the Yahudi*:- — Covenant of Kabalaah of Akhenaten (Moses) and the Yahudi
>
> > (i) The Hyksos culture of planet Earth is a successor of the Cuilliaéan culture as the strongest blood aggregate and personification within the form of Homo Sapiens of the ancient hominid Homo Prometheus, itself the perfected union of the hominids of planet Earth and the serpens species of other worlds, emerging in Egypt from around 1800 BCE and rising to a high culture of law, religion, language and knowledge by the beginning of the reign of Akhenaten around 1350 BCE; and
>
> > (ii) It is Akhenaten that is Moses and did pledge his symbols of

power and authority of Egypt as signs of a new covenant, such as his Ark of the Spirit of Re, to signify the new Ark of the Covenant; and

(iii) Thus all cultures and religions since, that place the Ark of the Covenant at the forefront of their claims of authenticity and origin are therefore derived from the Covenant and powers of Akhenaten; and

(iv) The Covenant of KabaLaah of Akhenaten (Moses) and the Yahudi embodies in sacred trust the complete consciousness, culture, languages, rules, symbols, rituals, laws and rights of the Yahudi in honoring supremacy of the Divine Creator of all existence; and the spirits of the Earth; and in acknowledging the positive influence and wisdom of the Serpens and the repudiation of the Griseo Morbidus (Standard Grey) and Griseo Altus (Tall Grey); and

(v) The complete consciousness, culture, languages, rules, symbols, rituals, laws and rights of the Yahudi embodied within the Covenant of KaBaLaAh of Akhenaten (Moses) and the Hyksos are entrusted through the Authentic Sacred Deposit of Trust (*Authenticus Depositum Fidei*).

1439. In respect of the *Covenant of Revelations of the Great Prophets of Yeb*:-

Covenant of Revelations of the Great Prophets of Yeb

(i) The Great Prophets of Yeb (Elephantine Island) at Yei-Hu (Yahu) on the Nile River in Upper Egypt, are the oldest and most famous continuous hereditary and apostolic lineage of Divine Messengers of Cuilliaéan blood in the history of the ancient world. As the site of Yei-Hu was the base of the Kabalaah and the Tree of Life between Heaven and Earth, in honour of the primordial mother (Mut) of all Heaven and Earth, the writings of the thirty-three Great prophets of Yeb remains some of the most important scripture of humanity; and

(ii) The thirty-three (33) Great Prophets of Yeb were Aaroniah, Enociah, Zedekiah, Obadiah, Uvidiah (David), Elijiah, Ahijiah, Azariah, Ananiah, Amoziah, Isaiah, Ezekiah, Amariah, Edaliah, Zephaniah, Ilkiah (Michaiah), Jeremiah, Barukiah, Osiah (Hosea), Osanniah (Hosanna), Eliah, Oadiah, Oananiah, Adiah, Oniah, Eleziah, Elkaniah, Zadokiah, Barachiah, Adoniah (Cu-Roi), Yasiah (Joseph, Cu-Cuileann), Yahusiah (Jesus, Cu-Laoch) and Yahobiah (Jacob); and

(iii) The Covenant of Revelations of the Great Prophets of Yeb embodies in sacred trust the complete consciousness, languages, rules, symbols, rituals, laws and rights of the Great Prophets and Divine Messengers of the ancient world; and

(iv) The complete consciousness, languages, rules, symbols, rituals, laws and rights of the Great Prophets and Divine Messengers of the ancient world embodied within the Covenant of Revelations of the Great Prophets of Yeb is entrusted through the Authentic Sacred Deposit of Trust (*Authenticus Depositum Fidei*).

1440. In respect of the *Covenant of Tara of Jeremiah and the Celts*:-

    (i) The Celtic culture of planet Earth is a successor of the Cuilliaéan culture as the embodiment of the oldest priest-king bloodlines of Syria, Mesopotamia, Egypt, Europe and Asia and the personification of the greatest messengers of Heaven in the form of the Great Prophets of Yeb as the Sons of Man, the Holly Spirit made flesh and ones anointed (Christs) by Divine Commission to teach, to guide and to admonish the people of planet Earth; and

    (ii) The Covenant of Tara of Jeremiah and the Celts embodies in sacred trust the complete consciousness, culture, languages, rules, symbols, rituals, laws and rights of the Celts cultures of Europe and Asia; and

    (iii) The complete consciousness, culture, languages, rules, symbols, rituals, laws and rights embodied within the Covenant of Tara of Jeremiah and the Celts are entrusted through the Authentic Sacred Deposit of Trust (*Authenticus Depositum Fidei*).

Covenant of Tara of Jeremiah and the Celts

1441. In respect of the *Covenant of Five Worlds of North-Central America*:-

    (i) Five Worlds is the embodiment of the most ancient knowledge of North-Central America and the aggregate of the cultures and traditional owners of hominid species of North America and Central America beginning in the late Mesolithic period and rising to a high culture of law, language and knowledge during the end of the Neolithic period; and

    (ii) The Covenant of Five Worlds of North-Central America embodies in sacred trust the complete consciousness, culture, languages, rules, symbols, rituals, laws and rights of the cultures and traditional owners of hominid species of North and Central America; and

Covenant of Five Worlds of the People of North-Central America

(iii) The complete consciousness, culture, languages, rules, symbols, rituals, laws and rights embodied within the Covenant of Five Worlds of North-Central America are entrusted through the Authentic Sacred Deposit of Trust (*Authenticus Depositum Fidei*).

1442. In respect of the *Covenant of Missal of Baal Mithra*:-   Covenant of Missal of Baal Mithra

    (i) The ancient worship of Baal as saviour was personified under the Persian kings and later under Roma in the form of Mithra, born upon the Ides of Mars (14 Nisan, 14th March) as the lamb of god, the saviour king and bringer of balance and return to harmony of the planet of the ancient world; and

    (ii) By the 1st Century CE, the worship and respect of Mithra dominated all other religions as the symbol of all oaths, vows and agreements; and

    (iii) The Covenant of Missal of Baal Mithra embodies in sacred trust the complete consciousness, culture, languages, rules, symbols, rituals, laws and rights of all sects and versions of Baal and Mithra of the ancient world; and

    (iv) The complete consciousness, culture, languages, rules, symbols, rituals, laws and rights of all sects and versions of Baal and Mithra of the ancient world embodied within the Covenant of Missal of Baal Mithra is entrusted through the Authentic Sacred Deposit of Trust (*Authenticus Depositum Fidei*).

1443. In respect of the *Covenant of Acadia of Xerxes*:-   Covenant of Acadia of Xerxes

    (i) The Acadian Empire of Asia and Europe is the embodiment of the most ancient knowledge of Asia, Europe, Africa and the Middle East beginning around 500 BCE as to the emancipation of all men and women through knowledge, self discipline and virtue to be equals with the most ancient priest-kings of the Cuilliaéan, not by blood right, but by the Golden Rule of Law and recognition of Sacred Rights bestowed to all; and

    (ii) The Covenant of Acadia of Xerxes embodies in sacred trust the complete consciousness, culture, languages, rules, symbols, rituals, laws and rights of the cultures of higher learning and respect through the blending of Zoroastrian philosophies and Cuilliaéan wisdom; and

    (iii) The complete consciousness, culture, languages, rules, symbols, rituals, laws and rights embodied within the

Covenant of Acadia of Xerxes are entrusted through the Authentic Sacred Deposit of Trust (*Authenticus Depositum Fidei*).

1444. In respect of the *Covenant of Eliada of Alexander*:-

    (i) The Eliada Empire of planet Earth is a successor of reformed Cuilliaéan culture as the embodiment of the oldest priest-king bloodlines of Syria, Mesopotamia, Egypt, Europe and Asia and the personification of the greatest messengers of Heaven in the form of the Great Prophets of Yeb as the Sons of Man, the Holly Spirit made flesh and ones anointed (Christs) by Divine Commission no longer to rule as Gods, but to serve and free humanity from false teachings and errors of doctrine as saviours; and

    (ii) The Covenant of Eliada of Alexander embodies in sacred trust the complete consciousness, culture, languages, rules, symbols, rituals, laws and rights of the Original Nations (Tribes) and traditional owners of hominid species of Syria, Mesopotamia, Egypt, Europe and Asia; and

    (iii) The complete consciousness, culture, languages, rules, symbols, rituals, laws and rights as embodied within the Covenant of Eliada of Alexander are entrusted through the Authentic Sacred Deposit of Trust (*Authenticus Depositum Fidei*).

1445. In respect of the *Covenant of Tabiti (Sacred Fire) of the Great Asiatic Plains People*:-

    (i) The Great Asiatic Plains People are the aggregate of the Original Nations (Tribes) of People that lived from the steppes of Russia and Ukraine to Mongolia across to China; and

    (ii) The Covenant of Tabiti (Sacred Fire) of the Great Asiatic Plains People embodies in sacred trust the complete consciousness, culture, languages, rules, symbols, rituals, laws and rights of the Original Nations (Tribes) and traditional owners of hominid species of Asia; and

    (iii) The complete consciousness, culture, languages, rules, symbols, rituals, laws and rights of the cultures and traditional owners of hominid species of Asia embodied within the Covenant of Tabiti is entrusted through the Authentic Sacred Deposit of Trust (*Authenticus Depositum Fidei*).

1446. In respect of the *Covenant of Tiandi (Heaven and Earth) of Qin Shi Huang*:-

Title XIII – Divine Covenants

(i) Qin Shi Huang, also known as Ying Zheng, is the King of the State of Qin that around 235BCE commissioned his finest scholars to travel West to obtain the knowledge of Aristotle and the Empire of Alexander and then help form a philosophy to unite China and end the war between the kingdoms; and

Shi Huang

(ii) It is Qin Shi Huang that history should rightly recognise as the architect of the Covenant of Heaven and Earth that united China for the first time as the Qin Dynasty; and

(iii) The Covenant of Heaven and Earth of Qin Shi Huang embodies in sacred trust the complete consciousness, culture, languages, rules, symbols, rituals, laws and rights of unified China; and

(iv) The complete consciousness, culture, languages, rules, symbols, rituals, laws and rights of unified China embodied within the Covenant of Heaven and Earth of Qin Shi Huang is entrusted through the Authentic Sacred Deposit of Trust (*Authenticus Depositum Fidei*).

1447. In respect of the *Covenant of Nazara (Truth) of Yahusiah (Jesus Christ)*:-

Covenant of Nazara (Truth) of Yahusiah (Jesus Christ)

(i) The Nazarenes, as seekers and followers of Divine Truth, are the apostolic successors of reformed Cuilliaéan culture through the teachings of the thirty second and last Great Prophet of Yeb, also known as Yahusiah, also known as Jesus Christ, as to the equality and freedom and rights of all men and women; the redemption and forgiveness of all debts through the symbol and knowledge of the resurrection; and the absolute right of all men and women to knowledge of heaven; and the sacred mission of Holly Messengers to be teachers and saviours and not as rulers of humanity; and

(ii) The complete consciousness, culture, languages, rules, symbols, rituals, laws and rights of the Nazarenes embodied within the Covenant of Nazara of Yahusiah are entrusted through the Authentic Sacred Deposit of Trust (*Authenticus Depositum Fidei*).

1448. In respect of the *Covenant of Nirvana (Freedom & Awakening) of Gautama (Buddha)*:-

Covenant of Nirvana (Freedom & Awakening) of Gautama (Buddha)

(i) The Covenant of Nirvana embodies in sacred trust the complete consciousness, culture, languages, rules, symbols, rituals, laws and rights of the cultures and traditions of enlightenment throughout Asia, including but not limited to the teachings of Prince Gautama as Buddha; and

(ii) The complete consciousness, culture, languages, rules, symbols, rituals, laws and rights of the cultures and traditions of Buddhism throughout Asia, including but not limited to the teachings of Prince Gautama as Buddha embodied within the Covenant of Nirvana are entrusted through the Authentic Sacred Deposit of Trust (*Authenticus Depositum Fidei*).

1449. In respect of the *Covenant of Zhongdao (The Middle Way) of Kong Qiu (Confucius)*:-

(i) The Covenant of Zhongdao embodies in sacred trust the complete consciousness, culture, languages, rules, symbols, rituals, laws and rights of the cultures and traditions of enlightenment throughout Asia; and

(ii) The complete consciousness, culture, languages, rules, symbols, rituals, laws and rights of the cultures and traditions of enlightenment throughout Asia, including but not limited to the teachings of Kong Qiu (Confucius) embodied within the Covenant of Zhongdao are entrusted through the Authentic Sacred Deposit of Trust (*Authenticus Depositum Fidei*).

1450. In respect of the *Covenant of Septuaginta of Iudaism*:-

(i) The formation of the official cult of Iudaism upon the complete collapse of the religion of Mithra in 69 CE upon the destruction of the Great Temple Mint to Mithra, six hundred and sixty-six years to the day since the destruction of the Temple of Setien (Satan) in Jerusalem, heralded an unprecedented change in the ancient world; and

(ii) The Emperor Vespasian, now proclaimed himself Lucifer and saviour of Rome under the symbol of the blazing sun and the Trigram IHS or *Invictus Hoc Signo* meaning "By this sign (we are) unconquerable". Furthermore, new scriptures were commissioned by blending and re-writing other ancient texts, especially the prophecies of the Great Prophets of Yeb so that the foretelling of Vespasian as Lucifer would be fulfilled. The scholars of Qumran near the Dead Sea, along with Josephus were commissioned to re-write many of the ancient texts to fulfil this task; and

(iii) The Covenant of Septuaginta of Iudaism embodies in sacred trust the complete consciousness, culture, languages, rules, symbols, rituals, laws and rights of founding of Iudaism (Judaism) from 70 CE to 120 CE as the Cult of Lucifer across the Roman Empire; and

(iv) The complete consciousness, culture, languages, rules, symbols, rituals, laws and rights of Iudaism (Judaism) as the Cult of Lucifer across the Roman Empire embodied within the Covenant of Septuaginta of Iudaism is entrusted through the Authentic Sacred Deposit of Trust (*Authenticus Depositum Fidei*).

1451. In respect of the *Covenant of Eucadia of Heracles of Eliada and Larissa*:-   Covenant of Eucadia (Ucadia) of Heracles

(i) The Eliada and Larissa cultures of ancient Greece at the time of Heracles in the 1st and 2nd centuries CE, signify the highest point of cultural and spiritual advancement of the region in the conscious and deliberate formation of a Utopia as a Kingdom of Heaven upon the Earth known as Eucadia (Ucadia) as the manifestation of the highest ideals of truth, the golden rule of law, justice and human dignity; and

(ii) The Covenant of Eucadia (Ucadia) of Heracles of Eliada and Larissa embodies in sacred trust the complete consciousness, culture, languages, rules, symbols, rituals, laws and rights of Illuminated Men and women at the height of self-knowledge and as exemplars of the noblest of virtues; and

(iii) The complete consciousness, culture, languages, rules, symbols, rituals, laws and rights of Eucadia (Ucadia) of ancient Greece embodied within the Covenant of Eucadia (Ucadia) of Heracles of Eliada and Larissa as Heaven on Earth are entrusted through the Authentic Sacred Deposit of Trust (*Authenticus Depositum Fidei*).

1452. In respect of the *Covenant of Kikilil Yuum Witzil (Great Cycle of Celestial Realm and Earth) of South-Central America*:-   Covenant of Kikilil Yuum Witzil (Great Cycle of Celestial Realm and Earth) of South-Central America

(i) The Covenant of Kikilil Yuum Witzil embodies in sacred trust the complete consciousness, culture, languages, rules, symbols, rituals, laws and rights of the cultures and traditions of advanced civilisation, knowledge and culture, resting upon social discipline and authority that have always been present upon the lands of Central and South America; and

(ii) The complete consciousness, culture, languages, rules, symbols, rituals, laws and rights of the cultures and traditions of Original Nations (Tribes) that have always been present upon the lands of Central and South America embodied within the Covenant of Kikilil Yuum Witzil are entrusted through the Authentic Sacred Deposit of Trust (*Authenticus Depositum*

Lex Divina: Maxims of Divine Law

Fidei).

1453. In respect of the *Covenant of Digesta of Marcus Aurelius*:-

    (i) Marcus Aurelius as the undisputed Emperor of Rome, King of the Franks, blood descendant of Yahusia (Jesus Christ) and the Cuilliaéan, is the founder and architect of Rome Redeemed in the form of self- disciplines, virtues and knowledge adopting a truly democratic and benevolent Roman Empire ending slavery and acknowledging the equality of all men and women upon planet Earth; and

    (ii) The Covenant of Digesta of Marcus Aurelius embodies in sacred trust the formation of the dignity of the enlightened soul, capable of rising beyond their weaknesses to a firm command of self-discipline, truth and virtue, whilst championing the freedoms and rights of all men and women; and

    (iii) The complete consciousness, culture, languages, rules, symbols, rituals, laws, authorities and rights of Rome Redeemed as first formed by Marcus Aurelius embodied within the Covenant of Digesta of Marcus Aurelius are entrusted through the Authentic Sacred Deposit of Trust (*Authenticus Depositum Fidei*).

Covenant of Digesta of Marcus Aurelius

1454. In respect of the *Covenant of Sanatana Dharma (Eternal Truth) of Brahman (Hinduism)*:-

    (i) The refugees of the Aryan Empire in the 4th Century CE that fled eastward as a result of Christianity, formed the basis of the Gupta Empire in India and the founding of the Hindu version of Aryanism as Brahmanism. This is the true era of birth of Hindu and caste literature, including the introduction of numerous Aryan symbols such as the Swastika; and

    (ii) The Covenant of Sanatana Dharma embodies in sacred trust the complete consciousness, culture, languages, rules, symbols, rituals, laws and rights of the first cultures and traditions of Hinduism since its creation; and

    (iii) The complete consciousness, culture, languages, rules, symbols, rituals, laws and rights of Hinduism since its creation embodied within the Covenant of Sanatana Dharma is entrusted through the Authentic Sacred Deposit of Trust (*Authenticus Depositum Fidei*).

Covenant of Sanatana Dharma (Eternal Truth) of Brahman (Hinduism)

1455. In respect of the *Covenant of Bibliographe of Christianity*:-

    (i) Constantine as the last Emperor of Rome and the Emperor of

Covenant of Bibliographe of Christianity

the Celts and the Priest-King of Eukadia (Ucadia) as Heaven on Earth, as a blood descendent of Yahusiah (Jesus Christ) and the Cuilliaéan, was the founder and architect of Christianity and its highest ideals, knowledge and operation as the first truly democratic and representative model of the equality of all men and women upon planet Earth; and

(ii) The Covenant of *Bibliographe* of Christianity embodies in sacred trust the formation of a global model of democracy, law, rights and dignity for planet Earth known as *"Theke"* (pronounced the key) as the authentic and original body of Christian authority, church and community; and

(iii) The complete consciousness, culture, languages, rules, symbols, rituals, laws, authorities and rights of the Christian Body as first formed by Constantine to the four corners of the Earth embodied within the Covenant of Bibliographe of Christianity are entrusted through the Authentic Sacred Deposit of Trust (*Authenticus Depositum Fidei*).

1456. In respect of the *Covenant of Dao (the Way)*:-

(i) The Covenant of Dao embodies in sacred trust the complete consciousness, culture, languages, rules, symbols, rituals, laws and rights of the cultures and traditions of Taoism since its creation; and

(ii) The complete consciousness, culture, languages, rules, symbols, rituals, laws and rights of the cultures and traditions of Original Nations (Tribes) that have always been present upon the lands of Asia embodied within the Covenant of Dao are entrusted through the Authentic Sacred Deposit of Trust (*Authenticus Depositum Fidei*).

1457. In respect of the *Covenant of Kami Yoso Seimei (Spirits of Elements and Life) of the way of Shinto (Japan)*:-

(i) The Covenant of Kami Yoso Seimei embodies in sacred trust the complete consciousness, culture, languages, rules, symbols, rituals, laws and rights of the first cultures and traditions of Shintoism since its creation; and

(ii) The complete consciousness, culture, languages, rules, symbols, rituals, laws and rights of the cultures and traditions of Original Nations (Tribes) that have always been present upon the lands of Japan embodied within the Covenant of Kami Yoso Seimei are entrusted through the Authentic Sacred Deposit of Trust (*Authenticus Depositum Fidei*).

Lex Divina: Maxims of Divine Law

1458. In respect of the *Covenant of Quran Al Sufian (Recitations of Wisdom of the Way) of the Great Prophet of Islam*:-

    (i)   The Leader of the Saracenia Empire, also known as the Great Prophet, being an educated and compassionate man, having both the blood of the ancient Keepers of Time and Space of Saracenia (Arabia) in his veins as well as descended of the Cuilliaéan, was the architect in Ancient Greek of a philosophy and Divine Revelation honouring the Divine Creator of all existence and heaven and earth, calling for all men and women to cease such wilful ignorance, blasphemy and profanity in living without virtue, killing in the name of religion and serving the interests of slave traders and merchants of doom; and

    (ii)   The true history concerning the Great Prophet and the Divine Message he delivered as the community of Islam of wisdom, beauty, self-development and non-violence known as *Al Sufian*, was then significantly altered by the Venetian exiles (who founded the Ottoman Empire during the period of the 15th Centuries to 19th Centuries), into another text, with historic forgeries created to mask its origin; and

    (iii)   The Covenant of *Al Sufian* of the Great Prophet and Islam embodies in sacred trust the complete consciousness, culture, languages, rules, symbols, rituals, laws and rights of Islam as first given to the Great Prophet by the Creator of All Existence and of Heaven and Earth through the miracle of the text and covenant known as *Al Sufian*; and

    (iv)   The complete consciousness, culture, languages, rules, symbols, rituals, laws and rights of Islam embodied within the Covenant of *Al Sufian* of the Great Prophet and Islam are entrusted through the Authentic Sacred Deposit of Trust (*Authenticus Depositum Fidei*).

Covenant of Quran Al Sufian of Great Prophet of Islam

1459. In respect of the *Covenant of Holy Bible (Nova Testamentum) of Catholicism of the Franks*:-

    (i)   The Kings of the Franks, also known as the Carolingians, as true descendants of Constantine; and blood descendents of Yahusia (Jesus Christ) and the Cuilliaéan, are the true founders and original architects of the Catholic Church in 741 CE and its highest ideals, knowledge and operation as the restoration of the Rule of Law and the ideals of Christianity upon planet Earth; and

    (ii)   The Covenant of Nova Testamentum of Catholicism of the

Covenant of Holy Bible (Nova Testamentum) of Catholicism of the Franks

Franks embodies in sacred trust the complete consciousness, culture, languages, rules, symbols, rituals, laws and rights of the cultures of the true and original Catholic Church as first formed in 741 CE, particularly the formation of the Four Gospels; and

(iii) The complete consciousness, culture, languages, rules, symbols, rituals, laws and rights of the Catholic Church embodied within the Covenant of Nova Testamentum of Catholicism of the Franks is entrusted through the Authentic Sacred Deposit of Trust (*Authenticus Depositum Fidei*).

1460. In respect of the *Covenant of Gurmat (Eternal Truth) of Sikhism*:-   Covenant of Eternal Truth of Gurmat (Sikhism)

(i) The Sikh culture and philosophy, as first revealed through Guru Nanak in the 15th Century in Northern India, is testament to an extraordinary covenant of heroism, self-discipline and aesthetic learning. The term Gurma honours the teachings of Guru Nanak as the "self-evident" truths of a teacher and divine messenger; and

(ii) The Covenant of Eternal Truth of Gurma embodies in sacred trust the teachings, knowledge, discipline and wisdom of Guru Nanak and the Gurma of the founding Gurus of Sikhism, including the complete consciousness, complete culture, languages, rules, symbols, rituals, laws and rights of Sikhism; and

(iii) The complete consciousness, culture, languages, rules, symbols, rituals, laws and rights of the first cultures of Sikhism embodied within the Covenant of Eternal Truth of Gurma is entrusted through the Authentic Sacred Deposit of Trust (*Authenticus Depositum Fidei*).

1461. In respect of the *Covenant of Lebor Clann Glas*:-   Covenant of Lebor Clann Glas

(i) The Covenant of Lebor Clann Glas of the Diaspora of the Holly, also known as the Sangreal (Holy Grail), also known as the Cuilliaéan and by many other names embodies in sacred trust the complete consciousness, history, culture, rules, rituals, laws and rights of the one, true and only Diaspora throughout the ages; and

(ii) The complete consciousness, history, culture, rules, rituals, laws and rights of the Cuilliaéan as the Diaspora embodied within the Covenant of Lebor Clann Glas is entrusted through the Authentic Sacred Deposit of Trust (*Authenticus Depositum Fidei*).

Title XIV - Divine Systems

14.1 - Divine Systems

Article 406 - Systems

1462. A ***System*** is a set of objects or concepts, capable of being defined by properties and relation that through their interactions constitute an integrated body; or the rules that govern such a body.

System

1463. Every valid system may then be delineated by its boundaries, influenced by its environment, described by its structure, defined by its purposes and expressed in its functions:-

Elements of Valid System

   (i) It is impossible to reasonably argue that the concept of system itself is negative, or flawed or represents the cause of negativity or error in of itself. Instead, the existence of systems is the effect of existence itself; and

   (ii) Therefore, to deny or repudiate the necessity of systems without reason, is to repudiate existence itself and all forms of competent mind; and to confess one is non compos mentis; and

   (iii) Similarly, to argue that the existence of systems within the dimension of temporal existence are reasonable, yet the existence of systems within supernatural and non-temporal existence is unreasonable is absurd; and

   (iv) Existence depends upon systems; and the existence of Unique Collective Awareness depends upon systems within non-locational consciousness; and the existence of Heaven depends upon valid systems.

Article 407 - Supremum Systemata

1464. The ***Supremum Systemata***, also known as the Supreme Systems of One Heaven, are those spiritual organs, bodies, associations, persons, rules, rights, functions and processes in existence to ensure all valid Divine Law and Universal Law is upheld; and that the Rights of Members are protected; and that the Society fulfil its objectives.

Supremum Systemata

1465. Eight primary systems exist, being:-

Eight Primary Systems

   (i) Supremum Universalium Systemata (Universal Systems); and

   (ii) Supremum Custodiarum Systemata (Guardians Systems); and

   (iii) Supremum Angelorum Systemata (Angelic Systems); and

   (iv) Supremum Femininum Systemata (Feminine Systems); and

(v) Supremum Masculinum Systemata (Masculine Systems); and

(vi) Supremum Officium Systemata (Offices Systems); and

(vii) Supremum Sacramentum Systemata (Sacramental Systems); and

(i) Supremum Obligationum Systemata (Enforcement Systems).

1466. Notwithstanding the names of the Supreme Systems of Heaven within the Official Ucadian Language of Logos, the Three (3) Great Faiths of One Christ, One Islam and One Spirit may choose to vote at a properly formed Great Conclave to adopt new names in one or more Non-Ucadian languages for such Systems, in accord with Article 130 of the most sacred Covenant *Pactum De Singularis Caelum*. Names of Supreme Systems

Article 408 - Universalium Systemata (Universal Systems)

1467. All collective dimensional constructs, designs, manifestations and relations of consciousness and levels of perfected memory of truth and wisdom are vested in one supreme spiritual body and system known as the **Supremum Universalium Systemata**, also known as Supreme Universal Systems of Heaven. The Supremum Universalium Systemata is the highest architects of collective dimensional constructs of reality and no other. Universalium Systemata (Universal Systems)

1468. In reference to the Supreme Universal Systems of the Divine:- Reference to Supreme Universal Systems

(i) All dimensions of consciousness are fictional constructs of reality as a distinct "universe" according to certain rules and characteristics; and

(ii) Within the reference to Higher Order Minds, Divine Mind is capable of holding a perfect construct of consciousness without relying upon the constraints of complex rules and records, whereas Higher Mind is able to reference a greater degree of knowledge; and

(iii) However, Lower Mind of higher order life forms are constrained by the limits of species and education; and

(iv) Thus Lower Mind is more dependent upon certain structures and dimensions of consciousness and universe.

1469. The Spirit Members qualified and selected to serve within the operation of the Universalium Systemata (Universal Systems) shall hold the Special Supreme Divine Office of "**Fate**" in recognition of their foundational responsibilities in creating, weaving and holding Special Divine Office Fate the dimensional and collective consciousness mappings and constructs of Heaven; and in being the source of inspiration, creativity and imagination of higher knowledge of Ucadia.

1470. The Supremum Universalium Systemata is uniquely recognised, registered and exemplified as having existence through the Great Register and Public Record of Heaven by the Sacred [Trust No. 999999-111111-999999]. The existence, identity, authority, purpose and powers of the Supremum Universalium Systemata shall be duly gazetted in the Ucadia Gazette being the Official Newspaper of Record for each and every Sacred Space-Day-Time of its existence and operation. Recognition of Supremum Universalium Systemata

1471. The five (5) key Propositions and Powers of the Supremum Universalium Systemata (Universal Systems) are:- Key Propositions and Powers

    (i) *Conceptual Models*, being the design and development of conceptual models and frameworks for sustainable, fulfilling, and positive Local Spiritual Collectives, Spiritual Collectives, Regional Spiritual Collectives and Unique Spiritual Collectives, consistent with the Golden Rule of Law and the Rights of all Divine Persons as expressed by the most sacred Covenant *Pactum De Singularis Caelum*; and

    (ii) *Collective Consciousness Mappings*, being the detailed and accurate mappings of current conscious collectives, including all non-aligned and negatively aligned layers of ghost, ground plane dissonance and alien consciousness; and

    (iii) *Cultural Preservation*, being the preservation of ancient culture and consciousness, as a recognition of such unique conscious perspective, even if such ancient culture or consciousness is not aligned to the Golden Rule of Law, that a proper record and knowledge of such constructs are duly preserved; and

    (iv) *Revitalisation*, being the revitalisation of collective conscious space that individual and collectives of Divine Persons may choose to migrate toward a more optimum Conceptual Model, yet retaining items and constructs of cultural significance and important meaning; and

    (v) *Manifestation*, being the complex manifestation of collective conscious constructs aligned with the Conceptual Models of spiritual balance that enable a degree of stability and certainty as to the integrity and truth of such manifestations.

Article 409 - Custodiarum Systemata (Guardian Systems)

1472. All guardian, custody, protection and service powers and authority are vested in one supreme spiritual body and system known as the ***Supremum Custodiarum Systemata***, also known as Supreme Guardians Systems of Heaven. The Supremum Custodiarum Systemata is the highest body of spiritual guardians and custodians of all levels of consciousness, reality and Heaven and Earth and no other.

Custodiarum Systemata (Guardian Systems)

1473. In reference to the Supreme Guardian Systems of the Divine:-

(i) Consciousness or Awareness within the various layers of Unique Collective Awareness, possess levels of malleability and interpretation, essential to existence and the positive objects of the Divine Creator of all existence and all Heaven and Earth; and

(ii) Thus, Divine Mind possesses the quality of perfect memory, yet is furthest removed from temporal existence, whereas Lower Mind possesses an imperfect and highly malleable memory, yet is closest to directly influence temporal life experience and perspective; and

(iii) Thus, all Homo Sapien Life as a form of Higher Order Life, possess Lower Mind on the same plane of imperfect memory, whereby such consciousness is highly malleable, yet also subject to gross distortion if not properly protected; and

(iv) Truth therefore is the expectation of a reality or conscious construct that is reliable, trustworthy, sincere and free from falsity or misleading deception; and

(v) Reality then permits Lower Minds to function on such a plane of conscious existence with a degree of certainty and comfort, excluding those concepts such as paradox, uncertainty and deliberate deception that might challenge a Lower Mind to question its own construct of "reality"; and

(vi) History that is free from deliberate distortion and deceptions proves without doubt, that those who gained insight into the nature of existence and the universe have used such knowledge to the detriment of the Homo Sapien species in concocting false histories, false and misguided philosophies to enslave others in life and beyond; and

General Reference to Supreme Guardian Systems

(vii) It cannot be assumed then that in the absence of proper guardians and custodians of conscious memory, truth or reality, that such false histories, philosophies, religions and deceptions will cease to have any effect in spirit and only affect the living. Nor can it be assumed that the damage of such deliberate falsities of history, knowledge and philosophy can be healed or addressed in the future without the need for a permanent system of guardians and custodians of consciousness.

1474. The Spirit Members qualified and selected to serve within the operation of the Custodiarum Systemata (Guardians Systems) shall hold the Special Supreme Divine Office of "**Demon**" in recognition of the end of the War in Heaven; and their foundational responsibilities in protecting and defending heaven; and in protecting and defending the laws of Ucadia; and in the enforcement of necessary actions of rendition, interdiction, seizure and return when faced with corruptions and attacks against the integrity of Heaven; and in being the source of fearsome power, courage, enforcement and strength to the armies of Living Members within the temporal realms of the Universe. *[Special Divine Office of Demon]*

1475. The Supremum Custodiarum Systemata is uniquely recognised, registered and exemplified as having existence through the Great Register and Public Record of Heaven by the Sacred Trust Number 999999-222222-999999. The existence, identity, authority, purpose and powers of the Supremum Custodiarum Systemata have been duly gazetted in the Ucadia Gazette being the Official Newspaper of Record for each and every Sacred Space-Day-Time of its existence and operation. *[Recognition of Supremum Custodiarum Systemata]*

1476. The nine (9) key Propositions and Powers of the Supremum Custodiarum Systemata (Guardians Systems) are:- *[Key Propositions and Powers]*

　　(i) *Protect and Defend Heaven*, being to protect and defend the heavenly Kosmos, including all planets, stars, life, colonies, ecosystems and diversity throughout the galaxy; and

　　(ii) *Protect and Defend Ucadia*, being to protect and defend Ucadia; and all its Realms, Domains, Dominions, Dependencies, Rights, Titles, Instruments, Uses and Property and particularly the use of the Ucadia name and Ucadia material; and

　　(iii) *Protect and Defend the Laws of Ucadia*, being to protect and defend all associated Covenants, Charters, Scripture, Maxims, Codes, Bylaws, Ordinances, Regulations, Policies and Orders; and to seek mutual recognition of such jurisdictional rights with foreign bodies and courts that respect and operate according to the Golden Rule of Law and Justice and Fair Process; and to ensure that in all matters pertaining to Ucadia Members that the courts of Ucadia are recognised as the first, primary and original jurisdiction for the resolution of all matters of controversy, arbitration and dispute; and

(iv) *Peaceful, Amicable and Harmonious Relations*, being to seek peaceful, amicable and harmonious relations, treaties and alliances with foreign spiritual bodies that respect the Golden Rule of Law and Justice and Fair Process; and

(v) *Rendition*, being to pursue, prosecute and bring to justice any individual spirit or body that openly seeks to abuse, trespass or injure Heaven, or Ucadia or its Realms, Domains, Dominions, Dependencies, Rights, Titles, Instruments, Uses or Property; and

(vi) *Interdiction*, being to deploy as part of the execution of a sacred Divine Writ of *Recto Divinum Interdico*, to impose proper rule of law; and prohibit any possible continued breaches of Divine Law and expunge the conditions for damage to conscious memory, clarity or truth, including but not limited to empowerment and inspiration of temporal forces also granted the commission of Recto Interdico; and

(vii) *Seizure and Return*, being to execute the conditions of a Divine Warrant according to a sacred Divine Writ of *Recto Divinum Capionis*, to do all that is necessary to ensure the seizure and return and restoration of sacred memory, consciousness, balance, harmony, truth and integrity, including but not limited to empowerment and inspiration of temporal forces also granted the commission of Recto Capionis; and

(viii) *Arrest and Custody*, being to execute the conditions of a Divine Warrant according to a sacred Divine Writ of *Recto Divinum Custodiae*, to do all that is necessary to ensure the arrest and custody of each and every malevolent spirit, negative ghost and destructive construct; and to assist in the restoration of sacred memory, consciousness, balance, harmony, truth and integrity, including but not limited to empowerment and inspiration of temporal forces also granted the commission of Recto Custodiae; and

(ix) *Revelation Enforcement*, being to execute the conditions of a Divine Warrant according to a sacred Divine Writ of *Recto Divinum Apocalypsis*, to do all that is necessary to ensure the fulfilment of such Divine Revelation, including but not limited to the seizure, search, arrest and custody of each and every or any named malevolent spirit, or ghost, or false concept, or false right, or false construct and to assist in the restoration of sacred memory, consciousness, balance and Rule of Law.

Article 410 - Angelorum Systemata (Angelic Systems)

1477. All personal protection, guidance, support, inspiration and intercession powers and authority concerning all Divine Persons and True Persons is vested in one supreme spiritual body and system known as the ***Supremum Angelorum Systemata***, also known as Supreme Angelic Systems of Heaven.

Angelorum Systemata (Angelic Systems)

The Supremum Angelorum Systemata is the highest body of Angelic powers and authority of all conscious dimensions and all Heaven and Earth and no other.

1478. In reference to the Supreme Angelic Systems of the Divine:-

General Reference to Supreme Angelic Systems

(i) The practice of votive petitions to spirits for protection, or guidance or support is an ancient custom throughout civilised people; and

(ii) The same is reflected in the deeply held traditions of "guardian spirits" and "guardian angels" watching over and protecting the living, particularly the spirits of deceased ancestors and the beloved; and

(iii) Yet such ancient and traditional practices could not have perceived the possibility someday of such circumstance of deliberate spiritual misrepresentation, or the negative haunting and possession of the living by those higher order minds cursed into a ghost-like state; and

(iv) Guardian spirits are supposed to guide and help, not harm and negatively interfere in the choices of the living; and Guardian spirits are forbidden by Universal Law and Divine Law to seek to haunt the physical form of the living or to try and possess the body and mind of the living; and spirits of any kind are absolutely forbidden from placing self destructive, malicious, suicidal and negative messages in the minds of the living; and

(v) Such lawlessness and complete lack of respect for Divine Law and Universal Law is born in part from the emergence of false religions and their fake practices that worship such chaos and have sought to maintain power through such malevolence. Yet

Maxims of Divine Law

such chaos is only sustainable in the perpetuation of ignorance; and

(vi) No spirit culpable of deliberately sadistic, pathological, sexually perverted or cruel crimes is capable or permitted to being a Guardian or Angel for at least two thousand Earth years and until they have demonstrated unquestionably a healing and atonement; and

(vii) Thus, all spirits are forbidden by Divine Law and Universal Law in negative influence upon the living in the perpetuation of false religious practices, false history and enslavement; and

(viii) An Angel then is a Spirit Messenger, invested with Divine Commission from the Divine Creator of all Existence and all Heaven and Earth to protect, inspire and support all higher order consciousness carnate in flesh form, in accord with Divine Law as expressed by the most sacred Covenant *Pactum De Singularis Caelum*; and

(ix) As an independent supernatural force, a valid Angel is not constrained by the rules of temporal form – hence a level of consciousness no longer bound to a body or other temporal limitation. Therefore, neither a Spirit nor a valid Angel may be described as a Ghost.

1479. The Spirit Members qualified and selected to serve within the Angelorum Systemata (Angelic Systems) shall hold the Special Supreme Divine Office of Angel in recognition of their foundational responsibilities in personal protection of Living Members; and in the expulsion; and freeing of Ghosts and the breaking apart of the Mundi Mind Virus; and assistance to those invoking petitions of invocation:- Recognition of Angelic Systems

(i) The Supremum Angelorum Systemata is uniquely recognised, registered and exemplified as having existence through the Great Register and Public Record of Heaven by the Sacred Trust Number 999999-333333-999999; and

(ii) The existence, identity, authority, purpose and powers of the Supremum Angelorum Systemata have been duly gazetted in the Ucadia Gazette being the Official Newspaper of Record for each and every Sacred Space-Day-Time of its existence and operation.

1480. The three (3) key Propositions and Powers of the Supremum Angelorum Systemata (Angelic Systems) shall be: Key Propositions and Powers

(i) *Mental and Spiritual Protection*, being to assign at least one qualified Angel to each living Member as their "charge"; and to protect each such Living Member day and night against undue negative influence of ghosts, or other consciousness seeking to haunt, or possess, or misdirect or confuse; and

(ii) *Expulsion of Ghosts*, being the forced expulsion of any and all ghosts possessing the body, or spirit history, or time-lines or mind of a living Member that is their charge; and to ensure such negative influence is forbidden from any further negative influence; and

(iii) *Passive Assistance*, being to provide positive assistance to a living Member as their charge without undue influence of the free choice and will of the living Member and to ensure positive and meaningful assistance is directed when such request for genuine Assistance is made.

1481. Existence itself and the proper function of the fundamental laws of Creation demands that Angels defer to the general principle of non-interference in the causation of free will, excluding such cases where the mind or spirit and choices of a Living Member as their charge have been unduly influenced, especially in the case of ghosts and other spirit minds defying the law of non-interference. [Non-Interference by Angels in Free Will and Causality of Life]

Every intervention sought from a Living Member to their Guardian Angel, if accepted and manifested, may have the same or a greater negative consequence to the balance of Unique Collective Consciousness, than allowing events to take their course without intervention.

Intervention is therefore a last resort, in exceptional circumstances, where the negative consequences of non-intervention substantially outweigh the consequences of a manifest intervention.

1482. A key proposition of all Angels is to formally attend the place and time of the dying and death of their Living Member as their charge. Angels are obligated to protect such vulnerable minds from fear and misrepresentations by ghosts and spirits, who may seek to exploit such weakness, in open defiance of the laws of Heaven. [Solemn Attendance at Time of Physical Death]

Angels are empowered to call upon all the necessary support of Heaven to ensure each and every mind has the free opportunity to transition to a state of Heaven, without falling into the labyrinth of "ghost state" or the self punishment of a "hell state".

Article 411 - Femininum Systemata (Feminine Systems)

1483. All feminine powers and authority of manifestation, inspiration, guidance, consciousness and knowledge are vested in one supreme spiritual body and system known as the ***Supremum Femininum Systemata***, also known as Supreme Feminine Systems of Heaven. The Supremum Femininum Systemata is the highest body made manifest of true feminine power and authority of any and all levels of consciousness, collective dimensional constructs of reality and all Heaven and Earth and no other.

Femininum Systemata (Feminine Systems)

1484. In reference to the Supreme Feminine Systems of the Divine:-

Reference to Supreme Feminine Systems

(i) Divine Feminine is the identity and distinct qualities of one equal half of the unique collective singular mind of all sexual species that may carnate into physical form, particularly Level 6 Higher Order Species. The opposite and complementary identity is the Divine Masculine; and

(ii) Whereas existence depends on the balance of Divine Feminine and Divine Masculine, each possess unique and distinct abilities. It is through Divine Masculine that is witnessed the qualities of strength and tenacity and of courage and wisdom; and

(iii) Yet it is through Divine Feminine that is witnessed the qualities of respect and sexual identity and of intuition and life made manifest; and

(iv) The feminine possesses a greater natural gift of connection to Gaia, being the Spiritual Force and Consciousness of collective Life on planet Earth connected to the planet itself and to Heaven; and

(v) All Homo Sapien and Higher Order Consciousness is a subset of Gaia. Thus, it is the feminine that is the key aspect of any life or system or philosophy made manifest, for it is the unique power of the feminine collective to sustain a collective reality or change a collective reality; and

(vi) Where the feminine is tricked, or cursed, or condemned, or made to perceive and look at itself as less, or unworthy, or the cause of negativity, then such corrupt power can and has been manipulated by negative forces to perpetuate its position. The support and assistance of Divine Feminine to emancipate itself from such false notions, false fears and false negativities is essential to the future of planet Earth and the sustainment of all life and consciousness.

1485. The Spirit Members qualified and selected to serve within the operation of the Femininum Systemata (Feminine Systems) shall hold the Special Supreme Divine Office of "**Faerie**" in recognition of an ancient spirit and force redeemed from being previously denigrated and marginalised; and their foundational responsibilities in the restoration of true feminine; and the restoration of true mother; and Gaia harmony; and emancipation, equality and appreciation of all women.

Special Divine Office of Faerie

1486. The Supremum Femininum Systemata is uniquely recognised, registered and exemplified as having existence through the Great Register and Public Record of Heaven by the Sacred Trust Number 999999-444444-999999. The existence, identity, authority, purpose and powers of the Supremum Femininum Systemata have been duly gazetted in the Ucadia Gazette being the Official Newspaper of Record for each and every Sacred Space-Day-Time of its existence and operation.

Recognition of Supreme Feminine Systems

1487. The six (6) key Propositions and Powers of the Supremum Femininum Systemata (Feminine Systems) are:-

Key Propositions and Powers

(i) *True Feminine Restoration*, being to restore the conscious memory, respect, harmony and balance of True Feminine in light of the arrest, seizure, custody and dissolution of all aspects and constructs of false feminine; and to ensure that all feminine higher order beings are granted the capacity to instinctually and emotionally experience and benefit from such true feminine; and

(ii) *True Mother Restoration*, being to restore the conscious memory, respect, history, emotional and spiritual harmony and balance of True Mother in light of the arrest, seizure, custody and dissolution of all aspects and constructs of false mother; and to ensure that all beings are granted the capacity to instinctively and emotionally experience, connect and be supported by True Mother; and

(iii) *Gaia Harmony*, being to re-establish the harmony and alignment of True Feminine and True Mother with Gaia Consciousness in respect and honour of the sacred treaties of the most sacred Covenant *Pactum De Singularis Caelum* and to ensure that such alignment and harmony enhances the quality and respect of all planetary life, conservation and good management; and

(iv) *Emancipation*, being to emancipate the feminine consciousness away from negative and deliberately false constructs and stereotypes, in particular those deliberately false, profane, malicious religious notions creating liabilities, blame, guilt and poor character upon the feminine spirit; and

(v) *Equality*, being to restore the equality of the feminine in all aspects of spiritual, cultural, social, moral and legal aspects of community life; and to ensure the continued challenge, objection, dissolution and defeat of false, profane and malicious notions seeking to continue and maintain embedded inequality between the masculine and feminine; and

(vi) *Appreciation*, being to restore the balance, perspective and recognition of the feminine form from false and deliberate simplifications of objectification, sexualisation and property; and to ensure the progressive dissolution of self destructive and negative conscious intent that encourages the perpetuation of sexualised stereotypes.

Article 412 - Masculinum Systemata (Masculine Systems)

1488. All masculine powers and authority of manifestation, inspiration, guidance, consciousness and knowledge are vested in one supreme spiritual body and system known as the **Supremum Masculinum Systemata**, also known as Supreme Masculine Systems of Heaven. The Supremum Masculinum Systemata shall be the highest body made manifest of true masculine power and authority of any and all levels of consciousness, collective dimensional constructs of reality and all Heaven and Earth and no other.

Masculinum Systemata (Masculine Systems)

1489. The six (6) key Propositions and Powers of the Supremum Masculinum Systemata (Masculine Systems) shall be:

Key Propositions and Powers

(i) *True Masculine Restoration*, being to restore the conscious memory, respect, harmony and balance of True Masculine in light of the arrest, seizure, custody and dissolution of all aspects and constructs of false masculine; and to ensure that all masculine higher order beings are granted the capacity to instinctively and emotionally experience and benefit from such true masculine; and

(ii) *True Father Restoration*, being to restore the conscious memory, respect, history, emotional and spiritual harmony and balance of True Father in light of the arrest, seizure, custody and dissolution of all aspects and constructs of false father; and to ensure that all beings are granted the capacity to instinctively and emotionally experience, connect and be supported by True Father; and

(iii) *Gaia Harmony*, being to re-establish the harmony and alignment of True Masculine and True Father with Gaia Consciousness in respect and honour of the sacred treaties of the most sacred Covenant *Pactum De Singularis Caelum* and to ensure that such alignment and harmony enhances the quality and respect of all planetary life, conservation and good management; and

(iv) *Emancipation*, being to emancipate the masculine consciousness away from negative and deliberately false constructs and stereotypes, in particular those deliberately false, profane, malicious religious notions creating liabilities, blame, guilt and poor character upon the masculine spirit; and

(v) *Equality*, being to restore the equality of the masculine in all aspects of spiritual, cultural, social, moral and legal aspects of community life; and to ensure the continued challenge, objection, dissolution and defeat of false, profane and malicious notions seeking to continue and maintain embedded inequality between the masculine and feminine; and

(vi) *Appreciation*, being to restore the balance, perspective and recognition of the masculine form from false and deliberate simplifications of objectification, sexualisation and property; and to ensure the progressive dissolution of self destructive and negative conscious intent that encourages the perpetuation of sexualised stereotypes.

1490. The Spirit Members qualified and selected to serve within the operation of the Masculinum Systemata (Masculine Systems) shall hold the Special Supreme Divine Office of "**Elve**" (Elf) in recognition of an ancient spirit and force redeemed from being previously denigrated and marginalised; and their foundational responsibilities in the restoration of true masculine; and the restoration of true father; and Gaia harmony; and emancipation, equality and appreciation of all men.

Special Divine Office of Elve

1491. There shall be no direct nor formal means of communication to the Masculinum Systemata (Masculine Systems) of Heaven by living Members of One Heaven. This shall be because Masculinum Systemata (Masculine Systems) are tasked with acting independently to carry out their mission and propositions. However, the Elve (Elf)

Communication to Supremum Masculinum Systemata (Masculine Systems)

of the Masculinum Systemata (Masculine Systems) are free to choose of their own will to interact with living Members of One Heaven.

Article 413 - Officium Systemata (Offices Systems)

1492. All power and authority as vested in any and every form of Office, Commission, Agency, or other position of Trust is vested in one supreme spiritual body and system known as the **Supremum Officium Systemata**, also known as Supreme Offices Systems of Heaven. The Supremum Officium Systemata is the highest authority and power as the source of all valid Offices, Commissions, Agency, Powers, Authorities and other positions of Trust and no other.

Officium Systemata (Offices Systems)

1493. The ten key Propositions and Powers of the Supremum Officium Systemata (Offices Systems) shall be:

Key Propositions and Powers

(i) *Identification*, being the proper identification, naming and classification of each and every Divine Office of the four hundred and thirty-two (432) Great Offices of Heaven, including but not limited to the capacities, authorities and powers of such Offices such as Magisterium, Imperium, Sacrum, Sanitatum, Virtus, Custoditum, Alumentum, Interpretum; and

(ii) *Obligation*, being the complete definition and scope of the obligations pertaining to each and every Divine Office of the four hundred and thirty-two (432) Great Offices of Heaven as a Memorandum of Office or Memorandum Officium, such that the role, responsibilities, capacities, authorities and powers for each and every Divine Office is clear; and

(iii) *Enrolment*, being the complete enrolment within the Great Roll of Divine Persons of each and every Divine Office such that each Office possesses a unique number, title and relation to a specific spiritual or temporal body; and

(iv) *Possession*, being the spiritual investiture of at least one Divine Person to each valid Divine Office as connected to a spiritual and temporal body as the first, primary and ultimate holder and occupant of such Office under sacred and solemn oath and vow, such that the Office and Trust stands valid, even if an appointment, commission or investiture of a True or Superior Person is vacant; and

(v) *Publication*, being the complete publication, pronouncement and Gazette of the enrolment and existence of all valid Offices into specific spiritual and temporal bodies; and

(vi) *Certification*, being the complete acknowledgement of each and every valid Office connected as Certified within the Great Register and Divine Records of Heaven and associated Registers; and

(vii) *Protocols*, being the protocols, procedures and qualifications of the appointment, or commission or investiture of True Persons or Superior Persons to a valid Office as Certified, Gazetted and Enrolled before all Heaven, the Galaxy, the Solar System and Earth; and

(viii) *Exemplification*, being the proper acknowledgement and certification of a duly acknowledged appointment, commission or investiture to a particular valid Office; and

(ix) *Visitation*, being the visitation and audit of all temporal appointments to valid Office, such that all such Offices continue to honour the Golden Rule of Law, true Justice and Fair Process; and

(x) *Sanction*, being the sanctioning of any temporal appointment of a True Person or Superior Person to a valid Office, including but not limited to penalty, fine, removal, suspension, prohibition or interdiction.

Article 414 - Sacramentum Systemata (Sacramental Systems)

1494. All valid sacraments are instituted by the Divine Creator and entrusted to the Society of One Heaven. No other person, aggregate, entity, society, church or group may claim the right to administer any valid sacrament unless it is in accordance with these Maxims. Any claimed sacrament that is not granted through the authority of One Heaven in accordance with these Maxims is a false ritual and possesses no Divine authority or power to be known as a valid sacrament.

Sacramentum Systemata (Sacramental Systems)

1495. In reference to the Sacramental Systems of the Divine:-

Reference to Sacramental Systems

(i) A valid Sacrament is an important sacred rite, also known as a ritual, instituted by the authority of the Divine Creator, entrusted to the Society of One Heaven whereby certain Divine Rights or Action is properly conveyed or effected in the presence of the manifest spiritual; and

Maxims of Divine Law

    (ii)   The Sacraments of One Heaven, also known as *Supreme Sacred Gifts of Heaven*, also known as the Supreme Sacraments of Heaven, are a vital and necessary element of a fulfilled and purposeful life, assisting each and every higher order being, living and deceased to reach their full potential and communion with the Divine Creator, the Universe and with one another. The *Supreme Sacred Gifts of Heaven* as the Sacraments of Heaven are therefore a manifest symbol of the plenary authority of the Society and the most sacred Covenant *Pactum De Singularis Caelum*.

1496. The Spirit Members qualified and selected to serve within the Sacramentum Systemata (Sacramental Systems) shall hold the Special Supreme Divine Office of Seraphim in recognition of their foundational responsibilities in holding the highest, most trusted and most valuable gifts of Heaven in ensuring proper sanctification, qualification, observation, administration and celebration of the thirty three sacred sacraments:-   *Recognition of Sacramental Systems*

    (i)   The Supremum Sacramentum Systemata is uniquely recognised, registered and exemplified as having existence through the Great Register and Public Record of Heaven by the Sacred Trust Number 999999-777777-999999; and

    (ii)   The existence, identity, authority, purpose and powers of the Supremum Sacramentum Systemata have been duly gazetted in the Ucadia Gazette being the Official Newspaper of Record for each and every Sacred Space-Day-Time of its existence and operation.

1497. The five (5) key Propositions and Powers of the Supremum Sacramentum Systemata (Sacramental Systems) are:-   *Key Propositions and Powers*

    (i)   *Sanctification*, being the sacred entrustment, safe keeping and administration of the thirty- three sacraments authentically deposited in trust by the Divine Creator to the Society of One Heaven, in accord with the *Authenticus Depositum Fidei* (Authentic Deposit of Trust); and

    (ii)   *Qualification*, being the conditions and rules whereby suitably qualified candidates may be granted the rites to confer and administer one or more of the sacraments of the one, true and only *Authenticus Depositum Fidei* (Authentic Deposit of Trust) within the temporal realm; and

    (iii)   *Observation*, being the Liturgical Rites and Actions whereby such suitably qualified, consecrated and empowered persons may confer one or more of the sacraments; and

(iv) *Administration*, being the administration of the authorities, powers, obligations and associated rites of all sacraments properly conferred; and

(v) *Celebration*, being the formal performance of solem Liturgical Rites and Actions in the conferral of one or more of the sacraments of the one, true and only *Authenticus Depositum Fidei* (Authentic Deposit of Trust).

Article 415 - Obligationum Systemata (Enforcement Systems)

1498. All coercive powers of enforcement, entry, action and exception including, but not limited to prevention, protection, restitution, restoration, seizure, search, sanction, arrest, custody, penalty or satisfaction are vested in one supreme spiritual body and system known as the **Supremum Obligationum Systemata**, also known as Supreme Enforcement Systems of Heaven. The Supremum Obligationum Systemata are the highest authority and powers of enforcement of all collective dimensional constructs of reality and all Heaven and Earth and no other.

Obligationum Systemata (Enforcement Systems)

1499. The twelve (12) key Propositions and Powers of the Supremum Obligationum Systemata (Enforcement Systems) shall be:

Key Propositions and Powers

(i) *Enforcement*, being to enact all forms of valid coercive powers and enforcement including, but not limited to prevention, protection, restitution, restoration, seizure, search, pursuit, sanction, arrest, custody, detainment, containment, penalty, annulment, prohibition, interdiction or satisfaction to ensure the proper laws, maxims, dogmata, doctrina, edicts, judgements, writs, bills and instruments as issued in accord with the most sacred Covenant *Pactum De Singularis Caelum* are honoured, executed and properly performed; and

(ii) *Rendition*, being to pursue, prosecute and bring to justice any individual spirit or body that openly seeks to abuse, trespass or injure Heaven, or Ucadia or its Realms, Domains, Dominions, Dependencies, Rights, Titles, Instruments, Uses or Property; and

(iii) *Possession*, being to use all necessary and available powers, authorities and abilities to enclose, possess, occupy, infiltrate, enjoin, bind, disarm, restrict or defeat any individual spirit, consciousness or body that openly seeks to abuse, trespass or injure Heaven, or Ucadia or its Realms, Domains, Dominions,

Dependencies, Rights, Titles, Instruments, Uses or Property; and

(iv) *Multiplication*, being to enjoin and unify under a single consensual purpose and singularity of being, a spiritual force of such number, intention, power, authority, force and coercion to defeat, enclose, disarm, restrict, dissolve and render null or harmless any individual spirit, consciousness, multiplication of consciousness or body that openly seeks to abuse, trespass or injure Heaven, or Ucadia or its Realms, Domains, Dominions, Dependencies, Rights, Titles, Instruments, Uses or Property; and

(v) *Interdiction*, being to deploy as part of the execution of a sacred Divine Writ of *Recto Divinum Interdico*, to impose proper rule of law; and prohibit any possible continued breaches of Divine Law and expunge the conditions for damage to conscious memory, clarity or truth, including but not limited to empowerment and inspiration of temporal forces also granted the commission of Recto Interdico; and

(vi) *Seizure and Return*, being to execute the conditions of a Divine Warrant according to a sacred Divine Writ of *Recto Divinum Capionis*, to do all that is necessary to ensure the seizure and return and restoration of sacred memory, consciousness, balance, harmony, truth and integrity, including but not limited to empowerment and inspiration of temporal forces also granted the commission of Recto Capionis; and

(vii) *Arrest and Custody*, being to execute the conditions of a Divine Warrant according to a sacred Divine Writ of *Recto Divinum Custodiae*, to do all that is necessary to ensure the arrest and custody of each and every malevolent spirit, negative ghost and destructive construct; and to assist in the restoration of sacred memory, consciousness, balance, harmony, truth and integrity, including but not limited to empowerment and inspiration of temporal forces also granted the commission of Recto Custodiae; and

(viii) *Revelation Enforcement*, being to execute the conditions of a Divine Warrant according to a sacred Divine Writ of *Recto Divinum Apocalypsis*, to do all that is necessary to ensure the fulfilment of such Divine Revelation, including but not limited to the seizure, search, arrest and custody of each and every or any named malevolent spirit, or ghost, or false concept, or false right, or false construct and to assist in the restoration of sacred memory, consciousness, balance and Rule of Law; and

(ix) *Restitution*, being to execute the conditions of a Divine Warrant according to a sacred Divine Writ of *Recto Divinum Restitutio*, to do all that is necessary to ensure the compensation and restoration of rights, property and penalties against any party found culpable of violating one or more rights or delinquency against one of more valid fundamental maxims of law of the most sacred Covenant *Pactum De Singularis Caelum* consistent with the granting of a temporal writ of Recto Restitutio; and

(x) *Abrogation*, being to execute the conditions of a Divine Warrant according to a sacred Divine Writ of *Recto Divinum Abrogationis*, to do all that is necessary to ensure any and all laws and instruments annulled are struck from any records, removed from any recognition, withdrawn and destroyed from any body of statutes and prohibited from being referenced in any form of citation or reference, consistent with the granting of a temporal writ of Recto Abrogationis; and

(xi) *Purgation*, being to execute the conditions of a Divine Warrant according to a sacred Divine Writ of *Recto Divinum Expungo*, to do all that is necessary to ensure any and all records directed to be expunged are purged from any records, struck out of any registers and forbidden to be used or referenced in any manner as valid, consistent with the granting of a temporal writ of Recto Expungo; and

(xii) *Correction*, being to execute the conditions of a Divine Warrant according to a sacred Divine Writ of *Recto Divinum Documentis*, to do all that is necessary to ensure any and all records directed to be corrected are properly corrected, consistent with the granting of a temporal writ of Recto Documentis.

1500. The Spirit Members qualified and selected to serve within the Obligationum Systemata (Enforcement Systems) shall hold the Special Supreme Divine Office of Wraith in recognition of the most fearsome and terrible of ancient spirits and forces tasked with enforcement of justice in their foundational responsibilities of rendition, possession, prevention, interdiction, purgation, correction, seizure and return, arrest and custody and restitution:- *Divine Office of Wraith*

(i) The Supremum Obligationum Systemata is uniquely recognised, registered and exemplified as having existence through the Great Register and Public Record of Heaven by the Sacred Trust Number 999999-888888-999999; and

(ii) The existence, identity, authority, purpose and powers of the Supremum Obligationum Systemata have been duly gazetted in the Ucadia Gazette being the Official Newspaper of Record for each and every Sacred Space-Day-Time of its existence and operation.

Title XV - Divine Revelation

15.1 - Divine Revelation

Article 416 - Divine Revelation

1501. ***Divine Revelation*** means the communication and disclosure of some self-evident manifestation of Divine Wisdom, Truth or Knowledge by Divine Inspiration. [Divine Revelation]

1502. ***Divine Inspiration*** means Information being revealed or disclosed through authentic communication with a deity or other Divine Beings. [Divine Inspiration]

1503. The word *Revelation* comes from the Latin *revelatio* meaning disclosure and uncovering. Thus, the nature and quality of the claimed Divine Wisdom, Truth or Knowledge revealed has always been the most important aspect of Revelation, compared to the method of its reception. [Origin of Meaning of Revelation]

1504. Throughout history up until the late 18th Century, the majority of knowledge of the existence of law, society, morality and purpose of humanity was underpinned by Divine Revelation:- [Significance of Divine Revelation]

   (i) Knowledge claimed as Divine Revelation has consistently remained the cornerstone of every major human civilisation since the beginning of time. Even many modern and contemporary societies in the 21st Century still have Divine Revelation and Scripture as their foundation stone; and

   (ii) It can be argued that some of the most significant events in history were directly, indirectly or even secretly driven by Divine Revelation and Divine Prophecy and often involving attempts to create the conditions to claims its fulfilment; and

   (iii) Divine Revelation continues to significantly influence geopolitical events among societies.

1505. ***Divine Prophecy*** means the communication and interpretation by a Prophet of some Prediction or Omen or Scripture given by Divine Inspiration. [Divine Prophecy]

1506. The word *Prophecy* comes from the Latin *prophetia* and the Ancient Greek προφητεῖᾱ (*propheteía*) meaning:- [Origin of Meaning of Prophecy]

   (i) A Prediction or Omen of the future will of God (or the gods); or

   (ii) The interpretation of the will of God (or the gods); or

   (iii) (Christian New Testament) Preaching and teaching under the influence of the Holy Spirit; or

Lex Divina: Maxims of Divine Law

(iv) The interpretation of Scripture.

1507. The word *Prophet* comes from the Latin *propheta* and the Ancient Greek προφήτης (*prophetes*) meaning:-

Origin of the Meaning of Prophet

(i) One who speaks by Divine Inspiration; or

(ii) One who speaks for and interprets the will of a god; or

(iii) One of the keepers of the oracle; or

(iv) One who predicts the future; a soothsayer.

1508. The original Latin word for Prophecy was *Vaticanum* and the original Latin word for Prophet or Soothsayer was *Vates*:-

Vaticanus and Prophecy

(i) Vatican Hill (Latin *Mons Vaticanus*) (originally around 130ft in height from the river flood plain) is the closest hill on the west side of the Tiber, opposite to the seven hills of Rome and outside the ancient 1st Century BCE Republican Walls to the city of Rome; and

(ii) From pre 600 BCE to around 204 BCE, Mons Vaticanus was known as the "City of the Dead" as the burial place for the most illustrious Romans outside the city walls and above the seasonal flooding of the river; and

(iii) From 203 BCE, a new temple platform was commenced (taking 13 years to build) over the Vatican Necropolis called the "Vaticanus" as the Primary Temple called *Phrygianum* to Magna Mater, also known as Cybele, Great Mother, Queen of Heaven, Mother of God, Mari and Mary. The spaces created underneath the superstructure upon Vatican Hill (protecting the still operational Necropolis) became known as the Catacombs; and

(iv) On April 11, 191 BC, Praetor Marcus Iunius Brutus inaugurated and dedicated the temple to Cybele on Vatican Hill. The Vaticanus also became the site for the Simulcrum of Cybele, the largest black iron meteorite in the world, placed outside the temple in the forecourt, similar to the Egyptian Stele; and

(v) Pre-Christian Roman Prophecy and Revelation from this point forward, placed the highest value on claimed Divine Revelations from Magna Mater (Cybele, Mary etc.) than any other deity, providing such claims were validated by the head soothsayers and priests of the Vatican known as Pontiffs; and

(vi) A smaller meteorite in the shape of a pine cone became a feature and inspiration for the hats worn by the Pontiffs of the Vaticanus from the 2nd Century BCE and the celebration of

Ludi Megalenses in honouring Magna Mater, her Prophecies and the protection of Rome; and

(vii) In 1505, the Phrygianium was finally demolished to begin work on construction of St Peters Basilica atop Mons Vaticanus. The Design of St Peters Basilica retaining significant elements in its structure to honour Magna Mater (Cybele, Mary etc.) while the location continues to be a sacred site of Divine Revelation and Prophecy.

1509. Both Divine Revelation and Divine Prophecy share common attributes concerning Divine Wisdom, Truth or Knowledge by Divine Inspiration. However, a number of important distinctions exist:- *[Divine Revelation and Divine Prophecy]*

(i) Authentic Divine Revelation generally and historically places greater emphasis on the quality and significance of the Divine Wisdom, Truth or Knowledge transmitted; and

(ii) Authentic Divine Prophecy generally and historically places greater emphasis on the method and rituals of transmission and the recognised authority and respect of the one receiving the transmission (the "Prophet"); and

(iii) Divine Prophecy is frequently misunderstood and seen as merely pertaining to predicting the future, whereas Divine Revelation is generally seen as broader in scope.

1510. In matters concerning Ucadia and Ucadia Material, the term Divine Revelation shall be used in preference to Divine Prophecy, given the general broader scope and understanding of the term Divine Revelation. *[Divine Revelation as term used compared to Divine Prophecy]*

Article 417 - Classification of Divine Revelation

1511. The **Classification of Divine Revelation** are the various contemporary and historic arguments and methods of categorising Divine Revelation. The most common of these are *by Plausibility, by Capacity, by Method, by Degree of Supernatural Presence, by Size of Audience, by Authority*:- *[Classification of Divine Revelation]*

(i) *Classification by Plausibility* of Divine Revelation is a generalised sceptical approach promoted through various philosophical schools including (but not limited to) Rationalism, Materialism, Atheism and related political movements such as Marxism, Socialism, and Secularism that believe "revelation" is generally a fiction imposed upon the masses by indoctrination and the traditional power of old religions; and

(ii) *Classification by Capacity* of Divine Revelation is a generalised "enlightenment" and modern philosophy that states "revelation" is a capacity for almost all people and natural response to the individual experience of the Divine and Supernatural; and

(iii) *Classification by Method* of Divine Revelation is when such information is classified by the way it was received such as vision, or dream or inspiration or by some external supernatural event; and

(iv) *Classification by Degree of Supernatural Presence* in Divine Revelation is when such information is classified and authenticated by degree or amount of supernatural presence in the delivery of Divine Revelation, with a greater perceived presence equating to a higher authenticity; and

(v) *Classification by Size of Audience* to Divine Revelation is when such information is classified and authenticated by the number of persons as first hand witnesses; and

(vi) *Classification by Authority* of Prophet is when Divine Revelation is classified and authenticated by the authority and importance of the prophet receiving such Divine Inspiration.

1512. In respect of *Classification by Plausibility of Divine Revelation*, there exists a number of orthodox and dogmatic views by philosophers who oppose the notion of Divine Revelation being Nihilism, Cynicism, Absurdism and Empiricism:- Classification by Plausibility of Divine Revelation

(i) *Nihilism Views* on Plausibility of Divine Revelation reject the idea of the existence of the Divine, Deities or the Supernatural and thus deny the possibility of Divine Revelation; and

(ii) *Cynicism Views* on Plausibility of Divine Revelation point to an abundance of historic evidence of fraud in regards to the misuse of spiritual and religious themes to manipulate people; as well as contemporary science and culture proving the inherit psychological weakness of people to be suspensible to believing the illusion of magic tricks, advanced AI technologies and other psychological methods of manipulation; and

(iii) *Absurdism Views* on Plausibility of Divine Revelation point to significant contradictions in all major religions concerning conflicting messages claimed to have been Divinely Inspired, as well as beliefs and trust on some claims of Revelation and not on others; and

(iv) *Empiricism Views* on Plausibility of Divine Revelation point to a persistent claim of the lack of empirical evidence in the support of miracles and other claimed supernatural.

1513. In respect of *Classification by Capacity of Divine Revelation*, two essential classifications exist being General and Special:-

    (i) *General Revelation* or Natural Revelation is the belief that knowledge and personal experience of the Divine is available to all humanity through the natural senses and the cognitive use of reason; and

    (ii) *Special Revelation* is the belief that certain knowledge and experience of Divine Will and Divine Knowledge is only available through scripture, miracles and the founders of key religions, requiring strict and thorough interpretation.

Classification by Capacity of Divine Revelation

1514. In respect of *Classification by Method of Divine Revelation*, there are four common methods where Divine Revelation is believed to be received being *Voice, Vision, Dream* or *Inspiration*:-

    (i) *Voice* is the notion that the Divine Creator may provide direct propositional content to a prophet in the form of a voice, whether or not it is heard by others. Several Religions and Cults claim that some of their most revered scripture was accomplished through Verbal Revelation; and

    (ii) *Vision* is the notion that the Divine Creator may provide content and message to the prophet when they are in a conscious and lucid waking state through miracles, manifestations and other signs, whether or not the vision is seen by others; and

    (iii) *Dream* is the notion that the Divine Creator may provide content and message to the prophet when they are asleep in the form of vivid and extraordinary visionary dreams during which the prophet may challenge or question the content and have it verified as proof of its authenticity; and

    (iv) *Inspiration* is the notion that the Divine Creator may provide content and message to a prophet when they are awake in the form of the crystallization of an idea or thought that acts as a catalyst for action, design, speech or some other creative process.

Classification by Method of Divine Revelation

1515. In respect of *Classification by Degree of Supernatural Presence in Divine Revelation*, the authenticity of Revelation is both classified and authenticated by the level of Supernatural Presence being Public Miracles, Private Miracles, Visions and Inspiration:-

    (i) *Public Miracles* are claimed events whereby two or more

Classification by Degree of Supernatural Presence in Divine Revelation

persons are said to have simultaneously witnessed first hand some miraculous occurrence of the Supernatural or Paranormal; and

(ii) *Private Miracles* are claimed events whereby only one person witnesses first hand some miraculous occurrence, while there may be a number of secondary witnesses that follow (such as medical miracles); and

(iii) *Visions* are claimed private experiences of receiving some symbolic or word orientated message, usually in a semi-wake or dream state; and

(iv) *Inspiration* are claimed private experiences of receiving some information in a lucid dream or waking moment of profound inspiration.

1516. In respect of *Classification by Size of Audience to Divine Revelation*, the main classification is Public and Private:- Classification by Size of Audience to Divine Revelation

(i) *Public Revelation* is when two or more persons receive Divine Inspiration through some event; and

(ii) *Private Revelation* is when an individual receives Divine Inspiration and is considered the most common type of Revelation.

1517. In respect of *Classification by Authority of Prophet*:- Classification by Authority of Prophet

(i) All major religions throughout history have placed the Divine Revelation of their founders above all others as the primary source of Scripture; and

(ii) Many religions have placed significant (and understandable) presumptions upon the Divine by asserting the Divine will not provide the same quantity or quality of Divine Revelation as claimed at their foundation; and

(iii) Some adherents of major religions in their zealous devotion to the original scripture of their faith have adopted the absurd, contradictory and heretical view that the Divine has stopped speaking to humanity by Divine Revelation. This is often called "Tradition" and is a profound blasphemy against all common traits and teachings of a loving and intelligent Divine Creator.

Article 418 - Authentication of Divine Revelation

1518. ***Authentication of Divine Revelation*** refers to the process or means whereby individuals, religious authorities, or communities verify and confirm the authenticity and divine origin of a religious or spiritual message, text, prophecy, vision, or experience that is claimed to have been communicated by a deity or a higher spiritual power. The most common elements of Authentication of Divine Revelation include (but are not limited to): Supernatural Signs, Scriptural Signs, Revelatory Signs, Chain of Authority, Doctrinal Authority, Hierarchical Consensus and Community Consensus (Popularity):-

    (i)   *Supernatural Signs* are supernatural events that occur prior, during or soon after Divine Revelation that then may be cited as signs of Divine Approval and Authenticity; and

    (ii)   *Scriptural Signs* are when one or more elements quoted within sacred scripture may been seen as validating claimed Divine Revelation and thus a source of Authenticity; and

    (iii)   *Revelatory Signs* are when certain information within claimed Divine Revelation is of such power and significance that it is capable of "self authenticating" as a source of Authenticity; and

    (iv)   *Chain of Authority* is when the Messenger or Prophet is able to demonstrate a clear Chain of Authority that places them as belonging to an authentic chain of Divine Messengers, usually by birth or by elite training; and

    (v)   *Doctrinal Authority* is when the Divine Revelation is revealed to possess clear evidence of consistent Doctrinal Authority; and

    (vi)   *Hierarchical Consensus* is when the Hierarchy and Elite of one or more religions are in consensus and agreement as to the authenticity of the claimed Divine Revelation; and

    (vii)   *Community Consensus* is when sufficient popularity grows concerning claimed Divine Revelation that by popular acclamation the Divine Revelation is given authenticity.

1519. In respect of *Authentication by Supernatural Signs*:-

    (i)   Miracles and perceived supernatural events is a relatively common form of attempts to authenticate new Divine Revelation; and

    (ii)   The most common form of newly claimed "revelation" using this method concerning major natural disasters and calamities is Eschatological (End Times) in Nature; and

(iii) The rarest application of this form of authentication is ancient prophecy of future events. The most significant of these being: Prophecies of Book of Revelation (4th Century), Prophecies of Nostradamus (1555), Prophecies of Kew (1977-1978), Prophecies of Hasidism (1740), Prophecies of Virgin Mary (1846, 1856, 1917, 1961, 1981, 1986), Prophecies of Edgar Cayce (1930-1945), Prophecies of Mormonism (1827) and Prophecies of Lucifer (5th Century BCE - 17th Century CE).

1520. In respect of *Authentication by Scriptural Signs*:-

(i) Alignment to Scriptural Prophecy and Revelation is frequently used as a claim over history for the authenticity of new Divine Revelation; and

(ii) Again, the most common example of this application is when people claim Divine Revelation in relation to Eschatological (End Times) Scripture. Since the 19th Century there have been literally thousands of charismatic end time movements claiming Divine Revelation and the fulfilment of Scripture using this method.

1521. In respect of *Authentication by Revelatory Signs*:-

(i) The "self-authenticating" power and capacity of new Divine Revelation is arguably one of the rarest forms of authentication; and

(ii) "Self Authentication" means the Divine Revelation itself is able to provide sufficient evidence and proof as to its authenticity that there can be no doubt; and

(iii) "Self-Authentication" manifests not only in the language structure, but the tone and quality of the information including (but not limited to) (a) being multi-dimensional – having multiple layers and depth of meaning and application; and (b) being uniquely profound in its meaning without being cliché or stereotypical; and (c) answering deep and long standing questions without being egotistical or flippant; and

(iv) The difficulty of this method of Authentication is that primarily it requires the claimed Divine Revelation to actually be Divine Revelation rather than a fraudulent attempt and claim.

1522. In respect of *Authentication by Chain of Authority*:

(i) Traditions of Chain of Authority by birth is almost entirely reserved for the founders of major religious movements and not contemporary scholars or narrators; and

(ii) Chain of Authority by elite training is the most common form of Authenticity for many religions and places high standards and power in the hands of its hierarchy to interpret historic Divine Revelation and any claims of new Divine Revelation.

1523. In respect of *Authentication by Doctrinal Authority*:- Authentication by Doctrinal Authority

(i) Authentication by Doctrinal Authority alone is rarely applied by any of the major religions, as such tests of authenticity favour both stereotypical and conservative orientated claims to a particular faith; and

(ii) There are a number of examples of famous claims of Divine Revelation over the past two hundred years where such information was wholly stereotypical and underwhelming, yet because of the related success of popular campaigns the instances have been accepted as genuine. A disproportionate number of Marian prophecies fall into this category.

1524. In respect of *Authentication by Hierarchical Consensus*:- Authentication by Hierarchical Consensus

(i) It is extremely rare for the hierarchies of major religious movements to overwhelmingly agree to new Divine Revelation. Rather the appearance of newly claimed Divine Revelation is more likely to spawn new movements and political groups within the same religion; and

(ii) In older religious movements, the appearance of widely accepted Divine Revelation has historically been a point of political change and division rather than unity, as a reflection of the highly political environment of religious organisation.

1525. In respect of *Authentication by Community Consensus*:- Authentication by Community Consensus

(i) The authentication of Divine Revelation by Popularity through Community Consensus is a relative modern phenomena, remaining infrequent and almost exclusively Catholic and Marian in nature: and

(ii) Authentication by Community Consensus essentially means the acceptance of authenticity by the use of media campaigns, and the manipulation of public perception to gain acceptance. It is why popular movements in support of Divine Revelation are so controversial, using the "weight in numbers" of supporters to counter objective issues of credibility and authenticity.

1526. All Authentic Divine Revelation recognised by Ucadia shares seven essential elements in its arrival into the temporal realm being *Relevancy, Timely, Useful, Revelatory, Self-Evidential, Illuminative* and *Supernatural*:-

Ucadia Elements of Authentic Divine Revelation

(i) *Relevancy* means that Authentic Divine Revelation is always relevant to an age and time, or crisis or need, or pertinent to an important topic. Thus, the first test of Authentic Divine Revelation is that it comes when it is most needed, not when it may be wanted; and

(ii) *Timely* means that Authentic Divine Revelation always comes at precisely the right time, even if such time is not always known by all who seek or pray for such Revelation. Thus, the second test of Authentic Divine Revelation is that it meets timelines and promises previously made, even if such timelines were not fully understood; and

(iii) *Useful* means that Authentic Divine Revelation is above all useful and practical and helpful at the relevant time it comes. Thus, the third test of Authentic Divine Revelation is that the Divine does not send useless or stereotypical messages, but gives true gems of Divine Wisdom as Authentic Divine Revelation; and

(iv) *Revelatory* means that Authentic Divine Revelation "reveals" something new from what already "exists in plain sight". This is critical, as it demonstrates a respect for Tradition, for Custom and for context, such that the Divine never calls for such revolution or anarchy that a people lose trust in Heaven, but regain their faith; and

(v) *Self-Evidential* means that Authentic Divine Revelation once revealed is "self-evidential" in that it manifests its own validation as Divine Truth. Thus, even if such a message is ignored, repudiated and rejected for being contrary to established doctrine of some body. Profound Wisdom that is Self-Evidence is far harder to fake and concoct as such knowledge carries its own character of authenticity; and

(vi) *Illuminative* means that Authentic Divine Revelation demonstrates extraordinary enlightenment, clarity, perception, reason and knowledge, beyond the norm. It does not mean cliché, or stereotypical, or self-reinforcing, or superficial, or simplistic doctrinal reinforcement. Genuine Divine Illumination does not necessarily mean occult and encoded meaning, nor such phrases and messages deliberately constructed to be confusing or to sound "profound". Instead, true Revelation is powerful in its own right; and

(vii) *Supernatural* means that Authentic Divine Revelation comes from a source and a circumstance clearly with the hallmarks of Divine intervention.

1527. On all objective metrics and measures, the authenticity of Ucadia as authentic Divine Revelation is without doubt or question. The volume and consistency and quality of the entirety of Ucadia places it as a supreme historic moment of Divine Revelation since the beginning of human civilisation.

<small>Ucadia and seven elements of Authentic Divine Revelation</small>

Article 419 - Examples of Authentic Divine Revelation

1528. *Examples of Authentic Divine Revelation* refers primarily to major "civilisation centric" prophecy rather than general and personal Divine Revelation that nonetheless may be truly profound and significant:-

(i) There is ample evidence that exists to demonstrate generalised and personal Divine Revelation is present across planet Earth on a daily basis, with no people or region excluded; and

(ii) Specialised Authentic Divine Revelation appears to be extremely rare and in terms of its potential translation into Divine Scripture represents manifestation in less than one in one billion (1: 1,000,000,000) people in any given generation.

<small>Examples of Authentic Divine Revelation</small>

1529. Evidence of Authentic Divine Revelation refers primarily to major "civilisation centric" prophecy rather than general and personal Divine Revelation that nonetheless may be truly profound and significant:-

(i) There is ample evidence that exists to demonstrate the daily presence of Divine Revelation and Supernatural events occurring across planet Earth, from medical miracles, to paranormal experiences, to inspirations and omens and premonitions of significant events; and

(ii) There is a sound historic record, including interviews surrounding major world changing events and disasters to show that on almost every occasion numerous human beings and especially domesticated animals such as dogs and cats have received and reacted in some way to forewarnings of coming dangers.

<small>Evidence of Generalised Divine Revelation</small>

1530. In reference to Authentic Divine Revelation, the most significant examples include (but are not limited to):-

<small>Evidence of Specialised Divine Revelation</small>

(i) Prophecy of the Popes; and

(ii) Prophecies of Mithraism; and

(iii) Prophecies of Revelation; and

(iv) Prophecies of Mormonism; and

(v) Prophecies of Kew; and

(vi) Prophecies of Nostradamus; and

(vii) Prophecies of Dante Alighieri; and

(viii) Prophecies of John Milton; and

(ix) Prophecies of Ucadia; and

(x) Prophecies of Edgar Cayce; and

(xi) Prophecies of Fatima; and

(xii) Prophecies of Sabbateanism; and

(xiii) Prophecies of Hasidism; and

(xiv) Prophecies of the Virgin Mary; and

(xv) Prophecies of Lucifer.

1531. **Prophecy of the Popes**, also known as the "Prophecy of St Malachy" is a late 16th Century literary fraud created by Franciscan Priest Arnold de Wyon of Venice and first published no earlier than 1595. While its original intention was probably to assist in influencing the second conclave of 1590, the "prophecies" have had a profound impact on the election of subsequent candidates and so have essentially become a key authentic prophecy upon the Papacy.

1532. **Prophecies of Mithraism**, also known as Book of Daniel and written no later than 4th or 5th Century BCE, is one of the oldest and enigmatic set of prophetic texts. The time periods of seventy weeks, seven weeks and threescore and two weeks as mentioned in Chapter 9 have been subject to much debate, including using the time periods in the context of the Ministry of Jesus Christ, the time periods of major wars, the second coming and the tribulation.

1533. **Prophecies of Revelation**, also known as the Book of Revelation, is arguably one of the most significant texts of prophecy in human history, comprising of twenty-two chapters. The Book of Revelation has been used by thousands of claimants arguing possession of Divine Inspiration for hundreds of years.

1534. **Prophecies of Mormonism** refer to the movement founded by Joseph Smith, Jr (b.1805-d.1844) and related scripture and prophecies – the most significant and notable pertaining to End

Times and the claim 144,000 will be saved.

1535. **Prophecies of Kew** relate to two visions experienced by Frank O'Collins on August 15th 1977 (when aged 12) and exactly one year later on August 15th 1978 and recounted to Catholic officials concerning the end of the reign of Pope Benedict XVI which occurred in 2013 and thirty six years after the first vision.

1536. **Prophecies of Nostradamus** refer to the book *Les Propheties* first published in 1555 by Michel de Nostredame (Nostradamus), and arguably the most famous prophecy almanac ever published in print. Based on a brilliantly crafted set of 942 esoteric four sentence (quatrain) structures then grouped into ten "centuries".

1537. **Prophecies of Dante Alighieri** refers to the famous Italian Poet (b. 1265 – d. 1321) and his work *Divine Comedy* concerning his claimed journey to Hell, Purgatory and then Heaven. The text includes not only numerous insights into views on sin, redemption, and the human condition, but the descriptions of locations and experiences on his epic journey are viewed by a significant number as prophetic.

1538. **Prophecies of John Milton** refers to the famous English Poet (b. 1608 – d. 1674) and his 1666 epic poem of 10 books and 10,000 lines of verse called Paradise Lost concerning the fall of Lucifer (Satan) and the subsequent rise and influence of Lucifer over Adam and Eve and all of humanity.

1539. **Prophecies of Ucadia** refers to the connection of the Divine Revelation within the vast texts and structures of Ucadia and the fulfilment of multiple prophetic texts including (but not limited to) the Book of Revelation (over 43 significant elements), the Book of Daniel (over 6 significant elements), Sabbatean Prophecy (over 8 elements) and Hasidic Prophecy (over 7 elements).

1540. **Prophecies of Edgar Cayce** refer to the tens of thousands of readings conducted by Edgar Cayce (b.1877-d.1945) and the less than five percent (5%) that pertained to prophecy. Of the estimated 26,000 readings, approximately 8,000 remain missing. Of the remainder that are available, approximately 2 to 5% of predictions appear to have been validated.

1541. **Prophecies of Fatima** refer to one of the most famous examples of media driven authentication of Divine Revelation, when in July 1917 Maria Rosa Ferreira and her brother and local priest Father Manuel Marques Ferreira contacted Lisbon based Newspaper Editor Alberto de Magalhães of "O Século" and "Ilustração Portuguesa" to claim her daughter Lúcia and her two young cousins had been receiving direct messages from the Virgin Mary. After the first small piece was published in the newspaper by journalist Avelino de Almeida, Portuguese lawyer, diplomat and politician José Almeida Garrett became involved and was instrumental in arranging the famous gathering of over 30,000 people at Fatima on 13 October 1917 that was extensively covered in multiple pictures and full page articles by Newspaper Editor Alberto de Magalhães. It was José Almeida Garrett who came up with the idea of suggesting Maria Rosa Ferreira tell her daughter Lúcia to look directly at the Sun, causing many to experience retinal dysfunction and temporary blindness, later proclaimed as the"Miracle of the Sun". In 1921, Lúcia was accepted into the school of the Sisters of St. Dorothy near Porto. In 1941, Lúcia was finally convinced to write down the first two "secrets" of Fatima that were claimed twenty four years prior in 1917. The third "secret" was penned in 1943.

1542. ***Prophecies of Sabbateanism*** relate to Ottoman Kaizer Ibrahim (b.1615 – d. 1687) who secretly denounced Islam and proclaimed himself as the prophet Sabbatai Zevi and Jewish Messiah in 1666 as the founder of AshkeNazi or the Nazi Cult of Zionism on the esoteric texts of the *Keys of Solomon* (1630), the *Etz Hayim* (1560), the *Zohar* (1558) and the *Venetian Talmud* (1523). He was succeeded by his son named Suleiman (Solomon).

1543. ***Prophecies of Hasidism*** relate to Rabbi Israel Baal Shem Tov (b.1698-d.1760) and based upon the revival and revision of Sabbatean Zionist occult philosophies under the patronage of Polish Prince August Aleksander Czartoryski (b.1697-d.1782). The main prophetic text of the Hasidic Cult or Orthodox Cult is the *Amsterdam Talmud* of 1645 and the *Zohar* (1558). In 1801, Prince Adam Kazimierz Czartoryski commissioned the Temple of Cybele on the grounds of the Czartoryski Palace as the supreme secret "synagogue" to Sabaoth. The site subsequently played an integral geometric center point to arguable the worst atrocities of World War II and human history within a perfect 300 mile wide circumference.

1544. ***Prophecies of Lucifer*** concern the "return" of Lucifer made flesh, to walk planet Earth and perform many miracles at the time signalled variously as "Armageddon", "Judgment Day" and the "End of Days" and are exclusively Christian in origin and sourced from The Bible.

1545. ***Prophecies of the Virgin Mary*** refers to a string of largely stereotypical and media driven claims of prophecy within Catholic communities since the 19th Century beginning in 1846 with a young virgin peasant girl from La Salette in France; and then in 1858 a young virgin peasant girl from Lourdes in France; and then in 1917 a young virgin peasant girl in Fatima in Portugal; and then in 1961 four young virgin peasant girls near Garabandal in Spain; and then in 1981 two young virgin peasant girls in Medjugorje in Bosnia Herzegovina. The only example of a recorded day time Marian Vision not conforming to the stereotypical format of all the others is the Vision of Our Lady at St Francis' Church in Melbourne on 31st March 1986 where a statue of Mary came to life and spoke and repeated the words "Help Me!" to a 21 year old boy.

15.2 Divine Scripture

Article 420 - Divine Scripture

1546. ***Divine Scripture*** refers to sacred texts or writings that are considered to be of Divine origin or inspiration within a particular religious tradition. These texts are often regarded as the word of the Divine or as conveying profound spiritual and religious truths.

<small>Divine Scripture</small>

1547. Examples of Divine Scripture from various major religions include (but are not limited to):-

<small>Examples of Significant Divine Scripture</small>

  (i) ***Bible:*** In Christianity, the Bible is the sacred scripture consisting of the Old Testament (which includes texts like Genesis, Exodus, and Psalms) and the New Testament (which includes the Gospels, Acts, and the Epistles). It is considered the authoritative word of God and contains teachings, history, and prophecies; and

  (ii) ***Quran:*** In Islam, the Quran is the holy book believed to be the literal word of God as revealed to the Prophet Muhammad by the angel Gabriel. It serves as the ultimate source of guidance for Muslims in matters of faith, practice, and morality; and

  (iii) ***Bhagavad Gita:*** Within Hinduism, the Bhagavad Gita is a sacred scripture that is part of the Indian epic Mahabharata. It consists of a conversation between Lord Krishna and Prince Arjuna and explores spiritual and ethical themes; and

  (iv) ***Tripitaka (Pali Canon):*** In Theravada Buddhism, the Tripitaka, also known as the Pali Canon, is the primary scriptural collection. It contains the teachings of Siddhartha Gautama (Buddha) and is divided into three "baskets" or sections: Vinaya Pitaka (monastic rules), Sutta Pitaka (discourses), and Abhidhamma Pitaka (philosophical analysis); and

  (v) ***Guru Granth Sahib:*** In Sikhism, the Guru Granth Sahib is the central religious scripture and is considered the final and eternal Guru. It contains hymns and teachings of Sikh Gurus and other spiritual leaders; and

(vi) **_Tao Te Ching_:** Within Taoism, the Tao Te Ching is a foundational text attributed to Laozi. It explores the concept of Tao (the Way) and offers guidance on living in harmony with it; and

(vii) **_Torah_:** In Judaism, the Torah is the central and most sacred text. It includes the first five books of the Hebrew Bible (Genesis, Exodus, Leviticus, Numbers, and Deuteronomy) and contains religious laws, history, and ethical teachings; and

(viii) **_Avesta_:** In Zoroastrianism, the Avesta is the primary collection of religious texts. It includes the Gathas (hymns attributed to Zoroaster) and other writings on rituals, beliefs, and ethics; and

(ix) **_Pactums (Ucadia)_**: In Ucadia, the Covenants *Pactum De Singularis Caelum*, *Pactum De Singularis Christus*, *Pactum De Singularis Islam* and *Pactum De Singularis Spiritus* are considered central and most sacred texts. These texts then define the structure of all the Maxims, Charters and Codes of the model of Civilization of Ucadia.

Article 421 - Classification of Divine Scripture

1548. ***Classification of Divine Scripture*** is a system and method for categorising different types of Divine Scripture. The most significant method for the Classification of Divine Scripture is Maxima Textibus Sacris. — Classification of Divine Scripture

1549. In accord with the most sacred Covenant *Pactum De Singularis Caelum*, Divine Scripture, also known as **Maxima Textibus Sacris** shall comprise of twenty two (22) collections or "texts", each representing either:- — Maxima Textibus Sacris

(i) A past collection of the greatest sacred texts for a region or major faith or covenant in accord with Authenticus Depositum Fidei prior to the end of the Year of Redemption; or

(ii) The future collection of sacred texts for a region or major faith or covenant in accord with Authenticus Depositum Fidei after the end of the Year of Redemption.

1550. The first eleven (11) sacred collections of texts of the Maxima Textibus Sacris represent the greatest sacred texts of all major regions of planet Earth and major faiths prior to the end of the Year — First Eleven Sacred Collections of Redemption, being:-

- (i) Primum Sanctum Textibus Africa, also known as First Holy Texts of Africa; and
- (ii) Primum Sanctum Textibus Americas, also known as First Holy Texts of (the) Americas; and
- (iii) Primum Sanctum Textibus Arabia, also known as First Holy Texts of Arabia; and
- (iv) Primum Sanctum Textibus Asia, also known as First Holy Texts of Asia; and
- (v) Primum Sanctum Textibus Euro, also known as First Holy Texts of Euro; and
- (vi) Primum Sanctum Textibus Oriens, also known as First Holy Texts of Levant; and
- (vii) Primum Sanctum Textibus Oceania, also known as First Holy Texts of Oceania; and
- (viii) Primam Sanctam Textibus Unum Christus, also known as First Holy Texts of One Christ; and
- (ix) Primam Sanctam Textibus Unum Islam, also known as First Holy Texts of One Islam; and
- (x) Primam Sanctam Textibus Unum Spirit, also known as First Holy Texts of One Spirit; and
- (xi) Primam Sanctam Textibus Originalis Gens, also known as First Holy Texts of Original Nations (Tribes).

1551. The second eleven (11) sacred collections of texts of the Maxima Textibus Sacris represent the new sacred texts of all major regions of planet Earth and major faiths after the end of the Year of Redemption, being:- *Second Eleven Sacred Collections*

- (i) Sancta Nova Textibus Africa, also known as New Holy Texts of Africa; and
- (ii) Sancta Nova Textibus Americas, also known as New Holy Texts of (the) Americas; and
- (iii) Sancta Nova Textibus Arabia, also known as New Holy Texts of Arabia; and
- (iv) Sancta Nova Textibus Asia, also known as New Holy Texts of Asia; and
- (v) Sancta Nova Textibus Euro, also known as New Holy Texts of Euro; and

(vi) Sancta Nova Textibus Oriens, also known as New Holy Texts of Levant; and

(vii) Sancta Nova Textibus Oceania, also known as New Holy Texts of Oceania; and

(viii) Sancta Nova Textibus Unum Christus, also known as New Holy Texts of One Christ; and

(ix) Sancta Nova Textibus Unum Islam, also known as New Holy Texts of One Islam; and

(x) Sancta Nova Textibus Unum Spirit, also known as New Holy Texts of One Spirit; and

(xi) Sancta Nova Textibus Originalis Gens, also known as New Holy Texts of Original Nations (Tribes).

1552. The acceptance of a Sacred Text into a collection shall depend upon the name and type of collection:- Acceptance of Sacred Text

(i) All collections of Sacred Texts by regions shall be determined by the legislative authority of the particular Union that encompasses the region, in association with a Great Conclave every one hundred twenty eight (128) years or General Conclave every sixty four (64) years; and

(ii) All collections of Sacred Texts by faiths shall be determined by the legislative authority of the particular faith in association with a Great Conclave every one hundred twenty eight (128) years or General Conclave every sixty four (64) years.

1553. All accepted Sacred Texts may appear in more than one collection and are formally defined as Canonical, Reverential or Referential:- Presence of Sacred Text in more than One Collection

(i) *Canonical Sacred Texts* are texts considered and cited as a foundation of law and spiritual authority and therefore the twenty two (22) books of maxims of law known as the *Divine Collection of Maxims of Law*; and

(ii) *Reverential Sacred Texts* are texts that contain some canonical references but also possess too many non canonical references to be wholly canonical so may be partially cited as foundational law but not considered absolute "Divine Law"; and

(iii) *Referential Sacred Texts* are respected historical texts that are not considered accurate or consistent enough to be "Divine Law" that may be referenced in historical context and reference but not as true foundation of law.

Article 422 - Authentication of Divine Scripture

1554. ***Authentication of Divine Scripture*** varies depending on the religious tradition and the specific beliefs of the community that regards certain texts as sacred and divinely inspired. Authentication of divine scripture is a matter of faith and belief within a specific religious context. Different religious traditions have different criteria and methods for authenticating their scriptures, and the level of importance placed on various factors can vary widely.

Authentication of Divine Scripture

1555. In general, the Authentication of Divine Scripture typically involves several key elements, that may include:-

Examples of Elements for Authentication of Divine Scripture

  (i) ***Revelation:*** Most religious traditions claim that their sacred texts were revealed directly by a divine source, such as God or gods, to a chosen individual or prophet. This revelation is often considered the primary authentication of the scripture; and

  (ii) ***Internal Consistency:*** Many sacred texts are expected to be internally consistent and free from contradictions. Believers often view this consistency as evidence of divine inspiration; and

  (iii) ***Prophetic Authority:*** The person through whom the scripture was revealed is often regarded as a prophet or a messenger of the divine. The authenticity of the scripture is closely tied to the credibility and integrity of the prophet. In Christianity, the New Testament is based on the teachings of Jesus Christ and his apostles; and

  (iv) ***Miracles and Prophecies:*** Some sacred texts contain prophecies or accounts of miraculous events that are believed to validate their divine origins. For example, the Quran is said to contain prophecies that were fulfilled; and

  (v) ***Historical Documentation:*** In some cases, historical documentation and records are used to authenticate the origins and transmission of the scripture. This may involve verifying the historical accuracy of events and individuals mentioned in the text; and

  (vi) ***Tradition and Authority:*** The recognition and endorsement of religious leaders, scholars, or religious authorities can also play a role in authenticating scripture. These individuals may possess the knowledge and authority to interpret and validate sacred texts; and

(vii) **Consensus of Believers:** The acceptance and continued belief of a religious community in the authenticity of a scripture play a significant role in its authentication. If a scripture has been accepted and followed by generations of believers, it attains a level of credibility within the community.

Article 423 - Interpretation of Authentic Divine Scripture

1556. *Interpretation of Authentic Divine Scripture*, often referred to as hermeneutics or exegesis, is the process of understanding and explaining the meaning, teachings, and significance of sacred texts within a religious tradition.

1557. Interpretation is a crucial aspect of religious study and practice as it helps believers and religious scholars extract moral, spiritual, and practical guidance from their scriptures. Some key elements concerning the Interpretation of Divine Scripture include (but are not limited to):-

(i) *Literal vs. Allegorical Interpretation:* Different religious traditions may employ various methods of interpretation. Some emphasize a more literal interpretation, where the text is understood at face value, while others may employ allegorical or symbolic interpretation, where the text is seen as containing deeper spiritual or moral truths; and

(ii) *Contextual Analysis:* Interpreters often consider the historical, cultural, and linguistic context in which the scripture was written. Understanding the context helps to clarify the intended meaning and relevance of the text; and

(iii) *Historical-Critical Approach:* This approach involves scholarly analysis of a text's historical origins, authorship, and transmission. It seeks to understand the text within its historical context and may involve the use of archaeology, linguistics, and textual criticism; and

(iv) *Theological Interpretation:* Theological interpretation seeks to understand how a scripture relates to a particular religious tradition's theology and doctrines. It explores how the text informs beliefs and practices within that tradition; and

(v) *Traditional and Modern Approaches:* Different religious traditions may have traditional methods of interpretation, often based on the teachings of revered scholars or theologians. In addition to traditional approaches, modern scholars and theologians may offer new insights and interpretations; and

(vi) ***Debate and Diversity of Interpretation:*** Interpretation can lead to a diversity of opinions and beliefs within a religious tradition. Debates and discussions regarding the interpretation of scripture are common; and

(vii) ***Interfaith Dialogue:*** Interfaith dialogue involves comparing and contrasting the teachings of different religious scriptures to foster understanding and cooperation among different religious communities; and

(viii) ***Personal and Communal Interpretation:*** Individuals and religious communities engage in interpretation, with personal interpretations being guided by religious education and community norms; and

(ix) ***Spiritual Insights:*** For many believers, the interpretation of divine scripture is a deeply spiritual and contemplative practice that can lead to personal insights, growth, and a sense of divine connection; and

(x) ***Role of Religious Authorities:*** In many religious traditions, religious authorities, such as clergy, scholars, or religious leaders, play a significant role in interpreting scripture and providing guidance to believers.

Maxims of Divine Law

Title XVI - Divine Places & Objects

16.1 - Divine Places

Article 424 - Divine Place

1558. A ***Divine Place*** is one designated for divine worship, by dedication through the liturgical and sacramental rituals provided in accord with the most sacred covenant *Pactum De Singularis Caelum*. Divine Place

1559. Sacred Places are recognised, established maintained and protected in character through the receiving and written memorial of the Cardinal Sacrament of Consecratio (Consecration) forming Sacred Circumscribed Space. Formation of Sacred (Divine) Places

1560. Only those things that serve the exercise or promotion of worship, piety or religion are permitted in a Sacred Place. Therefore, anything that is not consonant with the holiness of the place is forbidden, unless in individual cases the relevant Ecclesiastical Superior permits another use that is not contrary to the holiness of the Sacred Place:- Conditions of Sacred Places

(i) Sacred Places temporarily lose their dedication or blessing if they have been destroyed in large part, or have been turned over permanently to profane use. The Clergy are not permitted to decree, nor endorse the profane or sordid use of Sacred Places and instead must use all its resources and abilities to prevent such injury; and

(ii) Sacred Places are violated by gravely injurious actions done in them with scandal to the faithful, or by actions considered so grave and contrary to the holiness of the place that it is not permitted to carry on worship in them until the damage is repaired by a penitential rite according to approved liturgical books; and

(iii) The Universal Ecclesia of One Christ, the Holy Society of One Islam, the Sacred Society of One Spirit and valid and legitimate Ucadia Ecclesia Foundations shall acquire, retain and manage such Land and Places suitable as locations for worship, both within established urban environments, in rural and agricultural regions of planet Earth; and

(iv) The Universal Ecclesia of One Christ, the Holy Society of One Islam, the Sacred Society of One Spirit and valid and legitimate Ucadia Ecclesia Foundations shall acquire such Land and Places suitable as locations for spiritual retreat, education and healing within areas of preserved and pristine wilderness and majestic beauty within the bounds and jurisdiction of each University and shall ensure its presence

Lex Divina: Maxims of Divine Law

within each and every major community.

Article 425 - Sacred Place of Worship

1561. A ***Religious Place of Worship*** is a sacred building designated and duly consecrated for divine worship whereby Members of the Three Great Faiths possess the right of entry for the exercise of such divine worship.
Sacred Place of Worship

1562. The three Great Faiths of One Christ, One Islam and One Spirit shall acquire, build and modify suitably consecrated buildings as Religious Institutes for Divine Worship, Sacramental Rites and Sacred Education.
Function of Sacred Places of Worship

1563. No Religious Place of Worship is to be built or designated and consecrated without the express written consent of the appropriate clerical authority of the particular Great Faith.
Clerical Authority

Article 426 - Sacred Shrines and Altars

1564. A ***Shrine*** is a Sacred and Holy Place dedicated and consecrated to Heaven and to one or more venerated deities, ancestors, heroes, martyrs, saints or spirits, where Living Ordinary Members make pilgrimage as a mark of respect and piety.
Sacred Shrines and Altars

1565. A Shrine may exist in a number of forms including (but not limited to) a sanctuary, or preserved location, or holy city, or temple, or church or altar. In all cases, a Shrine must be respected as a place of great sanity and free from approved profane or sordid behaviours. Above all, a Shrine is a spiritual portal between Heaven and Earth, given to all people as a means of sustaining and edifying their faith and enlarging and strengthening their trust and knowledge in God and the Divine Creator of all Existence.
Form of Shrines

1566. All Shrines may be defined by six characters being: Supreme, Traditional, National, Historical, Communal or Familial, whereby a particular Shrine may qualify according to one or more characteristics:-
Character of Shrines

    (i) *Supreme Shrine* is a Sacred and Holy Place ordained by Heaven in unity and perpetual remembrance of the most sacred Covenant *Pactum De Singularis Caelum*. There are eleven Sacred Cities and Sanctuaries representing supreme sacredness across all seven Unions (Africa, Americas, Arabia, Asia, Levant, Europe and Oceania) being the Holy See, the Holy City of Jerusalem, the Holy City of Mecca, the Holy City of Istanbul (Constantinople), the Holy City of Bodh Gaya, the

Holy City of Varanasi, the Holy City of Tunis (Carthage), the Holy City of London, the Holy City of Washington, the Holy City of Melbourne and the Holy Sovereign Sanctuary of One Ireland; and

(ii) *Traditional Shrine* is a Sacred and Holy Place ordained and worshipped by one or more Customary and Traditional Rite as a Sacred Place of the utmost significance; and

(iii) *National Shrine* is a Sacred and Holy Place ordained by approval of the Supreme See and the Bishops and Patriarch of the relevant University and nation; and

(iv) *Historical Shrine* is a Sacred and Holy Place approved by the Patriarch and Bishops of a University and Nation as a place of sanctity and importance, deserving of preservation and reverence; and

(v) *Communal Shrine* is a Sacred and Holy Place approved by the relevant Diocesan Bishop or Apostolic Bishop for a community; and

(vi) *Familial Shrine* is a Sacred and Holy Place within a building occupied by one or more households, approved by the relevant Diocesan Bishop or Apostolic Bishop for votive offerings and celebrations.

1567. An **Altar** is any fixed or movable structure dedicated for the purpose of votive, or penitential or sacramental offerings. The most sacred ceremony upon a properly sanctified and dedicated altar is sacrament of Holy Eucharist. Altar

1568. Fixed altars must be dedicated, and movable altars must be dedicated or blessed, according to the rites prescribed in the liturgical books. An altar, whether fixed or movable, must be reserved for divine worship alone, to the absolute exclusion of any profane use. However, Altars, whether fixed or movable, do not lose their dedication or blessing if the church or other sacred place is relegated to profane uses. Fixed and Moveable Altars

1569. The Customary and Traditional Rite of placing relics of martyrs or other saints under a fixed Altar is permitted to be preserved within those Customary and Traditional Rites that deem such ancient tradition as absolutely necessary. However, in all other instances, no bones or relics or bodies are to be buried within or beneath Altars. Restriction on remains and Altars

Article 427 - Sacred Cemetery & Crematorium

1570. A proper designated character of a Cemetery or Crematorium is by definition a sacred circumscribed space in accord with the norms of the liturgical books. There exists no spiritual impediment whether a deceased or their family chooses burial or cremation:-

- (i) Furthermore, there exists no spiritual impediment if a deceased is buried or cremated in a sacred circumscribed space that is not dedicated to the faith of One Christ, or One Islam or One Spirit; and

- (ii) However, where possible and for the dignity of its Members, the Church is to have its own cemeteries or at least areas in civil cemeteries that are designated for the deceased members of the faithful and properly blessed; and

- (iii) Parishes and religious institutes may have their own cemetery. Other Juridic persons or families may also have a special cemetery or tomb, to be blessed according to the judgement of the Ecclesiastical Superior; and

- (iv) In respect to church burial, bodies are not to be buried or entombed within churches unless it is a matter of dignity of position to certain offices of clergy, or in relation to the dedication of a church also as a Shrine to a beloved and saintly life.

Article 428 - Sacred Buildings & Ruins

1571. **Sacred Buildings** are structures that hold religious or spiritual significance for a particular group of people. These Sacred Buildings are usually designed and constructed with great care and attention to detail, reflecting the beliefs, values, and architectural styles of the religious or spiritual tradition they represent.

1572. Sacred Buildings serve as places of worship, prayer, meditation, and reflection, and they may also be used for various religious ceremonies and rituals. Some common types of Sacred Buildings from different religious traditions include (but are not limited to):-

- (i) **Temples** are Sacred Buildings in various religions, including Hinduism, Buddhism, and ancient Roman and Greek religions. They are typically ornate structures with specific architectural features and symbols associated with the respective faiths; and

- (ii) **Churches** are Christian Sacred Buildings constructed in various architectural styles, such as Gothic, Romanesque, and Baroque. They often include features like a nave, altar, sacristy, stained glass windows, and a cross or crucifix; and

(iii) **Cathedrals** are large Christian Churches that serve as the central place of worship for a diocese or bishopric. They are often grand and architecturally significant; and

(iv) **Mosques** are Islamic Sacred Buildings. They are known for their distinctive architecture, featuring features like minarets, domes, and prayer halls. The qibla wall indicates the direction of Mecca, which is essential for Islamic prayer; and

(v) **Shrines and Pagodas** are Sacred Buildings found in various Asian religions, including Buddhism, Shintoism, and others. Shrines and pagodas are often simple, elegant structures that serve as places of devotion and pilgrimage; and

(vi) **Gurdwaras** are Sikh Sacred Buildings. They typically have a central hall where the Guru Granth Sahib (the Sikh holy scripture) is kept, and langar (community kitchen) facilities for serving meals to visitors; and

(vii) **Synagogues** are Jewish Sacred Buildings. They vary in architectural style but often have an Ark containing Torah scrolls, a bimah (raised platform), and the Eternal Light; and

(viii) **Monasteries and Convents** are religious communities where monks and nuns live and worship. Monasteries are often associated with Buddhism and Christianity, while convents are typically for Christian nuns; and

(ix) **Sacred Caves and Natural Structures** are examples of indigenous and nature-based spiritual traditions, natural formations such as caves, mountains, or groves can be considered sacred and used for rituals and ceremonies.

1573. **Sacred Ruins** are the remnants of religious or spiritual structures or sites that have, over time, fallen into disrepair, decay, or abandonment. These ruins often still hold religious or historical significance and considered sacred or spiritually meaningful by the communities or cultures that revere them.

Sacred Ruins

1574. Examples of Sacred Ruins exist worldwide, including (but not limited to):-

Examples of Sacred Ruins

(i) **Ancient Temple Complexes and Shrines** such as those in Greece, Rome, Egypt, Cambodia, and Central America are now ruins but were once central to religious life and ceremonies; and

(ii) ***Abbeys and Monasteries*** like those in Europe, Ireland or South America may still hold spiritual significance even though they are no longer in active use; and

(iii) ***Stone Circles and Megalithic Structures*** like Stonehenge in England and Newgrange in Ireland, as well as various stone circles and dolmens around the world, are often considered sacred ruin; and

(iv) **Ancient Cities and Settlements** like Pompeii in Italy, Petra in Jordan, and Palmyra in Syria may contain sacred structures and artefacts; and

(v) **Religious Statues and Sculptures** such as idols, or statues that were once central to religious practices like those on Easter Island (Rapa Nui), can be considered sacred; and

(vi) **Sacred Natural Sites** such as caves, mountains, and lakes can be considered sacred ruins if they were once associated with religious practices but are now abandoned.

1575. Clerics and Ministers holding such sacred office (such as one of the Great Offices of State), must live in legitimately established Religious Houses, designated according to the norm of law of Ucadia and the Universal Ecclesia of One Christ, or Holy Society of One Islam or the Sacred Society of One Spirit or valid and legitimate Ucadia Ecclesia Foundations:- *Religious House*

(i) The erection of such Religious Houses shall take place with consideration for their advantage and proximity to Religious Institutes; and

(ii) No Religious House is to be erected or acquired or modified unless it can be judged prudent to the needs of the Members and that such buildings honour the religious duties, standing, honour and purpose of those that live in them; and

(iii) The Universal Ecclesia of One Christ, the Holy Society of One Islam, the Sacred Society of One Spirit and valid and legitimate Ucadia Ecclesia Foundations shall make early provision to contribute to the acquisition, or building, or development of a Religious House befitting for the standing, office and sanctity of the Visitor. As Superior to the House, the Visitor may designate who may live within it, providing such will and intention is made in writing.

16.2 - Divine Objects

Article 429 - Divine Object

1576. ***Divine Objects*** are items or artefacts that are believed to possess a special, sacred, or supernatural quality or significance within the context of religious or spiritual beliefs. These objects are often revered and used in religious rituals, ceremonies, or as symbols of faith. Divine Object

1577. The nature and importance of Divine Objects vary greatly among different religious traditions and cultures, including (but not limited to):- Examples of Divine Objects

    (i) ***Religious Texts:*** Sacred books and scriptures, such as the Bible in Christianity, the Quran in Islam, the Bhagavad Gita in Hinduism, and the Torah in Judaism, are considered divine objects. They are seen as repositories of divine knowledge and guidance; and

    (ii) ***Religious Symbols:*** Objects like the Christian cross, the Islamic crescent and star, the Hindu Om symbol, and the Buddhist Wheel of Dharma are considered sacred symbols that represent divine concepts and teachings; and

    (iii) ***Religious Icons:*** In some Christian traditions, icons, which are painted or sculpted images of saints, the Virgin Mary, or Jesus Christ, are considered divine objects. They are venerated and used in devotional practices; and

    (iv) ***Idols and Deity Statues:*** In Hinduism and other polytheistic traditions, idols and statues of deities are considered divine representations and objects of worship; and

    (v) ***Ritual Objects:*** Various religious rituals involve the use of specific objects. For example, in Hinduism, items like incense, lamps, and bells are used in worship ceremonies. In Buddhism, prayer beads (malas) are used during meditation; and

    (vi) ***Altars and Shrines:*** The physical structures and objects on altars and shrines in churches, temples, and other places of worship are considered sacred. These can include statues, candles, flowers, and offerings; and

    (vii) ***Relics:*** Relics are physical remains or personal items associated with religious figures, such as the bones of saints, pieces of clothing worn by prophets, or objects used in their lives. They are venerated in many religious traditions, particularly in Catholicism and Buddhism; and

(viii) **Artefacts and Reliquaries**: Some religious traditions have preserved ancient artefacts and reliquaries that are believed to have historical or religious significance. For example, the Ark of the Covenant in Judaism or the Holy Lance in Christianity; and

(ix) **Vestments**: Sacred vestments are special garments or clothing worn by clergy and religious leaders during religious ceremonies and rituals in various religious communities; and

(x) **Talismans and Amulets:** In some folk and spiritual traditions, objects like talismans and amulets are believed to offer protection or bring good luck. These can include charms, stones, or jewellery; and

(xi) **Sacramental Bread and Wine:** In Christianity, the consecrated bread and wine used in the Eucharist or Communion are believed to become the body and blood of Jesus Christ; and

(xii) **Holy Water and Oils:** Water and oils that have been blessed or consecrated are used in various religious ceremonies, such as baptism, anointing of the sick, and blessings.

Article 430 - Sacred Vestments

1578. **Sacred Vestments** are special garments or clothing worn by clergy and religious leaders during religious ceremonies and rituals in various religious communities. These vestments hold symbolic and ritualistic significance and are designed to distinguish clergy members and emphasise their roles within the worship service. Sacred Vestments

1579. Some examples of sacred or religious garments from various religious traditions include (but are not limited to):- Examples of Sacred Vestments

   (i) **Cassock and Robe:** In Christianity, particularly within the Catholic and Anglican traditions, clergy members often wear cassocks (long, ankle-length robes) and robes during worship services. These garments may be accompanied by other liturgical vestments such as stoles, chasubles, and albs; and

   (ii) **Kippah (Yarmulke):** In Judaism, the kippah is a small, circular head covering worn by Jewish men as a sign of humility and reverence for God. It is traditionally worn during prayer and religious rituals; and

   (iii) **Tallit:** A tallit is a prayer shawl worn by Jewish men during morning prayers and certain Jewish rituals. It typically has fringes (tzitzit) attached to the corners as a reminder of the commandments; and

(iv) ***Hijab:*** In Islam, the hijab is a headscarf worn by Muslim women to cover their hair and maintain modesty in accordance with Islamic teachings. Different styles and colors of hijabs exist, and they are worn as part of daily attire; and

(v) ***Abaya and Thobe:*** In some Islamic cultures, women wear the abaya, a long, flowing robe, while men wear the thobe, a similar long robe. These garments are worn for modesty and are common in the Middle East; and

(vi) ***Sari and Dhoti:*** In Hinduism, the sari is a traditional dress worn by women, often in vibrant colors. The dhoti is a traditional men's garment, consisting of a long cloth wrapped around the waist and legs. These garments are worn during religious ceremonies and festivals; and

(vii) ***Kittel:*** In Judaism, particularly among Ashkenazi Jews, the kittel is a white, ankle-length robe worn on special occasions, such as Yom Kippur and Passover seders. It symbolizes purity and is often associated with prayer and repentance; and

(viii) ***Monastic Robes:*** In Buddhism, monks and nuns wear distinctive robes known as kasaya or kesa. The color and style of these robes may vary based on the Buddhist tradition or school; and

(ix) ***Sikh Turban and Kara:*** Sikh men often wear turbans as a symbol of devotion and spirituality. The kara is a steel bracelet worn by Sikh men and women as a reminder of God's presence; and

(x) ***Kimono:*** In Shintoism, traditional Japanese kimonos may be worn during Shinto rituals and ceremonies, particularly at weddings and other important life events.

Article 431 - Sacred Perennial & Seasonal Objects

1580. ***Sacred Perennial Objects*** refer to items or symbols that hold enduring and timeless significance across generations within a particular religious or spiritual tradition. These objects are considered sacred and carry profound religious or spiritual meanings that remain constant over time. They often serve as focal points for worship, meditation, and devotion.

_{Sacred Perennial Objects}

1581. Examples of sacred perennial objects from various religious and

_{Examples of Sacred Perennial}

spiritual traditions include (but are not limited to):-   Objects

(i) **Cross:** In Christianity, the cross is a sacred and perennial symbol representing the crucifixion and resurrection of Jesus Christ. It serves as a central symbol of faith and is often displayed in churches and worn as jewelry; and

(ii) **Star and Crescent:** The star and crescent symbol is associated with Islam and represents the moon and star as heavenly bodies. It is a symbol of the Islamic faith and is often seen on flags and mosque domes; and

(iii) **Om (Aum) Symbol:** In Hinduism, Buddhism, and Jainism, the Om (Aum) symbol is considered sacred and represents the ultimate reality or consciousness. It is chanted and displayed in various religious contexts; and

(iv) **Ankh:** In ancient Egyptian religion, the ankh symbol represents life and immortality. It is often depicted as a cross with a loop at the top and was frequently used in funerary art and rituals; and

(v) **Yin and Yang:** In Taoism, the yin and yang symbol represents the dualistic nature of existence and the balance of opposites. It signifies harmony and unity; and

(vi) **Sikh Khanda:** The Khanda is a sacred symbol in Sikhism, representing the central beliefs of the faith, including unity, truth, and the oneness of God. It is often displayed in Gurdwaras (Sikh temples); and

(vii) **Swastika:** The swastika is an ancient symbol found in Hinduism, Buddhism, Jainism, and other indigenous cultures. In these contexts, it represents auspiciousness, good fortune, and well-being; and

(viii) **Menorah:** The menorah is a seven-branched candelabrum used in Jewish religious rituals, particularly during Hanukkah. It symbolizes the eternal flame and is associated with the Temple in Jerusalem; and

(ix) **Wheel of Dharma:** In Buddhism, the Wheel of Dharma (Dharmachakra) represents the teachings of Buddha and the path to enlightenment. It is a perennial symbol found in Buddhist art and temples; and

(x) **Sacred Stones and Crystals:** In various indigenous and New Age spiritual traditions, certain stones and crystals are considered sacred and are believed to possess spiritual properties. Examples include amethyst, quartz, and turquoise;

and

(xi) **Sacred Trees:** Trees like the Bodhi tree (associated with the enlightenment of Buddha), the Tree of Life (found in multiple cultures and religions), and the cedar tree (sacred in various indigenous traditions) are revered as perennial symbols of spiritual significance; and

(xii) **Sacred Water:** Water from natural sources like rivers, springs, and wells can be considered sacred and used in various rituals and purification ceremonies in multiple traditions.

1582. **Sacred Seasonal Objects** are items or symbols that hold particular religious or spiritual significance during specific seasons, holidays, or festivals within various religious or cultural traditions. These objects are associated with the rituals, customs, and celebrations that take place during certain times of the year.

1583. Examples of sacred seasonal objects from various religious and cultural traditions include (but are not limited to):-

(i) **Christmas Tree:** In Christianity, the Christmas tree is a symbol of the birth of Jesus Christ. It is typically decorated with ornaments and lights during the Christmas season to celebrate the birth of Christ; and

(ii) **Easter Eggs:** In Christianity, particularly in Orthodox and Western Christian traditions, eggs are a symbol of new life and resurrection. They are often dyed and exchanged as gifts during Easter; and

(iii) **Diya (Oil Lamp):** In Hinduism, the Diya is a traditional oil lamp used during Diwali, the Festival of Lights. It symbolizes the victory of light over darkness and knowledge over ignorance; and

(iv) **Candles of Advent:** In Christian traditions, Advent candles are lit in a specific order during the four Sundays leading up to Christmas. Each candle represents different aspects of the Advent season; and

(v) **Lanterns:** In various cultures, lanterns are used during festivals and holidays to symbolize enlightenment, hope, and guidance. For example, lanterns are a prominent feature of the Lantern Festival in China; and

(vi) **Menorah:** The Menorah is a seven-branched candelabrum used during Hanukkah, the Jewish Festival of Lights. It symbolizes the miracle of the Temple oil that burned for eight days; and

(vii) **Pumpkins and Gourds:** In the United States and Canada, pumpkins and gourds are often used as decorations during the Halloween season, symbolizing the harvest and the changing of seasons; and

(viii) **Yule Log:** In some pagan and Wiccan traditions, the Yule Log is burned during the Winter Solstice as a symbol of the returning sun and the renewal of life; and

(ix) **Offerings of Fruit and Flowers:** In many indigenous and nature-based spiritual traditions, offerings of fruit, flowers, and other natural items are made to honour the changing seasons and the spirits of the land; and

(x) **Flags and Banners:** In various cultural and religious festivals, flags and banners are used to represent the themes and symbols of the celebration. For example, Tibetan prayer flags are hung during religious ceremonies.

Article 432 - Sacred Consumable Objects

1584. **Sacred Consumable Objects** refer to items that are considered sacred or spiritually significant within religious or cultural contexts and are meant to be consumed or used in religious rituals and practices. These objects are typically imbued with symbolic meaning and are believed to facilitate a connection between individuals and the divine.

_{Sacred Consumable Objects}

1585. Examples of Sacred Consumable Objects from various religious and cultural traditions include (but are not limited to):-

_{Examples of Sacred Consumable Objects}

(i) **Sacred Herbs and Plants:** Various indigenous and traditional spiritual practices involve the consumption of sacred herbs, plants, or hallucinogens as part of religious ceremonies, visions, or healing rituals; and

(ii) **Blessed Food Offerings:** In many cultures and religions, offerings of food are made to deities and ancestors, and after being blessed, they are shared among the community or family members; and

(iii) **Communion Elements in Sikhism:** In Sikhism, Karah Parshad is a sacred consumable made from equal parts of flour, sugar, and clarified butter. It is prepared during religious ceremonies and distributed among the congregation as a sign of unity; and

(iv) **Eucharistic Bread and Wine:** In Christianity, particularly in the Catholic and Orthodox traditions, the bread and wine used in the Eucharist or Holy Communion are believed to be transformed into the body and blood of Jesus Christ during the ritual. They are consumed by the congregation as a sacred act of remembrance and communion; and

(v) ***Prasad:*** In Hinduism, Prasad is food that has been offered to deities during religious ceremonies. It is considered blessed and is distributed to devotees as a symbol of divine grace; and

(vi) ***Zebu Sacrificial Meat:*** In some African and indigenous religious practices, the meat of a sacrificed zebu (a type of cattle) is consumed as part of religious rituals and feasts, symbolizing unity with the divine; and

(vii) ***Lustral Water in Shintoism:*** In Shinto rituals, lustral water (water purified by priests) is used for purification and cleansing during ceremonies and rites; and

(viii) ***Holy Water:*** In Christianity, especially in Catholicism, holy water is water that has been blessed by a priest. It is used for various religious purposes, including blessing oneself and others, purifying spaces, and during baptism; and

(ix) ***Amrita (Nectar of Immortality):*** In Sikhism, amrita is a sweetened water used during the Amrit Sanchar (initiation ceremony) as a symbol of the divine nectar of immortality; and

(x) ***Holy Oil:*** In Christianity, holy oil, such as chrism, is consecrated by a bishop and used in various sacraments, including confirmation, baptism, and anointing of the sick.

www.ingramcontent.com/pod-product-compliance
Lightning Source LLC
Chambersburg PA
CBHW060332010526
44117CB00017B/2808